Histories of Perplexity

By combining chronological coverage, analytical breadth, and interdisciplinary approaches, these two volumes—*Histories of Solitude* and *Histories of Perplexity*—study the histories of Colombia over the past two centuries as illustrations of the histories of democracy across the Americas.

The volumes bring together over 40 scholars based in Colombia, the United States, England, and Canada working in various disciplines to discuss how a country that has been consistently presented as a rarity in Latin America provides critical examples to re-examine major historical problems: republicanism and liberalism; export economies and agrarian modernization; populism and cultural politics of state formation; revolutionary and counterinsurgent Cold War violence; neoliberal reforms and urban development; popular mobilization and counterhegemonic public spheres; political ecologies and environmental struggles; and labors of memory and the challenge of reconciliation. Contributors are sensitive to questions of subjectivity and discourse, observant of ethnographic details and micro-politics, and attuned to macro-perspectives such as transnational and global histories.

These volumes offer fresh perspectives on Colombia and will be of great value to those interested in Latin American and Caribbean history.

Lina Britto is Associate Professor of History at Northwestern University. She is the author of *Marijuana Boom: The Rise and Fall of Colombia's First Drug Paradise*.

A. Ricardo López-Pedreros is Professor of History at Western Washington University. He has been a Leverhulme Trust Visiting Professor at University College London. He is the author of *Makers of Democracy: A Transnational History of the Middle Class in Colombia*.

Routledge Studies in the History of the Americas

36 A Plurilingual History of the Portuguese Language in the Luso-Brazilian Empire
Luciane Scarato

37 Remaking Indigeneity in the Amazon
Christianity, Colonization and the State
Esteban Rozo

38 U.S. Public Diplomacy Strategies in Latin America During the Sixties
Time for Persuasion
Edited by Francisco Rodríguez Jiménez, Lorenzo Delgado Gómez-Escalonilla and Benedetta Calandra

39 Fashioning Society in Eighteenth-Century British Jamaica
Chloe Northrop

40 Reterritorializing the Spaces of Violence in Colombia
Constanza López Baquero

41 Histories of Solitude
Colombia, 1820s–1970s
Edited by Lina Britto and A. Ricardo López-Pedreros

42 Histories of Perplexity
Colombia, 1970s–2010s
Edited by Lina Britto and A. Ricardo López-Pedreros

For more information about this series, please visit: www.routledge.com/Routledge-Studies-in-the-History-of-the-Americas/book-series/RSHAM

Histories of Perplexity
Colombia, 1970s–2010s

Edited by Lina Britto and
A. Ricardo López-Pedreros

First published 2024
by Routledge
605 Third Avenue, New York, NY 10158

and by Routledge
4 Park Square, Milton Park, Abingdon, Oxon, OX14 4RN

Routledge is an imprint of the Taylor & Francis Group, an informa business

© 2024 Taylor & Francis

The right of Lina Britto and A. Ricardo López-Pedreros to be identified as the authors of the editorial material, and of the authors for their individual chapters, has been asserted in accordance with sections 77 and 78 of the Copyright, Designs and Patents Act 1988.

All rights reserved. No part of this book may be reprinted or reproduced or utilised in any form or by any electronic, mechanical, or other means, now known or hereafter invented, including photocopying and recording, or in any information storage or retrieval system, without permission in writing from the publishers.

Trademark notice: Product or corporate names may be trademarks or registered trademarks, and are used only for identification and explanation without intent to infringe.

Library of Congress Cataloging-in-Publication Data
Names: Britto, Lina, editor. | López, A. Ricardo, 1974–, editor.
Title: Histories of perplexity : Colombia, 1970s–2010s / edited by Lina Britto and A. Ricardo López-Pedreros.
Other titles: Colombia, 1970s–2010s
Description: New York, NY : Routledge, 2024. | Series: Routledge studies in the history of the Americas | Includes bibliographical references and index.
Identifiers: LCCN 2023047784 (print) | LCCN 2023047785 (ebook) | ISBN 9780367499365 (hbk) | ISBN 9780367499372 (pbk) | ISBN 9781003048152 (ebk)
Subjects: LCSH: Colombia—History—1946–1974 | Colombia—History—1974–
Classification: LCC F2278 .H57 2024 (print) | LCC F2278 (ebook) | DDC 986.106/34—dc23/eng/20231220
LC record available at https://lccn.loc.gov/2023047784
LC ebook record available at https://lccn.loc.gov/2023047785

ISBN: 978-0-367-49936-5 (hbk)
ISBN: 978-0-367-49937-2 (pbk)
ISBN: 978-1-003-04815-2 (ebk)

DOI: 10.4324/9781003048152

Typeset in Sabon
by Apex CoVantage, LLC

To our fellow Colombians and Colombianists

Contents

List of Figures	*xi*
List of Tables	*xiii*
List of Maps	*xiv*
Acknowledgments	*xv*
List of Contributors	*xviii*
Preface: Colombia Revisited	*xxvi*
LINA BRITTO AND A. RICARDO LÓPEZ-PEDREROS	

Introduction: Histories of Perplexity   1
LINA BRITTO AND A. RICARDO LÓPEZ-PEDREROS

**PART 1
Identifying Multiculturalism**   21

1 A Conversation with an Afrodiasporic Humanist: Manuel Zapata Olivella in His Own Words   23
    WILLIAM MINA ARAGÓN

2 Black Upward Mobility, Neoliberal Multiculturalism and Social Whitening in Colombia   44
    MARA VIVEROS VIGOYA

3 From Native to Raizal: Indigeneity and the Anglophone Afro-Caribbean Heritage of San Andrés, Providencia, and Santa Catalina   65
    SHARIKA D. CRAWFORD

4 Campesino: A Contested Identity, a Vibrant
  Subjectivity in Colombia   84
  DIANA BOCAREJO AND CARLOS DEL CAIRO

PART 2
Surveying the Territorial State   107

5 A Country of Forests: Territorial State Building
  in Colombia   109
  CLAUDIA LEAL

6 Collective Land Titling and Neoliberalism in the
  Colombian Pacific Region   127
  MARTA ISABEL DOMÍNGUEZ

7 From Carbon Extraction to Blue and Green Extractivism:
  Demands for Radical Socio-environmental
  Transformations in La Guajira, Colombia   148
  ASTRID ULLOA

PART 3
Unpacking Drug Trafficking   167

8 Diplomacy, Drug Trafficking, and Political Repression:
  César Gaviria's Administration in Colombia, 1990–1994   169
  EDUARDO SÁENZ ROVNER

9 Narcotrafficking, Immigration, and Salsa Music:
  The Cali-New York Connection   185
  ALEJANDRO ULLOA SANMIGUEL

10 Mona®co: Conversations on Narco-Phenomena
   and Contemporary Art in Colombia   206
   SANTIAGO RUEDA AND HAROLD ORTIZ

PART 4
Watching the Media 227

11 The Accidental Persona: The Media and Pablo Escobar 229
CATALINA URIBE RINCÓN

12 The Moral Vision and Moral Performance of
Photojournalist Jesús Abad Colorado 252
ALEXANDER L. FATTAL

13 Community Radio Stations and the Construction of
Modern Indigeneity in Cauca, Colombia 273
DIEGO MAURICIO CORTÉS

14 Social Media and the Musical Nation: Hegemonic
Cooptation and the Making of a National Repertoire 292
HÉCTOR FERNÁNDEZ L'HOESTE

PART 5
Revisiting the Armed Conflict 311

15 Gendered Activism and Elite Formation on the
Colombian Frontier: Lessons from the Life of
Fátima Muriel 313
WINIFRED TATE

16 Coercive Brokerage: The Rise and Fall of the Colombian
Paramilitary Hernán Giraldo, 1976–2006 331
FRANCISCO GUTIÉRREZ SANÍN

17 The Conflicts of Coca: Women's Struggles for Economic
Autonomy in Colombia's Coca-Growing Regions 351
ESTEFANÍA CIRO

PART 6
Laboring with Memory 375

18 Fluctuations and Paradoxes in Colombia's Long Cycle of
   Historical Memory, 2005–2022 377
   MARÍA EMMA WILLS OBREGÓN

19 Rendering the Unheard-of Believable: On *Fragmentos* by
   Doris Salcedo and *Duelos* by Clemencia Echeverri 398
   MARÍA DEL ROSARIO ACOSTA LÓPEZ

20 "We Gave Them Names": Exhumations, Peace
   Agreement, and Social Reparation in Bojayá, Chocó, Colombia 419
   PILAR RIAÑO-ALCALÁ IN COLLABORATION WITH JOSÉ DE
   LA CRUZ VALENCIA, NATALIA QUICENO TORO, AND CAMILA
   ORJUELA VILLANUEVA

Bibliography 442
Index 487

Figures

1.1	Manuel Zapata Olivella holding a globe with the map of Africa	26
3.1	English and Spanish Catholic missionaries in Providencia, circa 1930s	75
3.2	San Andrés Island Mural	78
4.1	*The Story of Beto and the Jungle*, children's book	89
4.2	Postcard "Sumapaz, Peasant Reserve Zone"	98
5.1	"Under the oaks, Quercus Humboldtii, near Viotá"	111
7.1	Cerrejón coal mine, La Guajira	153
7.2	Transformations of Wayuu territories, *Ranchería Provincial*, La Guajira	155
9.1	Flyer announcing a Cali salsa show at El Abuelo nightclub, Sunnyside, Queens, NYC	198
9.2	Flyer announcing a Larry Landa Show at a nightclub located on the highway that connects Cali with the Pacific Coast, circa 1978	201
10.1	*Funerals vs. parties*, political cartoon, circa 2000	210
10.2	*Colombia land, guerrilla fighter with a bouquet of poppies*, 2005	214
10.3	*A ToN Of Coke*, 2021	219
10.4	*Horizontes*, 1999	222
11.1	"His cup is now filled," political cartoon, 1983	235
11.2	*Pablo Escobar's Real Estate*, 1988	238
11.3	*Esprit de corps*, political cartoon, 1992	241
12.1	*The Bride of Granada*, 2000	258
12.2	*Peace on the River*, 2002	262
12.3	*Christ in Pieces*, 2002	263
13.1	Drawing of ACPO class with Guambiano students for collaborative research project on historical memory	278

xii *Figures*

17.1	A child guides the author through the *plante* explaining how to take care and cultivate coca	361
17.2	Meeting with government representatives to discuss point four of the peace agreement on Illicit Crops Substitution with peasant women and *cocaleras*'s organizations	369
18.1	Human Rights defender Iván Cepeda with a portrait of his murdered father at the Oval Room while a group of paramilitary commanders addressed a congressional hearing	380
18.2	Some of the FARC commanders at the first acknowledgment of responsibility hearing, Special Jurisdiction for Peace (JEP)	393
19.1	Detail of Doris Salcedo's *Fragmentos*	405
19.2	*Fragmentos*, room view	407
19.3	Detail of dump truck in Clemencia Echeverri's *Duelos*	411
19.4	Detail of stones in Clemencia Echeverri's *Duelos*	412
20.1	Boat on the Atrato river carrying the coffins of the victims of the massacre of Bojayá	421
20.2	Ritual performed in Pogue before the exhumation begins	432
20.3	Relatives carrying the remains of their loved ones toward the temporary vaults	434

Tables

18.1 Fault Lines of the Primal Rift of Historical Memory   384

Maps

0.1	Map of Colombia today	xxvii
5.1	Forest Reserves, 1959	117
20.1	Bojayá and the Middle Atrato Region, Chocó	423

Acknowledgments

The idea for this project has its roots in two panels organized as part of the Gran Colombian Studies section and the Conference of Latin American History of the American Historical Association Annual Congress in New Orleans in 2013 and Washington, DC, in 2014. The project then got further traction as the editors continued discussions with some contributors to these volumes at several conferences in the following years. The task at hand seemed important yet daunting. At first, we wrote a book proposal with a limited chronological scope, but after we received feedback from anonymous readers, it became clear that it was imperative to expand the chronological coverage and the conceptual depth of the project.

It has not been an easy task. The two volumes that the readers now hold in their hands or screens have required not only lots of labor but also time, as they have taken longer than expected because we worked under conditions that were far from ideal. Despite our best efforts, we struggled to secure all the resources needed for the project to materialize, and that was even before the COVID-19 pandemic made our teaching responsibilities and individual research agendas—let alone our personal lives—incredibly difficult. The usual inequalities in an academia governed by a neoliberal mandate of productivity became more salient and evident under a "new normal": who gets what and under what circumstances, how resources get allocated, what topics become marketable, who can afford to buy expensive books on Colombia, and so on. Our way to deal with some of these challenges was to make this project a truly collective effort. Our profound gratitude goes first to all the contributors for their willingness to participate in what at first seemed like an impossible task, their good-natured responses to suggestions and criticisms, and their commitment in making these two volumes a reality. We also want to thank colleagues who helped at crucial junctures: Catherine LeGrand offered insightful comments on most of the content of the two volumes; Ann Farnsworth-Alvear provided early criticism on our editorial styles and reminded us of the need to showcase only scholarship of the highest caliber; Max Novick, editor of

Routledge Studies in the History of the Americas, believed in this project from the very beginning and has been a source of encouragement along the way; and Louise Ingham has worked on all kinds of details to transform two thick manuscripts into readable books. Several colleagues and friends graciously agreed to participate as peer reviewers in a week-long online conference in the middle of the pandemic: Íngrid Bolívar, Constanza Castro, Valeria Coronel, Angélica Durán Martínez, Hernán Pruden, Paul Gillingham, Mark Healey, Kendra McSweeney, Mary Roldán, Karin Alejandra Rosemblatt, Barbara Weinstein, and María Emma Wills. It is a platitude to say that without their work and intelligence, these two volumes would have not been at all possible, but it is so true that is almost an understatement. The detailed questions, thoughtful comments, and bibliographical references that they offered substantially improved the two volumes. We also want to reiterate our deepest gratitude to Íngrid Bolívar, Mary Roldán, Catherine LeGrand, Catalina Muñoz, Francisco Ortega, and Paul Gillingham for reading the Preface and the Introduction to each volume and providing critical feedback. *Eternamente agradecidos*. Finally, thanks to Sofía Jarrín-Thomas for working with us on some of the original essays and translations from Spanish as editor of English as a Second Language (ESL), as well as Lorena Iglesias and Gabe Levine-Drizin for their work on footnotes and bibliographies. Our thanks to Bill Nelson for his diligent work on producing the map that appears in the Preface.

These two volumes are in close dialogue with a similar effort in progress in Colombia—*Historias de lo político: Ilusiones nacionales y disputas por el orden*—under the intellectual and editorial leadership of Íngrid Bolívar, Franz Hensel Riveros, Margarita Garrido, and Francisco Ortega. We have found inspiration in what they are doing and share the spirit of the task at hand: thinking the histories of Colombia otherwise. We very much look forward to continuing working together in this endeavor. In our scholarly lives, we approach teaching as researchers and research as teachers so we would like to offer these two volumes as teaching and research tools for readers—broadly defined—to discuss the histories of Colombia as histories of democracy. It is indeed our hope that these two volumes soon become available in paperback so that they are more affordable and accessible.

Apart from the debts of gratitude that we accrued as a team, each one of us counted on a support net that helped us go through the finish line. I, Lina Britto, want to thank first and foremost my coeditor, friend, and ally *Richi*. If all these years of arduous work and unexpected obstacles were in fact an edifying experience, it was thanks to his generosity, reflexivity, kindness, and sense of humor. All the credit goes to him. Likewise, several of my colleagues at Northwestern University have taught me how to hold my ground under pressure: former Chair of History Deborah Cohen and current Chair Kevin Boyle have consistently led by example with grace and poise and encouraged me to follow my career instincts; Paul Gillingham has participated in this project at several steps; and the staff, faculty, and graduate students affiliated to the Latin American and Caribbean Studies program, LACS, have created and sustained a little universe that permanently reminds me of the importance of the silent work that we do. My greatest luck, however, has been having the honor of working closely with a group of talented young Colombians doing graduate school. María Camila Palacio, Christian Vásquez, Sofía Sánchez, Felipe Gutiérrez Franco, Daniel Ospina, Mariana Charry Esguerra, Usdin Martínez, and Leonardo Gil Gómez (now a professor in his own right) have taught me more than I have managed to teach them. My infinite gratitude to them for bringing the best of Colombia to the Great Lakes and serving as ideal readers. But none of this project would have been possible without my husband Seth Gransky—and our Coco *loco*—because his discipline and commitment sustain our domestic life, and his warmth and light are constant sources of strength, and hope.

I, A. Ricardo López-Pedreros, wish to thank my coeditor and friend—Lina Britto—in writing. I have learned so much in the making of these two volumes, but my experience working with Lina has made clear how collective endeavors like this one depend upon care, reciprocity, and solidarity. Indeed, knowledge production is a labor of friendship. All the credit goes to her. *¡Gracias parcera!* I also want to recognize the institutional support offered by the Department of History at Western Washington University (WWU). The Office Research and Sponsored Programs at WWU also offered funding for the materialization of the volumes. Some of the early but critical work on this project was done while I was Leverhulme Trust Visiting Professor at University College London. I would like to offer my gratitude to Paulo Drinot, Patricio Simonetto, Kesewa John, Néstor Castañeda, and Jonathan Bell for the discussion on the Americas, Latin America, and Colombia. I also want to thank my friends and colleagues at WWU: Blanca Aranda Gómez García, Pedro Cameselle-Pesce, Alex Czopp, Steven Garfinkle, Luis Gonzalo Portugal, and Jennifer Seltz. They have been a welcome source of ideas, encouragement, and support throughout this process. And, as always, I am immensely grateful to María Isabel Cortés-Zamora for everything in this world we shared. Last, but certainly not least, I thank Valentina López Cortés and Abdur-Rahman Abdus Salaam for the new experiences in life.

Lina Britto
Medellín, Colombia; Chicago, Illinois, USA

A. Ricardo López-Pedreros
Bogotá, Colombia; Bellingham, Washington, USA

Contributors

María del Rosario Acosta López is Professor of Latin American Studies in the Department of Hispanic Studies, University of California, Riverside. She teaches and conducts research on aesthetics, critical theory, political philosophy, and, more recently, decolonial studies, with an emphasis on questions of memory and trauma in the Americas. Her most recent publications are devoted to the aesthetics of resistance in Latin American art, decolonial perspectives on memory and history, and epistemic injustice and epistemic violence. She is currently working on the manuscript of her next book, *Grammars of Listening: Philosophical Approaches to Memory after Trauma* (forthcoming in Spanish with Herder and in English with Fordham UP).

Diana Bocarejo is a Colombian anthropologist. She holds an MA in social sciences and a Ph.D. in anthropology from the University of Chicago. Her main areas of study are political and legal anthropology and socio-environmental studies. She also works on multiculturalism (the legal articulations between minority rights and indigenous territories), collective forms of land and environmental management, and environmental conservation in different *campesino* and fishing communities.

Lina Britto is Associate Professor of History at Northwestern University. She holds a Ph.D. in history from New York University and was a postdoctoral fellow at the Harvard Academy for International and Area Studies, Harvard University. Her work situates the emergence and consolidation of illegal drug smuggling networks in Colombia in the context of a growing articulation between the South American country and the United States during the Cold War. She is the author of *Marijuana Boom: The Rise and Fall of Colombia's First Drug Paradise* (University of California Press, 2020), which is also published in Spanish with the title *El boom de la marihuana: Auge y caída del primer paraíso de las drogas en Colombia* (Crítica and Editorial Uniandes, 2022).

Estefanía Ciro is director of the Centro de Pensamiento desde la Amazonia Colombiana AlaOrillaDelRío. She has a Ph.D. in political and social sciences from the Universidad Nacional Autónoma (México). In 2018, she was awarded the Premio Unesco a la Investigación Social Juan Bosch. She is the author of *Levantados de la selva: Vidas y legitimidades de la actividad cocalera en el Caquetá* (Ediciones Uniandes, 2020). She has been a professor at the Instituto Tecnológico de Estudios Superiores de Monterrey (México). She has published in the *Journal of Political Power*, *Colombia Internacional*, and *La Revista Colombiana de Sociología*. She coordinated the research section on cocaine and marijuana economies, drug policy, and armed conflict at the Comisión para el Esclarecimiento de la Verdad (Colombia).

Diego Mauricio Cortés is Assistant Professor of Global Media at the University of Oregon's School of Journalism and Communication. He is an intercultural communication scholar who inquires on the formation of contemporary indigeneities in the Andes, alternative and development media, mass media representations and indigenous peoples as well as transnational evangelicalism. He has also done research on American whiteness and media representations of the War on Drugs. He is working on his book manuscript exploring the repercussions of the rapid expansion of American Christian fundamentalism among Andean indigenous communities in Colombia, Ecuador, and Bolivia.

Sharika D. Crawford is Professor of History at the United States Naval Academy. She is the author of *The Last Turtlemen of the Caribbean: Waterscapes of Labor, Conservation, and Boundary Making* (University of North Carolina Press, 2020). This work received an Honorable Mention from the Association of Caribbean Historians 2021 Elsa Goveia Book Prize in Caribbean History. The National Endowment for the Humanities, the Fulbright U.S. Scholar Program, and the American Philosophical Society generously supported research for the book. In 2022, she was awarded the United States Naval Academy's Civilian Research in Excellence Award.

José de la Cruz Valencia is a member of the Committee for the Rights of the Victims of Bojayá, comprised by various Indigenous and Afro organizations. He participated in the dialogue between the people of Bojayá and the peace negotiation team integrated by the Colombian government and the Revolutionary Armed Forces of Colombia (FARC), and the first act of acknowledgment of responsibilities for the massacre by the FARC. Along with Pilar Riaño-Alcalá, he led the collaborative project "Exhumations and Burial in Colombia: Strengthening Forensic Practices through Knowledge Transfer" and the online project

Los muertos de Bojayá son nuestros muertos: Exhumar, identificar, enterrar y acompañar en Bojayá, Chocó.

Carlos del Cairo is Professor in the Department of Anthropology, Pontificia Universidad Javeriana in Bogotá. He is an anthropologist specialized in political ecology and socio-environmental dynamics in the northwest Colombian Amazon. His research focuses on environmental conflicts among peasant and indigenous communities and their interactions with development/conservation initiatives promoted by institutions and international cooperation agencies. Del Cairo obtained his BA in anthropology from the Universidad del Cauca, MSc in anthropology from the University of Montréal, and Ph.D. in anthropology from the University of Arizona.

Marta Isabel Domínguez is Professor of Sociology at the Universidad de Antioquia, Medellín. She obtained a BA in sociology from the University of Cambridge, a master's degree in gender studies from the London School of Economics and Political Science, and Ph.D. in sociology from El Colegio de México. Her recent research is on everyday forms of state formation, processes of collective titling of Black communities in Antioquia, and technologies of order in Medellin in the 1960s (control over space, body, and ideas). She is the author of *Territorios colectivos: Proceso de formación del Estado en el Pacífico colombiano, 1993–2009* (Universidad de Antioquia, 2017).

Alexander L. Fattal is Associate Professor of Communication at the University of California, San Diego. He is the author of *Shooting Cameras for Peace: Youth, Photography, and the Colombian Armed Conflict/Disparando cámaras para la paz: Juventud, fotografía y el conflicto armado colombiano* (Harvard University Press, 2020) and *Guerrilla Marketing: Counterinsurgency and Capitalism in Colombia* (University of Chicago Press, 2018). He is also the director of two short films *Limbo* and *Trees Tropiques*.

Héctor Fernández L'Hoeste, Ph.D., Stony Brook University, 1996, is Professor of Latin/x American cultural studies at Georgia State University in Atlanta, Georgia. He is the author of *Lalo Alcaraz: Political Cartooning in the Latino Community* (University of Mississippi Press, 2017) and *Narrativas de representación urbana* (Peter Lang, 1998) and coeditor of *Digital Humanities in Latin America* (University of Florida Press, 2020); *Sound, Image, and National Imaginary in the Construction of Latin/o American Identities* (Lexington Books, 2018); *Sports and Nationalism in Latin/o America* (Palgrave Macmillan, 2015); *Cumbia!* (Duke University Press, 2013); *Redrawing the Nation* (Palgrave Macmillan, 2009); and *Rockin' Las Americas* (University of Pittsburgh

Press, 2004). He coedits two academic series: with Pablo Vila, he edits the Music, Culture, and Identity in Latin America series for Lexington Books; and with Juan Carlos Rodríguez, he publishes Reframing Media, Technology, and Culture in Latin/o America for the University of Florida Press.

Francisco Gutiérrez Sanín is a researcher at the Institute of Political Studies and International Relations at the Universidad Nacional de Colombia, Bogotá. He has a Ph.D. in political science from Warsaw University. Throughout his career, he has worked and published on civil war, patterns of violence against civilians, statehood and state fragility, political indicators, political parties, and clientelism. Some of his publications include *¿Un nuevo ciclo de la guerra en Colombia?* (Debate, 2020); *Clientelistic Warfare: Paramilitaries and the State in Colombia (1982–2007)* (Peter Lang, 2019); and "Politicians: The Sinews of Counterinsurgent Governance in Colombia," *Third World Quarterly*. He participated in the Comisión Histórica del Conflicto y sus Víctimas summoned by the Colombian government and FARC peace talks.

Claudia Leal is Professor in the Department of History and Geography, Universidad de los Andes. She holds a Ph.D. in geography from the University of California, Berkeley. She has published various books on environmental history, including the edited volumes *Fragmentos de historia ambiental colombiana* (2020); (with John Soluri and José Augusto Pádua) *A Living Past: Environmental Histories of Modern Latin America* (Berghahn Books, 2018); and *Landscapes of Freedom: Building a Postemancipation Society in the Rainforests of Western Colombia* (University of Arizona Press, 2018). She is working on a history of Colombian national parks and conducting research on the history of animals.

A. Ricardo López-Pedreros is Professor of History at Western Washington University. He has been a Leverhulme Trust Visiting Professor at University College London. He is the author of *Makers of Democracy: A Transnational History of the Middle Classes in Colombia* (Duke University Press, 2019), which was translated to Spanish as *La clase invisible: Género, clases medias y democracia en Bogotá* (Universidad del Rosario/Crítica, 2022). With Mario Barbosa and Claudia Stern, he co-edited *The Middle Classes in Latin America: Subjectivities, Practices, and Genealogies* (Routledge, 2022) and with Barbara Weinstein, *The Making of the Middle Class: Toward a Transnational History* (Duke University Press, 2012). He is the editor of the series Social Movements in the Americas (Rowman &Littlefield/Lexington Books) and is currently writing a biography of Colombian sociologist Gabriel Restrepo. He is also working on a history of domination in Colombia during the second half of the twentieth century.

William Mina Aragón is Professor of Law, Political and Social Sciences at the Universidad del Cauca, Colombia. He is also a member of the research group Actores, Procesos e Instituciones Políticas at the same university. He obtained a BA in philosophy from the Universidad del Valle and a Ph.D. in sociology and political science from the Universidad Complutense de Madrid. He has interviewed Fernando Savater, Edgar Morin, Alain Touraine, and Cornelius Castoriadis. He has written for *Afro-Hispanic Review*, *Claves*, *Communitas*, *Crítica*, and *Palara*. Some of his publications include *La imaginación creadora afrodiaspórica* (Editorial Universidad del Valle, 2022); *Manuel Zapata Olivella: Un humanista afrodiaspórico* (Poemia Editorial, 2020); *El escritor y la política* (Samava Ediciones, 2019); *Manuel Zapata Olivella: Un legado intercultural* (Fundación Universitaria de Popayán and Ediciones Desde Abajo, 2016); *Las gestas del afro por la libertad* (Editorial Universidad del Cauca, 2011); and *Poesía y filosofía política* (Artes Gráficas del Valle, 1999). He was the coordinator of the Biblioteca Afrocolombiana de las Ciencias Sociales (2022) and director of the research program "Trayectorias políticas de la Diáspora Africana," supervised by the Universidad del Cauca.

Camila Orjuela Villanueva is a social worker and has a master's degree in social anthropology. She has worked for more than 14 years in community research projects on the Colombian armed conflict and historical memory reconstruction as well as in the accompaniment of communities in the design, implementation, and evaluation of social projects and public policies. She has participated in several collaborative knowledge production processes including the exhumation, identification, and burial of the victims of the 2002 massacre in Bojayá.

Harold Ortiz is an artist and curator. He obtained a BA of fine arts at the University of Antioquia (Medellín, Colombia). His research and artistic practice focus on illegal ecosystems and the strategies of resistance and adaptation developed by different communities. He is also the founder and artistic director of Timebag Art Project, which has produced curatorship in Colombia, Aruba, and the United States. His work has been exhibited at the Museum of Modern Art of Medellín (2023, 2017), the Museum of Antioquia (2021), the Gilberto Alzate Avendaño Foundation (2019), and Pereira Museum of Contemporary Art (2019), among other venues.

Natalia Quiceno Toro is Associate Professor at the Institute of Regional Studies at University de Antioquia and a member of the Culture, Violence and Territory research group. She is an anthropologist with a master's degree in Political Science from the University de Antioquia and a Ph.D. in social anthropology from the Federal University of Rio de Janeiro, National Museum. Since she first arrived to the Atrato River in 2010, she has continued learning how to practice what people in the region call "accompaniment" and "embarkment." Her research addresses the experiences of violence, as well as the strategies that people create daily to dignify life in a country traversed by a long-term armed conflict.

Pilar Riaño-Alcalá is Professor at the Social Justice Institute at the University of British Columbia, Vancouver, Canada. She is an anthropologist and interdisciplinary scholar examining the afterlives of political violence, the traces of memory and social repair, oralities and sound memory, and social practice art. She is the author of *Poniendo tierra de por medio: Migracion forzada de colombianos* (University of British Columbia and Corporación Región, 2008) and *Dwellers of Memory: Youth and Violence in Medellín, Colombia* (Routledge, 2006). Currently, Riaño-Alcalá is working on two book manuscripts, *In the Interstices of War and Peace: Memory and Social Repair in Colombia*, and with Erin Baines she is editing *How Do We Be Together? Transformative Memory in the Wakes of Political Violence*. Her articles have appeared in *Memory Studies*, *The International Journal of Transitional Justice*, *Anthropology Quarterly*, *Revista Colombiana de Antropología*, and *Estudios Políticos*, among others.

Santiago Rueda is a researcher, curator, and historian of art and photography. He is the author of *Plata y plomo: Una historia del arte y las sustancias (i)lícitas en Colombia* (Crítica, 2019), among other books on Colombian art and photography. He has curated exhibitions about drugs, the environment, and the armed conflict in Colombia that have been presented in Argentina, Brazil, Bolivia, Colombia, the United States, Ecuador, Mexico, Spain, and Uruguay.

Eduardo Sáenz Rovner is Professor Emeritus at the Facultad de Ciencias Económicas, Universidad Nacional de Colombia, Bogotá. He has published extensively on the economic histories of Colombia and Latin America. His books include *Conexión Colombia: Una historia del narcotráfico entre los años 30 y los años 90* (Crítica, 2021); *The Cuban Connection: Drug Trafficking, Smuggling, and Gambling in Cuba from the 1920s to the Revolution* (University of North Carolina Press, 2009); *Colombia, años 50: Industriales, política y diplomacia* (Universidad Nacional de Colombia, 2002); and *La ofensiva empresarial: Industriales, políticos y violencia en Colombia en los años 40* (Tercer Mundo Editores, 1992).

Winifred Tate is Professor of Anthropology at Colby College. She studies struggles for democracy, citizenship, and political change in the wake of more than a century of prohibitionist drug policy regimes. Her research in Colombia examines community responses to illegal drug trafficking and political violence along the southern border, and in Maine, she studies the evolving opioid drug crisis. Her books include *Drugs, Thugs, and Diplomats: U.S. Policymaking in Colombia* (Stanford University Press, 2015), published in Spanish as *Drogas, bandidos y diplomáticos* (Editorial University del Rosario, 2015), and the award-winning *Counting the Dead: The Culture and Politics of Human Rights Activism in Colombia* (University of California Press, 2007).

Astrid Ulloa is Professor in the Department of Geography at the Universidad Nacional de Colombia, Bogotá. She is an anthropologist from the Universidad Nacional de Colombia, Bogotá, and received her Ph.D. from the University of California, Irvine. Her main research interests include indigenous movements, indigenous autonomy, gender, climate change, water, territoriality, extractivisms, and feminist political ecology. Ulloa's current research is about gender and territorial indigenous feminisms, as well as just transitions and indigenous territories in Latin America. She has published several books, chapters, and articles on indigenous peoples and women, as well as on environmental issues and extractivism.

Alejandro Ulloa Sanmiguel is Professor at the School of Communication, Universidad del Valle, Cali. He obtained a BA in literature and a master's degree in linguistics and Spanish. He also holds a master's degree in anthropology. His publications include *La salsa en tiempos de nieve: La conexión latina Cali-Nueva York, 1975–2000* (Editorial Universidad del Valle, 2020), which received the national book award by the Alejandro Ángel Escobar Foundation in the category of Social Science and Humanities, 2021; *Salsa Barrio Cultura—Convergencia Digital* (Editorial Universidad del Valle, 2018); *"Mi segunda piel": La pinta y el vestuario en el baile de la salsa en Cali* (Ministerio de Cultura, 2015); *La salsa en discusión: Música popular e historia cultural* (Editorial Universidad del Valle, 2009); *El baile: Un lenguaje del cuerpo* (Imprenta Departamental del Valle del Cauca, 2005); *Globalización, ciudad y representaciones sociales: El caso de Cali* (Universidad Pontificia Bolivariana, 2000); *Pagode, a festa de samba no Rio de Janeiro e nas Américas* (Multimais, 1998); and *La salsa en Cali* (Universidad Pontificia Bolivariana, 1988).

Catalina Uribe Rincón is Assistant Professor at the Center for Journalism's Studies at the Universidad de los Andes, Bogotá. Her research focuses on political communication, visual rhetoric, and journalism studies. She has a special interest in the power of the media and the construction of public characters through media narratives. She has published articles on media and disinformation, presidential rhetoric, and public opinion in Latin America, as well as on government communication and media coverage during war times, especially during the Colombian armed conflict. She has been a weekly columnist for *El Espectador* newspaper since 2013.

Mara Viveros Vigoya holds a Ph.D. in anthropology from the École des Hautes Études en Sciences Sociales (EHESS-Paris). She is a professor at the Faculty of Human Sciences at Universidad Nacional de Colombia, Bogotá. She has taught in the Department of Anthropology (1998–2017) and the School of Gender Studies at the same university. She is the cofounder of the school and has been its director three times. She has been guided in her career as a researcher and lecturer by the theoretical, political, and ethical dimensions of critical feminism; her research has focused on the intersections of gender, sexuality, class, and race and ethnicity in the social and cultural dynamics of Latin American societies.

María Emma Wills Obregón holds a Ph.D. from University of Texas, Austin, and an MSc in political science, University of Montreal. She has been an associate professor and director of the Department of Political Science at the Universidad de Los Andes; she has also been a researcher, associate professor, and director of the master's program of the Institute of Political Studies and International Relations at the Universidad Nacional de Colombia, Bogotá. From August 2012 to August 2018, she served as an adviser to the General Directorate of the National Center for Historical Memory. In 2014, she was part of the Historical Commission on the Conflict and its Victims, created during the negotiation of the peace agreement between the government and the FARC.

Preface

Colombia Revisited

Lina Britto and A. Ricardo López-Pedreros

Colombia is one of "the least studied of the major Latin American countries, and probably the least understood," stated historian David Bushnell in *The Making of Modern Colombia*, a book published in 1993 and still considered the standard reference text in English on this South American country.[1] Although Bushnell's groundbreaking work put Colombia back on the map for English-writing scholars, it has continued to be an uncommon topic of research in universities in the Global North, at least when compared to other major Latin American countries such as Brazil, Argentina, or Mexico.[2] Recently, an important textbook for instructors and students restated that "despite its size, wealth, and geopolitical importance, [Colombia] remains one of the least known and most misunderstood countries in Latin America."[3] At first glance, these statements could be interpreted as mere rhetorical devices. However, they do shape, and in some cases exhaust, how Colombia is discussed. Indeed, when the country is examined, scholars tend to portray its trajectory as so unique that it hardly parallels others.[4] How else can we explain that counterintuitive combination of a strong constitutional system and alarming levels of violence if not as a rarity, an anomaly, or an exception? Colombia is usually presented in academic and popular literatures as a "labyrinth," a country of "cities without citizens," a "democracy without the people," an "impenetrable thing," a "narco-democracy," a society in which modernity is forever "deferred" or "elusive," a "comedy of errors," and a "country of bullets" where an idiosyncratic political culture produced a "modernization [that] works against modernity."[5] In short, as Bushnell unwittingly put it, "a nation in spite of itself."

Time is ripe to reconsider these dominant narratives and ask instead how Colombia illustrates fundamental questions about the modern histories of the Americas. Located in the northernmost section of South America, between two geostrategic regions, the Panama Canal and Venezuela's oil district, Colombia has been a long-standing bridge between the Caribbean, the Andean, the Pacific, and the Amazon basins, and a key ally in the consolidation of a U.S. hegemonic project in the hemisphere.

Preface xxvii

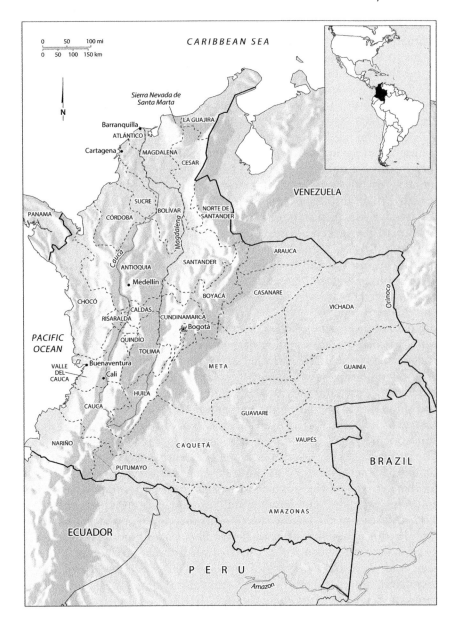

Map 0.1 Map of Colombia today, designed by Bill Nelson

By paying attention to this important role as a node connecting different regional histories, as well as its centrality to U.S.-Latin American relations, these two volumes—*Histories of Solitude* and *Histories of Perplexity*— offer histories of Colombia as *sites of democratic struggles*, not as examples of democracy's negation or deviation, as it has often been conceptualized. Our suggested focus comes at a moment when democracy seems to have entered a permanent state of emergency. From the discovery of thousands of unmarked graves across Canada that confirmed state-perpetrated genocide against indigenous peoples, and protesters storming the Capitol to prevent a peaceful transition of power in the United States—a tactic later copied by right-wing groups in Brazil—to immigration camps along Mexico's northern border where the human rights of thousands of asylum seekers are violated daily, and the self-coup attempt that justified a militarized government that is tearing Peru apart, at the moment of this writing, democratic orders all over the Americas have revealed their anti-democratic side. "What have we done to democracy? What have we turned it into?," South Asian intellectual and activist Arundhati Roy asked at the dawn of the twenty-first century.[6] Two decades later, Roy's questions echo more loudly, even in the United States, the world's self-proclaimed "beacon of democracy," where a powerful sector of the political class is currently seeking "a return to oligarchy."[7] Then and now, democracy seems to be unraveling, and these are the debates we seek to contribute to.

Each volume invites readers to explore the relevance of Colombia for a better historical understanding of democratic orders, from various angles and perspectives. In *Histories of Solitude: Colombia, 1820s–1970s*, we begin by inquiring how different actors imagined a republic after the wars of independence, and how they inserted themselves in political, scientific, and diplomatic vanguards of their times. We then move on to examine how dissimilar sectors engaged in processes, through the legislature, the educational system, and the domestic market, to build a public sphere. The irruption of the masses in that public sphere, created in the nineteenth century, is the main topic of the following section, where we shed light on the struggles of the popular sectors to craft citizenship vis-à-vis local and national elites. The legacies and consequences of these conflicts are studied further in the last two sections of the volume, in which we untangle the transnational history of development as a paradigm invented by a constellation of historical actors to craft a modern Colombian democracy, and we analyze the radical practices that social movements utilized to subvert orders, respond to, and remake modernizing reforms. In *Histories of Perplexity: Colombia 1970s–2010s*, we scrutinize the origins of neoliberalism in the all-encompassing crisis of the 1970s, and its unfolding until our present times. We start the journey by identifying multiculturalism as one of neoliberalism's greatest achievements, meaning, as a tool for the redefinition of categories used to organize hierarchically intrinsic differences between people. Then, we survey the territorial state and how specific regions participated in the making of extractivism as a means to an end, that is, for re-envisioning the state's role in the economy and in society. One of the most enduring forms of extractivism is examined in the next section, where we unpack drug trafficking to showcase the many approaches currently used to study Colombia's most problematic export economy. By connecting the illegal drugs business with public discourses, we offer various angles to watch the media and question how representations, routines, strategies, and participants have actively contributed to the tensions between peace and war in the last decades. The persistence of violence is the theme of the following section, where authors, through ethnographic research and social and cultural analysis, revisit the armed conflict and consider everyday practices of resistance and accommodation by variegated local actors. We conclude the volume by focusing our attention on recent social and artistic movements and efforts to labor with memory and make remembering and retelling crucial practices in the struggle for justice and reconciliation.

"Unthinkable" as it sounds, our invitation to reframe these histories of Colombia as histories of democracy withstands readymade notions.[8] For decades, historians and social scientists have criticized the study of democracies for its focus on the experiences of Europe and the United States, from where democracy has long been understood to have originated.[9] Eurocentric interpretations have routinely perpetuated a teleological narrative of an exclusively Western and universal democracy that other regions are found wanting and have thus copied; in fact, democracy is usually depicted as a selfless gift from "the West" for the rest of the world.[10] Under this model of mimesis and transplantation, divergent historical realities can only be understood as deviations, failures, or, at best, derivatives.[11] Although recent studies have criticized this normativity by examining multiple experiences in Latin America, we still tend to particularize, even exoticize, those cases perceived to be outside the putative norm.[12] Thus, the task for us has been to question precisely what are considered *universal* and *local* versions of democracy, dissolve hierarchical distinctions between the two, dispute teleological definitions that presume a linear progression according to which societies experience democratization as they move forward in history, thus deprovincializing the histories of Colombia by connecting them with global and transnational processes.[13] In the words of Colombian sociologist María Teresa Uribe de Hincapié, we abandon "that vocation of insularity and isolation, that quasi-narcissist fascination with our image, that is so present in Colombian intelligentsia."[14] Our critical reading also includes a degree of skepticism toward some decolonial approaches, which have become the hegemonic language that translates an "authentic" representation of a Latin America subalternity to the world, while tending to theorize democracy in the region as the result of an all-powerful colonial matrix of power imposed from above, reinscribing it as a reality of the "West" and erasing the historical experiences of democracy fought over in Latin America.[15]

Instead, the chapters in these volumes explore the tensions between the authoritarian and emancipatory roots of democracy.[16] The authors rescue several democratic experiments in various places and moments in time in Colombia that have been forgotten or silenced as unreasonable, impracticable, and disposable. They also historicize how certain definitions and practices of democracy have gained normativity and legitimacy while eclipsing others. In so doing, the authors distance themselves from the idea that democracy is a "given," and instead of taking it for granted, they recognize that "it requires conflict."[17] That is, they consider that advances and setbacks, expansions and contractions, inclusions and exclusions, and processes of hierarchical ordering are foundational to democracy. As Wendy Brown once said it, this type of approach "challenges conceits of purity" and forces us to accept that democracies encompass imperialism, slavery, genocide, class dominance, and punishment and are "saturated with these legacies in the present."[18] As we elaborate further in the introductions to each volume, the authors face the "unthinkable," in the sense that, by interrogating the frameworks used to conceive and write about the histories of Colombia, they examine "suppressed dimensions of past [and present] struggles" and offer case studies to illustrate democracy's heterogeneity.[19] Collectively, this endeavor proposes to bring democracy to the historical terrain, see it as contingent rather than preordained, and illustrates how multiple groups have fought over the meanings, subjectivities, practices, institutions, politics, economies, and rationalities of democracy. In this sense, the histories of Colombia, far from being unique or exceptional, are part of worldwide historical struggles over what it means to be part of a democratic society. By taking an intersectional approach, these volumes move away from assessing the quality of democracy to proposing a critique of its multiple histories.

The Colombian Paradox

This collective effort seeks to deepen a renewed international interest in Colombia that began a decade ago. The peace negotiations and accords between the government of Juan Manuel Santos (2010–2018) and the Revolutionary Armed Forces of Colombia (FARC) prompted a public debate about the causes, dynamics, and consequences of war and peace in the country. With the signing of an agreement in November 2016, the last and longest Cold War–era armed conflict in the Western hemisphere officially came to a close, setting an example on "how to end a civil war when neither side is vanquished on the battlefield," and generating international attention.[20] Then, the COVID-19 pandemic pushed millions of

Colombians below the poverty line and sparked the largest social protests in recent history, contributing to the rise to national power of a leftist coalition for the first time. Meanwhile, the Special Jurisdiction for Peace (JEP in Spanish), the transitional justice system investigating war crimes, began to charge responsible parties to bring them to trial. In this context of profound changes, new interpretations of Colombia's pasts and presents are imperative. These two volumes are intended to enhance such conversation.

Democracy, however imagined or idealized, has been one of the most discussed topics when studying Colombia, one often presented as a paradox between a perceived "vulgarity" of domination that is antidemocratic and a "properness" of power that is seen as inherently democratic.[21] The idea of "a country racked by chronic sociopolitical violence rooted in, among other things, inherited partisan hatreds; severe social inequities; a weak, corrupt state; and, not least, the influence of a vast, insidious, and illegal drug industry," readily contrasts with another set of representations of Colombia as a vibrant society, with a small but solid state in search of political legitimacy, economic prosperity, and social peace and inclusion.[22] Each narrative mirrors the other as if they were intrinsically opposed.

When explaining the Colombian paradox, scholars have developed three lines of analysis. The first type of narrative argues that the bipartisan system composed by the Liberal and Conservative parties, which dominated the political landscape from the mid-nineteenth century until the first decade of the twenty-first century, made Colombia "one of Latin America's longest-functioning democracies, with a lasting record of usually fair and regular elections and respect for political and civil rights."[23] The National Front (1958–1974), a political agreement between Liberals and Conservatives to put an end to a war by sharing the state apparatus and alternating power for two decades, established the foundations of a political system that, unlike other places in Latin America, provided crucial spaces for ideological dissent, political stability, economic growth, and a significant period of sustained peace.[24] Indeed, compared to other nations in the continent, Colombia lacked "revolutionary tumult and military governance."[25] A second line of interpretation contends that the history of the country has been paved by social exclusion, regional fragmentation, concentration of land in a few hands, unequal distribution of wealth, political repression, and oligarchical rule from the nineteenth century to the present. In short, a "manorial republic."[26] In this failed democracy, omnipotent oligarchies secured a social order for their own benefit since independence until today, by relying on coercion and repression, and limiting "any gains by urban and working classes."[27] In recent times, criminality associated with illicit drug trafficking, guerrilla insurgencies, and paramilitary squads dwarfed the absent state—weak, corrupt, oligarchic (adjectives vary)—making Colombia a noteworthy case of a "failed nation."[28] Last, a third explanation asserts that Colombia's history is the result of an unresolved tension "between legitimacy and violence," or in the picturesque expression of one of the greatest Liberal politicians of the twentieth century, Darío Echandía, an "orangutan in a tailcoat."[29] In other words, multiple forms of terror, domination, and repression dressed as civilian democratic governments, functioning under a constitutional order that holds presidential elections every four years, have generated impressive macroeconomic indicators and supported the rise of the urban middle class that enjoys cultural development.[30]

During the past decades, historical analyses based on these three lines of interpretations and formerly confined to the realm of the experts began to circulate in the public sphere thanks to the significant role that scholars—some of whom are contributors to these volumes—have played in projects of historical memory resulting from the peace negotiations.[31] Despite their different terminologies and methodologies, most of these projects shared the idea that Colombia is a deeply fractured democracy.[32] We simply need to cite, as an example, the most recent historical memory report that highlights the "geological faults" in the "construction of the nation," that is, the unresolved agrarian question, the chronic weakness of the state, deepening economic inequality, and the persistence of violence as a political recourse.[33] Colombia's social organizations and movements, leaders, and activists have offered proof of these "geological faults" by denouncing different forms of violence against them and their communities, as concrete evidence of anti-democratic practices. Leaders and representatives of right-wing political parties and socioeconomic sectors have reacted by celebrating a country of exuberant beauty, respect for the law, and national cohesion that has fallen victim to a "terrorist threat."[34] The latter discourse translated into the language of advertising in the slogan *Colombia es pasión* (Colombia is passion), and a nation-branding publicity campaign planned by the private sector that became corollary to Plan Colombia, the U.S.-financed counterinsurgent and anti-narcotics military initiative launched in 2000, and a key component of president Álvaro Uribe's Democratic Security (2002–2010), a state policy to save the country from the "youthful idealism" of a handful of revolutionaries.[35] Indeed, it was during the Uribe administration—while elsewhere in South America, the left was achieving important levels of legitimacy and winning election after election, in what later came to be known as "the pink tide"—that political radicalization in Colombia came to be seen as an archaic and colossal mistake.[36] More recently, when the Santos administration established peace talks with the FARC in Havana, Cuba, and especially after the signing of a peace agreement in 2016, the idea of "Colombia is passion" gained further traction under the new term of "post-conflict," a concept coined by a series of state-sponsored projects that promised a neoliberal future of peace and prosperity for a middle-class society, supported by extractivism and tourism.[37]

In short, the idea of a "Colombian paradox" and its multiple interpretations have reflected the power dynamics of the internal armed conflict. Whereas social movements led by victims of the war, and their allies in leftist organizations and parties, have emphasized the "vulgarity" of domination because it resonates with their lived experience, right-wing leaders and parties have weaponized the "properness of power" in their fight for the defense of their interests. In the end, the imaginary of Colombia as paradoxical—a unique and exceptional nation, violent and magic country, vibrant and conservative society—appears as hardwired in public opinion and common sense as it is fundamental in scholarship.[38] However, behind the many grains of truth in these interpretations, there lies a problem: the discourse of uniqueness bestows "apartness" in relation to Latin America and the world.[39] To paraphrase the famous words of our most celebrated author, Gabriel García Márquez, Colombia's exceptionalism is "the crux of our solitude."[40] Furthermore, our particularism ossifies democracy, making it a yardstick to be used in a transhistorical manner that quantifies how democratic or antidemocratic the country has been, usually in comparison with other places in the world.

As we explain in more detail in the introductions to both volumes, we have avoided tracing a sharp distinction between an ideal of democracy and its many realities to examine the mutual constitution, the continuum, the coexistence, the interplay, the tensions, and the conflicts between "vulgarity" and what is considered "proper" to move beyond the paradox. We thus unearth multiple histories of Colombia to illustrate the *abigarramiento* (motley reality) through which the definitions, structures, subjectivities, ideologies, technologies, institutions, and rationalities of living in a democracy, and what democracy is supposed to do, have been intensely fought over.[41] This pluralism should not be read as a reflection of Colombia's proverbial fragmentation but rather as an indication of the various struggles over the granular meanings and contested practices of democracy. We concur with truth commission and historical memory reports that have argued in recent years that Colombia's histories of violence are the result of disputes over power, not the manifestation of transcendental features of the country's ethos. Hence, we also pay attention to "some structural [forms of] violence whose connections with the armed conflict have been rendered invisible until recently: patriarchy, racism, multiple forms of discrimination based on class, regional origins, or ideological currents."[42] Notwithstanding, unlike those reports, we do not conjugate democracy in a conditional past tense—as in, had this ideal been achieved, no conflict or violence would have existed. Instead, we invite readers to de-idealize democracy and question it historically.

Motivations and Methods

Books are born from "an intense and pressing questioning that pushes oneself towards writing: not to say what one knows, but to try to know something," Cameroonian author Léonora Miano reminds us.[43] These volumes are no exception. They have been in the making for a long time, shaped by our own research agendas and professional trajectories, conditioned by how we have embodied and resisted the foundational narratives and silences that we question here, and organized according to our capacities to make sense of them in hindsight.

As children of the 1970s and 1980s, we the editors are members of a generation that witnessed the collapse of the dominant liberal consensus worldwide, and the beginning of a "tremendously ideologized era" in Colombia, after the end of the National Front.[44] I, Ricardo, was born, raised, and educated as a middle-class mestizo man in Bogotá, the country's capital. I, Lina, was born in Medellín and raised with a double regional identity, by a *paisa* mother and a *guajiro* father climbing their way into the middle class. By the time we were old enough to get a formal education, the "coffee republic" had metamorphosed into a cocaine powerhouse in a permanent state of war. However, at school, we learned *historia patria* (history of the fatherland), more specifically *la patria boba* (the foolish fatherland), a simplistic narrative about the first attempt at crafting a republic in the early nineteenth century, according to which meaningless fights between federalists and centralists and popular groups' political immaturity weakened the effort from within.[45] When we were teenagers, the cocaine cartels' brand of explosive violence dominated national life, yet at school, the *patria* was still *boba*. Although, a new historiography emerged under the name of Nueva Historia de Colombia (New History of Colombia) to introduce economic, social, and cultural approaches to the curriculum, private high schools insisted on patriotic accounts and avoided teaching recent history.[46] At the end, each detonated car bomb seemed to confirm that the history of the country was just a never-ending failed attempt at inventing a nation.[47]

If history felt static inside our classrooms, it was no stagnant outside school. Still too young to understand its depth, we witnessed a successful peace agreement between the government and the guerrilla group M19, which mandated writing a new constitution, and a movement of college students calling for a plebiscite to ratify it under the name of *séptima papeleta* (seventh ballot).[48] Despite the progressive new Constitution of 1991, *no futuro* (no future) was the vibe of our coming of age.[49] After the killing of cocaine kingpin Pablo Escobar on December 2, 1993, his former enemies took over Medellín's underworld and, using the political connections they had forged while hunting him down, financed paramilitary armies to vie for the control of the state.⁵⁰ Our youth coincided with their ferocious advance from Antioquia to the rest of the country where a scorched-earth war ensued against real and perceived guerrillas, whose exponential growth—as a result of the taxes guerrillas imposed on coca and cocaine production—made them indomitable enemies.⁵¹ I, Ricardo, found sources of inspiration and a formative experience in the Department of History at the Universidad Nacional de Colombia in Bogotá, by reviewing social histories from below, Marx and Freud, feminist theories and labor studies, writing on gender and labor relations for a student journal, learning sociology and anthropology, and developing my passion for the twentieth century. In the Department of Social Communication and Journalism in the Universidad Pontificia Bolivariana in Medellín, I, Lina, found that history classes at a private university sanctioned by the Vatican in the city where the paramilitary project originated were nothing but Eurocentric accounts of Western civilizations. Thus, I also enrolled in the Department of Anthropology at the Universidad de Antioquia, the city's main public university, and between the two worlds prepared myself for a year of fieldwork for an honors thesis on immersion journalism in the Darién rainforest on the Caribbean border with Panama. The daring curiosity of our youth and the vigorous cultural and artistic scenes that characterize Colombia were the lifesavers that helped us all survive a national cataclysm. "Nosotros de rumba y el mundo se derrumba" (we party and the world collapses) was the chorus of a punk-cumbia song by a rock band whose name poked fun at the Search Bloc created by the National Police to catch Escobar dead or alive. It soon became a motto for a generation that "luxuriating between cynicism and indifference" adjusted to the shipwreck the best we could.⁵² Traveling unexpected paths of despair and hope, we discovered our vocations and, ultimately, went into exile.

Knowing that the past matters for what it teaches us about the present, we left the country at the turn of the new millennium and began our lives inside an empire. By the time the world as we knew it came to an end with the 9/11 attacks, I, Ricardo, was a graduate student in Maryland learning that Colombians could not be true Colombianists because they lacked the neutrality necessary to produce objective knowledge. I, Lina, was part of the anonymous mass of immigrants working at restaurants in New York City, staring in shock from the rooftop of my apartment in Spanish Harlem at the mushroom cloud of dust, debris, and remains that arose from the Twin Towers. During the following decade, as we went through the taxing rite of passage of graduate school in the United States, we were introduced to a robust literature on Latin America and the Caribbean that considers the role of the dispossessed and destitute as historical actors in the formation of different countries in the region, making it possible for new interpretations about the nation, the state, citizenship, and democracy. Nevertheless, our country barely figured in our curricula. Furthermore, as we spent part of each year in Colombia conducting research for our doctoral dissertations—and witnessed the maturation of the Frankenstein of the War on Terror and the War on Drugs that Washington financed under Plan Colombia and beyond—we understood that the conspicuous absence of our country in the classroom transcended to the media. The confirmation that invisibility is the price to pay for being a repository of uncomfortable truths about U.S. power in the Americas has shaped our professional lives. As tenured professors in U.S. universities working on the transnational histories of illicit drugs and the middle classes, we now find ourselves racialized under the sweeping category of Latinx faculty.[53] However, no matter how important transnational approaches are in the current academic climate, or how diluted our national identities are in the ocean of diversity politics, Colombia is still our primary framework of inquiry. We have embraced such a realization as a constitutive aspect of our *destierro* (uprooting/exile), and with the modicum of safety and comfort that comes from our current class privileges, we have embarked on the collective effort of reclaiming our "multi-belonging" to recognize the centrality of our emotions, collective memories, lived experiences, and interpersonal and social relationships in the production of knowledge.[54]

What could the histories of Colombia explain about Latin America and the world, if anything at all? What does it mean to work on Colombia in an increasingly globalized planet? Who is entitled to tell the histories of Colombia? In a neoliberal society defined by a "carceral conception" of identity, these questions have led us to interrogate an assumption we have often encountered in our careers: the perceived hierarchical distinction between being a Colombianist and being a Colombian.[55] The former, a scholarly identification, is presumably the product of a metropolitan experience, a manifestation of an impersonal understanding of the country, since "perhaps only a foreigner could be so objective" as to comprehend our realities to explain them to an international audience.[56] The latter, a national identity, can only produce subjective and subordinated knowledge, accounts of raw experiences to be theorized and finalized by somebody else.[57] Some scholars, Colombianists themselves, would be quick to let us know that this distinction does not apply anymore, and we would partially agree with them. Since at least the 1990s, most historical and social science research on Colombia has been done by Colombians working in the country and elsewhere. Still, we wonder why those who are considered Colombianists get asked how their scholarly interest in the country emerged, while Colombian scholars are never asked such a question, as if our dedication to study Colombia were our only option, the natural consequence of our national identity.

To examine the imperial politics behind these hierarchies is beyond the pale of this preface.[58] We highlight them not to indict them or try to reverse them, but to reclaim a genealogy of collaborative research in (and on) Latin America in which Colombians have been protagonists, one that "sought to erase the subject-object distinction" and re-signify our craft "as a dialogue between equals."[59] As Colombian sociologist Orlando Fals Borda, "an important forebear" of this intellectual tradition, once wrote, "the commitment-action" during "transcendental political changes pushes [social] scientists to evaluate their discipline and reorient it."[60] Like Fals Borda and many others, we participate in networks that extend in all directions, South-North and South-South. In our particular case, we work in northern academic institutions while recognizing that the essence of our task is to struggle "agonistically and agonizingly, with and against humanism from within."[61] The production of knowledge on Colombia is a multi-situated practice that takes place in different geographical locations and its results ought to be discussed and criticized on equal terms across regional and national boundaries, regardless of the unequal material conditions within and across different academic universes.[62] This project is thus a collective effort among scholars to materialize a dialogue among multiple positionalities and interdisciplinary perspectives, to open up a space for contested forms of knowledge about the histories of Colombia.[63]

With this in mind, we embarked on the task of coediting two volumes despite these types of publications are strongly discouraged in the U.S. historiographical market. When it comes to tenure and promotion, they "count" significantly less, if at all, and they do not carry the same prestige as monographs, peer-reviewed journal articles, or special issues. However, in Colombia and in Latin America, edited volumes are still an important format to collect original points of view on a particular topic by multiple authors, under the leadership of one or several editors. Our project seeks to celebrate this type of sociability that is common to Latin America and exhibits the vitality of Colombian studies at home and abroad. Hence, we assessed the quality and merit of the different essays in a more social way. The collegial and rigorous peer-review process we undertook involved several stages. First, after reading all the works to provide meticulous comments, we the editors organized 11 virtual panels according to disciplinary similarities and topics, which eventually became the 11 sections for the two volumes. Motivated by the truncated project of Colombianist Michael Jiménez, who in the late 1990s was writing an essay titled "Colombia: The Latin American Paradigm," we invited renowned scholars working on similar themes on other places in the continent to engage in an open peer review of the essays in their designated panel.[64] This process became a week-long virtual conference full of lively discussions that helped the authors make final revisions and allowed us, the editors, to clarify overarching themes. Not taking for granted the assumption that critical knowledge is only possible as a result of double-blind reviewing procedures, we intend to set up an example on the importance of solidarity, friendship, and critical collegiality in academia.[65]

Another important methodological objective was to establish an intergenerational dialogue to avoid presenting "old works" as passé, while elevating recent scholarship as "pathbreaking." When production of knowledge is predicated upon the desires of a market that is driven by an individualized entrepreneurial spirit, scholars are inclined to assign newness to their arguments to become competitive in a contest over the ownership of ideas.[66] "Pioneering," "trailblazing," and other superlatives proliferate in prologues, blurbs, and reviews. Of course, we have participated in such trend, and it would be easy to continue the practice. But here our task has been to invite scholars at different stages of their careers to build upon the works of previous generations, and ultimately embrace a process of "reassertion and reformulation through evocation" of past and present scholarship.[67] In that spirit, the titles of each of two volumes—*Histories of Solitude* and *Histories of Perplexities*—evoke a conversation that Marco Palacios and Frank Safford had when they were crafting their coauthored book in the late 1990s, a collaboration between a Colombian and a Colombianist.[68] An anecdote between two seasoned historians who wanted to amuse each other with inside jokes inspired us to approach and unpack the canons through which Colombia has been read and interpreted in the world. Solitude, as Frantz Fanon conceptualized it from a historic-psychoanalytical perspective and Gabriel García Márquez popularized it in his literary work and Nobel Prize Lecture, is the emotional legacy of colonialism. Solitude is a residual sentiment that arises out of the invisibility of subaltern lives in the victorious narrative of the empire, a perceived state of isolation due to "a lack of conventional means to render our lives believable," the supposedly essence of Latin American and Caribbean modernity.[69] Perplexity, on the other hand, is a state of puzzlement and alienation that surfaces when one is confronted with deep changes or at an impasse, an "epistemic emotion" that can be either paralyzing or a catalyst for transformation.[70] Both terms encapsulate the sensibilities that historians and social scientists have to work through when looking for categories to decipher the realities of the postcolonial societies we seek to understand. It also condenses the spirit of our invitation to revisit major narratives of the histories of Colombia, that is, the "solitude" of nation-state formation that we examine in Volume 1, and the "perplexity" of the neoliberal turn that we study in Volume 2, in the hope of denaturalizing clichés and patterns of thinking and pushing ourselves out of our rut to ask new questions.

Histories of Solitude and *Histories of Perplexities* are histories of democracy in Colombia. To understand democracy as a multidimensional question rather than as a final answer, we looked for a plurality of voices and narratives. Therefore, we have replaced the concept of *Colombian history* for *histories of Colombia* to invite readers to think of the analyses contained in the chapters as reflections on universal questions and as descriptions of a reality belonging to a specific place. We also invited authors working on various disciplines, academic fields, regions, and topics, and who are based at institutions in Colombia, the United States, England, and Canada, public and private, big and small, from capital cities and more peripheral urban areas. In our search for variety, we have engaged in "the politics of translations" to question the assumption that knowledge produced in the Global North in English is by definition universal and applicable to any social reality, while the academic production from the Global South in any other language is particular and only pertinent to localized conditions.[71] Our aspiration is that our effort to translate into English research originally written in Spanish will contribute to a critical dialogue of divergent and contested knowledge(s) across regions in a "co-productivity of thinking."[72] The "necessary yet impossible effort" of translating worldviews, as Gayatri Spivak has argued, asked from us a more careful work alongside an editor of English as a Second Language (ESL) to make sure we kept nuances, subtleties, and idiomatic expressions alive.[73] Inspired in Ariel Dorfman's lifelong mission to raise awareness about the intrinsic connection between identity, language, and ideology, we practiced producing knowledge through difference rather than through the purification and domestication of language.[74]

Are the histories of Colombia a compass to the unknown? Do we need to find the future in the past? Colombian philosopher Estanislao Zuleta warned us about the risk of a "global doctrine that accounts for everything," one that presumably allows us to understand *colombianidad* (Colombianness).[75] Listening to him and those before us, we have been more interested in being provocative than authoritative. Ultimately, we have taken on this challenge as a double opportunity: to process our witnessing the fierce struggles and bloody conflicts among competing visions of democracy that have defined and redefined Colombia; and to foster a dialogue among a group of scholars breaking with the commonplaces used to narrate and analyze our pasts and presents, to tackle universal questions. The histories of Colombia contained herein seek to participate in the "planetary" discussion of ideas, realities, practices, and multifaceted taxonomies of what it means to live in a democracy, the worldliest question of all.[76]

xl *Preface*

Notes

1 David Bushnell, *The Making of Modern Colombia: A Nation in Spite of Itself* (Berkeley: University of California Press, 1993), vii. The translation to Spanish has several editions, each with a different preface by a different author. To our knowledge, the last one came out in 2021 with Crítica and a prologue by Álvaro Tirado Mejía.
2 For factors that explain this disparity, see Victoria Peralta and Michael LaRosa, *Los colombianistas: Una completa visión de los investigadores extranjeros que estudian Colombia* (Bogotá: Planeta, 1997), 16–17.
3 Pamela Murray, "Foreword" to Michael LaRosa and Germán Rodrigo Mejía Pavony, *Colombia: A Concise Contemporary History* (Lanham: Rowman & Littlefield, 2017), xiii.
4 For notable exceptions that analyze Colombia in a Latin American context or as part of transnational processes, see Catherine LeGrand, *Frontier Expansion and Peasant Protest in Colombia, 1850–1950* (Albuquerque: University of New Mexico Press, 1986); Ann Farnsworth-Alvear, *Dulcinea in the Factory: Myths, Morals, Men, and Women in Colombia's Industrial Experiment, 1905–1960* (Durham: Duke University Press, 2000); Mary Roldán, *Blood and Fire: La Violencia in Antioquia, Colombia, 1946–1953* (Durham: Duke University Press, 2002); Nancy Appelbaum, *Muddied Waters: Race, Region, and Local History in Colombia, 1846–1948* (Durham: Duke University Press, 2003); and Forrest Hylton, *Evil Hour in Colombia* (London: Verso, 2006).
5 Jenny Pearce, *Colombia Inside the Labyrinth* (London: Latin America Bureau, 1990), 207; Javier Almario, "Colombia: The Genesis of the World's First Narco-Democracy," *Executive Intelligence Review* 9, no. 30 (1992): 41–42; John Sweeney, "Colombia's Narco-Democracy Threatens Hemispheric Security," *The Heritage Foundation Backgrounder*, no. 1028 (March 21, 1995); Marco Palacios, *Between Legitimacy and Violence: A History of Colombia, 1875–2002* (Durham: Duke University Press, 2006), 228; Rubén Jaramillo Vélez, *Colombia: La modernidad postergada* (Bogotá: Editorial Temis, 1998), 3–50; Sergio Zubiría Samper, "Dimensiones políticas y culturales en el conflicto colombiano," in *Contribuciones al entendimiento del conflicto armado en Colombia*, ed. Comisión Histórica del Conflicto y sus Víctimas, CHCV (Bogotá: Ediciones Desde Abajo, 2015), 230; Ricardo Arias Trujillo, *Historia de Colombia contemporánea, 1920–2010* (Bogotá: Universidad de los Andes, 2019), 120; LaRosa and Mejía Pavony, *Colombia*; Juan Guillermo Gómez, *Colombia es una cosa impenetrable: Raíces de la intolerancia y otros ensayos sobre historia política y vida intelectual* (Medellín: Diente de León, 2006); Victoria Kellaway and Sergio J. Liévano, *Colombia: A Comedy of Errors* (Independently Published, 2020); Juanita León, *Country of Bullets: Chronicles of War* (Albuquerque: University of New Mexico Press, 2009); Sandra Borda, *¿Por qué somos tan parroquiales?: Una breve historia internacional de Colombia* (Bogotá: Crítica, 2019).
6 Arundhati Roy, *Field Notes on Democracy: Listening to Grasshoppers* (Chicago: Haymarket Books, 2009), 2.
7 Nancy MacLean, *Democracy in Chains: The Deep History of the Radical Right's Stealth Plan for America* (New York: Penguin Books, 2017), xxxiv.
8 Michel-Rolph Trouillot, *Silencing the Past: Power and the Production of History* (New York: Beacon Press, 1995), 70–107.

9 Julia Paley, "Introduction," in *Democracy: Anthropological Approaches,* ed. Julia Paley (Santa Fe: School of Advance Research Press, 2008), 3–20.
10 For a critique of teleological narratives, see A. Ricardo López-Pedreros with Barbara Weinstein, "We Shall Be All," in *The Making of the Middle Class: Toward a Transnational History,* eds. A. Ricardo López-Pedreros and Barbara Weinstein (Durham: Duke University Press), 1–11. For democracy as a "gift," see Chakrabarty who advocates for the provincialization of Europe in an "anticolonial spirit of gratitude"; see Dipesh Chakrabarty, *Provincializing Europe: Postcolonial Thought and Historical Difference* (Princeton: Princeton University Press, 2008), 255.
11 For mimesis and transplantation, see Manu Goswami, "The Modular Nation Form: Toward a Sociohistorical Conception of Nationalism," *Comparative Studies in Society and History* 44, no. 4 (October 2002): 770–799; for deviation, failure, and derivative, see Paley, "Introduction."
12 Good examples of this criticism are collected in Julia Paley, ed., *Democracy: Anthropological Approaches* (Santa Fe: School of Advance Research Press, 2008).
13 Patrick Riordan, "Crisis of Democracy: Practice and Theory," *An Irish Quarterly Review* 106, no. 423 (Autumn 2017): 298–307; see also Laura Alejandra Buenaventura Gómez, Andrés Jiménez Ángel, and Sven Schuster, *Colombia conectada: El "Tibet" de Sudamérica" en perspectiva global, siglos XIX y XX* (Bogotá: Universidad del Rosario, 2023). The task is not only to include Colombia into a global history paradigm but also to question the global histories of democracy by interrogating the histories of Colombia.
14 María Teresa Uribe de Hincapié, *Nación, ciudadano y soberano* (Medellín: Corporación Región, 2001), 129.
15 Walter Mignolo and Catherine E. Walsh, *On Decoloniality: Concepts, Analytics, Praxis* (Durham: Duke University Press, 2018). We find the call to return to the historical archive by Luciana Cadahia and Valeria Coronel important to historicize democracy in Latin America; see Luciana Cadahia and Valeria Cornel "Volver al archivo: De las fantasías decoloniales a la imaginación republicana," in *Teorías de la república y prácticas republicanas,* ed. Macarena Marey (Barcelona: Herder, Colleción Contrapunto, 2021), 59–98. See also Pablo González Casanova, *Explotación, colonialismo y lucha por la democracia en América Latina* (CDMX: Ediciones Akal, 2013).
16 For the relevance of Barrington Moore's *Social Origins of Dictatorship and Democracy* (1966) in Latin America, see Evelyn Huber and Frank Safford, eds., *Agrarian Structure and Political Power: Landlord and Peasant in the Making of Latin America* (Pittsburgh: University of Pittsburgh Press, 1995).
17 Geoff Eley, *Forging Democracy: The Left and the Struggle for Democracy in Europe, 1850–2000* (Oxford: Oxford University Press, 2002), 4. See also Paley, ed., *Democracy*; Greg Grandin, *The Last Colonial Massacre: Latin America in the Cold War* (Chicago: The University of Chicago Press, 2011); Greg Grandin, *Empire's Workshop: Latin America, the United States, and the Rise of New Imperialism* (New York: Holt, Henry & Company, 2007); and Breny Mendoza, *Colonialidad, género y democracia* (Madrid: Akal, 2023).
18 Wendy Brown, *Politics Out of History* (Princeton: Princeton University Press, 2001).
19 Trouillot, *Silencing the Past,* 82. For Walter Benjamin's idea of "suppressed dimensions of past struggles," see Goswami, "The Modular Nation Form," 781–782.

20 Indira A. R. Lakshmanan, "Colombia Sets an Example for Peace and Reconciliation," *The Boston Globe*, September 29, 2016.
21 For "vulgarity," see Michael-Rolph Trouillot, "The Vulgarity of Power," in *Trouillot Remixed*, eds. Yarimar Bonilla, Greg Beckett, and Mayanthi L. Fernando (Durham: Duke University Press, 2021), 97–102; and Achille Mbembe "The Banality of Power and the Aesthetics of Vulgarity in the Postcolony," translated by Janet Roitman, *Public Culture* 4, no. 2 (1992): 1–30. For the notion of "properness," see A. Ricardo López-Pedreros, *Makers of Democracy: A Transnational History of the Middle Classes in Colombia* (Durham: Duke University Press, 2019).
22 For the quote, see Murray, "Foreword," xiv. For Colombia as a vibrant society, see also Álvaro Tirado Mejía, "Presentación," in Bushnell, *Colombia*, 11–14; Ann Farnsworth-Alvear, Marco Palacios, and Ana María Gómez López, eds., *The Colombian Reader: History, Culture, Politics* (Durham: Duke University Press, 2017), 8–9; Jorge Orlando Melo, *Colombia. Una historia mínima: Una mirada integral al país* (Bogotá: Crítica, 2021), 383–384; Rob Karl, *Forgotten Peace: Reform, Violence, and the Making of Contemporary Colombia* (Oakland: University of California Press, 2017); LaRosa and Mejía Pavony, *Colombia*; and Harvey Kline, *Colombia: Democracy under Assault* (London: Routledge, 2020).
23 Rex A. Hudson, *Colombia: A Country Study* (Washington, DC: Federal Research Division, Library of Congress, 2010), li.
24 James Henderson, *Modernization in Colombia: The Laureano Gómez Years, 1889–1965* (Gainesville: University of Florida Press, 2001); Eduardo Posada Carbó, *La nación soñada: Violencia, liberalismo y democracia en Colombia* (Bogotá: Grupo Editorial Norma, 2007); Malcom Deas, *Del poder y la gramática: Y otros ensayos sobre historia, política y literatura colombianas* (Bogotá: Taurus, 2006); Carlos Caballero Argáez, Mónica Pachón Buitrago, and Eduardo Posada Carbó, eds., *Cincuenta años del regreso a la democracia: Nuevas miradas a la relevancia histórica del Frente Nacional* (Bogotá: Universidad de los Andes, 2012); Pablo Jiménez Burillo, Eduardo Posada Carbó, Jorge Orlando Melo, and Alejandro Gaviria, *La búsqueda de la democracia, 1960–2010* (Madrid: Taurus, 2015).
25 LaRosa and Mejía Pavony, *Colombia*, 218.
26 Antonio García, "Las clases medias y la frustración del Estado representativo en América Latina," *Cuadernos Americanos* 1 (January–February 1967): 37–38. See also Palacios, *Between Legitimacy and Violence*, 180; Amparo Murillo Posada, "La modernización y las violencias," in *Historia de Colombia: Todo lo que hay que saber*, ed. Luis Enrique Rodríguez Baquero et al. (Bogotá: Editorial Taurus, 2007), 278; Fernán González, *Poder y violencia en Colombia* (Bogotá: CINEP, 2014), 324; Álvaro Tirado Mejía, *Los años 60: Una revolución en la cultura* (Bogotá: Debate, 2014); Centro Nacional de Memoria Histórica, *Basta Ya! Colombia: Memories of War and Dignity* (Bogotá: CNMH, 2013); Fernando Guillén Martínez, *El poder político en Colombia* (Bogotá: Planeta, [1979] 1996), 445–469; Zubiría Samper, "Dimensiones políticas y culturales en el conflicto colombiano," 224–230 in *Contribuciones*; María Clemencia Ramírez, "Maintaining Democracy in Colombia through Political Exclusion, States of Exception, Counterinsurgency, and Dirty War," in *Violent Democracies in Latin America*, eds. Enrique Desmod Arias and Daniel M. Goldstein (Durham: Duke University Press, 2010), 84–107; Hylton, *Evil Hour*; Hernando Gómez Buendía, "Décalogo para entender este país," *El Malpensante*, no. 125

(Noviembre 2011); Malcom Deas, *Intercambios violentos y dos ensayos más sobre el conflicto en Colombia* (Bogotá: Taurus, 2015), 108–109.
27 Bushnell, *The Making of Modern Colombia*, 284–285. See also Daniel Pécaut, *Crónica de dos décadas de política colombiana, 1968–1988* (Bogotá: Siglo Veintiuno Editores, 1989); and James A. Robinson, "Another 100 Years of Solitude," *Current History* (February 2013): 43–48; Renán Vega Cantor, *La oligarquía colombiana: Una belicosa marioneta del Tío Sam* (Bogotá: Teoría and Praxis, 2022).
28 Philip McLean, "Colombia: Failed, Failing or Just Weak?" *The Washington Quarterly* 25, no. 3 (Summer 2002): 123–134; and James A. Robinson, "La miseria en Colombia," *Desarrollo & Sociedad* 76 (January–June 2016): 9–88.
29 Palacios, *Between Legitimacy and Violence*; Francisco Gutiérrez, *El orangután con sacoleva: Cien años de democracia y represión en Colombia, 1910–2010* (Bogotá: Debate, 2013); Jennifer S. Holmes, Sheila Amin Gutiérrez de Piñeres, and Kevin M. Curtin, *Guns, Drugs and Development in Colombia* (Austin: University of Texas Press, 2009); and Hernando Gómez Buendía, *Entre la independencia y la pandemia: La guerra más larga del mundo y la historia no contada de un país en construcción* (Bogotá: Fundación Razón Pública y Rey Naranjo Editores, 2021).
30 Marco Palacios and Frank Safford, *Colombia: Fragmented Land, Divided Society* (Oxford: Oxford University Press, 2001); and Charles Bergquist, Ricardo Peñaranda, and Gonzalo Sánchez, eds., *Violence in Colombia: The Contemporary Crisis in Historical Perspective* (Wilmington: Scholarly Resources, 1992)
31 Jefferson Jaramillo, *Pasados y presentes de la violencia en Colombia: Estudio sobre las comisiones de investigación, 1958–2001* (Bogotá: Editorial Pontificia Universidad Javeriana, 2014).
32 Take as examples CNMH, *¡Basta ya!*; CHCV, *Contribución al entendimiento del conflicto armado en Colombia* (Bogotá: Ediciones Desde Abajo, 2015); and Comisión para el Esclarecimiento de la Verdad, la Convivencia y la No Repetición, *Hay futuro si hay verdad* (Bogotá: CEV, 2022). For truth commission reports and the problem of "historical truth" in Latin America, see Greg Grandin, "The Instruction of Great Catastrophe: Truth Commissions, National History and State Formation in Argentina, Chile and Guatemala,"*The American Historical Review* 110, no. 1 (February 2005): 46–67.
33 Comisión para el Esclarecimiento de la Verdad, la Convivencia y la No Repetición, *No matarás* (Bogotá: CEV, 2022), 6. Because authors have used a variety of terminology, such as "factors" (Molano, 1), "knots" (Wills, 1), "triggers" (Fajardo, 3), and "multiplicity of causes" (de Zubiría, 4), the metaphor of "geological faults" served as lingua franca. The term is taken from an analysis of Chile's dictatorship; see Eduardo Pizarro Leongómez, "Una lectura múltiple y plural de la historia" in *Contribución al entendimiento*, 20; and Raúl Urzúa y Felipe Agüero, eds., *Fracturas en la gobernabilidad democrática* (Santiago de Chile: Universidad de Chile, 1998). Notice that the introduction to *Hay futuro si hay verdad* picks up the concept of "geological faults." See also Gómez Buendía, *Entre la independencia y la pandemia*.
34 Posada Carbó, *La nación soñada*; Isidro Vanegas Useche, *Todas son iguales: Estudios sobre la democracia en Colombia* (Bogotá: Universidad Externado de Colombia, 2011); and Jonnathan Jiménez, Juan Sebastián Bernal, David Leonardo Carmona, "La amenaza terrorista en el postconflicto" in *Políticas públicas de seguridad y defensa: Herramientas en el marco del postconflicto en Colombia*

eds., Carlos Alberto Ardila Castro and Vicente Torrijos Rivera (Bogotá: Libros Escuela Superior de Guerra, 2017). For popular literature, see Luis Alfonso Plazas Vega, ¿Desaparecidos? El negocio del dolor (Bogotá: Dipon, 2011); and Fernando Londoño Hoyos, Con licencia para hablar (Bogotá: Penguin Random House, 2004).

35 For advertising in Colombia's armed conflict, see Alexander L. Fattal, *Guerrilla Marketing: Counterinsurgency and Capitalism in Colombia* (University of Chicago Press, 2018). For "Colombia es pasión," see Lina María Echeverri, Eduardo J. Rosker, and Martha Lucía Márquez Restrepo, "Los orígenes de la marca país Colombia es pasión," *Estudios y perspectivas en turismo* 19, no. 3 (2010): 409–421. For Plan Colombia, see Eduardo Pizano, *Plan Colombia: The View from the Presidential Palace* (Carlisle: Strategic Studies Institute of the U.S. Army War College, 2001); Forrest Hylton, "Plan Colombia: The Measure of Success," *The Brown Journal of World Affairs* 17, no. 1 (Fall 2010): 99–115; and Jonathan Rosen, *The Losing War: Plan Colombia and Beyond* (Albany: SUNY Press, 2014). For Uribe's Democratic Security, see Pablo Emilio Angarita Cañas, *Seguridad Democrática: Lo invisible de un régimen político y económico* (Bogotá: Siglo del Hombre Editores, 2011); and Neyla G. Pardo, "The dual causes of fragmentation: Democratic Security and the Communitarian State in Colombian Politics," *Discourse & Society* 31, no. 1 (2020): 64–84. For armed struggle in Colombia as "youthful idealism," see Gustavo Duncan, "Exclusión, insurrección y crimen," in *Contribución al entendimiento*, 7–8; and Jorge Giraldo Ramírez, "Política y guerra sin compasión," in *Contribución al entendimiento*. For armed struggle in Latin America as failed romanticism, see John Beverly, *The Failure of Latin America: Postcolonialism in Bad Times* (Pittsburgh: University of Pittsburgh Press, 2019), 134–136; and Grandin, *Last Colonial Massacre*, 15.

36 For "the pink tide," see Steve Ellner, ed. *Latin America's Pink Tide: Breakthroughs and Shortcomings* (New York: Rowman and Littlefield, 2020).

37 For "post-conflict" as a problem of transformation of the rules on the use of violence rather than as a moment of peace, see Manuela Trindade Viana, *Post-conflict Colombia and the Global Circulation of Military Expertise* (Gewerbestrasse: Palgrave Macmillan, 2022). For extractivism and tourism, see Diana Ojeda and Eloísa Berman-Arévalo, "Ordinary Geographies: Care, Violence, and Agrarian Extractivism in 'Post-Conflict' Colombia," *Antipode* 52, no. 6 (2020): 1583–1602; and Diana Ojeda, "War and Tourism: The Banal Geographies of Security in Colombia's 'Retaking'," *Geopolitics* 18, no. 4 (2013): 759–778.

38 It is this uniqueness that recently gets mobilized as a gerund—*colombiando* (colombianizing)—to describe paradoxical realities. In this case, a country uniquely characterized by violence and magic features. See, for example, Eduardo Galeano, *Colombiando: Palabras sentipensantes sobre un país violento y mágico* (Bogotá: CEPA Editores, 2016). Since the beginning of the century pundits across the Americas has coined the term colombianization, as a manifestation of a drug-related violence, presumably a Colombian reality, to justify multiple situations of violence elsewhere. For a critique of these discourses, see Teo Ballvé and Kendra McSweeney, "The 'Colombianisation' of Central America: Misconceptions, Mischaracterisations and the Military-Agroindustrial Complex," *Journal of Latin American Studies* 52, no. 4 (2020): 805–829.

39 For "apartness" and uniqueness in historical interpretations, see Michel-Rolph Trouillot, "The Odd and the Ordinary: Haiti, the Caribbean and the World," in *Trouillot Remixed*, 85.
40 Gabriel García Márquez, *The Solitude of Latin America*, Nobel Lecture, December 8, 1982. www.nobelprize.org/prizes/literature/1982/marquez/lecture/
41 For *abigarramiento*, see René Zavaleta Mercado, translated by Anne Freeland, *Towards a History of the National-Popular in Bolivia, 1879–1980* (Calcutta: Seagull Books, 2018). In this book, *abigarramiento* is translated as motleyness. We prefer motley reality. See also Sinclair Thomson, "Self-Knowledge and Self-Determination at the Limits of Capitalism" in Zavaleta Mercado, *Towards a History of the National-Popular in Bolivia*, xxiii.
42 CEV, *No Matarás*, 9.
43 Léonora Miano, *Vivir en la frontera* (Madrid: Los libros de la catarata, 2016), 65. Our translation.
44 César Augusto Ayala Diago, "Colombia en la década de los años setenta del siglo XX," *Anuario Colombiano de Historia Social y de la Cultura* 30 (2003): 319–338, 326. See also Bruce J. Schulman, *The Seventies: The Great Shift in American Culture, Society and Politics* (Cambridge: Da Capo Press, 2001); "AHR Conversations: Each Generation Writes Its Own History of Generations," *The American Historical Review* 123, no. 5 (December 2018): 1505–1546; Bobby Duffy, *The Generation Myth: Why When You're Born Matters Less than You Think* (New York: Basic Books, 2021); and Stephen Katz, "Generation X: A Critical Sociological Perspective," *Generations, Journal of the American Society of Aging* 41, no. 3 (Fall 2017): 12–19.
45 On *la patria boba*, see Indalecio Liévano Aguirre, *Los grandes conflictos sociales y económicos de nuestra historia*, Vols. 1 and 2 (Bogotá: Imprenta Nacional, 1996 [1960, 1966]).
46 Diego H. Arias Gómez, "Pasado cercano de la enseñanza de la historia reciente en Colombia: Los ochenta y noventa del siglo XX" in *Pasados violentos en la enseñanza de la historia y las ciencias sociales: Colombia, Argentina y Chile*, eds. Diego H. Arias Gómez, Sandra Patricia Rodríguez Ávila, María Paula González, and Graciela Rubio (Bogotá: Editorial Universidad del Rosario, 2022).
47 On Nueva Historia de Colombia, see Ayala Diago, "Colombia en la década de los años setenta del siglo XX," 330–331.
48 Ricardo Zuluaga Gil, *De la expectativa al desconcierto: El proceso constituyente de 1991 visto por sus protagonistas* (Bogotá: Editorial Universidad Pontificia Javeriana, 2006).
49 Héctor D. Fernández L'Hoeste, "Rodrigo D. No Futuro by Víctor Gaviria and Focine," *Film Quarterly* 48, no. 2 (Winter 1994–1995): 48–51; and Erna von der Walde, "La novela de sicarios y la violencia en Colombia," *Iberoamericana* 1, no. 3 (2001): 27–40.
50 Gustavo Duncan, *Los señores de la guerra: De paramilitares, mafiosos y autodefensas en Colombia* (Bogotá: Debate and Penguin Random House Grupo Editorial, 2015); and Gustavo Duncan, *Más que plata o plomo: El poder político del narcotráfico en Colombia y México* (Bogotá: Debate, 2014).
51 Charles Bergquist, Gonzalo Sánchez, and Ricardo Peñaranda, eds., *Violence in Colombia, 1990–2000: Waging War and Negotiating Peace* (Wilmington: Rowman & Littlefield Publishers, 2001).
52 Lina Britto, "Generation War," *NACLA. Report of the Americas*, October 18, 2016. For punk-rock-cumbia band Bloque de Búsqueda (Search Bloc) see

Héctor Fernández L'Hoeste, "On How Bloque de Búsqueda Lost Part of Its Name: The Predicament of Colombian Rock in the U.S. Market" in *Rockin' Las Américas: The Global Politics of Rock in Latin/o America*, eds. Deborah Pacini Hernandez, Héctor Fernández L'Hoeste and Eric Zolov (Pittsburgh: University of Pittsburgh Press, 2004).

53 Nana Osei-Kofi, "Junior Faculty of Color in the Corporate University: Implications of Neoliberalism and Neoconservatism on Research, Teaching and Service" and Denise Sekaquaptewa "On Being the Solo Faculty Member of Color: Research Evidence from Field and Laboratory Studies," in *The Truly Diverse Faculty: New Dialogues in American Higher Education*, eds. Stephanie A. Fryberg and Ernesto Javier Martínez (New York: Palgrave Macmillan, 2014); Sarah Ahmed, *On Being Included: Racism and Diversity in Institutional Life* (Durham: Duke University Press, 2012), 51–82; and Raymond V. Padilla and Rudolfo Chávez Chávez, *The Leaning Ivory Tower: Latino Professors in American Universities* (Albany: SUNY Press, 1995).

54 Miano, *Vivir la frontera*, 48.

55 Achille Mbembe, *Critique of Black Reason* (Durham: Duke University Press, 2017), 157.

56 Harvey Kline, "Review of *Violence, Conflict, and Politics in Colombia* by Paul Oquist," *The Journal of Politics* 44, no. 1 (February 1982): 282–283, 283.

57 For example, Peralta and LaRosa, *Colombianistas*, only features foreign researchers. For a different perspective in tune with what we argue here, see Jonathan Andrés Montoya Correa, "¿Profesión? ¡Colombianistas!," *El Efaitense*, no. 109 (2015-2): 168–173.

58 For a critique of the political economy of knowledge production, see Silvia Rivera Cusicanqui, "Ch'ixinakax utxiwa: A Reflection on the Practices and Discourses of Decolonization," *South Atlantic Quarterly* 111, no. 1 (2013): 95–109.

59 Joanne Rappaport, *Cowards Don't Make History: Orlando Fals Borda and the Origins of Participatory Action Research* (Durham: Duke University Press, 2020), 7–8.

60 For "forebear," see Rappaport, *Cowards Don't Make History*, 10; for Fals Borda's words, see Orlando Fals Borda, *Ciencia propia y colonialismo intelectual* (Bogotá: Editorial Nuestro Tiempo, 1970), 75.

61 Anthony Charles Alessandrini, *Frantz Fanon and the Future of Cultural Politics: Finding Something Different* (London: Lexington Books, 2014), 73.

62 For the notion of multi-situated knowledge and intersectionality, see Mara Viveros Vigoya, "La interseccionalidad: Una aproximación situada a la dominación," *Debate Feminista* 52 (December 2016): 1–17; Rivera Cusicanqui, "Ch'ixinakax utxiwa;" Carola Dietze, "Toward a History on Equal Terms: A Discussion of Provincializing Europe," *History and Theory* 47 (2008): 69–84.

63 Mauricio Archila, Zohanny Arboleda, Sergio Coronado, Tatiana Cuenca, Martha Cecilia García, and Luis Emiro Guariyú, *"Hasta cuando soñemos": Extractivismo e interculturalidad en el sur de La Guajira* (Bogotá: CINEP, 2015).

64 Peralta and LaRosa, *Colombianistas*, 203.

65 Nathan F. Alleman, Cara Cliburn Allen, and Don Haviland, "Collegiality and the Collegium in an Era of Faculty Differentiation," *ASHE Higher Education Report* 43, no. 4 (2017): 7–122; Jolanta Bieliauskaité, "Solidarity in Academia and its Relationship to Academic Integrity," *Journal of Academic Ethics* 19 (2021): 309–322; Diane (DeDe) Dawson, Esteban Morales, Erin McKiernan, Lesley A. Schimanski, Meredith T. Niles, and Juan Pablo Alperin, "The Role of

Collegiality in Academic Review, Promotion and Tenure," *PLoS ONE* 17, no. 4 (2022): e0265506.
66 Alpesh Maisuria and Sveja Helmses, *Life for the Academic in the Neoliberal University* (New York: Routledge, 2000).
67 Lewis R. Gordon, *What Fanon Said: A Philosophical Introduction to his life and Thought* (New York: Fordham University Press, 2015), 112.
68 As it was told by Frank Safford to Peralta and LaRosa, *Colombianistas*, 169.
69 Frantz Fanon, *Black Skins, White Masks* (New York: Grove Press, 2017 [1952]); and García Márquez, "The Solitude of Latin America."
70 Helen de Cruz, "Perplexity and Philosophical Progress," *Midwest Studies in Philosophy* 45 (2021): 209–221.
71 Sonia Álvarez, "Introduction to the Project and the Volume/enacting a Translocal Feminist Politics of Translation," in *Translocalities/Translocalidades: Feminist Politics of Translation in the Latin-a Américas*, eds. Sonia Álvarez, Claudia de Lima Costa, Verónica Feliu, Rebecca Hester, Norma Klahn, and Millie Thayer with Cruz C. Bueno (Durham: Duke University Press, 2014), 2. See also Kiran Asher, "Spivak and Rivera Cusicanqui on the Dilemmas of Representation in Post-Colonial and Decolonial Feminism," *Feminist Studies* 43, no. 3 (2017): 512–524.
72 Emily Apter, "Forward" to *Gayatri Chakravorty Spivak Living Translation*, eds. Emili Apter, Avishek Ganguly, Mauro Pala, and Surya Parekh (London: Seagull Books, 2022), viii.
73 Apter et al., *Living Translation*, 157.
74 Ariel Dorfman, "If Only We All Spoke Two Languages," *The New York Times*, June 24, 1998; Ariel Dorfman, *Heading South, Looking North: A Bilingual Journey* (New York: Penguin Books, 1999); Ariel Dorfman, "The Nomads of Language," *The American Scholar* 71, no. 1 (Winter 2002): 89–94.
75 Estanislao Zuleta, *Elogio a la dificultad y otros ensayos* (Bogotá: Ariel, 2020), 16.
76 For "planetary imaginings" on democracy, see Gayatri Spivak, *An Aesthetic Education in the Era of Globalization* (Cambridge: Harvard University Press, 2012), 335–350.

Introduction
Histories of Perplexity

Lina Britto and A. Ricardo López-Pedreros

Volume two, *Histories of Perplexity*, experiments with the possibility of not only telling different stories about Colombia but also telling stories differently.[1] As historians, we believe that it is impossible to write histories of the present without being in close conversation with colleagues from other disciplines. Thus, this volume fully embraces inter- and multi-disciplinary approaches to examine the last quarter of the twentieth century and first decades of the new millennium when national life transformed in unexpected ways after the two-party system came to a definite end; the neoliberal agenda reshaped the economy, politics, and society; illicit drug export economies consolidated; and the internal armed conflict intensified. In close conversation with the preface to both volumes, this introduction identifies main historiographical problematizations to highlight the contributions made by the authors featured herein on the histories of democracy since the 1970s. Furthermore, as it was the case with volume one, *Histories of Solitude*, we implement what Jacques Rancière calls an "ontological indeterminacy" between histories and theories to explore how historical realities invite us to embrace new theoretical approaches, and how these theoretical approaches call upon us to see historical realities under a different light.[2]

In the past half a century, Colombia has been conceptualized as a singularity, a "failed nation," and a "failed state" that has little to teach beyond serving as a cautionary tale. Thus, the opening chapter tackles the production of knowledge paradigms behind assumptions that Colombia and similar countries have a limited—nonuniversal—relevance beyond a localized place of enunciation.[3] In the first of the two conversations included in this volume, philosopher, sociologist, and political scientist William Mina offers an excerpt of a longer interview he conducted with legendary intellectual Manuel Zapata Olivella in 2001, in which they call for a versatile understanding of the multiple forms of power relations delineating the history of the world and the Americas. Zapata Olivella shares his philosophy and experience as an Afro-Colombian man who is predestined to be seen

DOI: 10.4324/9781003048152-1

and understood in relation to his "terminal identity" and local reality.⁴ In conversation with Mina—and by reviewing his multidisciplinary works in anthropology, history, literature, cultural criticism, journalism, theater, and screenwriting—Zapata Olivella breaks the mold by reclaiming a universal aspiration and a "vagabond" or "wandering" identity in constant search for inspiration locally and internationally.⁵ He thus seeks to understand how the world is an integrated unity, defined simultaneously by differences and numerous hierarchies resulting from historical exploitation. An Afrodiasporic humanist, Zapata Olivella engages with African diaspora literature, Black Atlantic thought, Caribbean theories of modernity, liberation philosophies, and uses Spanish, the language of the colonizers, as a tool of resistance. In so doing, Zapata Olivella models how to embrace an *abigarrada*—motley—reality, imagines a different humanity, and materializes an alternative conception of freedom other than the individualistic version of the dominant Western epistemology.

Zapata Olivella's courage and creativity in asking big questions about our globalized societies inspire us to interpret *Histories of Perplexity* as a critique of what it means to live under neoliberalism, even if Colombia remains the subject of our inquiry. Scholars have explained the origins of neoliberalism in Latin America as the product of "shock therapies."⁶ Neoliberalism, they argue, was a policy crafted by U.S.-trained economists and first implemented as a political project by Latin American military regimes, thanks to the capitulation of national elites, and used since then by governments as a facade for anti-democratic practices.⁷ Because scholars tend to see neoliberalism as an imperial imposition, or at least as a calculated strategy created through international institutions and ideas, disseminated globally from Europe and the United States, the origin story sounds like a "master plan," as Marta Isabel Domínguez calls it in her chapter.⁸ Therefore, the only options left for Latin American societies seem to be either to embrace it or effusively reject it.⁹ Equally polarized are the historical interpretations about neoliberalism's endurance. Some scholars have explained the crystallization of a neoliberal democracy in terms of its capacity to provide the conditions to overcome the interventionist state that limited economic freedom in market-driven societies.¹⁰ Others rationalize its longevity in ideological terms, that is, neoliberalism's power to advance the interests of transnational financial elites as they created a "supranational state" capable of inoculating "capitalism against the threat of democracy" from below.¹¹ As James Ferguson said, scholars have become accustomed

> to a debate pitting triumphalist accounts of the global spread of 'free market' capitalism (decreeing the end of history or telling us the world is flat) against critical accounts of that same ascendancy that tell a formally similar story but with the moral polarity inverted.¹²

In the process, we have produced an "enduring episteme."[13]

In the case of Colombia, most interpretations of neoliberalism explain its dominance in terms of its malleability for renewing oligarchical rule.[14] Recent works have demonstrated that Colombian policymakers and economists, like everywhere else across the Americas, selectively "sorted out" the economic functions, resources, and practices that could work for a neoliberal society during the overarching crisis of the 1970s, before dismantling the active role of the state to promote industrialization, development, and modernization.[15] These studies thus rescue the agency of national elites and demonstrate how neoliberalism was not a complete break with the past nor an imposition from abroad, but the political product of the continued consolidation of a "mixed economy" and the result of local initiatives to address national needs.[16] *Histories of Perplexity* builds upon this new literature to explore some overlooked questions about the making of this political economy and rationality, predicated on the belief that democratic well-being is best achieved through entrepreneurial efforts, private property rights, everyday financialization, and deregularized state functions.[17] First, how has neoliberalism sheltered a degree of legitimacy and consent to become the main source of inspiration to organize societies? Second, how has a neoliberal democracy, which works as a dictatorship of capital rooted in an intersectional diversity of hierarchies and founded on vast material inequalities, been produced, reproduced, and sustained? And last, what are the multiple and fragmented social foundations of neoliberalism as a system of domination?

Using interdisciplinary and historically grounded approaches, ethnographic research, and discourse analyses, *Histories of Perplexity* brings to light a multiplicity of actors whose alternative definitions of democracy have been disregarded for being *inauditas* (unheard-of and inadmissible), as María del Rosario Acosta López argues in her chapter, and thus targeted with violence.[18] Part 1 of this volume, Identifying Multiculturalism, expands on the themes introduced by the conversation between William Mina and Manuel Zapata Olivella to underline some of the racialized discourses and social practices in the workings of neoliberalism and its efforts to reorganize political identifications, reconfigure different notions of cultural difference, reshape multiple senses of community belonging, and promote new ways of thinking about the role of Colombia in the world. The four chapters in this part question the teleological narrative according to which there was a clear-cut transition between the mid-century developmentalist state that promoted mestizaje as a national identity and the multicultural neoliberal nation of the last quarter of the century. Whereas the conversation between Mina and Zapata Olivella revisits the tension between Blackness and mestizaje, in the next chapter, anthropologist Mara Viveros Vigoya further scrutinizes the critique of neoliberal multiculturalism through detailed biographical accounts of Afro-Colombian men and women.[19] Viveros Vigoya argues that since the late 1980s, when the Colombian neoliberal state gave greater recognition to multiculturality and multiethnicity in response to pressure from social movements, middle-class professionals have been able to reclaim their Black identities to achieve certain level of upward mobility, or "become someone," in neoliberal parlance. But possibilities were predicated upon the expansion of class hierarchies between a privileged minority and most of the country's Black population. Viveros Vigoya concludes that by making upward mobility possible for some Afro-Colombians, who later became "agents of neoliberal capitalism," multiculturalism has attained a degree of consent, while concurrently reinforcing various forms of structural racism, material inequalities, and economic precarity.

The next two chapters continue exploring how multiculturalism is not merely an act of camouflage to disguise the realities of neoliberalization but a common "language of contention" used by various actors when engaging with the state.[20] Since the Constitution of 1991, which was partially a product of neoliberal rationality, multiculturalist discourses have become a lingua franca that allows social groups to enter in negotiations with the state over issues of autonomy, recognition, and representation. Historian Sharika D. Crawford takes us to the Caribbean islands of San Andrés, Providencia, and Santa Catalina to trace the islanders' *longue durée* efforts to carve out a distinct space within the multicultural landscape of the Colombian nation. Crawford focuses on the ethnic term *Raizal* (from the root) that community leaders use to claim a particular form of indigeneity that does not seek to evoke pre-Columbian indigenous ancestry but an Afro-Caribbean Anglophone Protestant identity. They use *Raizal* to resist efforts of a "Colombianization," legitimize demands for ethnic rights and political self-determination, and defend their Creole language and other communal cultural practices, despite the national governments' refusal to grant them the same protections offered to other indigenous populations. Tracing another *longue dureé* struggle for recognition, anthropologists Diana Bocarejo and Carlos del Cairo offer a critical analysis of how multiculturalism has reshaped not only racial and ethnic identities but class-based identities such as campesinos.[21] They assert that the Colombian state used the principle of multiculturalism in the Constitution of 1991 to disavow this "contentious and contested political category" of collective rights. The *Zonas de Reserva Campesina* (Peasant Reserve Zones, ZRCs), a political-territorial land management strategy reactivated after the 2016 peace agreements between the national government and the Revolutionary Armed Forces of Colombia (FARC), illustrates the political disputes between campesino movements and the state. It also reveals an unresolved contradiction of the neoliberal model of democracy. Bocarejo and del

Cairo ultimately argue that while campesinos have fought to be recognized as multidimensional political subjects in relation to their territoriality (land tenure and environmental conservation), the state continues to impose a multiculturalist lens that only recognizes ethnic identities to delegitimize their material demands. Their chapter gives context to the legislation recently approved by Congress that modifies Article 64 of the Constitution to allow the state to recognize campesinos as subjects of rights and grant them special protections.[22]

Part 2 in this volume, Surveying the Territorial State, further elaborates on the logic behind some of the Colombian neoliberal state practices and the grassroots responses to them. Geographer Claudia Leal dissects "the territorial character of the state" and "the materiality of the national space" by examining several land regimes in the spatial organization of the republic, from the end of the nineteenth century up to the 1990s. Leal argues that the initial regime of forest reserves, when nature became a source for extraction and income for the state, overlapped with a new type of territorial organization in the mid-twentieth century, the national parks for the conservation of natural resources, and both regimes reinforced the idea that the state must oversee the "management of nature." This apparent contradiction between extraction and conservation is what ethnic groups and Black rural communities operationalized during the decline of the developmentalist state in the 1970s—but more decisively after the introduction of multiculturalism in the new Constitution of 1991—to reclaim their ancestral territories and question the separation of humanized and natural spaces. Leal's genealogy invites us to reevaluate neoliberalism as an economic system for the deregulation of the state to conceptualize it instead as a process of creating a managerial state for a free-market economy that is oriented toward resource extractivism.[23]

The remaining chapters in the part offer close-up analyses of grassroots strategies of adaptation and resistance to the neoliberal managerial state. By examining the Pacific coast of Chocó, sociologist Marta Isabel Domínguez complements Leal's analysis with an ethnographic account on how Black and indigenous communities fought for their territorial and citizenship rights to be recognized within neoliberal parameters.[24] Focusing on "projectism," a political practice in which local actors are constantly vying for state resources and active participation in decision-making processes, Domínguez demonstrates that the neoliberal state is not a totalizing or finished entity but a field that is continuously redrawn and reshaped, locally and nationally, in uneven struggles. Domínguez concludes that communities have consolidated a fragile but important "grassroots neoliberalism" to advance their interests, through a creative use of all the mechanisms at their disposal. Next chapter takes us to the country's northernmost coast on the Caribbean region, in La Guajira Peninsula, where the largest open-pit coal mine in the world is located, and where anthropologist Astrid Ulloa examines extractivism as a central logic of the neoliberal managerial state. Ulloa argues that the "energy transition" from fossil fuels to renewable sources, such as solar and wind energy, constitutes a "green pretext" to impose a new form of "green capitalism" in the geostrategic Guajira.[25] The effects of deterritorialization, dispossession, and violence brought upon indigenous and Black people in the peninsula by this "energy transition," however, have also led to "radical socio-environmental transformations." For example, a set of practices around environmental-territorial autonomy, the recognition of human and nonhuman relations, and the promotion of local knowledge in pursue of "other ways of living" to confront the global climate crisis in one of the most vulnerable corners of the planet. Both coastal regions, the Chocó and the Guajira, are two of Colombia's most vulnerable territories and ecosystems, areas that have been deeply affected by climate change and the brutal dynamics of the internal armed conflict, including the many illegal economies that finance it. People's resistance strategies to survive and thrive in these regions, under dire conditions, constitute powerful lessons for other parts of the world where environmental, political, economic, and social forms of violence intersect.

Another heated global debate in which Colombia has figured prominently is the subject of Part 3 in this volume, Unpacking Drug Trafficking. When narcotrafficking became one of Colombia's largest export sectors in the 1970s, during the decline of the coffee economy, governmental priorities weighed heavily in the academic works of economists, political scientists, and sociologists, pioneers of the scholarship on drugs.[26] Their analyses on the structural factors behind the rise of the marijuana and cocaine export sectors, the surge of the narco-elites in Medellín and Cali, and the impacts of the illegal trade on macroeconomics and U.S.-Colombia foreign relations delineated public policy and shaped public opinion.[27] The killing of cocaine drug lord Pablo Escobar in 1993 changed the terms of the debate. Since then, historians and anthropologists have joined the conversation with a different set of tools and concerns. For the rest of the decade, scholars tried to elucidate how the production, traffic, and exportation of drugs intensified the long-running internal conflict, and what roles governments, traffickers, guerrillas, and paramilitaries played in the making and unmaking of the illicit economy.[28] After the implementation of Plan Colombia at the turn of the millennium, and its subsequent failure in ending the business, practitioners of humanities and other hybrid disciplines began to explore the social and cultural depths that accounted for the resilience and elasticity of the drug trade.[29] At the end, as Colombian economist Francisco Thoumi postulated, it was clear that "a multidisciplinary approach is necessary to answer basic questions about the illegal drug economy."[30]

The chapters in Part 3 offer examples of a wide range of methods used today to study drug trafficking in the country, which is still one of the world's main producers of illegal narcotics and stimulants. Historian Eduardo Sáenz Rovner begins the discussion by revisiting Colombian and U.S. governmental archives and declassified documents on the violent conjuncture of the early 1990s, when the country became the world's main theater of the War on Drugs. By meticulously combing official sources, the author is able to uncover the connections between president César Gaviria's (1990–1994) neoliberal agenda and the U.S.-financed hunt for Escobar and his associates. Sáenz Rovner argues that the Gaviria administration took advantage of the War on Drugs to secure commercial and financial support from Washington to privatize and liquidate state companies, implement new health and pension systems, dismantle protectionist import tariffs, and deregulate labor markets. Sáenz Rovner's scrupulous archival research and analysis of state documents reveals how crucial anti-narcotic policies were in the consolidation of neoliberalism in Colombia, and the specific ways in which operations and campaigns against drug cartels facilitated the reconfiguration of the counterinsurgent logic of an "internal enemy" to simultaneously wage a war against drug traffickers, armed insurgencies, and social movements.

In contrast, the next two chapters pay attention to the social fabric that sustained the illegal drugs political economy from below in the 1970s, as well as current efforts to desecrate the symbols of success associated with "the mythology of the *narcotraficante*" (drug trafficker) and to create counternarratives to the drug trade.[31] Anthropologist and communication scholar Alejandro Ulloa Sanmiguel demonstrates that far from being "the other economy," which social scientists who pioneered the study of drug trafficking conceptualized, the illegal drugs export business was not peripheral but central to establishing the foundations of a new neoliberal society.[32] Through oral history and ethnographic work, Ulloa Sanmiguel disentangles "the Latin connection," the webs of friends, relatives, and neighbors that connected Cali and New York under one single circuit of profitability, and illuminates the linkages between the salsa music industry, the cocaine export business, and the dynamics of migration through which a generation of *caleños* (people from Cali) materialized their aspirations for upward mobility. By offering an on-the-ground perspective, Ulloa Sanmiguel expounds the notions of entrepreneurial individualism that granted legitimacy to this novel economic activity and the compatibility between its promise and what neoliberalism had to offer. The shared ethics and aesthetics of narcotrafficking and neoliberalism are the central themes of a series of conversations in this section's final chapter. Historian and curator Santiago Rueda and artist and curator Harold Ortiz brought together groups of artists, curators, journalists, and cartoonists from various regional and ethnic backgrounds to explore the concept of "*narco* phenomena," a wide diversity of art, architecture, fashion, music, and cultural manifestations associated with this illegal business. Through an impromptu oral history of the drugs business in Colombia, this collective exercise of memory advances a critical view of how the violence associated with this industry has been commodified as a spectacle. Irony, humor, wordplays, slang, and works of art weave together different conversations, which as a whole question the idea of culture as property of a selected few. The marginalized *saberes* (wisdom and knowledge) and experiences of indigenous peoples, underground urban cultures, and counterhegemonic artistic and intellectual circles take center stage to reclaim their place in the nation.

The competing roles of cultural and media production in shaping a neoliberal public sphere are the themes of Part 4 in this volume, Watching the Media. Communication scholar Catalina Uribe Rincón's analysis of Pablo Escobar's public image offers a bridge with the previous section. Introducing the concept of "accidental persona," Uribe Rincón explains how the print media created a two-faced character from the real Escobar, which "once it is 'alive,' so to speak, [it] acquires its own inertia." A Robin Hood persona in the early 1980s, Escobar was represented as a masculine popular hero of humble social origins whose ingenuity made him a wealthy entrepreneur and a savior of the poor. In the early 1990s, he then became a *narco*, a monstrous drug lord that challenged the legitimate monopoly of violence exercised by the state and became a threat to the nation. Uribe Rincón's examination of headlines, ledes, photographs, and caricatures demonstrate how media routines, rather than "any preconceived plan or strategy," are what breathed life to both versions of Escobar, which continue to coexist ambiguously until today in films, TV shows, tours, souvenirs, t-shirts, Halloween customs, and other forms of paraphernalia and memorabilia, as it was previously discussed in Rueda and Ortiz's chapter. The part moves from an analysis on the evolution of an "accidental persona" to an examination of the making of an "intrepid witness," thanks to anthropologist and documentary filmmaker Alexander L. Fattal's examination of photojournalist Jesús Abad Colorado's works. Fattal critically reflects on Abad Colorado's role of documenting the silenced horrors of war at the core of Colombia's neoliberal democracy, and his partnership with the religious left, which enabled him to become "a spokesperson for collective struggles," a storyteller whose visual narrative "cuts against the grain of class-based structural invisibilities" of the armed conflict. "The mix of moral vision and moral performance" in Abad Colorado's "entwined personal and professional trajectories" broke the silence that "structurally muffled and muted" many voices through the conflict and into the post-peace agreement period. Fattal's analysis of Abad Colorado's photographs and the extensive public record of exhibitions, speeches, and interviews sheds light on the fundamental role that the media—with religious ideological underpinnings—have played in documenting human resilience of violently repressed communities that have dared to imagine alternative political horizons.

Yet, the media has also been an active agent of neoliberal legitimacy. Until the end of the twentieth century, mainstream media in Colombia were "mixed systems"—public and private, polarized, and pluralistic—that depended on a low level of development and selective state regulation. Additionally, a long partisan tradition made the public sphere of the media instrumental to the machinations of political power and conducive to the formation of private media monopolies.[33] Until the materialization of the internet, national newspapers were essentially family businesses supported by political alliances. Their purpose was to defend partisan ideology rather than to generate profits, while the local press was in the hands of a few owners who controlled newspapers in various regions.[34] Thus, as Jesús Martín Barbero long ago argued, these private interests played a fundamental role in defining what it meant to belong to Colombia as a regionalized nation—materialized in a public media sphere composed by news outlets, editorial pieces, music production, educational programs, radio melodramas, and television soap operas—and naturalized the notions of happiness, enthusiasm, and melancholia as essential features of the national culture.[35]

The next two chapters invite us to explore specific examples on the role of radio educational programs and musical production in neoliberal reforms. Communication scholar Diego Mauricio Cortés focuses on the Cauca region and argues that since the 1970s, state-sponsored or privately funded community radio stations, such as the Catholic Acción Cultural Popular Radio Sutatenza (ACPO) or the Evangelical Indigenous Radio Stations (EIRS), worked toward two opposite goals. On the one hand, they created channels to advance a "neoliberal governmentality" based on the notion of an individual economic subject with rights and specific obligations, legal restrictions, and dependence on external funders. On the other hand, ACPO and EIRS provided basic and vocational education, offered essential services to those affected by gender-based violence and alcoholism, facilitated the emergence of organic leaders, and inspired alternative popular media projects, all of which were important instruments for the formation of a combative indigenous movement in the Cauca region. Cortés concludes that this counterpoint made religious radio stations important social spaces for the articulation of "modern indigeneity" and hybrid identities to navigate between their incorporation into the capitalist logic and their opposition to it. Cultural studies scholar and media theorist Héctor Fernández L'Hoeste examines similar tensions around diversity and difference in the section's last chapter. Analyzing official efforts to give musical culture new meanings, such as a recent playlist released by the Ministry of Culture and associated website SIMUS and hashtag #*ColombiaCreaTalento*, Fernández L'Hoeste offers evidence of "hegemonic cooptation" in the making of a national repertoire. His study casts light on the ideas of inclusion behind a "more quantifiable manner, following the conjectures of technocrats" of producing, circulating, and appreciating the country's musical patrimony. Although these official efforts have incarnated "a brazen neoliberal take on culture," Fernández L'Hoeste shows that they have also been conducive to a certain degree of legitimacy for the neoliberal state in promoting an idea of a cohesive nation comprised by a diversity of actors coexisting in peace. It also serves the neoliberal state to project an image of an inclusionary Colombia for consumption in the international cultural markets, thus eliciting foreign interest and investments.

As we discussed in the preface, state-sponsored cultural initiatives that celebrate Colombia's *pasión* emphasize an exclusionary definition of the nation. On the one hand, they tend to eclipse the realities of a war as it were in the "distant past" and, on the other hand, justify an "extractivist aesthetic" of an imagined Colombia: Conflictless, unanimous, and peaceful, one that offers the ideal conditions for foreign investment, and international tourism.[36] This approach is the product of a thick genealogy. It is inspired in the National Security Doctrine that accompanied the developmental projects of the 1960s and got more traction in the late 1970s, when president Julio César Turbay Ayala (1978–1982) launched the Security Statute, a comprehensive program of state repression to respond to the massive political mobilization from below and the middle that challenged the exclusionary politics inherited from the National Front.[37] Following the example of authoritarian governments that ruled across Latin America at the time, Turbay Ayala administration revamped security by annihilating radical politics, curtailing civil liberties and personal freedoms, and granting major political roles to the military.[38] The constitutionally authorized state of siege under which the Security Statute legally incarcerated, tortured, disappeared, and, if necessary, killed Colombians who were perceived as "threats" to democracy normalized an ample repertoire of violent practices "to attack and erase what is considered dysfunctional, different or uncomfortable for the idealized nation."[39] Radical subjectivities associated to labor unions, student organizations, and leftist parties were presented in the public sphere as anti-democratic.[40] This Cold War counterinsurgency logic achieved such a degree of sacredness that served to legitimize parastate violence for decades. While peace talks proceeded between the guerrilla organizations and the state in the early 1980s, paramilitary groups financed by the rising cocaine Mafias expanded from the department of Antioquia and the nearby middle Magdalena valley region to the rest of the country.[41] Paramilitary ideal of social harmony was predicated on the elimination of class struggle and social conflict, and their sources of inspiration in ideology and radical politics. The parastate campaigns to eradicate an ever-growing collection of enemies, "bolstered the configuration of regionally based, reactionary blocs" and in alliances with state officials and security forces "push[ed] the insurgencies out of resource-rich areas of the country and destroy[ed] any organization deemed sympathetic to them."[42] The "fragmented regional sovereignties" or parastates regenerated a "labor-repressive mode of capital accumulation" best characterized as "a rentier-based political economy," which became central to the administration of a neoliberal society.[43] It is not a coincidence that Carlos Castaño, one of the founders of the paramilitary armies, characterized their project as the "armed wing of the middle-class" and justified their massacres as a defense of the sanctity of the free-market spirit.[44]

The chapters in Part 5 of this volume, Revisiting the Armed Conflict, take us to three different battlegrounds for the configuration of "resilient regimes of accumulation and rule" to explain how local actors negotiated possibilities within insurgent and paramilitary "orders" and "disorders," achieving positions of leadership as either part of the resistance or as agents of violence.[45] By looking at Fátima Muriel's experiences of political and social activism in the department of Putumayo, anthropologist Winifred Tate reconstructs the multiple strategies that this power broker, in a region that is considered a frontier, used to carve out a political space and redefine democracy as a human rights issue. Thus, in the section's first chapter, Tate's ethnographic analysis traces Muriel's use of her class position as a member of the local elite to channel resources in favor of women organizations that mobilized mothers and peasant farmers against different violent regimes. "Gender was foundational for the innocence that Fátima and other women activists in Putumayo needed to project for both their safety and for political legitimacy," Tate argues. Her sharp observations reveal how Muriel catalyzed a catholic-gendered discourse, according to which women became embodiments of "proper politics"—inherently peaceful, dedicated caretakers, non-ideological citizens—to sustain networks of solidarity for the implementation of social projects that were often funded by international allies.

The notion of peace as neutrality in contexts of systemic violence is not exclusive to Colombia, neither are "the synergies between illegality, capital accumulation, violence and state formation" that many scholars have exposed as "constitutive parts of actually existing democracies and free-market economies the world over."[46] However, due to the length and intensity of the armed conflict, pacification through violence has been even more critical in Colombia for the neoliberalization of state and society.[47] Paramilitarism, a "multidimensional entity" that is concurrently economic, political, and military in nature, has been the main vehicle for the dispossession and labor repression, which are indispensable for capital accumulation: a "strategy of the state-capital alliance" rather than an unintended outcome of a weak or absent state.[48] Drug trafficking has made possible such alliance. It gave paramilitary commanders the financial muscle and social capital needed to dispute the power of the traditional elites, by bringing about their "dilution" and merging with them, under certain conditions, or completely replacing them, under others.[49] In the next chapter, political scientist Francisco Gutiérrez Sanín studies one of those cases, the paramilitary regime of Hernán Giraldo in the Sierra Nevada de Santa Marta between the late 1970s and 2006, when he demobilized as a result of a peace agreement with the national government. Gutiérrez Sanín studies the judicial records and court rulings of the transitional justice system created during the demobilization proceedings and conceptualizes "coercive brokerage" to explain the complex system of intermediations between different territorial levels—local, regional, national, and global—that Giraldo instituted and the multiple forms of violence he used to maintain such system. Despite being "brutal and extraordinary," and counting on the support of the local elites, Giraldo's rule was also "intrinsically unstable" because of his impossibility to "align the central concerns of key coalitions" on which his reign rested. Demonstrating that Giraldo's localism was simultaneously a source of power and fragility, Gutiérrez Sanín's insightful finding invites scholars to scale down the importance of narcotrafficking in relation to the rise of "fragmented regional sovereignties," and consider instead political negotiations and intermediations as the most critical resources for control.

While the chapter on Giraldo places narcotrafficking in its proper place, sociologist and historian Estefanía Ciro's detailed ethnographic work centers the analysis of the armed conflict on the War on Drugs. Ciro's chapter offers a radiography of "communicating vessels" that connect the terror of the War on Drugs, as a force directed against "the bodies, territories and lives" of those situated at the lowest echelons of the transnational drug business, with policymaking.[50] By "listening to the lives of *cocaleras*" of the Caquetá region—women who grow coca used to process cocaine—Ciro reveals a "triad" of oppression endured by these women: the state's legal and political criminalization of their livelihood and ways of living; the economic hardships that come along with rural exclusion; and the daily patriarchal violence that shaped their family and personal lives. Ciro's extensive oral history and politically engaged participant observation transcends the critical analysis of structural violence to give account of the various forms of resistance that cocaleras have developed to advance their own notions of economic success, as a right and as a collective endeavor. Such efforts help them secure land ownership and economic autonomy, to fight against the lack of distinction between civilians and combatants, and to reconfigure women's traditional roles in rural politics and economics.

While the chapters in Part 5 of this volume conceptualize the internal conflict beyond armed confrontations, to examine the nuts and bolts of everyday life in the war zones, Part 6 rejects narrow definitions about the conflict to scrutinize instead the ins and outs of political struggles over historical memory. Laboring with Memory closes the volume by analyzing the highly contested ways in which multiple actors have engaged in disputes and struggles over the narratives of Colombia's recent past. First instituted in Bolivia in 1982, followed by Argentina in 1983, state-sanctioned investigations into previous episodes of political terror have been powerful mechanisms to distill a chaotic past into a "lucid story, one that portrays terror as an inversion of a democratic society" in an attempt to avoid repetition and "forget acts of violence central to state formation."[51] In the 1980s and 1990s, case after case in the Southern Cone and in Central America attested the impossibility to construct an "emblematic memory," that is, a "framework that organizes meaning, selectivity, and countermemory" and receives public acceptance and validation as all attempts to do so were always incomplete.[52] Most national projects of historical memory are fragmented, plural, and contentious because the "active political struggle [is] not only over the meaning of what took place in the past but over the meaning of memory itself"; hence, the outcomes of those struggles thus become "key elements in the processes of (re)construction of individual and collective identities in societies emerging from periods of violence and trauma."[53]

The opening chapter by political scientist María Emma Wills Obregón traces high-stakes negotiations over Colombia's historical memory about the conflict, since the institutionalization of a transitional justice legislation in the early 2000s. Wills Obregón offers a chronological framework, divided into three periods, to understand how the contention over memory has become central to the very definition of what it means to live in a democracy. During the first period between 2005 and 2010, "heroic memories of powerful actors" dominated the conversation alongside a plurality of grassroots movements contesting such narratives. In the second period between 2011 and 2018, in the context of peace negotiations between the Juan Manuel Santos's administration and the FARC, "a primal rift" emerged in the gaps separating different readings of the past, and a pernicious polarization anchored in irreconcilable interpretations. The third period, between 2018 and 2022, a new right-wing government attempted to bottleneck the work of state institutions leading historical memory projects, while victims' organizations responded by opening alternative spaces against official oblivion. A new moment initiated in 2022 after the first leftist government in the history of the country announced during its inauguration that a "new period in the making" had begun, when "memory is once again associated with the fate of victims." Tracing the evolution of the "field of memory" during the last two decades, Wills Obregón sheds light on a diversity of actors, strategies, and goals that have defined it, while highlighting the peculiarities of the Colombian case within the Latin American context, where "memory agents" must work amid an ongoing armed conflict.

As an active participant of many of the memory projects she analyzes, Wills Obregón sets the tone for the rest of the part comprised by works of collaborative research and politically engaged scholarship. In the next chapter, philosopher María del Rosario Acosta López, working in close collaboration with internationally renowned artists Doris Salcedo and Clemencia Echeverri, examines two of their artworks—*Fragmentos* and *Duelos*, respectively—as materializations of "non-institutional modes of memorialization" and "resistance to forgetting." What role has contemporary art played in Colombia amid the normalization of violence during the country's armed conflict? Acosta López asks this question to find "alternative grammars of listening" as part of her answer. Defined as new frameworks of meaning that are both perceptual and semantic, artworks by Salcedo and Echeverri bring that which is *inaudito* (unheard-of and inadmissible) into "audibility." Salcedo's counter-monument—a jagged horizontal plane made out of seventy tons of melted weapons surrendered by the FARC and molded by female survivors of sexual violence during the armed conflict—and Echeverri's installation—a looping video of a dumping ground that hides a yet-to-be-determined number of disappeared young people from Medellín's paramilitary war in the early 2000s—do not offer closure or resolution to the problem of historical memory, concludes Acosta López. Rather, they constitute "sites for believability," where the truth is not "something to be proven but rather something to be experienced" with all the "interruptions, subversions, and contradictions" that populate "the threshold between life and death, past and present, pain and resilience."

Whereas Salcedo's and Echeverri's artworks were exhibited at a Ministry of Culture-operated gallery in downtown Bogotá, the memorialization project that the last chapter of this volume addresses happened in Bojayá, Chocó, in the middle of the Pacific rainforest, thanks to a prolonged struggle for visibility and justice. For years, anthropologist and interdisciplinary scholar Pilar Riaño-Alcalá accompanied the tireless efforts of a community that survived a massacre perpetrated by the FARC in 2002, when 102 children and adults were killed inside of a Catholic Church, to get the bodies of their loved ones exhumed, identified, and properly buried in their territory following their "ancestral knowledges and practices to care for the dead." Riaño-Alcalá argues that their demands became a critical component of the peace negotiations between the government and the FARC, setting a precedent for the search and exhumation of the victims as "practices of historical clarification, peace sustainability, and justice in the afterlives of mass violence." Her collaborative ethnography, which involved 22 members of the community and knowledge keepers as well as one social leader and two other scholars, examines how mortuary rituals and ancestral knowledge intersected with forensic procedures, scientific expertise, and transitional justice interventions. This critical incorporation of the community's vision and practices of care for the living and the dead "showed a way to work towards decolonizing forensic, psychosocial, and judicial protocols" at the local, national, and international levels.

The creative, and sometimes conflictive, tension that characterized the search for those missing in Bojayá echoes a dynamic of antagonism and solidarity that paves processes of historical memory, clarification, justice, and reparation worldwide. This case of community activism and resilience after an unthinkable act of terror serves as evidence that the histories of democracy are also histories of genocide, war, torture, land dispossession, and forced displacement. Based on this idea, the last chapter of the volume takes us back to the first, in which one of Latin America's greatest thinkers invites us to embrace the *abigarramiento* (motley reality) of our modern histories. When Manuel Zapata Olivella educates us in *muntu*, philosophical tradition of African origins in defense of a fraternity of all of nature's kingdoms (plants, animals, and humans), living in intimate connection with those who are not alive (the dead, the ancestors, and the deities), he endows us with a powerful utopia.[54] Perhaps his hope was that those ancestral beliefs that have been preserved and reconstituted by peoples whose dehumanization and exploitation was crucial for the formation of a global capitalist system could help us envision "emancipatory alternatives" to the "current and imminent crisis [that] poses a planetary predicament."[55] His ideal of harmony coming out of heterogeneous, dense, messy, and contradictory histories has inspired us to hold the more modest hope that by recasting Colombia's pasts and presents as histories of "solitude" and "perplexity," our readers would be reminded of the transformational power of narratives and critical storytelling.

Notes

1 Clare Hemmings, *Why Stories Matter: The Political Grammar of Feminist Theory* (Durham: Duke University Press, 2011).
2 Jacques Rancière, *The Names of History: On the Poetics of Knowledge* (Minneapolis: University of Minnesota Press, 1994), 7. See also Mark Thurner and Andrés Guerrero, *After Spanish Rule: Postcolonial Predicaments of the Americas* (Durham: Duke University Press, 2003), 7.
3 Gary Wilder, *Concrete Utopianism: The Politics of Temporality and Solidarity* (New York: Fordham University Press, 2022), 66.
4 For "terminal identity" see Paul Gilroy, *Darker than Blue: On the Moral Economies of Black Atlantic Culture* (Cambridge: Harvard University Press, 2010), 156.

5 See also William Mina Aragón, "Manuel Zapata Olivella: A Wandering Thinker (1920–2004)" in *Routledge Handbook of Afro-Latin American Studies*, eds. Bernd Reiter and John Antón Sánchez (New York: Routledge, 2022).
6 Naomi Klein, *The Shock Doctrine: The Rise of Disaster Capitalism* (New York: Henry Holt and Company, 2010).
7 Luis Rojas Villagra, ed., *Neoliberalismo en América Latina: Crisis, tendencias y alternativas* (Buenos Aires: CLACSO, 2015); Greg Grandin, *Empire's Workshop: Latin America, the United States, and the Rise of New Imperialism* (New York: Holt, Henry & Company, 2007); Robert Jordan, "Neoliberalism and Free Trade in Latin America," *Oxford Research Encyclopedia of Latin American History*, published online on September 29, 2016. https://doi.org/10.1093/acrefore/9780199366439.013.227; Luis Bértola and José Antonio Ocampo, *The Economic Development of Latin America since Independence* (Oxford: Oxford University Press, 2012); Carlos Brando, *The Political Economy of Financing Late Development, Credit, Capital and Industrialization, Colombia 1940–67* (Ph.D. thesis, The London School of Economics and Political Science, 2012), 14–15, 98–99.
8 Gerard Dumenil and Domique Levy, *The Crisis of Neoliberalism* (Cambridge: Harvard University Press, 2013), 22. See also David Harvey, *A Brief History of Neoliberalism* (Oxford: Oxford University Press, 2007), 15, 19; Felipe Burbano de Lara, "El nacimiento de un nuevo sujeto político," *Íconos: Revista de Ciencias Sociales*, no. 15 (enero 2003): 7; and James Ferguson, "The Uses of Neoliberalism," *Antipode* 41 (2009): 166.
9 Philip Mirowski, "The Political Movement that Dared Not Speak its Own Name: The Neoliberal Thought Collective Under Erasure," *Institute for New Economic Thinking Working Paper Series*, no. 23 (September 2014). https://ssrn.com/abstract=2682892 or http://dx.doi.org/10.2139/ssrn.2682892
10 Michael Raid, *The Forgotten Continent: A History of the New Latin America* (New Haven: Yale University Press, 2017); Christopher Guilluy, *No Society: El fin de la clase media occidental* (Barcelona: Taurus, 2019).
11 Quinn Slobodian, *Globalists: The End of Empire and the Birth of Neoliberalism* (Cambridge: Harvard University Press, 2018), 2.
12 James Ferguson, *Give a Man a Fish: Reflections on the New Politics of Distribution* (Durham: Duke University Press, 2015), 1.
13 V. Y. Mudimbe, *The Invention of Africa: Gnosis, Philosophy, and the Order of Knowledge* (Bloomington: Indiana University Press, 1988), x.
14 For example, Renán Vega Cantor, *Capitalismo y despojo: Perspectiva histórica sobre la expropiación universal de bienes y saberes* (Bogotá: Impresol Ediciones, 2013); Renán Vega Cantor, *Los economistas neoliberales-Nuevos criminales de guerra: El genocidio económico y social del capitalismo contemporáneo* (Bogotá: CEPA, 2010); Juan Ricardo Aparicio Cuervo and Manuela Fernández Pinto, eds. *Neoliberalismo en Colombia: Contexto, complejidad y política pública* (Bogotá: Ediciones Uniandes, 2022).
15 Amy Offner, *Sorting Out the Mixed Economy: The Rise and Fall of Welfare and Development State in the Americas* (Princeton: Princeton University Press, 2020).
16 Offner, *Sorting Out the Mixed Economy*. See also Eduardo Dargent, *Technocracy and Democracy in Latin America: The Experts Running Government* (Cambridge: Cambridge University Press, 2015); Luis Bernardo Flórez Enciso, "Colombia: Economy, Economic Policy and Economists," in *Economists in the*

Americas, eds. Verónica Montecinos and John Markoff (Cheltenham: Edward Elgar, 2009), 197–226; César Miguel Torres del Río, *Colombia siglo XX: Desde la Guerra de los Mil Días hasta la elección de Álvaro Uribe* (Bogotá: Grupo Editorial Norma, 2010), 253; Carlos Caballero Argáez, *Economía colombiana en el siglo XX: Un recorrido por la historia y sus protagonistas* (Bogotá: Debate, 2016); and Jamie Peck, "Explaining (with) Neoliberalism," *Territory, Politics, Governance* 1, no. 2 (2013): 133.

17 For multiple definitions of neoliberalism see Harvey, *A Brief History*, 3–4. See also Stuart Hall, "The Neoliberal Revolution," *Soundings* 48, no. 1 (2011): 9–28; Carla Freeman, *Entrepreneurial Selves: Neoliberal Respectability and the Making of a Caribbean Middle Class* (Durham: Duke University Press, 2014); Verónica Gago, *Neoliberalism from Below: Popular Pragmatics and Baroque Economies* (Durham: Duke University Press, 2017); Heidi Tinsman, *Buying into the Regime: Grapes and Consumption in Cold War Chile and the United States* (Durham: Duke University Press, 2014); and Wendy Brown, *Undoing the Demos: Neoliberalism's Stealth Revolution* (New York: Zone Books, 2015).

18 See also María Teresa Uribe de Hincapié, *Nación, ciudadano y soberano* (Medellín: Corporación Región, 2001), 134.

19 See also Nancy P. Appelbaum, Anne S. Macpherson, and Karin Alejandra Rosemblatt, *Race and Nation in Modern Latin America* (Chapel Hill: University of North Carolina Press, 2003).

20 William Roseberry, "Hegemony and the Language of Contention," in *Everyday Forms of State Formation: Revolution and the Negotiation of Rule in Modern Mexico*, eds. Gilbert Joseph and Daniel Nugent (Durham: Duke University Press, 1994), 355–366.

21 See also Marta Saade Granados, *Elementos para la conceptualización de lo campesino en Colombia* (Bogotá: Editorial ICANH, 2018); and Soraya Mayte Yie Garzón, "¡Vea, los campesinos aquí estamos! Etnografía de la (re) aparición del campesinado como sujeto político en los Andes nariñenses colombianos" (Ph.D. dissertation in Social Science, Institute of Philosophy and Human Sciences, Universidad Estadual de Campiñas, Brazil, 2018).

22 Ministerio de Agricultura, "El campesinado será sujeto de derechos: Aprobado definitivamente en el Congreso el proyecto que lo reconoce," June 13, 2023.

23 See also Macarena Gómez Barris, *The Extractive Zone: Social Ecologies and Decolonial Perspectives* (Durham: Duke University Press, 2017).

24 See also Kiran Asher, *Black and Green: Afro-Colombians, Development, and Nature in the Pacific Lowlands* (Durham: Duke University Press, 2009); Claudia Leal, *Landscapes of Freedom: Building a Postemancipation Society in the Rainforest of Western Colombia* (Tucson: University of Arizona Press, 2018); Ulrich Oslender, *Geographies of the Social Movements: Afro-Colombian Mobilization and the Aquatic Space* (Durham: Duke University Press, 2016).

25 For more on extractivism in Latin America see Mark Goodale and Nancy Postero, eds., *Neoliberalism Interrupted: Social Change and Contested Governance in Contemporary Latin America* (Stanford: Stanford University Press, 2013).

26 For more on the early scholarship on drugs see Lina Britto, *Marijuana Boom: The Rise and Fall of Colombia's First Drug Paradise* (Oakland: University of California Press, 2020), 9–10.

27 Álvaro Camacho Guizado and Andrés López Restrepo, "Perspectives on Narcotics Traffic in Colombia," *International Journal of Politics, Culture, and Society* 14, no. 4 (2000): 151–82; and Alejandro Gaviria and Daniel Mejía, eds., *Anti-Drug Policies in Colombia: Successes, Failures, and Wrong Turns* (Nashville: Vanderbilt University Press, 2016).
28 Andrés López Restrepo, "Narcotráfico, ilegalidad y conflicto armado en Colombia," in *Nuestra guerra sin nombre: Transformaciones del conflicto en Colombia*, eds. Francisco Gutiérrez, María Emma Wills and Gonzalo Sánchez (Bogotá: IEPRI, Universidad Nacional, 2006).
29 For more on the most recent scholarship see Lina Britto, "The Drug Wars in Colombia," *Oxford Research Encyclopedia of Latin American History*, published online on September 28, 2020. https://doi-org.turing.library.northwestern.edu/10.1093/acrefore/9780199366439.013.504
30 Francisco E. Thoumi, *Illegal Drugs, Economy, and Society in the Andes* (Baltimore: The Johns Hopkins University Press, 2003), 3.
31 For "the mythology of the *narcotraficante*" see Luis A. Astorga, *Mitología del narcotraficante en México* (México D.F.: Plaza y Valdés, 1995), 12–13; for counter-narratives of the drug business see Gabriela Polit Dueñas, *Narrating Narcos: Culiacán and Medellín* (Pittsburgh: University of Pittsburgh Press, 2013).
32 Roberto Junguito and Carlos Caballero, "La otra economía," *Coyuntura Económica* 8, no. 4 (1978). For more on drug trafficking and drug wars as key to the transition between developmentalist to neoliberal states see Dawn Paley, *Drug War Capitalism* (Oakland: AK Press, 2014); Jasmin Hristov, *Paramilitarism and Neoliberalism: Violent Systems of Capital Accumulation in Colombia and Beyond* (New York: Pluto Press, 2014); Britto, *Marijuana Boom*; and Teo Ballvé, *The Frontier Effect: State Formation and Violence in Colombia* (Ithaca: Cornell University Press, 2020).
33 Daniel C. Hallin and Stylianos Papathanassopoulos, "Political Clientelism and the Media: Southern Europe and Latin America in Comparative Perspective," *Media, Culture & Society* 24, no. 2 (2002): 176–182.
34 Catalina Montoya-Londoño, "In Search of a Model for the Colombian Media System Today," in *Media Systems and Communication Policies in Latin America*, eds. Manuel Alejandro Guerrero and Mireya Márquez-Ramírez (London: Palgrave Macmillan, 2014), 67–68.
35 Jesús Martín-Barbero, *De los medios a las mediaciones: Comunicación, cultura y hegemonía*, 6th ed. (México D.F: Anthropos, Universidad Autónoma Metropolitana Azcapotzalco, 2010). Óscar Hernández Salgar has shown how the production of music has been connected with emotional and regionalized categorizations in which specific regions are imagined as the representation of the nation; see Óscar Hernández Salgar, *Los mitos de la música nacional: Poder y emoción en las músicas populares colombianas* (Bogotá: Universidad Javeriana, 2016). See also Peter Wade, *Music, Race, and Nation: Música Tropical in Colombia* (Chicago: University of Chicago Press, 2000); and Íngrid Johanna Bolívar Ramírez, "El oficio de los futbolistas colombianos en los años 60 y 70: Recreación de las regiones, juegos de masculinidad y vida sentimental" (Ph.D. dissertation, Department of History, University of Wisconsin, 2016).
36 Gómez-Barris, *The Extractive Zone*.
37 Comisión para el Esclarecimiento de la Verdad, la Convivencia y la No Repetición, *Hay futuro si hay verdad* (Bogotá: CEV, 2022), 91–96; and Comisión

para el Esclarecimiento de la Verdad, la Convivencia y la No Repetición, *No matarás* (Bogotá: CEV, 2022), 149–159.
38 Vilma Liliana Franco Restrepo, *Orden contrainsurgente y dominación* (Bogotá: Siglo del Hombre, 2009); and Renzo Ramírez Bacca and León Darío Marín Arenas, "Seguridad e ideología en Colombia, 1978–1982: Análisis crítico del discurso de Julio César Turbay Ayala," *Anuario de Historia Regional y de las Fronteras* 20, no. 2 (July–December 2015): 241–269.
39 Our translation of Juan Pablo Aranguren Romero, *Cuerpos al límite: Tortura, subjetividad y memoria en Colombia, 1977–1982* (Bogotá: Ediciones Uniandes, 2023), 10–12.
40 Mauricio Archila Neira, ed., *Violencia contra el sindicalismo, 1984–2010* (Bogotá: CINEP/Programa por la Paz, 2012); Lesley Gill, *A Century of Violence in a Red City: Popular Struggles, Counterinsurgency and Human Rights in Colombia* (Durham: Duke University Press, 2016).
41 Mauricio Romero, *Paramilitares y autodefensas, 1982–2003* (Bogotá: IEPRI and Editorial Planeta, 2003); and Gustavo Duncan, *Los señores de la guerra: De paramilitares, mafiosos y autodefensas en Colombia* (Bogotá: Planeta, 2006).
42 Gill, *A Century of Violence in a Red City*, 18. See also Forrest Hylton, "The Experience of Defeat: The Colombian Left and the Cold War that Never Ended," *Historical Materialism* 22, no. 1 (2014): 67–104.
43 Nazih Richani, "Caudillos and the Crisis of the Colombian State: Fragmented Sovereignty, the War System and the Privatisation of Counterinsurgency in Colombia," *Third World Quarterly* 28, no. 2 (2007): 403–417.
44 "El rostro de Carlos Castaño," *El Tiempo*, March 5, 2000. See also Fernando Estrada, "La retórica del paramilitarismo: Análisis del discurso en el conflicto armado," *Análisis Político* 44 (2001): 39–57.
45 For "resilient regimes of accumulation and rule" see Ballvé, *The Frontier Effect*, 5. For a theory of "order" and "disorder" in the Colombian armed conflict see Ana Arjona, *Rebelocracy: Social Order in the Colombian Civil War* (Cambridge: Cambridge University Press, 2017), 9–13.
46 Ballvé, *The Frontier Effect*, 102–103. See also Béatrice Hibou, ed., *Privatizing the State* (New York: Columbia University Press, 2004); and Enrique Desmond Arias and Daniel M. Goldstein, *Violent Democracies in Latin America* (Durham: Duke University Press, 2010).
47 For a radiography of peace as violence at the core of new reconfigurations of the paramilitarization of society see Javier Giraldo Moreno, Leonardo Luna Alzate, Ferdinad Muggenthaler and Stefan Peters, eds., *¿Del paramiltarismo al paramilitarismo? Radiografías de una paz violenta en Colombia* (Quito: Rosa Luxemburg Stiftung, 2023).
48 Hristov, *Paramilitarism and Neoliberalism*, 160–168.
49 Juan David Velasco, Gustavo Duncan, and Felipe Lopera, "Oligarquía, poder político y narcotráfico en Colombia: Los casos de Medellín, Santa Marta y Muzo," *Colombia Internacional* 95 (2018): 167–201.
50 For the War on Drugs as a combination of terror and policymaking see Paley, *Drug War Capitalism*, 16.
51 Greg Grandin, "The Instruction of Great Catastrophe: Truth Commissions, National History and State Formation in Argentina, Chile and Guatemala," *American Historical Review* 110, no. 1 (February 2005): 47–48.
52 Steve Stern, *Remembering Pinochet's Chile: On the Eve of London 1998* (Durham: Duke University Press, 2003), 105.

53 Elizabeth Jelin, *State Repression and the Labors of Memory* (Minneapolis: University of Minnesota Press, 2003), xviii. See also Juana Acosta López and María del Rosario Acosta López, eds., *Justicia transicional en Colombia: Una mirada retrospectiva* (Bogotá: Ariel/Universidad de la Sabana, 2023).
54 For more on muntu and ubuntu in Colombia see Natalia Quiceno Toro, *Vivir sabroso: Luchas y movimiento afroatrateños, en Bojayá, Chocó, Colombia* (Bogotá: Universidad del Rosario, 2016).
55 Wilder, *Concrete Utopianism*, 1–2; Massimiliano Tomba, *Insurgent Universality: An Alternative Legacy of Modernity* (Oxford: Oxford University Press, 2021); Robin D. G. Kelley, *Freedom Dreams: The Black Radical Imagination* (Boston: Beacon Press, 2022 [2002]). For a study on the conditions of recent social protest and its struggles over the definitions of democracy, see Juan Carlos Celis Ospina, ed., *Estallido social 2021* (Bogotá: Siglo Editorial, Editorial Universidad del Rosario, Collectivo La Maria Cano, Rosa Luxemburg Stiftung, 2023).

Part 1
Identifying Multiculturalism

1 A Conversation with an Afrodiasporic Humanist
Manuel Zapata Olivella in His Own Words

William Mina Aragón

This dialogue with Manuel Zapata Olivella—physician, writer, anthropologist, intellectual, activist, novelist, and autodidact from the African diaspora in the Americas, who was born in the Colombian Caribbean (in Santa Cruz de Lorica, department of Córdoba) in 1920 and died in Bogotá in 2004—introduces readers to his humanistic knowledge. Although he has been made invisible in Latin American scholarly circles, Zapata Olivella is one of the most significant and relevant intellectuals of Afro-Latin American thought. This chapter covers a wide range of topics on diversity, multiculturalism, empirical-magical literature, identity, and *mestizaje* in the Americas from a human, anthropological, and literary sciences perspective.

As a writer, Zapata Olivella created a wide range of novels and stories with Afro and indigenous characters who dignify their ethnicity, race, and culture in the face of an exclusionary and racist paradigm, one that is still alive in Latin American and Caribbean societies. Within this prolific ensemble, we have novels such as *La calle 10* (1960), *Detrás del rostro* (1963), and *En Chimá nace un santo* (1964). He defined himself as a vagabond, and his traveler's testament was the wandering trilogy titled *Pasión vagabunda* (1949), *He visto la noche* (1953), and *China 6 a.m.* (1955). He cultivated all genres: short story, theater, chronicle, novel, folk tales, poetry, and even scripts for radio and television, in addition to a beautiful autobiographical text called *Levántate mulato* (1990). His distinguished work is *Changó . . . el gran putas* (1983), a monumental and fundamental work about the African diaspora literature and libertarian thought in the Americas, an Afrocentric and decolonial epic that narrates the fight for freedom of Africans, an Afrodiasporic tale along the vein of Cedric Robinson's "Black radical tradition." His posthumous works, *Deslumbramientos de América* (2017) and *Africanidad, indianidad y multiculturalidad* (2017), deal with his concerns with the cosmic, humanistic, and planetary mestizo of the Americas, one without ethnic-racial prejudices. He received awards in a series of literary competitions (Premio Literario Esso, Prêmio Literário Francisco Matarazzo Sobrinho, Premio Nuevos Derechos Humanos);

worked as a journalist in Colombia, Mexico, and the United States; and was the director of the magazine *Letras Nacionales* between 1965 and 1985, where many Colombian writers forged their careers in what he called "literary nationalism," a movement opposed to the Latin American literary boom.

As an activist, Zapata Olivella was a member of the Afro social movement and in the 1940s helped found the Club Negro de Colombia, an intellectual and anti-racist organization in Bogotá, together with Natanael Díaz, Diego Luis Córdoba, Marino Viveros, and others. He organized three congresses of Black cultures of the Americas in Cali, Panama, and São Paulo, following the libertarian, organizational, and intellectual tradition of the Pan-Africanist movements of W. E. B. Du Bois, Marcus Garvey, George Padmore, and Henry Sylvester Williams.

He was a friend of great Africanists such as Léopold Sédar Senghor, Léon-Gontran Damas, Michel-Rolph Trouillot, Kwame Anthony Appiah, and Langston Hughes. He also interacted in congresses and symposia with renowned writers such as Alejo Carpentier, Miguel Ángel Asturias, Ciro Alegría, Pablo Neruda, Martín Luis Guzmán, Mariano Azuela González, and "Gabito" García Márquez. In his work flows the Caribbean of C. L. R. James and Aimé Césaire; the Africa of Shaka Zulu and Cheikh Anta Diop; the rebellion of Afro-North Americans like Malcolm X and Angela Davis, as well as the philosophy of nonviolence of Martin Luther King and Rosa Parks; the Brazil of Nganga Nzumbi and Abdias do Nascimento; the Colombian Pacific of Rogerio Velásquez and Arnoldo Palacios; and the aesthetic and ancestral artistic spirit of all the traditions of the African diaspora in the Americas, in a creative song of freedom and deeds to recognize our dignity as intellectual and academic forgers of a great homeland called Colombia and of an immense continent called Afro-America.

As a self-taught ethnologist of the world's plural cultures, Zapata Olivella sought to answer questions of who we were and what our position was as Colombian citizens. He devoted his careful research to understand Colombia's African cultural heritage and answered by saying that it was not savages nor barbarians who came from Africa, but creators. They were not merely "Blacks," as the colonial narrative of theologians, chroniclers, and travelers wanted them to be known. Zapata Olivella was also interested in the second legacy of our diverse identity, the constitutive heritage of a non "slaver" Spain that gave us Spanish, which we learned to impulse our own freedom and enrich it with countless linguistic meanings that helped not only shape Castilian but also in the construction of creole languages like Palenquero. The legacy of Juan de Castellanos and Miguel de Cervantes Saavedra is what allowed the creation of other languages that writers like Candelario Obeso and Jorge Artel will learn to diversify Spanish through our own interpretations and musicality in Colombia. The third element of diverse identity and mestizaje, as thought by Zapata Olivella, was one constituted by indigenous cultures of the Americas, their love of nature, their myths and legends, their artistic and architectural creations, their oral traditions, and their ontological worldview toward their gods and ancestors. Faced with the existence of indigenous, European, and African gods, Zapata Olivella highlighted the true mestizo religion, one without the hegemony of any particular religious symbol but rather a heterogeneity of them, in a space of autonomous faith and libertarian projects such as voodoo, Santería, candomblé, and Rastafarianism, among others.

According to Zapata Olivella, the discourse and the colonial intelligentsia fabricated and built a conceptualization of races, genes, and classes where "whiteness" supposedly was superior to Blackness and indigenousness (indianidad). The Afro-Colombian thinker will dedicate himself to demystify this perverse heritage in many of his works, such as *El hombre colombiano* (1974), *Las claves mágicas de América* (1989), *La rebelión de los genes* (1997), and, posthumously, *Tambores de América para despertar al viejo mundo* (2020). Faced with the racist myths and ideologies that ran through history, from the colonies to the present day, Zapata Olivella proposed in his lucid work a multiculturalism where Afro and indigenous people are equal vis-à-vis Europeans, although they have always been unequal economically, legally, politically, and socially under the purview of the constitution and the nation-state.

One of his dreams was precisely that we could recognize ourselves as brothers and sisters following the traditions of the African *muntu* and *ubuntu*.[1] Since 1974, he has aspired to a racial democracy in the following terms: "Let us face the historical fact of our mestizaje as a presupposition that it can become the first step towards a real cultural democracy."[2]

This conversation, a fragment of a longer interview published in Spanish and conducted in Bogotá between July and August 2001, takes up the Socratic method of dialogue to address diverse anthropological, psychoanalytical, and literary topics, such as mythical realism, Colombia and Americas' mestizo triethnicity, and Afrodiasporic identity and culture understood as the hybridity of multiple linguistic, religious, and racial family trees and roots, emphasizing the African legacy, the European uniqueness, and the autochthonous nature of the Amerindian world.[3] In this conversation, as well as in his work, Zapata Olivella immerses us in his wisdom of African *griot* (oral historian) to dis-alienate us from our psychic and historical-social conditioning, as the doctor and intellectual Frantz Fanon did so in the past. In this dialogue, the teacher proposes an autonomous culture, unique in each tradition, while at the same time affirming the mestizo diversity, or what he liked to call the muntu of the Americas, the fraternity between all beings of creation and their articulation with other living beings, where the human being is only one more piece within the

26 *William Mina Aragón*

Figure 1.1 Manuel Zapata Olivella holding a globe with the map of Africa. No author, no date.

Source: "Photographs, Portraits," box 241, folder 23, MZO Papers. Courtesy of Vanderbilt University Library, Special Collections.

logic of life. This is the lucidity, originality, and creativity of this thinker and citizen who lived philosophy as a life practice, both in conversation and in writing. Here are the words of an Afrodiasporic humanist, for us to grasp the simplicity and depth of his work and his thought.

William Mina Aragón (WMA): And the primary sources of inspiration that marked your life as a writer, what were they?

Manuel Zapata Olivella (MZO): For me, the sources of inspiration or creation were determined by the cultural environment in which I lived, which was in my family. Fortunately, I could rely on my father being a schoolteacher, who had turned his home into a place where children with few economic resources in the town of Lorica would come to learn. And also, the regions' peasants, artisans, illiterates, including of course adults, women, and young people. In these circumstances, my learning, within the customs and habits, was already linked to expressions that depended on the social condition of dad's students, that is, those children who came from well-off families and had "appropriate" behavior and dress habits, in a way of speaking, appropriate habits in the way of communicating with others, but, at the same time, the manners of peasants, of fishermen, of farmers, almost always badly dressed, some barefoot.

The important thing, surely in my training, was what dad taught in front of a chalkboard for everyone, for children, adults, young people, and women. I believe that this double dimension of perceiving culture in relation to literature gave me at first a multifaceted vision of being, of being Loriqueño and, therefore, of myself. This experience occurred throughout my first seven years. In 1930, dad and our family moved to Cartagena de Indias, where the environment and cultural influences were totally transformed.

We left a riverside village for the city of Cartagena, with all its historical past and its legacy, where dad reopened his school with the same name it had in Lorica: Colegio de la Fraternidad. That is, this name was a principle of every civility, of every community, and it meant that we lived in a world of fraternity, that we had to prepare ourselves as students, as relatives, to live in a fraternal world. To understand fraternity as a concept conceived by my father implied that society as a whole should have these values.

My father was Frenchified, a free thinker who expressed the fundamental principles of this culture through the texts of Montesquieu, Rousseau, and Voltaire. Of course, the essence of this information entered my head leaving some traces, such as the aphorisms of Nietzsche, of *Thus Spoke Zarathustra*, "You will write with blood and you will know that blood is spirit," which at the time I did not understand.[4] And it is also perhaps because my family in the Caribbean was also the product of mestizaje: A great-grandfather who descended from Europeans, an Afro grandfather, a mulatto grandfather of Santa Marta, in an inescapable context such as Cartagena. It was all these familiar, intellectual, and regional circumstances that marked and will mark my literary life.

WMA: Where are the sources of magical realism in your work? In the African animism or in the literary experience of some Latin American novelists, which García Márquez exemplifies very well, specifically in *Cien años de soledad* (*One Hundred years of Solitude*)?

MZO: First of all, you talk about the concept of magical realism. To address this, it is a priority to locate the context in which this concept is currently being used. As is known, in the mid-twentieth century, some concepts related to this question began to originate as literary movements. So, before talking about magical realism, there was talk of the "real wonderful," introduced by Carpentier, and surely already present in Asturias and Borges, those who previously referred to the wonderful within the literary context that you mention, related to poetry, the story, the novel. To find the concept of magical realism—based on man's attitude when faced with reality and wanting to transcend it—we would have to go back to the first works of the researchers and precursors of what we today call cultural anthropology, as is the case of the English Taylor and Morgan, who raised concerns and wondered what were the behaviors that primordial men had to be able to express their ideas, as much in words as in pictographs, in their songs, in their invocations, and so forth. From that recreational context of man, of his reality, a magical response of man to the facts of Nature and life began to be known. What I mean is that possibly these first allusions to the magical knowledge of the human being, within what we could call anthropological sciences, could have taken place at the beginning or middle of the last century with the elements that I have pointed out. From this century hereon, some authors began to appear who understood empirical elements within the process called "magic," that is, that man was passing the threshold of Nature to create a new cultural landscape. And the concept of "magical empiricism" began to be used to unite the experiences that man had accumulated in his historical dynamic and that he used to survive, such as the creation of instruments, the invention of fire, the development of the word itself, the practices of agriculture, the knowledge of the cycle of seeds, and the management of the elements of Nature used not in the way they appear within nature but as survival resources, such as for building, digging a hole, covering with branches, and pushing or moving animals so that they did not fall into those holes and other elements that are found in cave paintings of the Quaternary.

Man began, at that moment, after a time of extracting anilines, vegetables, minerals, and so forth to paint the rocks on those caves. All that world that we are now calling "magical," in reality was only a material—not magical—response of man to interpret the natural phenomena that influenced his life, reproduction, diseases, and death, which were elements that were already beginning to plant a series of puzzles of transcendental character in him; and that "transcendental" response was what was meant to be called a "magical" expression. Therefore, the concept of magical empiricism was grasping in a way all that material experience of man but also his interpretations of the magical, in the sense of giving a "philosophical reason" to the "why" of things.

In a book published by Freud, *Totem and Taboo*, the psychoanalyst referred to the empirical-magical conception as a philosophical system of primordial man to know and respond to the world around him, abstract responses through the word. And Freud has the brilliant vision—in this case it is worth saying so—to use his intuition, on the one hand, and on the other to prove through his observations that this philosophical method (the empirical-magical environment) was the most natural and logical method of interpretation of reality that would have been known up to the moment in which he was expressing himself, which goes back to the cultures of Mesopotamia, Greece, and Rome, and all those thinkers who are considered the fathers of Western wisdom. Freud considers that the most important element of interpretation of knowledge of that reality is the empirical-magical foundation created by primitive man, based on the fact that man used his senses to perceive his reality, and through that perception, he elaborated his ideas, with which he expressed a discourse; and through that discourse, he had a worldview of the environment that surrounded him, together with the appearance of the cultural elements of the man who was contributing to nature.

We must not forget that Freud was a physician and was trying to find a method that would allow him to find the roots of some psychiatric diseases, which at that time caused many speculations (some idealistic and others materialistic), and based on all of that, he considered that psychological diseases could be considered non-illnesses, because they were barely genetic or experiential forms that the individual had to appreciate reality, such as the concept of love, the concept of freedom, the concept of power, literature, and so forth. It is through the development of that empirical-magical method that all his ideas regarding psychoanalysis came from, in the sense that this practice first explores the psyche, that is, the mind of the individual to find through these perceptions of human thought some elements directly related to vital functions such as life, death, sex, and so forth. And that—as a result of these conceptions, of those relationships that arose through parents and children and also inherited from the cultural past—a series of literary contexts and behaviors were built and are still considered mythical, which were ways to memorize and codify experiences that the primordial man and the evolved man had no other way of relating to but with that imaginative conception.

WMA: And of the "imaginary" content of the Colombian Caribbean in your work, what is the magical content of man's thought in this region?

MZO: Just a few months ago I wrote a lecture that I want you to read, with the title "El substrato empiro-mágico en la obra de García Márquez,"[5] in which I did not refer exclusively to Gabo's work [García Márquez was affectionally called Gabo by friends and readers], but talked about the global context from an empirical-magical point of view, in order to be able to orient ourselves in the correct understanding of what more than 500 years of European and Spanish colonization in Latin America means, and of Colombian-Caribbean culture. We have to start from a base point, from the roots that defined the process of cultural mestizaje. In other words, we are referring to a very characteristic context of a region of the world, of a region of America, of a region of Colombia, in which the aboriginal, Amerindian, and Spanish roots, the millennial tradition of Africa, have intervened as fundamental roots in the formation of cultural thought.

Only on the basis of a multiethnic and multicultural consideration can we address a "genetic" consideration of the social, cultural, political, and religious behavior of the Caribbean man. But it is one thing to accept it and another to be able to calibrate it, to understand which elements of that culture were contributed by each of the continents that make it up. I believe that is the case of the culture in the Americas, in which our roots are combined, and we would have to assume that none of the three cultures that we believe provide the basic elements of our ethnic and cultural identity, none of them can be classified as an independent culture, as a specific culture, as a culture without a link between them. On the contrary, we would have to consider the three cultures that built the formation of the American man, of the Colombian man, and of the Caribbean man. We would have to add the Syrian-Lebanese immigration to this mestizaje. In other words, both the Amerindian and the other cultures mentioned are multi-ethnic and multicultural.

The Americas began to be populated in the Quaternary, when the so-called Eurasian peoples arrived; in that same continent, there is the evolution of the human species and there are great manifestations of the creativity of the peoples that constitute that geography. Some currents, the best known, came from that watershed, but they were just some of the currents that arrived, which we could call into question when comparing it to, say, the ethnic group of the Eskimos, who possibly originated from Eurasian cultures. They also penetrated the southern part of our continent, which constituted the primitive inhabitants of Patagonia and Tierra del

Fuego. So, even though they both came from frozen regions, from regions near the poles in the Arctic and in the Antarctic, they did not have the same customs nor the same languages. Neither did they have the same philosophical conceptions, nor the same behavior toward the environment, toward life, toward social organization, and so forth. And much less could we say that there is identity between the peoples who came from the different archipelagos that make up Oceania, New Zealand, in short, so many populations and navigators who came before the Americas were populated, carried by the currents toward the Pacific coast. It was a long process, centuries before the expeditions of Columbus.

It was part of the nomadic instinct of the peoples of the world, always in search not so much of acquiring new lands, not at all, but of going after scarce food sources, which could have pushed the inhabitants of Europe, Eurasia, and the inhabitants of Africa, to engage in hunting, fishing, or what was available. In addition to the Eurasian peoples, trans-Pacific currents also brought in peoples derived from human populations that arose before the Quaternary in this region of Oceania, among which the most important, and surely the first, was a "negrito" group of the primordial cultures of Africa. That group was related, in fact, through the diminutive term of "negrito," to the Pygmies, the small Bantu man known as "negritos," differentiating them thus from the other Afro, but who, in turn, come from a [family] trunk that multiplied and diversified in Africa before moving to the European continent and before moving to Oceania in that migration process. These "negritos" have a special characteristic, very defined by cultural anthropology, and they were undoubtedly the most important roots in the population of Oceania. But they were not the only ones; there were also the Mongolians and, on the other hand, people who came from Mesopotamia who inhabited all the part of the South Asian continent through the equatorial zone. That is how they are known since remote antiquity, corresponding to that time of possible migrations toward the Pacific of peoples called *Melanesian*, which means of Black skin, and others *Polynesian*, which means of mixed skin.

In such a way, the Americas were filling up, it was populating from north to south with its different migrations. It should not be forgotten that anthropological studies have been able to determine with some certainty who came from Polynesia and who from Melanesia, peoples that occupied northern Colombia and the rest of the southern Pacific continent: Ecuador, Peru, Chile, and so forth. That is, similarities can be found between the peoples that inhabit the Americas and the ancient peoples that inhabited Oceania. For this reason, it is very superficial to give the name of "indians" to the inhabitants of the Americas, since they had the oldest roots of humanity. If we start from this base, we are going to find the Amerindian roots of the Colombian peoples, of the peoples of the Caribbean, which in one way or another would have been formed by peoples who had contact between each other before, or if they did not, began to have them in this continent and particularly in this region of Colombia. Because we must not forget that it is an isthmic region, and this means that the peoples of Oceania arrived from the Pacific coast and continued their migrations, some toward the Amazon, looking for food wealth (vegetables, fish, and animals that were in that area); others stayed in Mexico in the plains of North America that, at that time, were not as devastated as today. Those peoples continued their journeys to the Caribbean, and there are those who suspect that the inhabitants of the Canary Islands, the Guanches, were somehow related to the migrations that left the Americas for Europe, in the opposite direction from what Columbus had done.

WM: So, would that be the component of Afro-Amerindian mestizaje in the diversity of Colombia?

MZO: No, that would be the Amerindian component. Elements were added from the Spanish colonization: European, where the Hispanic, Gaul, English peoples, etc., came from. They constitute another root that is going to merge with the Amerindians and the other contingent of Africans will come later, transported as prisoners to our lands and converted into another new human branch, which is going to be merged with some ancestors who in one way or another came through the part of Oceania, both from the European and Eurasian side, as well as on the African side. That is, the man of the Caribbean, the man of the Americas, is a man influenced many times by mestizaje.

I have always recalled the terms used by José Vasconcelos when he says that the "cosmic man" has been formed here in the Americas, a man that has all the antecedents of what we say when we talk about the cosmic presence of the human being. This related to not only the biological but also the cultural context. Each of these elements found in the Americas bring together a cultural past, skills of material creativity that are going to overlap through a process that has been called "acculturation," "transculturation," and "enculturation." All these phenomena are present there in the Caribbean, so it is not so easy to define—in the case of the Caribbean, or in the case of Chile, or in the case of the Argentines, and so forth—what could be found within that context of possible influences from Europe, Asia, and Africa. What we do know is that there were very important currents in the formation of the man of the Americas from the time of the conquest.

Referring exclusively to the African contribution, we can say, according to the most studied anthropologists in the field, approximately 50 million arrived here to the Americas, and those were the ones who survived the manhunt and the journey. The former president, philosopher, and Senegalese poet Léopold Senghor says that 200 million kidnapped prisoners were plundered from Africa, a figure that is yet to be verified, but in any case, the African presence in the formation of the Americas and the Caribbean man is very visible, very significant—although the intention has been to systematically ignore it, for political, social, and economic interests.

On the other hand, I also rely on the theses of historical materialism of Karl Marx applied to society, but to societies that act because of the evolution of material manifestations, which are not related to the biological phenomenon, as Charles Darwin applied them. In this case, it would be better to speak of the natural manifestations of the historical evolution of natural societies: the family, the horde, the clan, to properly establish the well-organized society, feudalism, capitalism. This conception of the evolution of society, from a Marxist point of view, is what I use as a basis to interpret the struggles and social and cultural reforms that were taking place on this continent, at a moment when different forms of thought came together here, in the Americas, based on these facts and on the historical evolution of men who evolved from primitive communism, to a more differentiated society when feudalism, capitalism, and colonialism appear, especially in the Americas and later in Asia.

Since the sixteenth century, the peoples of the modern age had already established codes and procedures for appropriating the peoples of Africa and the Americas through discriminatory, derogatory policies to diminish the human condition of the oppressed peoples, and it is this point of reference or interpretation that allows us to understand the society in which we have lived. With Latin American and African societies being the most harmed in this imperialist policy of divvying up the world with intimidating armament. These realities have made me understand the political reasons behind why Latin American countries, in this case Colombia, are living under external forces within an international framework where we are weak nations, we must be dominated by other more powerful nations that have not valued the human but have destroyed it. Therefore, my commitment to literature in the genres I have cultivated—such as essay, short stories, theater, chronicle—have always been based on the historical and sociological conditions of alienation of the oppressed.

WMA: Maestro, let's talk a little about Frantz Fanon and his contribution to the decolonization of the Afro-Amerindian psyche and history.
MZO: Look, it is necessary to create an awareness among all *ekobios*,[6] whatever their "race" might be here in Colombia, of the need to make an inner self-reflection of Fanon's theses, which allows us to carry out a process of dis-alienation to make us aware of the elements of cultural domination imposed by the slavers during the time

of slavery, and by their heirs in power after independence. Because 150 years after the so-called emancipation of the "enslaved" in Colombia, we behave as if we still had our bodies in chains, assuming patterns of behavior that were imposed on us. Generally speaking, we could say that we have not been able to recover our ancestors' memories as free men of Africa, but that we have the tragic history of manhunting on the continent, who brought us as prisoners and subsequently enslaved us here in the Americas.

From that process of bringing our ancestors here and enslaving us, we must reclaim the memory that none of those ancestors came here, to the Americas, without chains, that is, they were prisoners who did not accept slavery nor to be subdued in chains. When we talk about chains, we are thinking about not simply the ankles but also chains for their neck, for their fists, and muzzles for their mouths. That is why they were called muzzles, because they were so resistant to the condition of prisoners that the slavers did not trust themselves to leave their mouths without a muzzle and much less to leave their fists free, because they would punch, and much less free their feet and ankles, because they would run and kick. They never accepted the condition of being enslaved, and what Fanon points out is that now, after emancipation, after we have removed our chains, in the case of Colombia, we have been in chains for another 150 years. Fanon warns us that we have—engraved in our minds with fire—the mutilation of limbs, whippings, and shootings, that dependence on the colonizer who no longer acts today but continues with his heirs in power, in the economy.

Another phenomenon within this context is the conceptualization of the society we live in, and some acts of survival that our grandparents had to undertake for living with bare feet, in an environment of illiterates. We continue to behave under the idea that we must get any woman who walks by pregnant and not assume the responsibility of a constituted household. All these elements that Fanon and others point out, and that you know, are the themes we have to pass on in order to radiate that consciousness of free men. Within that process, we are talking about facing "a notion of ethnicity," of belonging to a very ancient culture, cultures that had as their basis sacred conceptions. Among them, I want to point out the conception of *kulonda* within the Bantu philosophy, name given to the seed that an ancestor deposits in the womb of a couple to give it the gift of fertility, committing that ancestor to give life to the protégé of his ethnic group.[7] The kulonda gave the individual the word and intelligence. The condition of humanization is given by that ancestor. His responsibility was to preserve the life he had received and to use intelligence to enrich the life of his community, and the gift of the word for creative activity. We say that the gifts received by the future product of gestation, the kulonda sowed the ancestor from any member of the couple. When he was born with the gift of life, speech, and intelligence, the protégé had to preserve these gifts. Life above all, intelligence, and the word to enrich the community.

We have here a whole muntu philosophy, which means the oldest ethnicity of the ontogenetic evolution of man in Africa.[8] For this very reason, the other ethnicities that exist in Africa are all participants in this philosophy, because it is not a philosophy of a controlled group but a product that is at least a million years old, of man having acquired those notions. If we make a reflection of the conditions our grandparents were subjected to in the trafficking of prisoners during slavery, to erase the religious notion of family, to do even the impossible for it to multiply, to snatch their children from their mothers so that they would never see each other again . . . all these aspects, point by point, marked the Afro as if they had been engraved with steel brushes in their conscience, in the unconscious of the enslaved, which have produced in the mentality of the enslaved a profound alienation in which they do not manage to glimpse with their conscience that they have gone from the condition of enslaved to that of citizens of independent republics, and continue to behave with that submission, with that mendicant attitude toward the "master," with that unwillingness to make decisions, with that abstraction to create autonomous values of their own, outside those imposed by the "master." These conditions have been introduced into the unconscious and into the consciousness of the colonized, and do not allow him to reconstruct the memory of the condition of free man in Africa, owner of his destiny, member of an urban or rural community of his tradition, is the loss to some extent of the kulonda concept and the obligation that the protégé has with his protector to preserve life and enrich it with his acts.

WMA: An integral notion of what the family should be on a spiritual, moral, social, and physical level in all areas of life?

MZO: And also, the desire to be unified with the woman, but in the certainty that those children would not become a family because they were going to be sold, the mother would not meet with her son again, or the son with the father. In short, all these elements are what we must overcome, all these alienations, all these negative aptitudes, all this loss of personal pride, of will, of sense of a stable herd family. It is what we must reintegrate into a national movement with all those who, one way or another, have had a process of mestizaje by which the African was present, or in those mestizos who do not have African blood but who also had family and tribal or social community, religion and concepts, which allowed them to identify themselves as entities of a community within a social context of mestizaje.

That is to say, what we are saying does work not only for the African but also for the son of the Spanish, who they considered of lineage but often did not recognize as sons, and so forth. And the same with the indigenous people, who they also tried to break from their cultural traditions and were broken within a society imposed by the colonizer or in the indigenous *resguardo* supervised by those colonizers. The only ones who could acquire an absolute awareness of their memory and language were those who escaped into the rainforest, but they were not men of the rainforest, as we see today in the way they identify the Indian with a wild man. They were men who lived in Santa Fe de Bogotá, in the Plaza de Caicedo, in the Plaza de Caldas; that is, they were citizens of the nation, who had been conquered, men were [living] by the banks of the rivers, in the rainforest region, but in some way [were] connected with some concept of nationality.

All that was erased and the descendants, whether African or Spanish or indigenous, are suffering that process of self-forgetfulness. I think that the indigenous people are doing so the least, but also the most, to the extent that they were the most marginalized voluntarily and lost all contact with the rest of the country's socialization. They are self-marginalized, and it is more difficult for them to try to join national society than any of the other African descendants who, in one way or another, were linked to the urban centers, and even when we were set aside for the exploitation of mines, we had contact with the administrative center of those mines and with the foremen of those mines and the children of those mines, and so forth.

I am pointing out this difference because at this moment we are seeing that the values have changed. We see that it is the indigenous who are defending their traditions, their customs, their habits, because in some way, since they were already in the rainforest, the indigenous people always protected them. That is why we find that many of the indigenous communities can identify with carrying out common defense programs, and are linked with indigenous organizations throughout the continent, and are also linked with defenders of human rights and with nongovernmental organizations that defend the preservation of indigenous cultural values, and so forth. On the other hand, we, the descendants of Africans, mulattos, and zambos, have not been able to rescue the ancestral heritage of the muntu, we have not fulfilled or do not always accomplish the mandate of enriching life as imposed on us in the past by the ancestors.

WMA: After listening to you, I understand that you are not part of those Latin American writers alienated by the artistic models imposed by the colonizer, because they ignore the richness, complexity, and mestizaje that are characteristic of our peoples, manifested in their culture and in their genes, in their ideas and in their thoughts.

MZO: I believe that we must re-channel them into our own roots. For example, the line of thought of some authors who say that it is necessary to intervene in the cultures of these peoples in order to put an end to barbarism and adapt them to the needs of development.[9] All of this reasoning appears throughout the historical development of the Americas. Instead, I demonstrate with our literature how concepts such as freedom, equality, and fraternity—brandished at the time by the European bourgeoisie—should be understood as part of what we call "democracy in the Americas." These bourgeoisie concepts, considered very democratic and just, were already present here when that same bourgeoisie, owners of power, kings, and crowns imposed their rule here and the concepts of equality, freedom, and fraternity among the peoples colonized by Europe.

This two-faced attitude, one consistent with the development of the peoples that they dominate and the other consistent with the ideas that the dominating peoples had, is the determinant for today's colonized peoples in the modern era, and those exploited since antiquity, to rise up against the principles of the bearers of civilization, technology, and democratic capital. Because these elements have led to the imposition of certain values on oppressed peoples, on peoples who have not developed the same degree of technology, using the power of capital as an element of diffusion of the imposed values that they preach. Today, we cannot lose tradition against those who conspire hegemonic power in the world, although we no longer live in the Cold War but in a much cruder, much crueler globalized world. Confrontations are not only today between technologized and non-technologized peoples, as it was before, but in a ruthless way among the technologized. And, as these countries confront each other, they are, in turn, developing their own ways of thinking, and this consists of depriving others of the possibility of accessing the instruments of technology so that they can develop. Today, we must take into account this vision, and this is what I have already included in my last novel, which I have titled *Itxao, el inmortal*, which is the conscience of all peoples of the world fighting so that the common good of civilization, humanity, and culture cannot be fractioned or enjoyed exclusively by those who have enough money to buy technological development, but must be the same for everyone.

WMA: I am surprised that a writer as universal and encyclopedic as García Márquez [known as Gabo] recognizes that only until 1978, when he traveled to Angola, did he become aware of his Afro legacy. This is truly surprising, right? If García Márquez said this, what could we expect from other writers?

MZO: Yes, there is a terrible alienation. Gabo's case is very surprising because he includes the Massacre of the Banana Fields [in his novel], and most of the dead were Afros, but he does not say so.[10]

WMA: Would this be related to the phenomenon you have called the "decolonization of Latin American literature?"[11]

MZO: Yes, that is what needs to be done.

WMA: The precise question, maestro, upon reading various texts, is that I have noticed that there was always an alliance, a co-belonging of mestizo authors of Portuguese language, such as Jorge Amado; of French language in the Antilles, such as René Depestre; of Hispanic America, such as Carlos Fuentes, Octavio Paz, Mario Benedetti, Uslar Pietri, and yourself, among others. The link between literature and politics, between the intellectual and social commitment, is insistent. How has this historical relationship shaped your actions, your novel, and to what tradition does it belong?

MZO: If you do not approach the issue from Fanon, you will never understand the differentiation between Octavio Paz, Fuentes, Manuel Zapata Olivella, and Domingo Faustino Sarmiento. The basis is that the project of slavery, colonization, the annihilation of the indigenous and Afro peoples by the Spaniards, the Anglo-Saxons, was a transgression of the natural concept of development of the cultures of the world. And there is no historical factor (technological superiority and development) that says a culture must oppress and impose its criteria on other cultures. What would have become of the Europeans—and I have wanted to write a novel on this issue—if the Indians were the ones who "discovered" them? At the time when Columbus arrived here, in the Americas, what would have been the design of humanity or Europe? What would it have been like if the Aztecs had the weapons of the Spaniards when they arrived here? Then you realize that to make these reflections it is not enough to have read this or that book or text. There is a need to have a system of knowledge, of a sociological, philosophical, scientific, and psychological nature, to understand the ground we are walking on. To consider and answer your question, not too long ago here in the Americas, the first steps of an autonomous and autochthonous thought had been emerging and began to take place. It started from the time of independence of the countries of the Americas, from the north to the south, but it did not germinate from slavery in any of these countries, but under the technological development of the Industrial Revolution that England had made. And they took advantage of those goods, those tools that the English had discovered, and which they used to dominate India and civilizations much older than the European ones.

WMA: I think, maestro, that you misunderstood me, or I misrepresented the question. In a word, why can not we understand Latin American writers without the idea of power, without politics?

MZO: It is what I am proposing, but I understand it my own way. If the conquistadors had arrived here without politics, without the interests of those regimes, things would pipe a different tune. There would have been a distinction between the political regime of the Aztecs, the Incas, and that of the Europeans. But that is not what happened. There was, therefore, a system of colonization with an imposed system of domination. So, it is not that politics is used capriciously, but that politics, in any society, occur in acts, and these are political acts. When this begins to be questioned, that is when an Americas' political thought begins to be forged faced with a political thought of the colonizer, which does not mean that it [political thought] appears at the moment of independence, because we have precedents like the indigenous revolutions throughout the colonial era.

And that was questioning the political system because indigenous revolutions were political, not just religious as they are often seen. When you come back, I would like you go to the Instituto Distrital de Cultura y Turismo [Culture and Tourism Municipal Institute] of Bogotá, and see the paintings of Sergio Trujillo, who more than a painter was a fighter, and much of the art he captured is reproduced on those walls. There, you are going to find representatives of Viceroy Amar y Borbón, in El Socorro and in San Gil, when the people rose up and came out to the streets, the way they are on their knees in front of one who is barefoot, they are *comuneros* [commoners] asking for accountability of the political system. This was in 1781; we are talking about the Rebellion of the Comuneros that, among other things, was widespread throughout all Latin American countries (there was a previous history in the creole struggles of Benkos Biohó in the Montes de María in 1605).

I feel I am the heir of all those thinkers, intellectuals, politicians, and citizens who fought and continue to fight against the domination of the European and Anglo-Saxon thought here in the Americas. I feel heir to Túpac Amaru, Piar, Padilla, Louverture, Dessalines, Martí. I belong to that heritage.

WMA: What was your personal, cultural, and academic relationship with what was called the "Latin American boom" in the 1960s? And what impact did the literary magazine *Letras Nacionales* have on this phenomenon?

MZO: We are again slaves to words. This word "boom" has a literary connotation in the sense that a series of prominent writers appeared in the Americas who, for the first time in history, had the literary experience for their books to transcend the regional sphere, and they began to be sold massively, in series. A great influence of the media, press, and radio appeared in literature. The word "boom," together with the knowledge of many books and many contemporary intellectuals that were taking place in Latin America, is only part of a technological process used by those who directed and coordinated it to sell more books.

A somewhat more acute analysis of this circumstance allows us to study how, from that moment on, only those names linked to the interests of the publicists have been written about, and have been selling and have been promoted, while others who were just as talented, and so were their works, were hardly known because they have different "styles" and published small editions through the sweat of loans. Faced with this circumstance, the magazine *Letras Nacionales* was born, and we wanted to give the opportunity to young people who were not published in the newspapers.

The presence of these intellectuals in *Letras Nacionales* was not because we joined the boom, it was because we took advantage of the boom of those famous intellectuals who arrived in Bogotá, where we had to grab them practically by the tie and ask them to come to our newsroom so that they could meet these boom monsters, whom they only knew through books and not personally.

This situation of the boom of the 1960s persists today and is one of the biggest impediments for us writers who unfortunately do not share these themes, these styles, to be able to join the great harvest of values that propagate and spread. There are a few who could make their books known in each country, and others that could not. *Letras Nacionales* wanted to bring writers from the Colombian provinces to make them known through those newspapers, in such a way that eventually *Letras Nacionales* stopped being published, but the task we carried out must be continued now with more insistence. We thus have literature that is based on that glorification of power that imitates European literature models and titles, while at the same time ignoring its own history, ceasing to tell its own oppression. On the other hand, there is a positive aspect that today in our literature, in an effort to face this situation, we see authors who do not allow themselves to be dominated by the guidelines drawn up nor join in being preachers of the known guidelines.

And I do not want to set myself as an example in that situation because I am not the only one but I have lived that circumstance personally, and it has affected me. Much of my life has been devoted to literature, but in order to find my books you need to go and look for them in the drawers of the sellers of old books, because there is no publisher who is interested in publishing the latest edition of my books, in an artistic market of insignificance. All of the above is enclosed in a situation that I consider to be most critical: we live in a culture of non-readers, a country with a high degree of illiteracy. And what is the point for a writer to write a book in a culture that does not read, that is not self-critical?

WMA: You know, maestro? Sometimes I have come to think that we are lost, because it is not only the Afro who is alienated, but the anthropos in general, alienated from the pedagogical, economic, political, and cultural structures.

MZO: This is one of the elementary principles of ethnology, which assumes that the human presence in the environment is the first alienation and depends on it; for example, he cannot live in an environment where there is no oxygen. If he demands water to live, it is essential, and he cannot live in an environment where there is no water. There and then is where the alienation begins already, the one that living beings have in the natural world. The second alienation is that which man creates for himself, at the moment when man begins to transform the environment with tools, because he cannot live without that cultural environment that he has created for himself. From there we can categorically affirm that man is not going to change his role of being alienated in the face of the environmental conditions that surround him. We can say that those who are most alienated from technology are the men who have developed it, and that is why today there is a fundamental conflict between those men who have been alienated by Nature and those who have been alienated by Culture but who have not had to suffer the violent technological impact that we are suffering at this time (and who are the ones who are alienating our oppressors). The social and cultural alienation of these oppressors by their technological means can be said to be expressed basically at the moment when you do not want to provide those technological tools for the service of humanity, but for the service of capital.

WMA: In this order of ideas, would the Marxist theses of development be valid here? What did lead man to become a "commodity" for certain purposes within a capitalist society?

MZO: It is from the capitalist economy, because we already know that before the emergence of class divisions in the evolution of a primordial community, society, the participants in this process had not become objects of commodification and trade. This appears when society is divided into classes to ensure the predominance of one class over another. Man not only becomes a commodity but a tool at the service of the economy.

WMA: How do you see the situation of human freedom ahead of the new millennium?

MZO: I start from an elementary base, simple, without dogmatic complications, neither political nor social. I start from the base of the construction of the muntu. Every being born is assured of his existence in complete freedom. We must demand, we must fight so that this embryo is given all the necessary tools for "development." Likewise, we must fight so that this individual is given all the necessary tools to express all his ideas through the technological means available to humanity. Keeping to the concept of the muntu, it is not conceivable at this time to be calm and peaceful, living in a society where each being and all living beings are not recognized, to enjoy in full equality of all the "goods" that society has produced throughout the ages, be them philosophy, science, technology. This is what the twenty-first century and human civilization is proposing in the future so that these rights are fulfilled, so that we are all equal according to the conception of the muntu, and so that life on the planet does not disappear. We have to revolutionize all the concepts that have existed throughout history to enrich them with all the knowledge of all cultures and to confront them at the crossroads where humanity is, of how to survive with this technological wealth and to survive here on earth.

Notes

1 Muntu: a political idea derived from West African Bantu philosophy, which holds that there is a brotherhood of man with all kingdoms of nature, plant, animal and human; a link between the living, ancestors, and deities. Ubuntu: this concept comes from the Zulu people of southern Africa, to refer to the fact that the collective is more than the individual; hence the ethical, philosophical, and communitarian motto "I am because others are."
2 Manuel Zapata Olivella, *El hombre colombiano* (Cali: Universidad del Valle, 1974), 12.
3 This interview is part of a project on the life and work of Manuel Zapata Olivella that includes previous research that I have carried out such as "Pensamiento, mestizaje e imaginación política" that served as a prologue to the book *El árbol brujo de la libertad* in 2002 (reissued in 2014); the article "Manuel Zapata Olivella: Writer and Humanist" (2006) published in *Afro-Hispanic Review*; the book *Manuel Zapata Olivella. Un legado intercultural: Perspectiva intelectual, literaria y política de un afrocolombiano cosmopolita* (2016); "Africanidad, indianidad y multiculturalidad," which was the prologue of the book *Africanidad, indianidad y multiculturalidad* (2017); "Estudio introductorio: Alienación y desalienación de la novela," which was the prologue of the book *Deslumbramientos de América, Manuel Zapata Olivella: Humanista afrodiaspórico* (2020); the virtual seminar "Intelectualidad, literatura y multiculturalismo en

Manuel Zapata Olivella (1920–2020)" lectured with George Palacios and Cristina Cabral for the Certificate in African American Studies of the Afro-Latin American Research Institute at Harvard University (2020); and the recent article "Manuel Zapata Olivella: Intelectual afrodiaspórico" published in *Revista Communitas* (2021). Likewise, methodologically and conceptually, Marvin Lewis's book, *Literatura afrocolombiana en sus contextos naturales: Imperialismo ecológico y cimarronismo cultural* (2019); and *Manuel Zapata Olivella (1920–2004): Pensador político, radical y hereje de la diáspora africana en las Américas* (2020) by George Palacios, contribute to give belonging and geographical and historical context to this interview that is more than twenty years old, but that is extremely topical.

4 Friedrich Nietzsche, *Thus Spoke Zarathustra* (London: Penguin, 1971), 22.
5 "The Empirical-Magical Substratum in the Work of García Márquez," lecture published by the Foro Internacional sobre la obra de Gabriel García Márquez, *Gabo: Ritmo, percusión y voces* (Valledupar: Fundación Festival de la Leyenda Vallenata, Ministerio de Cultura, 2001). See, also, William Mina Aragón, ed., *Deslumbramientos de América* (Cali: Asociación Iberoamericana de Filosofía Práctica, 2017).
6 A concept Zapata Olivella used to reclaim a bond of brotherhood based on African origins and shared experience.
7 See Manuel Zapata Olivella, *El árbol brujo de la libertad* (Bogotá: Ediciones Desde Abajo, 2014), 36.
8 See Manuel Zapata Olivella, *La rebelión de los genes* (Bogotá: Altamir, 1997), 363.
9 See the work of Sergio Marras, "Comedia de equivocaciones: Entrevista a Mario Vargas Llosa," in *América Latina: Marca registrada* (Santiago de Chile: Editorial Andrés Bello, 1992).
10 See Zapata Olivella, *La rebelión de los genes*.
11 I compiled all the essays on the decolonization of literature and the historical novel of the Americas, from 1947 to 2006, in the book titled *Deslumbramientos de América*.

2 Black Upward Mobility, Neoliberal Multiculturalism and Social Whitening in Colombia

Mara Viveros Vigoya

Daniela and Carlos, two successful Black professionals when asked what it would take to extend the better living conditions that a minority of Black people have to the majority, replied this way:

Daniela: A keyway to promote social mobility is by educating people, and I think for that we need affirmative action. . . . I don't like it as much in the work environment, because I think that you shouldn't get a job . . . because you're Black but because you're capable . . . and that there are positions that you have to earn, because if not, you'll make Black people look bad.
Carlos: Really, what Colombia needs is economic development, to somehow open up a space . . . with people who have managed to be successful professionally, . . . middle-class Afro-Colombians, who you can sit down with and say "Okay, you've been successful, what would you like to contribute to those who haven't been, which are 90% of Afro-Colombians". . . . What can we do, how can we share that success and privilege that these people have earned by themselves?

Daniela, from Cartagena, at the time of our interview, was 36 years old and living in Bogotá. She has been successful in her career and is a department director in the Ministry of Education. Carlos, around 50 years old at the time of the interview, is a biologist who has had a fruitful career both in Colombia and abroad as an expert researcher in both public and private institutions. They suggest, on the one hand, affirmative action in education and, on the other, economic development, two ways that would make it possible to confront the structural racism that has generated these inequalities.

However, I do not know to which model of economic development Carlos refers, although I suppose that it is one that would allow an increase in successful Black professionals. Nor do I know if the affirmative action

DOI: 10.4324/9781003048152-4

in education mentioned by Daniela endorses meritocracy, which equates talent with merit, "lack of talent" with demerit, and turns poverty into the fault of those who do not manage to get out of it. The implications of answers like those given by Daniela and Carlos have led me to wonder about the effects that neoliberal multiculturalism has had on Black people's social mobility in Colombia and the racial relationships in which they are immersed.

In the course of writing this chapter, as will be seen below, I seek to show that multiculturalism in its neoliberal incarnation paved the way for a more open and emphatic affirmation of Black identities. Before multiculturalism, Black people felt they had to conceal their background and "whiten" themselves if they wanted to move up the social ladder and into mainstream society, and it was difficult to create spaces of resistance to whitening. That said, today, neoliberal multiculturalism does not prohibit racial pride, but it does turn it into an individual endeavor. As Mary Pattillo et al. observed,[1] the Black middle classes in Cali, whilst being proud of their background, must not open their home to poor Black family members, nor set up a Black professional association in their workplace. If they do, their actions start to contradict their middle-class status, as these behaviors are perceived as separatist or "reverse racism," and as an undermining of the common good.

It is also important to keep in mind that in Colombia, neoliberalism was deployed relatively early—in the 1970s[2]—and that this neoliberalism has had to adapt to changes, with multiculturalism being one of the most fundamental. These adaptations and the fissures that have been generated in whiteness as a socio-racial order can be observed in the comments of some of the interviewees. As will be seen throughout this chapter, multiculturalism, in its neoliberal version, has offered up some opportunities for Black people, albeit always within certain margins, which have been widened by pressure applied by Black social movements. This is the dynamic that has operated within the Colombian socio-racial order, which, rather than a fixed hierarchical and exclusive structure, is a configuration of continual processes in which fissures can periodically open.

The Constitution of 1991 included, thanks to the struggles of indigenous and Afro-descendant social movements, demands for state protection to halt transformations of coastal lands and peasant communities associated with neoliberal reforms. However, this same constitution sought to cement the legal framework required by the new economic model, in order to open up the country to the market. Thus, a governance model guided by two contradictory notions began to take shape: one related to neoliberal social policies, and one aimed at defending the collective actions and rights of ethnic groups. In this ambivalent context, the middle classes, including the Black middle classes, have continued to struggle for a place in Colombian society. At the same time, they have lent political legitimacy and a social foundation to neoliberalism as a discourse and to their particular conception of democracy, centered on these same middle classes.[3] Carlos and Daniela, whose testimonies open this chapter, both move among these contradictions in their daily lives.

This chapter is based on information gathered from three research projects on the Black middle classes in Colombia, between 2008 and 2020. In the present chapter, I refer solely to the Bogotá-based interviewees.[4] A total of 18 three-generation family histories were collected, comprising 54 biographical accounts of men and women who identify as Black or Afro-Colombian and middle class, originally from the country's Pacific and Caribbean regions, but who have resided in Bogotá at some point.[5] In this chapter, only the middle and youngest generations are included. I have used pseudonyms for all of the interviewees quoted in this chapter.

Mestizaje, Neoliberal Multiculturalism and Colombia's Black Population

In the new millennium, neoliberal multiculturalism took on the function of governing difference that the discourse of *mestizaje* (race mixture) had fulfilled from the 19th century until the end of the 20th century in Colombia. Both of these racial regimes seek a way to lead countries made up of inhabitants of different races and cultures. Mestizaje, seeing the increasingly mixed populations as the antidote to barbarism and the basis of the modern Latin American republics,[6] set about governing difference by flattening it out and proclaiming that everyone was mixed, while still upholding enough of an idea of difference through an ideology of whitening to uphold social stratification and exploitation.

In the Colombian case, between 1930 and 1950, mestizaje is promoted by the country's elites and fluctuated between a Mexican model (which conceives mestizaje as the foundation of the nation and as an emblem of democracy) and an Argentine model (which seeks to change the racial composition of the population, progressively eliminating the Black and indigenous presence, strongly associated with backwardness and regression). In fact, beyond its egalitarian rhetoric, in Colombia, mestizaje has historically represented a whitening project whose objective has been the elimination of Black and indigenous minorities through their progressive mixture with the "superior" white element.[7] Despite the failure to meet this objective, the ideology of mestizaje wielded great influence until the end of the 20th century, when, according to the Constitution of 1991, the *mestizo* nation was replaced, at least in political discourse, by the recognition of the nation as "multiethnic and multicultural."

Multiculturalism took a different approach to "governing the Other"[8] by acknowledging difference on an ethnic and cultural level, which strengthened Black or Afro-Colombian identity. However, this has been accompanied by the rising social exclusion of Afro-Colombians, as the multiculturalist project has gone hand in hand with the neoliberal economic and political model. In the 1970s and 1980s, Afro-descendant social movements were involved in antiracist praxis.[9] Then, with the implementation of multiculturalism, from 1991 up until around 2010, the struggle was focused in large part on culture and recognition: ethnic identity, ethnoeducation, and collective land rights and titles. For Laó-Montes,[10] the multiculturalism of the 1990s in Latin America is, in reality, a multicultural neoliberalism that is, in essence, a racial project. This project, firstly, through a focus on ethnicity rather than race, renders the importance of racial configurations in the social fabric invisible, and secondly, portrays racism as discrimination, solvable through the provision of financial resources and technical assistance to communities, political representation, and educational programs.

In many cases, the advances were important, but did not go far enough. This is what our interviewee, Daniela, points out when she refers to Law 70. It recognizes the rights of Blacks Colombians to collectively own and occupy their ancestral lands, but since it is not accompanied by a clear policy of agrarian reform, it does not allow communities to prosper. In the same way, Carlos is aware, from his professional experience in the United States, that without "transforming institutional racism," it is impossible to "expect a real impact on the social fate of Black people." The tokenism of multicultural discourse also seems to be a problem, as Jane, born in 1977 and from San Andrés, who worked for many years as a university professor, explains. She remembers ironically an incident where, despite being regularly underestimated and excluded, she was picked to represent the university on a visit to the United States, in order to show off the "diversity" of the institution to potential funders: "They wanted me to go to Washington with [the directors] to receive the resources from the NGO, to prove there was a Black professor! [laughter]."

Another effect of neoliberal multiculturalism, which has been disastrous for the majority of Colombia's Black population, has been the widening gap between rich and poor. The combined circumstances of contemporary structural racism alongside a history of exclusion have meant that Afro-descendants are a persistent segment of Latin America's poor. In Colombia, there are significant gaps in key measurements of poverty and social disadvantage when Afro-Colombians and non-Afro-Colombians are compared, such as income, employment status and type, and education. This is exacerbated by additional factors that arise from the social circumstances of Afro-Colombians, such as living predominantly on the urban periphery.[11] Social mobility among Colombia's Black population (as well as the population at large) during this period has been minimal or even nonexistent.[12] A study on the intergenerational educational mobility of Afro-Colombians in urban areas, based on the National Household Survey of December 2000,[13] had already shown that Afro-Colombians face the highest levels of social immobility and short-distance mobility, compared to non-Afro-Colombians. Furthermore, this study found that the Afro-Colombian middle classes are subject to greater immobility than the bulk of the Afro-Colombian population.

My research has shown that the upward mobility of Black people in Colombia is mostly, but not always, generational. Some families had social trajectories that could be described as reproductive and began their social ascent as early as the beginning of the 20th century—Carlos' family is an example of this type of social mobility—but there are also examples of families who are part of the emerging middle classes, such as those that emerged as a result of multiculturalism. This is Daniela's particular case— her job in the Ministry of Education, working with Afro-Colombian populations, is a position closely linked to policies that set out a "differential approach" to multiculturalism. This labor niche that Black professionals have begun to occupy can favor social advancement. It also depends on the family and individual situation as to whether individuals experience their own social mobility generationally, that is to say, they imagine their family's past as working class and its present as middle class.

Karen, a university professor from Cartagena, born in 1981, notes the marked devaluation of academic degrees over time and the deterioration of the working conditions of the younger generations, attributing this to the international institutional machinery that has emerged as part of the neoliberal project. This has increased the lack of social mobility of Afro-Colombian teachers:

> A few years ago it was enough to graduate high school, then it was enough to get a degree. Now we are at the level of a doctorate, and if you have a master's it's not enough. Because of IMF policy, . . . our generation sees more short-term contracts, there is less job stability.

Afro-Colombians have also been disproportionately affected by the country's armed conflict. Its deterioration in the 1990s caused the forced displacement of around eight million people. With a high percentage of these being of African descent, it was a fiercely violent form of re-diasporization. The result was a sharp increase in Afro-Colombian populations in the country's major cities, many of whom settled in the marginalized urban periphery. The neoliberal mold for Colombian capitalism has failed to solve the dire situation in which these victims of the conflict find themselves, and their continued poverty and marginalization demonstrate the economy's persistent structural racism.[14] At present, communities continue to be banished from their collective territories by the combined effects of the armed conflict and mega-development projects—such as African palm plantations, large-scale mining and corporate tourism—promoted by the neoliberal establishment.

A huge question in all of this is whether the signing of the peace accords between the state and the FARC has had any effect on violence in rural areas inhabited by Black populations, in particular, if it has made any significant difference to the operation of paramilitaries, involved with the promotion and protection through violence of the economic interests of multinationals and the Colombian elite. The picture, though, is not optimistic. Since 2016, 81 Afro-descendant social leaders have been assassinated, 71 of them after the signing of the peace agreement in November of that year, and 21 during the presidency of Iván Duque (as of August 13, 2020).[15] Nevertheless, it is important to stress that Black movements have not kept quiet about these injustices. Although in the last ten years racism has been spoken about more explicitly by nongovernment organizations (NGOs), the media, and even the state, it is almost always direct racism or racial discrimination that is alluded to. Today, the historically accumulated, structural and racialized inequalities of society as a whole must be challenged through diverse means.

In sum, a nuanced analysis is needed to transcend a wholesale condemning of the neoliberal multiculturalist project, and oversimplifying its successes or failures as far as its effects on Afro-Latin Americans must be avoided. The issue is complex because, in terms of Afro social movements, the proliferation of sources of funding has brought resources to communities, promoted organization, facilitated projects with positive cultural and economic results, and raised the level of civic and political activity. However, this funding has had negative effects in that it has encouraged partial and subordinate integration into the prevailing regimes of power and has turned some leaders into agents of neoliberal capitalism. Dependence on external funding can also make organizations more aid-oriented and demobilize and depoliticize Afro-descendant civil society. Daniela, from her experience liaising with these organizations as part of her job, is skeptical, and said that the people running them are more worried about how they will benefit personally, than the good that they are doing for Afro-Colombians in general.

Mónica Moreno Figueroa and Peter Wade point out that challenging racialized stereotypes and creating space for Black and indigenous people that they have traditionally been denied—such as in higher education or the middle class—means questioning structures, both symbolic and material, rooted in inequality and difference.[16] For these authors, recognition (culture) and redistribution (political economy) are not only necessary components of progressive social change but also intrinsically linked to each other. In this sense, some of the actions implemented as part of multiculturalism, while not completely transformative, are certainly "better than nothing," in that they allow their meanings and effects to be defended, rather than be fixed from the start.

It is also true that making structural changes, no matter how small, is difficult to achieve, because of how unquestionable the idea has become that free and unhindered expansion of the market would be the solution to all economic, social, ecological and legal problems.[17] The supporters of neoliberalism have long presented it as an object of consensus and without alternative, since to oppose it would be proof of an archaic mentality. Now, what are the implications of neoliberal multiculturalism for the social ascent of Black people after the 1990s? What effects has it had on racial prejudice, racial discrimination and the social whitening that the Black middle classes grapple with? In the next section, we will see how the new era of multiculturalism may have introduced new ways in which upward mobility affects Black identities.

Upward Mobility and Social Whitening in Neoliberal Multiculturalism

Social whitening refers to the effect that the social ascent of non-white people has on the way they are received by white society[18] and the way white and elite spaces may start to open up to them.[19] This whitening is sustained by what Eduardo Bonilla-Silva[20] calls racial grammar, that is, the way that white supremacy and racial domination are made invisible through naturalization; likewise, the presentation of whiteness as inherently relevant makes it seemingly desirable and universal. In Latin America, even after the shift toward multiculturalism, and although whitening is not explicitly idealized either at the national or individual level, "the value of the white category as superior and most desirable continues to shape policies and social interactions in the region."[21]

In this section, I will look at social whitening through three lenses: ideological, social, and personal. Whitening's ideological lens is manifested, over the long term, through the erasure of Blackness and Afrodescendant people from the national identity. This has been the case for multiculturalism as much as mestizaje. Although Latin-American societies seem to be more tolerant of ethnic diversity, racial grammar still naturalizes certain occupations and spaces as white, and therefore Black people in higher-status roles are seen as interlopers. This creates an "expectation of whiteness,"[22] in which people are surprised and even disconcerted when encountering Black professionals in white spaces. It has happened to Carlos many times: "what is strange and rather curious to me about Bogotá is that people are surprised, middle-class Bogotanos are surprised to meet an educated Black man. It's appalling!"

The expectation of whiteness is also manifested by Black professionals being mistaken for staff working in lower-status jobs, for example, doctors being mistaken for nurses. In the same vein, several interviewees referred to being treated badly by service staff—such as porters, cleaners and wait staff—who they felt, in some cases, do not recognize them as customers to be served, and in others, were purposefully disrespectful. For example, Daniela laughs about a time that her apartment block's receptionist mistook her for the maid, rather than a resident, and asked to speak to her employer.

A particularly neoliberal layer has been added to the expectation of whiteness, wherein Black professionals must be seen to be competitive, enterprising, and pragmatic, lest they be labeled as backward-looking, ungrateful or out-of-touch. The old adage, "work twice as hard to get half as far" still applies: the effort required to be accepted, never mind successful, can be grueling. Daniela points out that not everyone is willing to take on the self-sacrifice that professional recognition requires: "Others don't want to get here at six in the morning and leave at nine at night, work on a Saturday. . . . You have to earn your place, earn the job, earn the space, earn respect." Despite this, Daniela says she has used the expectation of whiteness to her advantage, using it to confound assumptions and make a bigger impression.

Social whitening is expressed through the need for Black people to adapt and integrate into white culture and spaces on a social or community level. For older generations of Black middle-class Colombians, living under mestizaje, society demanded that they erase their Blackness as far as they could and integrate into white/mestizo society. Ana, an IT manager, born in 1958 in Chocó but brought up in Bogotá, narrated how her family, on arrival in the capital, were keen to integrate, choosing a middle-class neighborhood to live in, private schools for their children, and eventually cutting ties with contacts from their community in Chocó, to better adapt and help their children adopt the customs of the capital. There has been a change in the generation that follows Ana, who similarly, grew up in white/mestizo cities, but were born around the time of the Constitution of 1991 and so came of age in a different racial regime. These middle-class Black millennials are keener to return to their ethnic-racial roots, and explore their ancestry through their elder relatives and by appropriating the food, music and culture of their homelands, even without ever having visited these places. Ana's niece, Soraya, a 20-year-old marketing student at the time of our interview, cites the presence of the extended family as a huge part of what ties her to her roots and her identity as a Chocoana.

Moving in white-majority circles has also had an effect on the Black middle classes' romantic relationships and Black women seem to be desired by no-one and everyone at the same time, being the subject of stereotypical sexual fantasies and desires but excluded from stable sexual relationships which fall outside of these.[23] Ana spoke about the paradox of the middle-class Black female experience in terms of romantic relationships. They encounter few Black men in their professional lives and in their social circles, and those that they do meet tend to prefer lighter-skinned woman that better correspond to their ambitions for social mobility. Karen, who is younger than Ana, puts a more positive spin on her singledom. This could be because of her age, but also due to differences between the Caribbean and Andean cultures in which the two women are immersed. She describes her life and that of friends in Cartagena as a world of free, single, professional women who have short-term relationships with men who they do not depend on for their material well-being. In opposition to Ana, she is not necessarily looking for someone from a similar professional sphere.

Black men are also subject to stereotypes that come into play in the world of sexual and romantic relationships. This phenomenon has been studied especially in the context of interracial relationships between Black men and white women. Moutinho has shown how this process leaves Black Brazilian men, like Black women, excluded from the idea of a long-term partner and relegated solely to being sexual objects.[24] Hellebrandova has documented for Bogotá the performative use of spaces such as nightclubs by young Afro-Colombians from the middle classes who show off their dance skills in front of their white girlfriends.[25] Hamilton, Ana's younger brother born in 1964, remembers similar circumstances in his youth, where his dancing skills were his main resource for winning over girls.

As has been documented in many Latin American societies, beautifying is equated with whitening.[26] In addition to skin color, hair texture, body shape, facial features and clothes can be 'whitened' to increase physical capital. The gendered nature of skin color stratification in Latin America means that, in general, the aesthetic manifestations of white privilege are more damaging to non-white women.[27] Hair continues to be contentious for Black women, as "natural" Black hair and hairstyles are seen as ugly, unfeminine, and unprofessional. In Colombia, how a Black woman wears her hair is not only a marker of race but also of class. In other words, having your hair straightened, blow-dried or styled is a symbol of adhesion to modernity and the incorporation of aesthetic values and models associated with social mobility and insertion in the labor market.[28]

While Afro-Colombian women must go to some lengths to modify their natural hair, for their male counterparts, the solution is somewhat easier: all of the 15 men we interviewed had short hair and two of these had shaved heads.[29] This, because "Black men are expected to wear their hair in its natural state—though the expectation is for keeping it short and conservatively groomed."[30] This is reflected in the experiences of the women and men we interviewed—when men talked about their hair (if at all), they would relate isolated incidents, whereas the women we interviewed would be able to talk about their relationship with their hair as a journey that started from very young age, and was intimately related to their happiness.

Where men and women face similar choices is in their style of dress, where, for those working in a professional setting, tailored suits in neutral colors, smart shoes and discreet jewelry are a way of blending into the expectations of capital-city, white/mestizo style, rather than being singled out for a more "exotic" way of dress. Leandro, for example, interviewed in 2010, at the time, a 33-year-old electrical engineer from Buenaventura, explains why he avoids attire that would draw attention to him: "Ethnicity should not be seen much; because I notice that the treatment you receive is different if one day you show up in an African shirt. . . . I wanted to dress like they do on television." It is interesting that Leandro references the television as his guide or standard of how to dress, as Bonilla-Silva cites that the media, especially the news, film and television are principal conduits for the racial grammar, which, in this case, universalizes a specific style of dress and personal presentation as the "proper" way.[31]

The choice faced by Afro-Colombians in white/mestizo professional and social circles presents them with a serious dilemma.[32] That is, to conform to mainstream expectations and shed their ethnic identity comes with certain benefits in terms of being taken seriously by the white/mestizo world, but with accusations by Black voices of being pompous or pretentious[33] and even labels such as "self-hating" or "race traitor."[34] Embracing an African or "ethnic" identity expressed through personal style risks the opposite: being seen as "authentically" Black, but with more difficulty in accessing the elite, white spaces. Furthermore, Mariano, 38 years old at the time of the interview, a university professor originally from Santa Marta now living in Bogotá, is aware that wearing a more informal or "ethnic" style of clothing invites judgment from fellow Black people. Being authentically Black is not possible however, because, as Fanon (1986 [1952]) posits, Blackness only exists in negation to whiteness, which created it, because it defines it.[35] Both are the opposite faces of the same dialectical process of racialization.

Black and Middle Class: No Longer a Contradiction in Terms (for Some)

Multiculturalism has allowed a small proportion of the population to ascend socially, independent of, to a certain extent, their ethnic/racial background, meaning that today, there is a small number of Afro-Colombians with a high standard of living who are part of the country's elite. What is new, with respect to the mestizaje regime—in which social ascension was conditional on adopting the social and cultural codes of the dominant group—is that, in the post-1991 era, a Black middle-class person has more leeway to express their Blackness and in fact, a Brazilian study has shown that they are more likely to reject whitening, assuming a Black identity as they move in white-majority circles and identify themselves in contrast to those around them.[36]

In Colombia, race awareness has become more widespread in the context of multiculturalism and the creation of new nation-building narratives that promote Black identity popularized by Black-consciousness movements.[37] Nevertheless, in Colombia as in Brazil,[38] middle-class Black identity has become somewhat disconnected from any reference to Black struggles or social inequalities, rather, opting for an identity that rejects discrimination against them as an individual rather than as part of a racial group that could be mobilized. The Colombian interviewees expressed this through a wish to live in a post-racial world where they would be able to escape the pigmentocracy so that they could "universalize themselves" and want "more than to fight for the Afro community." This explains Hamilton's view that affirmative action for people of African descent should be a temporary measure ("these are laws that eventually have to disappear"), and his desire not to be associated with them, to be singled out as disadvantaged and in need of help. Many express they would like "to receive treatment that is equal to that of the rest of the Colombian population," "to be one of the crowd," and to "forget that they are black." Nevertheless, the social reality makes sure to remind them of these things, as in the case of Leandro. He feels he has to leave off the fact he was born in the Pacific from his resumé "in order not to single himself out" during his job search. His behavior shows his awareness of the way whiteness is perceived as the norm.

My research shows that the middle-class identity of the interviewees is organized around the distinction between being educated and uneducated, which is the class dividing line. They reproduce the class distinction between the mental and the manual, but in the way that having a university education allows engagement in intellectual rather than manual labor. Being "educated" also implies the adoption of certain cultural markers that create distance from the Black or Afro-descendant lower classes; in showing your education, you can rid yourself of the burden of the stereotypes heaped upon Black people that paint them as uncivilized, savage or barbaric. Some interviewees, like Carlos, are quite optimistic about how a small number of "outstanding" Black middle-class Colombians could normalize Black people's successes and, at the same time, make a difference for the rest of Colombia's Black population. At the time of the interview in 2008, he was a member of the Color Foundation, an association whose objective was to promote the strategic interests of Afro-Colombians, seeking equality, recognition, and integration; primarily through the promotion and circulation in elite circles of what he calls "the gifted ten percent": Black Colombians who have excelled in a competitive field. For Carlos, if you want to "promote social progress," you must use "economic power, since it opens doors." The organization's founders were thinking along the same lines, to use "[their] privilege . . . to position the cultural values of the black population." When Carlos advocates for individual and family success, recognizing the privileges that have made it possible, he seeks not only to use this success as a platform to support other (individual) Black people, but also to highlight this success in society at large, and recognizing people who have been largely ignored. His proposal seeks to vindicate their integration into society based on their socioeconomic condition, in order to eliminate surprise when society's expectation of whiteness is not met.[39]

Despite some indisputable benefits of this goal for those who have managed to excel and as a stimulus for the younger generations, one wonders how much they can help the vast majority of the Afro-Colombian population. It is difficult to ignore that this objective conforms to an individualist neoliberal vision in which the political is reduced to the "pure administration" of cultural issues.[40] In this way, and regardless of their intent, positions such as those of Carlos and the Color Foundation end up legitimizing the depoliticization of these achievements and with it the maintenance of racial inequality. And they resemble what Clay calls Black resilience neoliberalism, which establishes structural racism as "a constant that is taken for granted" and, therefore, normalizes the individual's ability to overcome it, undermining organization in the face of state violence and Black oppression.[41]

In the past 20 years, compared to previous decades, there have certainly been more visible Black faces high up in Colombian society. For example, of a total of nine Afro-descendant government ministers, five have been appointed since 2000. However, the presence of a greater number of Black politicians in the cabinet does not mean a greater debate in the council of the problems that afflict Black people. To be accepted by the mainstream, they have had to adapt their political orientations. In contrast, Black public figures who question the status quo are, as Ana asserts, often treated brutally, with racial under (and over) tones, referring to the unjust attacks that a political figure like Piedad Córdoba has constantly been subjected to. Ana points out: "Other congresspeople, regardless of the difficulties they find themselves in, are never referred to by the color of their skin." The Black political elite that has gained acceptance has done so by supporting free trade agreements and participating uncritically in neoliberal governments. And they have equated Black empowerment with the growth of a middle and political class. In this political framework, the fight against racism is only associated with projects for the modernization and social mobility of Afro-descendants, rather than initiatives that would see the bulk of the Afro-descendant population mobilized.[42]

Resistance to White Cultural Domination

Over the last five years or so, there has been greater attention and discussion around structural racism which is evident in organizations such as the National Association of Displaced Afro-Colombians (AFRODES), in their arguments and demands on the state to eradicate the structural racism that makes Black communities in the armed conflict more vulnerable to displacement and confinement and by extension the loss of their culture.[43] More recently, in the peace process, there has been evidence of an anti-racist turn in some areas, such as the incipient technical work group "Racism and the armed conflict in Colombia: Approaching the truth," although Cárdenas sees more potential for anti-racism in actions outside of state recognition.[44]

For example, the civic strike in Buenaventura in May 2017 clearly illustrated Colombia's race problem and the state's role in it, although the motivation of the strike was not the denouncing of racism but rather its effects. Through widespread street protests, the movement threatened serious economic consequences for the country, as more than half of its exports and imports move through this port city. Its commercial importance and the increased investment in nationally important megaprojects in this area are contrasted against the dire poverty, displacement, violence and state abandonment suffered by its 400,000 Afro-descendant residents, who have no access to, among other basic services, drinking water. While the strike produced concrete results—such as the construction of a retaining wall for a secondary school, the installation of a water tank for the storage and supply of drinking water to the city and the inauguration of an intensive care unit for the hospital—these are still insufficient to meet the reported needs.

And although structural racism has been more widely discussed in recent times, it is so deeply rooted in Colombian society that it remains difficult to recognize and therefore to resist. In this context, our interviewees have been successful in indirectly undermining racism by challenging racialized stereotypes, strengthening their self-esteem or providing alternative images of Black people that are detached from connotations of poverty, unattractiveness or lack of education. Along these lines, new generations of Afro-Colombian women and a microcosm of high-profile media figures have sought to change attitudes toward Black hair. Events such as *Tejiendo Esperanzas*, a Black hairdressing event held since 2004 in Cali by the Afro-Colombian women's collective Amafrocol, use the contest as an opportunity to vindicate and dignify the craft of braiding and to promote Black beauty micro-enterprises that use traditional ingredients grown by small local farmers to make their products. Along with YouTube channels for

Black hair care, these types of events respond to changing attitudes around Black women's hair.⁴⁵ High-profile Black women, such as television news anchor and reporter Mabel Lara, have spoken in the media about their decision to appear on screen with their natural curly hair as a political statement and a way to make Afro-Colombians visible to the nation.⁴⁶

In another field, visual artist Liliana Angulo has taken the violence directed at Black hair and, through exaggeration and parody, redoubles it in her series "*Pelucas porteadores*" (Wig Carriers), in which Black models, both men and women, wear huge wigs made of steel wool scourers molded into a single spiraling dreadlock, which connect the models to each other in solidarity and shared history.⁴⁷ The reference to porters evokes "colonial subjects who carried the baggage of white colonizers and the wig represents figurative baggage that [Black people] continue to carry today."⁴⁸

Carlos Valderrama has documented that social movements in Colombia have not been the only scenario in which Black identities are built and in which their political agendas and collective interests are mobilized.⁴⁹ Since the 1940s, cultural expressions have played a very important role in the construction of meaning about what it means to be Afro-Colombian and to make visible what mestizaje had hidden the Black presence in Colombian dance, literature, music and folklore. It also helped redefine the existence of an Afro-descendant community beyond its physical characterization. With an orientation to multiculturalism, policies were developed to recognize the diversity and cultural contributions of ethnic groups that structured and strengthened discourses of political, historical and cultural vindication.

An example of this has been the presence of Pacific folklore in popular music, introducing new sectors of the population to this Black musical tradition.⁵⁰ Thus, today, groups such as *Chocquibtown* or *Herencia de Timbiquí* have taken up the musical legacy of the Colombian Pacific, and have fused it with elements of contemporary urban music creating a sound that is global yet rooted in the unequivocally Black Pacific Coast. Through lyrics, music and dance they affirm racial pride and strength of the collective, and the need for a post-racial world. Their songs are also an invitation to use music as a resource for plural political mobilization. Thus, the double consciousness, which constitutes the founding experience of the Afro-American diaspora, assigns a double value to these songs that have become representative of both Black music and the country that produced it, Colombia.⁵¹ Due to its character of "escape" or "*cimarronería*" (marronage) in the face of western hegemonic values, Black music represents an opportunity to democratize social relations. Freedom and spontaneity in the combination of rhythms and dance as well as the dialogical and heterogeneous composition present a new type of anti-individualist sociability that challenges the verticalist and meritocratic democracies and install new models of citizenship.⁵²

Looking again at the fine arts, artistic works such as those of Liliana Angulo or Fabio Melecio Palacios are demonstrating that it is possible to redefine Blackness and subvert the socio-racial order from different creative actions that appropriate the possibility of self-representation of Blackness. Melecio Palacio's work, in particular a video named "*Bamba 45*," recreated his own family history to tell the story of the harsh working conditions experienced by Black men who work in the sugar plantations, one of which is his father. He uses the sounds produced by the *Bamba 45* machetes of a group of sugarcane cutters, producing rhythmic music. The video was part of an installation that won the 6th Luis Caballero Award, the country's most important fine arts prize, and so the artist managed to use his new-found position in the prestigious, white arts world to denounce the precarious conditions of these workers, and talk about a way of life, a cultural space and a Black aesthetic, opposed to the context in which it is exhibited, which echoes what some of our interviewees say: wishes of staying true to their roots.

Through tactics that use parody, as in Angulo's case, to make explicit both the epistemic violence that many representations conceal and the performative effect of race, these proposals have radicalized the kind of self-recognition that multiculturalism offers. The space that has been opened to think about racism allows us to hope that it will be possible to generate political mobilizations around demands that do not revolve around a single and rigid definition of Blackness and a critical mass of professionals capable of challenging the risk of converting the Black middle classes into a new elite.

Conclusion

In this chapter, I have attempted to identify advances for Afro-Colombians under multiculturalism, ranging from "better than nothing" to positive changes toward greater cultural recognition and Black consciousness. However, against the backdrop of neoliberalism, it is difficult to see these advances amid the dire and worsening circumstances that include the murder of community leaders and the shocking statistics of the pandemic. At the heart of this ambivalence is the neoliberal promotion of individualism, and its understanding of racism as the racial discrimination of individuals rather than structural/systemic racism. It is far less costly to recognize and attempt to redress racial discrimination compared to systemic racism. Nevertheless, it should not be ignored that recognition contains "an indispensable emancipatory moment."[53] From a dualistic and interdependent perspective of justice that integrates both recognition and redistribution, it is important that the successes of the Colombian Black middle class in terms of cultural recognition lead to a serious transformation of the social and economic conditions of the majority of the Afro-descendant population.

In this context, I have analyzed the connections between upward mobility and social whitening, finding many common threads in the lived experience of the Black middle-class interviewees, showing how the Black middle classes constantly oscillate between resistance and adaptation. The way in which this is expressed has changed over time, and today, in a context that is more sensitive to racism, there is more room to maneuver, especially in cultural circles. This has facilitated the emergence of artists resisting white cultural domination in innovative and engaging ways. Buenaventura's civic strike, on the other hand, showed that there is the potential and a desire to challenge racist structures, but that these objectives are more difficult and more dangerous to achieve.

The balance of the achievements of the age of neoliberal multiculturalism against racism is ambivalent. There has been greater attention and discussion around structural racism in some organizations and some social movements have made demands on the state, linking problems such as violence and deterritorialization with structural racism. Research that seeks to show correlations between ideas of race (mainly skin color), mobility and social exclusion is more frequent than before. Affirmative actions and inclusion programs have been carried out for Afro-descendant populations in the field of higher education. There have been legal advances such as the creation and implementation of laws that criminalize racial discrimination, and some use of them to denounce racism. Media campaigns on racism awareness have been broadcast in the public and private media, and in social media too. Artistic and aesthetic interventions have been carried out aimed at the visibility and empowerment of people of African descent. Various Black organizations have also mobilized empowerment associated with beauty, racial visibility and body positivity.[54]

But at the same time, as Laó-Montes has pointed out elsewhere,[55] there are key questions that must continue to be asked, such as whether we are advancing toward a global agenda of social justice or if we are simply opening some spaces for social and political mobility that serve largely to reproduce the status quo in the name of racial equality. Considering the problems reported in this chapter, we cannot affirm that the living conditions of the majority of Afro-Colombians are improving or that their political autonomy has increased. Nor can we conclude that we are in the same situation as 30 years ago. The awareness of racism is more widespread in the Black middle classes, although this has not resulted in the emergence of a generalized anti-racist activism among them. Middle-class factions closest to power or with higher economic incomes have discouraged disruptive anti-racist positions. And the social ascent of Black people remains as precarious and individualized as it was before multiculturalism, which is why it does not have redistributive effects. Some government and civil society policies and programs have undoubtedly contributed to greater cultural recognition, and in the field of culture, the frontiers of the imagination have been expanded to forge new anti-racist scenarios and possibilities.

Our current outlook of post-pandemic, post-*paro nacional*[56] and post-election of the *Pacto Histórico*[57] party holds important questions about the place of racism in Colombia's structural inequalities. In this regard, I wonder for what and for whom we are building our present and future, and what shape it will take? After the international outrage and protests in response to the murder of George Floyd in the United States in May 2020, and the abuses and violence that the Minga Indígena[58] endured in Colombia as they participated in the *paro nacional* (national strike) in 2021, we began to speak openly about structural racism in Colombia.[59] We also recognized the role that the state has played in the production and reproduction of racism. Encouraging floodgates have been opened in the response that these attacks and deaths have provoked: expressions of solidarity; the nationwide street protests challenging the police that went ahead even during the midst of the pandemic; the increasing political mobilization; the refusal to bury news stories that cover atrocities such as the death of Anderson Arboleda,[60] the political assassinations of Afro-descendant leaders, the precarious conditions in which Black communities faced COVID-19; and the 783,160 votes for Francia Márquez in the presidential elections. All these acts are forms of resistance against indifference to death and the naturalization, denial or minimization of systemic and everyday racism.

The discussions taking place in response to these actions are part of a transnational/international effort to widen the fissures that have already started to appear in the structural racism that sustains neoliberal capitalism. Paradoxically, online communities on social networks (a central aspect of the neoliberalization of society) have become promising arenas for contesting structural racism and exposing the workings of its processes. Social media platforms emerged as powerful tools for documenting and challenging police brutality and ending the mainstream media's silence and misrepresentation of negatively racialized people. At the same time, an important point to consider is the way social media have provided strategic spaces not only to question the long-established state violence but also to contest the racialized devaluation of Black bodies.[61] The users of social networks have employed their platforms to expand the public sphere and at the same time evidence the social and political relationships that sustain racist practices both nationally and internationally. Black and other ethno-racial movements and their allies, globally and locally, are advancing against the outrageous injustice that weighs us down and leaves us gasping for air.

Acknowledgments

I would like to thank Grace Acosta for her support during the writing process in English and help in honing the content of this chapter.

Notes

1 Mary Pattillo, Rosa Emilia Bermúdez, and Ana María Mosquera, "Estamos distanciados: The Black Middle Class and Politics in Cali, Colombia," *Du Bois Review* (2021): 1–24.
2 A. Ricardo López-Pedreros, *Makers of Democracy: A Transnational History of the Middle Classes in Colombia* (Durham: Duke University Press, 2019).
3 López-Pedreros, *Makers of Democracy*.
4 The bibliographic research for this chapter was carried out between August 2019 and February 2020, while supported by a grant from the Center of Advanced Latin American Studies (Centro de Estudios Avanzados Latinoamericanos CALAS) for the production of a piece of research titled "Las clases medias 'negras' en Colombia: Desigualdades sociales, identidades étnico-raciales y experiencias de interseccionalidad."
5 The word Afro-Colombian is linked to the adoption of the Constitution of 1991, and to the legal provisions that recognize cultural diversity in all political, economic, and cultural matters. National Day of the Afro-Colombian was formally established through Law 725 of 2001 and has been commemorated annually since May 21, 2002. This language is linked to neoliberalism through the particular confluence of multiculturalism and neoliberalism that took place in Colombia at the time. But multiculturalism is not inevitably neoliberal.
6 Lourdes Martínez-Echazábal, "*Mestizaje* and the Discourse of National/Cultural Identity in Latin America, 1845–1959," *Latin American Perspectives* 25, no. 3 (1998): 21–42.
7 Axel Rojas, "Subalternos entre los subalternos: presencia e invisibilidad de la población negra en los imaginarios teóricos y sociales," in *Conflicto e (in)visibilidad: Retos en los estudios de la gente negra en Colombia*, eds. Eduardo Restrepo and Axel Rojas (Popayán: Editorial Universidad del Cauca, 2004), 157–172. https://biblio.flacsoandes.edu.ec/libros/digital/41087.pdf; Peter Wade, *Blackness and Race Mixture: The Dynamics of Racial Identity in Colombia* (Baltimore: Johns Hopkins University Press, 1993).
8 Guillaume Boccara, "The Government of 'Others': On Neoliberal Multiculturalism in Latin America," *Actuel Marx* 50, no. 2 (2011): 191–206. https://doi.org/10.3917/amx.050.0191.
9 Santiago Arboleda, *Le han florecido nuevas estrellas al cielo: Suficiencias íntimas y clandestinización del pensamiento afrocolombiano* (Cali: Poemia, 2016); Carlos A. Valderrama, "La diferancia cultural negra en Colombia. Contrapúblicos afrocolombianos," *Revista CS* 29 (September 2019): 209–242.
10 Agustín Laó-Montes, *Contrapunteos Afrodiaspóricos: Cartografías políticas de nuestra Afroamérica* (Bogotá: Universidad Externado de Colombia, 2020), 249.
11 Fernando Urrea Giraldo, Carlos Viáfara López, and Mara Viveros Vigoya, "From Whitened Miscegenation to Tri-Ethnic Multiculturalism: Race and Ethnicity in Colombia," in *Pigmentocracies: Ethnicity, Race, and Color in Latin America*, ed. Edward Telles (Chapel Hill: The University of North Carolina Press, 2014).

12 OECD, "A Broken Social Elevator? How to Promote Social Mobility" (Paris: OECD Publishing, 2018). https://doi.org/10.1787/9789264301085-en.
13 Carlos Augusto Viáfara López, Alexander Estacio Moreno y Luisa María González Aguiar, "Condición étnico-racial, género y movilidad social en Bogotá, Cali y el agregado de las trece áreas metropolitanas en Colombia: Un análisis descriptivo y econométrico," *Revista Sociedad y Economía*, no. 18 (June 2010): 22.
14 Laó-Montes, *Contrapunteos Afrodiaspóricos*, 248.
15 Leonardo González Perafán, "Líderes Afrodescendientes Asesinados," *INDEPAZ* (August 13, 2020). www.indepaz.org.co/lideres-afrodescendientes-asesinados/.
16 Mónica Moreno Figueroa and Peter Wade, eds., *Against Racism: Organizing for Social Change in Latin America* (Pittsburgh: Pittsburgh University Press, 2022).
17 Pierre Bourdieu, "L'essence du néolibéralisme," *Manière de Voir* 8, no. 112 (2010): 11. www.cairn-int.info/magazine-maniere-de-voir-2010-8-page-11.htm
18 Tanya Golash-Boza, "Does Whitening Happen? Distinguishing between Race and Color Labels in an African-Descended Community in Peru," *Social Problems* 57, no. 1 (2010): 138–156. https://doi.org/10.1525/sp.2010.57.1.138; Wade, *Blackness and Race Mixture*.
19 Graziella Moraes Silva, Luciana Souza Leão, and Barbara Grillo, "Seeing Whites: Views of Black Brazilians in Rio de Janeiro," *Ethnic and Racial Studies* 43 (2020): 632–651.
20 Eduardo Bonilla-Silva, "The Invisible Weight of Whiteness: The Racial Grammar of Everyday Life in America," *Michigan Sociological Review* 26 (Fall 2012): 1–15. www.jstor.org/stable/23292648.
21 Moraes Silva, Souza Leão, and Grillo, "Seeing Whites," 633.
22 Moraes Silva, Souza Leão, and Grillo, "Seeing Whites," 644.
23 Mara Viveros Vigoya, "Más que una cuestión de piel: Determinantes sociales y orientaciones subjetivas en los desencuentros heterosexuales entre mujeres y 'negros' y no 'negros' en Bogotá," in *Raza, etnicidad y sexualidades: Ciudadanía y América Latina*, eds. Fernando Urrea, Peter Wade, and Mara Viveros Vigoya (Bogotá: Universidad Nacional de Colombia, 2008), 247–279; Fernando Urrea Giraldo, Jeanny Lucero Posso Quiceno, and Nancy Motta González, "Sexualidades y feminidades de mujeres negras e indígenas: Un análisis de cohorte generacional y étnico-racial," Informe Técnico Final (Cali: Centro de Investigaciones CIDSE, Facultad de Ciencias Sociales y Económicas, Universidad del Valle, 2010). http://etnicoraciales.univalle.edu.co/InfinalSexualidades.pdf.
24 Laura Moutinho, "Raza, género y sexualidad en el Brasil contemporáneo," in Raza, etnicidad y sexualidades, eds., Wade, Urrea Giraldo, and Viveros Vigoya, 223–245.
25 Klára Hellebrandová, "Escapando a los estereotipos (sexuales) racializados: El caso de las personas afrodescendientes de clase media en Bogotá," *Revista de Estudios Sociales*, no. 49 (May 2014): 87–100. http://journals.openedition.org/revestudsoc/8441
26 Erynn Masi de Casanova, "Beauty Ideology in Latin America," *DObra [s]: Revista Da Associação Brasileira de Estudos de Pesquisas Em Moda* 11, no. 23 (2018): 10–21. https://dialnet.unirioja.es/servlet/articulo?codigo=6543800.
27 Nilma Gomes, "Trajetórias escolares, corpo negro e cabelo crespo: reprodução de estereótipos ou ressignificação cultural?" *Revista Brasileira de Educação*, no. 21 (2002): 40–51. https://doi.org/10.1590/S1413-24782002000300004; Moraes Silva, Souza Leão and Grillo, "Seeing Whites."

28 Kristell Andrea Villarreal Benítez. "Trenzando la identidad: Cabello y mujeres negras" (Master's thesis, Universidad Nacional de Colombia, 2017). https://repositorio.unal.edu.co/handle/unal/63160.
29 Mara Viveros Vigoya, "Social Mobility, Whiteness, and Whitening in Colombia," *The Journal of Latin American and Caribbean Anthropology* 20, no. 3 (2015): 496–512.
30 Ashleigh Rosette and Tracy Dumas, "The Hair Dilemma: Conform to Mainstream Expectations or Emphasize Racial Identity," *Duke Journal of Gender Law & Policy* 14, no. 1 (2007): 409.
31 Bonilla-Silva, "The Invisible Weight of Whiteness," 1–15.
32 Rosette and Dumas, "The Hair Dilemma."
33 Peter Wade, *Blackness and Race Mixture*.
34 Viveros Vigoya, "Social Mobility."
35 Frantz Fanon, *Black Skin, White Masks* (London: Pluto Press, 1986 [1952]).
36 Moraes Silva, Souza Leão, and Grillo, "Seeing Whites."
37 Edward Telles and Tianna Paschel, "Who Is Black, White, or Mixed Race? How Skin Color, Status, and Nation Shape Racial Classification in Latin America," *American Journal of Sociology* 120, no. 3 (2014): 864–907.
38 Angela Figueiredo, "Fora do jogo: A experiência dos negros na classe média brasileira," *Cadernos Pagu*, no. 23 (2004): 199–228.
39 Mara Viveros Vigoya et al., "Grandes Esperanzas. Memorias de raza, género y clase en familias afrodescendientes del siglo XX," Manuscript for the Orlando Fals Borda research grant—2017, Apoyo a Proyectos de investigación docentes, 2019.
40 Chantal Mouffe, "Política y pasiones: Las apuestas de la democracia," in *Pensar este tiempo: Espacios, afectos, pertenencias*, comp. Leonor Arfuch (Buenos Aires: Paidós, 2005); Ernesto Laclau, "Identidad y hegemonía: El rol de la universalidad en la constitución de lógicas políticas," in *Contingencia, hegemonía y universalidad: Diálogos contemporáneos en la izquierda*, eds. Judith Butler, Ernesto Laclau, and Slavoj Zizek (Buenos Aires: FCE, 2003), 305.
41 Kevin L. Clay, "'Despite the Odds': Unpacking the Politics of Black Resilience Neoliberalism," *American Educational Research Journal* 56, no. 1 (2019): 78.
42 Agustín Laó-Montes, "Neoliberalismo racial y políticas afrolatinoamericanas de cara a la crisis global," in *Afrodescendencias: Voces en Resistencia*, ed. Rosa Campoalegre Septien (Buenos Aires: CLACSO, 2018), 245–265.
43 Roosbelinda Cárdenas, "Multicultural Politics for Afro-Colombians: An Articulation 'Without Guarantees'," in *Black Social Movements in Latin America: From Monocultural Mestizaje to Multiculturalism*, ed. J. M. Rahier (New York: Palgrave Macmillan, 2012), 113–134.
44 Roosbelinda Cárdenas, "The Anti-Racist Horizon in Colombia's Peace Process," *NACLA*, March 23, 2017. https://nacla.org/news/2017/03/23/anti-racist-horizon-colombia%E2%80%99s-peace-process.
45 Mara Viveros Vigoya and Krisna Ruette-Orihuela, "Care, Aesthetic Creation, and Anti-racist Reparations," in *Care and Care Workers: A Latin American Perspective*, eds. Nadya Araujo Guimaraes and Helena Hirata (New York: Springer, 2020).
46 "'Dejarme el pelo crespo es un acto político'," *Revista Semana*, May 12, 2018. www.semana.com/enfoque/articulo/mabel-lara-habla-de-dejarse-el-pelo-crespo-como-acto-politico/566901.
47 Sol Astrid Giraldo, "Si los héroes fueran negros: Liliana Angulo y los debates de la masculinidad afrocolombiana," in *La negritud y su poética: Prácticas artísticas y miradas críticas contemporáneas en Latinoamérica y España*, ed.

Andrea Díaz Mattei (Montevideo/Sevilla: BMR Cultural/Publicaciones Enredars, 2019), 295–310.
48 Jill Lane, "Hemispheric America in Deep Time," *Theatre Research International* 35, no. 2 (2010): 121.
49 Valderrama, "La diferancia cultural."
50 See for example Juan Pablo Estupiñán, "Marimba en 'la nevera': Tránsitos sonoros de la música afropacífica colombiana," *Revista de Estudos e Investigações Antropológicas* 6, no. 2 (2019).
51 Mara Viveros Vigoya, *Les couleurs de la masculinité* (Paris: La Decouverte, 2018).
52 Ángel G. Quintero Rivera, *La danza de la insurrección. Para una sociología de la música latinoamericana: Textos reunidos* (Buenos Aires: CLACSO, 2020).
53 Nancy Fraser, Hanne Marlene Dahl, Pauline Stoltz, and Rasmus Willig, "Recognition, Redistribution and Representation in Capitalist Global Society: An Interview with Nancy Fraser," *Acta Sociológica* 47, no. 4 (2004): 376. www.jstor.org/stable/4195051.
54 Moreno Figueroa and Wade, eds., *Against Racism:*
55 Laó-Montes, *Contrapunteos Afrodiaspóricos.*
56 The 2021 *Paro nacional* (national strike) in Colombia was one of the biggest and most important social protests in the country's history. Triggered in April of that year by government plans to reform tax policy, the manifestations took up the banner of the previous *paro* from November 2019 that demanded government action on social inequality, police violence, the non-implementation of the peace accord and the widespread murder of leaders of social movements. Hundreds of thousands of people took to the streets in urban centers across the country, and at the *paro*'s height, there were marches almost every day for two months, and highways and ports were blocked by workers.
57 Pacto Histórico is a political coalition composed mainly of left and center-left political parties and movements.
58 Collective of indigenous organizations, which is called Minga, referring to an act of community work.
59 See, for example, in the mainstream media, "¿Tiene Colombia un problema de racismo estructural en la sociedad?" *Hora 20*. https://caracol.com.co/programa/2020/06/06/hora_20/1591408757_605249.html; Olga Lucía Martínez Ante, "Creadores afro dan su opinión sobre la discriminación y el racismo," *El Tiempo*, June 15, 2020. www.eltiempo.com/cultura/arte-y-teatro/racismo-y-discriminacion-hablan-cuatro-creadores-afro-507006.
60 On May 19, 2020, Arboleda, a 19-year-old Black youth from Puerto Tejada, Cauca, died after receiving blows to the head from police after they accused him of violating lockdown rules.
61 Yarimar Bonilla and Jonathan Rosa, "# Ferguson: Digital Protest, Hashtag Ethnography, and the Racial Politics of Social Media in the United States," *American Ethnologist* 42, no. 1 (2015): 4–17.

3 From Native to Raizal
Indigeneity and the Anglophone Afro-Caribbean Heritage of San Andrés, Providencia, and Santa Catalina

Sharika D. Crawford

The Archipelago of San Andrés, Providencia, and Santa Catalina is one of the least visible parts of Colombia.[1] Situated in the southwestern Caribbean and nearer to the Nicaraguan coast, these tiny islands have a long history that connects them to the Caribbean coast of Central America and the wider Caribbean. Moreover, the cultural, linguistic, and racial makeup of the island population reflects the origins of settlement patterns across the past three centuries: Jamaican planters, Dutch smugglers, enslaved Africans, Miskitu fishermen, and Caymanian turtlemen formed an Anglophone island culture different from mainland Colombia with its majority Spanish-speaking *mestizo*, *mulato*, and white counterparts. These distinctions have long captured the attention of visitors; both state and non-state actors. During the first half of the twentieth century, most visitors—foreign merchants, newly appointed administrators, and religious missionaries—all observed, commented on, or were alarmed by islanders' cultural differences and attitudes toward Colombia, viewing it as a lack of loyalty. In response, state officials in Bogotá pursued a set of policies to assimilate the island population into Colombia known as Colombianization. One of these policies led to the arrival of new migrants from mainland Colombia to San Andrés Island in the 1950s. This dramatic demographic shift prompted islanders to draw sharper distinctions with the new island residents and continually adopted terminology to define themselves.

By the 1990s, San Andrés, Providencia, and Santa Catalina islanders had created a new term to describe themselves against other social groups in Colombia and reclaim a sense of ethnic pride. Drawing on the Spanish word *raíz*, meaning source or origin, they created the term *Raizal*. It distinguished islanders who descended from the population to settle permanently on these islands in the eighteenth century from islanders who had arrived more recently in the late twentieth century. In doing so, Raizals adopted a non-traditional form of indigeneity that made no claims to pre-Columbian indigenous ancestry.[2] Dissimilar to mixed Afro-indigenous populations

DOI: 10.4324/9781003048152-5

in Latin America like the Garífuna and some Miskitu, the indigeneity of Raizals is rooted in an Anglophone Afro-Caribbean Protestant identity forged in engagement with and opposition to mainland Colombians. Some scholars have argued that the adoption of a Raizal identity is simply a political strategy to advance contemporary cultural politics in response to Raizal displacement since the 1960s and was incongruent with the inherent hybridized nature of Caribbean identity formation.[3] Such exclusive definitions of Raizal identity have also been contested and undercut by Raizals of mixed heritage of Raizal and non-Raizal ancestry known as "the fifty-fifties."[4]

Instead, I argue that the recent adoption of the term "Raizal" to define their identity is the culmination of a century's long struggle for ethnic rights and self-determination reflective of their tenuous and unclear position within the multiracial landscape of Colombia and marginal place within the broader Caribbean. Combining an array of sources such as travel accounts, official correspondence, newspaper articles, diplomatic reports, and published oral histories, I develop this argument across three sections. First, I briefly trace the ethnogenesis of Raizal identity explaining its Anglophone Afro-Caribbean roots. Since Raizal identity is based on ancestral claims of being descendants of the "original" permanent settlers, it is necessary to introduce this wider context. Then, I introduce and examine the state project to assimilate islanders into Colombia that began in 1913 and culminated in the years after establishing a free port on San Andrés in 1953. In doing so, I show the rhetorical and concrete ways islanders gradually claimed a unique space vis-à-vis Colombians including Afro-Colombians and indigenous peoples. Finally, I conclude with some final considerations on the effects of the Constitution of 1991 on Raizal ethnic mobilization and visibility within Colombia and the greater Caribbean.

A Brief History of the Raizals of San Andrés, Providencia, and Santa Catalina

The ancestral origins of the Raizal population on the archipelago are deeply rooted in twin processes: The ongoing arrival of mostly English-speaking peoples to settle permanently on the island from the late seventeenth century onward and the multiple occupations and invasions from outsiders seeking to control these islands. These twin processes have shaped the memory and formation of a Raizal identity that has privileged their Anglophone Caribbean ancestry and differentiated them within a multiracial Colombia. What remains clear is that Raizals descended from the fourth wave of people who settled permanently on the Archipelago of San Andrés, Providencia, and Santa Catalina from the late eighteenth century onward.

Thus, the invention of themselves as autochthonous or indigenous to these islands reflects the local history of repeated series of population settlements and displacement.

Scholars have found identifying the first permanent settlers an easier task said than done, given the archipelago's multiple waves of population settlement and the lack of interest in early European encounters with it. While the Miskitu of Central America frequently visited and built temporary turtle-hunting stations on one or more of the adjacent cays near San Andrés and Providencia Islands, European newcomers found the islands without any permanent settlements suggesting that it was unoccupied.[5] While some Colombian historians like Félix Díaz Galindo have claimed that Christopher Columbus visited the islands during his fourth voyage and was responsible for naming San Andrés and Santa Catalina after Catholic saints, American historical geographer James J. Parsons considered such a supposition erroneous.[6] What we do know is that Europeans knew of these islands as early as 1500 as noted in cartographical maps and guidebooks. The earliest known European settlements may have been Dutch adventurers who lived temporarily on the islands during the late sixteenth to early seventeenth century since the 1604 expedition of Juan Díaz Pimiento did not result in Spanish colonization.[7] As a result, scholars agree that European newcomers were the first to establish permanent settlements on the island.

Until the end of the eighteenth century, the archipelago continued to receive multiple waves of mostly European settlers and occupiers. While it remains unknown the reasons the Dutch withdrew from the islands, they were soon replaced with a second wave of settlers: English-speaking Puritans from Bermuda and the United Kingdom in 1629.[8] Spanish authorities took the islands, confiscated and sold their enslaved African laborers, and expulsed the Puritans to St. Kitts, Tobago, the Bay of Honduras, and Mosquitia in 1641.[9] With the expulsion of the Puritans, the third wave of settlers, a small Spanish garrison that was even more transient and less stable than the Puritans, came to reside on the islands. With limited resources or protection from the Viceroy of New Granada, they confronted several attacks from buccaneers from Edward Mansvelt to Henry Morgan.[10] Despite the lack of attention and resources to the faraway archipelago, San Andrés, Providencia, and Santa Catalina Islands remained Spanish territories despite the ongoing challenges of populating and administering it with loyal Spanish subjects.

It was the fourth wave of newcomers to settle permanently on San Andrés and Providencia Islands who resolved Spain's long-term problems of establishing settlements there and to whom Raizals trace their ancestry. Beginning in the late eighteenth century, sporadic sightings and reports of mostly Anglophone settlers living on the islands circulated across the

Spanish- and English-speaking world.[11] When the Spanish tried to expulse them, in 1789, after signing a treaty with England, the mostly English-speaking population of farmers and fishermen petitioned to stay on as loyal Spanish subjects.[12] Without a plausible colonization scheme, the Spanish government agreed initially to place it under the Viceroyalty of New Granada and the purview of authorities in Cartagena to the chagrin of officials in Guatemala. As English-speaking subjects under the Spanish Crown, they experienced few benefits. Within a decade of petitioning to become Spanish subjects, New Granada like other places in the Americas became embroiled in the independence struggles. Cartagena officials neglected the island population without appointing a new official to administer them. As a result, prominent men on both islands ruled through municipal councils.[13] With several families and their bondsmen mostly cultivating cotton, islanders remained vulnerable to outsiders who robbed them of their goods and property—human and nonhuman—occupying them without the threat of state presence.[14] It was under such conditions that the islands became drawn into the age of Atlantic Revolutions eventually gaining independence from Spain.

There is some debate as to whether islanders joined freely or were annexed to the newly formed Republic of Gran Colombia in 1822. Given the paucity of written sources for this period, doubts were raised about the voluntary nature to which islanders agreed to join the newly independent state of Gran Colombia.[15] What is known is that the French corsair Louis-Michel Aury and later Scottish adventurer Gregor MacGregor along with their multiracial crews occupied Providencia, Santa Catalina, and San Andrés Islands from the years of 1818 to 1821. The legendary privateer Aury used Providencia Island as a base to attack Spanish ships in the name of Spanish American independence, a tactic used by authorities of the former independent republic of Cartagena just years before.[16] While no longer an ally to Simón Bolívar, Aury insisted that he shared Bolívar's vision for freedom.[17] MacGregor also had an extensive experience with the Spanish American wars of independence and even a closer relationship with the Great Liberator. Married to the cousin of Simón Bolívar, MacGregor had supported the Venezuelan patriot leader's cause across the Atlantic world as much as his own. With grander projects to pursue, MacGregor left San Andrés for the Caribbean Coast of Central America, whereas Aury later died after falling from a horse.[18] Their remnant forces later turned themselves over to Simón Bolívar and oversaw public ceremonies where islanders swore allegiance to the new Constitution of Cúcuta of 1821 at Providencia and San Andrés Islands on June 23 and July 12, respectively.[19]

As citizens of the newly independent Colombia, San Andrés and Providencia islanders lived far removed from many of the processes undergirding the social, political, and economic lives of their counterparts.

In some ways, the island population shared more in common with its Anglophone Caribbean neighbors. They also drew on enslaved labor. In the 1810s, an American trader noted "thirty families of free people of different nations and colors, and from five to thirty slaves to every free person in the island."[20] San Andrés Island had over a thousand enslaved men and women. Like their regional neighbors, slave resistance also occurred on these minuscule islands from insurrections to maroonage until it fully ended in the 1850s.[21] Much is still unknown about slavery on the islands as few scholars have attempted to examine this period closely. This historic moment has been immortalized in fictional accounts, however.[22] What is better understood is the way slave emancipation undergirded other social and economic transformations. Without forced labor, landowners swapped cotton for coconut cultivation, which offered newfound opportunities for the recently enslaved.[23] The coconut trade linked San Andrés to the United States with merchants regularly visiting the island. By the end of the nineteenth century, most islanders were members of the First Baptist Church, which Philip Beekman Livingston founded in 1847. The main church, plus its affiliates across both islands, became a central community institution.[24]

While little scholarly attention has been given to the archipelago's experience during the early national period, it remained a marginal territory vulnerable to the political upheavals in mainland Colombia. After a brief period of military commanders governing the archipelago through 1833, the islands became organized into a canton to be administered under the auspices of the Province of Cartagena until 1868. Thereafter, the islands became one of six national territories governed directly by the presidency.[25] This administrative shift reflected an acknowledgment of the archipelago's significance. In 1867, Colombian intellectual, journalist, and politician José María Samper explained the strategic importance of San Andrés and Providencia "by virtue of their position in the middle of the Panama Isthmus, the islands of Cuba and Jamaica, and the coasts of Central America. They need the presence of the federal authority, making itself felt directly and energetically."[26] Such a mission angered local notable and on a few occasions resulted in the assassination or attempted assassination of mainland authorities.[27] This administrative arrangement, however, was short-lived. When a civil war ended the radical Liberal wing's hold on the Colombian government, a unified centralist state replaced a federalist republic in 1884. Two years later, Article 185 in the Constitution of 1886 returned all national territories to their former political units and the Department of Bolívar with its headquarters in Cartagena again administered the archipelago.[28]

The nearly 30 years of departmental rule from 1886 to 1912 set the stage for massive administrative, cultural, and economic transformations on the archipelago in the future, which intersected with and diverged from changes occurring nationally on the mainland. While the Regeneration politics of Rafael Núñez and Miguel Antonio Caro sought political centralization, departmental rule failed to bring greater administrative oversight, financial support, or even state protection over the islands. San Andrés and Providencia islanders grew weary of *costeño* [from the mainland coast] prefects whom they saw as only concerned with self-aggrandizement in the face of deteriorating material conditions.[29] International threats, however, nudged departmental and central authorities to turn their attention toward the islands.

Each instance, in different ways, threatened Colombian sovereignty over the islands. In 1894, Nicaraguan authorities launched a campaign known as "Reincorporation" to assert control over Mosquitia where the Miskitu and Afro-creole residents enjoyed political autonomy and formerly British protection.[30] Nicaraguan authorities claimed their mission extended not only to the coastline but as far as the offshore Caribbean territories of Corn Islands and the Archipelago of San Andrés and Providencia. This situation caused alarm and opportunity. Since the islands lacked any true protection from Colombian defense forces, they were quite vulnerable. On the other hand, Colombian officials like the governor of Bolívar and the minister of foreign relations received the go-ahead to take Corn Islands. Receiving a petition from eighty Corn Islands residents, they insisted that they were also Colombians, "which can be proven by authentic documents, such as grants and deeds for landed property given by the Governor Tomás O'Neille then residing in the islands of Saint Andrews."[31] Whether Colombian authorities sought to take the Corn Islands is unknown, but it is clear that Managua officials understood these faraway islands as part of a greater Mosquitia and proved it by sending armed soldiers to occupy them even building a fort to prevent Colombian forces from taking the islands.[32] The securing of these offshore islands did not satiate Nicaraguan authorities. On the contrary, it kick-started future territorial disputes with Colombia, which spanned into the twenty-first century.

In addition to Nicaraguan aggression, other movements threatened Colombian sovereignty over these islands. The 1903 secession of Panama nearly led to the loss of the islands. Panamanian and American authorities consulted on whether the archipelago should join Panama given its strategic location and potential as coaling stations on the route to the interoceanic canal. The idea carried favor with some San Andrés islanders who may have sent a petition asking the new Panamanian authorities to annex them. When Colombian authorities heard of such developments, they sent troops to occupy San Andrés and prevent further defections. Those troops used the threat of force to keep islanders from following the Panamanians but also maltreated many causing some of them to flee to Bocas del Toro in Panama.³³ This situation only further embittered islanders who were already unhappy with Colombian governance.

From Native Islanders to Raizals

Drawn into a process of greater political integration, the archipelago converted from a province of the Department of Bolívar to a National Intendancy controlled by the Ministry of Government in Bogotá under Law 52 of 1912 under the Conservative government of Carlos E. Restrepo. It would begin a process of more sustained contact between the archipelago and mainland Colombia than in the previous centuries. The arrival of officials and newcomers from various parts of mainland Colombia, however, drew into light the stark contrasts between the island and mainland Colombians.³⁴ Throughout the century, central authorities in the capital ordered investigations to collect basic facts about the islands' populations, history, society, and economy to better incorporate them into Colombia. These reports and memoranda honed in on the distinctive characteristics of the island population that unsettled them: their Anglophone Protestant culture. Drawing inspiration from the culturalist project of Regeneration—unified Colombia under the Spanish language, Hispanic customs, and Catholicism—Colombian central authorities regularly sought to convert them into Spanish-speaking Catholic Colombians. Such culturalist projects faced tremendous resistance and had various degrees of success but were an essential component of the Colombianization project.³⁵ Beginning in 1912 and intensifying in the third quarter of the twentieth century, this project triggered a chasm between native islanders and continental Colombians.

Colombian officials have consistently expressed anxiety over the cultural and even racial differences between island and non-island Colombians. In the months before the passing of Law 52 of 1912, which converted the islands into a National Intendancy, president Carlos E. Restrepo ordered Santiago Guerrero to conduct a census. Guerrero had previously worked in San Andrés and had some familiarity with the archipelago and its people. The Colombian president also gave him the task to report on the conditions and central concerns of San Andrés and Providencia islanders. For Guerrero, the most important issue regarding governance of the island population was the cultural distance between Colombians on the mainland and the island. "The religion, the language, the customs, everything is absolutely contrary to us," explained Guerrero.³⁶ For Guerrero and many others like him at the time, Colombian nationality assumed a common culture, language, and religion: homogeneity.

The lack of a shared historic, cultural, and even racial experience with San Andrés and Providencia islanders threatened mainland Colombians. Emilio Eitón, a sea captain contracted to transport a group of men who came to build a wireless station on San Andrés Island in 1913, wrote an eye-opening account of his time on the island. In explaining the origins of the island population, an aggrieved Eitón admitted:

> We must not speak of race because we must accept, as painful as it is, the difference in genealogical origin of the archipelago's inhabitants with the rest of Colombia. Accept that the racial difference had the reason to be and exist as the result of the historical events that brought settlers to the islands. Hispanics were not the first to come.[37]

But the acceptance of the different ethnogenesis of the islanders proved difficult for most mainland Colombians who observed the English-speaking islanders gravitate toward people from other parts of the Caribbean and more so to the United States. Since the middle of the nineteenth century, the islanders had formed close ties to Americans because of religion and commerce. Most islanders were Baptists and, in San Andrés, their economy depended on the exportation of coconuts with American merchants as their principal buyers.[38]

These international connections confused and concerned mainland Colombians trying to understand where islanders had an affinity. In an *El Porvenir* editorial, a Cartagena-based newspaper, former public employee Rafael de Morales described the island population in simple terms. "Truly the islanders are English (not American) in their ideas, religion, language, tendencies, and aspirations. The reason is obvious; they are the majority from the English Antilles or descended from them."[39] The reality was islanders likely reflected an affinity for both England and the United States in ways that complicated their understanding of themselves as Colombian nationals. Writing to president José Vicente Concha (1914–1918), intendancy employee Luis Mateus acknowledged:

> In the archipelago today for there are but Anglo-American-Panamanian natives: when a foreigner asks them where they come from, they respond that they are English from San Andrés, and many instances they say that they are under the Colombian flag.[40]

Such anecdotes noting islanders' cultural differences amplified growing concerns about the islands and national authorities' tenuous administrative grasp over the archipelago.

In the wake of the Panamanian secession in 1903, Colombians grew particularly wary of the U.S. presence in coastal Colombia but also the archipelago.[41] Mateus's anecdote conjured up the similarities between the archipelago and Panama: governing faraway places poorly connected to Colombian central authority and the looming presence of the United States.

However, intendant Carlos M. Hernández cautioned against such claims of strong American affinity among islanders. In his report to the ministry of government, the intendant reminded them, "it is certain that the knowledge of how Americans treat people of color, keeps islanders on guard." But he agreed that "the ties that unite the archipelago to a Colombian nationality are, in reality, very weak and if the National Government does not take effort to strengthen them, in a few years, the fatherland will lose this territory."[42] Like Eitón, Mateus, and Guerrero, Hernández emphasized the cultural differences of San Andrés and Providencia islanders refusing to accept a pluralistic notion of the Colombian nation.

Elite islanders, however, insisted that they were islanders by birth and suggested they were Colombians by choice. Since the late nineteenth century, islanders adopted a rhetorical strategy of calling themselves native.[43] Europeans increasingly used this term to identify non-Europeans whom they viewed as uncivilized or inferior to them. While the growing use of native in the Anglophone world has a racially charged origin, San Andrés and Providencia islanders may have co-opted the meaning of the term to highlight their deep connection to these islands. Repeatedly in the first half of the twentieth century, islanders commonly addressed themselves as "natives of the island."[44] Other times, they wrote, "the undersigned Colombians, natives, and residents of this island" in their petitions to Bogotá officials.[45] Both instances suggest a privileging of their claims of belonging to the islands. As a group of petitioners further explained, "these islands, ours by right of birth."[46] It is also clear that these prominent islanders—pastors, merchants, and political figures—adopted a Colombian identity that overlapped but was distinct from their native islander identity.

Colombianization occurred slowly and with uneven success. San Andrés and Providencia islanders largely resisted state efforts to convert them to Catholicism. The Baptist Churches had long dominated the religious landscape on both islands. This is partly because Philip Beekman Livingston helped to bring an end to slavery at San Andrés and successfully proselytized to emancipated slaves.[47] Livingston later opened up sister churches on Providencia, which he and his son Brockholst oversaw into the turn of the twentieth century without an effective state presence, the Baptist pastors filled the vacuum. They registered births, marriages, and deaths.[48] The Livingstons demanded Baptist fealty, which upset some but often effectively competed against new religious communities such as Catholics and Adventists to whom they lost congregants.[49]

Moreover, English-speaking Catholic missionaries from the United States and later England led the evangelization efforts on the islands for the first quarter of the twentieth century. Many Colombian officials, however, felt they were unsuitable for the task. Writing to the police director in Cartagena, postmaster Raimundo Ayure noted, "The priests that reside there are Protestants and, in their talks, and meetings always speak of England and the United States instilling a patriotic love for these nations, but never anything about Colombia." The postmaster further explained that "even when there are English Catholic priests, these do not deal with the patriotic love for our country."[50] He proposed that the government bring in priests who knew both English and Spanish to inculcate islanders with religious sentiments and contribute to the teaching of Spanish.

The Colombian government responded favorably to the calls of men like Ayure and eventually found Spanish-speaking Catholic missionaries to takeover. In 1926, the Vatican sent four Spanish priests from the Capuchin religious order to lead the Catholic mission. Upon arrival, the missionaries quickly learned the true scope of their mission. One of the priests explained:

> The [mainland] Colombians have visited me since they are all very dear and good and more so with us. The Colombians only speak Spanish; the others, English. The natives are in everything Yankee. This explains such a cold character that we must change with our mission to make them love Colombia and the Catholic religion.[51]

Despite their prior experiences in the Caribbean coast of Colombia, an area fighting for popular religious expression, the Spanish missionaries confronted significant challenges. Initially, the Capuchin missionaries spoke little English.[52] It appeared that early calls for missionaries that spoke English and Spanish fell on deaf ears. As a result, the Capuchin priests initially could not complete their daily duties of listening to confession, leading catechism, visiting the sick, or recruiting islanders into the church. Figure 3.1 shows seated in the front row from the center-left the three British missionaries alongside Capuchin priest Cristóbal de Canals and to the right-side veteran Capuchin missionary Eugenio de Carcagente. They received support, including English language lessons, until all of the English priests departed in the following year.

Moreover, the Capuchin missionaries inherited the dismissal record of student enrollment in the Catholic-run government schools. Islanders sent their children to Protestant schools—either Baptist or Adventist to resist the Colombianization project. In 1928, the Intendancy opened a girl-only government school in The Hill community on San Andrés with a beginning enrollment of 50 students later dropped to ten after a Protestant school opened.[53] The following year, a new Protestant school opened in one of the communities on Providencia and again enrollment dropped at the government school. José Munévar, the school inspector on the islands, explained the reasons for these enrollment changes. "It is only for religious reasons [and] not because the government-run schools are inferior to the Protestant

Figure 3.1 English and Spanish Catholic missionaries in Providencia, circa 1930s. Courtesy of Centro Cultural Banco de la República, San Andrés, CCRBSAI.

ones; completely to the contrary."[54] Munévar and many others recognized that islanders refused to relinquish their religion or language to fit into mainland notions of Colombian identity.

Yet the Colombianization project was not quite dead. The Capuchin missionaries eventually made headway with conversions. Frustrated with island resistance, the Spanish missionaries worked with the Intendancy to forcibly close all the Protestant schools and deny non-Catholic islander students' scholarships to study on the mainland.[55] Islanders bitterly remember when neighbors, friends, and family converted to Catholicism to obtain opportunities for further study or to obtain a government job. Some islanders chided these converts calling them "job Catholics."[56] While they eventually learned Spanish, many recalled the hardship of attending school completely in Spanish. "The nuns did not understand English and prohibited speaking Creole, they didn't have to run over a community. On more than one occasion they told me to stop speaking it because it was cause for disciplinary [action]," remembered one islander woman.[57] Despite these personal challenges, some islanders assessed such efforts to enforce the use of Spanish as a successful part of the Colombianization project. "At present, all public schools teach in Spanish, and all public events are rarely done either in English or Creole, but only in Spanish," conceded one

Raizal.[58] Some scholars make similar conclusions noting that the intensification to organize challenges against these efforts reflects a conscious and unconscious social integration into mainland cultural norms.[59]

To Colombianize the Anglophone Protestant population on the archipelago required more than the united efforts of Intendancy officials and Catholic missionaries, arguably the most successful aspect of Colombianization was the arrival of migrants, the fifth wave of newcomers, from mainland Colombia to San Andrés Island in the immediate years after establishing a free port on the island. The largest number of migrants likely came between 1962 and 1977.[60] What is clear is that these newcomers competed with islanders in the employment market with the introduction of tourism and the free port. With the bulk of the tourists coming from mainland Colombia, hotel and restaurant employers sought out employees who spoke Spanish. Raizals were a minority in three sectors of the economy: Commerce, construction, and hotels/restaurants.[61] Moreover, some of these new arrivals helped to infuse cultural norms from the mainland through radio and television programs.[62] Unable to secure a foothold in this service industry and feeling culturally displaced, some English-speaking San Andrés and Providencia islanders increasingly felt threatened by these mainlanders. In turn, they created pejorative terms to describe them such as *champetudos, sharkheads*, and *chambucús*.[63] But the most enduring term that Raizals used to describe Spanish-speaking mainland Colombians was *paña* or *pañamanes* short for *españoles*. "In historic times, this pejorative term was used for the despised Spaniards who continually molested islanders. Now, it became a generalized term for any Colombian continentals, who proved to be dishonest," explained one Raizal.[64]

In addition to rising resentment toward the Colombian government and Spanish-speaking migrant newcomers, some San Andrés islanders organized themselves into separatist or greater autonomy movements. In 1964, San Andrés islander Marco Polo Britton wrote to the United Nations and even the U.S. secretary of state soliciting support in separating the island from Colombia to become the "Federal Republic of San Andrés," a sovereign territory administered jointly with the United States. News of this declaration embarrassed some Raizal and Colombian officials who called it a "joke" but were privately alarmed by the development.[65] While Britton proved unsuccessful, others joined him in calling for separation or even greater administrative autonomy within Colombia. Islanders in Bogotá formed the United Archipelago Club (UAC), composed of some 20 Raizal professionals and numerous university students. Seeking to divert from politics from their Raizal elders and mainland newcomers, they envisioned the youth leading the reforms.[66] They called on self-determination from the perspective of "Islanderism" and "the island for islanders."[67] Due to decades of governmental neglect and cultural differences, some UAC members argued that islanders must separate from Colombia. Mauricio McNish, a San Andrés lawyer and activist, championed such a position. "You and I are fundamentally different. You are from the mainland, Catholic, white and speak Spanish; we are islanders, black, Protestant, and speak English. You will continue being *pañamanes*."[68] While some returned to take public office and professional work on the islands, their movement to demand greater administrative autonomy only grew.

By the 1980s and 1990s, an array of groups had formed from the Sons of the Soil (SOS) to the Archipelago Movement for Ethnic Native Self-Determination (known as AMEN-SD). In 1984, SOS was formed to protect the cultural and land rights of native islanders as well as address issues such as overpopulation. In approach, they were integrationist, however. With the growth of such movements came an insistence to use the term "native islander" to describe them as the descendants of the original population to settle permanently on the islands. But some began to chalk at such a generic term since "it is so general as to be applicable to all island people of the globe and so 'fails' to define boundaries necessary for the construction of a separate and unique identity."[69] While the main division between the population of San Andrés and Providencia was between mainlanders and islanders, it proved insufficient since it could include islanders born to parents who arrived on the islands after the Free Port or those of mixed ancestry.[70]

The shift to the term "Raizal" emerged likely in the 1980s. One scholar has argued that two twin processes pushed islanders to not only emphasize their Anglophone but also African heritage. With the global spread of reggae music, native San Andrés and Providencia islander audiences came to engage with reggae artists' calls to understand their ancestral roots. It was also in the 1980s that the Spanish translation of Alex Haley's book *Roots* and the broadcast of its 1977 television portrayal of the story arrived in Colombia and the islands.[71] Activists in San Andrés took on this concept of roots to formulate their own ethnicity. "Since the 1980s we began to use the term Raizal to refer to our ethnic group. We want, well, our own name like the indigenous from Colombia have it."[72] Even more than fully adopting a Black identity, activists turned their attention to the local culture, particularly, the English and creole languages. Visual depictions of Raizal traditional culture decorate the downtown as seen in Figure 3.2. With the creole, Raizals began to acknowledge openly the African elements within creole and other cultural practices, which had been demonized in the past.

By 1990, native islanders had an opportunity to make some political gains. To resolve the protracted armed conflict and broaden democratization, the Colombian government started a constitutional reform process to restore legitimacy to the nation's democratic institutions. In doing so, the constitutional reform opened a pathway for various constituents to raise their voices in the political sphere including native San Andrés, Providencia,

Figure 3.2 San Andrés Island Mural. Photograph by the author.

and Santa Catalina islanders. Like in other parts of Latin America, racial and ethnic minorities sought to secure ethnic and indigenous rights.[73] In Colombia, native islanders drew heavily on regional and national indigenous movements like the Regional Indigenous Council of Cauca (CRIC) to the National Indigenous Organizations of Colombia (ONIC) who called on unity, land, culture, and autonomy in securing their ethnic rights and greater administrative autonomy.[74] But like other Black communities in Colombia that had to align with indigenous activists and intellectuals involved in the constitutional reform, not a single member of the Raizal community was invited to participate in the National Constituent Assembly.[75] Such organizational strategies proved somewhat effective. Decree No. 2762 of 1991 requires the regulation of migration to the island whereas Law 47 of 1993 makes creole a co-official language of the archipelago.

Conclusion

The Constitution of 1991 has secured legal protections for the Raizal population including seeing them as an ethnicity due to their distinct ethnogenesis. As a result, Raizals have successfully argued for greater protections to preserve their indigenous language of creole (or Kriol) and cultural practices. Yet, the Colombian government has not fully accepted their indigeneity claims and continues to place them alongside other Afro-Colombian communities.[76] The result is that Raizals are now more visible within the multicultural landscape of Colombia, at least at a juridical level, but the government continues to deny them the same protections as other indigenous populations in Colombia or recognizes Raizals continual calls for administrative autonomy from Colombia. With these demands still unmet, diverse yet disparate Raizal movements continue to organize to fight for better conditions on their islands.

Notes

An earlier draft of this chapter was presented at the Many Worlds of British Mainland Latin America Workshop held at Rutgers University where I received thoughtful comments from Camila Townsend. I also appreciate the feedback from the volume editors as well as Francisco Javier Flórez Bolívar and Karin Rosemblatt.

1 Santa Catalina is the smallest of the three islands connected to Providencia by a bridge. Generally, the inhabitants of Santa Catalina are usually lumped into Providencia. For the duration of the chapter, I will not refer much to Santa Catalina. Scholars have largely ignored or given scant coverage to the archipelago when surveying the history of Colombia. For a discussion of this absence in Spanish, see Inge Helena Valencia P., "Lugares de las poblaciones negras en Colombia: La ausencia del afrocaribe insular," *CS*, no. 7 (January-July 2011): 313–349. For English-language scholarship, see Ann Farnsworth-Alvear, Marco Palacios, and Ana María Gómez-López, eds., *The Colombia Reader: History, Culture, Politics* (Durham: Duke University Press, 2017); Michael J. LaRosa and Germán P. Mejía, *Colombia: A Concise Contemporary History* (Lanham: Rowman & Littlefield, 2017); Marco Palacios, *Between Legitimacy and Violence: A History of Colombia, 1875–2002*, trans. Richard Stoller (Durham: Duke University Press, 2006); Peter Wade, "Colombia," in *Africana: Encyclopedia of the African and African American Experience*, eds. Kwame Anthony Appiah and Henry Louis Gates Jr. (New York: Basic Civitas Books, 1999), 475–477.
2 Robert Sierakowski, "Central America's Caribbean Coast: Politics and Ethnicity," *Oxford Research Encyclopedia of Latin American History*, published online on September 29, 2016. https://oxforde.com/latinamericanhistory/view/10.1093/acrefore/9780199366439.001.0001/acrefore-9780199366439-3-372, accessed July 1, 2022; Mark Anderson, *Black and Indigenous: Garifuna Activism and Consumer Culture in Honduras* (Minneapolis: University of Minnesota Press, 2009).
3 Silvia Elena Torres, "Los raizales: cultura e identidad angloafrocaribeña en el Caribe Insular colombiano," *Revista Cuadernos del Caribe* 16, no. 1 (2013): 23.
4 Dano Ranocchiari, "Música urbana en San Andrés Isla: ¿hacia una etnicidad más inclusiva," *Cuadernos del Caribe* 19 (ene.–jul. 2015): 11–23; Sally Taylor, "Los 'Half & Half o Fifty-Fifties' de San Andrés. Los actores invisibles de la Raizalidad" (MA thesis, Universidad Nacional de Colombia, 2010).
5 Wenceslao Cabrera Ortiz, *San Andrés y Providencia: Historia* (Bogotá: Editorial Cosmos, 1980), 9; Félix Díaz Galindo, *Monografía del archipiélago de San Andrés* (Bogotá: Ediciones Medio Pliego, 1978), 12.

6 Díaz Galindo, *Monografía*, 41; James J. Parsons, *San Andrés and Providencia: English-Speaking Islands in the Western Caribbean* (Berkeley: University of California Press, 1956), 4.
7 Karen Ordahl Kupperman, *Providence Island, 1630–1641: The Other Puritan Colony* (New York: Cambridge University Press, 1995), 40; Cabrera Ortiz, *San Andrés y Providencia*, 20; Díaz Galindo, *Monografía*, 41; Parsons, *San Andrés and Providencia*, 5.
8 Lorraine Vollmer, *La historia del poblamiento del Archipiélago de San Andrés y Vieja Providencia y Santa Catalina* (San Andrés: Ediciones Archipiélago, 1997), 30; Walwin G. Petersen, "Cultura y tradición de los habitantes de San Andrés y Providencia," in *San Andrés y Providencia: Tradiciones culturales y coyuntura política*, ed. Isabel Clemente (Bogotá: Ediciones Uniandes, 1989), 115; Parsons, *San Andrés and Providencia*, 9.
9 Parsons, *San Andrés and Providencia*, 9.
10 Parsons, *San Andrés and Providencia*, 9.
11 Parsons, *San Andrés and Providencia*, 14.
12 Antonino Vidal Ortega, "Noticias de San Andrés e islas vecinas 1789," *Memorias: Revista Digital de Historia y Arqueología desde el Caribe Colombiano* 8, no. 14 (jun. 2011): 280.
13 Parsons, *San Andrés and Providencia*, 18.
14 Manuel Peralta, *Límites de Costa Rica y Colombia: Nuevos documentos para la historia de su jurisdicción territorial, con notas, comentarios y un examen de la cartografía de Costa Rica y Veragua por Manuel María de Peralta* (Madrid: M.G. Hernández, 1890), 178–189.
15 Martin Alonso Pomare Howard, *Clamor of the Islands: Saint Andrew and Old Providence under Colombian Rule*, ed. Jorge Duchesne Winter (Pittsburgh: Instituto Internacional de Literatura Iberoamericana, 2021), 120; Enrique Pusey, "Los eventos de 1822: Vistos por un raizal," in *Memorias, historias y olvidos: Colonialismo, sociedad y política en el archipiélago de San Andrés y Providencia*, eds. Raúl Román Romero and Antonino Vidal Ortega (Bogotá: Editorial Universidad Nacional de Colombia, 2019), 249.
16 Vanessa Mongey, *Rogue Revolutionaries: The Fight for Legitimacy in the Greater Caribbean* (Philadelphia: University of Pennsylvania Press, 2020), 29.
17 Jacob Dunham, *Journal of Voyages: Containing an Account of the Author's Being Twice Captured by the English and Once by Gibs the Pirate* (New York: Huestis & Cozans, 1850), 144.
18 Dunham, *Journal of Voyages*, 144.
19 Mongey, *Rogue Revolutionaries*, 34; Cabrera Ortiz, *San Andrés y Providencia*, 91.
20 Dunham, *Journal of Voyages*, 39.
21 Ángela Rivas Gamboa, "Anansi en el mar de los siete colores: Historia, memoria y cultura en el Archipiélago" (BA tesis, Universidad de los Andes, 1995), 46; Peralta, *Límites de Costa Rica y Colombia*, 177–178.
22 Keshia Howard Livingstone, *San Andres: A Herstory* (San Andres Island: Casa Editorial Welcome, 2014); Hazel Robinson Abrahams, *No Give Up, Maan!* (Bogotá: Editorial Unibiblos, 2002).
23 Parsons, *San Andrés and Providencia*, 30.
24 Loren Turnage, *Island Heritage: A Baptist View of the History of San Andrés and Providencia* (Cali: Colombian Baptist Mission, 1975).
25 Petersen, "Cultura y tradición," 48–49.
26 José María Samper, "División Territorial de Colombia," *El Republicano*, no. 22 (October 2, 1867), 88.

27 On assassination attempt against Prefect Polídoro Martínez, see Polídoro Martínez to Secretary of the Interior and Foreign Relations, March 28, 1870, Archivo General de la Nación (thereafter, AGN), Ministerio de lo Interior y Relaciones Exteriores, Tomo 78, Folios 492–493. For Prefect Leonidas Toledos' assassination, see "South American News," *New York Times*, New York City, December 5, 1883. Mark and Francis Bent were later identified as the culprits of Toledo's death, see Rodrigo Sánchez to Secretary of the Bolívar Government, January 17, 1912, AGN, Sección Primera, Tomo 698, Folios 361–362.
28 William Gibson, *Constitutions of Colombia* (Bogotá: Biblioteca Popular de Cultura Colombiana, 1951), 251.
29 For island complaints about departmental rule, see Pedro Pablo Restrepo to President Carlos E. Restrepo, 25 August 1910, in Colombia, AGN, Ministerio de Gobierno, Sección Primera, Tomo 650, Folio 238; Gabriel O'Byrne, "Lo que pasa en San Andrés: los habitantes se quejan," *El Porvenir*, May 5, 1911.
30 Robert Naylor, *Penny Ante Imperialism. The Mosquito Shore and the Bay of Honduras. A Case Study of British Informal Empire* (Rutherford: Fairleigh Dickinson University Press, 1989), 204–205.
31 Martin D. Schwartz, James Downs, Elisha Tucker, Elias A. Camble, John Campbell, John Rigby, Edward A. Downs, and 76 signatures to Governor of Bolívar, September 4, 1895, AGN, Ministerio de Relaciones Exteriores, Sección Primera, Diplómatica y Consular. Correspondencia con Gobernación de Bolívar, Transferencia 10, Caja 2, Carpeta 10, Folios 146–147.
32 Eduardo B. Gerlein to Colombian Minister of Foreign Relations, February 5, 1897, AGN, Ministerio Relaciones Exteriores, Sección Primera, Diplómatica y Consular. Correspondencia con Gobernación de Bolívar, Transferencia 10, Caja 2, Carpeta 12, Folios 9–10.
33 Sharika Crawford, "Panama Fever and Colombian Fears of Secession on San Andrés and Providencia Islands, 1903–1913," *The Global South* 6, no. 2 (Fall 2013): 15–38.
34 Law 52 of 1912 decreed the Archipelago of San Andrés, Providencia, and Santa Catalina to become a National Intendancy. For an English translation of the law, see Oswald L. Robinson, "Intendency," *The Searchlight*, December 2, 1912, 1.
35 Ana Milena Rhenals Doria and Francisco Javier Flórez Bolívar, "Marginados, pero no marginales: Negros, mulatos y sus disputas por la autonomía en Chocó, Colombia (1903–1947)," *Anuario de Historia Regional y de las Fronteras* 24, no. 2 (2019): 125–149; Jane Rausch, *Colombia: Territorial Rule and the Llanos Frontier* (Gainesville: University of Florida Press, 1999).
36 Santiago Guerrero to Carlos E. Restrepo, July 8, 1912, AGN, Ministerio de Gobierno, Sección Primera, Legajo 698, Folio 455.
37 Emilio Eitón, *El Archipiélago Lejano* (Barranquilla: Mogollón, 1913), 61.
38 Parsons, *San Andrés and Providencia*, 30; Alfred Tremble, "Among the Coconuts: A Jaunt through the Island of St. Andrews," *Leslie's Popular Monthly* (1877): 691; Dunham, *Journal of Voyages*, 134–135.
39 Rafael de Morales, "Nuestras Islas," *El Porvenir*, December 8, 1911, 2.
40 Luis Mateus to President José Vicente Concha, August 25, 1915, AGN, Ministerio de Gobierno, Sección Primera, Legajo 734, Folio 356.
41 Stephen J. Randall, *Colombia and the United States: Hegemony and Interdependence* (Athens: University of Georgia Press, 1992), 91.
42 Carlos M. Hernández to Minister of Government, October 9, 1923, AGN, Ministerio de Gobierno, Sección Primera, Legajo 886, Folio 45.

43 For an example, see See Brockholst Livingston, Rupert O'Neile, DC May, Fillmore Manuel, Joseph James, Thomas Forbes, and 88 signees to Governor of Cartagena, June 13, 1897, AGN, Ministerio de Relaciones Exteriores, Sección Primera, Diplomática y Consular. Correspondencia con Gobernación de Bolívar, Transferencia 10, Caja 2, Carpeta 10, Folio 42.
44 For examples, see F. A. Howard, Ellit Robinson, Phillip Hawkins, Julius C. Robinson, Cleveland H. Hawkins, and 185 additional signatures to President, February 18, 1924, AGN, Ministerio de Gobierno, Sección Primera, Legajo 906, Folio 210.
45 Thomas B. Livingston and 150 signatures to President Carlos E. Restrepo, January 4, 1912, AGN, Ministerio de Gobierno, Sección Primera, Legajo 698, Folios 405.
46 F. A. Howard, Ellit Robinson, Phillip Hawkins, Julius C. Robinson, Cleveland H. Hawkins, and 185 additional signatures to President, February 18, 1924, AGN, Ministerio de Gobierno, Sección Primera, Legajo 906, Folio 210.
47 Petersen, "Cultura y tradición," 124–126.
48 Raymond Howard Britton, "Religión y política eran una sola cosa," in *Textos y testimonios del archipiélago: Crisis y convivencia en un territorio insular*, eds. Socorro Ramírez and Luis Alberto Restrepo (San Andrés Isla: Universidad Nacional de Colombia Sede San Andrés, 2002), 108–110.
49 Interview by the author with Hazel Robinson Abrahams, Bogotá, December 13, 2005.
50 Raimundo Ayure sent this communication to the police commissioner Solomon Correar who forwarded it to the Ministry of Government. Salomón Correar to the Minister of Government, November 17, 1917, AGN, Ministerio de Gobierno, Sección Primera, Legajo 780, Folio 75.
51 Manuel Benlloch Castellar, *San Andrés y Providencia: Cincuenta años de misión bien cumplida* (Bogotá: Editorial Andes, 1976), 38.
52 Richard Turner to Superior General Joseph Biermans, 24 March 1927, Banco de la República, Centro Cultural San Andrés Isla (thereafter BR-CCSAI).
53 Memoria de Instrucción Pública (1928), Carpeta 546, BR-CCSAI.
54 Memoria de Educación (1929), Carpeta 547, BR-CCSAI.
55 Pomare Howard, *Clamor of the Islands*, 56.
56 Thomas J. Price, "Algunos aspectos de estabilidad y desorganización cultural en una comunidad isleña del Caribe Colombiano," *Revista Colombiana de Antropología* III (jul.–dic. 1954): 11–54.
57 Yasmine Dau, "El lamento sustituye el afán de pensar el futuro," in *Textos y testimonios del archipiélago: Crisis y convivencia en un territorio insular*, eds. Socorro Ramírez and Luis Alberto Restrepo (San Andrés Isla: Universidad Nacional de Colombia Sede San Andrés, 2002), 68.
58 Pomare Howard, *Clamor of the Islands*, 102.
59 Carlos Andrés Charry Joya, "Movilización social e identidad nacional en el Caribe insular colombiano. Una historia social contada desde el diario de campo," *Historia Crítica*, no. 35 (January-June 2008): 58–81.
60 María Margarita Ruiz, "Vivienda, asentimientos y migración en San Andrés Isla," 1950–1987," in *San Andrés y Providencia: Tradiciones culturales y coyuntura política*, ed. Isabel Clemente (Bogotá: Uniandes, 1989), 229.
61 Adolfo Meisel Roca, "La continentalización de San Andrés Islas, Colombia: Panyas, Raizales y Turismo, 1953–2003," in *Economía y medio ambiente del archipiélago de San Andrés, Providencia y Santa Catalina*, eds. Adolfo Meisel Roca and María Aguilar Díaz (Bogotá: Banco de la República, 2016), 33–34.

62 Orlando Javier Trujillo Irurita, "Integración nacional y pluralismo cultural en la radio y la televisión de San Andrés Isla: La configuración histórica del campo periodístico," *Historia Crítica*, no. 28 (2004): 153–169.
63 Inge Helena Valencia P., "Identidades del caribe insular colombiano: Otra mirada hacia del caso isleño-raizal," *CS*, no. 2 (July-December 2008): 51–73.
64 Petersen, "Cultura y tradición," 252.
65 "Una 'declaración de soberanía' de San Andrés," *El Tiempo*, April 29, 1964, 1; 7; "Correo del Intendente Isleño," *El Tiempo*, May 26, 1964, 4; "Los isleños rechazan la falsa 'declaración de independencia'," *El Tiempo*, May 24, 1964, 9.
66 Natalia Guevara Jaramillo, "Redes Isleñas del Archipiélago a la Capital," unpublished, 2009.
67 Islanderism is a translation of "isleñoismo." See, "Habla la juventud sanandresana: La isla para los isleños," *El Tiempo*, October 18, 1970, 3.
68 Juan Gossain, "Los pañamanes y San Andrés Isla," *El Espectador*, October 27, 1969.
69 James Ross, "Routes for Roots: Entering the 21st Century in San Andrés Island, Colombia," *Caribbean Studies* 35, no. 1 (January–June 2007): 25.
70 Taylor, "Los Half & Half."
71 Ross, "Routes for Roots," 27.
72 Valencia P., "Identidades del caribe insular colombiano," 60.
73 Juliet Hooker, "Afro-descendant Struggles for Collective Rights in Latin America: Between Race and Culture," *Souls* 10, no. 3 (2008): 279–291.
74 Virginie Laurent, "Multiculturalism in Colombia: Twenty-Five Years," *Global Center for Pluralism* (January 2008): 6–7.
75 Tianna S. Paschel, *Becoming Black Political Subjects: Movements and Ethno-Racial Rights in Colombia and Brazil* (Princeton: Princeton University Press, 2016), 105–107.
76 Torres, "Los raizales," 23.

4 Campesino
A Contested Identity, a Vibrant Subjectivity in Colombia

Diana Bocarejo and Carlos del Cairo

In 2013, during a growing popular mobilization against the poverty and precarity of the Colombian countryside, president Juan Manuel Santos uttered a controversial phrase that mass media echoed for days: "The so-called national agrarian strike does not exist." Santos was trying to minimize the protest led by different campesino organizations across the country in the public sphere. During the more than 30 days of the strike, the national government reacted by criminalizing social mobilizations and delegitimizing its motivations. Santos's declaration, a common attitude shared by other presidents, reveals a historical tendency of politicians to ignore, simplify, or criminalize campesinos' struggles. Instead of ameliorating the tense political atmosphere, Santos fueled massive discontent. Consequently, other sectors of the population, including urban organizations, joined the strike and the repertoires of protest intensified.[1] After a month full of tensions, the government had no alternative but to negotiate with campesino organizations.

The strike of 2013, also known as the *paro agrario*, became a milestone of the campesino social mobilization in recent decades, and it is one of many examples that confirm how the history of Colombian campesinos is full of complexities. In fact, campesinos are one of the populations most affected by different types of violence; they have had to struggle continuously to legitimize their place in society and before the Colombian state. Often translated as peasant in English, the term campesino represents a dynamic, contested, historical, and complex subjectivity until today. Currently, new social and legal scenarios are opening in Colombia for the political recognition of campesinos but getting to this point has not been easy.[2] Tensions, ambiguities, violence, bureaucratic obstacles, exclusions, and profound silences have paved the road. Campesinos' struggles today include at least four main claims: access to and formalization of land rights, a process of political representation and legitimacy, the recognition of a collective cultural identity, and their inclusion into political spaces through the acknowledgment of local forms of territorial governance and autonomy. The articulation of those demands shows the complex ways in which campesinos, vis-à-vis other social forces, have shaped their own political, economic, and cultural subjectivity well beyond their economic characterization as farmers.[3]

At the core of these struggles are the meanings of *campesino* as a political category. In fact, for decades, campesinos have played a crucial role in economic growth, modernization, and development state programs. However, the historical conditions shaping such subjectivity also involve diverse forms of campesino collective organizations in confronting violence, struggling for their rights and political spaces of representation, and forging multiple forms of belonging and rootedness in their rural territories within complex and unstable social and political processes. This chapter explores how *campesino* is a contentious and contested political category that could not be easily reduced to a unified or homogeneous economic activity. Our task in this chapter is to understand campesino as a category composed of different layers of political sensibilities, social mobilizations, and legal frameworks, which reveal agency, history, and political imagination. Given the fact that campesinos have usually been represented, if not fixed, according to certain economic criteria,[4] we will explore recent struggles and political-economic and cultural projects by campesinos to be recognized as legal and political subjects. By discussing Guaviare, a region located in the northern Amazon and conceived as an agrarian frontier since the mid-twentieth century, we first show some of the meanings and changing representations attached to the notion of campesino by both state and non-state actors. We then explore recent calls from campesino organizations and different academic and NGO sectors to mobilize historical notions of belonging and community forms of territorial management, as well as the (im)possibilities of doing so after the multicultural turn of the 1990s. In this section, we focus on peasant mobilizations of the 2010s to illustrate the power and potential of campesino organizations, which are expressions of a long history of peasant and agrarian struggles in various regions of the country. Finally, we analyze the case of the *Zonas de Reserva Campesina* (Peasant Reserve Zones), a political-territorial land management design that lays claims to a multi-dimensional understanding of campesino subjectivity, and the challenges that have emerged following the signing of a peace agreement in 2016 between the national government and the Revolutionary Armed Forces of Colombia (FARC).

What we are after here is a contextualization of some of the paradoxes and complexities that campesinos face in Colombia, and how they mobilize an ample repertoire of political discourses that seek to articulate old disputes, such as those related to land tenure, and new ones, such as environmental conservation. At the core of these struggles, we find a subjectivity that simultaneously seeks to advance conversations and consolidate gains for greater equity in terms of class and culture.

The Case of Guaviare and Campesino as a Contested Category

As many scholars have made it clear, the "agrarian question" has been central in shaping visions of how Colombia could achieve economic growth and development. Elites, state policies, and different governments have sought to intervene and reform what is perceived as campesinos' lifestyles, the question of land distribution, and the governance of rural areas in general. Through these processes, the very notion of the category campesino has historically been defined and redefined. Despite historical and regional variations, campesinos have been objects of multiple narratives and representations that tend to simplify—and homogenize—the diversity they embody.[5] In the case of Guaviare, the category of campesino gains or loses political visibility based on changing contexts and processes vis-à-vis other categories such as *colono* (settler) or *indígena* (indigenous person). For generations, thousands of campesino families migrated to Guaviare from the Andean region in search of land and a dignified life, and to escape violence. Over time, some of them have participated in a wide variety of activities such as exploiting natural resources (land, timber, skins), working in illegal economies linked to coca crops, and engaging in struggles for land. In such a volatile context, changing notions of campesino or colono have achieved (or not) political recognition and legitimacy before the state.[6] Until the mid-1990s, it was very common for rural migrants, who were recognized as campesinos in their regions of origin, to define themselves as colonos in the new lands. Identifying oneself as a settler implied to deploy specific practices such as *fundarse* or adapt plots (*fundos*) of logged forests and prepare the soil for cultivation. For that reason, colono was used as a category to describe men (a narrative with an explicit patriarchal bias) devoted to expanding the agricultural frontier through their labor force. The image was fixed: colonos were men in a process of civilizing wild lands. In the 1960s, official discourses praised the "civilizing" efforts of settlers who domesticated forests to make them productive for the nation's progress. The ax in a man's hands was a popular image that conveyed a wide variety of narratives disseminated in state policies, official documents, anthems and hymns, popular music, paintings, monuments, and so on.[7]

In colonization areas like Guaviare, the category of colono gained visibility in contrast to that of indígena, which was used to describe the region's native peoples. The binary opposition colono-indígena was a racial and cultural one expressing a social hierarchy upon which the distribution of economic and territorial resources or access to them was contingent. The relation with land was constructed as a social marker in public and official narratives. Colonos were men who could transform land into productive landscapes, and their correlation to productive practices was solidly established by the 1990s, even expressed in self-identification representations. For example, a settler said that "the land . . . is a source of survival; one cannot live without land. . . . The only thing I know is to work the land."[8] In contrast, indigenous people were conceived as unproductive and uncivilized. Their ancestral territories were occupied by colonos, which transformed further indigenous' territorialities that had been already drastically shaped and reduced by administrative legal institutions such as *resguardos*.[9]

During the 1990s, after the consolidation of an illicit drug economy in the region, there were also important mobilizations of coca farmers protesting the state's repressive measures implemented as part of the War on Drugs. In the mid-1990s, one of the largest mobilizations of coca farmers in the history of the western Colombian Amazon took place,[10] with demands, among other things, to be recognized by the state as "displaced campesinos ruined by fumigation and not guerrilleros and drug traffickers as we are labeled."[11] What is important here is that the category of campesino was mobilized for political action in response to the notion of colono, which was traditionally depicted as a "civilizing" force. It is also in this context that the category campesino was deployed to gain political legitimacy by tracing a clear distinction between campesino and guerrillero, between campesino and drug trafficker, to avoid being targeted in counterinsurgency or antinarcotics strategies.

A decade later, in the 2000s, with the consolidation of environmental conservation narratives and policies in the Colombian Amazon, the challenge for many was to mobilize a narrative of themselves as campesinos and avoid being identified as colonos, in a new context of increased sensitive for the protection of the rainforest.[12] In a place like Playa Güío, located on the banks of the Guaviare River, many of its inhabitants narrate how they or their parents or grandparents who arrived in the 1960s used to *tigrillear* (hunt for *tigrillos* or *leopardus tigrinus*) to sell their skins, which were highly valued in international markets. Also, they used to log the forest to plant corn, plantain, and cassava as part of *fundarse*. By the 1970s, marijuana appeared in the region, but it was soon replaced by coca crops. In the mid-1980s, the FARC began to regulate coca cultivation and commerce. This transition from hunting activities to coca cultivation in a region disputed for control by the FARC and the Colombian state, forged a stereotype of the colonos as predators of ecosystems, and sympathetic to the leftist guerrillas.[13]

The environmental conservation narratives that gained strength in the first decade of the twenty-first century served to generate new forms of territorial regulation through environmental protection policies. Conservation and securitization became part of a complex strategy of the

Colombian state to control biodiverse regions and populations associated to them. Also, the state designed strategies such as the "Programa Familia Guardabosques" (Family Forests Warden Program) to stimulate campesino communities to substitute cultivating coca for other legal crops. Instead of "illegal" economies, this program promoted "sustainable" economies such as ecotourism, but simultaneously prompted a new social practice that created the fragmentation of social networks and its social fabric—the mutual surveillance among campesino families to control who continued cultivating coca.[14] Environmental policies restricted campesino activities to those clearly aligned with conservation strategies. In this context, ecotourism was an alternative that many campesinos embraced, given the potential of their surroundings, but required them to participate in formalization and formation programs oriented to their entrepreneurialization through training in management techniques. These programs, however, promoted very narrow understandings of environmental conservation.[15] By doing so, the recognition of complex reciprocity practices of campesinos with nonhuman entities remained illegible as sustainable practices. The agency, emotions, and intentionality of and toward certain animal species such as tufted capuchin, oncillas, or pink dolphins were out of the scope of the hegemonic environmental conservation script.[16] From an institutional point of view, certain practices of environmental conservation became markers of what a campesino should be in biodiverse areas. These practices included not cutting trees, not hunting, not sowing coca crops, and reframing their local economy toward ecotourism, including learning technical notions of environmental conservation promoted by the state. This behavior became a way of measuring, through an institutional lens, how campesinos gained or not the right to keep living in the area, now valuated as biodiverse. The symbolic and material interactions with the environment that they had forged for decades remained illegible and ignored in the face of dominant narratives of market-oriented ecotourism. The challenge became how to make visible their sustainable practices to fit into the narrow political spaces that the Colombian state had opened for them in these biodiverse areas.

The case of the Guaviare, in which campesinos originally coming from the Andean region redefined their identities as colonos and later revendicated their identity as campesinos, cannot be extended mechanically to other parts of the country. However, it illustrates well the importance of understanding how the definition of campesino must be critically assessed in its specific historical and social processes to acknowledge how these definitions are contested and change over time when we move throughout different temporal and social scales. While situated meanings of campesino respond to specific spatial-temporal dynamics, generic definitions tend to be delocalized and, to some extent, lack an appreciation for the richness of everyday life. Instead of providing a sociological index of what the

Figure 4.1 La historia de Beto y la selva, cuento para niños. (*The Story of Beto and the Jungle*, children's book). Author: Nathalí Cedeño, Comunidad de Playa Güío in *Playa Güío: Ecoturismo y esperanza* (Bogotá: Editorial Pontificia Universidad Javeriana, 2016), 26–27.

campesino is supposed to be, we invite scholars to see the historical tensions between these top-down scripts and the social and historically situated understandings of what campesinos are, revealing how it is a complex, relational, and vibrant category. What it meant to be a campesino was contested precisely because it was contingent upon their rights over material resources, cultural recognition, and political participation.

The Constitution of 1991 and the Reframing of Political Subjectivities

Beyond the situated and changing understandings of the definition of campesino in contexts like Guaviare, there are broader scales that shape these definitions. In fact, the history of the peasant movement in Colombia shows an ample variety of aspirations and demands that include, but are not limited to, the formalization of property rights. There has been a growing interest in recent decades to show how the peasantry is a political subjectivity driven by cultural practices that in turn are defined by historical notions of belonging and community forms of territorial management. In Colombia, we have witnessed in recent decades a significant shift toward a new political understanding of campesino that goes beyond the rhetoric of the peasant as an economic subject, devoid of ethics of rootedness and care for their territory. This gradual change came about as a result of the limited recognition of campesinos as political subjects in the Constitution of 1991, which opened unprecedented spaces and mechanisms for political participation of historically marginalized populations. Simultaneously, neoliberal policies were introduced to open the Colombian economy and natural resources to global markets. These measures accentuated the precarity of rural populations, including campesinos, and came into tension with the purpose of improving living conditions sought in the new constitution.

The Constitution of 1991 also introduced a multicultural perspective. Colombia, like many other Latin American democracies, changed its political framework and followed the multicultural turn to incorporate minority rights for recognized ethnic groups such as indigenous peoples, Afro-descendant populations, and Rom people. Campesinos remained legally illegible as a collectivity and subjectivity with no cultural recognition.[17] During the decades thereafter, it was not unusual for governments, state and non-state officials, and academics to feed the imaginary of a peasant economic subject opposed to a cultural ethnic one. Hence, in the contemporary political imagination, campesinos tend to embody individual claims while ethnic groups embody collective ones: a contrast that has enormous consequences in relation to territorial governance because campesinos are seen as migrants and settlers, and as having mainly an exploitative relationship to the land. In other words, campesinos are usually portrayed as people who value land as individual property, and when required, can be easily removed to other rural or urban settings (since they lack the cultural territorial grounding associated with ethnic groups). They are rarely portrayed as a collective, as is common in the case of indigenous and Afro-descendant peoples. Since the 1960s, the state has acknowledged some forms of collective property for campesinos, such as the case of the *común y proindiviso* (joint community ownership), but these are focalized in a few rural areas of the country.[18]

As in many other countries of Latin America, in Colombia, the distinction between indigenous peoples and peasants is not a rigid one. However, in many regions of the country, such a political divide, especially when addressing campesino collective claims along the lines of territorial organization, land titles, and governance, has increased long-standing conflicts or created new disputes over state resources and public policies. These disputes have had tremendously negative impacts on both indigenous and campesino populations and their organizations precisely because they have exacerbated that separation while leaving regional and national (elite) powers intact.[19] The old adage "divide and conquer" seems to be the intended strategy or unintended consequence of the binary division between indigenous peoples and campesino.

Although the Colombian Constitutional Court has recognized, in recent decrees, that the Constitution of 1991 gives campesinos special protection by the state (Sentencia 2028 of 2018), their territorial rights do not have the scope nor the legal power that the indigenous resguardos and Afro-Colombian collective territories have. In the case of campesinos, a crucial legal status for collective land rights is the *Zonas de Reserva Campesina* (Peasant Reserve Zones, ZRC in Spanish), which were sanctioned by the Law 160 of 1994, but lacked the political will to be fully implemented. By acknowledging uneven territorial rights for different kinds of rural populations, the Constitution of 1991generated an asymmetrical terrain of territorial rights among campesino, indigenous, and Afro-Colombian populations.[20] This asymmetry has contributed to the emergence of new "horizontal territorial conflicts" between them for the control of territories in various parts of the country.[21] Additionally, the constitution reproduced the old economic reductionistic vision of campesinos as "agrarian workers," a kind of worker that "is associated with a production scheme that positions peasants as a labor force in a model of agro-industrial character, which ignores peasant identity, culture and economy, among other aspects."[22]

The disparity between campesinos and ethnic populations in terms of territorial rights marginalized the former, along with the political and cultural dimension of their experiences when interacting with their environments. For example, the current legal system resolves the tensions of campesinos living within indigenous resguardos under *saneamiento* (formalization of property rights), which converts the

> peasant subject as a third party from the perspective of civil law, which implies the disregard of their fundamental right to territoriality and to a life plan linked to a specific territory. In effect, there is no obligation to inquire into the pre-existing relationships in the territory between the different communities present or the social and cultural practices of the peasantry that inhabits it.[23]

Apparently, this perspective is part of a moment of "early jurisprudence" closely linked to the multicultural sensibilities that predominated in the early 1990s. This perspective seems to be revaluated now:

> In recent pronouncements, the [Constitutional] Court seems to move away from that paradigm and, instead, presents some sketches—still initial—of what could be a turn towards intercultural dialogue. From this perspective, the territorial rights of the subaltern subjects of rurality deserve equal protection when they come into conflict with each other, so the constitutional judge should seek their harmonization, as far as possible, instead of prioritizing some over others.[24]

Culture and Local Strategies of Territorial Management

Critical analysis of the effects of multicultural policies on the ethnic dynamics in Colombia leads us to think about the unintended effects of articulating cultural narratives to promote campesino political and territorial claims.[25] That is, the risk of embracing a culturalist narrative of the peasantry mobilizes a notion of culture based on static and "romantic" traits already present in the process of ethnic recognition in Colombia. In fact, multiculturalism—understood as a set of legal normativities that recognize and promote minority rights—and ethnic differences have had complex political repercussions in Colombia. For example, urban indigenous populations have trouble promoting their rights since their presence in the city contests the notion of cultural alterity that places them in rural areas. Similarly, people who have radically different ways of life, such as nomad groups, lack the necessary forms of political organization to mobilize their rights. Broadly speaking, there are legal complexities in addressing ethnic heterogeneity in a country with more than eighty indigenous groups with different forms of political organization and land tenure.[26] Many academic works analyze these and other political openings and closures of multicultural rights for marked (ethnic) and unmarked populations in Colombia and Latin America.[27] In sum, deploying cultural narratives in relation to campesino political and territorial claims places them in a broader political landscape in which they could be seen as not sufficiently "traditional" to warrant political acknowledgment vis-à-vis ethnic peoples, or when measured against the yardstick of "traditionality" in the context of disputes. In doing so, a "true" campesino culture would take form, placing populations that come closest to such parameters in primordial positions, while other populations would face the challenge of making themselves visible using the cultural and political resources available.

How to consider these challenges when reshaping the legal definitions of campesinos? One way is to recognize the relationship between organizational, cultural, and economic dimensions without treating them as separate spheres. This involves showing how, historically, economic practices that have been used to characterize campesinos are inserted in forms of rootedness, belonging, territorial management, and ethics. For instance, drawing on the contemporary literature about ethics, we have worked to show how campesinos define good and bad and, more specifically, how they try to live a good life, or the best possible life, within complex contexts of war, exclusion, and inequality. This can mean a range of things, from "thinking of the ethical as made up of judgments we arrive at when we stand away from our ordinary practices to that of thinking of the ethical as a dimension of everyday life."[28] For instance, in periods of strong violence, some campesinos in the Sierra Nevada de Santa Marta explained how they were able to live and survive by having *un buen juicio como campesino* (good judgment as a campesino), by knowing how to move and react, teaching children and youths to mind their own business, moving cautiously and with confidence, not being too greedy and ambitious, and especially not aspiring to the fame, money, and vices associated with local power figures (paramilitary, drug traffickers, and intermediaries for coca-paste transactions).[29] In other contexts, the ethical dimension also implies establishing, or deepening, and taking care of interconnections with nonhumans, following prescriptions that go far beyond economic exchanges to create a productive nature.

In general, talking about the rootedness and belonging of campesinos in their territories involves discussing not only the roughness of daily work and life but also the wide variety of strategies and agreements adopted to live in very different areas and ecosystems. In fact, as the Colombian Institute of Anthropology and History (ICANH) recently suggested, campesinos are historical beings that can only be understood through their origins and relationship with agricultural production, political processes, and the phenomena of violence. ICANH's analysis was written to provide the necessary analytical support to include campesino as a census category, therefore, one used to understand the several different dimensions of contemporary peasantry: sociological-territorial, socio-cultural, economic-productive, and organizational-political. This work is a call to understand campesino economic trajectories and the management and care of their livelihoods as part of multilayered political, social, and cultural discussions.[30] This is not a minor issue given the history of violence in the country. In fact, campesino organizations and territorial forms of management have encountered serious political bottlenecks and rejection as a consequence of having to exist within the territorial domains of guerrilla and/or paramilitary groups. It has been precisely in the context of a long war, fought mainly in rural areas, that campesinos have created local strategies for managing their territories and confronting its effects. There are many examples of campesino normativity that dictate where to live, how to organize collective duties such as access to water, opening and maintaining roads, where to cut trees to define agricultural production areas, or how much is *decente* (acceptable) to fish or hunt. Many peasant areas have been viewed as subversive and as the cradle of guerrilla warfare. However, as a campesino from Caquetá explains:

> We had to act according to each public order situation, for example, when there were guerrilla or military blockades, or when they prohibited us from moving through certain areas, we had to be strong and talk to them, and most of the time the guerrilla commanders were more open to talk than the military.[31]

Violence has had an enormous impact on the dissolution of peasant sociability networks, the fracturing of territorial ties, and the possibility of ensuring the improved wellbeing of future generations. The convergence of all these factors continues to be a stimulus for urban migration, for intense intergenerational tensions over the possibility of aspiring to a dignified life in rural Colombia, for the constant expansion of the agricultural frontier, and for the concentration of rural property.[32] That is, even if "conventionally war zones are described as chaotic areas," in reality they can be quite orderly.[33] The logistics of taking care of rural territories have included diverse arrangements to keep roads open, to define areas and types of crops, to generate alliances and support in times of illness through structures such as *compadrazgo* (parents-godparents relationships) or social institutions such as the *mano vuelta* (collective work based on solidarity networks), in educational and childcare processes, and in the management of forests and rivers, among other things. It is within the framework of the very many life histories of campesinos, who face very volatile contexts of violence and social inequality, that a multiplicity of management forms has emerged to embody territorial and organizational practices, which are often invisible or unknown to the state.

Zonas de Reserva Campesina and the Socio-environmental Agenda

Even today it is difficult to find in political scenarios an openness to recognize campesino organizational and political demands as stemming from territorial rootedness and life ethics, which suggest that their forms of "territorial imagination" challenge state prescriptions on what a campesino territory should be or look like.[34] These tensions have been addressed in recent scholarship through the analysis of how affects, ethics, and territorial ontologies have been created in contexts of complex histories of violence and social inequality.[35] The quest for visibility includes trying to override the statistical invisibility of campesino as a collective identity, creating knowledge and evidence of peasant territorial management practices, and theorizing about culture as a substantial aspect of campesino organizational processes. Colleagues who are actively trying to mobilize the political recognition of campesinos are working in a wide variety of settings: on advisory committees that seek to create or reform various public policies, on the political agendas of some state representatives, in specific litigation processes, and in international support agencies and NGOs.[36]

A campesino territorial legal status is still one of the most complicated demands. In fact, the way states classify campesino organizations is based on three levels: those oriented to production and commercialization, those oriented to the development of the productive environment, and those oriented to the sustainable management of natural resources (the latter are interesting given the persistent imaginary of peasants as destroyers of nature).[37] Traditionally, these levels have been used to articulate a platform for political participation aimed at discussing the country's agricultural management and rural development policies, but also to promote new value chains nationally and internationally. All these organizational forms also have implications for ways of thinking about and managing livelihoods and the environment, and, more broadly, are part of community arrangements and territorial aspirations. In fact, peasant associations, federations, unions, and organizations cannot be understood as mere economic actors. Rather, the economic dimension is only one element of their political claims, an attempt to organize the territory and social life autonomously.[38] Moreover,

> Campesino territoriality constituted by these associations is a social and political bet to allow greater access to land, first of all, but, and above all, a bet to open possibilities of autonomous development where it is possible to decide what is cultivated, how it is cultivated, and for what purpose all this effort is made.[39]

A key to open broad discussions of territorial management have been the Peasant Reserve Zones (ZRCs in Spanish), a legal status that brings together the work of diverse community structures for the institutionalization and demarcation of a territory. The ZRCs emerged as a result, among other processes and claims, of the struggles of coca farmers in the 1990s, whose social mobilizations led to the enactment of Law 160 of 1994, which created the ZRCs and consolidated the first pilot ZRCs in the Pato River basin and the Balsillas Valley, in the department of Caquetá.[40] There are currently six ZRCs and another seven in the process of being established.[41] ZRCs have seven specific objectives: to control the expansion of the agricultural frontier; to avoid land concentration; to create the basic conditions for the sustainable development of the peasant economy; to regulate the use of vacant lands; to build a proposal for integrating human development that includes land management, environmental sustainability, and political management; to facilitate the implementation of rural policies; and to strengthen spaces for dialogue between government institutions and local communities.[42] Reasons for claiming a ZRC legal status are diverse and show the intertwining of the many dimensions by which campesinos aspire to live in a territory.

In Sumapaz, at the heart of the country's Andean region, and where ZRCs have yet to be recognized, claims for recognition are explained on the basis of how peasants' daily life is rooted in a territory that was built through intense struggles in the face of war and the disappointments of the Green Revolution. "The *sumapaceños* (Sumapaz people) have always belonged to the *páramo* (moorland)," and for this reason, the organizational history and the day-to-day struggles of women, men, and children are what have built the Sumapaz territory. The ZRC and efforts for state recognition have been derived from many Sumapaceños who are trying to learn from their grandmothers' and grandfathers' experiences to invent better ways of cultivating and safeguarding the well-being of both the moorland and its inhabitants. The Sumapaz ZRC is rooted in its ecosystem, its *frailejones*, aromatic plants, guinea pigs, water, soil, bees, rabbits, and cows.[43] Interestingly, the demands tend to mobilize a collective connotation of management and protection of the territory, as well as integrated claims for autonomy, property, and the promotion of socio-environmental care practices, including agroecology, the preservation and use of native seeds, and the possibility of living in peace in their territories.

In December 2020, four peasant organizations represented by the nonprofit legal organization Dejusticia—they were the Union of Agricultural Workers of Sumapaz (SINTRAPAZ), the Environmental Peasant Association of Losada Guayabero (ASCAL-G), the Peasant Association for Organic Agriculture and Fair Trade (Agrogüejar), and the National Association of Peasant Reserve Zones (ANZORC)—filed a constitutional injunction to claim protection for the rights of three peasant communities to equality, peasant territoriality, and due process in the establishment of their ZRCs.[44] In fact, although the organizations had complied with state requirements for several years, none of the three ZRCs had been officially established. The injunction requested the Agencia Nacional de Tierras (National Land Agency) to proceed with the selection and delimitation of the ZRCs, to update or adjust their sustainable development plans, to take the necessary measures to guarantee sustainable development in articulation with other local and regional planning institutions, and to guarantee resources and coordinate with other entities for their establishment.[45] Although on April 26, 2021, the Superior Court of Bogotá ruled in favor of the establishment of the ZRCs, the rights of the campesino communities to territoriality and material equality—as special subjects of protection—were not recognized. That is, the judge ordered the establishment of the three ZRCs within a maximum period of six months from the ruling because due process had not been respected in the face of the claims of the peasant organizations, some of which had been fulfilling the necessary requirements for more than ten years.[46] However, the judge did not rule on the conceptual basis of the lawsuit, which, among other things, defended the establishment of the ZRCs as a special way to protect the rights of peasant communities in the face of inequalities, injustices, and problems they have historically suffered in the country. What campesinos and their legal partners and experts were expecting, beyond the establishment of the ZRCs, was a legal precedent to strengthen the jurisprudence on the protection of campesinos in Colombia.[47] Such processes show the complexities of open political and jurisdictional spaces to a broader, deeper understanding of campesinos, usually labeled merely as a form of economic production, in legal and political terms.

As in Sumapaz, campesinos' political agendas are actively including strategies of environmental care linked to food sovereignty. Many of the leaders working to diversify their farms explained how "quail, flowers, efforts to build a beautiful and very diverse farm, among trees, flowers and animals, are also an environmental commitment [of ours]."[48] For several years, they have been building live fences and alder trees in the farms to try to enrich the soil and avoid cutting down trees. There are also pine trees, but there are no foreign pines because, according to one of the leaders, "those trees are like the Colombian oligarchy: everything [is] for them and the rest can die."[49] As Figure 4.2 shows, the issue of environmental management is becoming increasingly relevant in Sumapaz and elsewhere, particularly because, like indigenous and Afro-descendant peoples, many campesino communities live in or around environmental hotspots and conservation areas. Public environmental policy does not allow campesinos to live in conservation

Figure 4.2 Postcard "Sumapaz, Zona de Reserva Campesina" ("Sumapaz, Peasant Reserve Zone"), 20 × 13.5 cm. Author: Rafael Díaz Vargas.

areas, which have caused a wide variety of conflicts. In fact, the creation and amplification of conservation areas in many regions have been a source of tension between campesino communities and environmental authorities. For example, the right of these communities to live inside areas declared as national parks has been a crucial topic in recent decades. "Parks with campesinos" is a social movement motto demanding recognition for their legal presence inside national parks. However, to this day, according to national environmental laws, the only people who can live inside national parks are indigenous or Afro-descendant people when their territories are formally recognized by the state as resguardos or *consejos comunitarios* (legally recognized Afro-Colombian collective territories) and are superposed on national parks. Campesino communities are no longer allowed to live there even if, as in many cases, they have lived on the land for decades before it was declared a national park.

Solutions are hard to find in a context where criminalization of campesino communities is regularly used to remove them from protected areas. Deforestation, illicit crops, illegal armies, or unstable political conditions after the 2016 Peace Agreement are some of the reasons deployed by the national government to justify punitive strategies for controlling these areas, while the structural causes behind such issues are not tackled.

In other regions considered strategic due to their ecological value, such as the Colombian Amazon, the political spaces in which the presence of campesino populations can be acknowledged are increasingly narrow, while non-participatory conservationist strategies maintain their prevalence within national institutions. Campesinos have not been actively included in environmental strategies nor is the political language of environmental conservation available to them. Nevertheless, they are actively showing a commitment to work for environmental conservation and to engage in a wide variety of sustainable and bioeconomic strategies, such as community-based ecotourism. However, one crucial concern remains: the few spaces for including campesinos within environmental movements and strategies risk disarticulating the ways in which environmental concerns and conservation initiatives are immersed in territorial forms of governance and long-standing claims for land access. The conflicts and contradictions show how campesinos have been recognized as subject of rights only in a fragmented, discontinuous, partial, and limited manner. Some legal tools—like the Constitution of 1991, the Law 160 of 1994, or the specific guidelines included in the 2016 Peace Agreement—have opened spaces for their political recognition, but these have been contested by many government and elite groups through political inaction, thus becoming an obstacle for their implementation.

Campesino protests during the last decades opened a new cycle of social mobilizations at the regional and national levels, creating political spaces for campesino demands in the struggle to stop the increasing precarity of campesinos' ways of life. In an unexpected way, these mobilizations have also been demanding recognition of the cultural dimensions of campesino lives, in a political context dominated by multicultural rights granted to ethnically marked populations. Despite the challenges, campesino movements are looking for a full, dynamic, versatile, and nonessentialist recognition of what it means to be a campesino in Colombia today.[50] Their claims also imply a rupture from external views that reduce campesinos to an economic condition, as a sector with no capacity to act, so that others must guide their destiny.[51] On the contrary, placing culture and autonomy at the core of the campesino political project is an expression of their capacity for resistance and creativity. As Carlos Duarte and Camilo Montenegro suggest: if the socio-political contexts vary, so will the campesinos' repertoires of struggle.[52]

Conclusion

The social mobilization of Colombian campesinos has deep roots in attempts to reconfigure their marginal and precarious political and social position in the country. The category of campesino is a heterogeneous subjectivity as they mobilize dynamic understandings of culture drawn from networks of sociability, politics of place, and local and national economies woven around state agrarian politics in very unstable and violent contexts. The agency of campesino communities has been crucial in promoting political and identity projects that go against monolithic and reductionist definitions and that seek to introduce nuances to reflect how campesino identity is more mobile, versatile, and complex.

Indeed, campesino organizations have mobilized in recent decades to broaden the legal and political understandings of campesino as a contested category. An important part of this effort has to do with positioning their cultural dimension; however, this purpose cannot be understood as a simple political instrumentalization of identities. It must be seen as a complex process that sediments and dynamizes political struggles with deep roots in time, as well as a critical reading and positioning in the face of changing political-economic and legal conditions that pose new challenges for these sectors of the population. The tensions and dynamics that arise around the notion of campesino is not a minor issue, because "the strength of names depends not only on what people intend to do with them today, but also on the experiences they evoke. We make history with language, but with a language with history."[53] Thus, campesino organizations have been promoting for many decades the self-management of political spaces and their claims through legal, political, and direct actions to become legible in their own terms and not in the register of stagnant and reductionist visions, usually promoted from outside. In doing so, they seek to gain legitimate spaces, manage special policies for populations that self-identify as such, and enjoy effective and differentiated recognition and inclusion by the state.

Contemporary claims regarding campesino culture emerge as a new political language that, in addition to environmental conservation, opens new possibilities for political recognition. Nevertheless, these claims ought to be understood within the long historical processes of land tenure claims and political struggles over equality, interconnected with the different forms of campesino territorial governance, including local environmental forms of management. Campesinos' aspirations toward a better life encompass a wide array of analytical discussions around justice, equality, local development, and ethics. The ways in which campesino organizations widely promote a multidimensional understanding of their subjectivity pose enormous challenges to state policies and conceptions on what campesinos can or cannot have in terms of access to prior consultation protocols, community forms of *veedurías* (citizen oversight), and so forth. The old quest for campesino land tenure now revolves around struggles for the uses, meanings, and aspirations of diverse territories.

These are cultural practices immersed within complex webs of historical violence and state formation. The complex history of exclusion and political marginalization experienced for centuries by campesinos, along with other rural populations, has been confronted, continuously, through social mobilizations, creative thinking, and political experimentation. It is a powerful testimony that democracy cannot be built based on injustice, exclusion, and misrecognition. Hence, the complex political subjectivity of campesinos opens a window for understanding some of the analytical challenges of thinking about the articulation of class, culture, and rurality in Latin America. An articulation filled with contrasts between political silences and the vibrant endurance of campesinos for defending their territories.

Notes

1 Edwin Cruz Rodríguez, "La rebelión de las ruanas: El paro nacional agrario en Colombia," *Revista Análisis* 49, no. 90 (July-December 2017): 83–109.
2 Vladimir Montaña, Natalia Robledo and Soraya Maite Yie, "La categoría campesino y sus representaciones en Colombia: Polisemia histórica y regional," *Revista Colombiana de Antropología* 58, no. 1 (2022): 9–24. Instituto Colombiano de Antropología e Historia, ICANH, *Elementos para la conceptualización de lo "campesino" en Colombia* (Bogotá: ICANH, 2017). Diana Güiza et al., *La constitución del campesinado. Luchas por reconocimiento y redistribución en el campo jurídico* (Bogotá: Colección Dejusticia, 2020).
3 Odile Hoffmann, "Divergencias construidas, convergencias por construir: Identidad, territorio y gobierno en la ruralidad colombiana," *Revista Colombiana de Antropología* 52, no. 1 (2016): 17–39. Maite Yie, "Aparecer, desaparecer y reaparecer ante el Estado como campesinos," *Revista Colombiana de Antropología* 58, no. 1 (2022): 115–152.
4 Hoffmann, "Divergencias construidas."
5 Jairo Tocancipá-Falla, "El retorno de lo campesino: Una revisión sobre los esencialismos y heterogeneidades en la antropología," *Revista Colombiana de Antropología* 41 (January-December 2005): 7–43. Yie, "Aparecer."
6 María Clemencia Ramírez, "Genealogía de la categoría de colono: Imágenes y representaciones en las zonas de frontera y su devenir en campesino colono y campesino cocalero," *Revista Colombiana de Antropología* 58, no. 1 (2022): 29–60.
7 Gabriel Cabrera, "El monumento al colono en tres localidades de la Amazonía colombiana. Historia de un objeto, representaciones de una idea," *Cadernos do LEPAARQ* 18, no. 36 (2021): 203–228. https://doi.org/10.15210/lepaarq.v18i36.21074.
8 Colono of Bocas de Aguabonita, 1997, referenced in Carlos del Cairo, "Tucanos y colonos del Guaviare: Estrategias para significar el territorio," *Revista Colombiana de Antropología* 34 (1998): 66–91.
9 The resguardo is a legal institution of territorial collective ownership for indigenous peoples formally recognized by the Colombian state. Resguardos are inalienable, indefeasible, and immune to seizure.

10 María Clemencia Ramírez, *Between the Guerrillas and the State: The Cocalero Movement, Citizenship, and Identity in the Colombian Amazon* (Durham: Duke University Press, 2011).
11 Comité Coordinador quoted in Carlos del Cairo, "Selvas y gentes (in)cultas: Políticas de la cultura y poblaciones amazónicas en los diseños de intervención estatal," in *Cultura: Centralidad, artilugios, etnografía* (Popayán: Asociación Colombiana de Antropología, 2019), 117.
12 Carlos del Cairo and Iván Montenegro-Perini, "Espacios, campesinos y subjetividades ambientales en el Guaviare," *Memoria y Sociedad* 19, no. 39 (2015): 49–71.
13 Del Cairo and Montenegro-Perini, "Espacios"; Del Cairo, "Selvas y gentes (in) cultas."
14 Carlos del Cairo, Iván Montenegro-Perini and Juan Sebastián Vélez, "Naturalezas, subjetividades y políticas ambientales en el noroccidente amazónico: Reflexiones metodológicas para el análisis de conflictos socioambientales," *Boletín de Antropología* 29, no. 48 (2014): 13–40.
15 Del Cairo and Montenegro-Perini, "Espacios campesinos."
16 Juan Vélez, "Entre la selva y el Estado: Políticas públicas medioambientales, comunidades campesinas y prácticas cotidianas en la Amazonía noroccidental colombiana" (BA thesis, Pontificia Universidad Javeriana, 2015).
17 Diana Bocarejo, *Tipologías y topologías indígenas en el multiculturalismo colombiano* (Bogotá: ICANH, Pontificia Universidad Javeriana, Universidad del Rosario, 2015); Del Cairo and Montenegro-Perini, "Espacios campesinos"; Carlos Duarte, "(Des)encuentros en lo público: Gobernabilidad y conflictos interétnicos en Colombia" (PhD dissertation, Université Sorbonne Paris Cité, 2015).
18 Juana Camacho and Natalia Robledo, "Indivisos, esquema colectivo y prácticas de propiedad campesina en Colombia," *Antípoda. Revista de Antropología y Arqueología* 40 (July 2020): 29–51.
19 Diana Bocarejo and Eduardo Restrepo, "Introducción: Hacia una crítica del multiculturalismo en Colombia," *Revista Colombiana de Antropología* 47, no. 2 (2011): 7–13. https://doi.org/10.22380/2539472X.952.
20 Güiza et al., *La constitución del campesinado.*
21 Carlos Alberto Benavides, "Sujeto y vida campesina: Reflexiones en torno al texto para la caracterización del campesinado," in *Conceptualización del campesinado en Colombia: Documento técnico para su definición, caracterización y medición*, ed. Marta Saade Granados (Bogotá: Instituto Colombiano de Antropología e Historia, ICANH, 2020), 79–80.
22 Carlos Duarte and Camilo Montenegro, "Campesinos en Colombia: Un análisis conceptual e histórico necesario," in *Conceptualización del campesinado en Colombia: Documento técnico para su definición, caracterización y medición*, ed. Marta Saade Granados (Bogotá: ICANH, 2020), 133.
23 Güiza et al., *La constitución del campesinado*, 226.
24 Güiza et al., *La constitución del campesinado*, 237.
25 Bocarejo and Restrepo, "Introducción."
26 Bocarejo, *Tipologías y topologías*; Carlos del Cairo, "Las jerarquías étnicas y las retóricas del multiculturalismo estatal en San José del Guaviare," *Revista Colombiana de Antropología* 47, no. 2 (2011): 123–149.

27 Charles R. Hale, "Neoliberal Multiculturalism: The Remaking of Cultural Rights and Racial Dominance in Central America," *Political and Legal Anthropology Review* 28, no. 1 (2005): 10–28; Eduardo Restrepo, "Imaginando comunidad negra: Etnografía de la etnización de las poblaciones negras en el Pacífico sur colombiano," in *Acción colectiva, Estado y etnicidad en el Pacífico colombiano*, ed. Mauricio Pardo (Bogotá: ICANH, Colciencias, 2001), 41–70; Eduardo Restrepo, ed., *Estudios afrocolombianos hoy: Aportes a un campo transdisciplinario* (Popayán: Editorial Universidad del Cauca, 2003).

28 Veena Das, "Ordinary Ethics: The Perils and Pleasures of Everyday Life," in *A Companion to Moral Anthropology*, ed. Didier Fassin (Hoboken: John Willey & Sons, 2012), 134; see also Webb Keane, "Minds, Surfaces, and Reasons in the Anthropology of Ethics," in *Ordinary Ethics: Anthropology, Language, and Action*, ed. Michael Lambek (New York: Fordham University Press, 2010), 64–83; Michael Lambek, *Ordinary Ethics: Anthropology, Language, and Action* (New York: Fordham University Press, 2010).

29 Diana Bocarejo, "Thinking With (Il)legality: The Ethics of Living with Bonanzas," *Current Anthropology* 59, no. S18 (2018): 48–59.

30 ICANH, *Elementos*.

31 Interview by authors, November 2018.

32 Fernán E. González, *Poder y violencia en Colombia* (Bogotá: Observatorio Colombiano para el Desarrollo Integral, la Convivencia Ciudadana y el Fortalecimiento Institucional, 2014); Daniel Pécaut, *Orden y violencia: Colombia 1930–1954* (Bogotá: Siglo XXI, 1987).

33 Ana Arjona, *Rebelocracy: Social Order in the Colombian Civil War* (Cambridge: Cambridge University Press, 2016); Nicolás Espinosa, *Política de vida y muerte: Etnografía de la violencia diaria en la Sierra de la Macarena* (Bogotá: ICANH, 2010); Diego F. Silva Prada, "Construcción de territorialidad desde las organizaciones campesinas en Colombia," *Polis* 15, no. 43 (2016): 633–654.

34 Hoffmann, "Divergencias construidas."

35 Andrea García, "Mujeres campesinas, afrodescendientes e indígenas en Colombia: Prácticas políticas y cotidianas del cuidado," *Pensares y Quehaceres: Revista de Políticas de la Filosofía* 4 (2017): 131–152; Kristina M. Lyons, *Vital Decomposition: Soil Practitioners and Life Politics* (Durham: Duke University Press, 2020); Daniel Ruiz-Serna, "El territorio como víctima. Ontología política y las leyes de víctimas para comunidades indígenas y negras en Colombia," *Revista Colombiana de Antropología* 53, no. 2 (2017): 85. Natalia Quiceno Toro, *Vivir sabroso: Luchas y movimiento afroatrateños, en Bojayá, Chocó, Colombia* (Bogotá: Universidad del Rosario, 2016).

36 Álvaro Acevedo Osorio and Nathaly Jiménez Reinales, comps., *Agroecología: Experiencias comunitarias para la agricultura familiar en Colombia* (Bogotá: Universidad del Rosario, 2018). Darío Fajardo, "Colombia: Dos décadas en los movimientos agrarios," *Cahiers des Amériques Latines* 71 (2012): 145–168. Ministerio de Agricultura, *Agricultura Campesina, Familiar y Comunitaria ACFC* (Bogotá: Ministerio de Agricultura y Desarrollo Rural, Unión Europea, 2012). Maite Yie, *Del patrón-Estado al Estado-patrón: La agencia campesina en las narrativas de la reforma agraria en Nariño* (Bogotá: Pontificia Universidad Javeriana, Universidad Nacional de Colombia, 2015); García, "Mujeres campesinas."

37 Food and Agriculture Organization of the United Nations, *Organización para la producción y comercialización* (Bogotá: FAO, n. d.). The first-level organizations include, for example, agricultural peasant associations and corporations, peasant cooperatives, and mutual associations. Second-level organizations have been regulated since 1989 and must be made up of at least 25 people. These have the same functions, duties, and rights as peasant associations (first level), but they usually have a greater negotiating capacity in markets and political institutions. Federations and societies are classified as third-level organizations made up of at least two second-level associations with national and international representation. There are antecedents dating back nearly a century, such as the National Federation of Coffee Growers and the Society of Farmers of Colombia.
38 Luis Carlos Agudelo Patiño, "Campesinos sin tierra, tierra sin campesinos: Territorio, conflicto y resistencia campesina en Colombia," *Revista NERA* 16, no. 13 (2013): 81–95. Diego Fernando Silva Prada, "Construcción de territorialidades desde las organizaciones campesinas de Colombia," *Polis* 15, no. 43 (2016): 633–654.
39 Silva Prada, "Construcción de territorialidades," 649.
40 González, *Poder y violencia*.
41 Food and Agriculture Organization of the United Nations, FAO, *Las Zonas de Reserva Campesina: Retos y experiencias significativas en su implementación* (Bogotá: FAO, 2019); Alejandra Osejo Varona et al., "Zonas de Reserva Campesina en el escenario del posconflicto: Una herramienta comunitaria para el manejo de la biodiversidad," in *Biodiversidad 2017: Estado y tendencias de la biodiversidad continental de Colombia*, eds. L. A. Moreno, C. Rueda, and G. I. Andrade (Bogotá: Instituto de Investigación de Recursos Biológicos Alexander von Humboldt, 2018).
42 FAO, *Las Zonas de Reserva Campesinas*.
43 Mateo Vásquez, María Galvis, and Diana Bocarejo, *Sumapaz: Zona de Reserva Campesina* (Bogotá: Universidad del Rosario, Sintrapaz, 2019).
44 Dejusticia, "Acción de tutela de asociaciones campesinas contra la ANT y del Consejo Directivo de la ANT ante la dilación en el proceso de constitución de las ZRC de Sumapaz, Losada—Guayabero y Güejar—Cafre," December 16, 2020. Dejusticia, "Presentamos una tutela para exigir que se garantice el derecho al territorio campesino," December 22, 2020.
45 Dejusticia, "Acción de tutela" and "Presentamos una tutela."
46 Tribunal Superior del Distrito Judicial de Bogotá, Sala Penal. Radicación: 110013187008202000077 02 [072], Magistrado ponente: Juan Carlos Garrido Barrientos, April 26, 2021.
47 Dejusticia, "Corte Constitucional selecciona tutela para constituir tres ZRC," September 20, 2021.
48 Vásquez, Galvis, and Bocarejo, *Sumapaz*.
49 Vásquez, Galvis, and Bocarejo, *Sumapaz*.
50 Marta Saade, ed., *Conceptualización del campesinado en Colombia: Documento técnico para su definición, caracterización y medición* (Bogotá: ICANH, 2020).

51 Mauricio Caviedes, "Obstáculos al desarrollo: La influencia del lenguaje del Frente Nacional en *El Campesino* (1961)," *Anuario Colombiano de Historia Social y de la Cultura* 49, no. 2 (2022): 159–186.
52 Duarte and Montenegro, "Campesinos en Colombia," 121.
53 Yie, "Aparecer," 144.

Part 2
Surveying the Territorial State

5 A Country of Forests
Territorial State Building in Colombia

Claudia Leal

In August 1984, in the context of president Belisario Betancur's peace process, the representatives of 39 Community Action Councils of Caguán, department of Caquetá, met with FARC commanders and officials from three state institutions to discuss strategies for regional development. The peasants decided to create a committee in charge of overseeing the settlement process of that jungle area, which began two decades earlier. They determined that properties should not exceed 200 hectares, and that they would strive for the rational management of natural resources by conserving the vegetation growing close to water springs and courses, as well as on steep slopes, and by safeguarding mineral licks frequented by wild animals. However, their main goal was to achieve the titling of their lands, for which they run against a major obstacle: titles could only be issued if the area was formally withdrawn from the Amazonian Forest Reserve.[1] By virtue of the establishment of the reserve, which covered the entire Colombian portion of Amazonia, the region was to be conserved for the development of a forest economy, that is, for the extraction of natural resources based on the precepts of scientific forestry. Therefore, those public lands were not to be titled for setting up farms, but granted temporarily in concession.

The Amazonian Forest Reserve is part of a form of territorial state building that was defined based on the natural vegetation of the country. Andrés Etter and his peers have estimated that over 80 percent of the area now known as Colombia was once covered by forests; the rest were lowland savannas, in the Eastern Plains and parts of the Caribbean, and above the tree line, *páramos* (moorland). The vast majority of forests lay on humid lowlands, that is, were (and still are) tropical rainforests. Their predominance has been strengthened by the fact that, by 2000, the two other forest types—dry forests and highland Andean or cloud forests—had been reduced to less than 10 and 40 percent of their estimated original cover.[2] Most of the country's rainforests lay within the seven forest reserves established in 1959, which extended over almost two-thirds of Colombia's

DOI: 10.4324/9781003048152-8

continental landmass. According to this designation, they were to remain forested and preferably in the public domain, with the extraction of its valuable resources—timber, saps, barks, seeds, and animal skins—regulated by the state.

These reserves were superimposed on municipalities and departments, the administrative units that constitute the quintessential form of territorial state building in Colombia, which cover the entire national territory. These units had been instituted since the inception of the republic in the early nineteenth century and acquired different names and limits throughout the years. Created around towns and cities, municipalities expressed a vision of the country based on agrarian—rather than forested—landscapes. Crops, pastures, and settlements defined the areas most densely populated, where private property was common, and over which the state exercised some measure of control. The meeting in Caguán in 1984 reflected the tensions between these two ways of conceiving the territory. Peasants in this region wanted to, and eventually succeeded in removing the official forested status of their lands so that these could revert to what we could call the agrarian realm.

This dichotomous view of the national space—based on two types of landscapes and administrative units—distinguished a humanized territory from another one conceived as natural. Such distinction did not only rest on the abundant forest cover that characterized Colombia and the whole of Latin America but also on entrenched ideas of nature. The agrarian ideal, which emerged first and is still dominant, was buttressed by a view of *montes*, that is, jungles, as places of doom, which runs deep in Western culture and has been influential across Latin America.[3] It should not surprise that the idea that civilizing the land meant transforming wild forests into croplands took hold in this sparsely populated country since colonial times.[4] An alternative view of forests, according to which they should be wisely managed to harvest their resources, rather than conquered through annihilation, gained force with the Enlightenment project and the development of forestry. In Mexico and Chile, which have homogenous temperate forests, similar to those of Europe where the tenets of scientific management developed, this science began its ascent in the late nineteenth century. In Colombia, with its diverse jungles, forestry took off in the middle of the twentieth century and enjoyed limited influence.[5]

However conceived, forests constitute a conspicuous part of the spatiality upon which the Colombian state is grounded and over which it operates. Addressing the territorial character of the state can lead to the recognition of this and other aspects of the materiality of the national space. Unlike many of their predecessors, modern states are territorial, that is, they are sovereign within clear demarcated boundaries.[6] Max Weber's often-quoted definition of the state—as a human community that

A Country of Forests 111

Figure 5.1 "Under the oaks, Quercus Humboldtii, near Viotá," watercolor.

Source: Édouard François André, *L'Amérique Équinoxiale (Colombie-Equateur-Pérou)*. (Paris: Librairie Hachette, 1869), 201. Courtesy of Banco de la República, Bogotá.

successfully claims the monopoly of the legitimate use of physical force within a given territory—acknowledges the spatial dimension of modern statehood. Yet, this dimension is downplayed or ignored in most studies about the state. In Colombia, whenever the territory is considered in the analysis, it tends to be in the form of the regional variations of the kind of non-spatial phenomena that political scientists and sociologist usually take into account. The best examples come from some outstanding analyses of the Colombian armed conflict. In response to the notion of a partially collapsed state, which derives from recognizing the power of illegal actors, Fernán González developed an influential view that proposes examining how state institutions have been built differently in various locales.[7] Other researchers have followed suit by exploring and comparing the reach of the state in various parts of the national territory, trying to explain where and why its authority is stronger.[8] In these important analyses, the landforms, vegetation, soils, and nonhuman populations that make up territories remain out of sight.

By acknowledging the relevance of biophysical realities for the emergence of some institutions of governance, this chapter breaks new ground. Following a basic tenet of environmental history—that the natural and human worlds are interwoven—it forces us to realize that material realities affect social processes, widening our range of vision and producing a more holistic understanding of our past and present. Since Independence, nature, and the ways in which it has been perceived, has shaped the formation of the territorial administrative units of government that comprise our national geography. This chapter proposes a view of state building in Colombia based on the analysis of four of these kinds of units. It starts with departments and the like, those basic entities of territorial state management established in the early nineteenth century. It then moves to the second half of the nineteenth century, but especially to the first half of the twentieth century, to explore the antecedents that in 1959 led to fully identifying forests as the basis for spatial units of state development. It continues with national parks, largely established between 1960 and 1990, which strengthened the spatial definition and management of nature. And it ends with ethnic territories, which starting in the 1970s, but more decisively in the 1980s and 1990s, departed from the previous forms of territorial management by coupling nature and culture in the same realm. This history has resulted from particular views of different landscapes that attempt to regulate the relation of various social groups with the resources these contain. Hopefully, it will stimulate social researchers who study Colombia to notice ever more often elements of the infinite nonhuman world and establish connections that might help them provide more comprehensive answers to their questions.

The Agrarian Ideal

After Independence, creoles had the challenge of building a republic, the main guidelines for which were expressed in the constitution. The first of these documents, which dates from 1821, outlined the principal strategy for territorial management: "The territory of the Republic will be divided in Departments, the Departments in Provinces, the Provinces in Counties (*Cantones*), and the Counties in Parishes."[9] Law 25 of 1824 specified the 12 departments and their capital cities, all the provinces and their capitals, as well as the cantones with their *cabeceras* (principal settlements). Cities and settlements constituted the basis for designating areas whose precise limits, in the absence of accurate maps, remained ill-defined. With time, provinces, cantones, and parochial districts disappeared; autonomous states, as well as second-class *intendencias* and *comisarías*, emerged and then ceased to exist; while municipalities became the basic territorial unit of the Colombian state. The names, numbers, and limits of these divisions also suffered multiple transformations.[10]

These units defined, at different moments in time, ideal forms of territorial administration—"utopian fictions," to borrow the expression used by Peter Vandergeest and Nancy Peluso when studying the territorialization of state power in Thailand.[11] They sketched goals to strive for and had designated authorities to achieve them. In the early nineteenth century, departments were run by intendants, provinces by governors, *cantones* by ordinary mayors, and parochial districts by parochial mayors. However, finding citizens to fill the posts of mayors was often an unmet challenge, even in the central province of Bogotá.[12] Other aspects of effective territorial administration were even harder to achieve. While well-populated *distritos* were relatively small, they became immense or rather nonexistent in regions where population density was low. These areas, which comprised more than half the alleged national territory, lied nominally within standard administrative units, but had virtually no state presence.

This blueprint for state formation was coupled with another ideal, that of state-sanctioned individual private property, which according to liberal ideology was the foundation for a flourishing economy. This form of land-ownership was "localized and precarious," often consuetudinary rather than backed by formal titles, and limited by areas belonging to indigenous and religious communities, as well as cities and towns. As Germán Palacio explains, the republican state strove to generalize private property and to stimulate the land market by abolishing communal properties, distributing public lands on an individual basis, and enacting, in 1876, a civil code based on this form of ownership. Like most of the aforementioned territorial administrative units, private property was seen as universal, a guiding principle for the building of a republican society throughout the totality of the national space.¹³

The farms and haciendas that epitomized private property were defined by a particular kind of landscape: agricultural fields and pastures. In the agrarian society of the early nineteenth century, prosperity was associated with the abundance of domestic plant and animal species. Vigorous agrarian landscapes had native cornfields or European wheat, as well as cattle, mules, horses, sheep, and goats, all of Old-World origin. Crops and domestic animals provided food, various materials, and services, and embodied the human labor that tamed the land. However, humid forests, and to a lesser extent dry ones, covered the majority of the mountains and plains that make up Colombian geography. While many private properties included forested areas, forests largely fell within the category of *baldíos*, that is, legally unclaimed lands that remained in the public domain.

The carving of agrarian landscapes out of jungles, and other native ecosystems, facilitated the extension of private property and the strengthening of municipalities. That was the case too beyond Colombia, for instance, in southern Chile and also in the Argentine pampas and in Patagonia, which were covered by grasses rather than by trees. Peasants often led the way in these processes of frontier expansion. Throughout the nineteenth century, settlers from the core of Antioquia, in the Colombian northwestern Andes, moved mostly south replacing native trees with corn, beans, coffee, sugarcane, and pastures, as settlements sprang up and new municipalities formed. In turning baldíos into productive private land, forests were seen mainly as obstacles to overcome, for clearing land by cutting down trees and burning them was hard work. However, peasants and entrepreneurs also valued forests for the resources they provided: nutrients that enriched soils after the vegetation was burned, firewood, timber for construction, and protein in the form of wild meat.¹⁴

Colombian legislation sanctioned the processes of frontier expansion by upholding peasants' right to the product of their labor, assessed largely through forest removal. Laws 61 of 1874 and 48 of 1882, which aimed at protecting migrant peasants from speculators, were based on the principle that crops and "artificial" pastures were the evidence needed for obtaining private property.¹⁵ These laws explicitly defined not only plantings but also clearings (*desmontes*) as improvements (*mejoras*) to the land. Furthermore, they acknowledged the right to own adjacent non-worked lands, anticipating future clearing or conceding the importance forests had for procuring construction materials and fuel wood in pre-industrial times. Subsequent agrarian legislation continued in the same spirit of sanctioning the conversion of forests into the private agrarian realm. Law 135 of 1961, enacted shortly after the triumph of the Cuban Revolution, when the U.S. government promoted agrarian reforms all over Latin America to hinder the advance of communism, aimed at fostering social justice and modernizing the countryside. It sought, among other things, to expand the area devoted to agriculture and cattle ranching by allocating property in baldíos to landless peasants.[16]

Forests receded slowly as crops but mostly African grasses colonized new areas, along with dwellings and new settlements. These settlements provided services, including stores, and also housed state institutions, especially mayors' offices and city councils that gave life to new municipalities. In this manner, the chief form of territorial state building expanded steadily. An alternative way of conceiving and designating parts of the national space, which assigned standing forests a central role, had to wait until 1959 for its most substantial development.

Forest Reserves

The awareness that forests were more than just land emerged slowly and derived from their economic potential as sources of export products and as protectors of water. Forest extractive economies developed since the late eighteenth century, when *palo de tinte* (dyewood) was exported from the Guajira peninsula. However, the importance of this kind of economic activities only became fully apparent in the late nineteenth and early twentieth centuries with the export of cinchona bark, rubber, and to a lesser extent vegetable ivory.[17] Then, the growth of some cities, as well as the development of commercial agriculture in certain parts of the country, drew attention to the role of forests for water conservation. These developments preceded the full-blown experiment of using forests to guide territorial state management.

National legislation demonstrates that, from the mid-nineteenth century on, congressmen recognized the potential significance of forests for public finances. Regulations from 1853 and 1865 implicitly acknowledge that these ecosystems were and should remain in the public domain by mentioning the possibility of renting out public forests as well as the need to obtain a license for extracting their resources. Although, in 1870, the radical liberal ideology that defined the federal period (1863–1886) led politicians to declare that the exploitation of public forests was free, soon after restrictions appeared. Licenses were reinstated in 1884, mainly seeking to guarantee resource conservation. Therefore, lawmakers not only recognized the convenience of public ownership but also the advantage of preserving forests so that the extraction of their resources would not be impaired. Forests were becoming more visible for state officials, even if regulations did not have strong impacts on their actual use.[18]

Conceptualizing forests in spatial terms by delimiting and reserving certain areas took longer. An important antecedent occurred in 1908 (and was reaffirmed in 1919) when, by law, forests containing hardwoods, vegetable ivory palms, cinchona trees and other exportable and marketable products were qualified as "national." This designation made some baldíos more concrete: not just forests, but particular kinds of forests. Yet a spatial understanding of these ecosystems developed somewhat later, around the need to conserve water. In the early twentieth century, Colombia's two main cities—Bogotá and Medellín—purchased the watersheds of the streams that supplied their aqueducts in order to eliminate productive activities (mainly agriculture, cattle ranching, and mining) and maintain the areas forested. In the case of Bogotá, the hills in question had been denuded; they were reforested mostly with pine trees and eucalyptus, while in Medellín plantings were combined with the protection of the remaining forest. In this latter city, the municipal council took a significant step by creating, in 1918, the "Bosque Municipal Piedras Blancas," that is, a protected area.[19]

In the 1930s and early 1940s, forest protection gained momentum through the establishment of a few reserved areas in the Cauca Valley, the Sierra Nevada de Santa Marta, and the environs of the cities of Pereira, Pasto and Villavicencio. Santa Marta led the way thanks to the influence of the banana plantation economy controlled by the United Fruit Company. In 1933, a "territorial state reserve" was created on the western flank of the Sierra Nevada, based on the Fiscal Code of 1912, which established this vague category for creating areas that should not be titled (including the headwaters of navigable rivers).[20] Reserving forests to protect watersheds received its firmest backing from the land regime law of 1936, which created and defined forest reserves as "private or public areas where forests must be conserved or replanted to maintain or increase water flow."[21] Shortly after, a succinct 1940 decree was entirely devoted to a new territorial unit called "zonas forestales protectoras" (protective forest zones), to be established in areas that "it is convenient that they remain covered with arboreal mass due to the action that these exert on the fluvial regime."[22] Based on these two laws, the Ministry of Agriculture and Commerce, renamed of National Economy in 1938, declared 14 reserves to conserve water for human consumption, agriculture, and the erection of the first hydroelectric plants in the country.[23]

About two decades later, in the post–World War II years, the special legal designation for forested areas went full swing. As Map 5.1 shows, Law 2 of 1959 established and demarcated seven forest reserves—over 58 percent of the national territory—"for the development of forestry [*la economía forestal*] and the protection of soils, water, and wildlife." These reserves would remain in the public domain and their resources could be extracted through concessions. At the time, forests still covered 61 percent of the national territory (representing 74 percent of their original expanse).[24] In the age of planning and development, under the aegis of the newly influential economic science, politicians and state officials realized that forests

A Country of Forests 117

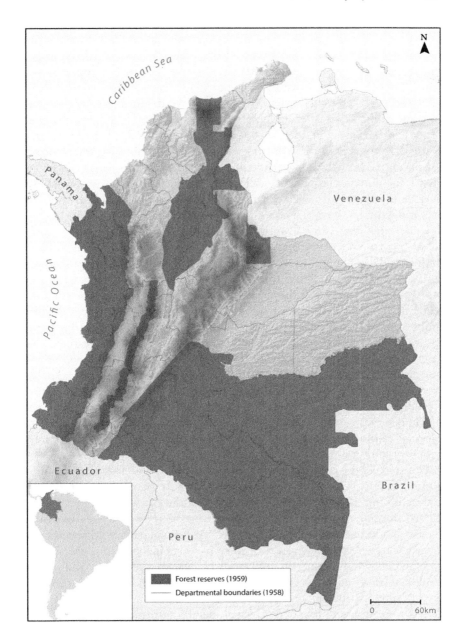

Map 5.1 Forest Reserves, 1959. Author: Christian Medina Fandiño.

Sources: Original map of Law 2, 1959, available at Unidad de Planeación Minero Energética www.upme.gov.co/guia_ambiental/carbon/areas/reservas/indice.htm and political map of Colombia, 1958, https://commons.wikimedia.org/wiki/File:Colombia_(1958).svg

needed to be marshaled in the drive for economic growth. The belated inception of scientific forestry in the country served as catalyst for devising a strategy, while state expansion and diversification provided the institutional backing for action. Forestry was one of the three programs with which Bogotá's public university (Universidad Distrital) opened its doors in 1950. A year later, the National University at Medellín created the Forestry Institute and started offering a degree in this science.[25] The establishment of these programs coincided with the creation, in 1952, of the Division of Natural Resources of the Ministry of Agriculture, following the reform of the executive branch of government proposed by North American economist Lauchlin Currie. He suggested that this new Division was needed to oversee the "rational development of natural resources, such as soils, forests and fisheries, with the goal of conserving them."[26]

Underlying the 1959 law promoted by this Division was the notion that—as products of nature—forests and their resources belonged to the nation and should be under state supervision. The Ministry of Agriculture was made responsible for overseeing forest exploitation within the reserves, which were mostly public lands, although the law conceded that some areas were held under private property. Reflecting their dichotomous view of the natural world, lawmakers established that if soils within the reserves were deemed "adequate for agriculture and livestock," the reserved status of those areas could be withdrawn. That happened in various places, which often—as in the case of Caguán that opens this article—were converted into private farmland. In 1974, the Code of Natural Resources reaffirmed this possibility but only after upholding the tenet of the reserves—"the area of the forest reserve may only be used for the rational exploitation of the forests"—and proscribing granting private property within it.[27]

Forest reserves necessarily overlapped everywhere with municipalities and departments, creating tension between these two forms of territorial state building. Reserves severely limited the uses of the areas they encompassed, forcing to relinquish in these places the long-held idea of taming the land, and building a prosperous society, by replacing wild species with domesticates. Moreover, reserves were to be managed from the nation's capital. Therefore, the potential control certain governors and majors could aspire to have over parts of the territories under their jurisdiction greatly diminished. However, as some critics warned, Law 2 of 1959 was issued to be ignored; it was not based on solid information, nor was there enough institutional expertise or strength to bring it into effect.[28] Thus, in parts of these reserves, peasants and entrepreneurs planted corn and raised pigs, and later diversified with cattle and coca, creating privately owned farms lacking legal titles. They were fulfilling the agrarian ideal in areas where it had been formally forbidden.

The indigenous groups living in Amazonia, the Pacific coast, and a few other parts of the country, as well as the Black rural people of this same coast, did not fit within either of the two landscape ideals: they tended to use forests rather than cut them down, and they were not entrepreneurs seeking concessions to extract natural resources. Titling their rather small plots would have not recognized their crucial access to forests, and although they inhabited the forest reserves, the law assumed they did not exist or, at least, had any rights over those areas. Therefore, Law 2 of 1959 reinforced their status as squatters in public lands. Despite long-term human habitation, the official conception of forests left little room for considering them as tamed environments or wild gardens. In the 1980s and 1990s, new kind of territorial units acknowledged indigenous and Black peoples' rights to forested lands; but before that happened, yet another dichotomous form of conceiving nature in spatial terms crystallized.

Precious Nature

National parks emerged in the wake of forest reserves as another way of conceptualizing parts of the national territory based on its biophysical features. Law 2 of 1959 also served as the initial legal basis for this other way of signaling and valuing nature; it charged the Ministry of Agriculture with the responsibility of declaring "natural national parks" aimed at conserving flora and fauna.[29] The law stated that areas designated as parks could not be privatized and that hunting, fishing, and all activities related to industry, ranching, and agriculture were prohibited within them; tourism was permitted as well as any other pursuit that the national government deemed convenient for conservation or beautification. That national parks were antithetical to private property and habitation was further stressed by authorizing the government to expropriate private lands and purchase any abodes, crops, or improvements settlers had in the designated lands.[30] A couple of years later, in 1961, the law that created the Colombian Institute for Agrarian Reform (INCORA in Spanish), in charge of managing public lands, gave it the authority to constitute "reserves destined to the conservation of natural resources."[31] With the exception of the first park, all others designated in the 1960s were the result of decisions taken by INCORA, upheld by the Ministry of Agriculture, and sanctioned by presidential decree.[32]

By the 1970s, a system of national parks had been instituted, and in the following decades it continued to expand. A variety of players—including Federico Carlos Lehmann, a well-known naturalist, and the *Corporación Autónoma Regional de los Valles Sinú y Magdalena* (CVM), one of the first regional corporations of the country—lobbied successfully for the pioneer parks. The exceptional institutional backing provided by CVM to the first Caribbean parks led to the development of two of them and the survival of all three. Lacking support and existence on the ground, six out of the 12 parks designated in the 1960s were short-lived. The environmental authority—that is, the Institute of Natural Resources (INDERENA), created in 1968—annulled them, while its specialized staff used ecological criteria for drafting a map with numerous areas worthy of protection. After INDERENA's responsibility for conserving nature was ratified by the 1974 Code of Natural Resources, and thanks to the pressure that its general manager exerted, the president approved, in 1977, the creation of 20 parks and similar areas. The need to conserve highland moors for water provision helped convince policy makers of the advantages of designating parks.[33] No matter the underlying appeal of each particular area—water storage, extraordinary landscapes, or representative life forms and communities—practically all of them included forests.

This kind of territorial state formation now covers over 14 percent of the country's continental mass, plus part of its maritime area. Its large expanse owes much to the establishment, mostly in the 1980s, of several very large parks in Amazonia (including the recent expansion of the largest of them, Chiribiquete). These parks were the result of the global attention paid to tropical rainforests, and the alarm caused by their accelerated destruction in the previous decades. The notion that their value resided in their extraordinary biodiversity represented a way of conceiving forests that departed from both the idea of obstacles to development that lay at the core of the agrarian ideal, and the belief that guaranteeing the extraction of its marketable resources was the fundamental reason for conserving them.

Parks sometimes overlapped with forest reserves, but always did with departments and municipalities, limiting the prospects of regional governance. Parks expressed and extended the power of both the executive branch and the central government as the president decided, without much consultation, which lands would be set aside for conservation. He followed the advice of a group of experts, best represented by naturalist Jorge "El Mono" Hernández, who used scientific knowledge to determine which places and ecosystems warranted special designation as national parks. The work of these life scientists contributed to the ideal of state autonomy, for they developed their own project without the interference of powerful vested interests or clientelistic networks.[34] Yet, by leaving Congress out of the picture, regional concerns represented there were sidestepped, just as municipal and departmental authorities were ignored. This imbalance of power between Bogotá and the regions was extended from designation to management. Since 1968, parks have been under the aegis of a specialized office initially housed within INDERENA and, after 1993, within the Ministry of the Environment. Ultimately, parks snatched from local and regional governments the possibility of shaping the use of natural resources in those areas and of benefitting from it.

The tensions that resulted from this state of affairs are expressed in the cases of the municipalities of Fómeque (department of Cundinamarca) and Vistahermosa (department of Meta). Half of the territory of the former is part of Chingaza National Park, which stores the water used by millions of people in Bogotá and its surroundings. While this half was the least peopled and productive of the municipality, it came to play a strategic role from which the municipality derives no benefit. Vistahermosa, for its part, represents an extreme version of a more frequent problem. Erected in 1969, its territory extended over La Macarena Mountain Biological Reserve, a protected area established in 1948 that preceded the park of the same name. This municipality resulted from the process of frontier expansion that contributed to build the agrarian ideal. In these and other public forests, landless peasants seeking a livelihood and national parks enacted to safeguard nature converged. Although legally antithetical, thousands of peasants live within national parks whose existence on the ground has been faulty, for reasons that range from lack of funds to violence. Peasants' productive activities often eliminate part of what national parks are set to protect, while the formal designation of those areas strip an already vulnerable population from the right to own the lands they work and to receive important state benefits, including credit, basic education, and transportation infrastructure.[35] Park legislation allows for human habitation, but only of indigenous communities, with whom tensions arise from overlapping governance logics. In a country that redefined itself as multicultural in the Constitution of 1991, ethnic groups have special rights, including communal ownership of their ancestral territories, many of which lie in tropical jungles. The collective property of forests came to bridge the normative separation between humanized and natural spaces.

In-between: Ethnic Territories

For thousands of years, humans have inhabited the forests that today make part of Colombia. For centuries, indigenous groups and Black communities have enriched them by, for instance, caring for useful species; they have also endowed those territories with meanings. Yet forest peoples had no rightful place in the dichotomous view of the national territory represented, on the one hand, by agrarian landscapes and, on the other, by nonhumanized nature. While they tend to have small family plots, they also use the surrounding forests as a source of construction materials and game, and sometimes the subsoil for mining. In the 1970s, the state started to recognize the territorial rights of indigenous forest dwellers, and in the 1990s followed suit with those of the Black communities living along the rivers of the Pacific coast. Considering these peoples as ethnic, that is, as culturally different, was the basis for endorsing collective rights over forested lands.

The titling of indigenous territories in lowland jungles was an unintended outcome of the struggle of Andean indigenous groups for their lands, which gained strength in the context of the agrarian reform movement of the early 1970s. While peasants fought for titles over family farms, indigenous groups sought to uphold their *resguardos*, collective lands of colonial origin, which, as we saw, had been under attack since at least the beginning of the republic. Anthropologists eased the move from defending long-established Andean resguardos to designating lowland ones by advancing a positive view of forest indigenous peoples. A few pioneer communities were granted *reservas* (reserves) that is, areas that remained in the public domain but whose usufruct their occupants enjoyed.[36] Creating reservas required INDERENA to withdraw those areas from forest reserves. Roque Roldán, a lawyer who championed indigenous rights, argued successfully that such a withdrawal was unnecessary because the kind of habitation in question did not conflict with the spirit of the forest reserves. Meanwhile, indigenous peoples contended that resguardos, which implied ownership, were the only appropriate form of recognizing their rights.[37] The reservas thus opened the way for the establishment of numerous resguardos in the 1980s.[38] Some of them were quite sizeable; the largest one—Predio Putumayo—measured over six million hectares. The recognition of ownership over extensive territories derived from conceiving indigenous peoples as stewards of nature. This notion followed the global concern for rainforests mentioned above and was made into policy through the collaboration of anthropologist Martín von Hildebrand, head of the Office of Indigenous Affairs, and Liberal president Virgilio Barco (1986–1990).[39]

The idea that forest dwellers take care of the environment also contributed to the granting of collective territorial titles to Black rural people in the Pacific coast. This right was first established in the Constitution of 1991 and developed subsequently in Law 70 of 1993, which identified these communities as an ethnic group. This development had its origins in the 1980s, when, backed by Catholic missionaries, Black people in the Middle Atrato region (department of Chocó) formed an organization that successfully defended their territory from the intrusion of timber companies.[40] They drew inspiration from the 169 Convention of 1989 on Indigenous and Tribal Peoples of the International Labor Organization, which encouraged governments to "identify the lands which the peoples concerned traditionally occupy, and to guarantee effective protection of their rights of ownership and possession." It also specified that the term lands "shall include the concept of territories, which covers the total environment of the areas which the peoples concerned occupy or otherwise use."[41] By 2005, 149 collective titles had been granted, covering over five million hectares.

The establishment of ethnic territories and conservation areas in rainforests undermined, but did not replace the idea that frontier expansion was the way to nationalize large parts of the country. Just as different kinds of administrative units overlap in a map, so too do bureaucratic and social practices aimed at building or sustaining the different environmental ideals signaled by those units. Thus, forests are areas where indigenous groups and their communal authorities encounter peasants and municipal officials, along with bureaucrats appointed in Bogotá, and entrepreneurs of various sorts; they negotiate their interests in a myriad of ways, leaving their imprint on Colombia's geography.

Conclusion: The Matter of History

Municipalities, departments, forest reserves, national parks, resguardos, and collective territories of Black communities constitute part of the intricate constellation of institutions and relations that we refer to with that generic and often obfuscating term "state."[42] Each kind of unit has its own regulations and forms of administration: National parks have a bureaucracy in charge of guaranteeing strict conservation, while ethnic authorities have numerous official responsibilities within their territories. The spatial character of these units makes them mappable, that is, easy to represent in visual form. Through them, the homogenous national space abstracted in a map is invested with specificities that make it legible and intend to direct and facilitate territorial management. Ultimately, these various kinds of areas must be understood as efforts to control people and their use of natural resources. And although reality never matches the ideals envisioned through these spatial artifacts, these not only reveal state rationalities but also have effects in the way different social groups and players interact in the lived space.

While the existence of all these units is well-known, they have rarely been subject of scholarly exploration as spatial constructs. This oversight speaks to the difficulties social scientists have had in thinking spatially, even in the case of the state, an influential concept and reality that is intrinsically territorial.[43] Furthermore, this chapter demonstrates that it is not just space that matters but also its very concrete material traits.[44] In the case of Colombia, forests are particularly relevant, given that they cover more than half of the country's continental area, a reality that is also true for other nation-states. For example, by the late nineteenth century, forests extended over around three-quarters of Thailand's territory. This reality was acknowledged by declaring, in 1896, that all unoccupied land was state forest, which fell under the jurisdiction of the Royal Forestry Department. Like in Colombia, enforcement largely failed, although after the 1930s, a process of demarcation of protected forests slowly unfolded.[45]

Forests are imposing. Defined and dominated by trees, they are complex worlds also formed by many other types of plants, a wide diversity of animals, and other life forms such as the ubiquitous fungi; soils and water, as well as rocks and relief are also integral to these environments. Forests' potent physicality and innate richness have greatly contributed to their cultural significance as places of origin, ruin, or hope. Although they occupy a privileged place in our imagination, and in the country's materiality, we have given our back to them as we sheltered ourselves in cities and surrounded our existence with domesticates. But they are there, shaping our worldviews, our future, and the institutions of government that define our nation.

Notes

1 Hilario Pedraza Torres, "El proceso de paz en Caquetá (El caso del Caguán)" (unpublished manuscript, 1986). I thank Leah Carroll for sharing with me this rich firsthand account of the process.
2 Andrés Etter, Clive McAlpine, and Hugh Possingham, "A Historical Analysis of the Spatial and Temporal Drivers of Landscape Change in Colombia since 1500," *Annals of the American Association of Geographers* 98, no. 1 (2008); Shawn Van Ausdal, "Pasture, Power and Profit: An Environmental History of Cattle Ranching in Colombia, 1850–1950," *Geoforum* 40, no. 5 (September 2009): 707–719.
3 Robert Pogue Harrison, *Forests: The Shadow of Civilization* (Chicago: The University of Chicago Press, 1992); Claudia Leal, "From Threatening to Threatened Jungles," in *A Living Past: Environmental Histories of Modern Latin America*, eds. John Soluri, Claudia Leal, and José Augusto Pádua (New York: Berghahn Books, 2018).
4 Edgardo Pérez Morales, *La obra de Dios y el trabajo del hombre: Percepción y transformación de la naturaleza en el virreinato del Nuevo Reino de Granada* (Medellín: Universidad Nacional de Colombia sede Medellín, 2011).
5 Thomas Miller Klubock, *La Frontera: Forests and Ecological Conflict in Chile's Frontier Territory* (Durham: Duke University Press, 2014); and Christopher Boyer, *Political Landscapes: Forests, Conservation and Community in Mexico* (Durham: Duke University Press, 2014).
6 Lars Bo Kaspersen and Jeppe Strandsbjerg, "The Spatial Practice of State Formation: Territorial Space in Denmark and Israel," *Journal of Power* 2, no. 2 (2009): 235–254.
7 Fernán E. González, "¿Colapso parcial o presencia diferenciada del Estado en Colombia? Una mirada desde la historia," *Colombia Internacional* 58 (2003): 124–158.
8 Mauricio García Villegas, Nicolás Torres, Javier Revelo, José R. Espinosa and Natalia Duarte, *Los territorios de la paz: La construcción del Estado local en Colombia* (Bogotá: Dejusticia, 2016).
9 Article 8, Constitution of 1821.
10 See, for instance, Title I of the Constitution of 1886.
11 Peter Vandergeest and Nancy Peluso, "Territorialization and State Power in Thailand," *Theory and Society* 24, no. 3 (Jun. 1995): 385–426.
12 Juan David Delgado Rozo, "La difícil instauración del gobierno republicano en el espacio local: Las municipalidades y los alcaldes parroquiales en la provincial de Bogotá, 1821–1830," in *La Independencia en Colombia: Miradas*

transdisciplinares, eds. John Jairo Cárdenas Herrera and Julián Augusto Vivas García (Bogotá: Universidad Antonio Nariño, 2015).
13 Germán A. Palacio Castañeda, *Territorios improbables: Historias y ambientes* (Bogotá: Editorial Magisterio, 2018), quote from p. 89. On the abolition of communal properties see Frank Safford and Marco Palacios, *Colombia: Fragmented Land, Divided Society* (New York: Oxford University Press, 2002).
14 James Parsons, *Antioqueño Colonization in Western Colombia*, revised ed. (Berkeley: University of California Press, 1968).
15 Catherine LeGrand, *Frontier Expansion and Peasant Protest in Colombia, 1850–1936* (Albuquerque: University of New Mexico Press, 1986).
16 Instituto Colombiano de Reforma Agraria, INCORA, *La colonización en Colombia, Una evaluación del proceso, tomos I and II* (Bogotá: Instituto Interamericano de Ciencias Agrícolas, IICA, 1974).
17 José Antonio Ocampo, *Colombia y la economía mundial* (Bogotá: Siglo XXI-Fedesarrollo, 1984); Camilo Domínguez and Augusto Gómez, *La economía extractiva en la Amazonía colombiana* (Bogotá: Tropenbos-Araracuara, 1990); Claudia Leal, *Landscapes of Freedom: Building a Postemancipation Society in the Rainforests of Western Colombia* (Tucson: The University of Arizona Press, 2018).
18 Juan José Botero Villa, *Adjudicación, explotación y comercialización de baldíos y bosques nacionales: Evolución histórico-legislativa, 1830–1930* (Bogotá: Banco de la República, 1994).
19 Luis Miguel Jiménez Ramos, "Unas montañas al servicio de Bogotá: Imaginarios de naturaleza en la reforestación de los Cerros Orientales, 1899–1924," in *Fragmentos de historia ambiental colombiana*, ed. Claudia Leal (Bogotá: Ediciones Uniandes, 2020); Néstor Javier Gamba Cubides, "El Bosque Municipal de Piedras Blancas: Primera iniciativa estatal de conservación de la naturaleza en Colombia" (Unpublished manuscript).
20 Chapter IX, law 110 of 1912. See Olga Fabiola Cabeza Meza, "Agua y conflictos en la Zona Bananera del Caribe colombiano en la primera mitad del siglo XX" (MA thesis, Instituto de Estudios Ambientales, Universidad Nacional de Colombia, 2014).
21 Article 10, law 200 of 1936.
22 Decree 1383 of 1940.
23 Néstor Javier Gamba Cubides, "Agua, energía eléctrica y caña de azúcar: Declaración de reservas forestales en el Valle del Cauca entre 1938 y 1943" (MA thesis in Geography, Universidad de los Andes, 2018).
24 Etter, McAlpine, and Possingham, "A Historical Analysis of the Spatial and Temporal Drivers of Landscapes in Colombia since 1500," 2–23.
25 Alberto Leguízamo Barbosa, ed., *Historia y aportes de la ingeniería forestal en Colombia*, Vol. I (Bogotá: Asociación Colombiana de Ingenieros Forestales, 2009).
26 Lauchlin Currie, *Reorganización de la Rama Ejecutiva del Gobierno de Colombia* (Bogotá: Imprenta Nacional, 1988 [1952]), 172; Manuel Rodríguez Becerra, "Ecología y medio ambiente," in *Nueva Historia de Colombia vol. IX: Ecología y Cultura*, ed. Álvaro Tirado Mejía (Bogotá: Editorial Planeta, 1998); *Memoria del Ministerio de Agricultura al Congreso Nacional, 1959* (Bogotá: Imprenta Nacional, 1959).
27 Title III, Chapter I, Decree 2811 of 1974.
28 Enrique Pérez Arbeláez, "Concepto del Doctor Enrique Pérez Arbeláez, acerca del proyecto de Ley sobre reservas forestales nacionales que propone el

Ministerio. 28-VIII-58," artículo no. 27, Libro 2, Fondo Enrique Pérez Arbeláez, Archivo General de la Nación, Bogotá, Colombia.
29 A precedent existed within a 1953 law (Decree 2278) that attempted to organize national forestry and stated that the Ministry of Agriculture would make a list of the places worth of becoming national parks and receiving special protection.
30 Articles 13 and 14. The law also established the possibility of designating "integral biological reserves," a provision likely inspired by the Macarena Biological Reserve where tourism was prohibited, and declared snow-covered mountains as national parks, but no development on this front ever happened.
31 Article 39, Law 135 of 1961.
32 What later became national parks started earlier with the establishment of the Macarena Mountain Biological Reserve, see Claudia Leal, "Un tesoro reservado para la ciencia: El inusual comienzo de la conservación de la naturaleza en Colombia (décadas de 1940 y 1950)," *Historia Crítica*, no. 74 (2019): 95–126.
33 Claudia Leal, "National Parks in Colombia," in *The Oxford Research Encyclopedia of Latin American History*, published online on March 26, 2019. https://doi.org/10.1093/acrefore/9780199366439.013.337.
34 On state autonomy see Theda Skocpol, "Bringing the State Back In: Strategies of Analysis in Current Research," in *Bringing the State Back in*, eds. Peter Evans, Dietrich Rueschemeyer, and Theda Skocpol (New York and Cambridge: Cambridge University Press, 1985).
35 www.parquesnacionales.gov.co/portal/es/mesacampesinos/actas/
36 Decree 2117 of 1969.
37 Interview by the author with Enrique Sánchez, Bogotá, August 18, 2015.
38 According to information provided by Incoder in 2015, between 1973 and 1979, five indigenous territories were established in the Pacific coast and four in Amazonia, those numbers increased to 60 and 53 in the 1980s. In the 1990s, the numbers were 53 and 62, but the total area was just a fraction of that of the previous decade.
39 Carlos del Cairo, "Environmentalizing Indigeneity: A Comparative Ethnography of Multiculturalism, Ethnic Hierarchies, and Political Ecology in the Colombian Amazon" (PhD dissertation, The University of Arizona, 2012); Martín Von Hildebrand and Vincent Brackelaire, *Guardianes de la selva: Gobernabilidad y autonomía en la Amazonía colombiana* (Bogotá: Fundación Gaia Amazonas, 2012).
40 Eduardo Restrepo and Alejandra Gutiérrez, *Misioneros y organizaciones campesinas en el río Atrato, Chocó* (Medellín: Uniclaretiana, 2017).
41 Articles 14 and 13, 169 Convention on Indigenous and Tribal Peoples, International Labor Organization, 1989.
42 The kinds of designations devised for territorial management are more complex and diverse than what I have explained here. There are conservation units at the departmental and municipal level, as well as *Zonas de Reserva Campesina* (Peasant Reserve Zones, ZRC in Spanish), mining and oil exploration and extraction areas, among others.
43 An important exception is Marta Herrera, *Ordenar para controlar: Ordenamiento espacial y control político en las llanuras del Caribe y en los Andes centrales neogranadinos, siglo XVIII* (Bogotá: Ediciones Uniandes, 2002).
44 A vast literature has developed in various disciplines on what has come to be known as the material turn. Relevant among these works is the book whose title I borrow: Timothy LeCain, *The Matter of History: How Things Create the Past* (Cambridge: Cambridge University Press, 2017).
45 Vandergeest and Peluso, "Territorialization and State Power."

6 Collective Land Titling and Neoliberalism in the Colombian Pacific Region

Marta Isabel Domínguez

In 1991, an elected and highly diverse national assembly sanctioned a new constitution in Colombia, with unprecedented recognition of citizens' rights and mechanisms for greater political participation for all.[1] As many constitutional and legal changes in Latin American countries at the time, the new constitution states that Colombia is a pluriethnic and multicultural nation, shifting away from the previous regional hegemony of *mestizaje* (race mixture) as the founding discourse of the nation.[2] Acknowledging ethnic and cultural diversity translated into the legal recognition of territorial rights for indigenous and Black rural communities, unprecedented autonomy over these territories and mechanisms of representation that guaranteed a voice in Congress, and the possibility of occupying a strategic place in the decision-making apparatus of the state.[3]

There has been much debate about the apparent contradiction between these new constitutional guarantees, in terms of citizens' rights, political participation and the recognition of diversity, and the simultaneous deepening of neoliberal policies that increase inequalities, particularly between urban centers and rural peripheries. These growing inequalities have to do with a central aspect of these neoliberal policies, clearly geared toward the "modernization" of the mining and energy sector as the new motor for a model of development that is based on the large-scale exploitation of natural and non-renewable resources, with massive profits for multinational corporations. In this sense, unprecedented gains in terms of territorial self-determination for ethnic rural communities are simultaneously coupled with an unprecedented pressure over those same territories through the implementation of an extractivist model of economic growth.[4]

Based on a multi-scale analysis of the process of collective titling of Black communal land in the Pacific coast, this chapter questions the apparent contradiction between the increased recognition of territorial rights and the increased pressure on these lands by large-scale extractivist models of development. It argues that, more than a contradiction, what we witness since the beginning of the 1990s is a new phase of neoliberalism that

DOI: 10.4324/9781003048152-9

operates through organized communities and requires clarity over citizens' rights and property of land. However, this chapter also argues against simple conspirative analyses of ethnic rights, where these are portrayed only as part of a "master plan" of dispossession and displacement of rural communities. A relational approach allows us to look at the struggles and triumphs of local communities to defend their land and livelihood as part of a contentious process that establishes local orders where the mechanisms of domination are not total or pre-set.[5]

This chapter displays this relational approach through the analysis of three different spatio-temporal processes. The first is the process of discussion and drafting of Law 70 of 1993. This law established the territorial rights of Black communities as well as their participation in different levels of government. It therefore defined who the Black communities were, according to law, and how they should organize to demand special rights and participate in the state. The Special Commission appointed to draft this law included representatives of rural Black communities, government officials, and academics specialized in Afro-Colombian studies. This part of the chapter will focus on the contentious process that resulted in these definitions of "Black communities" questioning the simplistic idea of a state imposition as a mechanism of domination.[6]

The second process develops on a regional scale and is centered in the procedures of collective land titling in the municipality of Buenaventura, one of the largest in the Pacific region. This part of the chapter will focus on the ways in which communities organized to legally own their land and the local and regional debates about autonomy and political participation and representation that this process generated. At the same time, it analyzes how collective land titling resulted in an overall transformation of local order and property rights, clarifying the land property map at the regional level, a fundamental factor for the implementation of extractive neoliberal policies. In looking at land titling at a local and regional level a key aspect of neoliberalism emerges; how rights that are embraced by local communities to protect their livelihoods generate procedures and overall results that may in fact facilitate the introduction of extractivist economies that destroy these ways of life.

The third process is mainly local, and it centers on the transformation of a single Black community that titled its lands in 2003. It looks into new local leaderships and the surge of "projectism," where local leaders center their action in drafting local development projects in order to access state resources to fulfil even basic needs in health, education, housing, and so forth. Much of the discussion about territorial autonomy seemed to have resulted in organized communities resuming local government functions, and unexpectedly furthering a neoliberal order at the local level, where even the most basic needs and services become the responsibility of local leaders and their capacity to negotiate with local and national bureaucracies.

Through a multi-scale ethnographic[7] approach to the complex process of collective land titling in the Pacific coast of Colombia, this chapter argues for the need to think of the state as a complex system, with porous borders, in which multiple actors converge, with very varied interests and political capacities, but a state that, in turn, manages to establish territorial orders at the local level, involving citizens in processes of simplification and readability of population, territory, and resources.[8] Understanding the state in this relational and multi-scale manner, in turn, allows us to understand the powerful and complex ways in which neoliberalism penetrates society, not only through direct imposition but rather through forms of domination that require organized communities at the local level doing the work of the neoliberal state.[9]

Debates and Contention in Drafting a Law for Afro-Colombians

> We have to make use of history when the present is bitter. History has ignored us as a people, as a community, as part of the State. This requires that, supported by the new constitution, they offer us guarantees that allow us to develop the only article that addresses the problems of the Black community. Therefore, it is not only the need for a bureaucratic assignment, or a purely administrative question that is being discussed.
> (Elver Montaño, commissioner representing the Black Communities of Cauca)[10]

As his words illustrate, most debates that arose in the drafting of Law 70 of 1993 had to do with the novelty of introducing "pluri-ethnic and multicultural" policies in context that characterized by a general sense of inclusion of previously excluded groups from the formal political and electoral arena at national and local levels, and by the deepening of a neoliberal model that aimed to increase national income through foreign investment in energy and mining sectors primarily, equating efficiency in state spending with privatization and mixed schemes for the provision of "services" such as education and health. Christian Gros wonders about the meaning of the recognition of the territoriality of indigenous and Black communities in this context of introduction of a neoliberal model that drastically worsened the situation of a large part of the population, posing new governance and legitimacy challenges to the state. According to Gros, the constitutional reforms of Bolivia, Peru, Colombia, and Mexico can be interpreted as searches for institutional solutions to the problems of governance and legitimacy that arose with the introduction of neoliberal models. Thus,

Gros argues that the legislative developments that promoted a decentralized political-administrative model and gave recognition to indigenous and Afro-Colombian territories with different degrees of autonomy can be interpreted as "a way to resolve the contradiction between political inclusion and economic exclusion, as a product of neoliberal policies."[11]

This chapter explores one of those legislative developments, looking closely at the dynamics of participation of those who were appointed to the Special Commission of Black Communities, to draft the law that granted special rights to Afro-Colombians, according to the spirit of the new constitution. Accordingly, in this chapter, the law will not be analyzed as a text, but rather as an arena of political debate, where each aspect of legislation was the result of contention between various actors with different interests. This contention was not always overt or displayed in public debates during the sessions, in fact a lot of the negotiating took place informally, between sessions. Both the minutes of sessions and in-depth interviews with Commission members were important sources of information for this analysis.

The Hegemonic Language of Participation

In his opening remarks as president of the Special Commission for Black Communities, the vice minister of government highlighted the novelty and importance of community participation in defining the paths of their own development. He emphasized that "the principles set forth in the Constitution of 1991 dictated that the communities had to be the motor, within a participatory process from the bottom up, where initiatives came from the communities and were not imposed by government officials."[12] The discourse and practices derived from this principle of citizen participation became a central aspect of the political transformations that followed the new constitution. Participation in this context meant not only being consulted in processes of law and policy making that concerned specific citizens or groups. It also meant entering the bureaucratic logics of the state, filling forms, registering communities and territories, complying with procedures for formal recognition and for some selected few, and becoming representatives of their communities within the bureaucracy of the state. It also implied that organized citizens would have to take on important aspects of state policies, designing projects and programs for their local communities, competing for resources, and implementing central aspects of social policy. As democratic as this may have seemed, in terms of citizens deciding on state policy, it also introduced new and more subtle ways in which citizens' demands and the realization of their rights were circumscribed. Greater citizen participation, coupled with the underlying neoliberal principles of reduction in state expenditure and privatization, meant that organized citizens would partner with the state to execute the meager and ever-decreasing budgets destined to social issues, unsuspiciously "sharing" responsibility for insufficient or inefficient state action on key social issues. Politically, this increased citizen participation in many cases had the indirect effect of de-politicizing citizens' demands. At best, the blurred responsibility of state action had local leaders grappling with state bureaucracy, project deadlines, and an endless search for co-financing. At worst, citizens that were involved in local politics became easy prey of clientelist relations, making a precarious living out of project scraps and state red tape, which, in turn, resulted in very precarious political action.

For ethnic groups, recognition and participation implied self-determination and territorial autonomy. It also implied that ethnic groups had to comply with definitions, forms of organization, and procedures that were defined by law. For Afro-Colombians in particular, this opened an arena for important debates about how they would be defined as an ethnic group, about territoriality, considering that the majority of Afro-Colombians lived in urban areas, and about the existence of a common shared culture. These issues were the main topics of debate in the Special Commission for Black Communities. The Commission had eight plenary sessions, chaired by the vice minister of government, with the Colombian Institute of Anthropology and History (ICANH) in charge of the technical secretariat. Three subcommittees discussed specific aspects of the law, one on territory and natural resources, the second on cultural identity, and the third on economic and social development. The Commissioners representing the communities carried out workshops in the rural areas of the Pacific coast, presenting the community's proposals to the Commission. In the first plenary meeting, one of the most debated issues in the Commission was introduced: What does it mean to give the Afro-Colombian population the status of an ethnic group? The issues of the internal functioning and the budget of the Commission dominated the second plenary meeting. The third plenary session was held in the city of Quibdó, capital of the department of Chocó. Multiple organizations participated in this session and voiced their complaints about the mining and logging concessions granted in the region. In the fourth session, again in Bogotá, a critical moment was reached in the conflict between the Commissioners representing the communities and the government representatives. Ignoring the complaints filed in Quibdó, the national government approved the logging concessions. Community representatives questioned the meaning of collective land ownership if government decisions did not consider the demands of the communities. Only until the fifth plenary session of the Special Commission, the content of the bill that would be presented to Congress was discussed. In the sixth session, the Commissioners representing the communities presented a full draft of the law. In the eighth plenary meeting, after eight months of work, the Commission approved the final draft to be presented in Congress in the 1993 legislature.

The Recognition of Afro-Colombians as an Ethnic Group

One of the most interesting aspects of the law is how it defines Afro-Colombians as an ethnic group with specific rights over land and special rights of representation in Congress and in various levels of state bureaucracy. Although today Afro-Colombians are undoubtedly considered an ethnic group, this was certainly not the case thirty years ago. At the time, indigenous communities were the ones who most successfully claimed their ethnic status, linking ethnicity with their struggles for the recognition and protection of their cultures and languages, the recovery of their ancestral lands, the expansion of *resguardos* (collective indigenous landholdings), and the autonomy to rule their territories through their own *cabildos* (indigenous councils). Ethnicity in the early 1990s in Colombia began to be strongly defined in cultural and territorial terms. The Afro-Colombian population, which, in contrast, was mostly urban, was therefore not so easily identifiable as a territorially defined ethnic group and culturally tended to be assumed as a specific segment within the broad spectrum of mestizaje.

The intervention of anthropologist Jaime Arocha in the first plenary session of the Special Commission started the debate about ethnic rights in the new constitution. Arocha illustrated the asymmetry of rights recognized for indigenous and Afro-Colombian populations. In the National Constituent Assembly, the three representatives of the indigenous movement played a central role in the incorporation of extensive provisions on indigenous law in the constitutional text. The pro-indigenous atmosphere during the sessions of the Constituent Assembly paved the way for the ratification of ILO Convention 169 of 1989 on Indigenous and Tribal Peoples. Together with Law 21 of 1991, Colombia produced the broadest legal setting in the continent to guarantee indigenous rights.[13] Afro-Colombians, in contrast, did not manage to elect a single representative to the Constitutional Assembly; yet, through intense lobbying, Afro-Colombian leaders managed a single Transitory Article that stated that in the following two years, a law should be drafted, recognizing Afro-Colombian territorial rights, the protection of their cultural identity, and the promotion of their economic and social development. During the first meeting to draft this law, anthropologist Arocha established his position: Afro-Colombians were, without a doubt, an ethnic group and the Commission had the task of correcting the asymmetries between ethnic groups in the Colombian constitution.

The comparison between Afro-Colombians and indigenous people was problematic for some members of the Commission that represented Black communities. Since the indigenous people were, at that time, the clearest example of an ethnic group that successfully claimed special rights, equating Afro-Colombians with indigenous people seemed an obvious move. However, some commissioners felt that this entailed complex limitations. The territorial and political rights of indigenous people were sustained on the idea of an essentially rural population, with a shared cultural identity rooted in a rural way of life; Afro-Colombians in general, and Afro-Colombian leaders in particular, had a strong bond with an urban existence. This does not mean that the indigenous peoples are a homogeneous ethnic group; however, the special rights they claimed as a collectivity are based on an existence linked to the territory under a common authority. For the Commissioners, the Afro-Colombians were much more heterogeneous, highly urbanized, and culturally diverse. As we will see below, the struggle to conceive the entire Afro-Colombian population as an ethnic group, with both rural and urban as beneficiaries of the law, made the representatives of the communities advocate a definition of ethnicity based on the idea of a common cultural identity and cosmogony. This, paradoxically, led them to argue that the entire Afro-Colombian population, rural or urban, shared a culture anchored on the practices, custom, and beliefs of a rural, riverside people, descended from enslaved Africans.

The commissioners representing the communities debated about the diversity of the Afro-Colombian population and the challenges this posed for the drafting of the law. The group of commissioners evidenced this diversity. Some were leaders from the rural Pacific, such as Trifilo Viveros, from the Naya River, and Jorge Aramburu, a schoolteacher from the Anchicayá river, both from the municipality of Buenaventura. However, the other commissioners were renowned Afro-Colombian activists; most of them were professionals that were part of an emerging Black middle class that lived in the urban centers of the Pacific such as Quibdó, Buenaventura, and Cali. Despite these differences, they built a strong consensus around the task in hand: given the limitations of Transitory Article 55, which defined Black communities as those that lived in the rural and riverside territories of the Pacific region, an attempt to stretch this definition too far risked that the bill would not pass in Congress, as it strayed too far from the constitutional mandate. The commissioners would therefore continue strengthening the regional ties between rural Black communities through workshops and meetings where the law was discussed. Although resources for this were scarce, and a constant reason of tension during sessions, many rural Black communities in the Pacific coast got involved in the debates about collective land titling, autonomy, and cultural identity. The commissioners continued to push for a broader definition of "Black communities" that could include the Black urban population, always maintaining the idea of a cultural unity that went back to rural life on the rivers of the Colombian Pacific.

It is common to find in the literature about collective land titling in Colombia the idea that Law 70 of 1993 reflects an essentialist interpretation of ethnicity by the Colombian state.[14] However, this is clearly not a straightforward state imposition, as most of the content of this essentialist interpretation was inadvertently supplied by the representatives of Black communities in an effort to establish a common ground for all Afro-Colombians to be recognized as an ethnic group, regardless of their urban or rural existence. The commissioners representing the communities were the ones that asserted the cultural unity of all Afro-Colombians and the need for legal backing to protect cultural identity. During the sessions of the Identity Subcommittee held on the 26th and the 29th of March, 1993, the commissioners explained this common culture, with close references to the shared history of enslavement and the shared ancestral experience of communal life along the rivers of the Colombian Pacific. Hernán Cortés, special commissioner for Nariño, pointed out the specificity of being descendants of enslaved Africans, as it "led to a different conception of life and death; the forms of organization based on solidarity and kinship were adaptations for survival in the Pacific jungle, and the particular conception of time and space, determined by the movements of the river and the sea."[15] Other commissioners spoke about the centrality of oral narration and the use of myths and legends in children's education. In these sessions, the commissioners evoked mythical creatures such as the Riviel, the Tunda, the Duende, the Mohana, the Catalina, the Encanto, the Patasola, the Madremonte, and the Marmaró. Jorge Aramburo, special commissioner for Valle del Cauca, spoke about traditional production cycles that alternated among agriculture, fishing, and forestry, with techniques that combined "the magical and the sacred, and labor was community based."[16] Hernan Cortés highlighted the importance of a lifestyle in harmony with nature:

> Black communities are not governed by the clock, but by the movements of the river or the sea. This, coupled with traditional production practices, means that territories are conceived in a harmonious relationship with nature, and an ethical coexistence and respect for all beings . . . demonstrating our own notion of development.[17]

Although this explanation of common cultural traits made direct reference to rural settings, the intention of the Commissioners was to emphasize a common memory and culture for all Afro-Colombians, rural or urban. This was expressed in various testimonies, registered in the minutes of the commission. Elver Montaño, special commissioner for Cauca, said:

> When these co-stories are referred to, we are doing nothing more than demonstrating that we Blacks in this country belong to a common world; we preserve a collective memory and share an imaginary linked to an African heritage that still persists and will continue to persist in our communities.[18]

Collective Land Titling and Neoliberalism 135

This is more explicit in the intervention of commissioner Cortés:

> The recognition of the rights of the black communities should not only be for the peoples of the Pacific, since we are all a family and therefore a culture. What has been said in this meeting is not open to discussion. The intention is for the government to understand some features of the Afro-Colombian culture, so they can show respect.[19]

The Commissioners' interventions weaved their narratives with hints of anthropological language, as an effective device in the context of the Commission. On one occasion, Rudesindo Castro, special commissioner for Chocó, read a fragment of a text by anthropologist Jaime Arocha on recent research in the Baudó river basin. The use of anthropology by those who had been the "object" of anthropological research, gave them legitimacy in the institutional context of the Special Commission. This combination of anthropological and experiential discourse drove the idea of a Black community that went beyond a rural setting. "Ethnicity" was constitutionally defined in cultural and historical terms, toning down a linguistic or racial construction, affirming that ethnic groups were those with their own differentiated culture that shared a common history. This had implications on the legal requirements and procedures that communities had to face to materialize these special ethnic rights; the evidence of "ancestry," of differentiated cultural traits, and in some cases even of "awareness of being descendants of slaves" became central in the reports of officials in charge of verifying the procedures for collective land titling. This may seem to impose a restrictive definition of ethnicity, one that the state could use to limit who would have access to special rights based on an essentialist check list that operationalized culture and history.[20] However, at that time, the cultural definition of ethnicity was seen as an important step toward a more inclusive conception of ethnic rights. It proposed sufficiently broad parameters of affiliation, which opened the way for the recognition of territorial rights, self-determination, and participation in important decision-making bodies.

In the Special Commission, the emphasis on a shared history of enslavement, the struggle for freedom, and the common culture that emerged from adaptation and proliferation of communities along the rivers of the Colombian Pacific became an important political statement, and a mechanism to broaden the limiting character of Transitory Article 55, which defined the beneficiaries of the law in geographical terms. In the Article, "Black communities" were defined as "families of African descent who occupied vacant public lands (*baldíos de la nación*) in rural and coastal areas of the Pacific."[21] The commissioners representing the communities initially spoke of "Black ethnicity" to refer to all Afro-Colombians, rural or urban, and they used the term "Black communities" to refer specifically to rural families from the Pacific. However, throughout the commissioners' interventions, these terms were switched and swapped: the common cultural traits of the entire "ethnic group" referred to rural life along the Pacific rivers; in turn, the "Black communities" could live in any area of the country, including cities. This had an influence on the final draft of the law, where Black Communities were defined in cultural and historical terms as "the families of Afro-Colombian descent that have their own culture, share a history and have their own traditions and customs within a country-town relationship, conserving an awareness of identity that is different from other ethnic groups." Although this did not mean that urban Afro-Colombians would collectively title urban dwellings, it did later result in mainly urban Afro-Colombians occupying positions of representation in the state.

The interest in promoting a broad-spectrum ethnic mobilization resulted in the formalization of many Afro-Colombian grassroots organizations, ranging from urban associations, sports and artistic groups, and cooperatives of piangua collectors and collectives that represented rural riverside communities. However, the sheer volume, diversity, and transient nature of many of these organizations has complicated the effective participation of an Afro-Colombian movement in electoral politics.[22] In congressional elections, the seats reserved for Black communities have been historically occupied by Afro-Colombians that are well-known for their accomplishments in sports and entertainment, but have little experience in the movement; many of them being backed by traditional parties. Their participation in Congress has had very little effect in advancing a collective agenda for Black communities. The efforts of the commissioners to broaden the spectrum of the beneficiaries of Law 70 of 1993 had the unintended effect of diffusing the political potential of the Afro-Colombian movement, particularly in electoral politics.

The Territorial Effects of Collective Land Titling

Historian Marta Herrera Ángel studies the spatial ordering of the Caribbean plains and the central Andes in the 18th century, stating that it is a process of political control, which is quite subtle and tends to go unnoticed.[23] Although it refers to a very different period and geography, the author's arguments are highly suggestive for any analysis on how spatial ordering structures daily life, shaping individual and collective behaviors. In March 2006, representatives of the Colombian government participating in a conference on agrarian reform policies in Porto Alegre, Brazil, announced that Colombia had titled five million hectares to Black communities, mostly settled in the Pacific region. Officials estimated that these five million hectares corresponded to 95% of the land that could be collectively titled, according to Law 70 of 1993.[24] The government's collective titling program for Black communities, partially funded by the World Bank, was presented as a success in terms of the fulfillment of goals and the execution of policies that realized the pluri-ethnic and multicultural character of the nation, embodied in Article 7 of the Constitution of 1991.

Those who fought for the recognition of the territorial rights of Afro-Colombians emphasized that collective titling was successful because it was achieved silently, without great media hype. It was a "silent revolution, behind the state's back."[25] According to these activists, this was done with hard work in two specific fronts: on the one hand, in the legal front, achieving the approval of laws and decrees that would regulate the collective titling of land, in such a way that the procedures were clear and feasible; on the other hand, in the territories, advising and accompanying the processes of rural Black communities, ensuring that they complied with the procedures and bureaucratic requirements for titling.

In both cases, the role of activists who served as government officials in different instances of state bureaucracy was fundamental. Those who speak of this "silent revolution" highlight the role of key figures of the Afro-Colombian movement who worked within the state apparatus, especially in the Ethnic Affairs Directorate of the Colombian Institute for Agrarian Reform, INCORA, the institution in charge of all the procedures of collective land titling and the Ethnic Affairs division on the Ministry of the Interior. These actors, in their role as state officials, managed to combine the government's concern to present an efficient bureaucratic apparatus—to meet goals and show results—with their political interests as part of the Afro-Colombian movement. This institutional affiliation allowed them to resolve obstacles, such as multiple oppositions to collective titles, with legal expertise, knowledge of the terrain and, above all, with the approval of the central government.

What does the expression "a silent revolution behind the state's back" mean then? In these narratives, the state appears both as the legal apparatus and bureaucracy that make collective titling possible, and as the accomplice of large-scale investors that have pushed an extractivist economy in the region against the interests of Black communities, and alongside (sometimes financing) the paramilitaries that caused several cycles of forced displacements sweeping the Colombian Pacific in the mid-1990s, just as Black communities were making efforts to title their land. Thus, in the activists' speeches, the idea of "silent revolution" implies a state that is not a monolithic actor, but a complex organization in which multiple individual and collective actors operate, with sometimes conflicting interests and with unequal capacities to influence multiple decision scenarios. The "silent revolution" refers to the capacity of the movement for collective titling to enter the bureaucratic game without raising suspicions from actors who opposed titling and had the political capacity to hinder it.

Undoubtedly, the magnitude of collective titling is due to the impetus of the Afro-Colombians who, in the 1990s, began to envision a national Afro-Colombian movement. However, given Colombia's history of failed agrarian reforms and of violent repression of social and political struggles for land redistribution, and given the renewed interest in the Pacific as a strategic region for mining, forestry, and port development, the titling of five million hectares for Black communities seemed like a paradox. The magnitude of collective titling requires an explanation that goes beyond the actors who have struggled for the territorial rights of Afro-Colombians, to understand how other interests, that could even be opposed to those of Black communities, may converge in benefitting from the collective titling of Pacific coast lands, allowing efforts to develop legislation to not remain on paper, but find the political will and resources for their execution. In what follows, I examine 21 land titling processes that were carried out in Buenaventura between January 1997 and September 2005, to understand the territorial organization and political transformations that collective land titling brought about. The fascinating documentation produced by this process is coupled with in-depth interviews with government officials and community leaders at the forefront of collective land titling, permitting an in-depth analysis of both local and regional repercussions, understanding the diverse, and often contradicting interests that coincide in this process.

The files of the collective titling of the municipality of Buenaventura contain privileged information on the qualitative and quantitative changes in the relationships and forms of communication between the state and rural communities. These files condense the coming and going of minutes, letters, forms, petition rights, and documentation required for collective titling. The creation and registration of community councils was the first step in the land titling process. In Buenaventura, Community Councils were quickly created. Between January 1997 and December 1998, 34 of them had been registered and had requested the collective title to their lands.

A typical collective titling file has six sections. The first section contains the documentation that each community council must present in order to request land titling: the minutes of the first general assembly must be submitted, stating that the entire community agrees with the creation of the community council, written evidence that this community council was registered in the municipality of Buenaventura, and the formal request for land titling, approved in the general assembly, authorizing the elected legal representative of the council to process the application. This first section also contains a general description of the community and its territory, its geographical location, usually enclosing maps that are collectively created.

The second section contains an "ethnohistorical report" where communities usually go through an unprecedented process of writing what has circulated through oral history as the origins of the community, the first settlers, where they came from, what they found on arrival, how they organized and what cultural, productive, and reproductive practices were of relevance for the community. There tends to be a certain structure to these reports, and there are always sections on traditional forms of production, individual and collective use of natural resources, local forms of land tenure, and territorial conflicts. Finally, a list of privately owned properties within the territory and "third occupants" is presented, a category that, in practice, has had multiple interpretations, but which in the law points to people who do not belong to the Afro-Colombian ethnic group but live within the community. These ethnohistorical reports also describe multiple developments in the region, and how they have transformed community life. Roads and railways, large-scale mining and forestry, and hydroelectric projects have been both a source of employment and of territorial conflict in the region. The reports evidence the importance of traditional forms of fishing, agriculture, and forestry, as well as the constant search for paid employment and higher education, which have meant a constant movement of family members between rural settings and urban centers in Buenaventura and Cali. In some ethnohistoric reports, there is a reference to the armed conflict and how it has affected rural communities, especially when there have been forced displacements during the process of land titling.

The third section contains documents produced by INCORA officials in Buenaventura and the technical visit they must conduct in each territory, georeferencing the land and meeting with local communities to verify all the submitted information.

The fourth section contains all documentation regarding boundary agreement meetings with neighbors. These include legal representatives of the adjoining Community Councils, governors of the indigenous resguardos or leaders of indigenous communities in the area, and in the case of Buenaventura, representatives of universities that hold permits for research in specific areas and officials of the navy, where coastal communities are adjacent to a naval base.

The fifth section contains oppositions to the collective titles. These are not common, but when they do exist, the reasons to oppose are diverse. On various occasions, these are presented by members of the community who do not agree with the collective title, or with the way in which it is being processed by a particular leader, as it is the case of Aribi in Llanobajo. Other oppositions are presented by people who identify themselves as settlers, but not as Afro-Colombians, and do not agree with their inclusion in the title as third occupants, as it is the case of San Joaquín in La Brea. Other oppositions are presented by organizations of a different nature, which consider that the collective titling is not taking into account their rights over the territory, as is the case of the Herencia Verde Foundation in Llanobajo, and the Universidad del Valle in Bahía Málaga.

The sixth and last section contains the official documentation issued by INCORA (later INCODER). A technical evaluation summarizes the collective titling process, contains the dates on which the different requirements were met and issues a concept about natural resources and traditional production practices in each territory. This important document became a standardized text that emphasizes the collective and sustainable practices of the communities. There is always mention of the strategic ecosystem of the Pacific region, due to natural resources and biodiversity. There is also emphasis on the nation's recognition of the ancestral knowledge of Afro-Colombian communities and their importance in the preservation of natural resources. Even where community reports and technical visits mention environmental problems, such as deforestation and water contamination from mining, technical evaluations leave these issues out, with a copy-paste concept that all communities have a sustainable use of natural resources.

Afro-Colombians as Owners of the Rural Pacific

Regardless of the diverse technical capacities of communities in creating maps and precising the location of their territories, all requested land was, in turn, georeferenced with global positioning systems (GPS) by INCORA officials. The process of collectively titling land resulted in the mapping of the territories of Black communities in the Pacific, having for the first time a precise map of land property in the region. In this new map of rural Buenaventura, there are three types of collective lands; there are six large collective titles that enclose whole river basins, each with a river that runs from the mountains to the coast. These territories are the property of the Community Councils of Naya, Yurumanguí, Cajambre, Mayorquín, and Raposo to the south, and Calima to the north. These territories are known as River Community Councils and are part of an effort by the Proceso de Comunidades Negras (PCN), a political organization that starts in Buenaventura with the land titling process, to constitute large territories and dynamize discussions on autonomy and political power in the region. To the north, there are many small collective titles that have maintained the territorial divisions of the villages that existed along the "old road" and the "new road" that go from Cali to Buenaventura. These are known as Road Community Councils and they include Agua Clara, Campo Hermoso, Llanobajo, San Marcos, Limones, and Sabaletas. The third type are those collective lands that run along the coast, in the north, and include La Barra, Juanchaco, Ladrilleros, Bahía Málaga, and Bazán La Bocana; these are known as Coast Community Councils. The different types of collective lands also reflected different organizational and political processes. In general, the large community councils that were part of the PCN had a stronger organizational trajectory, with river organizations that were motivated by the Catholic Church and the *Comunidades Eclesiales de Base* (Basic Ecclesial Communities) formed following the precepts of the Liberation Theology movement. These Community Councils had an internal political process with strong debates about autonomy and territory and the importance of titling entire river basins that included various interrelated Black communities, to constitute a strong regional political power. Most River and Coast Community Councils are part of this overall process. The large number of small titles along the roads and in the Anchicayá river basin tended to maintain the forms of village organization that originated in the 1960s with the Community Action movement,[26] and land titling did not necessarily trigger strong debates about territory and autonomy. Politically, the leaders of the land titling process were historical leaders that were part of the clientele of traditional political parties.

The mobilization to collectively title the rural lands of Buenaventura had an impact on the entire municipality. Today, all rural Black communities are part of a Community Council, and all rural lands are either titled or in the process. This represents an important change in terms of the territorial order of the municipality: the nation's lands ceased to exist, and the lands of Black communities emerged, with the Community Council as a new actor that must be consulted for any type of exploitation or productive activity in the area. This reflects a total formalization of land in the rural areas of the Pacific, where ambiguities in terms of property rights and occupation regimes have been substantially reduced.[27] From a local perspective, collective land titling significantly increases Black communities' possibilities of self-determination, and political leverage to control what happens within their territories. In some cases, like in the Raposo River, this meant bringing to a halt all large-scale mining concession, and prohibiting the use of dredgers, according to the internal regulations established by the Community Council. However, at a larger scale, only very few Community Councils have managed to take a strong stand in this direction. According to the law, the procedure of *consultas previas* (previous consultation) ensures that any form of exploitation affecting the collective lands of Black communities is approved by Community Councils. In practice, many Community Councils do not have the leverage to negotiate with large-scale mining enterprises, agreeing to very unfavorable deals at a very high cost for their immediate environment. As seen in the studies of Parra and Urán on gold mining in Chocó, the apparent greater control of Community Councils over their territories has actually increased mechanized gold mining at the expense of artisanal mining in ethnic territories.[28] According to the authors, this happens because of the way in which the gold production and trade network links traditional kinship bonds and precarious living conditions with the global dynamics of gold exploitation. On a regional scale, collective land titling has not been an effective way for Black communities to have control over their territories, and dictate the routes of their own development, as the vice-minister of government promised in his opening statement, when Law 70 of 1993 was being discussed. In fact, Black communities inadvertently invested time, efforts, and resources, doing most of the local work that resulted in the formalization of land property in the Pacific, an aspect that has in fact facilitated the introduction of large-scale extractivism in the region.

Previous consultation has become a formalized procedure in which private companies and the government subcontract, mainly anthropologists, to carry out the required visits, fill in the forms, and convince the communities that they cannot "stop progress." Thus, hydroelectric plants that affect the rivers have been approved, even if they do not provide electricity to the communities, large-scale mining and logging have the "go ahead" and the construction of seaports have not been stopped, even when proceeds do not benefit the neighboring population or are invested in the immediate environment. Land property, even collective titles, is not an issue for any of these enterprises, and consultation of communities seems to be a more straight-forward procedure than the previous government concessions. Not all cases have resulted in approval. Mechanized mining in Ovejas River in the north Cauca region, mining in Raposo River in southern Buenaventura, logging near Quibdó and palm oil plantations along the Atrato River have all been successfully stopped, not only due to a negative result during the previous consultation, but through large-scale mobilization and protest. However, on a regional scale, this procedure, that supposedly would empower local communities to decide on how they would conceive development and progress in their owned territories, has, in general, become a simple transaction, where communities receive a compensation, a couple of solar panels and computers, a new communal salon, in exchange for the deterioration or destruction of their environment.

On the other hand, the local process of land titling gave rise to Black community councils (*concejos comunitarios de comunidades negras*) as new and important political actors in the Colombian Pacific. At a local and regional level, this allowed for interesting discussions on political innovation, autonomy, and alternative conceptions of development that have had very interesting outcomes in Buenaventura. At the same time, at a regional level collective land titling "organized the map" of the Pacific coast of Colombia, reducing ambiguities and overlapping forms of land tenure and occupation. This, in fact, has facilitated large-scale extractivism in the Pacific, where formal national and transnational enterprises require formality and legal clarity in order to operate in the biodiverse and minerally rich region.

The Rise of "Projectism" and the New Leaders of Grassroots Neoliberalism

I arrived at Bazán-La Bocana for the first time in 2005, only two years after the collective land title had been issued by INCODER, the National Rural Development Institute in charge of collective land titles at the time. There had only been two *juntas*, which was the name given by law to the democratically elected governing bodies of Black community councils. La Bocana was not a typical community council in Buenaventura. It was one of the three costal territories, where communal life was not grounded by the river, but rather by the sea. La Bocana was not initially part of the Proceso de Comunidades Negras (PCN), the regional organization that articulated most of the river communities in Buenaventura, which explains their slightly late arrival to the discussions on autonomy, political innovation, and participation in the state. This became particularly interesting for fieldwork because hegemonic discourses on Black community politics developed by Afro-Colombian leaders in Buenaventura were not that common in La Bocana, making it somewhat easier to talk about people's perception, experiences, and expectations surrounding collective land titling. La Bocana was also atypical in that tourism was an important activity and source of income for the community, so discourses on traditional forms of production as grounds for collective titling were downplayed, and issues of sustainability and eco-tourism were quickly becoming central. In any case, fieldwork in La Bocana was focused on understanding what the process of collective land titling had meant to the community, especially in terms of local politics, decision-making, conceptions of autonomy, self-governance, and relations with the local and national state.

I spent a lot of time chatting with members of the *junta* (community board) as it was not evident how this governing body operated. There were no real meetings, no formal procedures, but rather a day-to-day fashion of dealing with upcoming issues. Observing the dynamics of each of the junta members, it was evident that they were, in turn, members of other local structures, each with its respective president and treasurer. The president of the association of artisanal fishermen was the legal representative; the chairman of the housing improvement committee was the outgoing chairman and current treasurer; the president of the water board was the secretary; and there were also committees for the elderly, a health committee, a tourism association, and a board for the management of garbage. The interaction between these groups and committees and the community council junta was informal but efficient. There were no reports of activities, decisions were not necessarily consulted or socialized, and there were no records of meeting or even a single document that formalized the existence of these groups and committees. However, the members of the board who were part of the groups served as a link in the few cases in which some formal endorsement was needed. It became clear that these groups, committees, and boards had a rather latent existence; however, I was curious to understand why they even existed, and why formal endorsement, the signing of letters, and the provision of official community council seals, stamps, and letterheads seemed to be the most important responsibility of the junta. During fieldwork, the water administration board was established, encapsulating the formation process of many of these groups. These began by initiative of the municipality of Buenaventura, or of any other organization that came to La Bocana to execute a project. The projects generally proposed participatory methodologies, where the community was invited to identify its own problems and suggest solutions. This usually culminated in the appointment of a committee or board for the self-management of the project to be implemented.

The arrival of representatives of the Corporación Autónoma Regional del Valle (CVC in Spanish), a powerful autonomous public corporation for the management of the resources of the Cauca river basin, and the Universidad del Valle, the region's main public university, called for the formation of the water management board. The final objective was to set up a "service provider company" that would manage the small aqueduct, establishing collection rates for drinking water and doing maintenance of the local water network. The project was implemented in accordance with the national policy of the time, following the recipe of "participation and decentralization": community participation was encouraged while freeing the state from the copious and expensive tasks involved in the provision of basic services, delegating these to the created community committees and boards.

Along with collective titling and the creation of the community council, a different way of relating to the state began to emerge in La Bocana. State resources went through a long process of subcontracting. In the case of the hydrographic basins management project, the Regional Autonomous Corporations were commissioned to design and execute the project with resources from the Ministry of the Environment and some international nongovernmental organization funding. The CVC, in turn, sub-contracted part of the design and execution with the Universidad del Valle. The people who ultimately had contact with the communities were CVC and university sub-contractors and state officials were rarely seen. These sub-contractors would guide the communities in the creation of the necessary structures for the self-management of the scarce resources that eventually, if ever, reached the communities. Finally, all these projects, contracts, and subcontracts had a timespan, and when deadlines were met, the work teams dissolved. The organized groups in the communities, in the best of cases, continued to search for more resources to give continuity to the work. Thus, they began to invest their own resources in the elaboration of projects to be presented through diverse "persons of influence" before the multiple government offices and NGOs. Even the fulfillment of basic rights to health, education, and housing began to show these dynamics. Rights became services, and state resources arrived intermittently, always mediated by the approval of community self-management projects.

Conclusion

This "projectism" had marked effects on the forms of local and community politics in La Bocana, which, not mistakenly, coincided with the process of collective land titling and creation of new forms of communal organization. State action was increasingly limited to the insufficient financing of small projects that were the responsibility, in terms of design, management and execution, of local democratically elected leaders. Thus, local politics was increasingly centered in leaders' ability to weave relationships of influence in government offices and negotiate crumbs to finance projects. Again, as rights become services, local politics move from the demand for the state to sanction rights toward the validation of managerial capacities and relations, effective to capture meager resources for partial projects. The withdrawal of the police station and the merger of all the local public schools into a single educational establishment were the local experiences of the "withdrawal of the state" in neoliberal key. The repeated creation of groups, committees, and boards for the self-management of the meager state resources is the other side of neoliberalism, which requires organized citizens in whom to delegate the responsibilities of the state.

Notes

1 In the drafting of the Constitution of 1991, National Constituent Assembly included certain groups and sectors of Colombian society that had been excluded from the formal political arena. The indigenous movement, that had gained visibility, especially in local and regional politics, and the former combatants of recently demobilized guerilla groups were particularly relevant new actors in the national political arena. Although the Afro-Colombian population did not have a single seat in the National Constituent Assembly, the new Constitution approved a Transitory Article that ordered the drafting of a law that would grant specific rights for Afro-Colombians. These were specifically directed towards collective land rights in the Pacific coast.
2 It is important to understand territorial ethnic rights as a transnational phenomenon. In the 1990s, Brazil, Ecuador, and Honduras underwent similar processes of constitutional and legal transformations that created the mechanisms for collective ownership of land by legally sanctioned ethnic groups. In many countries, including Colombia, the procedures to title land were financed by the World Bank. Many of the indigenous and Afro-Latin-American leaders from different countries communicate and learn from each other's strategies and

struggles in the process of materializing rights. In this sense, although this chapter concentrates on the connection between territorial rights and neoliberalism in Colombia, these processes are by no means unique or specific to Colombia.
3 Bettina Ng'weno, "¿Puede la etnicidad reemplazar lo racial?: Afrocolombianos, indigenidad y el Estado multicultural en Colombia," *Revista Colombiana de Antropología* 49, no. 1 (2013): 71–104; Eduardo Restrepo, *Etnización de la negridad: La invención de las comunidades negras como grupo étnico en Colombia* (Popayán: Universidad del Cauca, 2013).
4 Mayra Parra and Alexandra Urán, "Parentesco y precariedad en la minería de oro en Chocó, Colombia," *Revista Mexicana de Sociología* 80, no. 4 (September- December 2018): 801–826.
5 Viviane Brachet-Márquez, *El Pacto de la dominación: Estado, clase y reforma social en México* (México D.F: El Colegio de México, 1996).
6 Marta Domínguez, *Territorios colectivos: Procesos de formación del Estado en el Pacífico Colombiano (1993–2009)* (Medellín: Fondo Editorial FCSH, Universidad de Antioquia, 2017), 47–71.
7 In addition to a more conventional understanding of ethnography as "participant observation," I adhere to the methodological nuances by Ann Laura Stoler when she proposes an ethnographic approach to the archive. In this sense, my approach to archives on the procedures to design the law and on procedures to title collective lands is "ethnographic." For a comprehensive understanding of an ethnographic approach to the archive, see the special issue *Etnografía y archivo: Dossier especial Revista Colombiana de Antropología* 46, no. 2 (2010).
8 Alejandro Agudo Sanchiz and Marco Antonio Estrada Saavedra, eds., *Transformaciones del Estado en los márgenes de Latinoamérica: Imaginarios alternativos, aparatos inacabados y espacios transnacionales* (México D.F: El Colegio de México; Universidad Iberoamericana, 2011); Alejandro Agudo Sanchiz and Marco Antonio Estrada Saavedra, eds., *Formas reales de la dominación del Estado: Perspectivas interdisciplinarias del poder y la política* (México D.F: El Colegio de México, 2014).
9 Viviane Brachet-Márquez and Mónica Uribe Gómez, eds., *Estado y sociedad en América Latina: Acercamientos relacionales* (México, D. F.: El Colegio de México, 2016).
10 Colombian Institute of Anthropology and History (ICAHN), Minutes No. 002 of the Special Commission for Black Communities, Minutes of the Special Commission, Bogotá, September 3, 1992.
11 Christian Gros, "¿Cuál autonomía para los pueblos indígenas de América Latina?" in *Utopía para los excluidos: El multiculturalismo en África y América Latina*, ed. Jaime Arocha (Bogotá: Universidad Nacional de Colombia, Facultad de Ciencias Humanas, Departamento de Antropología, Centro de Estudios Sociales, 2004), 219.
12 ICAHN, Minutes No. 001 of the Special Commission for Black Communities, Minutes of the Special Commission, Bogotá, August 11, 1992.
13 Frank Semper, "Los derechos de los pueblos indígenas en Colombia en la jurisprudencia de la Corte Constitucional, in *Anuario de Derecho Constitucional Latinoamericano 2006, Tomo II* (Berlin: KONRAD-ADENAUER-STIFTUNG E.V.), 763. The indigenous people in Colombia did not lose the legal right to constitute themselves into special territorial entities despite the liberal reforms of the end of the 19th century, which had the objective, among others, of eliminating differentiated legal statuses, which were seen as an obstacle for the development of a modern society where individuals would coexist with equal rights

and duties. With Law 89 of 1890, the right to create reservations (resguardos) and indigenous councils (cabildos) was maintained, allowing the existence of territorial units that were governed by legal structures that were different from those that ruled the rest of the nation. This preservation of some aspects of 16th and 17th-century Spanish colonial legal philosophy regarding indigenous law is central in understanding the possibility of legally reproducing a similar principle for Afro-Colombians.

14 César Alejandro Cardona, "Proceso organizativo de las comunidades negras rurales de Antioquia. Ancestralidad, etnicidad y política pública afroantioqueña," *Estudios Políticos* 50 (2017): 180–202.

15 ICAHN, "[Cuarta] sesión de la subcomisión de entidades estatales y comisionados de las organizaciones populares [de la] Comisión Nacional Especial para las Comunidades Negras," Actas Comisión Especial, Bogotá, March 29, 1993, Actas Comisión Especial, f. 3.

16 ICAHN, "[Cuarta] sesión," f. 3.

17 ICAHN, "[Cuarta] sesión," f. 7.

18 ICAHN, "[Cuarta] sesión," f. 5.

19 ICAHN, "[Cuarta] sesión," f. 7.

20 As we will show in the following section, and as seen in separate research on land titling in Antioquia, this apparently essentialist definition of black communities was not, in practice, an obstacle for the collective titling of territories with very diverse occupation dynamics and production practices. For further reference see Marta Domínguez, "Comunidades negras rurales de Antioquia: Discursos de ancestralidad, titulación colectiva y procesos de "aprendizaje" del Estado," *Estudios Políticos* 46 (2015): 101–123.

21 "Baldíos de la nación" is the denomination given to lands that are owned by the state and can be adjudicated according to state policy.

22 Laly Catalina Peralta, "Curules Especiales para Comunidades Negras: ¿Realidad o Ilusión?" *Estudios Socio-Jurídicos* 7, no. 2 (2005): 147–172.

23 Martha Herrera, *Ordenar para controlar: Ordenamiento espacial y control político en las llanuras del Caribe y en los Andes centrales neogranadinos, Siglo XVIII* (Bogotá: Instituto Colombiano de Antropología e Historia, Academia Colombiana de Historia, 2002), 343.

24 Colombian Institute of Rural Development, INCODER, "Reforma Agraria y Desarrollo Rural para los Grupos Étnicos en Colombia," paper presented in the International Conference on Land Reform and Rural Development. Porto Alegre, Brazil, March 7–10, 2006.

25 Carlos Rúa, interview transcript by Marta Domínguez, Bogotá, March 26, 2006.

26 See Óscar Calvo Isaza's chapter in volume 1, *Histories of Solitude*, to understand the history of the Juntas de Acción Comunal in Colombia as a social technology for the organization and participation of civil society in the context of the Alliance for Progress and the Cold War.

27 Prior to the titling process, multiple property and occupation regimes coexisted. In some areas, natural reserves, natural parks, exploitation concessions, "baldíos de la nación," and lands occupied by Black and indigenous communities overlapped; see Claudia Leal's chapter in this volume.

28 Parra and Urán, "Parentesco y precariedad."

7 From Carbon Extraction to Blue and Green Extractivism

Demands for Radical Socio-environmental Transformations in La Guajira, Colombia

Astrid Ulloa

On January 11, 2021, United Nations Secretary-General António Guterres addressed the COP26 Virtual Roundtable on Clean Power Transition in these terms: "All countries need credible mid-term goals and plans that are aligned with this objective. . . . To achieve net zero emissions by 2050, we need an urgent transition from fossil fuels to renewable energy."[1] The imminence of climate change, the challenges of decarbonizing energy generation, and the reconfigurations of extractivist economic processes have generated global and national debates about alternatives to fossil fuels. The ecogovernmentality of climate change, through international organizations, contemplates options for nonconventional renewable energies or green (solar and wind), and blue (blue hydrogen) energies, based on technical processes and expert knowledge.[2] In Latin America, extractivism has increased with the corresponding effects of deterritorialization, dispossession, and conflicts, which have exacerbated social, intersectional, and socio-environmental inequalities. Grassroots organizations, nongovernmental organizations (NGOs), scholars, and stakeholders have proposed alternatives to extractivism to confront climate change and move toward decarbonization, generating debates and different energy transition alternatives. On their end, governmental institutions, in compliance with climate change agreements, have conceived energy transitions as a valid economic option. Meanwhile, national and multinational mining and energy companies have launched global-local projects of renewable energies, which include wind energy and the reconversion of coal mining into the production of blue hydrogen.

This diversity of perspectives on energy transition makes the debate on global environmental and climate crises a complex one. Companies, grassroots organizations, NGOs, and governments use similar terms with different meanings, often toward disparate goals. The concept of energy transition thus becomes an ambiguous and contradictory one, in permanent friction with the reality on the ground, one that requires analyzing its political, environmental, and territorial implications. To understand these terms better, it is necessary to explore how transitions are defined—ranging from economic to social, environmental, and territorial changes in situated contexts—while looking at their scope in the search for new conceptual reconfigurations. In other words, it is not only an issue of terminology but real implications of these transitions in the face of the irreversibility of environmental, social, and cultural transformations.[3]

In this chapter, I analyze La Guajira, Colombia, the northernmost region of the country's Caribbean coast, a place where all the complications related to extractivism and energy transition become evident. Here I use two perspectives. First, I build upon the work of Andrew Stirling to consider how in the context of global environmental degradation and demands of social justice, deep changes are needed in the form of "repeatedly unruly, bottom-up 'transformations' rather than top-down structured 'transitions.'"[4] Second, I resort to Leah Temper et al. to understand the need for radical systemic changes after analyzing various conflicts and demands for environmental justice and the transformation of the current economic, political, and social model.[5]

The case of La Guajira allows me to argue that energy transitions have become "green pretexts" to impose different development projects that give continuity to the accumulation of capital.[6] Although energy transition has offered a useful perspective to rethink extractive processes vis-à-vis social movements' struggles,[7] renewable and blue energy projects have also been instrumental for the accumulation of corporate capital and for the projection of a vision of sustainable development and prosperity by governmental institutions. This "green capitalism" offers a socio-ecological solution through novel forms of governance and new types of infrastructure.[8] Energy transition projects in places like La Guajira, that is, indigenous peoples' territories with unresolved structural inequalities, have generated territorial, environmental, and sociocultural effects that are similar to conventional forms of mining-energy extractivism. Additionally, energy transition projects led by companies and governmental institutions have neutralized and coopted the public debate, preventing efforts to rethink extractivism or transforming socio-environmental relations.

To understand these many layers of contradictions, I propose the concept of *radical socio-environmental transformations* to argue in favor of a profound change in capitalist structural relations—in terms of control of and access to nature as economic resources, and the territorial and environmental appropriation of such resources—in the struggle to position other ways of living[9] in pursuit of relational environmental justice.[10] In the case of La Guajira, these radical socio-environmental transformations call to reposition Wayuu people's ways of life to the center stage and to consider human-nonhuman relations under other ontologies, based on local practices and knowledges for the defense and continuity of life. Hence, this chapter is the product of multiple dialogues with Wayuu leaders and local grassroots and environmental organizations, such as Fuerza de Mujeres Wayuu, during two years of research in La Guajira, from 2018 to 2020. Based on ethnographic fieldwork, interviews, and analysis of narratives (videos, conferences, and political statements made by NGOs and Fuerza de Mujeres Wayuu), this chapter considers the perspective of different actors around socio-environmental conflicts and territorial transformations arising from Cerrejón coal mine and several wind farms. In other words, the process of exploring the region took place hand in hand with learning local perspectives and engaging with communities. I was also inspired by conversations that took place during several events about extractivism and energy transition, which were organized between 2020 and 2021, in the middle of the pandemic, and involved local organizations from all over the Colombian Caribbean coast. Finally, I take into consideration recent events related to the construction of a new wind farm in La Guajira.

Using ethnographic data and qualitative perspectives, I have structured this chapter into four sections. In the first one, I detail the complexities of La Guajira related to the reconfiguration of carbon and wind energy projects and processes of cultural and territorial dispossession. In the second section, I address the implications of institutional transition and their effects in the context of structural inequalities. In the third one, I return to the idea of radical socio-environmental transformations and consider local dynamics and demands for relational environmental justice from a Wayuu perspective, based on their ontologies on human-nonhuman relationships. Finally, I synthesize these ideas in the conclusion.

Carbon Extraction and Territorial and Cultural Dispossession

La Guajira is characterized by diverse ecosystems, from desert areas in the northern peninsula to fertile foothills along the southern Sierra Nevada de Santa Marta and the Serranía del Perijá. Various economic artisanal and commercial activities, such as fishing, agriculture, and tourism, coexist in this space. La Guajira has high levels of desertification due to trade winds that swipe the area. Within Colombia, it is one of the regions most affected by climate change and significant water shortages due to intense periods of drought.[11] Socially, it is a very diverse region: 44.9 percent of the population are Wayuu, Kogui, Wiwa, and Arhuaco indigenous peoples, representing 20.2 percent of the total indigenous population of Colombia. Additionally, 40.3 percent are mestizo or white, 14.8 percent Afro-Colombian, and 0.04 percent Romani people.[12] The largest population group, the Wayuu, whose territory spreads between Colombia and Venezuela, is composed of approximately 371,550 people. They have legal rights over 28 collective territories (called *resguardos*), which comprise approximately 1,084,027 hectares.[13]

Due to its ecological diversity and natural resources, La Guajira region has been the setting of many forms of extractivism as well as their reconfigurations toward green energies. During the first two decades of the twenty-first century, territorial, socio-environmental, and cultural conflicts have been exacerbated in this peninsula due to increasing coal mining and prospective projects related to fracking and other hydrocarbon extraction techniques. Governments and companies have restructured different forms of extractivism toward greener options as a response to international pressure, stemming from several climate change agreements that Colombia is signatory of. Hence, wind and solar photovoltaic energies have emerged as renewable alternatives and strategies for this energy transition.

These intertwined processes have deepened social, ethnic, gender, and geographic inequalities with profound implications for the Wayuu people, particularly in terms of territorial loss and displacement. These processes of dispossession have affected their food sovereignty and ways of living, denied them territorial rights, including access to water, and led to a lack of recognition of their concepts, knowledge, environmental and territorial practices, as well as their autonomy and self-determination. Thus, while governmental projections for coal mining and wind and solar energy in La Guajira have become central to the country's energy transition, the Wayuu people have engaged in serious debates about the implications of this transition and have demanded recognition of their ways of life and autonomy, and respect for their ancestral and legal rights over their territories. The political dynamics of their struggles and identities allow for a deeper notion of *relational environmental justice*, a perspective under which "environmental justice should be understood as an ethical, political, territorial and reciprocal action with the nonhumans and from territorial and cultural indigenous principles."[14]

Since the establishment of Cerrejón coal mine in 1983, and its official opening in 1986, various conflicts have emerged that have affected the social dynamics of the Wayuu people due to the impacts on their territory and territorial rights. The expansion of the mine has forced drastic changes in the ways they organized and located housing, neighborhoods, and cemeteries, based on clan relationships, and their access to water, among others. Health problems have also been common due to gas emissions from combustion and vibrations caused by explosives. Although both men and women have been affected, women have been the most harmed by processes of resettlement and relocation, as these have implied new cultural and spiritual relations to the land and those around them. Women use water daily to wash, cook, and care for humans and nonhumans, and have been forced to travel longer distances in search for new water sources.[15]

This territorial resettlement has caused intangible damages that cannot be measured in economic or material terms since they also imply emotional harms. Coal mining has led to socio-spatial segregation, destruction, hoarding of common goods, and the environmental suffering and lack of autonomy and self-determination of the Wayuu people.[16]

Promises of economic development through coal mining projects have remained unfulfilled at the local level; instead, Wayuu people have been directly affected by pollution, water scarcity, and undesired territorial and environmental transformations. Expectations of economic development focused on extractivist processes have been a mirage and have mainly benefited transnational capital. In fact, the department of La Guajira presents the highest levels of inequity in Colombia with a Gini coefficient of 0.553 in 2017, a poverty index of 55.8 percent, and with 25.7 percent of the population living under extreme poverty. Although the economic bonuses of the mining and energy sectors are an important source of fiscal revenue, La Guajira presents the highest proportion of Unsatisfied Basic Needs (UBN) at 44.6 percent, which is above the UBN of the Caribbean Region (26.9 percent) and the national average (14.6 percent).[17]

In response, the Wayuu people have opposed coal mining in their territories demanding socio-environmental and territorial justice. The closure of the mine is expected to happen in 2034, but there are no concrete plans in place for that to occur. Therefore, in the last five years, the Wayuu people, in association with Afro-descendant communities and the mine's labor union, have debated the implications of the mine's closure and have generated proposals for an energy transition. These debates have focused on life after coal, looking at the territorial, environmental, and social effects of the mine, and imagining a future away from extractivism. Their ideas for energy transitions are based on defending territorial and water rights as a central axis for their autonomy.[18] These crucial components of resistance for the Wayuu people against mining have led to discussions on territoriality for humans and nonhuman and water access rights for both. All of this has allowed researchers to rethink the notion of *common goods* and to expand our understanding of environmental and water justice, especially in semi-desertic areas with water scarcity, as it is the case of La Guajira.

Because coal mining and the extraction of hydrocarbons through offshore drilling, and more recent calls for fracking, has coexisted with alternative energy and extractive practices, such as the production of wind energy and solar energy, La Guajira offers a clear example of how structural inequalities can be unrelenting under both the extractivist and the energy-transition models.[19] Like Cerrejón coal mine, green and blue energy projects have disregarded the territorial rights and autonomy of the Wayuu people. Therefore, the Wayuu continue organizing resistance to these projects and demand the recognition of their rights in a context of irreversible territorial changes, as well as social and ethnic inequalities.

From Carbon Extraction to Blue and Green Extractivism 153

Figure 7.1 Cerrejón coal mine, 2018. Photograph by the author.

Force of the Wind and the Asymmetries of Power

Under the Kyoto Protocol agreement and The Clean Development Mechanisms, a project of wind energy called Jepirachi Wind Farm (JWF) was implemented in La Guajira in 2003. Located in the upper section of the peninsula, in the municipality of Uribia, between Cabo de la Vela and Puerto Bolívar, in the Wayuu *rancherías* (villages) of Kasiwolin and Arrütkajui in the Media Luna area, JWF was the result of the intervention of several actors, from the World Bank to the Colombian state and local Wayuu people.[20] The premise for its implementation responded to "two components: i) studies on the economic, technical, and environmental viability, ii) social management."[21] That is, the implementation of the project was externally legitimized under specific economic, technical, and political criteria. In other words, the JWF is the product of external territorial intervention and the presence of new actors responding to climate governance and international and national agreements, affecting the social relations and territorial and cultural processes of the Wayuu people. As stated by July Rojas,

> After the arrival of EPM [Empresas Públicas de Medellín, the company in charge of the JWF] and under the new dynamics based on JWF's presence, material conditions improved and the basic need for water was

satisfied. Along with this, however . . . the ways of exercising power and of decision-making among the Wayuu were altered, weakening social relations and family ties anchored on redistribution, solidarity, and complementarity of the *sukuipa wayuu* [the ways of acting through ancestral law, the word, and therefore determinants of Wayuu territoriality].[22]

Given that the Wayuu leaders did not have technical or financial information, nor did they have knowledge about carbon offsets, compensation was paid in kind, according to their own cultural laws but disregarding their territorial rights.[23] Finally, different infrastructures related to turbine platforms, substations, access roads, parking areas, construction offices, and other civil works generated significant spatial transformations, evidence of the territorial and cultural effects of green energy projects.[24] And this was only the beginning. Currently, "it is estimated that, with the programmed investments, in 2030, the production of wind energy . . . could be over 3000 MW, meaning, approximately 20 percent of the national total."[25] Diverse national and multinational companies have planned the infrastructure for 57 wind farms and 2,833 wind turbines expected by 2030 and 2040. They will be placed throughout the Wayuu landscape irreversibly altering the territory.

> Wind farms take around 45 thousand hectares to install towers of up to 120 meters high with blades between 100 and 140 meters in diameter; the area of each farm, besides including the polygon delimited by rows of towers every 300 meters and separated by an average of 500 meters between rows, contains roads, networks, and authorized activities in each phase of the project. With this many changes come, of course, the mobility of the Wayuu people and their customs of shared territories and for seasonal use.[26]

The process of implementation and development of some of these new wind energy projects was initiated through prior consultation in some communities under the modality of free, prior, and informed consent and in accordance with the rights of indigenous peoples in national and international legislation. However, the inquiries have been made in a fragmented manner and do not show all the impacts and territorial, social, and economic changes that the projects will entail. Additionally, the information has been provided gradually to the communities, and the environmental impact studies have not had local participation. Finally, the companies have outsourced many activities to subsidiary firms, which makes dialogue with the communities difficult. As stated by the NGO Nación Wayuu,

> Denys Velásquez Uriana, the authority of the Maleen indigenous community, jurisdiction on Cabo de la Vela, has denounced before national

From Carbon Extraction to Blue and Green Extractivism 155

and international public opinion, the arbitrary interference of the company ISAGEN on their ancestral territories. As well as the violation of sacred places such as ancestral burial grounds, where the company pretends to settle their wind farm projects in an arbitrary way and without consultation.[27]

On the other hand, companies do not always consider the internal processes of local community organizations nor their decision-making processes and territorial rights according to clan or ancestral authorities. There is no permanent or clear participation of the government in these processes, which leads companies to play the role of the state. These missed opportunities have prompted Wayuu organizations to demand that their rights and autonomy, in accordance with their social and political organization, are considered part of the decision-making process for current and future projects taking place on their territory.[28]

Last, but not least, Wayuu knowledge and their conceptions of nonhuman entities, specifically the wind, as well as their practices, lived experiences, and relationships with their territory were not considered in the

Figure 7.2 Coal excavations and transformation in water in the Wayuu territories have affected women the most. *Ranchería* Provincial, 2020. Photograph by the author.

implementation of JWF nor in future projects. Weilder Guerra Curvelo explains that according to the Wayuu worldview:

> Winds, whose mother is *Palaa* (the Sea), are beings with gender, masculine or feminine; they engage in alliances, love, or antagonistic relationships, and move through places and ancestral trails. Some are considered beneficial and loving such as *Jepirachi*, because of the cold that surrounds it . . . others, like *Joutai*, dry and hot wind from the east, are associated with hunger and drought; others are recognized tricksters, as *Jepiralujutu*, who pretends to be *Jepirachi*, wind of the northeast, to trick and get fishers lost. These were the first dancers of primordial humanity. *Tepichikua*, the small whirlwind, *Chiputna*, the strong hot wind that comes from the east, *Wa'ale* the ruthless wind that blows in gusts during storms, *Jepirachi* the soft wind as the breath of a sleeping person, and last, *Wawai*, the hurricane, that destroys everything that comes in its way.[29]

The failure to consider Wayuu knowledge and experiences of previous social and environmental inequalities affect not only Wayuu ways of life at different levels but also their interactions with nonhumans.

Structural Inequalities and Implementation of Institutional Transitions

As social, intersectional, and socio-environmental inequalities are perpetuated and the rights of the Wayuu people are disregarded on behalf of neoliberal dynamics, coal mining and wind energy projects constitute examples of energy transitions under the old extractivist logic. The changes in the materiality of energy sources—sunlight and wind—respond to the search for a socio-ecological solution that does not alter the capitalist model, but rather maintains and deepens it. The territorial and environmental impacts of extractive processes in Wayuu territory occurred under unequal relations of structural power. Energy transition projects reconfigure capitalism but do not transform existing underlying inequalities. The ideas, proposals, or ways of living of the Wayuu people in whose territories these transitions take place are not taken into consideration. Therefore, in a semi-arid ecosystem like La Guajira that, moreover, is going through climate change, wind farms are a way of legitimizing governmental, economic, and political actions. Moreover, governance operates through nongovernmental actors, in a privatized and commodified manner. This institutionalized governance works to increase the implementation of energy projects in specific territories, affecting decision-making processes within communities, and lead to environmental, territorial, and cultural transformations.

One example was the imposition of infrastructures on Cerrejón mine. In 2012, the company launched a project to extract the coal located under the stream bed of the Bruno Creek, one of the most important tributaries of the Ranchería River. The company built a canal simulating a new channel for the stream, in addition to a series of access roads, and a bridge over the said channel. Then, the company diverted the Bruno stream by 3.6 km. The final goal was to expand the production of coal in a place called La Puente, with endorsement from the national government's environmental authorities. The company thus implemented new technical and political mechanisms of water management infrastructures that affected not only the Bruno Creek but the cultural and territorial dynamics of the Wayuu people in that area.[30] This situation shows how socio-environmental solutions related to extractive processes can be seen more clearly through infrastructure.[31] In this case, the water infrastructure built by the mining company responded to technical and political considerations in pursuit of mining expansion, exacerbating inequalities regarding access to water and generating scarcity.

Similarly, the construction and implementation of wind farm infrastructures have generated different environmental and territorial consequences. On January 21, 2022, ISAGEN, a private company of energy generation and commercialization, inaugurated the wind farm Guajira 1. This project is the first of 16 wind farms in Wayuu territories. Local leaders questioned the existence of Guajira 1 due to the lack of recognition of their territorial rights. As the leader Denys Velásquez Uriana said in a letter that she sent to Colombia's president Iván Duque, on January 17, 2022:

> Mr. President! This park was built contrary to the fundamental right to the free, prior, and informed consent of my community and that of my two maternal uncles, it was built on top of our sacred sites, on top of our lives and our dignity.[32]

In other words, as Pablo Jaramillo observes in relation to JWF, the first type of consideration in cases of construction of infrastructure for the transportation and installation of wind turbines

> implies a definition of the potential area of affectation, whose inhabitants must enter into processes of consultation and negotiation, as they will end up involved in a long-term relationship with the infrastructure, its immediate effects of presence of a wind farm, operators, and transnational actors.[33]

These examples illustrate how companies have imposed infrastructures without local consent, prioritizing technical and economic interests.[34] The companies have thus transformed the territory insofar as the infrastructure becomes part of the landscape, in fact, it becomes the landscape, places where nonhumans and humans lose their territories and territorialities, while the relationships of the Wayuu people with the landscape and the ecosystem, defined by affections, emotions, and daily practices, are fragmented. As the Wayuu leader Jakeline Romero Epiayu explains:

> Confronted with this new global discussion on the issue of the energy transition, from what we have seen in our experience, in our work in the territory, we can start by saying that this dialogue has just begun . . . while the state's policy of concession of territories is moving fast . . . at an impressive speed, in the specific case of La Guajira, for example, where gigantic enclaves of other extractive projects are being built. In addition to mining activity, there is wind energy, for example, which is a monster already present in the territory.[35]

The governmental goal of moving away from coal mining to blue hydrogen, wind, and photovoltaic energy projects responds to extractivist capitalist socio-environmental solutions in the hope of addressing the environmental and climate crisis. Wind power and sunlight are now part of the commercialization of nature, turning them into abstractions through the creation of economic value, which denaturalizes them.[36] This leads to the appropriation of life through the market, while depoliticizing local environmental and territorial demands. From this valorization of nature, functional valorization processes have continued for carbon-markets and energy transitions. As Morgan Robertson argues,

> Nature is now encountered as ecosystems that consist only of services that already take the commodity form. The commodity form is not something imposed on it after it is extracted from a forest or a mine—it is now a precondition for an encounter with material nature.[37]

The construction of nature as a commodity has the consequence of its fragmentation, which results in specific policies for forests, water, ecosystem services, mining, and wind energy, among others.

Furthermore, infrastructures are the material and spatial expression of institutionalized governance that assumes territorial intervention as neutral, based on the notion of progress. But these interventions are not neutral, in fact, they generate lasting effects, such as those of JWF, which have caused territorial, social, and cultural impacts.[38] Similarly, wind turbines are embedded in the territory, changing the landscape due to technical and political needs.[39] Expert technical knowledge becomes functional in validating this process while minimizing the uncertainty, risk, and unsustainability of wind projects in La Guajira. These wind farms and their infrastructures will have unprecedented consequences, given the territorial transformations, dispossessions, displacements, territorial confinements, and cultural disruptions that will deepen the existing impacts of coal mining. Furthermore, the case of La Guajira adds evidence to the effects of the expansion of wind farms at a larger scale in other places in Latin America. For example, Alexander Dunlap analyzes the consequences of wind energy projects in the Isthmus of Tehuantepec, in the state of Oaxaca, Mexico, and asserts:

> Wind energy development in the *Istmo*, or renewable energy in general, continues to consolidate, intensify, and expand capitalist infrastructure and relationships, state violence and infrastructural development that, in its present form, is altering local livelihoods, cultures and ecosystems. If this present trajectory continues, it will lead to significant cultural and ecological degradation, if not destruction. Wind energy, in its current and industrial-scale manifestation, we see is renewing the destruction of the industrial-capitalist system and not de-growing, transitioning or repairing socio-ecological damages brought by industrial development (as it is popularly envisioned by the public).[40]

These transitions are taking place in the context of prior structural inequalities, and under a conception of development, "environmental" and "green" notions that are defined from an economic and capitalist perspective. As I have stated in previous publications, global policies for climate change, through new controls of nature, have allowed the consolidation of "neoliberal nature," unleashing the following processes of "the construction of a zero-carbon citizen, the control and fragmentation of nature, the symbolic and de facto appropriation of territories and nature, the local deterritorialization/territorialization, and the imposition of agendas for local participation."[41] Simultaneously, according to Dunlap,

> There are severe structural problems associated with wind energy development to centuries-old patterns of grabbing indigenous land, industrial development, and legally binding growth imperatives that mandate economic and material growth and . . . consequently, the increasing electricity demand from private sector industries.[42]

New scenarios of transnationalization of nature through their incorporation into green markets have thus generated the reconfiguration of territories, peoples, and the transnational and local relations regarding decarbonization and energy transition.

Radical Socio-environmental Transformations in La Guajira

In the context of La Guajira, radical socio-environmental transformations need to start from Wayuu people's conceptions of, and relationships with, nonhumans, as well as their political proposals for repositioning their ways of life, which are based on collaborative principles and intertwining of networks among different beings for the perpetuation and continuation of life. In Wayuu ontology, all living beings have the capacity for agency; therefore, they maintain affinity and kinship relations with all.[43] The worldview and practices of the Wayuu are embedded in their territory, which have different levels, both horizontally and vertically. This relational perspective conceives territories as living entities, to be recognized as political actors with rights, allowing for the continuity of spiritual and material life and guaranteeing the existence of humans and nonhumans. As such, their perspective poses a critique to projects of economic development based on the idea of nature as a commodity. The defense of their territories includes sacred places that connect diverse nonhumans at different levels. Wayuu leader Jazmín Romero explained it clearly when she talks about coal mining in Cerrejón and its effects on water sources:

> Territory, for us, is a living being and represents Wayuu women. Mna is a woman, she is earth, and Juyaá is the one who fertilizes her, he has to do with everything related to water, be it rain, water sources, rivers, streams, etc. The Bruno stream represents the veins, it is the vein of the Earth, it is the vein of Woumainkat; and for us, cutting a vein means death.[44]

This situated knowledge demands the recognition of Wayuu identities as linked to their territories. Their notions and practices imply cultural governance and collective rights and obligations because all living beings, including the wind, have the right to be and exist in the territory. Consequently, they have demanded active participation in energy transition processes, along with their forms of decision-making, from coal mining to wind energy. Their resistance revolves around the search for alternatives not only to extractivism but to accumulation by dispossession. They have fought to open spaces for their environmental and territorial policies, which are based on their ontology, epistemology, and ways of life, in the local-global political arena. Wayuu organizations and leaders are not against environmental projects or energy transition, but they are against the unequal processes that have ignored their fundamental rights, against the lack of recognition of their knowledge, territorialities, and interactions with nonhumans, and against the territorial transformations generated by infrastructures built by companies, which will remain with them for a very long time. In short, if they are against something is the reality that these projects are reproducing the structural inequalities, which they have had to live with for centuries.

Wayuu leaders have placed their territorial and environmental struggles against extractivism and new energy projects in the national and international contexts. They have generated a wide repertoire of actions, ranging from local protests and legal actions at the national level to the construction of transnational global networks. As Jakeline Romero Epiayu said in relation to the organizational process among Wayuu women to confront wind farm projects:

> This process of "Women Friends of the Wind" arises from concerns of women from different communities of La Guajira . . . where wind energy megaprojects will be implemented. And what we have done to date is a series of dialogues and conversations about the effects of climate change on the lives of women and on the lives of the communities, generated by extractive projects and megaprojects within [their] territories.[45]

The leaders at the forefront of these organizational processes have received death threats and have been subject of social and political persecution, which has ripped the social and territorial fabric that sustains their struggle. At the same time, these extractive activities have also generated social ruptures and conflicts within their communities due to the uneven distribution of economic benefits and the existence of different visions of progress and for the future. Given these divisions, Wayuu leader Jakeline Romero Epiayu has insisted on the urgency of collective action for the defense of their ways of life in order to be able to remain in their territories:

> On this issue, what our communities, people, and localities have done, has been to organize ourselves, in order to be able to stand up to this, but above all, to be able to care for each other, for that home, that body, which is the territory and life itself. Where will we all find ourselves when the territory is vulnerable and abused?[46]

Some of these collective actions include the protection of sacred places and spiritual practices, the development of political skills for community-based actions and advocacy, national and international mobilization. These strategies have to do with the collective territorial defense of men and women who seek to make their ways of life visible.

After years of resisting the expansion of Cerrejón, and even demanding the closure of the mine and the dismantlement of the infrastructure of coal extraction, Wayuu people now face the challenge of reconfiguring their lives in an irreversibly transformed territory with chronic water scarcity. They forecast that future wind farms in their territory will affect local organizational processes and alter the landscape, including their sacred places. Nancy Gómez, a Wayuu leader conveyed their concerns about wind energy with great clarity:

> Our territory is priceless. . . . They can give us all the thousands and thousands and millions [of Colombian pesos], but we will still not be well paid. Our wealth is in the land. Our wealth is in the sea. Our wealth is in the air. How are we going to get rid of what is ours? How are we going to allow them to come and fool us like that and talk about development?[47]

To put it simply, the restructuring of extractivism toward energy transition based on renewable green and blue energies cannot be implemented in La Guajira without the recognition of the Wayuu people's rights to autonomy and of self-determination. Their visions and demands go beyond the concept of energy transition; they ask for a profound transformation of development policies and the current economic model.

Furthermore, their decade-long territorial and environmental struggles, which are based on their ontology and conceptions of life, constitute a great contribution to the construction of what I call radical socio-environmental transformations. That is, their proposals, based on demands of relational environmental justice and their knowledge of and interaction with nonhumans, as in the case of the wind, reposition the relationships of humans and nonhumans under different ontologies. Their demands and proposals deal with questions at the center of national and international debates on the rights of nature and living beings. Taking Wayuu conceptions seriously would imply, in Stirling's words, *transformations* rather than *transitions*.[48] The extractive activities taking place in La Guajira, along with the political actions of the Wayuu people to address and resist socio-environmental conflicts generated by these activities—and proposed alternatives—evidence power relations in the struggle for environmental justice. The dimension of transformations demanded by social movements asks for profound changes of the ideals of environmental democracy.[49]

Conclusion: Transformations for the Continuation of Life

Local demands for change around environmental justice or fair energy transitions have been coopted by institutions and companies that depoliticize and give them new meanings, minimizing past environmental effects of extractivism. Institutionalized energy transition ends up reconfiguring capitalism through socio-ecological solutions as part of its own crises, which allows it to survive by compensating or complementing extractive processes. The dynamics reflected in La Guajira, where the transition from coal mining to blue hydrogen, as well as wind energy, respond to extractive capitalism's search for green capitalist socio-ecological solutions to the environmental and climate crisis. Meanwhile, social movements demand a radical transformation to the current economic, political, and social model.

The Wayuu people are making their demands visible to influence political and public decision-making on their territory and have joined local and transnational support networks for their struggle and to encourage respect for other ways of relating to nonhumans. They also seek to confront narratives around energy transition, sustainable development, and capitalist socio-ecological solutions that legitimize dispossession. These are only imagined realities because what we see are irreversible environmental changes and territorial effects. These socio-ecological solutions generate deterritorialization and fallout, not only of spatial practices but also of relations with nonhumans, while disregarding the rights of indigenous peoples. More recently, Wayuu people's demands have joined recent proposals for a fairer energy transition from Afro-descendant people and peasants from La Guajira and other regions of the Colombian Caribbean and the country.[50]

The Wayuu people are demanding relational environmental justice for the decades of environmental suffering caused by extractivism. The equal footing positioning of nonhuman rights with humans leads us to a new notion of environmental justice. Theirs are proposals that allow for the recognition of structural inequalities and the effects of extractive economic dynamics, while rethinking issues of use of, access, rights, and decision-making. The recognition of indigenous' territorial and environmental dynamics, including the interaction of humans-nonhumans and local practices, ontologies, and epistemologies, offers us a radical alternative to extractivism, allowing for transformations that drive the continuation of life.

Notes

1 United Nations, "UN Chief Calls for 'Urgent Transition' from Fossil Fuels to Renewable Energy," *UN News*, January 11, 2011.
2 Astrid Ulloa, "Geopolíticas del cambio climático," *Revista Anthropos: Huellas del Conocimiento* 227 (2010): 133–146; Astrid Ulloa, "The Geopolitics of Carbonized Nature and the Zero-Carbon Citizen," *South Atlantic Quarterly* 116 (2017): 111–120.
3 Astrid Ulloa, "Transformaciones radicales socioambientales frente a la destrucción renovada y verde, La Guajira, Colombia," *Revista de Geografía Norte Grande* 80 (2021): 13–34.
4 Andrew Stirling, *Emancipating Transformations: From Controlling 'the Transition' to Culturing Plural Radical Progress*, STEPS Working Paper 64 (Brighton: STEPS Centre, Economic & Social Research Council, 2014), 1. https://steps-centre.org/wp-content/uploads/Transformations.pdf.

164 *Astrid Ulloa*

5 Leah Temper et al., "A Perspective on Radical Transformations to Sustainability: Resistances, Movements and Alternatives," *Sustainability Science* 13 (2018): 747–764.
6 Diana Ojeda, "Green Pretexts: Ecotourism, Neoliberal Conservation and Land Grabbing in Tayrona National Natural Park, Colombia," *Journal of Peasant Studies* 39, no. 2 (2012): 357–375.
7 Catalina Caro, "Soñando futuros en la tierra del olvido: Trayectos co-laborativos para imaginar la transición," in *Energías para la transición. Reflexiones y relatos*, ed. Tatiana Roa Avedaño (Bogotá: CENSAT Agua Viva, Fundación Heinrich Böll, 2020).
8 Michael Ekers and Scott Prudham, "Towards the Socio-Ecological Fix," *Environment and Planning A: Economy and Space* 47 (2015): 2438–2445. James McCarthy, "A Socioecological Fix to Capitalist Crisis and Climate Change? The Possibilities and Limits of Renewable Energy," *Environment and Planning A: Economy and Space* 47, no. 12 (2015): 2485–2502. James Patrick Nugent, "Ontario's Infrastructure Boom: A Socioecological Fix for Air Pollution, Congestion, Jobs, and Profits," *Environment and Planning A: Economy and Space* 47, no. 12 (2015): 2465–2484.
9 Stirling, *Emancipation Transformations*; Temper et al., "A Perspective on Radical Transformations to Sustainability."
10 Astrid Ulloa, "Perspectives of Environmental Justice from Indigenous Peoples of Latin America: A Relational Indigenous Environmental Justice," *Environmental Justice* 10, no. 6 (2017): 175–180.
11 Institute of Hydrology, Meteorology and Environmental Studies (IDEAM), *Reporte de Avance del Estudio Nacional del Agua ENA* (Bogotá: IDEAM, Ministerio de Ambiente y Desarrollo Sostenible, 2018).
12 Gobernación de La Guajira, *Plan de desarrollo para La Guajira: Un nuevo tiempo 2017–2019* (La Guajira, Colombia: Gobernación de La Guajira, 2017). https://guajira360.org/wp-content/uploads/2018/09/PDG-Final-2017-2019.pdf.
13 Mauricio Archila, "Introducción," in *"Hasta cuando soñemos." Extractivismo e interculturalidad en el sur de La Guajira*, eds. Mauricio Archila et al. (Bogotá: Centro de Investigación y Educación Popular, Programa por la Paz, 2015).
14 Ulloa, "Perspectives of Environmental Justice," 179.
15 Yaneth Ortiz et al., *Agua y mujer: Historias, cuentos y más sobre nosotras, la Pülooi y Kasouolü en el Resguardo Wayúu Lomamato* (Bogotá: Centro de Investigación y Educación Popular [CINEP], 2018).
16 Mauricio Archila et al., *"Hasta cuando soñemos": Extractivismo e interculturalidad en el sur de La Guajira* (Bogotá: Centro de Investigación y Educación Popular, Programa por la Paz, 2015); Ortiz et al., *Agua y mujer*.
17 Gobernación de La Guajira, *Plan de desarrollo*.
18 Catalina Caro, "Horizontes y sentidos de las transiciones: Agendas y propuestas desde los territorios," presented at Diálogos del Caribe: Trayectorias extractivas y transiciones. Sesión 6: Transiciones para un Caribe post-extractivista, November 13, Facebook live, 1:13. www.facebook.com/915836611798896/videos/2561867754104422/.
19 Camilo González Posso and Joanna Barney, *El viento del Este llega con revoluciones: Multinacionales y transición con energía eólica en territorio Wayúu* (Bogotá: Indepaz, Fundación Heinrich Böll, 2019).
20 July Carolina Rojas Gómez, "Conflictos ambientales por medidas de mitigación al cambio climático en territorio Wayuu: el Parque Eólico Jepirachi,

1999–2011, Colombia" (MA thesis, Universidad Nacional de Colombia, Bogotá, 2012). https://repositorio.unal.edu.co/handle/unal/9676.
21 Rojas, "Conflictos ambientales," 2.
22 Rojas, "Conflictos ambientales," 104.
23 González Posso and Barney, *El viento del Este llega con revoluciones*.
24 Pablo Jaramillo, *Las servidumbres de la globalización: Viento, créditos de carbono y regímenes de propiedad en La Guajira, Colombia* (Buenos Aires: Centro de Estudios Legales y Sociales, 2013).
25 González Posso and Barney, *El viento del Este llega con revoluciones*, 158. Joanna Barney, *Por el mar y la tierra guajiros vuela el viento wayuu. En alerta la Püloui y Waneetu'unai, por el asedio de las multinacionales eólicas en territorio Wayuu* (Bogotá: Indepaz, 2023).
26 González Posso and Barney, *El viento del Este llega con revoluciones*, 34.
27 Cristian Avendaño, "ONG Nación Wayuu denuncia incursión arbitraria de la empresa Isagen en un territorio ancestral," *Diario del Norte*, March 18, 2021. www.diariodelnorte.net/?p=60124.
28 González Posso and Barney, *El viento del Este llega con revoluciones*.
29 Weilder Guerra Curvelo, "Ontología wayuu: Categorización, identificación y relaciones de los seres en la sociedad indígena de la península de La Guajira, Colombia" (PhD dissertation, Universidad de los Andes, Bogotá, 2019), 89–90. http://hdl.handle.net/1992/41315
30 Gerardo Damonte, Astrid Ulloa, Catalina Quiroga Manrique, and Ana Paula López, "La apuesta por la infraestructura: Inversión pública y la reproducción de la escasez hídrica en contextos de gran minería en Perú y Colombia," *Estudios Atacameños* 68 (2022): 1–32.
31 Ekers and Prudham, "Towards the Socio-Ecological Fix"; McCarthy, "A Socioecological Fix"; Nugent, "Ontario's Infrastructure Boom."
32 Camilo González Posso, "Guajira 1. Las verdades ocultas del único parque eólico instalado: 'Renovables Sí, pero no así,' dicen comunidades," *Revista Sur*, January 24, 2022. www.sur.org.co/guajira-1-las-verdades-ocultas-del-unico-parque-eolico-instalado-renovables-si-pero-no-asi-dicen-comunidades/.
33 Jaramillo, *Las servidumbres de la globalización*, 57.
34 González Posso, "Guajira 1. Las verdades ocultas."
35 Jakeline Romero Epiayu, Panelist at *Diálogos Caribe 6: Transiciones para un Caribe post-extractivista*, produced by Censat, Agua Viva, podcast, February 18, 2021, MP3 audio, 14:35. https://transiciones.info/podcast/dialogos-caribe/dialogos-caribe-6-transiciones-para-un-caribe-post-extractivista/.
36 Morgan Robertson, "Measurement and Alienation: Making a World of Ecosystem Services," *Transactions of the Institute of British Geographers* 37, no. 3 (2012): 386–401.
37 Robertson, "Measurement and Alienation," 12.
38 Julia Obertreis, Timothy Moss, Peter Mollinga, and Christine Bichsel, "Water, Infrastructure, and Political Rule: Introduction to the Special Issue," *Water Alternatives* 9, no. 2 (2016): 168–181.
39 Ashley Carse, "Nature as Infrastructure: Making and Managing the Panama Canal Watershed," *Social Studies of Science* 42, no. 4 (2012): 539–563.
40 Alexander Dunlap, *Renewing Destruction: Wind Energy Development, Conflict and Resistance in a Latin American Context* (London: Rownan & Littlefield, 2019), 3.
41 Astrid Ulloa, "Controlando la naturaleza: Ambientalismo transnacional y negociaciones locales en torno al cambio climático en territorios indígenas en Colombia," *Iberoamericana* 13, no. 49 (2013): 117–133.

42 Dunlap, *Renewing Destruction*, 3.
43 Guerra Curvelo, "Ontología wayuu."
44 Jazmín Romero, "¿Qué pasaría si se desvía el arroyo Bruno?" Interview by CINEP, Programa por la Paz, YouTube video, 2015, 1:58–2:52. www.youtube.com/watch?v=7jDDOaaOPCU, accessed June 1, 2021.
45 Jakeline Romero Epiayu, "Mujeres amigas del viento," *Noti Wayuu*, produced by Fuerza Mujeres Wayuu and Oxfam, June 29, 2022, YouTube video, 0:07–0:38. www.youtube.com/watch?v=gOd1toz_G_w.
46 Jakeline Romero Epiayu, "La movilización y la resistencia desde distintas latitudes: Reflexiones y herramientas para la acción colectiva," presentation at Quinto Conversatorio de la Universidad del Magdalena, YouTube video, 2021, 14:54, 16:08. www.youtube.com/watch?v=2XBL9YAxuW4.
47 Francesc Badia I. Dalmases, and Andrés Bernal Sánchez, "Fiebre eólica en La Guajira," *Open Democracy*, December 16, 2021. www.opendemocracy.net/es/fiebre-eolica-guajira-colombia/.
48 Stirling, *Emancipating Transformations*, 1.
49 Temper et al., "A Perspective on Radical Transformations to Sustainability."
50 Óscar Santiago Vargas Guevara et al., *Impulsos desde abajo para las transiciones energéticas justas: Género, territorio y soberanía* (Santa Marta: Fundación Friedrich Ebert Stiftung, 2022).

Part 3

Unpacking Drug Trafficking

8 Diplomacy, Drug Trafficking, and Political Repression

César Gaviria's Administration in Colombia, 1990–1994

Eduardo Sáenz Rovner

The year after the presidential candidate Luis Carlos Galán was murdered in an attack ordered by drug traffickers in 1989, a young politician who, like Galán, was a member of Colombia's Liberal Party, was elected president. César Gaviria, who had already served as congressman and cabinet member, had also worked as Galán's campaign manager until the day of his death. Gaviria's administration undertook a series of economic and social reforms, very similar to those pursued at the time by other Latin American governments, including the privatization and liquidation of state companies, the surrender of the health and pension systems to private capital, the dismantling of a protectionist system of import tariffs, and the "flexibilization" of the labor market.

Since the 1970s, after Richard Nixon had declared a War on Drugs, the illegal drug trade had gradually become a key concern in diplomatic relations between the United States and Colombia. A continuous pattern can be traced back to Misael Pastrana's administration (1970–1974): The United States would push its anti-drug policies and successive Colombian administrations would try to meet their demands, with occasional disagreements, as during the administrations of Alfonso López Michelsen (1974–1978) and Belisario Betancur (1982–1986). But Gaviria went further. The new president was able to take advantage of the War on Drugs and, using the fight against drug trafficking as a rhetorical device, sought to obtain commercial advantages and financial aid from the United States.[1] However, high officials in the U.S. government had reservations about Colombia's commitment to the fight against drugs under Gaviria, claiming that his administration's stance was not "aggressive" enough, and taking note of his willingness to enter into negotiations with drug lords and of the fact that state agents were behind severe human rights violations in Colombia.[2] The setting for these disagreements and diplomatic negotiations was determined by the promulgation of a new Constitution of 1991, which replaced the conservative one of 1886. This political event was framed by extreme levels of official repression, as duly reported by international human rights organizations.

DOI: 10.4324/9781003048152-12

This chapter reconstructs this story through unpublished documentation reviewed at the Fondo César Gaviria of the Archivo de la Presidencia de la República in Bogotá, and at the presidential archives of George H. W. Bush and William J. Clinton, in College Station, Texas, and Little Rock, Arkansas, respectively. These governmental and diplomatic sources reveal that in the early 1990s, Gaviria's administration used the War on Drugs, which Colombia engaged in under pressure from the United States, as a political tool to wage war against armed insurgent groups and civilian opposition movements.

Gaviria Seeks Commercial Advantages

On July 13, 1990, president elect César Gaviria and U.S. president George H. W. Bush met in the White House. While Bush was mainly concerned with the problem of illegal drugs, Gaviria's agenda was focused on requesting more trade with the United States. To that effect, he reminded Bush of the negative impact for Colombia of the termination of the International Coffee Agreement, and of ongoing difficulties for the flower export trade.[3] A few days later, Bush announced an "Initiative for the Americas" that would stimulate trade and foreign investment through market mechanisms.[4] In a later meeting, the Colombian ambassador Jaime García Parra brought up again the matter of trade with the United States, calling for a decrease in U.S. import tariffs and a free trade agreement between the two countries. García Parra stressed the fact that Colombia placed foreign investment under the same conditions as national investment, and that it had approved a labor bill that favored the interests of private investment. Gaviria also warned the United States that the extradition of Colombian citizens could not be the only tool in the fight against drug trafficking, and that the measure was extremely unpopular among his citizens.[5] For these reasons, his administration had offered terms of surrender for those accused of illegal drug trading, under which those willing to confess would receive reduced sentences and the promise that they would not be extradited.[6] Although U.S. Attorney General Richard Thornburgh had stated that he approved of the measure, with some reservations, the new U.S. Drug Czar Robert Martínez estimated that the decree would send the "wrong message to future generations."[7] Melvyn Levitsky, Assistant Secretary of State for International Narcotics Matters, stated that although Colombia had impounded large amounts of narcotics, its "political will was slacking" by engaging in negotiations with criminals like the Ochoa Vásquez brothers, from Medellín, "whose drug trafficking operations [would] remain intact."[8]

The presidents of Andean countries urged the United States to host an anti-drug summit, a request that was in sync with a shift in U.S. foreign policy for the region. While under Ronald Reagan the United States had directed its economic and military aid in the hemisphere predominantly toward Central America, during the Bush administration, its main recipients were South American countries that produced illegal drugs.[9] Bush accepted the invitation and suggested that the summit be held in Texas.[10] The San Antonio summit took place in late February, 1992, and its concluding statement "acknowledged the great importance of economic initiatives to lead the war against drugs successfully," and highlighted "the progress that Andean nations have made in restructuring their economies and instituting market-based reforms."[11] This approach continued even after Bill Clinton was elected. In private correspondence, Gaviria wrote to the new U.S. president to remind him that "the expansion of our bilateral trade and support for a new coffee agreement" would be the best line of support for Colombia.[12] Colombians soon found out that Clinton's anti-drug policy would be focused on persecuting drug traffickers in their places of origin, rather than on simply enforcing the interdiction of narcotics trading.[13]

The Colombian State Negotiates with Drug Traffickers

As with the Ochoa Vásquez brothers, the Colombian government negotiated Pablo Escobar's surrender and accepted Escobar's terms in order to put a halt to his ongoing campaign of car bomb attacks. Escobar turned himself in to Colombian authorities in June, 1991. Gaviria had called Bush to inform him about it and denied rumors that the location selected by Escobar for his incarceration, a building located in Envigado, one of the municipalities of Medellín's metropolitan area, known as La Catedral, was a "luxurious jail."[14] One year later, Gaviria summoned the National Defense and Security Council. The Attorney General, Gustavo de Greiff, confirmed rumors according to which Escobar was engaged in crimes and murders committed both out and inside the prison, and indicated that an escape attempt was very likely. The Council called on the National Army to guard the prison, both inside and outside, and studied the possibility of having Escobar transferred to a military garrison outside Medellín.[15] When he became aware of these plans, Escobar, along with his brother and lieutenants, escaped from the prison after holding two hostages, the general director of prisons and the vice minister of justice, both of whom were on the premises.[16] In a Cabinet Council, Gaviria explained that "[it was] very difficult to minimize the damage produced by this issue of a luxury prison in the eyes of international public opinion," adding that "what happened in Envigado was a generalized situation of corruption that reached up to very high [levels]."[17] The National Director of Prisons, the Commander of Medellín's Military Police Battalion, the Commander of the Army's Fourth Brigade in Medellín, and the vice minister of justice were all discharged.[18]

Soon, the drug war intensified when a group of drug traffickers who were enemies of Escobar, Los Pepes ("Persecuted by Pablo Escobar"), claimed a series of attacks in Antioquia against Escobar's properties and family members.[19] Lieutenants, associates, financial front-men and lawyers working for Escobar were also murdered.[20] Although there were more than a thousand police officers and soldiers involved in the search for Escobar, Los Pepes acted with complete impunity.[21] Escobar himself denounced Los Pepes and claimed that the group's leaders were drug traffickers from Antioquia, like the brothers Fidel and Carlos Castaño, as well as the brothers Gilberto and Miguel Rodríguez Orejuela and other criminals from Cali, working in tandem with members of the state's security apparatus.[22]

And he was right. Los Pepes collaborated with Colombian authorities, who in turn were getting a lot of help from the Americans. In September 1992 General George Joulwan, Chief of the Southern Command, traveled to Bogotá and met with César Gaviria. In a private communication, Joulwan noted that "Colombia was a savage place to operate. Witnesses and judges are just killed."[23] American military intelligence "doubted that Gaviria's government was sincere about cracking down on Castaño's gang" since they "shared a common enemy: Leftist Colombian guerrilla groups." According to American intelligence, General Miguel Antonio Gómez Padilla, Director of the National Police, had ordered one of his high-ranking officers "to maintain contact with Fidel Castaño . . . for the purposes of intelligence collection."[24] In 1991, another confidential report from U.S. Military Intelligence had called attention to the politician and lawyer Álvaro Uribe Vélez, described as a senator who was "dedicated to collaboration with the Medellín Cartel at high government levels," noting that he was one of those politicians who has "attacked all forms of the extradition treaty in the Senate."[25] Finally, Escobar was found hiding out in a house in Medellín and killed on December 2, 1993. The U.S. government congratulated itself: "The United States is proud of having cooperated with Colombia in the long effort to track down Pablo Escobar and bring him to justice."[26] As this was happening, U.S. anti-narcotics authorities were pressuring the Colombian government to go after the drug traffickers from Cali.[27] Noemí Sanín, Colombia's Minister of Foreign Affairs, acknowledged that "United States authorities [had] clearly started a wide-ranging campaign against the Cali cartel, especially directed against their image of 'non-violent businessmen.'"[28]

The American government had not liked Gaviria's surrender policy.[29] Attorney General Gustavo de Greiff jumped ahead of the U.S. shift in focus toward the Cali cartel and met with three of its members in his office to negotiate a surrender in exchange for a five-year prison term. As a sign of protest against this meeting, U.S. officials refrained from sharing narcotics-related information and evidence with Colombian officials.[30] Harsh words were exchanged between U.S. Attorney General Janet Reno and De Greiff, and the U.S. government issued explicit complaints against the Colombian government.[31] De Greiff continued to meet with the lawyers of Cali's drug lords, and received a surprise visit from the DEA's head officer in Colombia; De Greiff angrily protested that the U.S. government was "meddling in the process" expected to convince the drug traffickers to surrender.[32] John Kerry, acting as head of a U.S. Senate subcommittee, described De Greiff's contacts with the drug traffickers as a "capitulation" and echoed the description of Colombia as a "narco-democracy."[33] In his own defense, De Greiff remarked that he was working under the framework of the same decree that Gaviria had used to negotiate the surrender of the Ochoa Vásquez brothers.[34] As all of this was happening, secret reports from Colombia's own intelligence agency, the DAS, noted the growing presence of coca, poppy, and marihuana plantations all over the country (some coffee growers were even growing poppy among the coffee bushes), and an equally widespread upsurge in processing labs.[35]

The Domestic Economic Agenda

If the fight against the illegal drug trade was a central concern for Gaviria, his administration was just as intent on pushing forward a set of reforms aimed at the privatization of state companies, the "flexibilization" of the labor market, and allowing private capital to take over the health and pension systems. In response, Colombia's labor unions called for a general strike in November 1990. The labor federations met with the government's economic team but failed to reach an agreement: The presidential agenda was unshakeable and based on the alleged need to "remove distortions from the [labor] market."[36] Moreover, in internal discussions, Gaviria and his cabinet members claimed that guerrilla groups were behind the social protest movements.[37] Under such premises no negotiation was possible.

The government's response to the protests organized by social movements had the trimmings of a military operation. From November 8th to the 14th the National Defense and Security Council (CDNS), the Crisis Committee, and the Cabinet Council were in permanent sessions.[38] The government authorized company owners to fire those workers who joined the strike. The CDSN placed all units of the Armed Forces on alert and unit commanders were instructed to protect "critical points in which terrorist activity [was] likely to concentrate."[39] The strike included peasant marches, closures of hospitals, banks, and public service providers, energy cuts in the country's main hydroelectric plants, protests in the industrial enclaves of Bogotá and Yumbo, and strikes in two major state-owned companies: the oil company ECOPETROL and the country's sole provider of communication services, TELECOM.[40] The government opened disciplinary procedures against the strikers, and workers and union leaders were fired and imprisoned.[41] Through repression and its efforts to debilitate the labor movement, the government managed to push its agenda forward and ultimately presented the Senate with a bill proposal designed to undermine the rights and stability of workers. The Minister of Labor, Francisco Posada de la Peña, sent the bill to congress and Senator Álvaro Uribe Vélez was the proponent.[42]

A few weeks later, as Colombians were voting to elect the members of the National Constitutional Assembly, Gaviria ordered the bombing of a site known as Casa Verde in La Uribe, department of Meta, which functioned as headquarters for the leadership of the country's largest guerrilla organization, the Fuerzas Armadas Revolucionarias de Colombia (FARC). The Army occupied the camp, but the guerrilla leader Manuel Marulanda Vélez and his men escaped.[43]

While the search for Pablo Escobar was still underway, the Colombian government continued to treat social and civil protests as instances of subversive activity and escalated its offensive against the guerrillas. Although the Cabinet Council claimed that these measures were intended "to restore the peace that has been captured by guerrillas, drug traffickers, and common criminals," there was a high increase in the portion of the national budget assigned to the armed forces.[44] Under the screen of its efforts to track down drug traffickers and common criminals, the government was also escalating police and army operations against guerrilla movements while it pursued and arrested union leaders and left-wing politicians.[45] As a case in point, when the central workers' unions called for a new national strike in February 1993, the CDSN, again chaired by Gaviria, met to discuss a group of documents, among them a report by the DAS that examined the links between public workers' unions and social movements in a section titled "Subversive Influence. Working the Masses."[46] A few months later, in September 1993, when the unions organized a national day of protests, the DAS accused them once again of working in alliance with the FARC guerrillas.[47] In the eyes of the government, the labor movement and armed insurgency were the same thing.

State Violence

As the government advanced its economic agenda with such violent and militarist means, a few intellectuals who were both respected in the academic world and closely associated with the administration played a key role by crafting a discourse that justified the struggle against insurgents and rationalized human rights violations. One of them was the British historian Malcolm Deas, who was in contact with CDSN officials and advised them on security-related legislative projects.[48] As the CDSN described it, they had recruited Deas as an advisor in order to count on his experience "as a professor who specializes in military matters." Deas' task was to offer "recommendations as to how we can strengthen our approach to security and defense," based on his "indispensable . . . access to thorough international information regarding our national defense."[49] Apparently, to develop strong ties with intellectuals like Deas was an important component of the government's strategy. Ricardo Santamaría, director of the CDSN, suggested hosting an international seminar on security and defense, arguing as follows: "In addition to fostering closer ties between civilians and the military, it will be an opportunity to shift the trends, concepts, and attitudes that prevail in the media."[50] In another document, the objective was described in different terms: The seminar would be "a good occasion to promote Colombia's armed institutions."[51] This formal proposal was actually inspired by a suggestion from Deas, who had argued that an international event of this kind could be staged as a way to garner "support for the government's policies" and "give them greater publicity," "present new approaches and alter some doctrines," and "initiate a change in attitude among members of the press and reduce their ignorance."[52] Another intellectual, the historian Jorge Orlando Melo, presidential advisor on human rights, suggested that the seminar's theme should be "in tune" with U.S. foreign policy.[53] Eventually, the seminar was postponed as a result of Escobar's escape from prison.[54]

As much as the government endeavored to present human rights violations as legitimate uses of state force, several international organizations raised the alarm. Ian Martin, Secretary General of Amnesty International, went to Bogotá to address the National Constitutional Assembly in May 1991 and criticized the role of the military in Colombia. Martin also wrote a message to Humberto de la Calle, minister of government, with an unambiguous assessment of the situation:

> For years we have encountered convincing evidence that Colombia's military intelligence apparatus is involved in severe and persistent violations of fundamental rights, including the right to life. . . . Amnesty International believes, based on conclusive evidence, that paramilitary forces play an integral role in a counterinsurgency program deployed by Colombia's armed forces in order to eliminate its opponents, whether real or presumed.[55]

In response, De la Calle asserted that "Martin's presentation [contained] many unilateral and biased statements . . . many conclusions that yield a false image of our nation's reality," in a letter that had actually been written by Melo.[56] Speaking before the United Nations' Human Rights Commission, Melo stuck to the government's script, claiming that the ties between Colombia's Communist Party and the "FARC guerrilla were plain to see." Melo went on to assert that the murder of militants of the Unión Patriótica and Communist parties had been carried out by "drug traffickers and illegal armed groups" that only

> *in some cases, no doubt exceptional* . . . had received some support from members of military units, whose backing was occasionally based on the assumption that they were legal self-defense groups, but nearly always as a result of corruption and bribery among *a few* members of the military.[57]

In private, high government officials justified the creation of armed self-defense groups. Their line of argument is explicit in Santamaría's post-meeting remarks to Rafael Pardo, the first civilian to hold the position of Minister of Defense in over 40 years:

> I thought the issue that you discussed today in our meeting with Military and Police commanders was extremely important. . . . I believe that we should take advantage of the opportunity to find a new way of handling cooperation between the Public Force and citizens who are engaging in defense and security efforts. . . . As you pointed out, it is not just a matter of restoring the good name of the self-defense groups, we must also create a new awareness of the importance of security, the responsibilities that fall upon civil society in that regard, and the instruments that they can use to work in coordination with the Public Force, at different levels and for diverse purposes.[58]

The Colombian government was very concerned by the activities of the Andean Commission of Jurists, which had reached out to delegates from several countries to the UN's Human Rights Commission and urged them to support a resolution that would send an official rapporteur to Colombia. The government responded by contacting various embassies in Bogotá, and Melo was sent to Geneva to "hold a series of meetings with the delegations to the UN Commission to present Colombia's situation" from the official perspective.[59] Melo's task was not easy: The France Libertés foundation, founded and directed by Danielle Miterrand, the First Lady of France, had covered the travel and lodging expenses of a Colombian citizen whose husband had disappeared in Colombia, so that she could "speak before the UN's Human Rights Commission" in Geneva.[60]

In October 1994, the UN finally sent a commission to compile a report on Colombia's human rights situation. The report concluded that one half of the extrajudicial executions between January 1993 and March 1994 had been carried out by state forces and noted that "military operations leading to the death of civilians" included "indiscriminate bombing of civilian settlements and armed incursions into villages." Moreover, it stated that civilian casualties were often "presented to the public as guerrilla fighters who died in combat," after soldiers would "dress the cadavers with military clothes and place weapons and grenades in their hands."[61]

Amnesty International likewise issued a sequence of extremely critical reports. The 1993 report placed particular emphasis on the violent actions carried out by paramilitary groups in complicity with the State's security forces, specifically targeting Human Rights activists, left-wing militants, and the socially marginalized in "cleansing operations."[62] A year later, Amnesty International maintained its criticism, pointing out that military and police officers continued to carry out "arbitrary detentions, acts of torture, illicit killings, and forceful 'disappearances' of people in many regions of the country in their offensive against the guerrillas." The report also claimed that military officers were "creating new paramilitary structures in Colombia's central region and using them as an integral component of the army's operations against the civilian population."[63]

Yet another prestigious organization, Americas Watch, published a report titled *State of War: Political Violence and Counterinsurgency in Colombia*, which singled out mobile counter-guerrilla brigades as responsible for the majority of human rights violations and asked the American government to withhold aid to Colombian military officers who had moreover been trained by the United States.[64] William F. Schutz, executive director of Amnesty International USA, wrote U.S. Secretary of State Warren Christopher a message questioning American military aid to Colombia, which he claimed had been used "not only with antinarcotics purposes but also in antisubversive efforts."[65] Indeed, the State Department's report on human rights in Colombia in 1993 stated that members of Colombia's police and military "were responsible for extensive human rights abuses including extrajudicial executions, disappearances, torture, and arbitrary detentions," and that "right-wing paramilitary groups [acted] with the support or complicity of local or regional Army and Police units."[66]

Gabriel Silva Luján, Colombia's ambassador in Washington, worried over the fact that "that the State Department [had] been asked by the office of congressman Patrick Leahy . . . to initiate a review of the human rights situation in Colombia."[67] Critical remarks were also made by Democratic congresswomen Lita Lowey and Nancy Pelosi.[68] Meanwhile, Senator Russell D. Feingold and State Representative Tammy Baldwin, both from Wisconsin, questioned César Gaviria's election as OAS General Secretary, citing his administration's human rights violations and militarist policies.[69]

The Colombian government did not relinquish its efforts to defend its image and to protect members of its military responsible for human rights violations. On June 6, 1994, the General Assembly of the Organization of

American States (OAS) convened in Belém do Pará, Brazil, and approved the creation of an Inter-American Convention on Forced Disappearance of Persons. Colombia's Minister of Foreign Affairs, Noemí Sanín, wrote to Gaviria to express her opposition to the penalization of the forced disappearance of persons, since "the Colombian state would be obligated to categorize the forced disappearance of persons as a crime."[70] The Gaviria administration did not sign the convention.

Conclusion

The concerns raised by members of the U.S. Congress did not prevent the U.S. government from supporting Gaviria's election as Secretary General of the OAS. The determining factors in diplomatic relations between the United States and Colombia during Gaviria's administration were the commitment to reduce the trade of illegal drugs from Colombia on the part of two successive U.S. administrations, and the Colombian government's interest in augmenting trade and foreign investment. As for domestic policy, Gaviria successfully implemented his neoliberal economic agenda amid undisguised repression at the hand of the military forces and their paramilitary partners, a practice inherited from earlier administrations and through which Colombia became one of the world's worst offenders in the repression of social movements and the violation of human rights.

Notes

This chapter is based on documentation preserved at Archivo de la Presidencia de la República, Bogotá; George H.W. Bush Presidential Library and Archives, College Station, Texas; The National Security Archive, George Washington University. http://nsarchive.gwu.edu; William J. Clinton Presidential Library and Archives, Little Rock, Arkansas; *El Tiempo* (Bogotá); *The Washington Times* (Washington); *Voz* (Bogotá).

1 Martha Ardila, *¿Cambio de norte? Momentos críticos de la política exterior colombiana* (Bogotá: Tercer Mundo Editores, IEPRI—Universidad Nacional de Colombia, 1991), 217; Diana Pardo and Diego Cardona, "El procedimiento de la certificación y las relaciones entre Colombia y los Estados Unidos," *Colombia Internacional* 29 (1995): 3–6; Stephen Randall, *Frente a la estrella polar: Colombia y los Estados Unidos desde 1974* (Bogotá: Taurus, 2017), 129.
2 Randall, *Frente a la estrella polar*, 146, 159.
3 "Memorandum of conversation. Meeting with President-Elect Gaviria of Colombia," Washington, DC, July 13, 1990, George Bush Presidential Library, College Station, Texas (GBPL from here on), Mencons and Telcons. "The White House. Office of the Press Secretary," Washington, DC, July 13, 1990, GBPL, Pryce Files, CF 00724. "Risky Business. As Its Involvement in the Drug War Grows, the Pentagon Outlines a Plan to Crush the Cartels," *Newsweek*, July 6, 1990, press clipping, GBPL, WHORM, CO 035. "National Security Council, Memorandum for Johnson," July 12, 1990, GBPL, Pryce Files CF00724.

Diplomacy, Drug Trafficking, and Political Repression 179

4 Department of State, Division of Language Services (Translation), "Embassy of Colombia, Washington, Remarks by Ambassador Jaime García-Parra of Colombia upon the Presentation of His Letters of Credence to His Excellency George Bush President of the United States of America," GBPL, Gillespie Files, CF 01092. "Iniciativa de las Américas," undated, Archivo de la Presidencia de la República, Gobierno César Gaviria Trujillo, Bogotá (APR/CGT from here on), Consejería Presidencial para Asuntos Internacionales (CAI from here on), 1991, Box no. 26.

5 "Meeting with President Cesar Gaviria of Colombia," Washington, DC, February 26, 1991, GBPL, Memcons and Telcons. Eventually the United States relaxed import restrictions on Colombian textiles in 1992. See: "George Bush to Cesar Gaviria," Washington, DC, April 29, 1992, APR/CGT, CAI, 1990, Box no. 7.

6 "Acta no. 005 correspondiente a la sesión [del Consejo de Ministros] del día 5 de septiembre de 1990," APR/CGT, Secretaría General de la Presidencia (SG from here on). "Background information summarizing the Government of Columbia [sic] presidential decree relating to drug trafficking cooperation," GBPL, Pryce Files, CF 00724. Luis Fernando Jaramillo Correa, *Memoria al Congreso Nacional, 1990–1991* (Bogotá: Ministerio de Relaciones Exteriores, 1991), 39.

7 "Department of Justice. For Immediate Release," Washington, DC, September 6, 1990, GBPL, Pryce Files, CF 00724.

8 "Statement of Assistant Secretary of State for International Narcotics Matters Melvyn Levitsky before the House Select Committee on Narcotics Abuse and Control," Washington, DC, June 11, 1991, GBPL, Gillespie Files, CF 01013. "Statement of Assistant Secretary of State for International Narcotics matters Melvyn Levitsky Before the House Foreign Affairs Committee Task Force on International Narcotics Control," Washington, DC, July 10, 1991, GBPL, Gillespie Files, CF 01013.

9 "Amembassy Caracas to SecState Washdc," Caracas, May 23, 1991, GBPL, Gillespie Files, CF 01380. See also Lina Britto, "The Drug Wars in Colombia," *Oxford Research Encyclopedia*, September 28, 2020. https://doi.org/10.1093/acrefore/9780199366439.013.504; and Arlene Tickner, "U.S. Foreign Policy in Colombia. Bizarre Side Effects of the 'War on Drugs'," in *Peace, Democracy, and Human Rights in Colombia*, ed. Christopher Welna and Gustavo Gallón (Notre Dame: University of Notre Dame Press, 2007), 312.

10 "National Security Council, VMSMail User Morley," Washington, DC, October 28, 1991, GBPL, Gillespie Files, CF 01380.

11 "Declaration of San Antonio," San Antonio, February 27, 1992, GBPL, Gillespie Files, CF 01570.

12 "César Gaviria Trujillo a William J. Clinton," Bogotá, February 24, 1993, APR/CGT, CAI 1992, Box no. 40.

13 "Jaime García Parra, Embajador de Colombia, a Noemí Sanín de Rubio, Ministra de Relaciones Exteriores, Andelfo García, Viceministro de América y Soberanía Territorial, Gabriel Silva Luján, Consejero Presidencial para Asuntos Internacionales," Washington, DC, July 19, 1993, APR/CGT, CAI, 1993, Box no. 53. "Gabriel Silva Luján, Embajador de Colombia, a Señor Presidente, Martín Carrizosa, Consejero Presidencial para Asuntos Internacionales," Washington, DC, November 1, 1993, APR/CGT, CAI, 1993, Box no. 53. "Gabriel Silva Luján, Embajador de Colombia, a Martín Carrizosa, Consejero Presidencial para Asuntos Internacionales," Washington, DC, November 3, 1993, APR/CGT, CAI, 1993, Box no. 53.

14 "Telcon with Cesar Gaviria Trujillo, President of Colombia," Washington, DC, June 20, 1991, GBPL, Memcons and Telcons.
15 "Consejo Nacional de Seguridad. Martes 21 de julio de 1992, primera reunión, 10 a.m. a 12 p.m.," Actas Consejo Nacional de Seguridad, Tomo III, APR/CGT, Secretaría General Especiales 1991/94, Box 13647. "Consejo Nacional de Seguridad. Martes 21 de julio de 1992, segunda reunión, 3 p.m. en adelante," Actas Consejo Nacional de Seguridad, Tomo III, APR/CGT, Secretaría General Especiales 1991/94, Box 13647.
16 "Relación y cronograma de los acontecimientos ocurridos entre el martes 21 y el miércoles 22 de julio de 1992," APR/CGT, CAI, 1992, Box no. 36.
17 "Consejo de Ministros. Acta no. 054 correspondiente a la sesión del día 27 de julio de 1992," APR/CGT, SG, 1992, Box no. 132.
18 "Decreto número 1244 de 27 de julio de 1992. César Gaviria Trujillo, Presidente de la República, Rafael Pardo Rueda, Ministro de Defensa," APR/CGT, CAI, 1992, Box no. 36. "Cayó comandante de Cuarta Brigada," *El Tiempo*, July 28, 1992. www.eltiempo.com/archivo/documento/MAM-166209. "Decreto número 1263 de 28 de julio de 1992," APR/CGT, CAI, 1992, Box no. 36.
19 "Departamento Administrativo de Seguridad. Dirección. Informe evaluativo de orden público (periodo: ENE 25 al 31 del 93)," APR/CGT, SG, 1993, Box no. 157. "Ministerio de Gobierno. Oficina de Orden Público y Convivencia Ciudadana. Informe semanal de orden público. Periodo: 26 de enero al 1 de febrero de 1993," APR/CGT, CDSN, 1993, Box no. 37. "Ministerio de Gobierno. Oficina de Orden Público y Convivencia Ciudadana. Informe semanal de orden público no. 008–93. Periodo: del 16 al 22 de febrero," APR/CGT, CDSN, 1993, Box no. 37. "Ministerio de Gobierno. Oficina de Orden Público y Convivencia Ciudadana. Informe semanal de orden público no. 010–93. Periodo: del 22 al 28 de febrero [1993]," APR/CGT, CDSN, 1993, Box no. 37.
20 "Ministerio de Gobierno. Oficina de Orden Público y Convivencia Ciudadana. Informe semanal de orden público no. 011–93. Periodo: del 1 al 7 de marzo," APR/CGT, CDSN, 1993, Box no. 37.
21 "Ministerio de Gobierno. Oficina de Orden Público y Convivencia Ciudadana. Informe semanal de orden público no. 010–93. Periodo: del 22 al 28 de febrero [1993]," APR/CGT, CDSN, 1993, Box no. 37.
22 "Ministerio de Gobierno. Oficina de Orden Público y Convivencia Ciudadana. Informe semanal de orden público no. 020. Periodo: del 3 al 9 de mayo de 1993," APR/CGT, CDSN, 1993, Box no. 38. "Roberto Escobar Gaviria, siguen 15 firmas, a César Gaviria Trujillo," Itagüí, November 16, 1993, APR/CGT, CDSN, 1993, Box no. 32.
23 "AmEmbassy Bogota to SecState WashnDC, Immediate 1425," Bogotá, September 28, 1992, "Document 5" in "Colombian Paramilitaries and the United States: 'Unraveling the Pepes Tangled Web.' Documents Detail Narco-Paramilitary Connection to U.S.-Colombia Anti-Escobar Task Force. CIA Probed Whether U.S. Intelligence Was Passed to 'Los Pepes' Terror Group. Colombian Government Both Recipient and Target of U.S. Intelligence," National Security Archive Electronic Briefing Book no. 243, edited by Michael Evans, February 17, 2008. http://nsarchive.gwu.edu/NSAEBB/NSAEBB243/index.htm.
24 "Colombian Paramilitaries and the United States: 'Unraveling the Pepes Tangled Web . . .'"
25 "Subj: Narcotics—Colombian Narcotrafficker-Profiles," National Security Archive. https://nsarchive2.gwu.edu/NSAEBB/NSAEBB131/dia910923.pdf, accessed December 1, 2017.

Diplomacy, Drug Trafficking, and Political Repression   181

26 U.S. Department of State, Office of the Spokesman, "Statement by Christine Shelley, Acting Spokesman. Colombia: Killing of Pablo Escobar," Washington, DC, December 2, 1993, Clinton Presidential Records (CPR from here on), William J. Clinton Presidential Library, Little Rock, Arkansas (WJCPL from here on), OA/ID 1416, National Security Council.
27 "Lee P. Brown, Director, Office of National Drug Policy, Executive Office of the President, a César Gaviria," Washington, DC, August 25, 1993, APR, CGT, CAI, 1992, Box no. 40. "Embassy of the United States of America," no. 720, Bogotá, August 3, 1993, APR/CGT, CAI, 1993, Box no. 53.
28 "Ministerio de Relaciones Exteriores. Ayuda Memoria. Entrevista del Señor Presidente de la República, Dr. César Gaviria, con el señor Timothy Wirth, Subsecretario de Estado para Asuntos Globales," Bogotá, August 9, 1993, APR/CGT, CAI, 1992, Box no. 40.
29 Tickner, "U.S. Foreign Policy in Colombia," 315–316.
30 Douglas Farah, "Colombia Split Over Cali Cartel. Drug-Evidence Sharing Ends After Prosecutor Meets With Reputed King Pins," *The Washington Post*, March 8, 1994, press clipping, APR/CGT, CAI, 1993, Box no. 53.
31 "Janet Reno, Attorney General, a Gustavo de Greiff, Fiscal General," Washington, DC, August 27, 1993, APR/CGT, CAI, 1993, Box no. 56. "U.S. Department of Justice. Office of Public Affairs. Attorney General Delivers Firm Message to Colombian Prosecutor," Washington, DC, November 18, 1993, APR/CGT, CAI, 1992, Box no. 40. "Gabriel Silva a Señor Presidente [y] Martín Carrizosa," Washington, DC, August 31, 1993, APR/CGT, 1993, Box no. 53.
32 "Departamento Administrativo de Seguridad. Dirección. Informe evaluativo de orden público (Periodo: 14 a 20-FEB-94)," APR/CGT, SG, 1994, Box no. 193. "Departamento Administrativo de Seguridad. Dirección. Informe evaluativo de orden público (Periodo: 21-FEB- al 06-MAR-94)," APR/CGT, SG, 1994, Box no. 193. "Cali Cartel Attorneys on 'Surprise' DEA Visit to Prosecutor," Bogotá, March 9, 1994, CPL, WJCPL, F:\Cable\Data_Source\Cables\CD006\MAR94\MSGS\M0923661.html.
33 John F. Kerry, "Law Enforcement a Kingpin Could Love," *The Washington Post*, April 6, 1994, press clipping, APR/CGT, CAI, 1993, Box no. 53.
34 Gustavo de Greiff, "In Accordance with Colombian Law. Letters to the Editor," *The Washington Post*, April 14, 1994, press clipping, APR/CGT, CAI, 1993, Box no. 53.
35 See: "Informe[s] Evaluativo[s] de Orden Público de la Dirección del Departamento Administrativo de Seguridad," APR/CGT, SG, 1992, Box no. 114, passim. "Departamento Administrativo de Seguridad. Dirección. Informe evaluativo de orden público (Periodo: julio 13—ago 09/92)," APR/CGT, SG, 1992, Box no. 114. "Departamento Administrativo de Seguridad. Dirección. Informe evaluativo de orden público (Periodo: 03 a 09–MAY-93)," APR/CGT, SG, 1994, Box no. 157. "Departamento Administrativo de Seguridad. Dirección. Informe evaluativo de orden público (Periodo: 02 a 08-AGO-93)," APR/CGT, SG, 1993, Box no. 157. "Departamento Administrativo de Seguridad. Dirección. Informe evaluativo de orden público (Periodo: 16 a 21-NOV-93)," APR/CGT, SG, 1993, Box no. 157. "Departamento Administrativo de Seguridad. Dirección. Informe evaluativo de Orden Público (Periodo:20-SEP a 03-OCT del 93)," APR/CGT, SG, 1993, Box no. 158. "Departamento Administrativo de Seguridad. Dirección. Informe evaluativo de orden público (periodo: 16 a 21-NOV-93)," APR/CGT, SG, 1993, Box no. 157.

36 "En firme orden de paro," *El Espectador*, November 11, 1990, 14A, press clipping, APR/CGT, CDSN, 1990, Box no. 1. "Centrales obreras insisten en mantener orden de paro," *El Tiempo*, November 12, 1990. "Una protesta que comienza. Nov. 14, pese a las intimidaciones de las armas," *Voz*, November 15, 1990, separata, 2–3. Rudolph Hommes, *Memoria al Congreso Nacional, 1990–1991* (Bogotá: Ministerio de Hacienda y Crédito Público, 1991), 1.

37 "Consejo de Ministros. Acta no. 009 correspondiente a la sesión del día 13 de noviembre de 1990," APR/CGT, SG, 1990, Box no. 22. See also: "DAS. Dirección General de Inteligencia. División de Análisis, Informe evaluativo de orden público no. 207," November 2, 1990, APR/CGT, SG, 1990, Box no. 8. "Departamento Administrativo de Seguridad. Jefatura. Evolución de la jornada de protesta," Bogotá, November 13, 1990, APR/CGT, CDSN, 1990, Box no. 1.

38 "Acta Consejo Nacional de Seguridad. Jueves, 8 de noviembre de 1990," APR/CGT, CDSN, 1990, Box no. 1. "Acta, Consejo Nacional de Seguridad. 13 de noviembre de 1990," APR/CGT, CDSN, 1990, Box no. 1. "Consejería para la Defensa y la Seguridad Nacional. Comité de Crisis, Acta no. 1, noviembre 13, 1990," APR/CGT, CDSN, 1990, Box no. 1. "Acta no. 2. Informes y evaluación del paro nacional convocado por las centrales obreras," Bogotá, November 14, 1990, "Acta no. 3. Informes y análisis de la situación de orden público con motivo del paro nacional," Bogotá, November 14, 1990, APR/CGT, CDSN, 1990, Box no. 1.

39 "Paro: Declarado ilegal. Autorizan despedir a quienes participen," *El Tiempo*, November 14, 1990, 1A.

40 "Acta no. 2. Informes y evaluación del paro nacional convocado por las centrales obreras," Bogotá, November 14, 1990, APR/CGT, 1990, CDSN, Box no. 1. "Acta no. 3. Informes y análisis de la situación de orden público con motivo del paro nacional," Bogotá, November 14, 1990, APR/CGT, 1990, CDSN, Box no. 1.

41 "Sanciones y medidas impopulares. Tras el Paro Nacional del 14 de noviembre," *Voz*, November 29, 1990, 6.

42 "Bitácora. El paro nacional del 14 de noviembre," APR/CGT, CDSN, 1990, Box no. 1. "Balance 90. El año de la contrarreforma laboral," *Voz*, December 18, 1990, 12–13.

43 Édgar Téllez, "El Ejército ataca Casa Verde," *El Tiempo*, December 10, 1990, 1A, 18A. Manuel Cepeda, "Marquetalia 1964 . . . La Uribe 1990," *Voz*, December 13, 1990, 5.

44 "Ministerio de Gobierno. Oficina de Orden Público y Convivencia Ciudadana. Informe semanal de orden público no. 010–93. Periodo: del 22 al 28 de febrero [1993]," APR/CGT, CDSN, 1993, Box no. 37. While in the late 1970s President Julio César Turbay had militarized the war against drug trafficking, Gaviria—in spite of his anti-drug rhetoric—directed military spending mainly towards pursuing the guerrillas. On the Turbay administration and the militarization of the Guajira region, see Lina Britto, *Marijuana Boom: The Rise and Fall of Colombia's First Drug Paradise* (Oakland: University of California Press, 2020), Chapter 5.

45 "Ministerio de Gobierno. Oficina de Orden Público y Convivencia Ciudadana. Informe semanal de orden público no. 007'93. Periodo: del 8 al 14 de febrero de 1993," APR/CGT, CDSN, 1993, Box no. 37.

46 "Departamento Administrativo de Seguridad. Dirección. Informe evaluativo de orden público (Periodo: FEB 01/07 del 93)," APR/CGT, SG, 1993, Box no. 157.

47 "Departamento Administrativo de Seguridad. Dirección. Informe evaluativo de orden público (Periodo: 09 a 16 AGO- 93)," APR/CGT, SG, 1993, Box no. 157.
48 "Malcolm. Memo a Ricardo Santamaría, Javier Torres," December 16, 1991. APR/CGT, CDSN, 1991, Box no. 8. "Nota sobre conversación Control de Armas, 20 de diciembre 1991, Malcolm Deas, Javier Torres, Andrés Peñate," APR/CGT, CDSN, 1991, Box no. 6.
49 "Presidencia de la República. Programa de las Naciones Unidas para el Desarrollo. Proyecto COL/91/008. Apoyo al fortalecimiento y a la transparencia institucional de un modelo de gestión pública en Colombia," APR/CGT, CDSN, 1993, Box no. 37, Folder no. 5.
50 "Ricardo Santamaría Salamanca, Consejero Presidencial, a Rafael Pardo Rueda, Ministro de Defensa," Bogotá, May 4, 1992, APR/CGT, CDSN, 1992, Box no. 16.
51 "Consejería Presidencial para la Defensa y Seguridad Nacional. Seminario Internacional para la Defensa, Seguridad y Orden Interno. Noviembre 10 a 12 de 1992," APR/CGT, CDSN, 1992, Box no. 16.
52 "Malcolm. Marzo 1992," APR/CGT, CDSN, 1992, Box no. 16.
53 "Jorge Orlando Melo, Consejero Presidencial Derechos Humanos, a Ricardo Santamaría S., Consejero Presidencial para Defensa y Seguridad Nacional," Bogotá, July 23, 1992, APR/CGT, CDSN, 1992, Box no. 16.
54 "Mauricio Jiménez, Asesor Consejería Presidencial para la Defensa y la Seguridad Nacional, a Profesor Alain Joxe, EHESS," Bogotá, August 26, 1992, APR/CGT, CDSN, 1992, Box no. 16.
55 "Ian Martin, Secretario General, Amnistía Internacional, a Humberto de la Calle Lombana, Ministro de Gobierno," London, July 4, 1991, APR/CGT, Consejería Presidencial para los Derechos Humanos (CPDH from here on), 1991, Box no. 9.
56 "Humberto de la Calle Lombana, Ministro de Gobierno, a Ian Martin, Secretario General, Amnistía Internacional," Bogotá, August 28, 1991, APR/CGT, CPDH, 1991, Box no. 9. See also: "Juan Carlos Posada García-Peña, Asesor Ministro de Gobierno, a Jorge Orlando Melo González, Consejero Presidencial para los Derechos Humanos," Bogotá, July 26, 1991, APR/CGT, CPDH, 1991, Box no. 9; "Borrador. Jorge Orlando Melo González a Señor Ministro," receipt-stamped August 2, 1991, APR/CGT, CPDH, 1991, Box no. 9.
57 "Jorge Orlando Melo, Consejero Presidencial Derechos Humanos, Parte General de la Respuesta del Gobierno Colombiano al grupo de Trabajo sobre Desapariciones Forzadas e Involuntarias de las Naciones Unidas," Bogotá, November 9, 1990, APR/CGT, CAI, 1990, Box no. 5 (Italics are mine).
58 "Ricardo Santamaría Salamanca, Consejero Presidencial para la Defensa y la Seguridad Nacional, a Rafael Pardo Rueda, Ministro de Defensa Nacional, Ideas para una campaña de difusión sobre las empresas de seguridad," Bogotá, August 27, 1992, APR/CGT, CDSN, 1992, Box no. 12.
59 "Embajador Fernando Cepeda: Derechos Humanos, Posición Canadiense," Ottawa, February 16, 1993, APR/CGT, CAI, 1993, Box no. 43. "República de Colombia. Ministerio de Relaciones Exteriores. Ayuda Memoria. 49° periodo de sesiones de la Comisión de Derechos Humanos de la ONU, Ginebra, febrero-marzo de 1993," APR/CGT, CAI, 1993, Box no. 43.
60 "República de Colombia. Ministerio de Relaciones Exteriores. Ayuda Memoria. 49° periodo de sesiones de la Comisión de Derechos Humanos de la ONU, Ginebra, febrero-marzo de 1993," APR/CGT, CAI, 1993, Box no. 43.

61 "Visita de los Relatores Oficiales a la República de Colombia del 17 al 26 de octubre de 1994. Comisión de Derechos Humanos, 51°. Periodo de sesiones. Consejo Económico y Social, Naciones Unidas, E/CN.4/1995/111," January 16, 1995, APR/CGT, Consejería Derechos Humanos Área Política (CDHAP from here on), 1993, Box no. 4.
62 "Antonio Copello Faccini, Ministro Plenipotenciario, a Noemí Sanín de Rubio, Ministra de Relaciones Exteriores, Andelfo García, Viceministro de América y Soberanía Territorial, Rafael Pardo Rueda, Ministro de Defensa Nacional, Gabriel Silva Luján, Consejero Presidencial para Asuntos Internacionales, Carlos Vicente de Roux, Consejero Presidencial para los Derechos Humanos," Washington, DC, July 14, 1993, APR/CGT, CAI, 1993, Box no. 53.
63 Amnistía Internacional, "Colombia. Recomendaciones al gobierno colombiano," London, March 1994, APR/CGT, CDHAP, 1994, Box no. 9.
64 "Gabriel Silva, Embajador de Colombia, a Señor Presidente, Martín Carrizosa, Consejero Presidencial para Asuntos internacionales," Washington, DC, December 15, 1993, APR/CGT, CAI, 1993, Box no. 53.
65 "William F. Schulz, Executive Director, to Warren Christopher, Secretary of State," Washington, DC, April 14, 1994, APR/CGT, CDH-AP, 1994, Box no. 9.
66 U.S. Department of State, "Colombia Human Rights Practices, 1993," January 31, 1994. http://dosfan.lib.uic.edu/ERC/democracy/1993_hrp_report/93hrp_report_ara/Colombia.html, accessed May 6, 2017.
67 "Gabriel Silva Luján, Embajador de Colombia, a Martín Carrizosa, Consejero Presidencial para Asuntos Internacionales," Washington, DC, March 16, 1994, APR/CGT, CAI, 1993, Box no. 53.
68 "Gabriel Silva Luján, Embajador de Colombia, a Carlos Vicente de Roux, Consejero Presidencial para los Derechos Humanos," Washington, DC, April 15, 1994, APR/CGT, CSHAP, 1994, Box no. 9.
69 Russell D. Feingold, "Human Rights in Colombia," *The Washington Post*, April 5, 1994, press clipping, APR/CGT, CAI, 1993, Box no. 53. "Tammy Baldwin to Bill Clinton," Madison, February 28, 1994, CPR, WJCPL, OA/ID 23396, WHORM 0039.
70 "Noemí Sanín de Rubio, Ministra de Relaciones Exteriores, a César Gaviria Trujillo," Bogotá, July 12, 1994, APR/CGT, CDSN, 1994, Box no. 43.

9 Narcotrafficking, Immigration, and Salsa Music
The Cali-New York Connection

Alejandro Ulloa Sanmiguel

This chapter analyzes the relationship between salsa music, drug trafficking, and migration in the two-way Cali-New York connection during the last quarter of the twentieth century, when the Cali Cartel controlled 80 percent of the drug market in the "capital of the world."[1] Three parallel processes linked these two cities from the 1970s until the end of the twentieth century in what I call the *Latin connection*. First, the recording and entertainment industry of salsa music, led since 1964 by the Fania Records company in New York, which had in Cali one of its most important markets in Latin America. Second, the cocaine industry, administered from Cali since the 1970s, and also from Medellín, which had in New York its main worldwide market, as the center of consumption and distribution for other U.S. cities. Third, the migration of Colombians that included many people from the department of Valle del Cauca and its capital Cali, who traveled to the Big Apple during the same period. The following decades, thousands of immigrants, documented and undocumented, ended up working for the marketing and distribution of drugs in the United States, completely dedicated to the so-called big business, or by combining illicit activities with legal work, aspiring to the American way of life.

The convergence of these three processes had a great social, symbolic, and cultural impact on both Colombia and the United States, although it remains a taboo subject in Cali, one that is not talked about in the historical records of salsa nor of the city's. I ask: How were these three processes intertwined in their simultaneity and translocation? Moreover, in what ways do they determine the relationship between salsa and drug trafficking in the Cali-New York two-way connection during the last quarter of the twentieth century? To answer these questions, I conducted extensive fieldwork and ethnographic research in the cities that served as stopovers for this connection, which later extended to Miami and Los Angeles. I supplemented this research with a bibliographic study and by consulting several newspaper archives, including *El Diario La Prensa* and *The New York Times*. I have also relied on salsa songs that were created during the same

DOI: 10.4324/9781003048152-13

period. Hence, some verses are used in this chapter to illustrate the topics discussed, although I have already undertaken an analysis of these songs in the book from which this text is derived.[2] Finally, I relied on testimonies of 20 immigrants I interviewed over several years in the cities mentioned above. This sample is not intended to have statistical validity but rather to offer qualitative evidence for historical and cultural analysis. Each of those interviewed, on average, talked about ten more people with the same profile and whom they engaged with in both salsa and drug trafficking settings in either Cali or New York, or both. These stories offer a unique view, different from an academic one, which can facilitate the analysis of a social phenomenon of great magnitude.

Those interviewed were selected based on five criteria: They had to be *Caleños* (from Cali) or people from the Valle del Cauca who became *caleñized*; they had to be *salseros* (salsa fans and connoisseurs) and who self-identified as such, and who liked to dance salsa; they had to have been involved in drug trafficking in one or more of the links of production, transportation, storage, wholesale, or retail distribution chain; they must have participated in two or more cities of the drug connection; and they could offer testimonial, documentary, or other evidence (photographs, musical collections, paraphernalia, etc.) to be able to verify their profile. When referring to them, at their request, I have used pseudonyms or their name and surname initials to protect their identities. In the end, the research revealed that they all had something else in common: They came from Cali's working-class neighborhoods, with a relatively shared life experience, although they did not know each other; they belonged to poor families; they fought against adversity and socioeconomic limitations; they had little education but desired to get ahead in life, even via risk-taking; and they had a certain predisposition to adventure and transgressing the rules, oscillating between the legal and the illegal.

I should add that I am myself a *salsero de la mata*, that is, a salsa fan through and through, someone who has been imbued in salsa music since adolescence in my neighborhood, on my street, and in other spaces in different cities, in addition to doing research for this ethnography. This method has allowed me, on the one hand, to offer qualitative and contextualized descriptions of the observed phenomena. On the other hand, it has allowed me to make comparative approximations of different phases of the same social or cultural phenomena, by analyzing their development and revealing new facts and new relationships between them. Hence, I have been able to establish points of contact between the data found in my fieldwork and theoretical statements regarding social or cultural change. By discovering the simultaneities between the facts and the interdependencies between them, I offer empirical support to certain conceptual generalizations that are typical of critical social theory.

Historical Context: Some Background

At the beginning of the 1960s, Cali was already the third-largest city in Colombia, with a population of close to 500,000 inhabitants. Located near the port of Buenaventura on the Pacific Coast, Cali was experiencing a progressive industrialization along with the development of a diversified agro-industry, where sugar and coffee exports production were predominant. Overall, a working class emerged as a result of the modernization of this regional economy at a time when Colombia was moving from an agrarian society to an urban and industrialized one. At the same time, the conflict between members of the two main political parties, Liberals and Conservatives—which between 1948 and 1965 caused the deaths of more than 200,000 Colombians in a period known as *la Violencia*—produced an exodus of many people, mostly of peasant origin, toward urban centers. Cali became the most important recipient of displaced people in the country's southwest, attracted by the mirage of progress that was proclaimed. Cali grew rapidly in different directions as a new city that emerged from rough construction and informal settlements. This dynamic spurred the creation of marginalized neighborhoods in a process that modified the old town, which had been in existence for 400 years, into a new, unplanned, diffuse, and informal working-class city, the *Cali popular*. It was a sociospatial and cultural configuration that had its antecedents in the San Nicolás neighborhood—which had a long tradition of artisans dating back to the eighteenth century and a middle-class population in the twentieth century—and in the Obrero neighborhood, which was founded in approximately 1920.

In the 1950s, *Cali popular* spread out from the social marginalization of these working-class neighborhoods and their neighbors. Its cultural influence manifested in ludic and festive practices that transcended into the city's periphery. This refuge city was thus ruralized, and the rural consciousness of the masses became urbanized as it assimilated to the new rules of the game, fostered by the demands of its late modernization. Cultural expressions and agrarian trajectories began intermixing with elements of urban life—in particular soccer and tropical music and Afro-Caribbean rhythms and dance, which were already established in the aforementioned neighborhoods—to give rise in later generations to a new sensibility. In the collective construction of *Cali popular*—the former and the new—an open and spontaneous attitude developed within the "plebeian" social base. Locals and immigrants, having to fight for the occupation of urban territories, assembled and organized to solve the immediate problems imposed by their survival. The acceptance of other ways of being and other customs was integrated into the racial tolerance of this plebeian social base, which had its origins in the nineteenth century, a legacy of the abolition of slavery. According to Édgar Vásquez, during the colonial era in Cali:

> There was strong social and racial discrimination by the white elite of landowners, miners, and merchants against indigenous, Black, mestizo, and brown people; but there was no strong mutual racial discrimination within that plebeian base, white people included. Since no one had a pure white ascendant and had to exist at the bottom of the social pyramid, no commoner felt authorized to exercise a drastic and continuous attitude of racial discrimination.[3]

Immigrants became Caleños by adapting to these new living conditions and by adopting references of interaction in the spaces they occupied, such as dancing, walks by the city's rivers, and by playing soccer and other sports. Thus, a city that was different from the modern Cali of the elite was created, to the point that by the 1960s, two socio-spatially opposed cities coexisted, although in tension, as evidenced by the massive mobilization that took place as a result of the fall of General Gustavo Rojas Pinilla in 1957 and the historic "Sugar March" strike of 3,000 workers and their families in 1959 calling for better working conditions and to protest against the political situation that came to be known as la Violencia.[4] Products of the transnational cultural industry—radio broadcasts, the music industry, and cinema—would arrive to both "cities" in different ways. The Afro-Cuban and Puerto Rican rhythms, also known as the "Antillean music of the old guard," stood out. The plebeian masses found in the Afro-Latin culture a link to get together in their new environment, by taking advantage of the appeal of the body and the incitement to dance that ended up mediating their relationships and becoming a way of ritualizing social relations in *Cali popular*'s modern life. In the 1960s, this soundtrack expanded its repertoire with the advent of salsa music, created by Puerto Ricans and their descendants in the United States. Brought by sailors to the nearby Pacific port of Buenaventura, and some local and foreign immigrants who came from New York, Puerto Rico, or Panama, salsa music began to occupy the territory and to inhabit young people's hearts, memories, and bodies in Cali. That included middle-class rebellious, anti-establishment youth who were permeated by salsa's rhythms, as represented in the 1977 novel *¡Qué viva la música!* by Andrés Caicedo.[5] This new urban and low-income sensibility was connected with the refreshing airs of a cosmopolitan sound, open to different influences. However, both the old Afro-Antillean guard and salsa were stigmatized by the local elite as "bad taste" in music, and disparagingly ascribed it to the populace and to "the Blacks" from the city and the region.

In the fabric woven between the city's working class—product of structural exclusion—and the city's business class—the visible and hegemonic side of Cali—a school of crime was forged from which the most important drug lords emerged. For example, the brothers Gilberto and Miguel Rodríguez Orejuela—founders of the Cali Cartel and leaders of a criminal organization that developed into an industrialized and modern multinational company—arrived with their family in Cali as children around 1953. As immigrants displaced by *la Violencia*, they lived in the Obrero neighborhood and rapidly assimilated its idiosyncrasies. In their youth, they experienced Afro-Cuban music, salsa, dance, and soccer, which were their most cherished pleasures, as expressed by some of their closest friends, whom I interviewed for this research.[6] From the same sociocultural environment came the dancers of Antillean and salsa music who would later represent the city within and outside the country, as well as the first "made in Cali" salsa musicians, who followed influences from Cuba, New York, and Puerto Rico.

From these same neighborhoods came many of the immigrants who would arrive in the United States in the following decades in search for the "American way of life." Thousands of travelers ended up being linked as laborers in the drug marketing networks of the Cali-New York two-way connection. One of them was TRL, originally from Tuluá, and one of the people interviewed. He arrived with his family to a working-class neighborhood in Cali in approximately 1955. In 1968, he traveled to New York. He was then 22 years old and had a high school diploma. He worked in a can factory in Elizabeth, New Jersey, where he met people who would later be the leaders of the "big business," including MCF and RMZ. In 1974, he returned to Cali and in 1977, he became involved in drug trafficking with a group of friends:

> With one of them, we would travel to Ipiales, near the border with Ecuador, and would buy the [coca paste] base, which we would then bring to Cali, where we got the [chemical] supplies to extract the drug, cocaine. We performed the procedure in El Bolo, a rural area between Cali and Palmira where we had a small but functional "kitchen" [cocaine laboratory]. Another boy in the group made leather shoes, and we would stick the drugs between the soles of shoes to send them to New York. The one who carried [the drugs] had to wear the shoes for at least one day so that they looked used, because they were part of his luggage. He could carry a kilo inside three pairs. We had that line for a year, until it fell apart. Back then, people were still naive. Even the police didn't know about many things.[7]

With the gained experience, TRL decided to return to New York in 1978, but his visa had expired. Thus, he crossed the border illegally as a "mojado" ("wetback," slur used in the U.S. for undocumented immigrants). In New York, TRL reconnected with his old contacts:

> They were already connected with other people. . . . Since I already spoke some English and knew the Big Apple, they required me for various tasks. One of them was to receive "the merchandise" that was sent to us from Colombia. I worked with NG, MCF, and PZ; we would collect five kilos, "cut" them, and get ten. The quality was lower, but we increased its quantity and our profits. Other times, I would travel by car to Miami to receive "the errand" and take it to New York. We did the same thing—we would cut the *perico* [cocaine], increase its yield, and divide it into halves, quarters, and eights [one-eighth of a kilo], and we would distribute it to the *jíbaros* [drug dealers] who sold it on the street. Then, we would collect the money, return to Miami, and give it to NG's people. At one point I got to handle up to a million dollars per day, although it wasn't mine, it belonged to the people I worked for. They paid me well, regardless . . . I worked like that until the mid-80s. . . . With what I earned, I lived in the Yores [New York] and sent some money to Cali, thinking of investing it later.[8]

Colombian Migration to New York and the Narco-Entrepreneurs of Salsa

Several researchers have explored Colombian migration to the United States, mainly to New York during the second half of the twentieth century. This intensified when the U.S. government issued the Hart-Celler Immigration Act in 1965, which was prolonged for several years and stimulated migration.[9] However, this law is better understood within the framework of the redefinition of international capitalism, as explained by David Harvey:

> One of the main barriers to the continuous accumulation of capital and the consolidation of the power of the capitalist class during the decade of the sixties was the organized labor movement: there was a shortage of labor both in Europe and in the United States; the workers were well organized, reasonably well paid and had political influence. However, capital sought to have a more docile and inexpensive labor supply, for which there were several means. One of them was to encourage immigration; the Immigration and Nationality Act of 1965, which abolished quotas according to national origin, made it easier for American capital

to access the global surplus population (until then, European immigrants and whites in general had an advantage).[10]

According to figures from the U.S. Department of Justice, between 1965 and 1970, total 46,198 Colombians were admitted into the country. These figures also show that according to "the 1970 United States population census records, a total of 63,538 inhabitants were born in Colombia."[11] By January 1975, that figure had increased to 69,614 Colombians.

Now, how were the links between many of these immigrants initially established via the drug trafficking that originated in Cali and Medellín and then continued in Miami and New York? Among so many immigrants who were hooked on this "big business" for several years, not all came to occupy a leadership position in the organization that emerged from Cali, as did, for example, Benjamín Herrera Zuleta (also known as "El Papa Negro" [the Black Pope]), José "Chepe" Santacruz, and Hélmer "Pacho" Herrera, who became its leaders. According to Eduardo Sáenz Rovner,

> There were cases of mules that ended up being drug lords in their own right, [like] Benjamín Herrera Zuleta, captured in Miami in the mid-1970s while importing cocaine in his clothes. In 1973, Herrera escaped from a federal prison in Atlanta where he was serving five years in prison for drug trafficking.[12]

On the other hand, in his research on the collapse of the cartel, the journalist José Gregorio Pérez states that

> Herrera Zuleta managed to create in Cali a coca base distribution network that after being refined in laboratories was sent to the United States. There, the drug was received by administrators of small groups, or "cells," which were responsible for its commercialization in the streets of Miami, California, Houston, and Chicago.[13]

Moreover, the Latin connection was wide; according to Pérez,

> The members of one cell did not know anyone from another cell, which allowed them to maintain control of the networks. . . . Following the example of "El Papa Negro," Hélmer "Pacho" Herrera organized a network of distribution in New York for the Rodríguez Orejuela brothers and . . . controlled seventy cells, 55 of which were in charge of marketing the drug in New York.[14]

Herrera Zuleta is also mentioned in the memoirs of William Rodríguez Abadía, a son of Miguel Rodríguez Orejuela and one of the capos of the organization. According to Rodríguez Abadía, "El Papa Negro" commissioned his uncle Gilberto and "Chepe" Santacruz, members of the band "Los Chemas,"

> to transport coca paste to Cali from Bolivia and Peru to process it and send it to the markets in the United States. With this accumulated experience, "Los Chemas" became independent, took over the drug trafficking business in Cali and began to make its first shipments to the northern part of the country.[15]

Rodríguez Abadía adds:

> My uncle Gilberto and 'Chepe' decided to make their first trip with their first kilo, which at the time was a large amount. . . . A month after leaving Cali (traveling through Central America), the two partners arrived in New York, where they were surprised by the retail value. . . . A kilo in New York could be sold for between 50 thousand and 60 thousand dollars. In the jargon of the narcos, they always said that the important thing was the first kilo—from then on, everything would come to boot.[16]

According to the same author, at the time, a kilo in Bolivia had a price of 1,800 dollars, but

> with the arrival of Colombians to the business, it would cost between seven thousand and ten thousand dollars. . . . After that first kilo, my uncle began to perfect his business by dividing its functions. They went to buy coca sulfate in Peru or Bolivia, then others transported it; my father was in charge of converting it into cocaine hydrochloride in small laboratories in Valle del Cauca. Coca was transported to the United States in a thousand ways, and there were some people in charge of distributing it wholesale and others through retail, until it finally reached the discotheques, bars, and nightclubs of large cities in grams.[17]

Thus, the business was from its beginning a transnational company that started in three Andean countries in South America (Colombia, Peru, Bolivia) and ended in the streets of New York, Miami, and the most important cities in the United States, notoriously in the nightlife linked to the music scene, in general, and salsa, in particular.

The narrative by Rodríguez Abadía corresponds to Harvey's theoretical analysis of the dynamics of capitalism, although the latter does not refer to drug trafficking, much less to salsa. According to Harvey,

> The circulation of capital also involves its spatial movement; money is gathered in a particular place and taken to another to use the labor

resources that come, perhaps, from another place ... the means of production (including materials' premiums) have to be brought from somewhere else to produce a commodity that, in turn, is sold in a market perhaps very far from the place of production.[18]

The Cali Cartel in New York

As cocaine consumption and demand grew in the United States, the market expanded. According to Pérez,

> Specialized DEA reports pointed to the Cali Cartel as responsible for the introduction of 80% of the cocaine consumed in the United States between 1982 and 1995. Statistics indicate that the cartel obtained eleven billion dollars annually, of which it deposited two billion in Colombia. The rest remained in foreign bank accounts or was spent to pay for the infrastructure of the market.[19]

For his part, General Óscar Naranjo, who participated in the fight against drug trafficking in the 1980s and knew the Cali and Medellín Cartels closely, told journalist Julio Sánchez Cristo, "There was a market for everyone. In addition, the Medellín Cartel always recognized that New York was a plaza owned by José 'Chepe' Santacruz, one of the capos of Cali, who had opened that business and therefore they respected him."[20] In a recapitulation of the trajectory of drug trafficking in the Big Apple, *El Diario La Prensa* of New York argued on June 25, 1995,

> The Cali Cartel originated in Queens. The decade of the seventies was, without a doubt, the period when what would be later called the Medellín and Cali Cartels were born. It was the boom era of the prosperous business of transporting cocaine from Colombia to the United States. ... Gilberto and Miguel Rodríguez Orejuela set their roots in Jackson Heights, as well as José Santacruz Londoño and "Pacho" Herrera, who had their businesses on Roosevelt Avenue. The business was growing by leaps and bounds.

This is also evidenced by the story of Liza, another of my sources. She was one of the many women linked to the Cali Cartel who stood out in New York for her cunning, courage, and intelligence when performing different tasks in an environment dominated by men. Along with MV, "la señora de las caletas" [lady of the secret stash hideout], DZ, "La Flaca L," and "La Cachona," Liza "was the tough one in Queens," according to several of her colleagues. A neighbor of another working-class neighborhood in Cali, Liza—still a teenager—arrived with her family in New York in 1978. In Queens, she attended a public school, where she found the children of other Colombians immersed in a hostile environment of discrimination and rejection. Liza said:

> Out of thirty students in the classroom, 28 were Colombians, the majority from Cali and Medellín. . . . They taught us everything in Spanish, and the exams were done in English. In school, I fought with men; I learned to smoke marijuana and to play cops and robbers with friends. I was always on the side of the robbers. . . . In 1980, I traveled to Medellín to visit my mother's family, and in 1981, I married Frank, a 46-year-old merchant from Valle del Cauca who worked with Griselda [Blanco], "The Queen of Cocaine." He put me in charge of receiving the merchandise in Miami and then upload it to New York, where I was reunited with family and friends. I would travel to New York with 200 kilos, where I would deliver [the merchandise]. [Back then] a kilo of cocaine would cost in Colombia $400,000 pesos and in Miami US$ 40,000. . . . In Queens, I got involved more with "the people from Cali," and in the mid-80s, I was already working on my own. They were the ones who ran the business. I went from *rumba* to *rumba* [party to party] with my salsa friends. There were many salsa clubs in Queens. There I saw Willie Colón and Larry Harlow, Conjunto Clásico, Sonora Ponceña, Héctor Lavoe. . . . Most were on Roosevelt Avenue. The businessman Ralph Mercado also would show up there. . . . Everyone *embalaba* [snort cocaine] in the discotheques, but it was not well seen for traffickers to bring in the *perico*. . . . In the middle of everything, the salsa and the rumba were like an escape valve for us. I really liked to dance a lot because since I was little, I always wanted to be a dancer. . . . Queens was full of Colombians, especially Paisas [from Medellín and surrounding region] and Caleños. We Caleños went to the salsa discos and the Paisas went to their businesses. . . . There were also many Puerto Ricans and Dominicans; some worked for the Colombians. Back then people said that for every Colombian family that lived in New York, at least one of its members was linked to drug trafficking.[21]

Liza ended her story but later continued, "When the bonanza was going so well, I would invite my friends and paid the bills in the nightclubs. Once, I bought a coat that cost me 10,000 dollars and a jacket for 5,000 dollars." When referring to her tastes and consumption patterns, Liza stated,

> I always bought music; I collected approximately 5000 LPs. I bought them in a store in La Marqueta and also from OMZ, who was the *discómano* [DJ] of Espumas Club and owner of Z Records. One day, I paid $500 for an LP of salsa that I did not have.[22]

Later, Liza was jailed twice for drug trafficking. In 2020, she died of cancer in Miami.

On my part, when walking the streets and visiting some Colombian families in Queens in 1991 and the following years, I was able to observe that in different ways, all businesses, legal or not, had been inscribed in this "criollo" cultural environment where festive trajectories, gastronomic traditions, and other idiosyncratic traits were intermixed. This is indicated by a chronicle published in the *New York Times* on June 1, 1983, that talked about the Cali Viejo II Restaurant:

> It's 6 o'clock on a cool night and Jackson Heights is electric. Along Roosevelt Avenue, under the shadows of the elevated tracks of the train, the end of another school and workday in Queens is celebrated with a characteristic Latin impetus. Salsa music seems to come out in cascades from each entrance of the stores, and half a dozen adolescents with their characteristic *tumbao*, infected by the rhythm as they pass, begin to wiggle their body and move their limbs with great ease. A moment later, they calmly continue their walk toward the *bailadero* [dance club] on the sidewalk in front of the next venue. In Cali Viejo, a Colombian restaurant the size of a Volkswagen van, diners begin to arrive early, some of them attracted by the powerful smell of onions, garlic, and fried ripe plantains, which circulate at the entrance door and form a human barrier on 73rd Street. In an apartment several blocks away, TM Caicedo is cooking a beef tail in a large pot and chopping cilantro while preparing a traditional Colombian soup called sancocho.[23]

In addition to the *sancocho*, two characteristic elements of the popular culture of Cali stand out in this description—dance and the taste for salsa music, which young people used to take over a New York street, as if they were in their neighborhood of origin. Through them and their families, *Cali popular* extended to Queens.

Despite its plebeian origin, the Cali Cartel consolidated itself as a large transnational company with all its ramifications, precisely because it rested on the rails of a hegemonic culture and its rationality, which was based on strategic planning, calculation, ambition, labor exploitation, and profitability, combining legal and illegal activities and implementing different forms of social transgression that targeted accumulation as a strategic goal. However, at the same time, its leaders and most important members, as well as most of its subordinates, preserved features of the working-class culture from which they came and to which they belonged, since it was here that they had learned and developed the cunning of illegality. Long criminal records, including convictions in different prisons, enriched the experience of such transgression as a systematic behavior. However, it was the convergence and intersection between these two worlds—with their respective logics—that made it possible for Cali Cartel members to reach their destinations. As Gilberto Rodríguez Orejuela wrote in a letter to his grandchildren, "I am a rebel by conviction, a merchant and a businessman by vocation, and I was a drug trafficker by ambition; I am proud of my first two conditions and absolutely ashamed of my last condition."[24] His attachment to *Cali popular* and his criminal record were as important as his business vision to create an industry and control a large part of the global cocaine market. However, this was not only a product of violence and chance, as is to be expected. They created the cartel and dominated the New York market by confronting the governments of Colombia and the United States (which they bribed with their narco dollars) and while waging a war against Pablo Escobar. Thus, in addition to violence and bribery, they took advantage of their economic power, their financial and administrative knowledge, their technological ability and the structure of the social relationships they created with political and business leaders, police and military authorities, bankers and the media, legal institutions, musicians, soccer players, and ordinary people with whom they expanded the social base as necessary for the cartel's legitimation and enclosure. Simultaneously, the members of the cartel increased existing corruption to climb social hierarchies and manage a power parallel to that of the country's political power. Accordingly, they were able to develop their mafia enterprise, permeating all strata of Colombian society until they were taken to prison for the last time.

Without the rational logic of the capitalist economy that they had implemented, they would have been no more than a short-range criminal organization, like so many others. Moreover, without the cultural capital that included the cunning, learning—legal and illegal—and practices derived from social transgression as a matrix for what they had learned in the slums of *Cali popular*, such mafia entrepreneurship would not have prospered. They progressed while being trapped in structural ambiguity, by leading a public life as "good people" and projecting the image of successful entrepreneurs while their private life, shared with partners and friends, was marked by plebeian behaviors ranging from their experiences in prison to the settling the scores and other criminal procedures when necessary. The transactions between these two parallel modes of existence were inherent to the dynamics of their entrepreneurship, to "pretend the virtues and hide the vices," as a way of keeping the tension between the plebeian culture which they came from and the business culture in which they had enrolled.

The parallel occurrence of migration, the production of salsa music, and the growth of the cocaine drug industry determined the two-way connection between Cali and New York. As the Puerto Rican composer and singer

Raúl Marrero asked himself in one of his songs, "And how do they do it? I don't know. What is the business? You know. And how do they do it?"[25] These questions challenged his listeners, motivating a possible conversation and answer. According to the ethnomusicologist Christopher Washburne,

> The relationship between salsa and cocaine was facilitated in part by the synchronous appearance of this style of music and the drug industry. . . . Its first formal appearance in the United States [was] in 1972. This, of course, coincided with a vibrant period for salsa.[26]

However, this coincidence that historically came about by chance, strengthened both industries to the extent that thousands of Colombian immigrants in New York played a role as laborers in drug trafficking and to expand both the market and the consumption of salsa music. Based on sociodemographic data documented by different sources, Washburne estimates that by 1979, "Approximately 200,000 Colombians had settled in New York, the majority in the District of Queens. These new immigrants, who came mostly from the lowest economic sectors of society, constituted in large part the workforce necessary to manage the complexities of drug distribution networks (while significantly increasing the audience for local salsa)."[27] On the other hand, in her characterization of Colombian immigrants, Elsa Chaney states,

> Typically, the new immigrant creates a residual population with low training and working in low-paying jobs that cannot be automated—such as restaurant or construction workers, porters and guards, parking lot workers, baggage loaders, clandestine taxi drivers (those who drive without an official license from the city taxi commission), and some other similar jobs. Performing tasks that others disdain, the new immigrant performs very necessary and useful tasks that nevertheless provide him with little remuneration and little prestige or recognition.[28]

Under these conditions, it was possible for many immigrants to end up being linked to drug trafficking networks, as my sources have admitted, whose social profiles coincide with what Chaney described. Some even told me stories about how their activities in the service under the capos of Cali are mixed with their work as administrators of salsa clubs or establishments where drug trafficking and prostitution converged. This is what CHJ testified when he told me, "In addition to being in the 'business,' I managed, 'El Chorrito Musical,' a bar owned by O.O in Roosevelt [Avenue] and 69 in New York, I also worked in 'The Executive,' where there were women [prostitution] and the [drugs] arrived."[29] PCO, another of our interviewees who arrived in the United States in 1968, became involved in

198 Alejandro Ulloa Sanmiguel

trafficking and spent 20 years in prison for drug trafficking in that country. Regarding his activities, he said:

> We were in "El Calvario," a cemetery in Queens; we brought flowers as if we were visiting the deceased and we hid the merchandise. We gathered 15 or 20 kilos and negotiated quickly. Then, we would go to party at Aretama, a disco owned by another Caleño. . . . Our business colleagues sponsored salsa dance competitions in some places. Even CTCL, who was a great dancer and recognized in Cali, used to organize the competitions with several friends before going to New York. We would all go there to party and to see the dancers.[30]

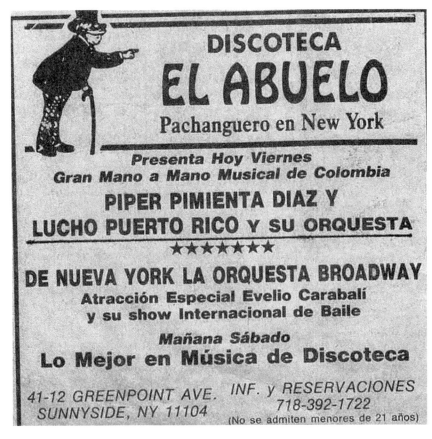

Figure 9.1 Flyer announcing a Cali salsa show at El Abuelo, nightclub located in Sunnyside, Queens, NYC. No date.

Source: Author's personal archive.

However, in Queens, there were also many professionals, university students, and legally established merchants, as shown by the studies of Ramiro Cardona and Silvia Rubiano de Velásquez, and other researchers.[31] According to Chaney,

> It is of note that Jackson Heights is a place of attraction for Colombians because there they find their culture and would stay there for some time, according to the "experts" ["informants"], even if their economic situation allowed them to move [to a different neighborhood].[32]

Here, Chaney refers to a commercial epicenter in that neighborhood known as "Chapinerito," which she describes as

> an inventory of businesses, restaurants and other agencies of Colombian interest in Chapinerito (for example, travel agencies that offered one-way or roundtrip excursions to Colombia for vacations, bookstores that sold Colombian magazines and newspapers, or record stores specializing in Colombian music) as well as a chain of regional clubs. . . . Moreover, Chapinerito is the place where Colombian food is offered as well as the ingredients to prepare it. On 83rd and Roosevelt Streets, you can find six Colombian restaurants, each one specializing in the cuisine of a different region of Colombia.[33]

Larry Landa, Narco Businessman in the Salsa Industry

Research studies on drug trafficking usually mention the trajectory of the most recognized drug lords, but they do not usually refer to Larry Landa, someone very important for the subject matter of our investigation, although he did not become a drug lord, as Lise Waxer argues in her research on Cali.[34] Landa was captured with drugs in Miami and died in a U.S. prison in 1984. His "stage name" was Larry Landa (also known as Lalá), and I have reconstructed his profile using different descriptions from 25 sources who knew him directly as friends or worked with him or for him. Due to his performance as a businessman and producer of salsa shows, he went head-to-head with his peers in a space that was as competitive as that of salsa in the capital of the world. He excelled in his activities, which in addition to the "big business," included tours, concerts, recordings, as well as music producer, as evidenced on several LPs where his name appears. Moving between the licit and the illicit, Larry Landa, a Caleño with working-class roots, salsero, and immigrant to New York and Miami, became a successful narco businessman with the ability and sufficient capital to articulate other actors in the United States. He became the most notable business leader in the entertainment industry in Cali between

1975 and 1983, along with the most important producers in New York, Jerry Masucci and Ralph Mercado, who also had problems with the U.S. authorities for their links with the mafia and the commercialization of narcotics in their clubs and discotheques. As Washburne states in his analysis as an insider:

> Jerry Masucci of Fania Records and Ralph Mercado—who before directing the RMM record company was the largest booking agent/manager/promoter of concerts in New York—coordinated the reservations for many salsa concerts during the 1970s and 1980s (both worked in close collaboration with Larry Landa, a reservation agent who often served as a liaison). Both Masucci and Mercado established relationships with drug trafficking organizations to organize tours. On the other hand, this symbiotic relationship between the salsa business and drug trafficking organizations was not limited to the borders in Colombia but extended to cities in the United States. . . . Throughout the 1970s and 1980s in New York, they opened many salsa clubs that served as money laundering fronts, where the proceeds of drug trafficking were channeled through the legal commercial transactions of the club.[35]

Larry Landa, along with his partners in New York and Cali, formed the Latin connection at a time when being a front man was not yet a crime in Colombia, and the domain extinction laws and Colombian Law 30 of 1986 on narcotics did not yet exist. With his companies, Productores Asociados in Cali and Latinoamerican Representations in New York, he acquired the power and prestige necessary to put Cali on the international map of salsa music, although salsa had not been born in this city, which was circumscribed as only a recipient of this music genre. As a mafia entrepreneur, he transformed the salsa scene in Cali; first, in 1976, he brought the first salsa orchestra from New York to the Feria de Cali, the city's carnival that takes place every December since 1958. Landa thus became the bridge that linked the salsa industry in New York and Cali with the cocaine drug industry. The Colombian composer Jairo Varela, director of Grupo Niche, alludes to this relationship in one of his songs:

> In New York City, something is contaminated; in the entire neighborhood, in all of Queens, people are complaining, "Bring Raphy Mercado, who lives calling the firefighters. Bring Raphy Mercado, who he lives dialing 911. . . ." It was on the corner of Roosevelt with 82. Could it be that in all of New York there is not a drop of? To calm the desire for, from Manhattan to the Bronx. Hey, what about the *jíbaro* [drug dealer]? The jíbaro missed the corner.[36]

Figure 9.2 Flyer announcing a Larry Landa Show with salsa orchestras from NYC and Cali at a nightclub located on the highway that connects Cali with the Pacific Coast, circa 1978.

Source: Author's personal archive.

Via Landa's management as a businessman, Cali became a producer and exporter of salsa music and not just of cocaine. In 1978, he brought to New York the first Cali—and Colombian—salsa orchestra (Fórmula 8 with singer Piper "Pimienta" Díaz) and a few dancers. He presented them in the clubs for his members in New York, thus inaugurating another path of the two-way connection (later, he took the group Fruko y Sus Tesos from Medellín to Madison Square Garden). In addition to hiring musicians in both cities, Landa linked them with small non-mafia entrepreneurs in Cali whom he placed at his service, some of whom were salsa radio programmers at local stations (such as Grupo Radial in Colombia, owned by the Rodríguez Orejuela brothers). He promoted his shows through the radio and the Cali press that "supported" him with publicity and the dissemination of his business and musical projects, for example, the inauguration of his Juan Pachanga Disco Club and the creation of the Juanchito Carnival. In both spaces, he presented local and foreign artists. Through his two companies, he hired 20 salsa groups from New York and Puerto Rico, which came to Cali between 1976 and 1983, including Fania

All-Stars in 1980. In this way, the cocaine industry stimulated the recording production of salsa and the promotion of shows with salsa musicians and orchestras, as well as the addiction of many artists and their followers to psychoactive substances. Under his auspices, Cali's image as the world capital of salsa was intensified while drug trafficking exacerbated corruption and increased violence.

Conclusion

Based on the empirical findings and the analysis and interpretation of the data, the relationship between drug trafficking and salsa at different points of the Latin connection materialized in several ways. It occurred through the patronage of some drug traffickers who sponsored musicians to form a music group, record an album, or finance a trip, which generated legitimacy in the salsa medium and a bit more than a "thank you" from the artists. They did not, however, become drug traffickers because of this. It also took place through the hiring of orchestras or private musicians accompanied by a music group for narcos' private parties or in their discotheques in Cali and New York, as well as in New Jersey, Miami, Los Angeles, and other cities. Likewise, this connection was consolidated because drug traffickers, as clients of clubs and discotheques in these and other cities, filled these establishments, paying high prices to see salsa orchestras and freely spending large amounts of money on the consumption of liquor and narcotics—elements inherent to the environment of the type of party they liked. The same happened in *casetas* [itinerant stages] during the Feria de Cali, at least since 1976, when producer/narco/businessman Larry Landa established the Toro Sentao caseta and presented the Conjunto Cachana with Joe Quijano and guest vocalist "Chivirico" Dávila, brought from New York. From that date on, the permanent hiring of such orchestras occurred at different times of the year, in the last quarter of the twentieth century, under the direct or indirect patronage of various members of the Cali and north of Valle del Cauca cartels.

The purchase of records for their discotheques or their private collections was another important mechanism with which the narcos contributed to the commercialization of salsa and the development of the industry and the market for this music. The large collections seen by the author in the aforementioned cities are just an indication, considering that such records were also bought as gifts for family, friends, radio stations, or even to sell them and thus take advantage of this business opportunity, in times of an economic emergency, as it actually happened. The purchase of these records not only boosted their commercialization but also the salsa entertainment industry, rendering it a sphere of production and consumption that encompassed multiple activities in which other social agents participated. This does not mean, however, that all the large acetate and vinyl collections of this music are owned by drug traffickers or were bought only with drug money. The relationship between drug trafficking, salsa, and migration has been represented in the lyrics of songs, composed by different authors in Cali, New York, and Puerto Rico. I collected a corpus of 50 songs that show different aspects of this relationship and analyze them in the book *La salsa en tiempos de nieve* that I published in 2020. Similarly, this phenomenon has been represented through graphic design, photography, and iconographic illustration on album covers, which I have also used as sources of information in my analysis. These forms of representation are a complementary product of the relationship between salsa and drug trafficking that express the equation under study.

Another link between drug trafficking, salsa, and migration that this chapter does not address, but that I develop in depth in my forthcoming book, is the issue of drug abuse and addiction, which led many salsa musicians to health and rehabilitation centers, as has been publicly recognized by different national and foreign artists.[37] Others died due to this cause. Additionally, several of them have been indicted or imprisoned for possession of narcotics or drug trafficking, as have several producers and composers linked to the salsa entertainment industry in the United States.

In sum, the Cali-New York two-way connection expresses other modes of insertion of Colombia in the globalized world, and what this insertion means in both the modernization of the country and the transformation of the Colombian state and its institutions, which have been eroded by narco dollars. Via the symbiosis between transnational migrations, drug trafficking, and the salsa industry, one can look at the processes of globalization from a different perspective, one in which the country is configured by rotating around an orbit through the accumulation of licit and illicit capital.

Notes

1 This chapter is derived from a broader investigation published in the book *La salsa en tiempos de nieve: La conexión latina Cali-Nueva York, 1975–2000* (Cali: Universidad del Valle, 2020). In this chapter—the result of new research developments—I follow some approaches from this earlier work, but I also deploy other arguments and propose new conclusions by presenting unpublished data and novel testimonies. This book is a product of the Salsa Barrio Cultura research program (phases I, II, and III), funded by the Universidad del Valle between 2012 and 2018, which I lead within the Palo de Mango group (urban musical cultures of the Afro-Latin diaspora), and which is part of the university's School of Social Communication. In addition to published books and articles, the digital platform Salsabarriocultura.univalle.edu.co was created as a result of this program.

2 *La salsa en tiempos de nieve*, I discuss the methodological aspects related to the use of songs as an object of analysis: Can lyrics be taken as valid sources

of information? Do they have the same value as what a journalist for *The New York Times* documents, for example? Or as historical or judicial archives? How can they be used for ethnographic and anthropological research? What are other legitimate sources, and how does one address them? Ulloa, *La salsa en tiempos de nieve*.
3 Édgar Vásquez, "Los Caleños, por qué somos así," *Revista Cali-Artes* 1 (1983): 4.
4 Alejandro Ulloa, *La salsa en Cali* (Cali: Editorial Universidad del Valle, 1992), 262.
5 See Alejandro Ulloa, *Salsa, drogadicción y oralidad en la narrativa de Andrés Caicedo: Un estudio sobre la transgresión social en la novela ¡Qué Viva la música!* (Popayán: Editorial Universidad del Cauca, 2022); Andrés Caicedo Estela, *¡Que viva la música!* (Bogotá: Grupo Editorial Norma, 2001).
6 In the late 1970s, Miguel Rodríguez Orejuela became the main shareholder of the Soccer Club América de Cali, and he remained so until he was arrested by the authorities in 1995. Soccer was another of his front businesses, behind drug trafficking. Thanks also to his passion for this sport, the love for his team, and the sense of belonging to the city that welcomed him, he led the América league, which became one of the most important teams in the continent. See: William Rodríguez Abadía, *No elegí ser el hijo del cartel* (Madrid: Ediciones Temas de Hoy, 2015) and Camilo Chaparro, *Historia del Cartel de Cali* (Bogotá: Intermedio Editores, 2005).
7 TRL, personal communication with author, Cali, 2017.
8 TRL, personal communication.
9 Ramiro Cardona, and Sara Rubiano de Velásquez, eds., *El éxodo de colombianos: Un estudio de la corriente migratoria de los Estados Unidos y un intento para propiciar el retorno* (Bogotá: Ediciones Tercer Mundo, 1980); Elsa M. Chaney, "América Latina en los Estados Unidos. Colombianos en Nueva York," in *El éxodo de colombianos: Un estudio de la corriente migratoria de los Estados Unidos y un intento para propiciar el retorno*, eds. Ramiro Cardona Gutiérrez and Sara Rubiano de Velásquez (Bogotá: Tercer Mundo, 1980); Eduardo Sáenz Rovner, "La participación de los cubanos, los colombianos y los chilenos en las redes del narcotráfico en Nueva York durante los años sesenta," *Innovar* 17, no. 30 (2007): 133–144; Eduardo Sáenz Rovner "Entre Carlos Lehder y los vaqueros de la cocaína: La consolidación de las redes de narcotraficantes colombianos en Miami en los años 70," *Cuadernos de Economía* 30, no. 54 (2011): 105–26; William Mejía, "Casi dos siglos de migración colombiana a Estados Unidos," *Papeles de Población* 24, no. 98 (2018): 65–101.
10 David Harvey, *El enigma del capital y las crisis del capitalismo* (Madrid: Ediciones Akal, 2012), 17.
11 Cardona and Rubiano de Velásquez, *El éxodo de los colombianos*, 58, 50.
12 Sáenz Rovner, "Entre Carlos Lehder y los vaqueros de la cocaína," 10.
13 José Gregorio Pérez, *Operación Cali Pachanguero* (Bogotá: Editorial Planeta, 2005), 15.
14 Pérez, *Operación Cali Pachanguero*, 15.
15 Rodríguez Abadía, *No elegí ser el hijo del cartel*, 35–36.
16 Rodríguez Abadía, *No elegí ser el hijo del cartel*, 37.
17 Rodríguez Abadía, *No elegí ser el hijo del cartel*, 37–38.
18 Harvey, *El enigma del capital*, 42–43.
19 Pérez, *Operación Cali Pachanguero*, 15–16.
20 Julio Sánchez Cristo, *Óscar Naranjo: El General de las mil batallas* (Bogotá: Editorial Planeta, 2017), 68.

21 Liza, personal communications, 2015, 2017.
22 Liza, personal communications.
23 Bryan Miller, "In Queens, a Medley of Latin Flavors," *The New York Times*, June 1, 1983, C1. Translation by Juan P. Jiménez y A. Ulloa.
24 *Semana*, "Una carta a sus nietos, la última comunicación de Gilberto Rodríguez Orejuela con su familia en Colombia," June 6, 2022. www.semana.com/nacion/articulo/una-carta-a-sus-nietos-la-ultima-comunicacion-de-gilberto-rodriguez-orejuela-con-su-familia-en-colombia/202255/.
25 Raúl Marrero, *El señor de la salsa*, Sello Salson 07(1431) 00006, LP, Álbum, Colombia, 1987.
26 Christopher Washburne, "Salsa y drogas en Nueva York: Estética, prácticas performativas, políticas gubernamentales y tráfico ilegal de drogas," in *Cocinando suave: Ensayos de salsa en Puerto Rico*, ed. César Colón Montijo (Caracas: Ediciones Callejón, 2016), 77. The date of 1972 is questioned by Saenz Rovner in his article "Entre Carlos Lehder y los vaqueros de la cocaína."
27 Washburne, "Salsa y drogas en Nueva York," 78. The figure of the 200,000 Colombians in New York—"the majority in Queens"—in that year, does not coincide with the figures provided by Mejía ("Casi dos siglos"), who suggests there were 150,000 in the United States by 1980. The figures vary according to the sources because of the difficulties in obtaining accurate information—even more so when registering "illegals." In any case, they all suggest that a considerable number of Colombians settled there. The truth is that "Jackson Heights in Queens became a favorite place of Colombian immigrants from 'low social strata' in the sixties," according to Eduardo Sáenz Rovner, "La participación," 137.
28 Chaney, "América Latina en los Estados Unidos," 228.
29 CHJ, personal communications, 2022.
30 PCO, personal communication, 2021.
31 Cardona and Rubiano de Velásquez, *El éxodo de los colombianos*.
32 Chaney, "América Latina en los Estados Unidos," 218.
33 Chaney, "América Latina en los Estados Unidos," 218.
34 Lise Waxer, *The City of Musical Memory: Salsa, Records Grooves, and Popular Culture in Cali, Colombia* (Middletown: Wesleyan University Press, 2002).
35 Washburne, "Salsa y Drogas en Nueva York," 83–84.
36 Jairo Varela, "No muero mañana," in *Señales de Humo* by Grupo Niche, CD, recorded at Estudios Niche, Cali: Sony Music Colombia, 1998. Varela was imprisoned in Cali in 1995 on charges of illicit enrichment and money laundering in the service of one of the cartel's kingpins. He was released in 1996, but in 1997, he was arrested again. In 1999, he was definitively released.
37 Ulloa, *Música salsa, drogadicción y oralidad en la narrativa de Andrés Caicedo*.

10 Mona®co

Conversations on Narco-Phenomena and Contemporary Art in Colombia

Santiago Rueda and Harold Ortiz

There are countless studies on Colombia's armed conflict, its history and evolution, its connection with the drug business, including recent developments such as the peace negotiations between the national government and the Revolutionary Armed Forces of Colombia, FARC, that took place in Havana, Cuba, between 2012 and 2016. However, the cultural, aesthetic, and artistic dimensions that have accompanied the emergence, consolidation, and persistence of the drug-producing and trafficking business in the country have not been sufficiently studied. This chapter reclaims these dimensions of what we call the *narco phenomena*—that goes beyond criminal acts to include a wide diversity of cultural manifestations in art, architecture, fashion, music, and behavior—using oral histories as methodologies and patching the voices of several cultural figures who are active in various territories.

The idea was born in 2019, after the authors of this chapter coordinated a collective exhibition for a research project on the aesthetics of illicit substances in Colombia inside an iconic hotel in downtown Medellín. Built in the 1940s and considered a symbol of the coffee and textile industries of the twentieth century, the Nutibara Hotel became the temporary headquarters of *A Line of Dust: Art and Drugs*, an exhibition curated by Santiago Rueda, which had previously toured throughout Latin America, from 2011 to 2018. The curatorship was invited as part of an initiative entitled *Welcome to Discomfort*, created by Harold Ortiz, artist, cultural manager, and coauthor of this chapter. *A Line of Dust: Art and Drugs* addressed issues of sacred and ancestral plants, the use and abuse of illicit substances, the (im)possible legalization of these substances, the urban transformations resulting from underground economies, and violence in drug-producing territories, among others. The same year, Ortiz received an invitation to reflect on the implosion of the Monaco building, the residence of drug lord Pablo Escobar and his family and symbol of his illegal empire in Medellín, which was imploded by orders of the municipal government to put an end to one of the hot spots of drug tourism, a flourishing industry at the time.

DOI: 10.4324/9781003048152-14

Ortiz, supported by the program "Medellín abraza su historia" (Medellín Embraces its History), created by administration, and with the support of the Museo de la Casa de la Memoria, decided to interview artists and use these conversations as a tool to bring back memories and reflections on Medellín's painful drug era. Ortiz accompanied Rueda during different versions of his *A Line of Dust: Art and Drugs* exhibit, which took place (with different names) in Bogotá, Pereira, and Cali. In those cities, Ortiz and Rueda started to make recordings of dialogues with local characters involved in the exhibition, in a free and spontaneous way, regardless of their ethnic origin, profession, age, or level of education. They captured the voices of artists and other people active in anthropology, journalism, education, human rights, cinema, music, and social leadership in indigenous communities. The set of voices reflected territorial and cultural diversity. Amid the energy of the moment, various topics arose, ranging from political humor and censorship to the impact of drug money on the art market, as well as the myth of Escobar, the narco aesthetic promoted by big media, the criminal underworld and its direct relationship with financial speculation, the differences between coca and cocaine for indigenous people, and the defense of indigenous territories against new transnational cartels.

A summary of these conversations, including more than eighty works of art, was recently published as *Mona®co* (ConTension Editorial, 2022), a title that plays with the name of the building, the term *narco*, and the trademark symbol to denote that this is also a history of neoliberal capitalism. In this chapter, only a few of these conversations are included. This short version does not attempt to give a complete vision of the effects of the narco phenomena but rather to offer a multiplicity of voices reflecting on impacts and legacies. It is a portrait of a very precise moment in time, just before the social demonstrations that began in November 2019. The thoughts expressed through these voices, the weaving of interpretations that build threads through closeness and friendship, and the desire to transmit those unique moments are essentially what we have tried to achieve in the following pages.

Bogotá, Principality of Monaco

Conventions:

H.: Harold Ortiz
S. R.: Santiago Rueda
O. R.: Omar Rincón
Ch.: Chócolo, alias of Harold Trujillo
B. J.: Benjamín Jacanamijoy

The first conversation takes place in Bogotá, with the participation of Chócolo, a cartoonist with more than 20 years of experience in major Colombian newspapers. He engages in conversation with Omar Rincón, renowned researcher, journalist, and media analyst, and Benjamín Jacanamijoy, an Inga indigenous artist from Putumayo, who knows the secrets of healing plants like ayahuasca (*Banisteriopsis caapi*) and *andaki borrachero* (drunken binge tree, *Brugmansia arborea*).

H.: We are going to have a conversation about the Monaco building, the tension caused by its recent implosion in Medellín, an attempt to "turn the page"—a popular phrase in Medellín—that seems to avoid wanting to understand the drug phenomenon. The people in Medellín stopped talking about Escobar for a couple of decades, but recently a Netflix series appeared and created a fictional story, which, no matter how extraordinary might be, does not come close to reality. The phenomenon of narco TV series has brought thousands of tourists from different parts of the world to the city, trying to find a rational explanation, or not, to the myth of Escobar and the narco phenomenon. In response, the local government tried to create a different history about the city, to erase the symbolism of Escobar in a series of actions that led to the demolition of Monaco. The detonation literally cleaned the dust from this conversation.

S. R.: An article in *El Espectador* [2019] joked about this being the "second bombing" of the building. The first one was on January 13, 1988, when Escobar's enemies attacked the building with 30–50 tons of TNT. The explosion opened the door to Pablo Escobar's art collection, an Ali Baba cave full of treasures. The press wondered whether all the cars and motorcycles that Escobar had in the parking lot were more valuable than his art, pre-Columbian ceramics, and Chinese jars collection. Shall we start there?

O. R.: Monaco seems a great place to start. Monaco is the place where no taxes are paid, where those with illegal fortunes live, where the world's royalty go. The name Monaco is total narco, total capitalism, the kingdom of the self, without the presence of the state but with money. We go from the "Principality of Monaco" to the "Principality of Pablo," a great metaphor. That show they put on [to demolish the building], the national joy through the sanitization of memory, the attempt to erase Pablo became the construction of a new national myth and the reaffirmation that we are drug traffickers. In Medellín, the park that was built after the disappearance of Monaco, is already being called "Pablo Escobar Park." The lesson is that things are not physically erased; they are transformed by a catharsis of reality. One can try to kill the symbol but that does not make the symbol die, and Pablo is a symbol, a myth, a legend, and a fiction. They want to kill the metaphor, and metaphors cannot be killed. And the Monaco building was and is a metaphor for Medellín. The daily life in Medellín is full of Pablo. The tours, the museums, the myths of Pablo keep going. The neighborhood that he built changed its name but is still called "Pablo Escobar's neighborhood."

H.: Victoria Henao, Escobar's wife, reconstructed the Monaco building's history in her autobiography. She married very young, when she was around fifteen years old. Not knowing what to do with her life, she travels to Europe to understand what high culture is like, and where it comes from, and is surprised by Monaco. She returns from Europe and finds out that Escobar had bought a building near the Club Campestre, right next to elite territory, and she decides to live there. This is like becoming Antioquia elite's neighbor, and art is her entrance ticket, as she starts buying art, guided by gallery owners and art dealers.

O. R.: Colombia is a society without symbols. But people create them because the elite has not been able to generate a national narrative, because they want to live in Miami. The people, the working class, need symbols to recognize and imagine themselves. We are a society without national symbols or rituals, and this is due to being a country that is governed by the right, whose only narrative is God, family, and property. And that is the brilliance of the narco, that in order to exist, it creates symbols. The Monaco building was just that, a symbol about how success has been achieved. With its destruction, a greater myth is born: The Monaco building becomes a story imagined by the taxi driver, by the head of tourism, by everyone. Before it was an ugly building, now it is a void to be filled with fantasies. It became a denser symbol. Next time you take a tour, you will say, "This is where Pablo Escobar's bunker was." Then, you imagine a building like the Trump tower, with the word "Escobar" in front of it, and you can say that it had a swimming pool on the top floor, and that it had a psychedelic disco. Everyone can expand that myth. In five years, that mental building will be more important than the physical building, which was in decline, had nothing of narco; it was gray, ugly, badly inhabited. That ruin lacked narco; it lacked neon; it lacked strength. Now it has all the magic of the narco. The Monaco was destroyed, but the oral and symbolic myths that were created are unstoppable. It has been a popular narrative and a work of a genius to knock down that building, which rather than closing a door on the past that wants to be forgotten, it opened an infinite machine of stories where everything

210 Santiago Rueda and Harold Ortiz

is possible. We are now narcos. And we must take advantage of the cultural legacy that the narco left behind for us to exploit it culturally and touristically. It is an opportunity to achieve a catharsis from the acts of brutality in order to move on to the future.

H.: If the absurd represents the narco, the exploration of humor then becomes necessary. Humor as a space that opens a universe of possibilities for self-criticism, and that teaches us to laugh at ourselves, despite the acts of brutality. Chócolo can tell us about how cartoons changed before and after drug trafficking. What happened there? What was a cartoonist like before and after Pablo?

Ch.: The cartoonist is a designer of memories, of the national reality and its setting. I belong to the generation that grew up during the '80s. I began to give my opinion and draw it on paper when Pablo exploded into the scene, in its literal sense.

H.: Could we then say that a completely different topic of conversation exploded into the world of humor and caricature?

Ch.: Yes, literally speaking. . . . He contributed a lot to the country's literature of comedy by popularizing his product and making us important on the global scene. It helped because drug trafficking—sociologists and historians say—permeated politics in Colombia,

Figure 10.1 *Funerales vs. fiestas* (funerals vs. parties): "Narcotrafficking is about creating funerals here to recreating parties over there." Author: Chócolo, published in *El Espectador*, circa 2000. Courtesy of the artist.

although several cartoonists think otherwise. Rather, it was politics that infiltrated drug trafficking. It exploded in themes, and its disastrous effects spread everywhere to create a *traqueta* [drug trafficking] culture that touched cartoonists too. As a folkloric fact, Escobar loved caricatures, he liked humor. I don't think he threatened any cartoonist, any artist; politicians did so later, in lurid events even against comedians, as it happened to Jaime Garzón.

S. R.: *Pablo Escobar en caricaturas* [Pablo Escobar in cartoons] was a book with scarce circulation, merely fifty copies were made. Escobar edits it while in the La Catedral prison, which he built for himself, and sends the book to certain political figures. Escobar was drawn extensively, especially after he escaped from La Catedral. Osuna drew ex-president Gaviria—this caricature was made after Escobar's escape from La Catedral—in shorts, as a small kid—his ministers were called "Gaviria's kindergarten"—showing an empty small bird cage in his hand to the Church patriarch García Herreros, the only one who Escobar surrendered to, and saying: "The little bird escaped." And the priest answers, "Because it's a good and a bad little bird."

H.: The book has a leather cover and a title in gold dust letters, and the autograph and fingerprint of the *Capo di cappi*. Inside the phrases: "This book was finished on June 2, 1992" and "Reproduction and sale prohibited," are, if not a death sentence, perhaps a warning. The book itself is not only a collection of caricatures. The object itself is an important part of our narco culture. Edited and published by Escobar to his liking, while in prison, it is a defeat of the judicial system and of institutionalism; it is a triumph of the Mafia over the state.

Ch.: I am not in that book because I grew up in Medellín in a neighborhood of bandits and to protect my life, I preferred not to touch that subject. When I arrived in Bogotá and started drawing for *El Tiempo* in 1992, Pablo was already in a cage, then he was free, on the run. Knowing how these things were handled in the neighborhoods of Medellín, I preferred not to comment. In any case, I had other themes to explore, political violence against union workers was the usual one. I have never seen the book, but I do believe that not only Pablo but also his entire entourage loved to be talked about. The ego was very high. I think it had to do with the money exchange rate at the time. Underneath Pablo's naivete, his disastrous personality turned Colombian society to shit—that is how youth and women were treated, turned everything to shit—he knew about the power of caricature and the power of humor, and he certainly understood them. I would have liked to draw him at a book fair and talk to him. Despite being a brute, with a lot of power and an iron fist—because you either had to be on his side or dead, like the politicians of today—I would have liked to meet him because there is a lot of strength and a lot of emotions there, a lot of script to draw from.

S. R.: We are talking about the past, the drug trafficking of the past: Escobar, the Monaco building. And yet we are exporting more cocaine than ever. The number of hectares planted with coca today, 200,000, is twice the maximum figure of the past. We are living in a narco empire that is hard to measure, thinking that this is in the past, that it only exists on Netflix and drug tourism. Where is that power now? How does it work? Who is exporting? Where is the profit, where is the laundering? Who and where are the owners of the business? We are mythologizing a past, but we cannot see the present.

Ch.: A few years ago, I drew a cartoon to represent what our country means to the United States. I don't remember who coined that phrase that Latin America is the backyard of the U.S., well, I accepted it and drew from it and wrote, "Violence remains the same or worse, but we are no longer the backyard of the United States, we are now its kitchen [*cocina* or illegal drug lab]." The price of cocaine continues to rise and is listed on the world's underground stock exchanges. Cocaine is becoming more and more expensive on the streets of New York and Europe, and we continue to produce it, we continue to be at the vanguard, we continue to be the best, the *jíbaros* [street slang for drug dealers] of the planet.

H.: This could be a good opportunity to introduce Benjamín Jacanamijoy, an artist from Putumayo, who is going to help us understand the connection between this conflictive universe in contrast to the universe of creation, of the earth, and of sacred plants.

B. J.: We, the Ingas and the communities of the Amazon, do not consider drugs as such. The Ingas belong to the culture of *yagé* [a variation of ayahuasca]. I am not speaking as a shaman, I am speaking as a member of a culture that is governed by its thinking, and above all, by thinking beautifully and *buen vivir* [living in harmony]. My parents, grandparents, and uncles practiced knowledge learned from yagé. From generation to generation and through oral tradition there has been this knowledge. Yagé is a leaf and a vine that is cooked near a waterhole or spring. Yagé or *yagecito*, as we call it with love, is emetic, a purgative. It cleanses the body and the spirit to remove the shit from the body and spirit, people say. Additionally, there are other plants that are called *binanes*, *chundures*, and *angiyos*. Binanes revive the spirit; the chundure is the root of

	knowledge; and the angiyos are plants for love or beautiful thinking. These plants come together, are intertwined to reanimate people's spirit, so they can feel happy and can go home peacefully.
S. R.:	We have been summoned by the Monaco building. We do not know if memory is under attack or if a new memory is being created; it is a question mark. We have talked about what it means, and we want to know what you think.
B. J.:	I heard you talking when I arrived, and it brought back a memory about those kinds of places. For the Ingas and other indigenous communities, the territory is made up of many places. Places of thought and orphan places, places of love, places of knowledge. Talking about this one day, I said: "What would be a heavy place?" And someone said, "Congress." I was remembering that, about how heavy or orphan places are dangerous, where you shouldn't walk at six in the morning or at twelve at night, because you can get sick. It is a sickness known among the communities as "bad air" or "bad wind." Imagine the territory, the forces of the territory. Those are the most privileged places, chosen by the *taitas* [elders in positions of political or spiritual authority] to sow those plants I was telling you about: Binanes, chundures. They even do science there by sowing plants and taking them from the paramo, from the jungle and trying to grow them there. I imagine that everything that happened with Monaco must have been like a plant that grows, dies, and grows again. That is what we call growing with another way of thinking or with another breath of the heart. Different people arrive, and they are going to make something new grow. Those are heavy places, but it depends on the breath of people's hearts. Bad places to live do not exist, what exists are bad people living in specific places.
S. R.:	What do you think, Benjamín, about how we have forbidden plants, how we sprayed and persecute plants?
B. J.:	Just like I told you about the places, there are no bad plants. What happens is that knowledge, the breath, as we say among the Ingas, does not understand their essence. And by not understanding their essence, you are harming yourself. There is a tree called *andaki borrachero* that works really well for sickness like stress. You can eat one leaf for one day, or three days, or five days, or seven days, always on odd days. But people say it's so good that you can say: I want another, and another. Because that is how humans are: They learn about something that is like knowledge, and they want more, they are eager for something, and they even don't know why in the end. Some people think that yagé is toxic and people wonder: How does a taita know? But it is not something that it has been done for twenty years, it has been done for more than a thousand years.

Figure 10.2 Colombialand, guerrilla fighter with a bouquet of poppies. Author: Nadín Ospina, 2005. Polyester resin, 70 × 100 × 60 cm. Courtesy of the artist.

Cali, *Minga*

Conventions:

H: Harold Ortiz
S. R.: Santiago Rueda
E. Q.: Edinson Quiñones
T. L.: Taita Lorenzo Tunobalá
M. K.: Governor Mauricio Kuchimba

The second conversation took place in Cali but has to do with the neighboring Cauca Region, the ancestral territories of various indigenous peoples where the population has suffered intensely different conflicts. Native populations have been hostages of illegal armed groups that struggle to control illegal crops, the drug processing and transportation on those territories, in addition to their criminalization by the state. Mauricio Kuchimba, a member of the Nasa people, an artist and former governor of Tierradentro, participates in this conversation with Lorenzo Tunobalá, a traditional and ancient medicine man, member of the Misak nation, and Edinson Quiñones, an artist who has worked using coca, cocaine, explosives, bullets, and human remains in his performances.

S. R.: We are going to start a dialogue with Taita Lorenzo Tunobalá, Mauricio Kuchimba, and Edinson Quiñones. The first two are representatives of the ancestral communities Misak and Nasa of Cauca. We are very interested to know what happens in Cauca. We've had the privilege of Edinson's presence in the last five or six years in the art world; he has brought us quite close to Cauca, as a performance artist and curator. Beyond drugs, we would like to talk about medicinal and sacred plants, as well as about the armed conflict that is still present there. Edinson, please give us an overview of the current situation.

E. Q.: We are here with two partners. One comes from the Pubenense Valley, Lorenzo Tunobalá. He has accompanied us in several processes related to spirituality, related to [ancestral] medicine. He is the one who helps us to harmonize spaces and artworks. Being a traditional doctor, I would like Lorenzo to talk about medicine, plants, and the coca leaf. And later, since we are brothers, ask Master Mauricio Kuchimba, governor of Cohetando, a Nasa indigenous reservation, to speak.

L. T.: My name is Lorenzo Tunobalá. I am from the Misak people and a traditional doctor, through dreams, plants, the paramo (highland moor), and the lagoons in the central mountain ranges of the world. We have been accompanying the process woven by comrade Edinson. When we say weaving, for our people it means weaving history, weaving and reviving the history that we, as indigenous peoples, have walked. When we talk about resistance, when we talk about the armed conflict, we do it from our homes; it is what we must do and what we must build. And when we talk about territory, we talk about spirituality. What we call the spiritual and the way we handle it, people in the West could call it art. For us, medicine is an art and is part of the culture of our people. Together with the Nasa people, we use the coca leaf, *mambeamos* [using *mambe*, coca leaf medicine for rituals], we use tobacco, and we know how to handle plants from the paramo. That is why when there are meetings, assemblies, or mobilizations, the elders tell us:

First, the medicine, and for us it is important in all stages of the process to use medicine and harmonize the territory and harmonize the house, harmonize what we are going to talk about. That is part of our culture and our worldview. There are different processes in the department of Cauca. With agriculture, we can say, "No to drug trafficking"; with art, we can say, "No to drug trafficking." The biggest problem, our elders have said, is leaving the "self" behind, only wanting the "self." The elders tell us that it must be about "us," where we all fit. That is the great task that we have been called to, the one that we assume with the Nasa nation, with the brother and sister peoples we share our existence with.

E. Q.: Master Governor Mauricio Kuchimba of the Nasa people is a great friend, a sensitive artist, he lives and works from the heart. He has a beautiful artistic process and different projects in his territory. He has a project with weapons that the town council and the *guardia indígena* [indigenous guard, unarmed security force] seize, destroy, and he decides to give them a new meaning.

M. K.: To speak of Cauca is to speak of an artistic environment, its lines, mountains and textures, its rivers, its native peoples. Unfortunately, it is one of the departments where the greatest social conflicts and violence have taken place, precisely because it is beautiful. For years we have been working on processes that have greater depths, connotations and readings that have yet to be discovered in the course of time, understood as past, present, and future. Faced with the situation we are experiencing, a friend said, "You go out *en masse* to claim for your rights." That mass is called *minga*, but minga must also be art, and I want to recognize the work that Edinson has done, because he gives a new meaning to the minga and puts it in the context of art. For us it is wonderful, a paradox: "An art piece that has the power of dissemination based on current events [that affect us all], can also be like a mass of people." It's good to do this type of metaphorical, aesthetic work. Truly political art that we can understand and reflect on. That's where we must work on and explore. To use metaphors for the state of violence to create awareness—that is a remedy, a remedy that heals the soul and cures the thought. Today, we are still looking for the end of that thread that unraveled at the time of the conquest and that we have been unable to put together again, that immense *jigra* [Nasa knitting with symbolic meanings] where we all fit. The idea is to reeducate ourselves and reconnect with our roots. We are merely talking about giving a new definition to our origins, where we come from . . . that is a beautiful story with a very long staircase, I would say.

S. R.: Cauca is a department where the drug problem has deep roots. Coca and marijuana plantations multiply there, and the government seems incapable of reducing them and solving the social issues generated by the illicit trade of substances. Since the drug problem revolves around plants, we want to know how you see coca, what it means for ancestral communities.

M. K.: Coca is a plant of feminine origin, for some feminine and masculine, but it is our people's worldview. The female plant is the one we use to do all the harmonization work, and there is the male coca, which is not used to practice medicine. Coca has been an energy enhancer, it has been and continues to be food for the indigenous people; and coca is also the little key we use to open the door to knowledge, to "open portals," to understand and raise awareness of the other world. The Nasa people always talk about three worlds: the world above, the world in the middle, and the world below. Chewing coca is to know those three spaces. Moreover, there is also a very beautiful connotation, the child coca, which is the plant's *cogollito* [little heart or seedling]; there is the teenager coca, the sweet fifteen coca, the little miss that is the immature plant; and the woman coca that one harvested for all type of work. Today, there is no respect for any of that. Everything is taken, the little miss coca leaf and the child coca leaf are scraped and violated with an open hand. The knowledge to exercise the *mambeo* or to chew the plant has been forgotten. For some it is the curse that was uncovered, the profanation, the looting, all those evils that came out and transformed it. And when they transform it, they blame the Indian. They do not realize that the blame is on those who transformed it, not whoever planted it, not whoever had it and used it for spiritual reasons. Coca has always been one of the most important spiritual and material foods of the indigenous peoples, not only for the Nasa. My Misak friend will have another perspective from his own spiritual understanding. That does not mean that coca is a problem for the indigenous peoples, no. It is a remedy, and it is the little key that opens the door to knowledge.

S. R.: Some people think that the solution to drug trafficking is legalization. Not only the legalization of marijuana but also of cocaine. We would like to know what you think of that and of the possibility that coca can be accessed without being punished.

L. T.: For us it is legal because those are plants. The Western world is the one that has a hard time understanding that. The one who sows the plant is not guilty. Those of us who are in the territory are not guilty. Guilty are those who have been making cocaine for 110 years. For us it is a sacred plant, we have always used it, we have always *mambeado*, it is part of our spirituality and legalization belongs to the state, not to us. The Nasa people are having a hard time, and the Misak people are not. I'll tell you why. Drug trafficking began in the '80s and '90s, my town was a garden of opium, which is the poppy. It was a garden. But what did the authorities in my territory say? The authorities appointed by the people said: "The Misak people are not going to accept that. That is a medicinal plant, we are not going to accept drug trafficking," and they did not allow it. Sure, a slaughter came between us, but it led us to reflect and conclude yes, we can end this. We are never going to eradicate it because it is a medicinal plant, but drug trafficking has been eradicated. Legalization belongs to the state, to understand things; we already understood ours, and now it is the responsibility of the state and its leaders. That's how it is for us.

M. K.: Drug shipments pass through the territories, but the police are not stopping them, even on the main roads. It's illogical. Who is buying it? Who really owns the business? The small consumer does not have the capacity to buy the tons of product that comes out. It is the direct responsibility of the state, which must create a social policy. The problem with the crops is that there's no equity and people are going to look for ways to earn their pesos, and if they have an income that meets their needs, then they'll do it, and they are going to support crime. But if there were equity, people would not opt for that illicit economic rent. There's a problem of conscience, but of social conscience.

E. G.: As a minga of thought, for example, in the workshops in Corinto [a town at the heart of the marijuana and coca producing areas in Cauca], we discussed chapter four of the peace agreement with FARC [Revolutionary Armed Forces of Colombia]. A chapter about drugs. Peasants told us that the government has not complied. The government promised subsidies, roads, and many types of aid that were never delivered. So, they said: How are we going to support our families? It's more expensive to live in Bolívar, Cauca, which is very far away, and one must carry a bundle of tangerines uphill to town to sell it. It is more expensive for us to transport it than to let it go to waste. We do not have anything else to survive, we have no option but to sow [coca]. If the Peace Agreements were signed, then, they must comply. There are places in Colombia that have been completely abandoned by the state, and then conflicts generated by their policies begin over land or plants.

S. R.: A few years ago [2013], in the Proartes art space here in Cali, Edinson performed a piece called *Between Dust and Skin*. He placed a big glass over a naked woman and made drawings with cocaine. It was a provocative gesture that bordered on the illegal. A reference to the nude on classical art, to Marcel Duchamp, to art history, but also a crude act that broke a taboo, the public appearance of cocaine in cultural spaces, as a work of art. As an artist with a long career working with the leaf, with the plant and with the alkaloid: what difference is there? What should we think of one or the other?

E. Q.: At first it was very natural for me to look at the process and the transformation of the coca leaf into an alkaloid; it was also very natural for me to see sowing from the seed. I come from two completely different backgrounds: from my father's side, from the coca boom in Bolívar, Cauca, one of the first coca base laboratories; and my indigenous mother is the spiritual side that lives within in the leaf. I grew up with those two worlds. I worked in a cocaine laboratory, understood all the processes and the alchemy of making the material. I tried both and both are like love: A mother's love and a whore's love. That is my relationship with the plant and with cocaine. Cocaine gives you a little bit of that love; it gives you an

Figure 10.3 A ToN oF coke, NFT collection of 1,000 one-kilo crypto-cocaine packages. Author: Camilo Restrepo, 2021. Courtesy of the artist.

instant comfort, right? And the other is uncomfortable, and what is uncomfortable costs money. . . . We don't have the notion of *mambear* [to chew the coca leaf], we want everything quickly. I classify it within these two notions. On a personal level, a mother's love, and then, that love that comes from a totally artificial thing. I wanted to break those myths. I simply broke myths to show that the state has shown us a false reality. I had to compare it, I had to understand it. And well, I'm more on the spiritual side, but I'm interested in understanding both worlds, both sides. I must understand it and live it to be able to communicate. I know it's negative, but negative generates something positive.

Medellín, Million-Dollar Apartments

Conventions:

H: Harold Ortiz
S. R.: Santiago Rueda
V. M.: Víctor Muñoz
J. A. Z.: Jorge Alonso Zapata
C. U.: Carlos Uribe

The last conversation, which took place in Medellín, where the project Mona®co started, was held on November 2019, after the recording sessions in Bogotá, Cali, and Pereira. Carlos Uribe participates in this conversation as an artist and curator for the Museum of Antioquia. Víctor Muñoz, an artist and curator, joined the session with Jorge Alonso Zapata, a self-taught artist who works in a poverty-stricken neighborhood that is considered dangerous.

H.: In this last session we return to Medellín, and by returning here we can give an account of what has happened this past year. We feel that the approach of the narco from Medellín speaks from the past, from elements and symbols embedded in our collective memory of the past. Today, the figures and data speak of the highest rate of cocaine exports in decades. Medellín is a city that by virtue of tourism allows and encourages consumption. Fortunately, today these issues are being conscientiously taken up again through projects such as those carried out by the Museo de Antioquia and the Museo Casa de la Memoria.

S. R.: It seems good to me to close the sessions where everything begins. It is a pleasure that Víctor [Muñoz], Carlos [Uribe], Jorge [Zapata] are here because it gives us the opportunity to delve into the city that has the most to say on the subject, that has the longest history, and that every one of you, as artists, have elaborated on in your work. Carlos, you were one of the first artists to work with Escobar's image, a figure difficult to deal with and a tragic symbol of Medellín. You were censored, and many people do not know what happened or have not heard you talk about it. Let's talk about how it was to expose Escobar in front of the building of the Centro Colombo Americano. What was it like to alter the image of the most famous painting of Antioquia's history?

C. U.: *Horizontes* [1999] is an appropriation of Francisco Antonio Cano's painting by the same name [1913]. Through digital alteration, I incorporated the issue of illicit crops to the painting, with a plane spraying glyphosate on a crop, to set it apart it from the picturesque and contemplative landscape of the original piece. In 2010 the Colombo Americano, through Juan Alberto Gaviria, invited artists, including myself, to create artwork about the bicentennial. He offered me the outside of the building that overlooks Maracaibo Street, a wide wall, eight meters long by four meters high. I began to work on a saga of *Horizontes*. A friend called me and said: "Have you seen the photo of Pablo Escobar mounted on his Jeep? It's just like the character in your painting." I started researching and found the book *La parábola de Pablo* by Alonso Salazar and in it, a very small photo. I kept digging through the archives; I didn't know whose photograph it was, and it didn't have the format for a mural. I wanted a digital print with direct applications on the wall, and from a Discovery Channel documentary we managed to download a better-quality image. In any case, *New Horizons* was made as a comment on the rise of drug trafficking. I didn't even gauge the consequences; it seemed very natural to me. The surprise came on the day of the inauguration when I was very happy, and they were very upset. They asked me to dismantle it, and I said no; they had invited me, and I was doing what was requested of me. Three days later, they dismantled it. I believe it is a vetoed theme of conversation in Medellín; it is an issue that has not been talked about enough. It is a silenced topic, nobody wants to talk about him, neither at home, nor among friends, the academy does not work on the issue either. It has been twenty-five years, more or less, since Pablo's death, and forty years of drug trafficking history. Part of it was activated a bit with "Medellín embraces its history." It activated the academic, artistic, and journalistic fields and showed that it is time for deeper work; it is time to make this conversation public, so that we can exorcise this narco mystery, so that the new generations can understand what the city really experienced.

The city has undergone positive transformations; it emerged from an abyss and from being a forbidden city. There was a social pact and alternatives for the future between businessmen, the state, academia, and civil society organizations. The cultural organizations in the neighborhoods helped a lot to get out of this impasse. But the theme is critical and necessary, especially in this city where it remained completely hidden.

V. M.: There is something related to "Pablocentrism" that is complex. Because when people talk about the narco is only the image, and how the image of Escobar is everywhere, even on t-shirts. I mean, yes, it is terrible, but I don't see it that way either, it doesn't seem like a loss of values. What about people who weren't born back then or who weren't affected? Pablo represents something important, his

Figure 10.4 Horizontes (Horizons). Digital print on canvas, 100 × 200 cm. Author: Carlos Uribe, 1999.

image. His condition and what he dynamized is something else, but from art we take care of dynamizing relationships, and that is what matters: to de-stipulate the stories of sin, the sinfulness associated with drug trafficking. This society must talk about drug trafficking, it is very important and necessary, and if artists tackle the issue and it becomes narco art, that is fine. They don't do it to put labels, but to talk out loud and create connections between those things and important and reflective aesthetic dimensions.

S. R.: Does the narco genre exist in the visual arts? People who visit exhibits like *A Line of Dust* for the first time say: "This is like a style, a movement. . . .. Is this just Colombian? Or does it occur in other countries?" And I usually say, no, artists like Carlos, Jorge Alonso, Víctor, Harold, are not defined by narco aesthetics or illicit substances.

V. M.: A narco aesthetic or narco art would be wonderful. Narco art is what the drug traffickers bought to hang in their homes. It would be wonderful to know what they bought, how they bought it, where they hung it, how they hung it, which artists they worked with. The narco is not an issue, is a condition, a condition that is entrenched in us. Meaning, it would be very nice if there was narco art. There is no incendiary way to provoke it. Narco crosses all scales of society, so an aestheticization or precariousness ends up being a euphemism, because the narco aesthetic is as precarious as it is sophisticated. And it would seem very interesting to me to be able to reveal those specters from each social class that take on their roles, co-responsible with and appropriating the narco. There are narcos with spectacular taste [laughs], with collections and the whole thing. So a "narco art" with a different sense is wonderful, one that distances itself but emanates into a narco art.

J. A. Z.: I am going to speak from my personal experience and what I have experienced with my artistic work, which has been a late vocation. From a young age I was permeated by the drug phenomenon. I lived on the Caribbean coast and the marijuana boom touched me. I toured the Sierra Nevada de Santa Marta and learned about deforestation to grow marijuana, and I also had to see when people began to grow coca and the environment permeated by drug trafficking at all levels. In Colombia almost all of us are or have someone very close to us who has been affected by drug trafficking or drug violence. We either have a family member or friend who is addicted to drugs, or we have a family member or friend who has been a victim to drug violence. Drug trafficking has dominated Colombian culture in the last 30 or 40 years. I made this decision to dedicate myself to tell stories through painting in Medellín, because the streets are where the phenomenon of micro trafficking is so palpable and evident in popular culture. It's an employment alternative for people who arrive by forced displacement, or by this new phenomenon of displacement of Venezuelans who add people to the long lines of unemployment. Drug trafficking becomes a source of employment, as dealers, as reducers [reducing the quality of drugs to double or triple the quantity], it generates dynamics in the informal economy of the city's downtown. Also, I see and paint human trafficking, child prostitution, hired killers, the strengthening of this paramilitary phenomenon within the city. There is the unknown for us as a society: How are we going to face this problem that is becoming much stronger? These people have been taking over downtown's real estate, spawned a number of extremely profitable businesses, developing a strong economy. We don't know what is stronger in Colombia, whether the formal economies or the informal economies that generate an impressive amount of employment and move so much money around. We really do not know how to deal with it.

S. R.: We are looking at one of your works now, a painting of disturbed intimacy and where each little scene is tragicomic: a clown sitting down smoking a joint; a man without legs and with only one arm hitting another; a man with a jacket bumping into another one who has a knife; a couple, the man is injecting himself, and the woman is walking down the street with a groceries bag. . . . There are many questions that come to mind with a painting like that.

J. A. Z.: The people who come to the city, who don't have a job, who arrive displaced, don't know how this city devours them, how to manage in it. The first job they get is as a drug dealer in a plaza where vice is everywhere, and with that money they manage to survive and generate their family's economy. But they live in an apartment complex where the Christian [preacher], the transvestite, and the prostitute also live. There is no employment for young people, but there is employment for them to work as drug dealers in a plaza. So, look at the dissonances. They say that crime doesn't pay, but when you're out of work, with no chances at all, it turns out you can work on vice plaza, distributing [drugs]. It became a duty to start telling these stories because nobody wanted to tell them. I live with these situations all the time, and I see the consumption phenomena twenty-four hours a day. A profitable and efficient market, the supply is there all the time. The police operatives arrive and ten minutes later, the business is up again and everyone already providing services; it is very efficient. What can I say? The images overflow, and it is impossible to be indifferent to all this.

I can't dedicate myself to paint flowers and cows. I want people to have a dialogue with these stories and, in one way or another, for this to become public and become a part of the public.

H.: Roberto Saviano writes in *Gomorrah*: "The centers of the world's financial power has been kept afloat with money from cocaine." It is an established, open subject matter, but here in Colombia is not "politically correct" to say those kinds of things. On a recent trip to Italy people asked me: "Is there a narco aesthetic in Medellín? What is the contemporary narco aesthetic?" And it made me think: Are we living so deeply in the narco aesthetic that perhaps we don't realize that the city itself is a narco aesthetic?

V. M.: I was up there in Envigado [a municipality in Medellín metropolitan area that used to be Pablo Escobar's stronghold] and saw a billboard that said: "Last apartments. One million dollars. On sale." And I was literally stunned. There is a lot of money here, right? But I said, "Fuck, to put it on a billboard!" How many executives do we have in Medellín who can buy million-dollar apartments? Who or which foreign capital or foreign investors? That seems very strange to me. But we are so involved that it seems wonderful to be able to talk about a public billboard that makes it explicit that, yes, a million dollars is a lot of money, and yes, these are the last ones left and are in promotion, because the other fifty have already been sold. It's a dynamic of latent drug trafficking, and so present and evident that they can put it on a billboard. That figure of a million dollars is like that historical picture of gangsters who would frame "my first million dollars." That's part of our present more than ever. For me, that's the current narco aesthetic today. The billboard is publicity, but it is also public policy, it is public as opposed to the invisibility of the drug trafficker. The narco aesthetic is current, it regenerates and reformulates itself and becomes publicity. But if we look at the other side, the image I'm left with is those boys standing on the corner, selling drugs, the eternal boys on the corner, standing twenty-four hours on a corner, moving the substance around but always in the same place, always there, with loud music, taking shifts.

Participants

Harold Ortiz: Artist, caricaturist, and curator. Creator and director of the *Timebag* project, exhibited in the United States and Colombia. He is currently a curator associated with *Memorias (il)lícitas*. His works and projects have been invited to different national and international exhibitions.

Santiago Rueda: Researcher, curator, and art and photography historian. Author of *Plata y plomo. Una historia del arte y las sustancias (i)lícitas en Colombia* (Silver and lead. A history of art and (il)licit substances in Colombia), among other books on Colombian art and photography. He has curated exhibitions about drugs, the environment, and the armed conflict in Colombia that have been exhibited in Argentina, Brazil, Bolivia, Colombia, the United States, Ecuador, Mexico, Spain, and Uruguay.

Omar Rincón: Associate professor at the Universidad de los Andes in Bogotá, and director of the Center for Studies in Journalism and the Master's Program in Journalism at the same university. He researches, rehearses, and writes about media cultures and entertainment aesthetics. He is director of the *Fesmedia* project of the Friedrich Ebert Foundation.

Chócolo—Harold Trujillo: Winner of the Simón Bolívar National Award for humor (2019), he has been a cartoonist for *El Espectador* for the past twenty years. He has participated in different national and international exhibitions.

Benjamín Jacanamijoy: Artist from the Inga community of Putumayo. He studied at the Universidad Nacional and is the author of the book *Chumbe arte Inga*.

Edinson Quiñones: Artist and cultural promoter. Founder of the *Popayork* project, he has been invited to participate in exhibitions in Norway, Germany, Spain, Mexico, Brazil, and Bolivia. He led the MINGA Regional Artists Salon, a project where former members of the FARC collaborated and that dealt with issues of ancestry, indigenous legacy, and mining.

Taita Lorenzo Tunobalá: Traditional doctor of the Misak community, Cauca. He worked together with Edinson Quiñones in the MINGA Regional Artists Salon (2018–2019).

Mauricio Kuchimba: Former Nasa governor of the Tierradentro reservation; he is an artist and a ceramist.

Víctor Muñoz: Artist and cultural manager based in Medellín. He has collaborated on several projects at the Museum Casa de la Memoria in Medellín. He has been a curator for several projects in Taller Siete, Casa Tres Patios, among others.

Jorge Alonso Zapata: Self-taught artist. His works are part of the Museum of Antioquia's permanent collection, where he has participated in the "La consentida" wing.

Carlos Uribe: Artist and historian. He is currently chief curator of the Museum of Antioquia in Medellín. He has been a jury for different national awards and curator of various exhibitions. Advisory member of the procurement board of Banco de la República.

Part 4
Watching the Media

11 The Accidental Persona
The Media and Pablo Escobar

Catalina Uribe Rincón

Pablo Escobar is not only part of Colombia's cruel past but also of its very difficult present. Escobar was one of the first major modern drug traffickers and the leader of the Medellín Cartel. He was responsible for more than 4,000 deaths. He had an incalculable fortune and appeared for seven consecutive years on the *Forbes* magazine's list of the ten richest men on earth. A fortune that he used to instill terror and corruption. Furthermore, a quarter century after his death, and despite his brutal and painful legacy, the capo seems more alive than ever. Items related to the kingpin of cocaine are produced on a massive scale, including films, biographies, tourist souvenirs, t-shirts, dolls, and Halloween costumes.[1] Some actual geographical spaces that bear the drug lord's mark attract millions of tourists and locals every year. Why? Why is his persona not completely censured? The short answer: Because his public persona was more morally ambiguous and layered than, most likely, the actual individual. It is Escobar, the persona not the person, that got entangled with some features of Colombian national identities; that is, with our self-understanding, and with the understanding others have of us.

What we know today about Escobar is in great part the result of a story that has been continuously reshaped by literature, art, and popular culture. The print media, however, were some of the first to put their ink to the service of the character. In this chapter, I discuss some aspects of the relationship between the drug kingpin and the print media. In particular, I examine how the interdependent relationship between public figures and the media creates, in its very practice, an "accidental" persona. That is, a persona, a character, that acquires a life of its own, in the absence of any preconceived plan or strategy, and once it is "alive," so to speak, acquires its own inertia. That is not to say that the different actors do not have an input. Pablo Escobar was self-absorbed. His egocentric personality reflected his will to use certain rhetorical strategies for crafting his public image. It was also well-known that Escobar and the Extraditables group were branding experts and had their own marketing and publicity strategies, which not

DOI: 10.4324/9781003048152-16

only included pamphlets that they distributed among the Colombian population but also terrorist actions intended to be replicated by the media.[2] The Medellín Cartel, as Alexander Fattal puts it, trafficked not only with cocaine but with televised horror images, corpses of notorious people, and dramatic press releases.[3]

The Colombian print media were key in helping Escobar cement his image. Before Escobar and the Extraditables made a conscious and systematic effort to control the narrative, Colombian media had partially, if unknowingly, cleared the path and prepared the ground for them. The print media constructed the character of Escobar, first through the framework of Robin Hood and then through the rhetoric of the narco, in a way that I call the accidental persona. Rhetorical and media scholars have widely discussed the concept of persona and have usually referred to it as something constructed by a speaker or writer on the individual's own behalf. Escobar's case, however, offers a clear example of how the media and the character of a public figure become interdependent and build a character in an unintentional manner, basically as they go along trying to figure out in real time what was going on. Again, this does not mean that Escobar did not have any input in the construction of the image. Nevertheless, I want to emphasize how there is an aspect of the communication that is accidental; that media and journalistic routines were essential in setting the ground for Escobar to build his "terrorist publicity agency."

To demonstrate these claims, I examine how four Colombian print publications, *El Espectador*, *El Tiempo*, *Semana*, and *El Colombiano*, covered the rise of Escobar as a drug lord. I focus only on print media because they were some of the most assiduous ones to report on Escobar and to denounce his nexus with drug trafficking and the mafia. Beginning in the 1970s and during the 1980s, the Colombian press stood out for exercising denouncing journalism. Several national and regional newspapers developed investigative journalism units that culminated in important denunciations against corruption, large oligopolies, and drug trafficking.[4] *El Espectador*, for example, was the first newspaper to report about Escobar and drug trafficking when he was still an unknown felon. Years later, when Escobar began to participate in politics, this newspaper published a piece that brought up the old article about Escobar's earlier conduct. Years before Escobar killed Guillermo Cano, *El Espectador*'s editor, Cano created a section in the newspaper called "Libreta de apuntes" ("Notebook") in which he denounced Escobar's activities and the relationship between drug trafficking and politicians. Cano accused politicians like Alberto Santofimio for having alliances with drug traffickers and for receiving money from the drug business.[5] In 1987, Fabio Castillo, a journalist from *El Espectador*, published a thorough investigation on the history of drug trafficking in Colombia. Consequently, Castillo received death threats and had to go into exile.

Despite low development and circulation, print media in Colombia were key for constructing Escobar's accidental persona.[6] Investigative journalism, which actively denunciates, evinces the spontaneity of the accidental persona by inadvertently reinforcing certain narratives around a public character. Escobar's case is especial because he was a public figure who, due to his outlaw status, had to hide from the public eye for most of his life. Escobar only had direct access to the public during 1982 and 1983 when he campaigned and was elected to Congress; after that, he spent most of the time hiding from authorities. The constructing of his persona felt largely into the hands of the people, and their imaginations, and, more systematically, into the hands of the media. In the following sections, I examine how the construction of Escobar's character through the print media moved between two rhetorical categories: first, the introductory and tangential category of Robin Hood and, second, the foundational category of the narco.

The Robin Hood

In April 1983, about a year after Pablo Escobar was elected alternate member of the House of Representatives, *Semana* magazine published a special issue with a focus on extradition. The cover read: "Extradition of Colombians: The Order of the Day?" In the inner pages, one could find an entire special report on the debate. With titles like "Extradition of Colombians, Unbelievable Case," "Colombia, Do Not Give Away Your Children: Let's Reject Extradition," "We Are Confusing State with Government," articles discussed why extradition should be spurned. The articles showed that in the 1980s when the Colombian Penal Code was modified, the United States was granted permission by the Colombian Congress to extradite Colombian citizens. Lawyers and politicians explained through *Semana*'s pages why the treaty was or was not biased, and whether it went against Colombia's Constitution or not. Among those articles was a peculiar one about a recent forum on extradition. The event, according to *Semana*, was presided over by the priest Elías Lopera, vice president of the Colombian Ecclesiastic Tribunal, and took place in one of the most luxurious nightclubs in Medellín, and hosted around 500 people. Among its important guests, one could find Pablo Escobar and Humberto Barrera Domínguez, ex-magistrate from the Colombian Supreme Court. The article quoted one of the assistants saying that "the problem is that 'gringos' are upset because we are bringing back the money that they took." When the forum addressed the topic about those whom the U.S. government was calling "cocaine cowboys," Escobar intervened: "It is false that Colombians are more dangerous than Sicilians. The United States is the one who has big problems. We are not poisoning chocolate bars in Halloween candy or Tylenol, as it occurs there."⁷ The ex-magistrate Barrera Domínguez pointed out that extradition not only affects drug traffickers but any Colombian who has committed the felonies that the extradition treaty considers. To this, he added: "If this goes on, Colombians are going to have to ask for asylum in Colombia." Moreover, Félix Vega Pérez, a senator for the department of Magdalena, said: "Gringos praise ratting on people while we Colombians despise that. Soon the United States will become the empire of snitches." Fabio Mejía, a law professor, said that extradition was against human rights because in Colombia life in prison and the death penalty do not exist. "Colombia would be giving up its citizens for another country to kill them." The forum was called by the assistants "an appointment with the nation."⁸

However, the irony in this situation comes not only from the fact that the magazine was giving voice regarding extradition to one who later would become the biggest drug trafficker, but also from the fact that in that same issue an article "Un Robin Hood paisa," a complimentary profile of Pablo Escobar, was published. The Robin Hood article has become iconic because it evinces how clueless some media were about who Escobar was and who he was to become. It also praised someone who had already started to trick the country with his underground businesses. But most important, it started the narrative about the Robin Hood *paisa* [from Medellín and surrounding region], the charming man who was helping the poor.

The Robin Hood paisa article introduced the capo as a savior. The publication opens describing the municipal landfill in Medellín, where 2,500 families have improvised their houses next to waste and foul smells. It narrates how people fight with rats, chickens, and stray dogs for food. After describing a Dantesque scenario, it narrates in a descriptive movie-style tone how people act when Escobar arrives in the neighborhood. The capo gets out of his Havana Renault 18, while the kids run toward him to say hi and hug him. They call him "don Pablo" as a sign of respect, while they praise and thank him for previous favors.⁹ Then the text raises the question that would give the nickname to the capo: "Who is don Pablo, the Robin Hood paisa, that elicits so much excitement and gives hope to these miserable people? A situation very hard to explain, taking into account how sordid the environment is." The article spends many paragraphs describing Escobar's wealth, by stating that the thirty-three-year-old "businessman" has already become one of the richest men on earth. It describes some of the most ostentatious properties, including the Hacienda Nápoles—a land then valued at $6,000 million pesos—around 200 apartments in the United States, ten airplanes and half a dozen helicopters, and a personal zoo with animals imported from Africa. When asked about the origin of his fortune, says the article, Escobar replied that he had a merchant vocation: "When

I was very young, I began a bicycles business, I then worked for the lottery, I then bought and sold vehicles, and now I work in land and real estate."[10]

But what is most striking is how after showing Escobar's enormous fortune, the article comments on Escobar's humility. It narrates how, despite a few extravagances like a watch with diamonds, his personal appearance and personality were surprisingly simple. Escobar, adds the article, preferred to spend his wealth in civic and political causes, while he advanced a program to build one thousand houses in a gigantic lot. Escobar bought the lot in order to build a neighborhood to transfer hundreds of families living in the slum area of Medellín. Escobar even employed some of the future beneficiaries in his construction company, the article stated.[11] The Robin Hood paisa article emphasizes the misery of the people and the magnanimous heart of Escobar and concludes that no other politician had provided this kind of financial support for civic work. People who knew him or received aid from him corroborated *Semana*'s version of Escobar. Some of them manifested the love they felt for the capo and the gratefulness for the wealth they received.[12] Joe Toft, former chief of the Colombia office of the U.S. DEA, referred to Escobar as a Santa Claus and asserted that the capo gave hope to those who did not have any.[13]

Throughout 1982 and 1983, the years of Escobar's short life in politics, the capo constructed his Robin Hood personality with the aid of the media. When asked in an interview what he thought about the fame of Robin Hood that he was earning, he responded with the leisurely speech that characterized him: "This is a very interesting qualifier because indeed he fought for and came out in defense of the popular classes."[14] As we later learned, throughout these years, Escobar had already begun his illicit activities, but *Semana*'s article evinces that not many people were aware of them. Colombians knew little about his business, and those who knew did not care. Poor people in some of Medellín's neighborhoods knew him not only because of the economic help he was providing for their families but also because he was making their lives happier, by constructing soccer fields and contributing to popular sports in general. Some video and audio reports that circulated in Antioquia's local TV and radio stations show how the drug lord inaugurated soccer fields in pompous events. At the inauguration of two soccer fields—one in Envigado's Flores neighborhood and the other in Medellín's Tejelo neighborhood—one could see people happy and cheering for Escobar.[15] The Colombian journalist Germán Castro Caycedo narrates one of these ceremonies as follows: "It must have been seven thousand people, the soccer field was dark, Escobar arrives [the field illuminates], he greets everyone, and people began crying 'Pablo, Pablo, Pablo.'"[16] According to witnesses, it was common for Escobar to intervene in these events to thank people, praise construction workers, and tacitly promote himself as a politician.

After Escobar's debut in the media, people began to wonder about his fortune. Other media outlets were not as benevolent as *Semana*. On August 22, 1983, the U.S. television network ABC broadcast a special about the "cocaine cartel" in its program *Close Up*. The show described the cartel as a group of "false social champions and heirs of the traditional American mafia." *El Espectador* wrote a note about the ABC program and how it described Colombian drug traffickers. Traffickers, according to the publication, seemed to be social champions earning their local power by building apparent social programs for poor citizens, and by bribing politicians. There was a focus on Escobar, a 33-year-old Colombian whose fortune reached two billion U.S. dollars. It described Escobar as "a typical Latin American with a dense mustache" and narrated how he was always surrounded by orphaned poor street kids. Escobar, concluded the note, wanted to help poor people after overcoming poverty himself.[17] Three days later, Guillermo Cano, *El Espectador*'s editor, published an article reminding readers that despite Escobar's constant denial of illicit activities, he had already been in jail for drug trafficking.[18] The article titled "In 1976 Escobar Was in Jail" republished Escobar's first appearance in the media. It reminded readers that the drug lord was busted with thirty-nine pounds of cocaine in Itagüí, a town in Antioquia. These publications, and many others denouncing Escobar, provoked the capo's rage, who in 1986 ordered to kill Cano. Some media praised Escobar, other accused him, but many referred to his social work, for good or ill. The *Semana* article set the precedent for other media to continue referring to Escobar as a Robin Hood, and the message has clearly resonated until today. Even in 1989, the *Sunday Times* of London published the article "Cocaine Baron Revered by Poor as Robin Hood." The publication, translated into Spanish and printed in *El Espectador*, talked about the capo's huge fortune, his involvement in drug trafficking, and his passing through politics as a benefactor of the poor. "He became Medellín's largest benefactor, building floodlights at soccer fields, as well as financing the construction of roller-skating rinks and 1,000 low-income houses," asserts the article.[19]

The category of Robin Hood introduced by the media set up the foundations for how the public assessed Pablo Escobar's significance. This mediating moral category set the ground for people tacitly interpreting and assimilating his illegal activities. The Robin Hood category took most of the moral weight away from the capo's character and prepared Colombian and international audiences for the category of the narco that was about to emerge. Without knowing it and perhaps because they had other investigative priorities, journalists defined Escobar in completely opposite terms to his criminal personality. For example, some of Escobar's images that appeared in the newspapers analyzed in this study situate Escobar in a sportive or familial atmosphere. They are relevant because they put him in

Figure 11.1 "His cup is now filled" read the caption of the photo of Pablo Escobar at an auto racing cup in Medellín.
Source: *El Espectador*, October 30, 1983.

a mundane environment but also show his power. One of the first images circulated in 1983 shows the drug baron dressed in car racing overalls holding a trophy in his hands.[20] This image is correlated with a later image of Escobar on a soccer field performing the ceremonial first kick. The latter shows a smiling Escobar wearing a striped polo, looking at the ball, while soccer players stand in line staring at him with a respectful attitude.[21] Another picture of Escobar attending a soccer game of Atlético Nacional, one of Medellín's teams, shows him relaxing on the platform next to Jhon Jairo Velásquez Vásquez, known as Popeye, one of the most terrifying hitmen in Colombian history.[22]

These pictures also evince ironic situations if analyzed next to their captions or the text that accompanies them. As Cara Finnegan points out, it is important to consider the hybrid nature of images and texts. Most images created for public purposes should be studied in terms of their "external dialogue" with their time in relation to visual culture and circulation.[23] Images purport to depict Escobar in mundane activities, but the captions show the perversity of what was happening in the drug war and in Colombian politics. Captions invite audiences to think about Escobar as an everyday man but also as a powerful one. The title accompanying the image with the trophy, "Se le llenó la copa" ["His cup is now filled"], tried to play a word game suggesting that justice was finally done.[24] Thus, the overall message is ambiguous, since the image, on the contrary, suggests that Escobar is a winner. It shows the drug lord in a situation of power. He appears triumphant even after just losing his seat in the Colombian Congress. The article in which the picture of Escobar appears doing the ceremonial kick is titled "Surrender Feints." It uses an analogy to feinting in sports, to "make as if to."[25] This was Escobar's attitude toward justice when he promised he was going to surrender after escaping prison; he never did it.

The Narco

Although the category of Robin Hood still accompanied Escobar, the new category of the narco soon emerged. In 1987, Escobar, a bandit, an outlaw, appeared in *Forbes* magazine as one of the richest men in the world along with a list of international billionaires. Escobar's exorbitant fortune and eccentric stories circulated in the Colombian press too. Journalists narrated and described in detail every asset belonging to the capo, contributing to the belief that no one could be richer than Escobar. In fact, the media constantly reminded Colombians how rich Escobar was. In 1988, when the drug baron was already known as the head of the Medellín Cartel, *El Espectador* published an article about Escobar's "legal properties," as absurd as that term can sound. The first part of the article was published next to another one linking Escobar with the assassination of Guillermo

Cano. The article had a picture of a helicopter, allegedly belonging to Escobar, that had recently crashed in "La Aguacatala," a 2,240-square-meter lot that belonged to the capo. The publication narrated that the helicopter had fake license plates and was carrying five hundred kilograms of cocaine; it also stated that the crew was able to escape with the majority of the cargo, leaving behind only 78 kilograms. The article questioned the fact that helicopters were able to fly with no license above Medellín's airspace. Since the moment Escobar decided to settle in the town, the article stated, "more than twenty applications for the construction of heliports have been submitted." Many of those applications were denied because the law forbade the granting of heliport licenses to people with drug-trafficking backgrounds. Nonetheless, "in the Poblado [Medellín's richest neighborhood] there are more than ten daily helicopter flights, which are not authorized, whose occupants and cargo are unknown."[26]

The article also included a list of each of Escobar's more than 300 "legal properties" with their value, including apartments, farms, houses, lots, garages, commercial premises, offices, and warehouses. The estimated value of all properties reached 560 million Colombian pesos. The text also asserted that one of Escobar's properties, the Mónaco, had different values. For the revenue department in Medellín, the Mónaco building was a single house with a pool that cost 35 million pesos. For the Metropolitan Planning office, it was a building with 8 floors, 13 rooms, and 39 parking spots with a value of 68 million pesos. In reality, the Mónaco was an anti-bomb construction with an estimated value of 500 million Colombian pesos. Even worse, Diego Londoño White, the owner of the construction company Londoño y Vayda Ltda, dedicated to luxury property and constructor of the Mónaco, used to be the chief executive officer (CEO) of the rail system in Medellín and was also the former chief of the Metropolitan Planning office. The article concluded that Escobar did not pay for many of the additional lots he owned; he paid taxes but not in the proportion that he should have.[27]

This publication made Escobar look like a wealthy entrepreneur who, like many other billionaires around the world, evaded and eluded taxes. In other words, he was a billionaire among others, sharing the ordinary practices of wealthy people. *El Espectador* also made explicit that he was using the same construction companies that other wealthy people used for building luxury real estate. Escobar's common use of legal construction companies demonstrated the relationship that the drug baron had with investment and the legal economy. Many Colombians knew about his illegal activities but accepted them precisely because he contributed to the businesses of Medellin's entrepreneurs. In addition, the article asserted that Escobar was making deals with people close to power and that corruption was evidently involved. Above all, the article suggested many of

Inmuebles de Pablo Escobar

Apartamentos:

—Calle 11, N° 30-21, primer piso	$ 1'055.274
—Carrera 32B sur, N° 16A-31, 401	$ 22'797.731
—Calle 47B, N° 93A-25	$ 1'755.695
—Calle 57, N° 43-58, 401	$ 2'165.000
—Carrera 63B, N° 35-70, 302	$ 5'187.219
—Edificio Mónaco	$ 67'584.300
TOTAL	$100'545.219

Fincas en El Poblado:

—Los Mangos y Santamaría	$ 32'843.946

Casas:

—Carrera 42 sur, N° 16B-50	$ 12'049.574
—Carrera 43, N° 14-129	$ 10'447.459
—Carrera 43 sur, N° 16A-442	$140'157.939
—Carrera 43A sur N° 6—15	$ 3'333.874
—Carrera 44 sur, N° 15—31	$ 35'537.991
—Carrera 81, calle 5ª	$ 164.893
—Carrera 88 N° 34-11	$ 2'061.167
—Casa sin identificación, El Poblado	$ 6'653.790
—Carrera 83A, N° 33AA-22	$ 1'539.580
—Carrera 44 sur, N° 15-31	$ 35'537.991
—Calle 18C sur, N° 41A-25	$ 2'817.500
—Carrera 45, N° 15 sur-72	$ 13'563.257
—Calle 56, N° 78A-26	$ 5'372.428
TOTAL	$266'830.756

Lotes:

—Calle 4A, carrera 29	$ 7'016.206
—Calle 10, N° 33-33	$ 50'945.838
—Lote sin identificación (con piscina)	$ 4'857.504
—La Mona, Aguacatal y Martarita	$ 18'359.517
TOTAL	$ 81'179.065

Garajes:

—Carrera 63B, N° 35)70, garaje N° 8	$ 581.065
—Calle 11, N° 30-21, garajes 5 y 9	$ 259.292
—Carrera 32B sur, N° 16A-31, 34 y 36	$ 3'990.467
—Sin identificación (calle 57)	$ 824.464
—001 a 039, Calle 50, N° 68-28	$ 40'063.286
TOTAL	$ 45'137.509

Locales:

—Carrera 43 N° 31-106, local N° 13	$ 4'259.200
—Carrera 43A, N° 10-47, 5 locales	$ 8'855.692
—Calle 50, N° 68-38	$ 1'774.957
TOTAL	$ 14'889.849

Oficinas

—Carrera 43A sur, N° 6-15, 228	$ 3'200.518
—Calle 50, N° 68-38, siete pisos	$ 40'063.286

Depósitos

—Carrera 32B sur, N° 16A-31	$ 537.034
GRAN TOTAL	$558'444.627

Figure 11.2 Pablo Escobar's Real Estate: "Apartments/Houses/Lots/Garages/Commercial Premises/Offices/Warehouses."

Source: *El Espectador*, in an article entitled "List of Escobar's 'Legal' Real Estate in Medellín," January 23, 1988.

the paradoxes that would accompany the narrative about Escobar in the media: How can a fugitive have legal properties? How can authorities be aware that the drug lord is based in a specific neighborhood without being able to do anything about it? How is it possible to have so much detailed information about Escobar and his estates without being able to capture him?

From the time that Escobar became a congressman in 1982, articles about his alleged criminal activities appeared in the print media. It was common to see the capo dressed in his classic beige suit or in a gray jacket without a tie smiling, as if the Congress belonged to him. One article, for instance, put as a caption under Escobar's picture: "Pablo Escobar in Congress: Representative of What? Questioning the irony and contradiction of having a criminal in a public institution."[28] While serving in Congress Escobar always denied every link to narcotics or illegal activities. On one occasion, for instance, he appeared in front of the media showing his passport stamped with a U.S. visa, to corroborate his claim that he was not wanted by the northern country. His disregard for the truth continued years later when he appeared in the press denying any participation in the murder of Rodrigo Lara Bonilla, one of his political opponents. The publication quotes Escobar asserting that "the fact that there are communication media that syndicate me as a drug dealer does not mean that I am. . . . My economic activity is construction and livestock."[29] Such an alteration of reality was one of his modus operandi. The media gave the drug lord a voice and a public platform every time that, despite the evidence, he cynically denied any accusation against him.

Escobar's world of lies and ambiguity in public discourse began to crumble when Guillermo Cano explicitly published the news about Escobar's being a drug trafficker.[30] The note that would cost Cano his life quoted Escobar denying again any link with narcotics: "We're going to end all the slander about me. . . . I don't register a history of drug trafficking." Next to the quote, the article summarized the first time that Escobar appeared in the media for trafficking 19,500 grams of cocaine inside a truck's spare tire. After the news was revealed, it was hard for Escobar to keep concealing his criminal status. However, for two months, he benefited from parliamentary immunity, which meant that ordinary justice was not able to prosecute him. But the media did not rest. Most print media continued to report regularly on congressional discussions and the continuing delays in deciding whether Escobar should lose his parliamentary privileges.[31] Escobar again showed his disregard for the law and common sense and decided to appear at public events as if nothing was happening. One editorial, for instance, questioned the narco's impunity, stating that Escobar was still not a fugitive because he "could go to Medellín's stadium to watch a soccer game in clear demonstration of defiance of justice."[32]

At the end of October 1983, the Congress finally decided to take away Escobar's immunity, issuing an arrest warrant for the assassination of two agents of the Colombian security service (DAS) agents.[33] Escobar went underground and detonated a terroristic wave that left Colombia devastated until the 1990s, with 1989 as the bloodiest year. Colombia suffered from nonstop killings, massacres, kidnappings, and bombings. Every day in the media you could read about "Escobar's bombs" and terror. But despite the efforts, and offerings of huge rewards, it was impossible to catch Escobar. Colombians saw every day the COL$100 million reward for anyone who gave information about the capo, while reading about shopping centers being destroyed by bombs and policemen being massacred.[34]

At the same time that Colombians read about terror, they learned about Escobar being the patron of justice. One 1989 publication narrates how Colombian narcos were able to control police and public service officers around the world. The article narrates that in a session of the U.S. Congress, Senator Joseph Biden denounced the illegal drug business for producing around US$500,000,000. In the same session, U.S. senators discussed how drug traffickers were paying most public workers around the world. The impunity and massive power of narcos and Escobar had led the Colombian government to negotiation instead of capture. For at least one entire year, the Colombian news reported that Escobar would submit himself to justice under certain conditions. One of them, of course, was for Colombia to eliminate extradition.[35] Another one included the construction of his own jail, with his own guards, in a territory chosen by him. The Catholic Church became the mediator for Escobar's surrender, while most Colombians were thinking that this was a joke. That is how the ludicrous story of La Catedral jail emerged. Escobar picked a drug rehabilitation center and offered to pay all the expenses for building his own detention center. One of the articles in *El Espectador*, titled "Envigado Prison Rented," had as a subtitle: "Drug Addicts Could Stay without Rehabilitation Center."[36] Despite many protests from "no face judges,"[37] those who had to conceal their identities to protect their lives, Escobar's prison was approved.[38] And just like that, drug addicts ended up without a place to rehabilitate in order to build Escobar's prison, better known as Club Medellín for all the luxury and eccentricities that you could find there. In June 1991, as *El Espectador* proclaimed "The Terror Won," extradition was eliminated, and Escobar submitted himself to justice.[39] As it was later reported, Escobar constructed a soccer field, a casino, a game center, and a bar. He brought women, singers, soccer players, and his own family without restrictions.

La Catedral made Colombia and president César Gaviria a laughingstock of the world. Media reported on how Escobar arrived in a helicopter like a patron with all journalists watching him.[40] After the surrender, most articles in the Colombian press denounced the comforts enjoyed by the

The Accidental Persona 241

capo and his henchmen in prison. Many times, Gaviria had to come out to explain why officials were being so permissive with the drug baron, clarifying that Escobar had the necessary security.[41] Everyone had an opinion about Escobar, including George H. W. Bush, who said he would prefer to have the drug lord in a U.S. jail.[42] Nevertheless, when the Colombian government learned about assassinations being committed inside La Catedral, Escobar's game could not go further. The news showed thousands of military personnel entering the huge resort club staged as a prison, with the purpose of capturing and finally giving a fair sentence to the worst terrorist in Colombian history. But the drug baron escaped without leaving a trace.[43] The papers showed soldiers trying to find the man who was again the most wanted man in the world, one man who was able to mock and dominate the Colombian state. Cartoons about the escape mocked the state's indulgency with Escobar.[44] And just like that, Escobar became again the guy who appeared every night on Colombian television in a wanted poster with

Figure 11.3 Esprit de corps: "How was he able to escape?" Author: Osuna, published in *El Espectador* after Escobar's escape from La Catedral prison, July 26, 1992. Courtesy of Osuna.

an reward of hundreds of millions of Colombian pesos that kept increasing over time. Terror and bombings started again, and Colombia became a "narco-estate" for the rest of the world.[45] Colombians then began reading articles about the country's narco-image, one that still haunts its citizens.[46]

The War on Drugs in Colombia became a war against one single man. The vagueness of this war allowed the synecdoche to occur. However, putting Escobar as the representation of a whole and complex enterprise made him symbolically more powerful. The unwinnable war was not against drugs but against a powerful capo who was capable of controlling and challenging the state and its institutions. From 1983 until 1991, the rhetoric against the trafficking of drugs switched to a discourse against the terrorism of Escobar and the implications of his violent power for Colombia's image in the world.[47] Escobar was depicted as controlling most of Colombian institutions and an even some authorities in foreign countries. Justice lost its face because of Escobar. The image of a judge "without a face" illustrates the perversity of the situation, not to mention the networks of locals who admired him and helped him hide throughout Medellín and its surroundings. That situation made it very difficult for authorities not only to catch Escobar but also to consider a fair trial for him and his associates. Moreover, every time journalists denounced Escobar and his domination of the state, they invited Colombians to think about the drug lord in terms of limitless power. They portrayed a man who was able to use money's buying power for becoming the head of a state; there was no law that could stop him, not because he was above the law, but because he was the law.

This narco category portrays the discourse of infinite wealth and power. The rhetoric about his persona showed an ambitious man who wanted to reinvent national leadership on his own terms. People perceived him not as an anti-establishment figure but as the all-powerful establishment, or, stated differently, as the founder of a new establishment, a new commerce, a new way of life. His fortune and defiant attitude made him stronger and admired by those who saw virtue in power. The story of Escobar is also that of the narco who incarnated the excesses and possibilities of the underground economy that threatened to free life from the normative order of the state.

Journalism Routines

The construction of the Robin Hood and the narco rhetorical categories evidence that symbolic narratives depend not only on audiences, speakers, and discourses but also on specific media dynamics. Media texts relied on media production choices that appear to be spontaneous but depend on routines, circumstances, moods, and power structures. As Stuart Hall and his colleagues put it:

> The media do not simply and transparently report events which are naturally newsworthy in *themselves*. 'News' is the end-product of a complex process which begins with a systematic sorting and selecting of events and topics according to a socially constructed set of categories.[48]

The assertion complements the "Agenda Setting" theory of media activity.[49] In other words, the media have the power to shape and filter what readers get and, in that sense, tell us what to think about. This does not mean that media tell readers or viewers what to think, but media practitioners select the degree of importance in the news. For instance, when the media focus attention on Escobar's personality, on the way in which he mocks the state, or on how the War on Drugs is failing, journalists decide to give importance to certain aspects of the capo's life, his environment, and his circumstances. The public, willingly or not, then considers those aspects to be important. Selecting the news is part of journalism routines that are determinant in how stories are constructed through the media. Journalism routines refer to the way in which mass media, in this case, print media, produce information in *real time*, with a certain *pace*, and subject to the newspaper's *periodicity*. Journalists have to face *gatekeepers* and limitations on *access* to information. Their success depends on *reliability* or reliable sources, and they have *limited space* for writing. Moreover, media institutions within the conglomerate system compete with each other, seeking *exclusiveness* by finding scoops. In addition, in order to catch the reader's attention, newspapers try to use a *personalized tone* and to cover *conflicts* or flashpoints in the story. Newspapers are also conditioned by events and topics related to their *staff organization*, such as specialist correspondents and departments, and the structural division of papers into *sections*. Finally, most newspapers resort to the *mirror effect* that consists in covering the same news that competing newspapers have already published.[50]

In other words, when we examine the construction of Escobar's character through the Colombian print media, we cannot forget that the narrative is subject to these "conditions" of journalism routines. The analyzed newspapers, for instance, publish daily, making the pace very quick and the analysis sometimes not as deep as it could be. Many times, the story covers just one angle, and the next day or next week the newspaper complements the story with a follow-up article. If the story breaks after the edition has been closed, then people learn about it by rumors, and when it finally appears in the papers the spark of the news is gone. The natural fragmentation of the news means that some readers might get only certain versions of the story because they do not follow the news every day, because they forget, or simply because, as with any speech act, they read partially what interests them. Some might read about how Escobar escaped prison and how he mocked the state but might ignore the following analysis of how narco-trafficking is bleeding the country dry. Moreover, as happened with determinative events like Escobar's death, newspapers decided to release a special edition about the capo that circulated the night of the killing. These special editions resembled sensationalist newspapers because they showed detailed images of the capo lying dead on the roof of the house where he was shot. They also described step by step and in detail, as in a thriller, what the detectives did and the efforts that led to Escobar's capture and shooting. The story was therefore constructed in partial chunks of information.

Reading about Escobar through the media was comparable to reading a comic book. Comic books are usually written and drawn by different writers and artists. These books have vignettes that sometimes abruptly change from one to another, giving the reader the freedom to imagine and contextualize the temporal gaps. Some vignettes are more significant, some have more text, and some have no text at all. Readers have to add a lot of context and imagination in order to give coherence and continuity to the story. Escobar's appearance in the news was fragmentary in the same way. Different journalists wrote about the capo. Narrative threads about Escobar were marked by events and not by the degree of importance for democracy of certain news items. In addition, there was a dissonance of sizes and foci in the news articles; some articles had more or fewer column inches depending on the limited space and prioritization of some information. This could provoke in the reader a simplification of thought and a way of thinking about the capo in terms of a Hollywood movie narrative.

The construction of Escobar's story was also influenced by gatekeepers, economic interests, and censorship. When Escobar was at the height of his violent power, self-censorship was the rule. Because the capo and the cartel routinely threatened journalists, many opted not to publish news about him to avoid being killed or putting their families in danger. Economic interests and alliances between some government officials who were allies of the narcos also barred access to sources and privileged information. Being a journalist in Colombia has always been very difficult. However, during the 1980s and 1990s, the profession of journalism was one of the riskiest trades, as the 1986 assassination of Guillermo Cano, *El Espectador*'s editor, bears witness. In this sense and at this time, Escobar's portrayal in the media could only be produced by heroic journalists who pursued their jobs against all odds, but also, there was a tacit acknowledgment that a lot of the information was nuanced or kept quiet by those who did not want to take the risks, or who wanted to remain moderate in order to stay in the fight.[51]

The worldwide fascination for one of the most powerful capos of all time produced in Colombian journalists a necessity for exclusivity and scoops. Stories about Escobar were tainted with a dramatic telenovela tone that forced journalists to seek new dramatic elements. In addition, the necessity for giving a personal and appealing tone in the news presented the capo as either an everyday character and a savior or as the evil villain who committed the worst atrocities and made fun of the Colombian state and international authorities. Moreover, the fact that all media wanted to cover everything about Escobar made the mirror effect and repetition the norms. Colombians read the same story in local, national, and international media.

The journalism routines were part of the reason why Escobar appeared through the media as he did. The newspapers did not have a purpose of neglecting some information and highlighting others. They were instead publishing according to historical context and circumstances that made them prioritize some information. The print media helped in building Escobar's character in a kind of accidental way, conditioned by their previous routine and practices.

The Accidental Persona

The concept of persona has been fruitful for a variety of rhetorical and media studies, and it is complicated when the media and processes of circulation are involved. Don J. Waisanen and Amy B. Becker, for instance, introduced the circulating persona for describing the different roles created and attributed to public figures across media spaces.[52] Waisanen and Becker use the case of former U.S. vice president Joseph Biden and his comedic representations to explore how circulation and recirculation bring agency to audiences in the construction of a public persona. The media indeed have played an important role in the construction of the persona of public figures. Traditional media and its infrastructure have been and are still essential in the process. Despite the proliferation of digital and social media, media conglomerates with their traditional TV channels and newspapers continue to be some of the main sources of information. The crisis of "fake news" and people not trusting random publications has also given strength to old-school media news enterprises that, despite their economic and political biases, are more or less trusted not to produce entirely false information.[53]

Information that comes from traditional media depends on journalism routines. Escobar's public persona was constructed by multiple agents, predominantly by the media due to his outlaw status. Because of the journalism routines and its practices, the media shaped Escobar in "accidental" or unintended ways. As it happened with *Semana*'s article about the

Robin Hood paisa, the media accidentally created the category of Robin Hood. Because the nickname fitted his narrative, Escobar decided to own the Robin Hood moniker and complemented the construction of his public persona by portraying his claim to similarities with other outlaw characters like the Latin American bandit Pancho Villa.[54] Simultaneously, the same media accidentally created the category of the powerful narco. The construction of public figures through the news media and its practices therefore originates what I call an accidental persona. This is an instance of a "first persona," in terms of rhetorical theory; it is also a figure created by multiple agents, both consciously and accidentally.[55]

Practices of journalism cause some public figures to appear by a mediated accident. It is mediated because what is said about the character does not come directly from the individual. It is instead an interpretation of journalists who are conditioned by the media infrastructure. And it is accidental precisely because it is generated through practices and routines that do not have specific objectives and are not controlled by an agent; further, the outcome of the public persona does not always coincide with the individual's own projection or historical facts about the person's character. The accidental persona obeys news production rhythms, agenda setting, time constraints, space limits, and censorship, among others. The accidental persona emerges in moments of transition in which a character or situation is still very hard or difficult to digest or understand. In some cases, like Escobar's, the difficulty in introducing the public figure has to do with lack of knowledge, priority with other news, little journalistic interest on the topic, and the most relevant: Restricted access to information. Journalists resort to a narrative with a lot of speculation that encourages audiences to construct an idealized or distorted representation of the person in question.

There were several specific consequences of journalistic practices in Escobar's case. One of them was the over-denunciation of the weakness of the state. The character of Escobar is strong because the state is weak was an underlying argument. A story that took hold because of other news. The context of Colombia is particularly interesting for understanding how the accident works. Because the country suffered and continues to suffer an internal conflict, a large portion of the news is always taken up with articles about war. It is normal that the agenda of a newspaper is determined by circumstances, but this situation is clearer and more explicit because of the guerrilla warfare. In other words, relevant news occupies journalists' mental space and newspapers' literal space, conditioning the treatment given to figures like Escobar, especially at the point of their emergence. Not enough attention was paid to him at the beginning, and then his story folded into the bigger one: The incapacity of the state to uphold its sovereignty. A line of argument that was political, but also moral. There is an inherent sadness and shame to acknowledge that your political community is not in control of its destiny. The emphasis on self-criticism also moderated the emphasis on the evilness of Escobar.

Also, there was always a "human interest" side to the story. Partly, of course, out of sincere curiosity: Who was this individual that many people adored? Partly, out of celebrity gossip. One of the most renowned faces of journalism, Virginia Vallejo, was dating him. What did she see in him? Could he be that evil? To the human side of the story, was the social side, which journalists tend to authentically pursue. The inequalities of opportunities in Colombia are profound, and the capacity of the state to address such realities has been insufficient, to say the least. To talk about and underscore the underlying and structural causes of crime is a common place in journalistic practice. Something that is generally regarded as good, as it points to the big picture. Although, as noted, in this story, Escobar's commitment with the poor, and his attacks to the corrupt establishment occluded the fact that he was causing death and poverty, and further corruption of the State. Still, at the end, there is a part of the story that has him as a Robin Hood.

But the Robin Hood was also a narco. When Escobar appeared in the media, the illegal drug business was just becoming the enterprise that it is today. For journalists, he was part of a mostly unknown world in budding. Colombia was just beginning to be known internationally as a drug producer country, with vast international networks. And for most journalists, the "relevant" and newsworthy story was local. Moreover, the language to talk about and narrate such story was not yet in place. Despite narcos being more than just smugglers, the imaginary that it was available was that of the smuggler. Should smugglers be given much thought or ink?

Conclusion

The practices of journalism can forge a persona through a mediated accident. It is mediated because what is said about the character does not come directly or only from the individual. And it is accidental precisely because it is generated through practices that do not have specific objectives and are not controlled by an agent; further, the outcome of the public persona does not always coincide with the individual's own projection or historical facts about the person's character. The accidental persona obeys to news production rhythms, agenda setting, time constraints, space limits, and censorship, among others. The accidental persona emerges in moments of transition in which a character or situation is still very hard or difficult to digest or understand. In some cases, like Escobar's, the difficulty in introducing the public figure has to do with lack of knowledge, priority with other news, little journalistic interest on the topic, and the most relevant: restricted access to information. Journalists resort to a narrative with a lot

248 *Catalina Uribe Rincón*

of speculation that encourages audiences to construct an idealized or distorted representation of the person in question. The media function with a structure, but the product, more times than not, is mostly unintentional, a creation of decentralized and relative unconnected decisions on decentralized and unconnected events.

Notes

1 See link to Redbubble and Escobar's products online: www.redbubble.com/shop/pablo+escobar+t-shirts, visited January 21, 2022.
2 Los Extraditables was an organization created by the Medellín Cartel in the early 1980s. Their most famous slogan was "We prefer a grave in Colombia than a prison in the United States."
3 Alexander L. Fattal, *Guerrilla marketing: Contrainsurgencia y capitalismo en Colombia* (Bogotá: Universidad del Rosario, 2019), 58.
4 Maryluz Vallejo Mejía, *A plomo herido: Una crónica del periodismo en Colombia (1880–1980)* (Bogotá: Planeta, 2006), 219–221.
5 "La manzana podrida," Libreta de Apuntes, *El Espectador*, December 16, 1984.
6 See Vallejo Mejía, *A plomo herido*, 337–348 and Catalina Montoya-Londoño, "In search of a Model for the Colombian Media System Today," in *Media Systems and Communication Policies in Latin America*, eds. Manuel Alejandro Guerrero and Mireya Márquez-Ramírez (London: Palgrave Macmillan, 2014), 67–68.
7 Escobar's comment alluded to stories that were circulating in the news during that time. In 1982, two days before Halloween, a series of weird episodes caused trick-or-treating to be strictly restricted or almost banned across the United States. Frank Comunale, a Long Island resident, found a straight pin inserted in his Cadbury Caramello bar, causing him to cut his cheek. In New Jersey, a group of schoolchildren were hospitalized for ingesting phencyclidine that had been sprinkled over their Tootsie Rolls. But one of most renowned cases of adulterated consumer products occurred in Chicago, where seven people were killed due to Tylenol laced with cynadine. "How the Tylenol Murders of 1982 Changed the Way We Consume Medication," *PBS*, September 29, 2014. www.pbs.org/newshour/health/tylenol-murders-1982, accessed June 24, 2022; "New Warnings of Tainted Candy Heighten Worries over Halloween," *New York Times*, October 31, 1982. www.nytimes.com/1982/10/31/nyregion/new-warnings-of-tainted-candy-heighten-worries-over-halloween.html, accessed June 24, 2022.
8 "Un Robin Hood paisa," *Semana*, no. 50, April 19–25, 1983.
9 In Spanish the word *don* is used before first names as a form of respect. In the past, it was reserved for people who had a higher social status.
10 "Un Robin Hood paisa."
11 "Un Robin Hood paisa."
12 See *Pablo Escobar, Ángel o demonio*, directed by Jorge Granier, Netflix, Sierralta Entertainment and Angostura Film Company, 2007.
13 *Countdown to Death: Pablo Escobar*, written by Pablo Martín Farina and Santiago Díaz, Netflix, 2017.
14 *Countdown to Death*.
15 Envigado is a town in the Departamento de Antioquia located southeast of Medellín.

16 *Countdown to Death*.
17 "Impulso a la inflación por 'cocadólares' en Colombia," *El Espectador*, August 22, 1983.
18 Escobar told the press that he was going to sue the ABC network because it was circulating false information about him: "We are going to end once and for all the slander against me, not only in Colombia but also abroad, because I do not register a history of drug trafficking either in the United States or in this country"; "En 1976 Escobar estuvo preso," *El Espectador*, August 25, 1983.
19 "Cocaine Baron Revered by Poor as Robin Hood," *El Espectador*, August 16, 1989. See also "Cocaine Baron Revered by Poor as Robin Hood: Pablo Gaviria Escobar," [London] *Sunday Times*, August 13, 1989.
20 "Se le llenó la copa," *El Espectador*, October 30, 1983; "El peor criminal de nuestra historia," *El Espectador*, December 3, 1993.
21 "Amagos de entrega después de la Catedral," *El Tiempo*, December 3, 1993.
22 There were rumors about Escobar giving money from the cartel to Nacional. There were also accusations of Escobar threatening referees to influence matches' outcomes; "Escobar Gaviria en su sitio," *El Espectador*, June 20, 1991.
23 Cara Finnegan, *Picturing Poverty: Print Culture and FSA Photographs* (Washington, DC: Smithsonian Institution Scholarly Press, 2003), vii.
24 "Se le llenó la copa" or "his cup is now filled" alludes to the Spanish saying "La gota que rebalsó el vaso" that in English is translated as "the straw that broke the camel's back." In this case the title points out that after *El Espectador* published the proof that Escobar had indeed smuggled drugs, the Congress could not handle any more rumors about Escobar's fortune so decided to impeach him.
25 In sports, feinting means to make a brief movement in a different direction from the one the player intends to follow for the purpose of confusing or deceiving the opponent.
26 "Las propiedades legales de Pablo Escobar en Medellín," *El Espectador*, January 23, 1988.
27 "Las propiedades legales."
28 "El primer artículo sobre Pablo Escobar: Un Robin Hood paisa," *Revista Semana*, no. 367, May 16–22, 1989.
29 "Yo no soy narcotraficante: Pablo Escobar," *El Colombiano*, June 20, 1991.
30 "En 1976 Escobar estuvo preso," *El Espectador*, August 25, 1983.
31 "Dilatan levantamiento de inmunidad a Pablo Escobar," *El Espectador*, October 20, 1983.
32 "Los fugitivos de la droga y sus derivados," *El Espectador*, October 1, 1983.
33 "Levantada inmunidad a Escobar," *El Espectador*, October 27, 1983.
34 "Asesinado Galán," *El Espectador*, August 19, 1989; "Asesinado comandante de la policía en Antioquia," *El Espectador*, August 19, 1989; "Seguimos Adelante," *El Espectador*, September 3, 1989; "107 inmolados en el aire," *El Espectador*, November 28, 1989.
35 "Narcos colombianos controlan a policías y a funcionarios," *El Espectador*, August 19, 1989.
36 "Contratada Cárcel de Envigado," *El Espectador*, June 2, 1991.
37 Escobar's terror produced a new category in justice: the "no face judges." This meant that judges could maintain anonymity and not disclose their identity during a trial in order to avoid threats and assassinations. Despite this effort, many judges were killed by Escobar, who managed to find out their identity.
38 "Juez pide a Escobar en la modelo," *El Espectador*, June 15, 1991.
39 "Ganó el terror," *El Espectador*, June 20, 1991.

40 "García Herreros narra la operación entrega," *El Espectador,* June 20, 1991.
41 "Solo se negoció la seguridad," *El Espectador,* June 20, 1991; "No tengo respuesta contundente," *El Espectador,* June 23, 1992.
42 "Bush preferiría ver a Escobar en E.U.," *El Espectador,* June 20, 1991.
43 ". . . Y se les voló," *El Espectador,* July 23, 1992.
44 "Escapó Escobar," *El Espectador,* July 23, 1992; "Espíritu de cuerpo," *El Espectador,* July 26, 1992.
45 "Bogotá estremecida por la violencia terrorista," *El Colombiano,* February 1, 1993; "Cuatro muertos y 100 heridos," *El Colombiano,* February 16, 1993; "Bogotá, escenario de 5 poderosas bombas," *El Colombiano,* February 16, 1993; "La violencia no se marcha," *El Colombiano,* February 21, 1993.
46 "Revive la narco-imagen colombiana," *El Espectador,* July 23, 1992.
47 "Escobar es el enemigo número uno de Colombia," *El Colombiano,* February 2, 1993.
48 Stuart Hall et al., *Policing the Crisis: Mugging, the State, and Law and Order* (London: Macmillan, 1978), 56.
49 The agenda setting was first introduced by Maxwell McCombs and Donald Shaw, who argued that media do not tell us what to think but what to think about; see Maxwell E. McCombs and Donald L. Shaw, "The Agenda-Setting Function of Mass Media," *Public Opinion Quarterly* 36, no. 2 (1972): 176–187.
50 Some of these elements are described in Stella Martini, *Periodismo, noticia y noticiabilidad* (Buenos Aires: Grupo Editorial Norma, 2000), chap. 4; and in Hall et al., *Policing the Crisis,* 55–58.
51 After Escobar's death and to this day, many journalists have published information that was impossible to publish when the capo was alive. For instance, the journalist Silvia Hoyos, whose uncle was murdered by Escobar in 1988, began some correspondence with the capo while he was in prison. She wanted to find answers about Escobar's violence and personality, and "surprisingly," as she argues, the capo answered her letters. The only condition was to keep the letters secret. Only in 2015 did Hoyos publish the book *Los días del dragon* that contained their correspondence. The letters from Escobar revealed personal information and were signed with his fingerprint.
52 Don J. Waisanen and Amy B. Becker, "The Problem with Being Joe Biden: Political Comedy and Circulating Personae," *Critical Studies in Media Communication* 32, no. 4 (2015): 256–271.
53 Gordon Pennycook and David G. Rand, "Fighting Misinformation on Social Media Using Crowdsourced Judgments of News Source Quality," *Proceedings of the National Academy of Sciences* 116, no. 7 (2019): 2521–26; "Old-School Media Is Pulling Way More Viewers Than You Think," *Wired,* February 16, 2017. www.wired.com/2017/02/daily-audience-numbers-for-big-media-outlets/, accessed May 19, 2020; Diana Owen, "El papel de los nuevos medios en la política," in *La Era de la Perplejidad. Repensar el Mundo que conocíamos* (Madrid, BBVA: 2017); Informa Dimensión 2019, Kantar. www.kantarmedia.com/dimension/es, accessed May 19, 2020.
54 Escobar's admiration for Pancho Villa is evinced in a famous picture in which the capo appears dressed up as the Mexican revolutionary. This image has circulated through the media, books, TV shows, and films about Escobar, making it one of the most iconic images of him. The image was taken in prison and displayed in Escobar's prison cell, it circulated in some newspapers after Escobar's death. "Con Escobar no muere el narcotráfico," *El Tiempo,* December 3, 1993;

James Mollison and Rainbow Nelson, *The Memory of Pablo Escobar* (London: Chris Boot, 2007), 148, 149.

55 In U.S. rhetorical studies, Edwin Black in the mid-twentieth century adapted the concept of persona to discuss characteristics of audiences. He differentiated between the concepts of first and second persona to talk about the voice of the rhetor and the implied audience, respectively. Discussions around first and second persona, specifically regarding elements like identity, subjectivity, and collectivity, inspired scholars to develop other angles on the persona concept, in order to discuss various characters implied within discourse; see Edwin Black, "The Second Persona," *Quarterly Journal of Speech* 56, no. 2 (1970): 109–119.

12 The Moral Vision and Moral Performance of Photojournalist Jesús Abad Colorado

Alexander L. Fattal

El Testigo (*The Witness*) opens with an empty window in front of the blue sky. Soon we see Jesús Abad Colorado taking pictures of abandoned buildings, vegetation crawling up the walls. He wobbles, weighed down by a backpack, as he zooms his lens in and out to compose a shot. He is squinting back sweat when a yellow butterfly zips past. The image cuts to a black-and-white photo of a space that is only recognizable as a classroom from the chalkboard on the wall. The voiceover—Abad Colorado's own voice—considers the trope of ruins. "[They] testify to the horror." He recalls peering into a classroom where the story of Cain and Abel was still etched onto the board and retells the biblical fable as it was written in white chalk. His voice emphasizes Cain's response to God: "I don't know where he is, I'm not my brother's keeper," and then recounts God's curse on Cain, leaving him to roam the earth for in a distraught search for forgiveness.

The video track returns to a closeup of Abad Colorado as he lowers the digital camera from his eye. He reviews the image that has just taken, and says, "In Colombia, I haven't been able to figure out who is Cain and who is Abel." The impact of the line, by then well practiced in Abad Colorado's public talks, resounds as the video track fills with his black and white photographs of human suffering, coffins and funeral processions, people in exodus, and people mourning. Backdrops of rivers and rubble frame figures left wandering and wondering in the wake of horrific violence. León Gieco's protest song, "Solo le pido a Dios (I only ask God)" fills the audio track as Abad Colorado's images roll. It is a rousing sequence that leads to the title card: *El Testigo: Cain y Abel*.

This chapter parses the public personae of Jesús Abad Colorado, a photographer who has made the unlikely transition from photographic witness to spokesperson for peace and reconciliation. I argue that as a visual storyteller Abad Colorado cuts against the grain of class-based structural invisibilities of the Colombian conflict in a way that transcends partisanship and strikes a clarion moral tone. The mix of moral vision and moral performance has emerged through his entwined personal and professional trajectories and

DOI: 10.4324/9781003048152-17

The Moral Vision and Moral Performance of Jesús Abad Colorado 253

reverberates with other moral voices such as Father Francisco de Roux and social leaders, voices that have been structurally muffled and muted through the conflict and into the post-peace accord period. In the end, I zoom in on Abad Colorado's decision to embrace religiosity in his public discourse, to further argue that this shift has been central to his metamorphosis from a documentarian to a megaphone for peace, whose message of reconciliation resounds across Colombia in a way that nimbly hops over partisan cleavages and echoes abroad in a humanist key.[1] While driving this line of argumentation, the chapter also strives to shed light on elements of conflict photojournalism as it evolved in Colombia through the 1990s and 2000s.

These dynamics are on full display in Kate Horne's 2018 film, *El Testigo*.[2] The film is part of a growing subgenre of documentaries about photographers that celebrate the life and work of an individual photographer. These are close collaborations between the filmmaker and the photographer that draw on his (they are most often men) images to pack an aesthetic and emotional punch. For example, *The Salt of the Earth* lionizes Brazilian photographer Sebastião Salgado[3] and *War Photographer* does the same for photojournalist James Nachtwey. Though the trope of the intrepid witness to human misfortune connects the three films, *El Testigo*, unlike the other two, does not foreground globetrotting but operates in a national context.[4] The film from this subgenre that *El Testigo* most closely resembles is *Pictures from a Revolution*, a documentary in which Susan Meiselas returns to Nicaragua to find the people who have featured in her photographs of the Sandinista uprising.[5] *El Testigo*, similarly, takes its structure from Abad Colorado's encounters with the people in his most iconic images. Some he has kept in touch with, others he is tracking down for the first time. Abad Colorado and Meiselas's ethical commitments are not to an abstracted humanity—pace discourses of photojournalism following World War II—but to individual humans.[6]

In both films, the motif of the photographer's return to the people who populate their archive serves as a weak corrective to the extractive dynamic of standard photojournalistic practice. Yet, these re-encounters often feel forced, even as they are generative of the insights that only the passage of time can produce. An important difference between the two films is that Meiselas is not from Nicaragua but the northeastern United States and *Pictures from a Revolution*, narrated in the first person, centers her own experience as an outsider. She, like Nachtwey and Salgado, is a liberal hero with whom western audiences can identify and admire for her adventurousness, compositional skill, and thoughtful reflections on her experiences. Abad Colorado, by contrast, derives his authority less from aesthetic virtuosity and more from his ethical commitment to document the plight of his compatriots and use his vision and voice to draw attention to their often-tragic experience.

It is this ethical disposition that has catapulted Abad Colorado to a level of recognition exceedingly rare for a photographer and it is that visibility that this chapter takes as its object of study. Why has a talented, though not technically masterful photographer, who has focused his career primarily in western Colombia achieved such renown? Stated otherwise, what accounts for Abad Colorado's outsized public voice on questions of peace and reconciliation? What I will suggest is that Abad Colorado's strategic partnership with social movements, especially the religious left, enabled him to transcend his position as a photojournalist to become a spokesperson for collective struggles to dignify and humanize the lives of the conflict's victims (as well as rank and file members of armed groups).

To understand how Abad Colorado has come to preach to larger and larger rapt audiences requires tracking his career. In what follows, I divide his trajectory, roughly chronologically, in two stages. The first explores the photographer as a young man, from his time as an undergraduate student at the Universidad de Antioquia in 1987 through his decision to abandon his media patron, *El Colombiano* in 2001. The second part, from 2001 to the present, traces the emergence of his status as a politically committed visual advocate for human rights as he takes commissions from international human rights organizations, builds his personal archive, and transitions to a public figure. In the second stage, I focus on how, in recent years, Abad Colorado has woven his Catholic background into his visual storytelling in a way that has enabled him to transcend predictable political formulas and strike a non-partisan profile. "Nobody can keep him quiet," is the way one of his colleagues synthesized his ability to avoid being hemmed in by the tendentious but entrenched logic of presumed alliance and enmity in the war.

For the last 20 years, I have followed Abad Colorado's career and, as a participant and observer in the world of documentary photography in Colombia, kept in episodic contact with him as his star has risen. This chapter draws on long-term research that reaches back to 2001–2002, a year that I dedicated to investigating photojournalism in Colombia. I intermix interviews from that year with close readings of Abad Colorado's photographs, and a detailed study of the extensive public record of Abad Colorado's exhibitions, speeches, and interviews in the last 20 years.

The Photographer as a Young Man

Abad Colorado grew up lower-middle class in urban Medellín, abutting Comuna 13, which in the late 1990s and 2000s became a hotspot of urban warfare. In 1960, seven years before he was born, his parents came to the city displaced from San Carlos in eastern Antioquia when conservative partisans killed Abad Colorado's grandfather and uncle. During one of our interviews, he described how his family was forced to sell their land "at the price of an egg," but emphasized how his parents refused to foster hatred and a desire for vengeance in him or his seven siblings. In 1981, the Colombian military disappeared his cousin, and in 1994, the FARC kidnapped another cousin, who ultimately died in captivity. These traumatic events place Abad Colorado in the capacious category of victim of the conflict, but in a way that does not immediately situate him politically—an ambiguous victimhood that exemplifies the complexity of the conflict often overlooked by media discourse. It is therefore not surprising that he decided to situate himself "on the side of the victims," as he is wont to declare. Logical as such solidarity is, it grates against not only common-sense ideas of journalism as a profession of objective reportage but also deeply classed structures of mediation, which Abad Colorado would ultimately rebel against. To understand his turn against the existing system of photographic patronage via newspapers, magazines, and wire agencies requires going back to his time as a student at the Universidad de Antioquia, where Abad Colorado became exposed to photography in the late 1980s.

Medellín was in the throes of violence from many actors, but predominantly paramilitary-aligned drug traffickers. The university was not immune to the bloodshed engulfing the city, to the contrary. In 1987, right-wing forces killed ten students and seven professors. The dead included Héctor Abad Gómez (no relation to Abad Colorado), a socially committed physician who published a biting weekly column in *El Mundo*. The impact of those murders, especially that of Abad Gómez, stoked Abad Colorado's indignation. He began to carry a camera with him everywhere, "an extension of his hand and mind," according to journalist Nelson Padilla.[7] While taking a photography course in 1990, he documented visits by two presidential candidates who would be assassinated only weeks after their respective visits, Carlos Pizarro Leongómez of the then recently demobilized M19 and Bernardo Jaramillo Ossa of the Unión Patriótica. Álvaro Sierra Restrepo compellingly argues that these experiences impressed upon Abad Colorado the importance of photography in keeping a historical record.[8] On the strength of his final presentation to that photography class, he was offered an internship at *El Mundo*.[9]

El Mundo was an upstart project, founded in 1979 by liberals in a conservative city and region. It set out to compete against Antioquia's only daily, the conservative *El Colombiano*. Beyond the fresh partisan perspective (a partisan press was a tradition going back to independence in Colombia),[10] the newspaper gained traction, thanks, in part, to an innovative photography department. When I interviewed León Darío Peláez, a long-time photo director at *Semana* who cut his teeth at *El Mundo* as a photojournalist, he described the use of telephoto lenses, unconventional cropping, and enlarging photographs beyond then-standard sizes as tactics that set *El Mundo* apart. I was surprised that this is what passed as innovation. He explained to me,

> [back then] you would stand up with a camera and press click, that's it. There was no searching around, no composition, no playing with foreground and background, no playing with light. There was always a flash because the camera came with flash.[11]

I interviewed Ricardo Mazalan, an Argentine photographer turned photo-editor, at the Associated Press in Bogotá in 2001 and he felt that not much had changed since the days Peláez described in the 1980s. Mazalan said that Colombian photojournalism was "underdeveloped" and was not on par with "the protagonistic role [that photography plays] in modern media."[12]

El Mundo began to combat this visual poverty and win top prizes in the annual Postobón (the largest brand of Colombian soda) contest for sports photography, one of the only prizes dedicated to photography at the time. The photographers would apply their skills of shooting contested headers and the outstretched arms of goalies to their other assignments, creating a more visually intriguing paper to hold. Peláez recalls how foreign magazines served as inspiration for this new look. Many of the photographers who trained in *El Mundo*, like Peláez, would go on to influence the photo departments of the largest newspapers and magazines in Medellín and Bogotá from the 1990s to the 2010s,[13] and some, like Albeiro Lopera, would cover the war for the likes of Reuters.[14] Those photographers' experience of navigating the conflict by banding together in caravans is something they have reproduced out of the ongoing necessity of war reporting in many of the photo-departments they later landed in—a degree of cooperation often elided by the focus on individual authorship expressed through bylines.[15]

Press photography remains an afterthought to the written word in Colombia, even as the country has experienced a veritable boom in creative documentary works that have found eager audiences online through the 2010s. Photojournalism for the corporate press remains, overall, illustrative rather than a form of reportage on its own merits. Such format bias is compounded by the press' long-standing class bias, a skewing in favor of elite sources and subjects exemplified by the "social" section that publishes photos of the who's who in high society while not giving social issues the weight they deserve given their urgency. Coverage of subjects of social concern such as poverty, health, and education among the working classes is also prone to slip into what filmmakers Luis Ospina and Carlos Mayolo have called "pornomiseria" [a pornographic view of poverty].[16] The class bias tracks with the ownership of the corporatized media system in the country. Colombian media scholars Jorge Iván Bonilla and Ancízar Narvaez Montoya examine the shifting terrain of elite control of the press, radio, and television, documenting how families at the core of the Liberal and Conservative parties have gradually diluted their influence by selling off to large corporate consortiums.[17] Whether ownership is by elite families or corporate conglomerates, class structure in the country is reproduced in editorial practice.[18]

Even though *El Mundo* had been the liberal newcomer that dedicated more space and resources to issues of concern to the popular classes, by the time Abad Colorado interned there in 1991, "it had already entered into a decline," in his words.[19] Like its competition, it also dedicated ample space to "social shots," those posed pictures from cocktail parties at embassies, art galleries, or opulent residences. Abad Colorado disliked the work, quit the internship, and finished his studies in "social communication" (the equivalent of journalism and media studies in the United States). While still an undergraduate, he had a solo show about cultural life in the comunas at Medellín's Chamber of Commerce, which Jesuit Priest Francisco de Roux brought to CINEP, the socially committed Jesuit research center in Bogotá. Upon graduation Abad Colorado took a job at *El Colombiano* that allowed him to lean into his youthful passion to document the conflict. The paper sent him through much of the country's northwest quadrant, areas that included eastern Antioquia, the southwestern Caribbean, Urabá, Chocó, and the middle Magdalena—regions where, and the moment when, paramilitarism was incubating and expanding. At *El Colombiano*, Abad Colorado had a press pass to document the human tragedy of the paramilitary movement as it came into conflict with guerrillas that were also expanding in the 1990s.

In addition to reporting on the war, the newspaper sent Abad Colorado and the other staff photographers to cover more mundane events. As he said in one of our interviews, "I even had to cover fashion shows and that stuff, even though my work and my trajectory was something else entirely."[20] Many of his most famous images date to his nine-year tenure at *El Colombiano* (1992–2001). On two occasions in this period, he was "detained" by the guerrillas, first in 1997 by the FARC and then in 2000 by the ELN. Both episodes were short-lived, eight and three days respectively, absurdly routine affairs for journalists covering the conflict in the late 1990s. In this period, his work began to gain recognition as he contributed to books and was featured in exhibitions.

On December 6, 2000, the FARC detonated a car bomb packed with 400 kilograms of dynamite outside of a police station, decimating an entire section of the town. It being the same region from which his parents had fled, Abad Colorado was especially motivated to cover the tragedy. *El Colombiano* refused to send him, concerned, allegedly, about the safety of

Figure 12.1 The Bride of Granada (Granada, Antioquia): "We all lose at war. Let's all help to build a peace process," December 9, 2000. Courtesy of Jesús Abad Colorado.

its vehicle, which armed groups might target. So, Abad Colorado linked up with a non-governmental organization (NGO) and traveled to Granada, ultimately getting the blessing of his bosses. There he would make one of his most famous series. It included a bird's eye shot of a marching mass carrying an enormous banner that read "Territory of Peace." Perhaps Abad Colorado's most reproduced image is of a woman walking with her head bowed as she enters the town's central cathedral to get married. In the image, the long train of her gown spills out behind her, the energy in the frame moving rightward toward a sign denouncing the war that rests at the base of one of the church's columns. Onlookers' shadows project on the ground as the Colombian Red Cross' truck sits parked across the frame. The image strikes a chord of grace, faith, and resilience.

The series would win him the Simón Bolívar Award for journalism, the most prestigious in the country. The experience of partnering with an NGO and winning the Bolívar Award gave Abad Colorado the confidence to take the leap to leave *El Colombiano*. In an interview back in 2013 with Marta Ruiz, a journalist who served as a member of the Truth Commission, Abad Colorado reflected on the image of the bride in Granada:

> That woman in the middle of ruins was like a monarch butterfly with wings. On the same contact sheet, I have photos of women crying. . . .

That woman needed to walk on top of the ruins of the town to get home. I understood that I also needed a drastic change, like those worms that turn into butterflies.[21]

Abad Colorado's Moral Vision

In the 20 years since Abad Colorado decided to go alone as a freelance documentary photographer, he has increasingly put down his camera and picked up a series of microphones. For the first decade after leaving *El Colombiano* he still acted as an itinerant witness to the conflict, inserting himself into the wake of the war's violent eruptions. His photographic work, however, has grown more episodic as he has assumed the role of unappointed spokesperson for victims of the conflict, using his stature to speak incessantly about injustice, indifference, and inequality. This section continues to track Abad Colorado's career and parses the way he has harnessed his unique celebrity as a photojournalist to craft a moral voice that he has intertwined with his photographic repertoire.

After Abad Colorado resigned from *El Colombiano* in 2001, he would rely on his resourcefulness to find a constellation of patrons and protectors in left-leaning and working-class civil society groups. He earned commissions from human rights organizations and partnered strategically with civilian groups and social movements, operating with the entrepreneurial savvy associated with his native Antioquia. When I met Abad Colorado at a conference about the photographic image at EAFIT University in Medellín in late 2001, peace negotiations between the Colombian government and the Revolutionary Armed Forces of Colombia (FARC) were falling apart. Waves of displaced people were fleeing regions that paramilitaries were moving into and that guerrillas were fighting to hold. A swath of the map that represented contested territory was ballooning. Abad Colorado's family was again ensnared in the violence. Between 2001 and 2002, his household in Medellín gave temporary refuge to family members leaving the same region that his parents had fled 40 years earlier; this time, however, it was his conservative relatives from his mother's side of the family that were on the run.

One of our conversations took place in February, just before the Colombian military retook the Caguán, the Maryland-sized piece of territory in the departments of Meta and Caquetá that President Pastrana had ordered the military to withdraw from to facilitate peace talks with the FARC. Recently independent, Abad Colorado did not feel safe traveling to the region. He said,

> I would like to be there, not to show the soldiers arriving to the demilitarized zone but to show what's happening to the people who live in the (demilitarized) zone, putting up their little white flags, their faces filled with worry about what is going to happen in this country.

He explained why he could travel, "I'm very scared, increasingly scared to cover everything right now. I don't work for a specific outlet. I don't have the backing where I can say, 'Look at this press card of *El Colombiano* or *El Tiempo* or from the magazine *Semana*' or 'I'm from *Caracol* or *RCN*.' "[22] Previously he not only had press credentials but also could insert himself in a pod of journalists working under the same constraints.

When I asked him whether he could rely on his growing reputation as a form of protection, he explained that such recognition might work in Antioquia but not in southern Colombia. As paramilitarism expanded from a regional to a national phenomenon, Abad Colorado was trying to figure out a way to do the same. Though he resisted his urge to document the dramatic unfolding in the Caguán, he was developing strategies to move around the country without press credentials, namely allying himself with international human rights organizations, church groups, and social movements. In one of our conversations in 2001–2002, he discussed his plans at the time:

> I'm about to sit down and work on a proposal for the International Committee of the Red Cross that needs some photographs for its web page. There's another possibility with the office of UNHCR [The United Nations High Commissioner for Refugees]. . . . I'm waiting for a representative from UNHCR to come to Medellín because we're going to work on the subject of border areas with Venezuela, Ecuador, and the border region with Panama. They're interested in me producing the photographic material, so I think there are some good possibilities. . . . These are things that will help me consolidate my work to be able to continue my personal projects.[23]

What is interesting is his commitment to "consolidate his work" and his "personal projects," shorthand for the development of his personal archive about the conflict over a *longue durée* rather than a singular publication or given event, a strategic projection that proved clairvoyant. Between commissions from large international organizations, Abad Colorado traveled on a shoestring with church groups, the women's movement, local pro-peace NGOs, or the Defensoría del Pueblo (the state's own human rights watchdog). Moving as a group provided both protection in numbers and moral support since most armed groups often avoided provoking a large public backlash to gratuitous violence against civil society organizations. Civil society accompaniment had replaced the pack of journalists of his days reporting on the war at *El Colombiano* and imbued his trips with an ethos of righteous indignation rather than journalistic norms of objective reporting.

One of the most tragic episodes of the war happened on May 2, 2002, about a year after Abad Colorado became independent, the massacre at

Bojayá. The event has been dissected in detail by the National Center for Historical Memory, among others, but for those unfamiliar, it ended in the death of 117 people—98 on May 2, 13 more before and after May 2, and 6 more over the next decade—and wounded more than 80 others, all Afro-Colombian residents of the area. The fighting between the FARC and the United Self-Defense Forces of Colombia (AUC), a federation of regional paramilitary groups in northwest Colombia, was part of a larger battle to control a strategic corridor for drugs and arms.[24] In an effort to repel the paramilitaries, the FARC launched a series of gas cylinder bombs, artisanal and notoriously imprecise weapons. One burst through the roof of the church where many people had gathered in the hope that the belligerents would respect their sanctuary. The scale and symbolism of the event punctured a collective callousness built up after decades of political violence.

Unlike most journalists who traveled to the region a week later in a convoy of government helicopters, Abad Colorado left almost immediately with a Spanish journalist to Quibdó to speak with the representatives of the diocese there. With the Church's support, they traveled by boat upriver. Abad Colorado's images document a man bent over the coffin of his wife, women gathered in contemplative disbelief, people leaving the area in motorized canoes. Two of the most emblematic images of this series is of a man in the front of one of those boats holding up a makeshift white flag (interestingly, this image resonates with the picture he imagined taking in the Caguán), and a picture of a shattered sculpture of Christ—no arms, no legs, no crucifix, just torso and head—in the destroyed church.

Abad Colorado's images are rawer, even as he is careful not to photograph the carnage directly. And unlike many of the journalists who came to document the tragedy, Abad Colorado would return, one month later, four months later, and again over the years.[25] It is hard to gauge the extent of connection between Abad Colorado and his subjects in Bojayá. In *El Testigo*, the relationships can feel forced and awkward (a dynamic likely exacerbated by the presence of the camera crew). Yet, relative to most of his colleagues, Abad Colorado is reflexive about his role as a documentarian and takes steps to work in a reciprocal way with his subjects and their communities. This comparative difference establishes Abad Colorado as an ethical witness among his peers, obliquely responsive to media critiques from the academy that are often felt but not acknowledged by media professionals hesitant to undermine their own authority.

The fact that the massacre at Bojayá was perpetrated by the FARC and occurred during the electoral rise of Álvaro Uribe, coincided with its scale and the symbolism of the failed sanctuary of the church, ensure that it resounded particularly strongly in the media and through the ensuing decades. Abad Colorado's image of the amputated Christ became iconic. The

262 Alexander L. Fattal

Figure 12.2 Peace on the River (Atrato River, Chocó), May 2002. Courtesy of Jesús Abad Colorado.

suffering symbol had itself been shattered, the beams of the crucifix and those of the church lay broken on the floor. The message was clear, no place was safe, no space sacred enough to provide protection, no savior could stop the carnage.

The Moral Vision and Moral Performance of Jesús Abad Colorado 263

Figure 12.3 *Christ in Pieces* (Bojayá, Chocó), May 2002. Courtesy of Jesús Abad Colorado.

Though a certain messianism was building around Álvaro Uribe, he would prove a polarizing persona. The country lacked a figure with a moral vision who was, or at least appeared to be, untainted by the partisanship of the conflict, except for Father Francisco de Roux. Gradually, Abad Colorado has stepped into that void by serving as a conduit for empathy. As he clicked the shutter of his camera with a mixture of indignation and compassion, he built an archive that served as the basis of compelling presentations that he would share with ever-larger audiences from podiums, radio booths, television sets, and in virtual forums.

From Moral Vision to Moral Performance

After documenting the massacre at Bojayá, Abad Colorado's reach extended. One year later, the Swiss government sponsored a large exhibition of his photographs, "Memoria, la guerra olvidada en Colombia" (Memory, The Forgotten War in Colombia), and took it on a two-year tour to Switzerland's main cities, including a showing at UN headquarters in Geneva. The Swiss government had been one of the "friendly countries" during the 1999–2002 peace talks. Through Abad Colorado's images, the Swiss highlighted what a missed opportunity those talks had been and suggested that Europe and the UN should remain attentive to the unfolding tragedy in Colombia. The exhibition validated Abad Colorado's role as an ethical witness and boosted his standing at home. The exhibit's framing, "against forgetting," a human rights slogan throughout Latin America, was by then a familiar trope in the framing of Abad Colorado's work. It simultaneously signals a call to slow down and recall horrific events and the suffering they have caused and a more general plea to refocus the public's attention on working-class people, peasants, who are the conflict's primary victims and fighters. Here Abad Colorado sets himself up to serve as a corrective to the structural invisibilities of the Colombian media system, inordinately focused on elite, urban, and intellectual perspectives.[26] He does not leave this critique latent, rather centering it in his public talks, imploring—often urban—audiences to not so easily dismiss, ignore, or consume and forget, snippets of suffering, and rather allow themselves to be affected.[27]

In an interview in 2015 about Abad Colorado's book *Mirar la vida profunda*, journalist Álvaro García asked Abad Colorado why his photographs did not include pictures of guerrilla, paramilitary, or military commanders. "Because they don't deserve it," Abad Colorado responded, continuing,

> This is a book that's about the victims. There are soldiers and rank and file guerrillas or paramilitary kids . . . but you won't find Mancuso (AUC leader) or Tirofijo (co-founder of the FARC) or Gabino, Antonio Garcia

The Moral Vision and Moral Performance of Jesús Abad Colorado 265

(ELN leaders) in any of my many exhibits, no big commanders on the left or the right, or important politicians.[28]

What Abad Colorado does not say, because he does not have to, is that the media has fallen into the trap of lionizing authority and privileging its competing discourses at the expense of the lived realities of common people.[29] In other instances, Abad Colorado is explicit when it comes to media criticism. As he said in one of our interviews, "Instead of producing news that helps understand the conflict, Colombian media produce news that fills the population with fear, that makes the people terrified."[30]

The producers of Álvaro García's television interview of Abad Colorado intersperse a montage of his photos as the two talk, as is common in Abad Colorado's media appearances. The combination is impactful but not as powerful as when Abad Colorado curates his own presentations in which he combines his own images and storytelling cum editorializing about those images to dramatic effect. The following excerpt is from his 35-minute presentation to the high-profile event *Hablemos de verdad* (Let's talk about truth), organized by *El Espectador* (and its E.U. sponsor) in May of 2019.[31] Commanders from the former FARC, former AUC, and the Colombian Army all attended.

> How many peasants have I seen flee from their territories? (*Image of people packed onto a giant canoe with their belongings, houses built on stilts over water in the background.*) In villages built on raised sticks, like Nueva Venecia, in regions like San Carlos where I saw a man, Misael, carry out his children, his refrigerator. (*Image of Misael carrying a large refrigerator on his back with a girl, presumably his daughter, running in front of him.*) But Misael—and please look at the photographs that should be viewed carefully—Misael carried out his refrigerator, his children, his chickens, but Misael also took out his pigs. (*Image of Misael carrying pig over his shoulder as it squeals.*) And this pig is crying for the peasants of this country (*image of woman and child fording a river on horseback*) that are fleeing war, who leave with chickens (*image of toddler kissing a chicken's head*), dogs (*image of dog stretching on street*), pigs (*image of girl trying to carry a pig*), monkeys, with all the animals (*image of child holding a large fish*). And I say, how much longer? (*Image of a small monkey holding onto the head of an indigenous child.*) That's why it's important to continue working for peace (*image of a child guerrilla fighter with a bandolier of heavy ammunition draped over his torso laughing*) and not continuing to divide us (*image of rifle tip pointing up the torso to the neck of someone in camouflage wearing a scapular*) because this can't go on in Colombia (*image of military landing via helicopter to prepare for a major operation*).

Who carries the guns in our country (*image of hundreds of paramilitary youths in formation with hands over their hearts*)? Who carries them (*image of boy peering from beyond a wall at a man carrying a gun*)? The children of the same peasantry (*image of young soldier crying with hand on forehead*), the same ones that I see crying (*repeat of image of child guerrilla fighter with a bandolier of heavy ammunition draped over his torso laughing*). Soldiers or children in the guerrilla. And it's reprehensible because the only thing that I want to make clear to this auditorium—and I apologize for the time that I'm taking—what I want to do here is talk about what's true—and the only truth that I know in this country is not red, blue, yellow, or green, no. This is how the photographs are. What you are seeing is in black and white but [the pictures] have many nuances. They have the heart and soul of a photographer, who, when he presses his finger what he feels is the pulse of the soul, the only thing I know. I can say it here to Luis Eduard Cifuentes (regional paramilitary leader), who I know, and to Mr. Timoleón Rodrigo Londoño (sic., the FARC's last commander) because I know you (*les conozco*): I don't lie—and General Colón, who I respect. I tell you, in war, it's *the youth* that die but *the arms* that survive. I'm tired of seeing mass graves in our country. A weapon passes from one hand to another (*slideshow reverses to review recent images*), which is why I always reject war. War enriches the entrepreneurs of death, those who manufacture arms, those who take over land. And we fill the country up to the sky, ocean, and land with war. And yes, it's a deeply religious country (*image of a paramilitary fighter with a small statue of the Divine Child Jesus latched into his vest next to the butt of his rifle*) but it doesn't even respect the commandment "thou shall not kill."[32]

You, the reader, may excuse the length of the quote. I include it because it encapsulates Abad Colorado's style of public speaking, which is primarily of a righteousness that shifts suddenly from compassion to indignation. It is also associative to the point of rambling, reliant more on an emotional combination punch of image and impassioned reflection than a logical argument. Abad Colorado leans into his natural talent as a storyteller and improvises around a loose script, staying within the parameters of a discourse that, though it has shifted slightly over time, has always emphasized: Non-partisanship and a refusal of vengeance, an orientation toward peasants and victims, attention to the ecological dimension of the conflict, outrage at elites for corruption and quietly fueling the war, and Colombia's deeply religious ideological underpinnings. He uses his images like bumpers in pinball, bouncing off them as he jumps around this constellation of themes. As his slideshow moves around the country in an emotionally charged photographic tour, the affective and moral impact of his presentations build gradually, with affective engagement and moral indignation mutually reinforcing the other.[33]

Conclusion: Preaching a Post-partisan Story Worth a Thousand Pictures

As his megaphone has grown over the past 20 years, Abad Colorado has become an expert photo-storyteller. He offers his own narratives of encountering the people in his photographs, fills out the context in which the images were made, recalls pieces of dialogue with his subjects, and injects elements of "color," to use journalistic parlance to refer to the instrumental anecdote, to enliven his mostly black and white images. This is not common among professional photographers operating within the professional norm of a gendered masculine reticence. In this professional code, the images are supposed to speak for themselves and for the odyssey that was required to make them. There are exceptions to the reigning ocularcentrism of the craft, when a photographer is implored to speak—upon winning an award, opening an exhibit, or being interviewed by the press—but even in such instances, there is professional pressure to keep commentary brief. Photographers are presumed to speak primarily through their eye and its mechanical extension.

In understanding Abad Colorado's decision to break this mold, his early influences are revealing. As a student at the Universidad de Antioquia, recalls, he stumbled into photography, having gravitated first to the acerbic critiques of Héctor Abad Gómez and Alberto Aguirre in their columns, both of which wrote harshly about the elite consensus. In a way, Abad Colorado's profile is better understood as part of the Colombian tradition of critical essayists and chroniclers who act as public intellectuals than within a photographic tradition (that he seems indifferent to if not casually ignorant of). It would only be after Abad Colorado established himself as a photographer that he began to speak of having been attracted to the work of Colombian photographer Leo Matiz or the likes of Henri Cartier-Bresson, a post-hoc emplotment into the most mainstream of photographic histories in Colombia and abroad. When we spoke in 2001, he played coyly ignorant of photographic traditions or theories, saying "I've recorded what I saw. In the style of—I haven't read much about Cartier-Bresson, I haven't read much—but simply and plainly know that the man said that things happen and you record them."[34] Though it is logical that Abad Colorado would be inspired by Leo Matiz's portraiture of the peasantry, Matiz's international focus and publicity work sits uneasily with Abad Colorado's trenchant nationalism and disdain for commercial work. When presented with the platitude "a picture is worth a thousand words," in an interview, Abad Colorado pushed back, "the photograph or video is important only insofar as someone tells the story. It's controversial, but an image isn't worth more than a thousand words. Photography and words need to come together for there to be a story."[35] This is where Abad Colorado has excelled.

The story that Abad Colorado tells through his archive has increasingly crystallized into: *Colombia is a country that has forsaken its Catholic foundation and descended into an inferno of tragedies; the peasantry bears the brunt of those tragedies while pockets of civil society resist the robust, fratricidal war machine.* Photographs may be the visible vehicle for telling this story, but it is the religious idioms that Abad Colorado has increasingly used that have enabled his visual work and public persona to bridge the partisan chasm that has marred Colombian history and been reconfigured since Álvaro Uribe reluctantly left office in 2010. Here we can see a longer thread of continuity with the religious peace movement, especially the work of the Jesuits in Colombia and the trajectory of Francisco de Roux who gave Abad Colorado's career an early boost. Interviewers who try to pin Abad Colorado as a leftist sympathizer—despite his kidnapping at the hands of the FARC and ELN in the late 1990s—find themselves outmaneuvered when he jumps over the divisive premise of the question by using his own biography and experiences to skirt the zero-sum logic of the war and move the question to ethical and humanitarian concerns.[36] As he does this, he claims a moral high ground with his voice and his vision and achieving what so few in Colombia are able to do: Undercut the partisanship that fuels the conflict.

His photographic eye for religious symbolism—not only in the churches of Granada and Bojayá but also evident in a series he made of religious symbols and charms worn by paramilitaries in the early 2000s—combines with his reflections on the religion-infused ideology of Colombian society. The latter gained prominence in Abad Colorado's public talks and media appearances through the 2010s. As he centered religion, specifically Catholicism, his ethical celebrity transformed into a moral performance. This growing emphasis on religiosity, more than any other element in his discourse, has enabled him to connect the left of human rights activism with political conservatism on the right, striking a profile that balances and transcends competing forces even as his critical disposition resonates with the left. Abad Colorado embodies a moral discourse that is often reserved for left-leaning clergy in conflict-ridden countries, figures that set an example of a righteous commitment to truth and reconciliation. In Colombia, he has hedged into that space by achieving a voice and influence exceedingly rare for a documentary photographer, let alone one who, since the late-2000s, has been surpassed by many of his peers in terms of technical mastery, compositional skill, and reflexivity about the genre itself. Though Abad Colorado is not ordained, his discourse, by now deeply familiar to those attentive to the Colombian public sphere has come to resemble a sermon, one that the country continues to ignore at its own peril.

Toward the end of *El Testigo*, Abad Colorado returns to Patio Bonito, the hamlet of San Carlos, where conservative partisans killed his grandfather and uncle with his now elderly aunt who witnessed the horrific event and is haunted by it. His father had said he never wanted to return and Abad Colorado confesses to coming close to the village many times but never having felt able to enter. His parents' farm is gone. A small church now stands on the property. Abad Colorado takes a portrait of his aunt holding a black and white portrait of his grandparents, her parents. He and his aunt light a candle and recite the Lord's Prayer before the alter. The edit of the film highlights the line "forgive our trespasses as we forgive those who trespass against us," looping the line as the audio track of another slideshow of Abad Colorado's images fills the screen—a man holding a cross up defiantly with the name of a deceased handwritten on it, a small girl walking past a soldier with handgun drawn, a coffin being handed over outstretched hands and into the chamber of a cemetery, women with hands over mouths in mourning in Bojayá.

The sequence segues into the final segment of the film in which Abad Colorado speaks to a university audience and tells the story of a guerrilla commander lecturing him about a woman, Camila. The commander speaks of Camila and introduces her as someone who lost her father and two siblings, one 20 months old and the other 5 years old, in the paramilitary massacre in San José de Apartadó in 2005. She had kept a press cutting from *Semana* in her pack since. Abad Colorado realized that he was the author and photographer for that story, having been the only journalistic witness to the massacre's immediate aftermath. When he returned to Medellín after his time with the guerrilla unit, he searched his archive for a picture of the guerrilla fighter and recognized her as an adolescent pictured in his image of a girl nailing a cross in the ground to mark the death of her father. The film then cuts to a trip Abad Colorado makes to the FARC transitional camp after the peace accord had been signed to see Camila again. Now she is ten years older than in the photo and has a toddler, her daughter, in her arms. She explains that the urge to avenge her family's murder drove her to join the FARC. Choking back tears, she reads an excerpt from the press clipping in which the paramilitary commander is quoted as saying that they had to kill the children because they would grow up to be guerrillas. When Abad Colorado asks, she responds that now, committed to the peace process, she would forgive her family's killers, even after all the suffering she has endured—and presumably also caused. With that message reverberating is how I will leave this story of Abad Colorado's moral vision and moral performance.

Notes

1 The author would like to acknowledge the help of Andrés Felipe Caicedo who served not only as a diligent research assistant but also a sounding board and critical colleague whose engagement has greatly enhanced this chapter, as well as Lina Britto, A. Ricardo López-Pedreros, Íngrid Bolívar, Catalina Uribe Rincón, María del Rosario Acosta López, and Héctor Fernández-L'Hoeste for their extraordinary feedback.
2 It is worth noting that Horne's only previous solo-directed documentary is about Colombian author and Nobel Laureate Gabriel García Márquez, *Gabo, la creación de Gabriel García Márquez* (2015). In both films she blends active interviews with archival materials to tell her story as a recomposition of the past in the present.
3 *The Salt of the Earth*, directed by Juliano Salgado and Wim Wenders (2014; Cannes, France: Decia Films, 2015) and *War Photographer*, directed by Christian Frei (2001; USA: Christian Frei Filmproductions/Swiss National Television).
4 In their unwavering celebratory tone, all three films hedge into the realm of sophisticated public relations.
5 *Pictures from a Revolution*, directed by Alfred Guzzetti, Richard Rogers and Susan Meiselas (1991; USA: GMR Films).
6 On the dynamics of post-war photojournalism, see Nadia Bair's extraordinary *The Decisive Network: Magnum Photos and the Postwar Image Market* (Oakland: University of California Press, 2020).
7 Nelson Padilla, "Jesús Abad Colorado: La mirada por excelencia," *Festival Gabo*, September 10, 2019. https://premioggm.org/noticias/2019/09/jesus-abad-Abad Colorado-la-mirada-por-excelencia/.
8 Carolina Ponce de León and Jesús Abad Colorado, *Mirar de la vida profunda* (Bogotá: Paralelo 10 Ltda., 2015), 16.
9 Ponce de León and Abad Colorado, *Mirar de la vida profunda*, 36.
10 For a great summary of the partisan press dynamics in the early republican period, see David Bushnell, "The Development of the Press in Great Colombia," *The Hispanic American Historical Review* 30, no. 4 (November 1950): 432–452; and Maryluz Vallejo's treatment of the same subject in the late 19th century in *A plomo herido: Una crónica del periodismo en Colombia, 1880–1980* (Bogotá: Planeta, 2006).
11 Interview by the author, November 8, 2001.
12 Interview by the author, December 6, 2001.
13 That is not to say that the photographers were on the same page. Abad Colorado described a sharp division between the purists, represented by Gabriel Buitrago, who took a strictly documentary line, and the montage-ists (*de montaje*) who had no scruples with manipulating or setting up images. Abad Colorado describes confronting Agudelo when he worked under him at *El Colombiano* and having barbed exchanges on the subject.
14 For a visual homage to Albeiro Lopera, known affectionately in Medellín as "el 9," see Alfonso Buitrago Londoño and Stephen Ferry, graphic editor, *El 9, Albeiro Lopera: Un fotógrafo en guerra* (Medellín: Tragaluz Editores, 2015).
15 Alfonso Buitrago Londoño describes this pod system of group protection, as exemplified by the crew that tended to travel in Natalia Botero's Jeep, in *El 9: Albeiro Lopera*, 94–100. A similar phenomenon played out at night in urban Cali where Óscar Muñoz, Fernell Franco, and Eduardo Carvajal would band

together; see Juanita Solano Roa, "Melodrama's Fictional System: Fernell Franco's Photography and the Golden Age of Mexican Cinema," *History of Photography* 44, no. 2–3 (2020): 185. For a discussion of a similar phenomenon in the context of civil war in El Salvador, see Mark Pedelty's *War Stories: The Culture of Foreign Correspondents*, (New York: Routledge, 2022), chapter 2.

16 Colombian filmmakers Luis Ospina and Carlos Mayolo coined the term *pornomiseria* in their 1978 manifesto, that accompanied their groundbreaking film *Agarrando Pueblo* (Vampires of Poverty).

17 Jorge Iván Bonilla and Ancízar Narváez Montoya, "The Media in Colombia: Beyond Violence and a Market-Driven Economy," in *The Media in Latin America*, ed. Jairo Lugo-Ocando (New York: Open University Press, 2008), 78–99.

18 For a recent reflection on how to characterize Colombia's media system, see Catalina Montoya-Londoño, "In Search of a Model for the Colombian Media System Today," in *Media Systems and Communication Policies in Latin America*, eds. Manuel Alejandro Guerrero and Mireya Márquez-Ramírez (London: Palgrave Macmillan, 2014), 66–81.

19 Interview by the author, February 22, 2002.

20 Interview by the author, January 29, 2002.

21 Lorenzo Morales and Marta Ruiz, *Hechos para contar: Conversaciones con diez periodistas colombianos* (Bogotá: Penguin Random House, 2013).

22 Interview by the author, February 22, 2002.

23 Interview by the author, January 29, 2001.

24 Comisión Nacional de Reparación y Reconciliación, *Bojayá: La guerra sin límites* (Bogotá: Ediciones Semana and Taurus, 2010).

25 For an insightful comparison between his works from different trips to Bojayá, see Julián Mejía Villa, "La fotografía violenta: Dispositivo alegórico y construcción emblemática de la masacre de Bojayá" (MA thesis, Universidad Nacional de Colombia, 2017), 39–41.

26 For a theoretically rich reflection on the structural invisibilities of the Colombian conflict, see Jorge Iván Bonilla Vélez, *La barbarie que no vimos: Fotografía y memoria en Colombia* (Medellín: Editorial Eafit, 2019). Bonilla Vélez dwells on what it means to claim "we didn't see" as a way of denying the proximity of the conflict (loc. 292). Abad Colorado's work as a witness relentlessly undercuts such deniability.

27 For more on the call to contemplation in Abad Colorado's work in Bojayá, see Mejía Villa, "La fotografía violenta," 63.

28 "Palabras más con Jesús Abad Colorado (2/2)," Palabras más, published on June 18, 2017, video, 24:27. https://youtu.be/ZAk7Qve9MD8.

29 Here Abad Colorado echoes the ethos of 1930s documentary photography in the United States, especially James Agee and Walker Evans' classic *Let Us Now Praise Famous Men*, though Abad Colorado gives no indication that he is aware or interested in this or other similar work.

30 Interview by the author, February 22, 2002.

31 To watch the full talk, which I highly recommend, see: www.youtube.com/watch?v=3m-62xqrW28&list=PLyO-gZSyewQhilMMooLTCkS6k1OXoq1CV.

32 Jesús Abad Colorado, "Jesús Abad Colorado: ¿Hasta cuándo la guerra? Es necesario trabajar por la paz," Colombia 2020, published May 29, 2019, video, 34:55. https://youtu.be/3m-62xqrW28

33 Although Abad Colorado has managed to maintain an impressive degree of coherence in his public personae, a contradiction emerges when he sells his

images for thousands of dollars. When I interviewed curator Carolina Ponce de León, she offered a glimpse into the opaquer realm of Abad Colorado's public personae, the sale of his photographs to the ultra-wealthy, raising the issue of the prickly ethics of turning human suffering into commodified art. She said, "Chucho is a cool guy and likes to infiltrate all types of spaces. You can buy a picture of his for $10,000, but he'll do an exhibit for a school in any hamlet. He has a fluidity with respect to the circulation of his images that's very cool." Interview by the author and Andrés Felipe Caicedo, January 28, 2022.
34 Interview by the author, November 3, 2001.
35 "Entrevistas con Hernán—Jesús Abad Colorado, Part 1," Entrevistas con Hernán, published July 7, 2020, video, 08:49. https://youtu.be/bsAPqC1LfQA.
36 A good example of this would be his interview with Claudia Palacios at *Canal Capital* in 2017. https://youtu.be/j4e__KSmfYI.

13 Community Radio Stations and the Construction of Modern Indigeneity in Cauca, Colombia

Diego Mauricio Cortés

During the last decades of the twentieth century, Latin American indigenous people became influential political actors by employing indigeneity as a tool for political organization. This move marked the transformation of the indigenous movement's strategy—by pivoting from a class to identity focus—as a means of political contestation.[1] In Colombia, the Misak and Nasa people from the department of Cauca pioneered this new type of political mobilization. They created the first regional indigenous organization, the Consejo Regional Indígena del Cauca (Indigenous Regional Council of Cauca or CRIC) in 1971,[2] coordinated the first uprisings for territorial reclamation,[3] and participated in drafting the Constitution of 1991 that recognized Colombia as a pluriethnic and multicultural nation.[4] They have also engaged with de facto and administrative autonomous practices to ensure local governance.[5] Nasa's and Misak's remarkable political achievements have resulted from a synergy of forces, among them, the modernization agendas of the Catholic Church, the neoliberal state, and Evangelical organizations.

By analyzing three community-oriented radio stations: The Catholic-sponsored Acción Cultural Popular (ACPO), the state-supported indigenous radio stations (IRS), and the Evangelical Indigenous Radio Stations (EIRS), this chapter illustrates how these external actors influenced the Nasa and Misak. These mass media have served as instruments for promoting Catholic, neoliberal, and Evangelical agendas. This case study helps to de-essentialize modern indigenous identities by illustrating how they are disputed grounds, constantly shaped by the interaction between indigenous cultures and multiple external actors.

ACPO, IRS, and EIRS represent three overlapping visions and periods of "indigenous modernization" that facilitated but also restrained indigenous people's cultural aspirations and political goals in the Cauca region. For example, from the 1960s to the 1980s, ACPO provided the Nasa and Misak access to basic education and training on community organizing, contributing to the development of indigenous institutional and political efforts.

DOI: 10.4324/9781003048152-18

However, ACPO also promoted modernizing developmentalist discourses and practices that replaced autochthonous technologies more suitable for people's cultural, geographical, and political realities.[6] Since the 1990s, the IRS has contributed to the indigenous movement by forging new leaders, promoting indigenous languages, encouraging political mobilization, and facilitating their democratic participation and articulation with the state. But these state-supported radio stations also facilitated a "neoliberal governmentality" by creating new economic obligations, legal restrictions, and dependence on external funders.[7] Meanwhile, EIRS have provided essential services to those affected by gender-based violence and alcoholism since the 1980s. Evangelical media outlets have also served as tools for religious recruitment by providing health and educational services.[8]

This chapter aims to conceptualize the relationship between modernization and indigenous identities, unveiling the intervention of the Catholic Church, the state, and Evangelicalism in the way the Misak and Nasa peoples forged their modern identities. Research results came from several periods of ethnographic field work in Cauca since 2008, a compilation of ACPO data from the Luis Ángel Arango Library in Bogotá, and interviews with state representatives, local academics, Evangelicals, indigenous leaders, and media practitioners. It includes a drawing that depicts Misaks receiving literacy and home improvement classes in an ACPO's radiophonic school, which was part of a 20-month collaborative research project on oral histories with the Misak by Rosa Montano, John Montano, and Liliana Camayo—three Misak students at the Misak University, a grassroots educational project. The ethnographic research and collaborative project led me to conclude that "modern indigeneity" is a hybrid identity that aims to keep an epistemic differentiation from mainstream capitalist forms of production and consumption.[9] Territoriality—an ontological space where people and the environment coproduce life—is fundamental for the construction of indigeneity.[10] This theoretical route has allowed me to analyze the paradoxical outcomes of the intervention of the Catholic, the neoliberal, and the Evangelical modernization agendas in the Cauca region. I argue that, on the one hand, these external actors have pushed for a process of incorporation into the capitalist logic through various methods—such as developmentalism, individuality, and multicultural citizenship—while, on the other hand, they have also contributed to the forging of indigenous identities and equipped Misak and Nasa with political and cultural tools to contest that incorporation.

Indigenous Peoples as Modern Subjects

According to Latin American elite discourses, outdated social, political, and economic practices have restricted indigenous people's access to the benefits of modernity.[11] Modernity's potential advantages include participating in the nation's democratic deliberation and decision-making,[12] the development of indigenous peoples as rational-secular individuals,[13] their participation in the market economy,[14] and access to essential services such as formal education and healthcare.[15] Despite these promises, the complete immersion into modern trends has reduced indigenous peoples, who practice non-Western spiritual rituals, languages, modes of production, and kinship relations, into consumers and cheap laborers.[16] Various decolonial scholars have deconstructed modernist developmental agendas by unveiling the historical fallacy that positions modernity as a European phenomenon that pursues human betterment at a universal scale.[17] These scholars have also linked modernity to colonial institutions that created concepts such as "indigeneity" to subjugate pre-Columbus cultures, and they have recognized that these subjugated peoples reappropriated the term "indigeneity" to transform it from a tool of domination into discourses of political resistance.[18]

Inspired by decolonial theory, critical approaches to modernity,[19] and the concept of hybridity,[20] the Chilean sociologist Jorge Larraín proposes a critical view of the relationship between modernity and identity formation.[21] Larraín and others criticize the "culturalist approach" that positions identities as "innate essences" without considering complex processes in their formation.[22] Larraín criticizes conservatives, liberals, and indigenists for their tendency to position Latin American indigeneity in opposition to modernity. Conservatives and liberals deem indigeneity as an obstacle to the advancement of the Euro-American path to progress, while indigenists advocate for a returning to indigenous traditions to prevent the encroachment of "foreign modernization."[23] In contrast, Larraín proposes understanding indigeneity and other Latin American hybrid identities as modern. These identities are composed of various attributes including solidarity, traditionalism, religiosity, clientelism, authoritarianism, legalism, exclusion, and hidden racism.[24] As an alternative, Larraín approaches identity as a social process shaped by many forces, including religion, sexuality, and ethnicity. According to Brian Stross, identities are recognized as "homogeneous," despite their multiple influences, due to "cycles of hybridity" or prolonged periods of reconfiguration.[25] Indeed, "cycles of hybridity" have homogenized Misak and Nasa identities, obscuring the influence of Catholicism, the state, and Evangelicalism in how indigenous people forged their own identities.

Hybridity does not make Latin American modernity inferior vis-à-vis the Euro-American model. The supposed secular, rational, bureaucratic, and egalitarian character of the latter becomes tenuous when, for instance, one scrutinizes the power of religion in the U.S. political culture,[26] the institutional dismantling of Western democracies,[27] and the structural racism against minorities in the United States[28] and Europe.[29] Indigenous and Euro-American modernities share—at least in theory—their pursuit of "development"—understood as the improving of living conditions for all—and "progress"—or their willingness to overcome current challenges toward a better future.[30] Based on these approaches, I claim that Misak and Nasa are "modern subjects." Different forces have shaped these identities, including their own "traditions" and the influence of external actors. This constantly transforming subjectification has created boundaries but also possibilities to resist, adapt, navigate, and project themselves into modern times. Such is the case of community-oriented radio stations in the Cauca region, led by the Catholic Church, the neoliberal state, and Evangelicals, which played an essential role in this indigenous people's identarian (re)construction.

The Catholic ACPO

Following efforts by the United States, Argentina, and Cuba to raise national literacy levels, the Colombian government employed a public radio initiative to promote literacy and a sense of national identity among largely isolated populations during the 1930s and 1940s.[31] As part of this program, the Catholic priest José Joaquín Salcedo founded Radio Sutatenza in 1947 to provide peasants of Sutatenza, an impoverished township located in the department of Boyacá, introductory lessons on Catholic faith, literacy, and math. This initial project would expand into ACPO's national multimedia educational project two years later, thanks to the support of the Catholic establishment and the Conservative Party government. ACPO exposed rural populations to "Integral Fundamental Education," a method grounded in five areas: spirituality, health, literacy, math, work ethics, and economics.[32] Based on the 1950s U.S. developmental views and conservative Catholicism, ACPO aimed to transform "backward" rural populations into "modern agents of national development," attuned to Catholic and capitalist principles, healthy habits, and anti-communism.[33] Developmental and private organizations, such as the United Nations Educational, Scientific and Cultural Organization (UNESCO) and Chase Group, provided ACPO with technical assistance and money to develop various multimedia initiatives, including radio broadcasting, *El Campesino* newspaper, booklets, and audio clips.[34]

ACPO's multimedia initiatives reached ordinary folks nationally through local organizations called radio schools. These schools consisted of groups of five to ten students led by a community member with basic literacy skills and guided by local parishes who followed ACPO's classes broadcasted three times per day. These classes were based on the ACPO's five study areas and organized into three educational levels—primary, progressive, and complementary.[35] La Voz de los Andes, a U.S. Evangelical missionary radio station, pioneered a similar long-distance educational format in the 1930s in neighboring Ecuador. In 1963, missionary nuns of the Madre Laura congregation, or Lauritas, organized the first ACPO radio schools in the Misak and Nasa territories. These radio schools were a continuation of local educational initiatives led by the Lauritas and other Catholic congregations, such as Vincentians and the Lazarists, who had promoted indigenous acculturation since colonial times. Catholic domination over indigenous people after the wars of independence in the 1810s was renewed during the Conservative counterreforms (1863–1886) that reversed the Liberal Party's secular educational policies. One of the most critical policies was the 1887 Concordat, which transferred the responsibility for national education to the Church, lasting until the Constitution of 1991 abolished it. The 1887 Concordat consolidated the power of Catholic missions that aimed to replace indigenous spiritual rituals, languages, and collective modes of production with Catholic practices, Spanish, "traditional" gender roles, and capitalist methods of production and ownership.

Correspondence between ACPO personnel at the local level—such as priests, organizers, radio schools' leaders, students, and national coordinators—between 1963 and 1976, shows the initial clashes between the Catholic organization, the Nasas and Misaks. For instance, ACPO local organizer Ángel Piedrahita complained to José Antonio Rodríguez, ACPO office coordinator, about the Misak's "apathy" and "reluctance to progress."[36] According to various testimonies from former participants, the leading reason for the initial indifference among the Misak was not a lack of interest to modernize their living conditions, but the authoritarian attitude of ACPO's leaders, especially over their religious affiliation. For instance, *taita* Mariano Cuchillo, who self-identified as Evangelical, remembered how ACPO leaders forced everyone to attend Catholic service every week, a situation he did not resist to gain access to technical training in agriculture and home improvement.[37] In addition to religious indoctrination, ACPO's training brought other challenges to these indigenous communities. For instance, the ACPO promoted the maximization of agricultural production through Green-Revolution technologies, such as massive irrigation, standardized seeds, and chemical fertilizers. According to taita Cuchillo, ACPO techniques initially increased production, cultivation in times of drought, and broadened access to technologies via education in geometry, and math. However, these positive outcomes became overshadowed by long-term negative consequences, such as dependency on agro-industrial products, the disappearance of local native seeds, new undiagnosed respiratory diseases, and the progressive desertification of farming areas.

Similar mixed outcomes resulted from ACPO's campaign for home improvement. ACPO followed other developmental agencies in promoting brick houses as signifiers of progress and prosperity, denigrating traditional materials such as *bahareque* (clay and canes) and adobe, which are less expensive and more suitable for the cold and rainy weather, as well as seismic-prone areas in the region.[38] Even though the brick houses were more durable, their higher cost pushed many Misak to acquire debts and engage in the illegal production of opium poppy, resulting in a social crisis partially resolved with self-eradication campaigns in the 1990s.[39] ACPO's "modern houses" had brick stoves with better ventilation and more comfortable cooking areas, yet they replaced the *fogón* (firepit), considered by the Misak as the most critical place for cultural reproduction.

Beyond agriculture and home improvement, literacy represents ACPO's most paradoxical intervention in shaping the Misak and Nasa political and cultural identities. For example, ACPO educated several individuals whose work became crucial in consolidating the indigenous movement in the 1970s. Javier Calambas of the Misak, Marcos Yule of the Nasa, and many others who founded the CRIC—the first and most militant indigenous organization in Colombia—accessed primary education through ACPO.[40] Also, ACPO's leadership school served as one of the first places for training several Nasa and Misak school teachers. One of them is *mama*

Figure 13.1 Drawing of ACPO class with Guambiano students for collaborative research project on historical memory. On the chalkboard: "Radio Sutatenza: Ignorance is a sin." Resguardo de Guambia (Silvia, Cauca), June 2015.

Source: Author's research archive.

María Rosa Tombé Tunubalá, recipient of the 2011 Compartir Award as the best teacher in Colombia for her pedagogy teaching children the Misak language, Nam Trick.[41]

ACPO, however, also reinforced modernist ideas that disregarded indigenous oral traditions by linking illiteracy and the use of Spanish as a second language with ignorance, sinfulness, and backwardness. The psychological affections of these stigmas continue to harm indigenous commoners until today. For instance, as part of our collaborative research with students from Misak University, we interviewed Misak elders María Elena Tombé Almendra and Sebastiana Guazá, who speak little Spanish and cannot read and write. They initially claimed a lack of knowledge because they had never attended school.[42] However, a few minutes later, they shared valuable insights about racial discrimination, medicinal plants, agriculture, moon phases, and territorial reclamation, among other socio-historic events. In addition to their lack of self-acknowledgment, they organized their narratives in a very particular way, by answering our questions indirectly, starting their historical recounts with their childhoods but unfolding them differently, nonchronologically. The conversation with Tombé Almendra and Guazá shows that illiterate people develop other memorization methods, contradicting modernist theories that degraded them as ignorant.

In sum, ACPO contributed, perhaps unintentionally, to the formation of the CRIC by providing primary education, leadership training, and access to modern technologies in agriculture and home improvement to the traditionally excluded indigenous communities of the Cauca region. However, this project also reinforced internalized stigmas by promoting developmental technologies as "superior" to indigenous people's agriculture, construction, and memory practices.

The State-Sponsored Indigenous Radio Stations

In the 1970s, scholars developed critical analyses of ACPO's developmentalism based primarily on theories endogenous to Latin America, such as Dependency Theory[43] and Liberation Theology.[44] Stefan Musto and Luis Ramiro Beltrán criticized ACPO's lack of connection with the social bases, insufficient commitment to structural change, and the absence of the rural population in its decision-making.[45] Yet, despite criticism, the power of ACPO and the Bolivian miner's union network of radio stations (especially Pio XII, supported by the Catholic Church), and their ability to reach wide audiences, inspired various popular sectors to develop their own radio stations.[46] Unlike ACPO, this new wave of community-oriented radio stations aimed for a more horizontal communication that responded to local political mobilizations instead of developmental agencies. One of the first radio stations of this type was Radio Eucha (good morning in Nasa Yuwe), founded in Tierradentro, Cauca, by Vincentian missionaries and Nasa leaders in 1987. This radio station, the first to broadcast in an indigenous language in Colombia, came to air after eight years of legal difficulties due to the lack of national legislation for alternative radio stations in the highly monopolized 1980s Colombian media landscape.[47]

The restrictive situation against indigenous radio stations radically changed in the following years. In 1990, the state recognized communication as a fundamental right, establishing the Ministry of Communication, the Direction of Social Communication, and the Division of Social Development—disbanded in 2009—to support popular media initiatives. Decrees 1900 and 1991 formed the basis of the right to communication that would be later stipulated in the Constitution of 1991. Based on these proclamations, the state provided licenses, legal frameworks, technical support, connections with international funders, and special programs, such as *Programa comunidad* (2000) and *Programa y radios ciudadanas: Espacios para la democracia* (2001–2010), that benefited the Misak, Nasa, and other dozens of IRS throughout the country.[48]

Four main factors influenced the radical change from state restrictions to support for IRS. First, one must consider the political engagement of indigenous people in the national arena at the end of the 1980s. Thanks to political alliances with other popular sectors, the indigenous movement gained three representatives among the 70 delegates in the National Constituent Assembly that drafted the Constitution of 1991. They were Lorenzo Muelas of the Misak, Francisco Rojas Birry of the Embera people, both elected through popular vote, and Alfonso Peña Chepe of the Nasa, who participated in exchange for the demobilization of the indigenous self-defense group Movimiento Armado Quintín Lame.[49] Along with representatives from progressive sectors, these delegates formed the "social democrat" block and achieved the nation's multiculturality and subsequent cultural and political rights for indigenous people and other minorities to be recognized. This multicultural citizenship has facilitated the indigenous people's political participation at the local, regional, and national levels. Still, it has also enabled the incorporation of indigenous people into neoliberal exploitative dynamics of global production.[50] Second, the institutional crisis in the 1980s resulted from the War on Drugs and neoliberal reforms. The Constitution of 1991 aimed to relieve this crisis through multicultural reforms[51] that included the right of communication, which facilitated the development of the IRS. These cultural rights represented a remarkable advancement of the indigenous political agenda, but they also served the political interest of traditional elite groups. For instance, having facilitated and benefited from the growth of narcoparamilitarism, a primary agent of violence against social sectors, elites often promoted cultural rights to improve their popular image.[52] Third, the shift from class-based to identity-based social movements during the 1980s contributed to the progressive deradicalization of social grievances, making the state and elites more receptive to IRS and other indigenous peoples' projects. Adrian Pulleiro illustrates how identity politics depoliticized popular media by explaining that "who is speaking" became more important than "what is being said."[53] Fourth, indigenous people represent less than 5 percent of the total population of Colombia, which facilitates state support for reforms that benefit them, such as developing IRS, and provision of special constitutional rights, insofar as they seem less disruptive than similar initiatives that would have benefitted larger disenfranchised groups, such as Blacks and peasants, who comprise more than 20 percent of the nation's population.[54]

In 1994, the state sponsored a radio station license, equipment, training, and infrastructure to an ambitious Misak media project, in exchange for participating in an eradication program of illicit crops called Plan Plante. This Misak media project included the establishment of Guambia Estéreo—the community's first licensed radio station—a newspaper, a video production facility, and a training program for indigenous media producers organized by the Misak *cabildo* (assembly) and the University of Valle's Department of Social Communication. Some years later, financial troubles due to electricity and tax costs led the Misak to close Guambia Estéreo and replace it with a new IRS called Namuy Wam, which also received economic assistance from the government and international aid programs.[55]

Nasas also founded various IRS in different locations throughout the department of Cauca, including in the cities of Toribio (Nasa Estéreo), Belalcázar (Radio Nasa de Tierradentro), Caldono (Uswal Nasa Yuwe), and Santander de Quilichao (Radio Payumat). In addition to the state and international aid programs such as UNESCO, the development of these media projects was possible thanks to Nasa's long-standing political processes supported by external *solidarios* (people in solidarity), *colaboradores* (collaborators), and members of progressive branches of the Catholic Church, including Nasa priest Álvaro Ulcué Chocué, assassinated by paramilitary groups in 1984.[56]

Indigenous organizations, state institutions, academics, and international sponsors have depicted the IRS as a solution to all sorts of problems. The list includes a lack of access to mass media production, indigenous peoples' low sense of trust in state institutions, racist representations in mass media, impunity for human rights violations and environmental crimes, and the loss of indigenous languages, spiritual beliefs, and healing practices.[57] Indeed, these projects have contributed to Misak and Nasa political and cultural agendas by forging new generations of indigenous leaders, promoting the use of indigenous languages, encouraging political organization and mobilization in times of unrest, and creating alliances with other popular organizations around the world. However, IRS's concrete outcomes are more nuanced than initial optimistic projections made by its supporters. Suffice to say, IRS created new financial burdens for organizations with already-weak finances, fostered new dependencies on external donors, and undermined horizontal communication methods. These media projects also augmented internal power conflicts between critical media producers and indigenous leaders, who deemed IRS as press offices that must work aligned with their personal interests.[58]

Ironically, many IRS's problems resulted from state's intervention and regulation. For instance, the law allows IRS news reporting but not the provision of analysis or political commentary. The law also permits "sponsors" but not the sale of advertising. It also limits the use of indigenous languages and networking. These restrictions reflect what Silvia Rivera Cusicanqui and Charles Hale have referred to as "policies of *indios permitidos*" through which the neoliberal multicultural state facilitates participatory venues, as long as they do not endanger its socioeconomic agenda.[59] Since indigenous media practitioners frequently violate restrictions that limit commercial advertising and freedom of speech, these laws ended up fostering a culture of illegality, which contradicts the original goals of IRS as a vehicle to promote citizenship and restore the fragile relationship between indigenous people and the state.[60]

IRS, in summary, have contributed to the consolidation of Nasa and Misak modern political identities, facilitating the indigenous people's political participation at the national, regional, and local levels. The development of these media projects has allowed indigenous people to learn about policymaking by participating in designing public policy on media and communication and negotiating vis-à-vis state institutions. IRS, especially those that resulted from long-lasting grassroots and progressive political processes, have also served as places for leadership formation, networking, and cultural reaffirmation. IRS have also become, however, a new venue for state control via draconian legal restrictions, cooptation, and dependencies to cover the high cost of IRS production and maintenance, among other expenses.

Evangelical Indigenous Radio Stations

EIRS have been present within the Misak territory since the 1980s. One of these radio stations is Srɪo Wam (good news in Nam Trick), the unlicensed radio network of the Comunidad Alianza Cristiana Misionera Guambiana de Colombia (CACMIGC), and the oldest Evangelical Misak congregation.[61] Srɪo Wam has played a fundamental role in the survival of CACMIGC, which has had to compete against an intense "religious market" of Catholicism, several Pentecostal and neo-Pentecostal organizations, Jehovah's Witness, and indigenous practices. Srɪo Wam promotes Evangelical advancement through a variety of programming, including "prosperity theology" that promotes wealth as a manifestation of God's grace,[62] spiritual and body healing relief, internationally and locally produced Evangelical music, and local religious and social events.[63]

Various scholars have extensively documented the role of Evangelical and related religious branches in advancing rightwing, racist, anti-homosexual, and anti-feminist political agendas. Such examples include the U.S. counterinsurgency campaign that killed hundreds of thousands of Mayans in Central America in the 1980s and the election of the ultra-right-wing Jair Bolsonaro in Brazil.[64] The relationship of Evangelicalism with rightwing politics inspired the available academic production on EIRS, resulting in an evaluation of these media outlets as inherently colonialist, conservative, and anti-democratic.[65] However, the Misak EIRS case shows a more nuanced picture of the role of Evangelical institutions in the ongoing construction of indigenous identity. These radio stations have allowed Evangelical organizations to expand their membership and internal influence, reconfiguring these indigenous communities' socioeconomic, political, and cultural practices and expectations. Even though the individualist ethos of Evangelical practice contrasts with indigenous collectivism, Evangelicalism has helped indigenous people navigate the neoliberal socioeconomic system by offering social and health services and creating venues for networking outside the community.[66]

A brief review of the history of Evangelicalism in the Cauca region is fundamental to comprehending EIRS's impact on the Misak. The Christian Missionary Alliance was the first U.S. missionary organization to reach the Misak and other Catholic-dominated indigenous populations in Cauca in the 1930s. It received support from members of the Liberal party, who sought to counteract the power of the Catholic Church, a traditional ally of the rival Conservative party, in rural areas.[67] Over time, these North American missionaries gained influence among the Misak due to their willingness to learn Nam Trick and to embrace Misak's daily routines. Evangelical interest in indigenous languages corresponds to Protestant's belief in individualist religiosity, which seeks to promote an active engagement with the Bible. The Evangelical support for indigenous languages contrasts with the Catholic tradition, which opposed its teaching and promoted biblical learning in Spanish, mediated by a priest. Evangelicals also gained supporters among the Misak due to their opposition to the historical abuse of the Catholic Church. These abuses include forced labor, exclusion of women from the few opportunities for personal growth, the prohibition of the Nam Trick language, and the mandatory participation in Catholic festivities for the Church's economic gain.[68]

The Evangelical presence continued to grow in the 1940s and 1950s, despite the opposition of the Catholic Church and the political conflict between Liberals and Conservatives known as *la Violencia* (1946–1964). During those years, Evangelicals established a bilingual educational center and a biblical institute in Misak's territory. They also promoted local women to positions of leadership within their organizations. The arrival in the 1960s of the Summer Institute of Linguistics (SLI), one of the world's most significant Evangelical educational projects for indigenous people, empowered Evangelical missional work among the Misak and several other indigenous communities. Although they were accused later of being agents of imperialism and cultural indoctrination,[69] the SLI invigorated the knowledge and use of Colombian indigenous languages by researching and producing hundreds of publications including 27 books in Misak. Despite such contributions, Evangelical missionaries' individualistic vision clashed with indigenous peoples' collective struggle for territorial reclamation during the 1970s, motivating the departure of U.S. missionaries. Evangelical Misaks, who shared the missionaries' faith but not their opposition to land seizure, assumed the control of Evangelical organizations. These local Evangelicals, led by taita Henry Eduardo Tunubalá, founded the CACMIGC. This organization initially promoted ecumenical activities with non-Evangelicals and participated in the community's political actions toward reclaiming territory.[70]

The Constitution of 1991, which proclaimed freedom of religion and stripped the Catholic Church of its power over indigenous subjects, facilitated the growth of Evangelical influence among the Misak. Ironically, once Evangelical organizations became a dominant socio-religious force, they discouraged participation in "traditional" rituals. This situation created conflicts between Misak Evangelicals and those who followed Andean spiritual beliefs. Guillermo Trejo[71] found a similar situation in Mexico, where low levels of competition between Catholics and Evangelicals resulted in religious intolerance from the dominant group. This phenomenon explains why, for instance, the Catholic Church became more supportive of social mobilization after the arrival of Evangelical missionaries in Cauca and why Evangelical presence in the Amazon, where the Catholic Church had less influence, resulted in more aggressive forms of Evangelical missionary actions.[72]

Despite the radicalization of Evangelical Misaks, institutions such as EIRS challenge the traditional dichotomy between "good Catholic" and "bad Evangelical" media. As many evangelical and non-Evangelical Misak women attest, EIRS provides a voice of relief and support to victims of gender-based violence.[73] Feminicides, intrafamily violence, and sexual assault mark high impunity levels among indigenous people due to the few economic and technical resources available to autonomous authorities for criminal investigation and prosecution. Evangelical radio stations also promote a culture of savings and money investments. They have launched campaigns against alcoholism, an acute problem affecting many elders involved in *terraje*, a semi-slavery production system that was abolished in the 1970s. As a result of Evangelical involvement in these types of social issues, the community often elected Evangelicals to lead internal positions related to processes of autonomous justice. Elizabeth Brusco found similar Evangelical interventions on behalf of peasants and working-class women in other areas of Colombia. She argues that Evangelical interventions have allowed women to contest *machismo* in their households and improve their economic situation.[74]

The progressive radicalism against other religious and traditional spiritual practices stemmed from the Evangelical dominance among Misaks, which has invigorated internal conflicts and obscured the positive Evangelical contributions to Misak society. These contributions include facilitating access to the capitalist market, essential services denied by the neoliberal state, and exercising their constitutional rights to autonomous justice despite the scarcity of resources. Misaks who want to access Evangelical services without renouncing their community's political and entertainment events have developed a flexible religious identity to bypass radical evangelization. As a result, many join Evangelical organizations while participating in carnivals and other traditional regional festivities. When their specific Evangelical organization condemns their actions, they switch to another of the dozens of Evangelical denominations within Misak territory.

Conclusion

The case of community-oriented radio stations sheds light on how Misak and Nasa indigenous identities are in constant reconfiguration. The hybridity between indigenous "traditions" and the practices and ideologies promoted by the Catholic Church, the neoliberal state, and Evangelical organizations constantly shape Misak's and Nasa's modern indigeneity. This conclusion contradicts culturalist, liberal, conservative, and indigenists approaches that evaluate indigenous identities as "premodern." This hybridity process is not absent of contradictions, restrictions, and resistances. As I have shown, the Catholic Church, the state, and Evangelical organizations have played various roles in forging the Misak and Nasa indigenous identities. They have facilitated educational opportunities, gave indigenous people access to new technologies, provided vital health care services, and encouraged self-produced media outlets. These contributions have allowed Misak and Nasa peoples to position themselves as influential political actors at the national level, an unthinkable situation before the 1970s due to historical segregation, exploitation, violence, lack of recognition, and exclusion.

The intervention of these external actors has also brought negative consequences, including the restriction of traditional practices, the dependency on the state and international cooperation, and the control of radio initiatives via legal regulations. These problems have also encouraged indigenous people to develop novel responses to overcome external limitations. As the Evangelical intervention among the Misak shows, sometimes indigenous people employ the tools provided by one of the external actors to overcome the limits imposed by others. We could also observe how the Misak forged highly volatile religious affiliations to confront Evangelical control. Evidence on the intervention of the state in shaping modern indigenous identities demonstrates, as I have documented elsewhere, that this has exacerbated local political conflicts.[75] Some consider accessing public funding as the best way to guarantee the fulfillment of constitutional rights. Others prefer self-financing and autonomous de facto practices to prevent state intervention in indigenous affairs. This case is one among many that show that interventions of powerful actors result in profound changes of indigenous communities and cultures. In other words, Misak and Nasa indigenous identities are sites of dispute, constantly shaped by the actions of indigenous people but also the interventions of external actors.

Notes

1 Arturo Escobar and Sonia E. Álvarez, "Theory and Protest in Latin America Today," in *The Making of Social Movements in Latin America: Identity, Strategy, and Democracy*, eds. Arturo Escobar and Sonia E. Álvarez (New York: Routledge, 1992), 367; Peter Wade, *Race and Ethnicity in Latin America* (London: Pluto Press, 2010).
2 Brett Troyan, "Ethnic Citizenship in Colombia: The Experience of the Regional Indigenous Council of the Cauca in Southwestern Colombia from 1970 to 1990," *Latin American Research Review* 43, no. 3 (2008): 166–191.
3 Rodolfo Stavenhagen, "Indigenous Peoples: Land, Territory, Autonomy, and Self-Determination," in *Promised Land: Competing Visions of Agrarian Reform*, eds. Peter Roser, Raj Patel, and Michael Courville (Oakland: Food First Books, 2006), 208–211.
4 Ángela Santamaría Chavarro, "Lorenzo Muelas y el constitucionalismo indígena 'desde abajo': Una retrospectiva crítica sobre el proceso constituyente de 1991," *Colombia Internacional* 79 (2013): 77–120.
5 Diego Mauricio Cortés, "The Quest for Indigenous Autonomy: Communication Media, Internal Conflicts, and Policy Reform in Colombia," *Journal of Latin American and Caribbean Anthropology* 26, no. 1 (2021): 84–103.
6 Diego Mauricio Cortés, "Foes and Allies: The Catholic Church, Acción Cultural Popular (ACPO), and the Emergence of the Indigenous Movement in Cauca, Colombia," *Latin American and Caribbean Ethnic Studies* 1, no. 2 (2019): 171–193. https://doi.org/10.1080/17442222.2019.1612828.
7 James Ferguson and Akhil Gupta, "Spatializing States: Toward an Ethnography of Neoliberal Governmentality," *American Ethnologist* 29, no. 4 (2002): 981–1002. See also Diego Mauricio Cortés, "Era mejor cuando éramos ilegales,"

Journal of Alternative and Community Media 4, no. 3 (2019): 28–42; and Diego Mauricio Cortés, "Foes and Allies."
8 Diego Mauricio Cortés, "Evangelical Indigenous Radio Stations in Colombia: Between the Promotion of Social Change and Religious Indoctrination," Global Media and Communication 16, no. 3 (2020): 313–328.
9 Jorge Larraín, "Globalización e identidad nacional," Revista Chilena de Humanidades 20 (2000): 21–42; Walter Moser, "Eulogy for Bolívar Echeverría," Anales del Instituto de Investigaciones Estéticas 32, no. 97 (2010): 195–203; Daniel Inclán, "La historia en disputa: El problema de la inteligibilidad del pasado," in Piel blanca, máscaras negras: Crítica de la razón decolonial, eds. Gaya Makaran and Pierre Gaussens (México City: Bajo Tierra, 2020), 59–60.
10 Martin Holbraad and Morten Axel Pedersen, The Ontological Turn: An Anthropological Exposition (Cambridge, UK: Cambridge University Press, 2017).
11 Larraín, "Globalización e identidad nacional," 5.
12 Ronald Inglehart and Christian Welzel, "Changing Mass Priorities: The Link between Modernization and Democracy," Perspectives on Politics 8, no. 2 (2010): 551–567.
13 Walter D. Mignolo, "Enduring Enchantment: Secularism and the Epistemic Privileges of Modernity," in Postcolonial Philosophy of Religion, eds. Purushottama Bilimoria and Andrew B. Irvine (Dordrecht, Netherlands: Springer, 2009), 273–292.
14 William M. Loker, "'Campesinos' and the Crisis of Modernization in Latin America," Journal of Political Ecology 3, no. 1 (1996): 69–88.
15 Gillette Hall and Harry Anthony Patrinos, "Indigenous Peoples, Poverty and Human Development in Latin America," in Indigenous Peoples, Poverty and Human Development in Latin America, 1994–2004, eds. Gillette Hall and Harry Anthony Patrinos (New York: World Bank, 2004).
16 Kyle T. Mays, City of Dispossessions: Indigenous Peoples, African Americans, and the Creation of Modern Detroit (Philadelphia: University of Pennsylvania Press, 2022).
17 Enrique Dussel, El encubrimiento del Otro: Hacia el origen del mito de la modernidad (Quito: Editorial Abya Yala, 1994); Arturo Escobar, La invención del Tercer Mundo: Construcción y deconstrucción del desarrollo (Bogotá: Editorial Norma, 1998); Walter D. Mignolo and Catherine E. Walsh, On Decoloniality: Concepts, Analytics, Praxis (Durham: Duke University Press, 2018); Aníbal Quijano, "Coloniality of Power and Eurocentrism in Latin America," International Sociology 15, no. 2 (2000): 215–232.
18 Les W. Field, "Who Are the Indians? Reconceptualizing Indigenous Identity, Resistance, and the Role of Social Science in Latin America," Latin American Research Review 29, no. 3 (1994): 237–248.
19 Stuart Hall, "Cultural Identity and Diaspora," in Contemporary Sociological Thought, ed. Sean P. Hier (Toronto: Canada Scholars' Press, 2005), 443–54; Peter Wagner, A Sociology of Modernity: Liberty and Discipline (London: Routledge, 2002).
20 Néstor García Canclini, Culturas híbridas: Estrategias para entrar y salir de la modernidad (Buenos Aires: Editorial Paidos SAICF, 2001).
21 Jorge Larraín, "Modernidad e Identidad en América Latina," Revista Universum (1997): 12–31; "Globalización e identidad nacional"; and "Modernity and Identity: Cultural Change in Latin America," in Latin America Transformed: Globalization and Modernity, eds. Robert N. Gwynne and Kay Cristobal (London: Routledge, 2004), 22–38.

22 Amanda Keddie et al., "Beyond Culturalism: Addressing Issues of Indigenous Disadvantage through Schooling," *Australian Educational Researcher* 40, no. 1 (2013): 92–93.
23 William H. Katra, *The Argentine Generation of 1837: Echeverría, Alberdi, Sarmiento, Mitre* (London: Associated University Presses, 1996); Octavio Paz, *The Labyrinth of Solitude* (New York: Grove Press, 1985); Héctor Álvarez Murena, *El pecado original de América* (Buenos Aires: Editorial Sudamericana, 1957).
24 Larraín, "Modernity and Identity," 32–38.
25 Brian Stross, "The Hybrid Metaphor: From Biology to Culture," *Journal of American Folklore* 112, no. 445 (1999): 254–267.
26 Guenter Lewy, *Why America Needs Religion: Secular Modernity and Its Discontents* (Cambridge: Cambridge University Press, 1996).
27 Ezra Suleiman, *Dismantling Democratic States* (Princeton: Princeton University Press, 2003).
28 Zinzi Bailey, Nancy Krieger, Madina Agénor, Jasmine Graves, Natalia Linos, and Mary T. Bassett, "Structural Racism and Health Inequities in the USA: Evidence and Interventions," *The Lancet* 389, no. 10077 (2017): 1453–1463.
29 Marc Verlot, "Understanding Institutional Racism," in *Europe's New Racism: Causes, Manifestations, and Solutions*, The Evens Foundation ed. (New York: Berghahn Books, 2002), 27–42.
30 Sarah A. Radcliffe, "Development for a Postneoliberal Era? Sumak Kawsay, Living Well and the Limits to Decolonisation in Ecuador," *Geoforum* 43, no. 2 (2012): 240–249; Olga Lucía Sanabria Diago and Arturo Argueta Villamar, "Cosmovisiones y naturalezas en tres culturas indígenas de Colombia," *Etnobiología* 13, no. 2 (2015): 5–20.
31 Mary Roldán, "Radio y Cultura Nacional: Años 30 y 40," in *Música, Radio y Documentos Sonoros* (Bogotá: Radio Nacional de Colombia, 2009), 16–25.
32 Luis Ramiro Beltrán, "Social Structure and Rural Development Communication in Latin America: The Radiophonic Schools of Colombia," paper presented at the Summer Conference on Communication and Group Transformation for Development, Honolulu, Hawaii, June 29–July 11, 1975. https://idl-bnc-idrc.dspacedirect.org/handle/10625/1663.
33 Colin Fraser and Sonia Restrepo-Estrada, *Communicating for Development: Human Change for Survival* (New York: Bloomsbury Academic, 1998).
34 Jorge Rojas Álvarez, "'Campesinos y radios': Aspectos sociales de la tecnología escuelas radiofónicas de Radio Sutatenza (1950–1970)" (MA thesis, Universidad de los Andes, Colombia, 2014). https://repositorio.uniandes.edu.co/handle/1992/12820.
35 Cortés, "Foes and Allies."
36 Cortés, "Foes and Allies."
37 "Taita" is a suffix commonly used to refer to Misak male adults. Men in positions of authority are called "Tata." Adult female authorities, and without authority, are called "Mamas." Kasucos/kasucas are young adults without previous experience in authority positions.
38 Manuel Francisco López, Julian Bommer, and Patricia Méndez, "The Seismic Performance of Bahareque Dwellings in El Salvador," presented at the 13th World Conference on Earthquake Engineering, Vancouver, Canada, August 1–6, 2004.

39 Santiago Villaveces Izquierdo, "¿Por qué erradicamos?: Entre bastiones de poder, cultura, y narcotráfico," *Journal of Latin American Anthropology* 7, no. 1 (2008): 226–253.
40 Álvaro Rodríguez Rueda, *Cómo vivían nuestros mayores* (Santander de Quilichao, Colombia: Asociación de Cabildos Indígenas de la Zona Norte del Cauca, 2001). https://isbn.cloud/pt/9789589704202/catedra-nasa-unesco/.
41 Fundación Compartir, *Nuestros mejores maestros* (Bogotá: Nomos Impresores, 2011).
42 Cortés, "Foes and Allies," 184–185.
43 Fernanda Beigel, "Crítica y teoría en el pensamiento social latinoamericano," in *Crítica y teoría en el pensamiento social latinoamericano*, eds. Fernanda Beigel et al. (Buenos Aires: CLACSO, 2006), 287–326.
44 Leonardo Boff and Clodovis Boff, *Como Fazer Teologia da Libertação* (São Paulo: Livraria Vozes, 1986).
45 Stefan Musto, *Los medios de comunicación social al servicio del desarollo rural: Análisis de eficiencia de "Acción Cultural Popular—Radio Sutatenza"* (Bogotá: Acción Cultural Popular, 1971); Beltrán, "Social Structure."
46 Alan O'Connor, *Community Radio in Bolivia: The Miners' Radio Stations* (Lewiston, NY: Edwin Mellen Press, 2004).
47 Mario García Isaza, "La perfectura apostólica de Tierradentro," in *Quinientos Años de Evangelización*, ed. Hernando Escobar (Bogotá: CLAPVI- Conferencia Latinoamericana de Provincias Vicentinas, 1992), 384–398. http://via.library.depaul.edu/cgi/viewcontent.cgi?article=1074&context=clapvi
48 Unidad de Radio del Ministerio de Cultura, *Memorias del Encuentro Internacional de Radios Indígenas de América* (Bogotá: Ministerio de Cultura, 2002).
49 Santamaría Chavarro, "Lorenzo Muelas y el constitucionalismo indígena."
50 Peter Wade, "Mestizaje, Multiculturalism, Liberalism, and Violence," *Latin American and Caribbean Ethnic Studies* 11, no. 3 (2016): 323–343.
51 Donna Lee Van Cott, "Constitutional Reform in the Andes: Redefining Indigenous-State Relations," in *Multiculturalism in Latin America: Indigenous Rights, Diversity and Democracy*, ed. Rachel Sieder (London: Palgrave Macmillan, 2002), 45–73.
52 Mike Gatehouse, "State Violence, Policing, and Paramilitaries," in *Voices of Latin America: Social Movements and the New Activism*, ed. Tom Gatehouse (Rugby: Practical Action Publishing, 2019), 173–97; Aaron Tauss, Daniel Pardo and David Graaff, "El bloque de poder contrainsurgente en Colombia y su papel en el resurgimiento de la derecha en América Latina," *Colombia Internacional* 99 (2019): 63–90.
53 Adrián Pulleiro, *La radio alternativa en América Latina: Debates y desplazamientos en la década de 1990* (Buenos Aires: Universidad de Buenos Aires, 2012), 92.
54 Carlos Agudelo, *Retos del multiculturalismo en Colombia: Política y poblaciones negras* (Medellín: Ed. IEPRI, IRD, ICANH, La Carreta, 2005).
55 Cortés, "Era mejor cuando éramos ilegales."
56 Mauricio Caviedes, "Solidarios frente a colaboradores: Antropología y movimiento indígena en el Cauca en las décadas de 1970 y 1980," *Revista Colombiana de Antropología* 38 (2002): 237–260.
57 Eliana Herrera Huérfano and Francisco Sierra Caballero, "Comunicación y pueblos indígenas en Colombia: Apuntes sobre la necesidad de una política pública," in *Miradas propias: Pueblos indígenas, comunicación y medios en*

la sociedad global, eds. Claudia Magallanes Blanco and José Manuel Ramos Rodríguez (Quito: CIESPAL, 2016), 45–57; Mario A. Murillo, "Weaving a Communication Quilt in Colombia: Civil Conflict, Indigenous Resistance, and Community Radio in Northern Cauca," in *Global Indigenous Media: Cultures, Poetics, and Politics*, eds. Pamela Wilson, Michelle Stewart (Durham: Duke University Press, 2008), 362; Clemencia Rodríguez and Jeanine El Gazi, "The Poetics of Indigenous Radio in Colombia," *Media, Culture & Society* 29, no. 3 (2007): 449–468.

58 Cortés, "Era mejor cuando éramos ilegales."
59 Charles R. Hale, "Rethinking Indigenous Politics in the Era of the 'indio permitido'," *NACLA* (September 25, 2004). https://nacla.org/article/rethinking-indigenous-politics-era-indio-permitido.
60 Diego Cortés, "Radio indígenas y Estado en Colombia ¿Herramientas 'políticas' o instrumentos 'policivos'?" *Chasqui. Revista Latinoamericana de Comunicación* 140 (April–July 2019): 59–74.
61 Íngrid Zacipa Infante, *La mujer pentecostal de la etnia Misak en Guambía, Cauca: El caso de la comunidad Alianza Cristiana Misionera Indígena Guambiana Colombiana* (Bogotá: Universidad Nacional de Colombia, 2019).
62 Jens Köhrsen, "Pentecostal Improvement Strategies: A Comparative Reading on African and South American Pentecostalism," in *"Pastures of Plenty:" Tracing Religio-Scapes of Prosperity Gospel in Africa and Beyond*, ed. Andreas Heuser (Frankfurt: Peter Lang, 2015), 49–63.
63 Cortés, "Evangelical Indigenous Radio Stations in Colombia."
64 Lauren Frances Turek, "To Support a 'Brother in Christ': Evangelical Groups and U.S.-Guatemalan Relations during the Ríos Montt Regime," *Diplomatic History* 39, no. 4 (2015): 689–719. https://doi.org/10.1093/DH/DHU039; Ronaldo De Almeida, "Bolsonaro Presidente: Conservadorismo, Evangelismo e a Crise Brasileira," *Novos Estudos CEBRAP* 38, no. 1 (2019): 185–213.
65 Susana Andrade, "Ethos evangélico, política indígena y medios de comunicación en el Ecuador," *Revista Cultura y Religión* 4, no. 1 (2010): 1–14; Alfonso Gumucio Dagron, "Call Me Impure: Myths and Paradigms of Participatory Communication," in *Community Media: International Perspectives*, ed. Linda K. Fuller (New York: Palgrave Macmillan, 2010), 197–207.
66 Cortés, "Evangelical Indigenous Radio Stations in Colombia."
67 Elizabeth E. Brusco, *The Reformation of Machismo: Evangelical Conversion and Gender in Colombia* (Austin: University of Texas Press, 1995).
68 Christian Gros, "Evangelical Protestantism and Indigenous Populations," *Bulletin of Latin American Research* 18, no. 2 (1999): 175–197. https://doi.org/10.1111/j.1470-9856.1999.tb00082.x.
69 Carlos Andrés Ramírez, "Indigenismo de derecha: La formación de la OPIC como 'revolución pasiva,'" *Revista de Estudios Sociales* 51 (2015): 89–104.
70 Juan Diego Demera Vargas, "Católicos y protestantes entre los indígenas guambianos: La adopción y transformación de nuevas nolectividades," *Ciências Sociais e Religião* 5, no. 5 (2007): 173–190.

71 Guillermo Trejo, "Religious Competition and Ethnic Mobilization in Latin America: Why the Catholic Church Promotes Indigenous Movements in Mexico," *American Political Science Review* 103, no. 3 (2009): 323–342.
72 Gerard Colby and Charlotte Dennett, *Thy Will Be Done. The Conquest of the Amazon: Nelson Rockefeller and Evangelism in the Age of Oil* (New York: HarperCollins, 1996).
73 Cortés, "Evangelical Indigenous Radio Stations in Colombia."
74 Brusco, *The Reformation of Machismo.*
75 Cortés, "The Quest for Indigenous Autonomy."

14 Social Media and the Musical Nation

Hegemonic Cooptation and the Making of a National Repertoire

Héctor Fernández L'Hoeste

On July 2, 2020, the Colombian Ministry of Culture (Mincultura) launched a list of 100 songs under the #ColombiaCreaTalento (Colombia Creates Talent) hashtag, seeking to promote the music of local artists and appeal to a sense of national pride in local cultural production. The main list is divided into four separate ones, grouped thematically: *Territorios sonoros* (Sonic Territories); *Rock, pop y rap* (Rock, Pop, and Rap); *Nueva música colombiana* (New Colombian Music); and *Música bailable* (Dance Music); each subset contains 25 songs. The list was publicized as the first of several efforts by the government in an attempt to increase the visibility of new sounds and novel ways of playing traditional music emerging across the country, as well as to contribute to the growing impression of a government seeking to explore remote corners of the national geography in its quest to do justice to a more comprehensive understanding of difference and cultural diversity. According to the accompanying release, it was produced with the support of the then minister of culture, Carmen Inés Vásquez, and Felipe Buitrago Restrepo, vice minister of creativity and orange economy, and curated by Luisa Piñeros (OneBeat), Felipe Grajales (Altavozfest.co), Juan José Peña (CD Baby), and Diego Maldonado (Onerpm).

The "orange" or creative economy represents an area of utmost interest for recent Colombian administrations. As defined by Howkins, it includes sectors whose goods and services are based on intellectual property.[1] It is important to note that while Howkins's contribution is from 2001, globally, states and societies have been aware of the key role of cultural industries for a long time, as the writings of Antonio Gramsci testify. With the emergence of more assertive positions, like the one adopted by French minister of culture Jack Lang (1988–1993), whose famous quote, "économie et culture, même combat" (economy and culture; it's the same fight), draws attention to the implications of cultural production, the interplay between culture and the economy came into the open. Former Colombian president Iván Duque Márquez (2018–2022) was a strong supporter of an orange economy since the day of his possession, in part as a continuation of his

DOI: 10.4324/9781003048152-19

work at the Inter-American Development Bank in Washington, DC, which included the publication of a rather schematic volume on the topic.[2] However, it is important to note that this effort to privatize areas of culture is part of the greater dynamics of neoliberalism, overtly manifest in Colombia since at least César Gaviria's administration (1990–1994) and the establishment of a National Constituent Assembly that, despite claiming to acknowledge difference, also provided new opportunities for the state to implement cosmetic measures—chiefly, through a focus on culture, along with realignments of Gramscian overtones—while avoiding profound structural change addressing social disparities.

Therefore, one must consider that Colombian governments and the private sector's drawn-out tradition when it comes to the engagement of the cultural industry as an element of policy. Initial stabs at the engagement of the cultural sector by the Colombian government were incomplete and forceful. On July 23, 1936, the Colombian government led by Alfonso López Pumarejo (1934–1938) attempted to nationalize the radio industry through a bill that sought to increase official control of radio programming.[3] However, the measure was defeated thanks to strong resistance by a group of radio stations, mainly led by those in Antioquia. In 1945, during López Pumarejo's second term, the government pushed forward a bill seeking the unification of communication industries.[4] In response, the radio stations circulated a memo in which they requested the organization of the Colombian radio industry to emulate the United States's model, which led to the demise of the bill. Following Jorge Eliécer Gaitán's assassination on April 9, 1948, Conservative President Mariano Ospina Pérez managed to accomplish what Liberals could not: The government suspended all licenses, effectively assuming control of the radio industry, which it held tightly by the leash through the issuing of successive temporary licenses. According to Óscar Hernández Salgar, the Conservatives did not seek direct intervention in the industry, but rather the implementation of self-censorship, hoping to benefit from enforced "neutrality."[5] These first attempts speak more of coercive measures, so clearly, the state had not yet embraced an approach bent on consent.

In comparison, the private sector's engagement with culture is far more sophisticated. Take, for instance, Medellín's music industry in the 1960s, whose rise resulted from the concentration of economic power in the Andean region in contrast with the Caribbean.[6] At this time, Medellín's novel music industry took advantage of the growing popularity of cumbia music in the 1940s and 1950s to create an international market and consolidate its position as arbiter of Colombian tropical music, eventually offering a sequel to the big band-style of Lucho Bermúdez and Pacho Galán and an alternative to more traditional acts (the so-called *sonido sabanero*) through the creation of a local sound: The *sonido paisa*.[7] The appeal of *música tropical* rooted in folkloric tradition seemed limited, so the need for a more commercial sound became apparent. Echoing the modern arrangements and instrumentation of Venezuelan bands like Los Melódicos or the Billo's Caracas Boys, the labels in Medellín—Codiscos (originally known as Zeida), Fuentes, and Sonolux—were able to cash in on the successful exportation of cumbia, giving way to greater popularity all over the Americas. In this sense, Medellín's industry played a significant role in the creation of a more contemporary "national" genre—as opposed to bambuco, the traditional Andean music championed by Colombia's establishment during the early twentieth century. In the 1990s, thanks to its endorsement of TV heartthrob Carlos Vives, this same industry—now sharing credit, given fluctuation between Sonolux and Sony Music Latin—even managed to update and launch vallenato music internationally, supplementing cumbia's reign.[8] These two latter developments, both spearheaded by private interests, insinuate the importance of the market in any definition of official cultural policies, given how the private sector modeled the extent to which culture may serve as a tool for hegemony. Having witnessed the efficacy of consent, one can only assume the Colombian establishment learned the lesson. Taken together, these episodes speak of how the Colombian state and the private sector, with a sort of orange-economy consciousness *avant la lettre*, have long engaged and influenced the cultural industry—the music industry, among others—bearing in mind its contribution to the national economy and culture. I write of radio and recording labels, but new technologies have always played a part in the definition of tension between culture and the state. It is now the time of the internet and social media, thus the need to embrace the orange economy as a MacGuffin.

Put succinctly, the orange economy is the latest stage in a long chain of events promoted by liberalism and neoliberalism, in which the market seeps into areas that were yet not entirely taken over. As part of a long-term process, the orange economy incarnates a rather brazen neoliberal take on culture, willing to quantify all innovative intellectual activity in terms of capital—not symbolically, à la Bourdieu, but strictly from an economic perspective. An event like the release of the playlist exemplifies the government's efforts to engage culture in a more quantifiable manner, following the conjectures of technocrats. Initially, the playlist served as a prelude to the celebration of a virtual concert sponsored by Mincultura during the following July 20, the national holiday for Colombian independence. As stated by the information shared by the Ministry, the concert would build bridges "across regions, genres, and generations, strengthening the sense of belonging to a collective project of nation."[9] To this extent, the playlist was publicly and unashamedly associated with the government's awareness of its role as guardian of a cohesive project of national identity. At first, the songs were simultaneously available on SIMUS, Spotify, and Deezer.

Ultimately, they also became available on Amazon Music, Apple Music, and YouTube.

The mainstay of the government's bet for the support of a seemingly more inclusive national musical repertoire is SIMUS, *Sistema de Información de la Música* (Music Information System), a massive database connected to Mincultura's website that maps out musical practices in myriad places of Colombia.[10] As of November 2023, its collection includes musical agents (2,415), groups (1,148), institutions (978), and schools (965) throughout the entire country. As a tool to define what belongs or does not within a certain idea of nation, SIMUS encloses formidable power. It even includes a graphic interface based on national geography—it shows dots in three colors (yellow, blue, and red, like the national flag) over a map—in which the list of musical resources connected to the government appears according to its physical location, creating an impressive portrayal in terms of the number and variety of musical acts documented in the database. Visually, SIMUS creates a striking representation of the breadth and span of sonic practices in the country. However, this is an image that, in many ways, reiterates the prevalent disparities in resources perceptible throughout Colombian geography. In the following paragraphs, I argue that, though they cater to the spirit of appreciation for difference and inclusiveness pioneered by the Constitution of 1991, SIMUS, the aforementioned playlist, and associated hashtags like #ColombiaCreaTalento constitute neoliberal policies on the part of the Colombian state to actually fortify and preserve numerous inequalities as well as the government's centrality, effectively curtailing efforts on the part of musical artists and producers to operate beyond the circuits of an officially sanctioned culture. By sanctioned culture I mean the set of practices and products advocated by the state as suitable ways of enacting Colombian identity, most of which never manage to question or undermine the hierarchical structures of Colombia's cultural, economic, and political order. In brief, the Colombian government is finding new ways of including and excluding through music. Technology like SIMUS, the playlist, or #ColombiaCreaTalento contributes to the consolidation of a neoliberal hegemony in Colombia along the lines of earlier government-sponsored educational programs that condoned inclusion and visibility only as long as they proved convenient to the order benefitting the state and elites. So, while favoring equity and inclusion, Colombia's government is refining its mechanisms of preserving systemic hierarchy. In the end, under the mantle of nationalism and at the cost of curtailing the musical imagination of the nation, measures like these continue to preserve the gap between the state and disenfranchised segments of the population. In *Music, Race, and Nation*, Peter Wade clarifies that, while elites effectively seek negation and marginalization of difference, they also seek to construct it in ways that allow for the preservation of hierarchies of class and culture, be it through transformation and appropriation or by enacting the tensions between standardization and diversification, that is, homogeneity and a transnationally constituted heterogeneity.[11] This is what is at stake here.

On Music and Hegemony

To paraphrase Benedict Anderson, quoted by Wade, music is capable of generating imagined communities.[12] As a tool to "invent" the nation, and thus define the relationship between the nation and the state, music conceals formidable power, particularly in a place as politically volatile as Colombia. The state's definition of a nation describes an idealized situation, idyllic under its own interests and constraints. Consequently, this view of a perfect model contains the will to control and organize communities by way of promising less disparity, which is never the same as achieving equality, and supporting empty slogans, such as *La cultura es de todos* (culture is for all), a questionable truth when conditions of production and consumption are inequitable and culture ends up belonging to those who can produce and/or consume it. Within this framework, musical repertoire alludes to an assortment of genres and practices that, thanks to many historical and social processes, have garnered significant value for and within its followers. In the end, these genres and practices, the products of specific cultural and social circumstances, contribute to the definition of national identity according to their very own cultural and social circumstances, thus offering the possibility of expanding the understanding of nationality.

This is one of the main reasons for Mincultura's focus on music via social media. The fact that the mechanics of the effort can be criticized as insincere does not necessarily mean that the components and ingredients of the strategy are based on insincerity. Many of these acts truly play with the best interests of the population at heart. After all, musicians are familiar with the intricacies of the market and remain fully conscious of the benefits and risks associated with collaboration with the state. They are not passive cultural actors. Engaging with the state includes the possibility of taking advantage of greater resources and even the possibility of identifying potential weaknesses within neoliberalism to negotiate more advantageous positions in future interactions with the state. If the state seeks to benefit from ideologies like nationalism, there are ways to play along without necessarily falling prey to governmental schemes or serving as accomplices to official diktats. Furthermore, state-sponsored initiatives contribute to the increased visibility and expanded international understanding of the country, very much in the spirit of acts like Shakira, Juanes, J Balvin, Totó La Momposina, Los Corraleros de Majagual, and the Gaiteros de San Jacinto. Nonetheless, these acts can also incarnate the objectification of their communities, unfortunately bypassing contact between them and the state. As a result, the state gains the ability to comment on and discuss communities in distant corners of national geography with relatively minimal contact and investment. As an exchange, it is an experience characterized by optimal mutual benefits at the expense of the communities and the nation.

The activities involved in the definition, dissemination, and preservation of a national musical repertoire tend to pay close attention to how categories like class, ethnicity, and gender contribute to a prevailing hierarchy. Along the same lines, individuals involved in these efforts and processes consider carefully how music, as a cultural product, has a proven record of transgressing boundaries implemented by these very categories of identity, therefore contributing to the illusion of inclusion in a significant manner. For this reason, given the immateriality of the musical practice—putting aside the billions in the industry—it serves as an ideal tool for the promotion of inclusion. While the music goes everywhere, it is just a small minority of individuals that gain access to space traditionally forbidden to people of its community. This is particularly apparent in the musical response resulting from the transition from the Constitution of 1886—the time of the acceptance of a whitened form of cumbia or vallenato in central parts of the country—which made no secret of its desire to homogenize the nation, to the Constitution of 1991—when musical genres like champeta or reggaetón, previously disdained and scorned by cultural elites gained visibility and acceptance throughout the entire country. This suggests greater governmental cognizance of the challenge to homogenize one of the most ethnically and culturally diverse populations in the region.

In truth, this shift—which is not a shift, but the refinement of previous forms of inclusion and exclusion—reflects the zeitgeist, having witnessed the advance of multiculturalism in other latitudes and consumed enhanced societal representation in global media. In this way, diversity and multiculturalism attain a rather "universal" quality that promptly impacts the desire of Colombian society to change, specifically amid a country immersed in conflict as the result of social actors bypassing the rather inadequate prospects of economic mobility. A hard reality prevails. For this reason, it becomes evident that a time-tested approach must be developed and embraced, one in which, by way of policy, it is possible to convince the diverse populations of the country of the sincerity of the attempt at inclusion. This is where awareness of the hegemonic potential of musical practices becomes apparent. After all, is the national anthem not one of the most embraceable symbols of the state? While a national musical repertoire is a communitarian expression, it also incarnates a hegemonic drive. Just as music by a minority is favored by many, it provides a way of imagining the nation. Suitably popularized, the way of imagining the nation of a few may become the way of imagining the nation of the many. This process literally embodies the experience of hegemony, justifying the government's concern for music as an element of the new economy. As many regimes with a national form have discovered—the case of tango in Argentina, samba in Brazil, merengue in the Dominican Republic, ranchera in Mexico—a musical genre is an ideal vehicle for the popularization and transmission of an aspirational model of nation promulgated by the state. In the case of Colombia, we no longer speak just of cumbia, but also of vallenato, which the population inside the country espoused eagerly since the 1980s. While many Colombians would argue vallenato represents the country as a whole, it is unquestionable that, in truth, it is a cultural expression proper of a very specific area: Not even the environs of the department of Cesar and the nearby departments of Guajira and Magdalena, as celebrated in conventional popular mythology, but rather the entire Colombian Caribbean, as there are forms of *música de acordeón* that emerge in what used to be the greater province of Bolívar (the Caribbean half west of the Magdalena river).

At a broad level, the national musical repertoire is viewed as a collective expression, yet, in truth, what it manages to express is the musical preferences of a few over those of the crowd. The national musical repertoire has always been about a musical repertoire supportive of a collective imaginary that does not contemplate the full range of options in terms of musical expression, but a mere sample of it, usually according to the views of experts connected to the government. The outcome of this officially sponsored normativity is not a national one—one fully representative of the range of musical expressions of the nation—but a partial and incomplete one, as advocated by its implicitly finite nature. Quite evidently, this is the result of state intervention in the process, as in the case of the then minister of culture and her team of advisors, and even the accompanying accumulation of information via SIMUS. By definition, their view of the musical map of the nation is subjective—ultimately influenced by the many factors contributing to the strengthening of regional stereotypes in a country as fragmented as Colombia. The incorporation of technology, be it via the list or SIMUS, only serves to feign objectivity. For this reason, despite the advances in technology, this kind of process still engages in an effort similar to previous ways of making of a repertoire during earlier periods of the nation when disparities in class, race, and gender were even more ubiquitous than at present. Hence, more so than in spirit, it still expresses the invention of a musical repertoire of the few, rather than the majority. That is to say, by definition, it embodies intranational hegemony. As Catalina Muñoz states, inclusion does not involve recognition as equal political subjects.[13] Within this scope, the main object and function of this national repertoire is to advance a cultural, economic, and political project, that is, supporting collective imaginaries of an ideal nation helps in the construction of a cohesive and socially unifying version of Colombia for the benefit of the elites.

A Hashtag, a Playlist, a Map

On June 4, 2020, roughly one month ahead of the release of the list with 100 songs, Luisa Piñeros, a journalist associated with Mincultura and a member of the OneBeat Colombia staff, purportedly held an interview with Vásquez titled "Entrevista: La *playlist* de la Ministra" (Interview: The Playlist of the Minister), under the hypothetical premise of discussing the Minister's personal playlist in a supposedly unrehearsed manner.[14] OneBeat is an initiative of the U.S. Department of State's Bureau of Educational and Cultural Affairs centered on the promotion of collaborative original music as a form of cultural diplomacy; in a nutshell, it is a tool of the United States' soft power arsenal. Given its object, an organization like OneBeat is made up of individuals cognizant of the political bearing of cultural forms, often employed to promote and support the governmental agendas of politicians in power. In the interview, Vásquez's repeated glances at the printed material in front of her reveal the manufactured nature of the event (the movement of her pupils betrays the fact that she is reading, unlike TV anchors, trained to conceal excessive eye movement), during which she already hints at the work being done to compile a musical selection promoted under the premise of support for national music. While the list includes staples and well-known groups, many lesser-known acts must have resulted from the curators' advice, hopefully expanding the envelope for what stands as representatively acceptable to many Colombian listeners. The quality of the music in the playlist is uneven—in my view, at least—but this is clearly beyond the point. The object of the event is to prepare the ground for the formal launching of the list later on in the year.

Nevertheless, the language favored by Mincultura to disseminate its efforts certainly does not help, as some of the material released and shared via the internet reveals an essentialist view of culture. In the Ministry's year-end report for Vásquez's term released in late 2019, containing a lengthy inventory of this entity's achievements, the phrase/slogan "Cultura, la esencia de un país que se transforma desde los territorios" (Culture, the essence of a country that transforms itself from the territories [provinces]) is displayed on the cover, framing the entire contents of the document.[15] The fact that a ministry conceives identity as essence, as though there were something congenital to being Colombian, is, in and of itself, problematic; it speaks volumes of lack of critical thought in the grasp of identity. The fact that the slogan alludes to the transformation of the country according to inertial impetus rising from the periphery, rather than the center, stands dramatically in contrast with the conventional sense of direction of the Colombian government, inured to centralism ever since the nineteenth century. The old Constitution of 1886, which stood the test of time for over a century, paid scant attention to cultural and ethnic diversity, shaping for decades the disposition of Colombian society toward difference. Nevertheless, while the Mincultura's slogan wishes to convey the willingness to accept a variety of identitarian versions and assign protagonism to cultural practices emanating from the periphery of the national territory, it reflects unapologetically the disposition of state bureaucracy in the capital city to confuse the bringing of difference to the center with the arrival of the state to distant corners of Colombia. Even this dynamic—the acknowledgment of other forms of Colombian culture than those envisioned by the country's elites—went sorely absent from the official national imaginary until the late twentieth century, when Bogotá was flooded with immigrants from all over the country (partly due to the armed conflict), forcing its inhabitants to face and embrace difference amid a country fragmented by topography. And even then, one could argue, the force field of centralism is so strong in Colombia, that the capital's inhabitants started mistaking Bogotá's diverse population for an actual incarnation of the nation, rather than just a synthesis of it. In a sense, it is the discrepancy between this dynamic and the actual expansion of the state to the most remote corners of Colombian territory to provide much-needed services like education and health what reveals how the state's current focus repeats and reinforces the customary tendency to bring everything within reach of a rather insufficient central bureaucracy, in an act of inclusion that neglects actual recognition.

To put it openly, what I contend is that the compilation of audio tracks and imagery from distant parts of the nation, to be incorporated into a database that will later serve as a launching pad for a more cohesive alliance between musical acts and the current administration, is a far cry from the tangible empowerment of communities and neighborhoods from where musical production originates. If anything, SIMUS just mirrors current disparity, highlighting a wealth of creativity in enclaves with high populations while simultaneously documenting and obscuring the scarcity of production in locations with fewer resources. The dots in distant corners speak of a presence, but they never hint at the degree of despair in these locations. After all, it is this state of affairs—and the thoroughly classist mindset of Colombian society—that empowers radical inequality in the country, proper of one of the highest GINI coefficients in the region. SIMUS serves as a tool for the construction of class according to the state, in which certain acts count with its approval—and thus brandish higher social standing—while others are mired in disregard and lowly status.

Overall, Mincultura's strategy is designed for inclusion—sonically and visually—which, in the context of the rampant inequalities apparent in terms of access to facilities of musical production, stands in stark contrast to the circumstances of acts absent from the playlist. In Colombia, as in many other places, despite the wider availability of technology, musicians still travel to key urban locations to mix and record. A quick search on the internet shows that, except for a couple of studios on the Caribbean coast and two or three in Cali, the majority are located in Bogotá and Medellín, preeminent enclaves of the national music industry, discounting the fact that most recorded acts may not be based or have emerged in any of these two locations. The history of the Colombian musical industry is the history of the displacement of musical groups and studios from their corresponding place of birth and practice to locations dictated by more centrally oriented economic interests—witness the move of Discos Fuentes from Cartagena to Medellín in 1954. Presence in the playlist, while not a guarantee of access to resources, certainly contributes to higher visibility, increasing the odds that these acts may gain popularity or even land a contract as the result of official endorsement. Inclusion in the list operates as an act of professional commendation, providing an indefinite degree of agency.

In terms of sonic territories, SIMUS divides the country into eight areas: (1) the sonic territory of *joropo*, the musical genre of Colombia's eastern plains, shared with Venezuela; (2) the sonic territory of the *marimba*, popular among communities of people of African descent along the Pacific Coast, from the southern port of Tumaco to the central port of Buenaventura; (3) the land of *trova*, comprising the region known for its cultivation of coffee: Antioquia and the nearby departments of Caldas, Risaralda, and Quindío; (4) the sonic territory of chants, horns, and drums, basically, the greater Caribbean region; (5) the sonic terrain of the *rajaleña* and *cucamba*, better known as the preferred musical genre and ensemble of the Upper Magdalena, respectively, represented by the departments of Huila and Tolima; (6) the land of *chirimía* or the department of Chocó along the northern Pacific coast; (7) the sound space of *torbellino*, a genre popular in the departments of Boyacá and Santander; and finally, (8) the land of southern flutes, strings, and drums, in the mountains close to Ecuador (Nariño, Cauca, Putumayo). The variety of genres underscores the wealth of musical heritage in Colombia. It also provides the state an ideal opportunity to taxonomize and hierarchize the culture according to political prerogatives dictated by economic interests. Most importantly, in a "country of regions" like Colombia, it provides a measure of division, allowing the government to underscore and substantiate differences contributing to the strengthening of centralism. To emphasize regional boundaries is akin to highlighting the limited nature—and thus weakness—of geopolitical constructs potentially contesting the national state.

Visually, the SIMUS interface, which includes a map of the country covered by dots, is the incarnation of taxing logic. Thanks to its interface, which represents the location of associated acts and entities, a graphic equivalent of overall inclusion is generated, even though the size and impact of many of these associates can be minimal in the context of the related area/region. The interface allows anyone with a general knowledge of Colombia to look at its representation of national geography and, given the accumulation of dots in the most inhabited locations or the presence of just a few in sparsely populated areas, conclude that official efforts have tried their best to include as many people as possible. Aside from the numbers or recordings at the heart of these circles, these dots do not convey much information about the relationship between these agents and their surroundings. Once again, a bonus of these visuals is the customary regionalization of the territory, further dividing and fragmenting the nation while simulating cohesion.

SIMUS contains many maps, accounting for music schools, performances, musical groups, entities associated with musical activities, and events. The view of the information is dictated by the extent to which the user zooms in on the map. Though arrangements may vary, the circles on most maps are colored like the Colombian flag. In its main version, red seems to point out nodes with high numbers (Andean cities like Bogotá and Medellín), while blue seems to indicate the nodes with the least associates (the basins of the Amazon and Orinoco rivers as well as the department of Chocó). Amazingly, in a hovering view, Barranquilla, Cali, and Cartagena do not bear circles; Cali is totally clear while the two Caribbean cities have an associated node between them. It takes some zooming in to see in more detail the arrangement of points around these cities. In any case, the main effect of the interface is to ratify the impression of equity and inclusion of official selection.

The main graphic interface, labeled *Mapa musical* (Musical Map), is ideal for this purpose, generating a feeling of identification between the public and the representatives of the state, whose efforts it supposedly represents. As a measure to render explicit the state's shift toward a model of government that attempts to reproduce in its structure and organization the multicultural and ethnically diverse nature of the nation after 1991, SIMUS's musical map is remarkably effective, offering a graphic equivalent for the "equitable and responsible" way in which musical affiliates of the state have been selected and identified. It should remain clear that the interests of any cultural actors in discord with the cultural elite in charge of selecting participants may remain unrepresented by this setup. For this not to be the case, the community of musicians and musical entities of Colombia would need to be consulted about any act's merit, so that the noncentralized nature of its constituency would bear some support over the development of a more genuinely equitable construct of a nation. A more open selection process, rather than outright government choice—this latter method usually betrays closer ties to economic, political, and societal hubs of power—would guarantee that one of the objects of belonging to this group would be a more authentic representation of the interests of its affiliates. This is how true accountability happens, through means of direct involvement rather than appointment. Most likely, through mechanisms of this nature, a list of musical acts representative of current production would be categorically different from the one put forward with the assistance of Mincultura's musical advisors, consequently extending beyond the reach of the customary state narrative. In sum, the playlist should not be associated with an individual, but with the institution, and the list should not result from a team of advisors, but from a selection process under the guidance of the many musicians and musical bodies available throughout the country, seeking a construct whose collective nature is more appropriate.

Moreover, a more problematic aspect may be the lack of a critical assessment not only of the officials involved in the creation of this interface—SIMUS was launched in late 2017, during the administration of Juan Manuel Santos (2010–2018), with Mariana Garcés Córdoba as Minister of Culture and Alejandro Mantilla as Music Coordinator for the Arts Directorate at Mincultura—but also of individuals belonging to bodies like the playlist's advisory committee, some of whom may be linked to other governments, interested in actions compatible with their concerns, logics, and versions of the state. After all, to a general public unaware of these ties, these individuals will come across as agents of good. What wrong could come from the support of national music? Is it not fine to feel pride in your place of origin? This is the habitual degree of reductive candor with which nationalism is embraced throughout Latin America thanks to official campaigns and programs. Never mind the actual quality of official proposals or the fact that many acts/practices/products serve as tokens in a game of representation, in the same spirit of members of underrepresented groups paraded by governments of wealthy nations to prove their commitment to inclusion and social equity. For the most part, this type of inclusion becomes appealing as the result of ostensible advantages emerging from the support of the state, through the gain of cultural, economic, or symbolic capital. As Wade emphasizes, a nationalist project does not just deny or suppress diversity; it actively seeks to reconstruct it.[16] As involved governmental agents, these cultural actors are responsible for the dissemination of a logic justifying the official assessment of cultural goods, that is, the fact that some groups are perceived as "worthy" of inclusion in collections promoted by the state. These logics consider a wide number of aspects, like the economic and political objectives of the corresponding administration and the development of an internal or external market for these goods, all within the possibilities of neoliberal capitalism.

In the end, like many other products that manage to transcend, eventually gaining recognition abroad, the people who benefit the most are not those involved in actual production, who gain increased economic retribution and visibility at the national level thanks to added presence online, but the ones in charge of distribution and marketing. In terms of direct economic capital, the participating actors may not be tied to the success of a specific cultural product, yet the amount of symbolic capital gained thanks to the circulation of their production more than compensates for any lack of reimbursement. It is very likely that the state benefits groups whose newly gained sense of agency may advance or be compatible with official interests. In this sense, it is important to reiterate how their actions may favor the elite, with which they are distinctly aligned, as well as themselves, regardless of awareness. In addition, they achieve agency in terms of promoting specific forms of national identity that, though associated with the state, may eventually bring forth a new understanding of Colombianness. In turn, elite sectors gain cognizance of their work, which they support in the hope of being able to dictate and/or influence what may be celebrated, preserved, or valued as a paradigmatic example of national identity alongside versions congruent with personal economic interests.

These logics are habitually designed to promote the impression not only that everyone is included but also that, most importantly, their choices personify the best interests of all nationals, even though in truth they just represent those of a minority. If the national musical repertoire were to be more authentically representative of all citizens, following closely the spirit of the multicultural and ethnically diverse nation documented in 1991, it would be germane to dwell for more than just a moment on the implicit inequalities across the land. Thus, it is not the same if the government includes a large number of acts from Bogotá or Medellín than if it manages to identify two or three acts along the Caribbean or Pacific coast, regions more traditionally ravaged by inequity and poverty. The inclusion of groups from more neglected areas of the country can even result from targeted efforts, willing to generate the impression of newly hailed recognition.

Nonetheless, a disturbing implication of the map is the following: To a large extent, it bolsters the inequality patent in the national territory. In other words, just because some locations are more inhabited and plentiful with infrastructure and others are scarcely inhabited and barely supported, the result mimics the degree of their importance under these circumstances, effectively normalizing negligence and indifference. Or to put it plainly, rather than granting greater visibility to sectors of the population that have stood ignored, a move that would be more representative of the spirit of the new Magna Carta, it keeps reinforcing disparity under official tutelage. In this way, regionalism, rather than working against the state, ends up working in its favor. In SIMUS, the graphic interface manages to accomplish two contradictory feats simultaneously: While it ratifies the official interest in inclusion (documented visually), it normalizes and substantiates the fact that, until this moment, fed by the spirit of an earlier construct of a nation, some areas have it better than others. When a citizen uncritically looks at SIMUS, rather than ask it to suggest a new order for the cultural output of the country, one that effectively defies the up-to-now customary narratives with Bogotá and Medellín at the heart of the country's music industry, what she/he will most likely do is endorse the government's version of piecemeal, state-of-the-art inclusion by way of technology.

A Flawed Strategy

Beyond these considerations, Mincultura's strategy is flawed on three points. First, it promotes inclusion by bringing the production of musicians to the capital, though rejecting the notion of wider availability of resources at the national level, that is, extending the actual presence of the state to the most remote corners of national geography. By rendering visible many acts from the periphery—virtually, of course—it appears further governmental engagement with outlying communities may not be necessary. This approach nourishes inclusion through media, though not through actual infrastructure contributing to a rise in the general standard of living of populations in many of these distant points. As suggested previously, there are ways in which cultural actors can challenge these claims, including underscoring the actual absence of the state in their home communities. Quite understandably, official inclusion prevails as long as the state gets to define what exactly is meant by "inclusion." In other words, it is by way of this type of exercise that the state legitimates its dominant role as arbiter of inclusion/exclusion. The nature of the artifice is anticipatory: Why ponder the lack of infrastructural involvement when it pays so much more to redefine how the general public gets to think about inclusion through the circulation and implementation of novel internet-based strategies?

Second, it officializes the use of cultural policy related to music production as a tool of hegemony, through musicians who internalize, popularize, and validate the discourse of an elite determined to ignore extensive inequality. By embracing heterogeneity through appropriations that devalue or deny contribution, the establishment thus achieves consensus thanks to many of these regional musicians seeking recognition and support.[17] For many of these acts, the fact that the central government includes them and grants some visibility may be interpreted as a significant achievement, since many do not play with a widespread commercially driven disposition, but rather as ethnic/folkloric groups with relatively limited projection. Then again, as mentioned earlier, there may be acts that, while participating in official initiatives, maintain a degree of intellectual independence and artistic honesty that allows them to not only not be complicit but perhaps even undermine official narratives. In the case of acts with a commercial disposition, dissemination of works by a branch of the government involves the incorporation of their material to the greater catalog of expressions of national identity sanctioned by the state, in other words, giving a seal of authoritative approval, a measure not to be underestimated amid populations seeking or in need of official endorsement.

And third, given the internalization of capitalism through media monetization, the distribution and sharing of a playlist underwritten by the government substantiate the most advantageous benefit of this strategy: The state's legitimacy as the party with the actual right to choose who stands in and out of its definition of the nation, effectively controlling the enactment of Colombianness. Admittedly, it remains the duty of cultural actors to formulate tactics that may question governmental single-handedness. Altogether, benefits resulting from the monetization of a list circulated by the government are viewed as a plus. To boot, these three schemes go along with the purported objects of the Constitution of 1991, which has resulted in many governmental campaigns, multifaceted nation-brand management, and endless slogans (*Culture is for all, Future is for all, Colombia is passion*, etc.), all advanced with the theoretical goal of generating more cohesion and sense of affiliation within the population.

At the heart of this project stands the notion of imagining music as a collective process engendering cohesion. The information distributed does speak about "the sense of belonging to a collective project of nation,"[18] so the state's intentionality is readily apparent. Within this framework, it is not only the music that is being imagined as "national," but also its capabilities, which include the ability to create a new, more equitable nation, serving as inspiration for the efforts of musicians, as well as the remote possibility of international projection once sanctioned with government approval. This is not a minor resource in a country where it is common that professional musicians face discrimination and stereotyping when they travel abroad. In many corners of the world, a Colombian passport, or several passports in the hands of artists with idiosyncratic appearances, is cause for alarm.

Culture, Infrastructure, and the Role of the State

In the times before the Constitution of 1991—when I was raised—hegemony was enacted following a more modest approach, seeking to conceal and erase national diversity. Occasional efforts to accept and celebrate difference, such as those studied by Catalina Muñoz during the Liberal administrations between 1930 and 1946, concealed the state's condescending and patronizing attitude, bent on viewing citizens as mendicants rather than equals. Undoubtedly, this is not the case anymore; the neoliberal state involves further sophistication. Hence, new strategies need to be implemented to attest to the government's efforts at inclusion and to treat the cultural production of diverse regions of the country in an accepting manner, brushing aside manipulation for political purposes. In this century, through the introduction of new guidelines, the state has been charged with the responsibility to value, protect, and disseminate the culture of the nation, at times, with a not-so-veiled economic agenda. These new guidelines are largely responsible for the Colombian government's adamant focus on culture, that is, a view of cultural industries as potential revenue-earning machines that may lift many out of poverty, but also feed the coffers of the state. Given the continuity of this focus, from the times of César Gaviria to the current administration, the nature of the Colombian neoliberal state becomes plain. So, what is initially portrayed as official efforts to be inclusive can, in the long run, be interpreted as attempts to co-opt and privatize cultural and musical production that, in the past, circulated more freely among the population.

The musical repertoire of the nation is made up of a collection of immaterial expressions and practices and material goods. Generally speaking, these are the products and representations of Colombian music—regardless of its actual connection to national soil; such is the case of Lido Pimienta, who, for all the Colombian value of her work, migrated to Canada at a very early age—which, to a fair degree, speak of music's participation and presence within the national imaginary. These are the cultural expressions that communities recognize and validate as crucial components of musical heritage, hence legitimating them as Colombian expressions while simultaneously embracing them to legitimate themselves as Colombians. These expressions and practices contribute to feelings of identity and posit affective bonds with regional and national memories. In sum, they talk about how people inhabit the land and document their presence in a place like Colombia, awarding special value to circumstances and surroundings. Since they account for practitioners, this is how they promote an acceptance of ethnic and cultural diversity.

Given the cultural landscape I have described, with the issuing of the Constitution of 1991, one could argue that this apparent interest in greater representation coincides with the will to voice concerns for previously excluded groups, for those who in the past never managed to have their voices heard or were even chastised—as in the case of champeta or tropipop in the late 1990s and early 2000s. Thanks to their presence in a list (or website), the object, it seems, is for the groups that support these practices to identify now with a government-sponsored lineup of officially sanctioned forms of Colombianness, supposedly because of its "authentically designated" national nature. That acts and musicians legitimate the government's right to develop a national musical repertoire is akin to their validation of the state's specific understanding of the nation—about who stands in or out of the nation, according to the state—which, in a place like Colombia, with groups involved in a peace process transitioning in and out of hiding, has serious implications in other fronts. Once institutional acceptance is granted, it extends to other areas of Colombian nationality, including, most pertinently, the governmental monopoly on violence.

This narrative, supportive of the notion that a "national" musical repertoire is more inclusive and consequently represents most genres and styles of music produced in the country (including accompanying populations), in truth waters down several forms of difference within national geography to the point of relegating actual celebration of diversity to the background. In addition, it is one thing to add and circulate a few videos and even to incorporate information into a database and another very different one is for the state to improve the living conditions of many forsaken territories, as in the case of the department of Chocó—home of renowned hip-hop group ChocQuibTown—which for decades has remained disconnected from the national highway network. That musicians from peripheral regions are included in a playlist does not mean the conditions of living in their communities are impacted by the presence of the government. It is not the act of being different that is being celebrated by the playlist, but that the state has managed to come up with a repertoire that, to the common citizen's eye, appears to include an enhanced catalog of Colombianness, playing down that much attention or depth is given to any of them. Within this repertoire, a group like Margarita Siempre Viva, a band of middle-class rock and pop from Medellín, one of the locations with the best infrastructure in the country, is at the same level as an act like Alexis Play, who comes from nearby Quibdó, Chocó, and has almost single-handedly revamped the musical scene at only 95 miles from Medellín. However, at 143 miles long, the currently unfinished road from Medellín to Quibdó is a testament to the true difference between locations, taking almost seven hours to cover as a result of its poor condition. Quibdó, which receives the most rain in the world among cities with over 100,000 inhabitants, has been consistently forsaken by national administrations in terms of infrastructure and social investment, so artists gain acclaim and recognition not thanks to official support, but despite official neglect. So, while inclusion in a playlist—or even positions on a map, which seem close—hides the differences between both locations, it is important to keep in mind the actual engagement of the government in the standard of living of each place, hinting at the degree of its more material relationship—rather than mediatic—with the state.

In this sense, not all acts confer the same degree of legitimacy to the government. Acts from places where the Colombian state has an established presence—Medellín—clearly do not embody the novelty of acts more recently included as the result of the state's change of strategy after the Constitution of 1991—evidently, the case of Quibdó, whose musical tradition stood ignored for decades. Consequently, more than an acknowledgment of their presence by a state adjusting to a reconfiguration and revamping of the idea of a nation, the inclusion of acts of this nature speaks of the government's willingness to update its conventional narrative of inclusion, so more will embrace it as patriotism, eager to support another form of national cultural production. This is how consensus is born.

In sum, Mincultura's playlist is a modern hegemonic stab, which may succeed or not, depending on the alertness of audiences. Through the circulation and sharing of these cultural forms, the general population can internalize the ideology, mores, practices, and values suggested by loosely associated official representatives. In this way, the followers of Mincultura's attempt to hegemonize the population by way of endorsing a specific idea of the national musical repertoire begin consuming music from acts not only because they are partial to their music but because they feel that, in the act of doing so, they are validating their sense and understanding of national identity while simultaneously legitimating the Ministry as a champion of Colombianness. Hoping to belong more to the nation—the imagined community they share in their minds— the followers of Mincultura end up validating the actions of the state. It appears a clear distinction between the two may not be plain. In this way, music, or rather the making of a national musical repertoire, becomes a new tool in the state's arsenal for the construction of hegemony. The risk apparent with these recently acquired mechanisms of validation is that, in the future, the number of the acts excluded and/or ignored by the government will inevitably increase— the population will soar, the number of acts will thrive, and the state's capacity to celebrate will saturate—fostering the government's stranglehold on the notion of a functional Colombian identity—and this, we all know well, is a clear path to authoritarianism/nationalism. Communities may feel encouraged to figure and participate in programs devised by the central government, duly convinced of the possibility of official recognition and celebration, only to find the numbers working against them. Nonetheless, this may not represent a problem to the political establishment because, by then, a majority of the inhabitants will have internalized the versions of identity and narratives favorable to the government, including the exercise of memory, which will discard any version of history contrary to the interests of a privileged few. This outcome may echo a doomsday scenario, yet the choice to resist is always a possibility.

Notes

1 John Hawkins, *The Creative Economy: How People Make Money from Ideas* (London: Allen Lane, 2001).
2 Carlos Ortega, "Qué es la economía naranja de la que habla Duque?" *El Tiempo*, September 4, 2018. www.eltiempo.com/economia/sectores/que-es-la-economia-naranja-que-promueve-ivan-duque-253254, accessed April 3, 2021; Felipe Buitrago Restrepo and Iván Duque Márquez, *The Orange Economy: An*

Infinite Opportunity (Washington, DC: IDB, 2013). Available for download at https://publications.iadb.org/en/orange-economy-infinite-opportunity.
3   Óscar Hernández Salgar, "Los mitos de la música nacional: Poder y emoción en las músicas populares colombianas 1930–1960" (PhD dissertation, Pontificia Universidad Javeriana, 2014), 148.
4   Hernández Salgar, *Los mitos de la música nacional*, 152.
5   Hernández Salgar, *Los mitos de la música nacional*, 161.
6   The move of Discos Fuentes from Cartagena to Medellín in 1954 is symptomatic of this shift. Previously, Barranquilla figured as the second most important Colombian city and Cartagena de Indias even served as forerunner and alternate capital to Bogotá. Many Colombian firsts—that is, the arrival of commercial radio (1929) and the birth of commercial aviation (1919)—took place in Barranquilla, given its status as main Colombian seaport and point of entry until 1941. Hernández Salgar, *Los mitos de la música nacional*, 176.
7   Juan Sebastián Ochoa Escobar, *Sonido sabanero y sonido paisa: La producción de música tropical en Medellín durante los años sesenta* (Bogotá: Pontificia Universidad Javeriana, 2018).
8   Manuel Sevilla Peñuela et al., *Modernity and Colombian Identity in the Music of Carlos Vives y La Provincia* (Lanham: Lexington Books, 2020).
9   "Mincultura, Mincultura lanza listado de '100 canciones #ColombiaCreaTalento' para promover a los artistas nacionales," Ministerio de Cultura, July 2, 2020. www.mincultura.gov.co/prensa/noticias/Paginas/Mincultura-lanza-listado-de-%E2%80%98100-canciones-ColombiaCreaTalento%E2%80%99-para-promover-a-los-artistas-nacionales-.aspx
10 Ministerio de Cultura, *Sistema de Información Musical* (SIMUS). Ministerio de Cultura. https://simus.mincultura.gov.co/, accessed August 20, 2020.
11 Peter Wade, *Music, Race, and Nation: Música Tropical in Colombia* (Chicago: The University of Chicago Press, 2000), 5–29.
12 Anderson in Wade, *Music, Race and Nation*, 25.
13 Catalina Muñoz, *A Fervent Crusade for the National Soul: Cultural Politics in Colombia, 1930–1946* (Lanham: Lexington Books, 2022), 25.
14 Ministerio de Cultura de Colombia, "Entrevista: La *playlist* de la Ministra," *Facebook*, June 4, 2020. www.facebook.com/MinisterioCultura/videos/entrevista-la-playlist-de-la-ministra/254784129274605/, accessed August 20, 2020.
15 Ministerio de Cultura de Colombia, *Informe de Gestión. Enero—Diciembre 2019*, Ministerio de Cultura. www.mincultura.gov.co/prensa/noticias/Documents/Patrimonio/INFORME%20GESTION%202019%20MINCULTURA%20V31012020.pdf, accessed August 20, 2020.
16 Wade, *Music, Race and Nation*, 7.
17 Wade, *Music, Race and Nation*, 9.
18 Language of this nature has been recurrent since it first appeared in the Plan Nacional de Cultura 2001–2010, under then Minister of Culture Araceli Morales López, part of Andrés Pastrana's administration (1998–2002). https://mincultura.gov.co/planes-y-programas/Planes/plan%20nacional%20de%20cultura/Paginas/default.aspx. It is no coincidence that it was precisely between 1997 and 1998, at the end of the Samper administration (1994–1998) and the beginning of Pastrana's, that Mincultura was born.

Part 5

Revisiting the Armed Conflict

15 Gendered Activism and Elite Formation on the Colombian Frontier
Lessons from the Life of Fátima Muriel

Winifred Tate

"I am Patricia Llombart, the ambassador of the European Union in Colombia and *pongo la cara* por Fátima Muriel," begins the 12th in a series of short videos produced in 2020 as part of governmental campaign in which high profile politicians and actors speak in support of threatened activists. "She is one of the leaders of the Women Weavers of Life in Putumayo . . . for me, they embody resilience [*son sinónimas de la resiliencia*], they are *berracas* [strong], they have been victims of the violences of war, of femicides, and because of all that, they are committed to building peace." Working in Putumayo in a context of criminalization, violence and political exclusion, Fátima adeptly mobilized political resources by claiming legitimacy for women as mothers and peasant farmers. This chapter explores her work as a power broker whose advocacy and activism used gender and class to mobilize national and transnational networks in the face of shifting forms of violence in southern Colombia over the past five decades. Her success hinged on her position in an emerging frontier elite as she catalyzed dominant gender ideologies that positioned women as inherently peaceful caretakers and non-political bystanders in the regional criminal economy, enabling women's solidarity to develop under the radar during the height of the conflict, while later allowing high-profile public protests, collective mourning and funding projects supported by international allies.

As a frontier region, Putumayo has been simultaneously remote and marginal, and deeply implicated in national and transnational projects. The region is lowland jungle with a minimal population of indigenous groups and poor *colonos* (settlers) that was made into a department in 1991. As such, it lacks an entrenched political and economic elite on the scale of those in urban areas or regions with longer histories of incorporation into the nation-state. Local political culture reflects an ethos of colonization, exploration, and creation. Waves of colonization have resulted in part from land policies as the area was designated as *"tierras baldías,"* or public

DOI: 10.4324/9781003048152-21

lands that were declared empty and available for settlers, the only requirement being a machete and a tolerance of backbreaking rural labor. The region played a central role as one of the "escape valves" for escalating land pressure in the context of Colombia's extreme land inequality and repeated waves of violence to dispossess small farmers from their holdings.[1] At the same time, historically Putumayo has been deeply enmeshed in transnational economic and political processes, including Catholic missionary efforts, quinine, fur, rubber, and oil exploitation, and coca paste for the illegal drug trade for the international market.[2] Beginning in the 1970s, the profits of dramatically expanded coca cultivation brought thousands of small farmers into the region, who created villages and began organizing to secure state services such as roads, schools, and health centers.[3] By the 1980s, however, residents were stigmatized as violent criminals intent on personal enrichment through the drug trade and associated with the guerrillas, considered throughout Colombia as a growing population excluded from citizenship and rights claims because of their assumed criminality.[4] Deadly conflict between guerrillas, the Colombian military, and their paramilitary allies escalated into the early 2000s. Following peace initiatives, violence targeting community leaders continues.

As Fátima and her allies navigated this complex political terrain, I am particularly interested in the ways in which gender was foundational for the innocence that Fátima and other women activists in Putumayo needed to project for both their safety and for political legitimacy. Innocence remains a critical ontological category for victims of human rights abuses to gain political and social legitimacy, complicating organizing efforts in Putumayo.[5] Throughout the Americas, populations criminalized for their identity, such as Black youths, or because they inhabit areas controlled by illegal actors are the target of state violence and prevented from participation in public life and policy debates.[6] Organizing as women, portrayed to be unconcerned with political attachments and focused on their domestic roles of kinship care, was one path to political legitimacy.[7] As the daughter of an *inspector de policía* [local state representative] and wife of a *terrateniente* [landlord], Fátima was connected through kinship to high-ranking politicians; through her work in the Ministry of Education, she was one of the first generation of educated women who worked salaried government jobs that connected them to national institutional networks.[8] Born to a local official married to an Inga woman in Puerto Limón, Putumayo, Fátima studied first at the new missionary school in Puerto Limón, and then in the *Normal*, a high school training teachers in Sibundoy. Her husband's family had fled Nariño during the mid-century conflict of *la Violencia*, accumulating more than 600 hectares of land for cattle ranching along the Caquetá River. During the years of domination of the Revolutionary Armed Forces of Colombia, FARC, when little international attention turned to Putumayo, Fátima mobilized her extensive social and kinship connections, the network of rural teachers she supervised, and Catholic institutional projects to channel low-profile activism work. As the region gained international attention while the violence waned, Fátima was able to turn her focus to public work bringing attention to different forms of violence against women, while using her international connections, particularly with the European Union diplomatic corps, to channel resources to women's small scale development projects. As founder and president of the Putumayo Women's Alliance Weavers of Life, Fátima has become an internationally recognized peace activist and spokesperson for women's rights and victims of the Colombian conflict. This work was profoundly local and largely invisible even to the armed groups during the initial years of FARC domination, and to a lesser degree during the height of the conflict. As the conflict faded, the 2000 United Nations Resolution 1325 transformed the international structure through which women's activism became visible. Calling for "gender mainstreaming" in peace and security, the resolution opened up funding opportunities, as well as greater attention from diplomats from the European Union.

Fátima and others strategically drew on the symbolic resources developed during decades of women's protests in the Americas. These histories continue to profoundly shape the forms of organization and the nature of the political claims produced by women within the network. A central thread of all their work is *visibilizar*, to make visible the suffering, and political demands, of women. Victimhood has become a deeply gendered category that is a central channel for state recognition and resources in contemporary Colombia.[9] Such dynamics are clearly at play in Putumayo as well. My analysis focuses on the ways in which local elites can broker such recognition in the name of women as a general category of victim, in contexts where perpetrators include the entangled actors of illegal narcotics trade, guerrillas, paramilitaries, and the state armed forces as well as women's intimate partners. Such activism can elide the myriad differences among women, as well as the ways in which women are also perpetrators of violence, while achieving greater public recognition.

I met Fátima more than 20 years ago when I began periodic research trips to Putumayo, documenting community responses to the illegal drug trade, political violence and U.S. intervention.[10] I was fascinated by her tales of contesting the rule of armed actors, inspired by her focus on the plight and activism of women, annoyed by her tendency to mock and belittle anyone doing something she did not approve of (including me). Her support was and is foundational to my ability to conduct ongoing research in Putumayo. Here, I focus on the shifting political possibilities for women embedded in elite formation in the region through the story of one woman. She is also, of course, part of a broader movement in which hundreds of women have collectively and individually worked for transformation in the region. While recognizing the limitations and contradictions she embodies, my focus here is on how Fátima was able to leverage her position to achieve significant recognition and support for women in the region, part of an ongoing book project focusing on her life and examining the past half century of women's activism in Putumayo. This chapter uses Fátima's life story to trace how particular kinds of violence in Putumayo became visible, the ways in which frontier class formation enabled Fátima's growing leadership, and how gendered innocence was central to the ways in which women became the subject and object of political interventions.

Indigeneity and Class Formation on the Frontier

In her conversations with me, Fátima begins the retelling of her life story with the violent abduction of her mother by her father. Rosana Silva Anacona was an Inga child stolen from her community at 14 by Luciano Muriel Pabón, a Spanish-descendent white man 20 years her senior. While her family protested, they were told there "was no law for the white man." Fátima's sister told me proudly that Luciano was tall, bearded, and from upper Putumayo, tracing his family to the part of Spain that is mixed with German, "where everyone is white, blond and blue eyed." The eighth of Luciano and Rosana's 12 children, Fátima was born on May 21, 1950, in Puerto Limón along the banks of the Caquetá River. Luciano was the local *inspector de policía*, the only state representative in rural areas, charged with maintaining public order and adjudicating disputes. Through the wealth guaranteed by his position and accumulated by selling supplies from the city and the cheese and bread made by his wife, he educated all his children through college, a rarity at that time. In response to one of my queries about how she was so brave in standing up to local powerful actors, Fátima responded that she was inspired by her father, who laid down the law in Puerto Limón and used his power to protect the weak, including women beaten by their husbands.

Throughout her childhood, Fátima both identified with her Inga friends while existing in a privileged class apart. Fátima recalled that the first floor of their two-story mud-plaster house was filled with her mother's extended family, cooking communal meals and telling stories. Rosana raised Fátima to speak Inga. "We did it precisely because we knew [my father] couldn't understand us, a form of feminine complicity," Fátima recalled. Once after hearing them talking in *Ingano*, her father realized what was happening and threatened them, saying he never wanted to hear them speaking like *indios* again, telling them, "dialect has no future." She attended an elementary school newly founded by Catholic missionaries to evangelize indigenous children, and assisted in their recruitment efforts, accompanying a nun in her search for indigenous children hiding along the river. After they succeeded in gathering 50 children, classes started with haircuts and pesticide sprays to kill lice with traditional clothes (a black tunic) replaced with a school uniform ("white shirts, with blue pants for the boys and blue skirts for the girls"). Fátima's father bought her shoes and nicer clothes, but she recalled a small act of solidarity with her classmates: "Because everyone went without shoes, I didn't wear mine either. It was something that I now understand as a way to not renounce my identity, which was built around this community." With her father's support, Fátima was able to resist the nuns' harshest punishment. On Monday mornings, those who missed mass were punished by being shut in a coffin to signify their "death in life." After her father was informed that she had fled the coffin, to her surprise, he chastised the nuns and threatened to report them to the Bishop of Sibundoy. As a result, the nuns refused to let Fátima play with other children at school; "the nuns said I was very disobedient and that I was teaching the *indígenas* to protest."

Fátima left her teacher training school at 17 to marry 30-year-old Julio Flórez and begin her life as a wife of a local *terrateniente*. However, she was not content to remain in the domestic sphere. At 23, with two small children, Fátima began teaching school; she later finished a college degree and a master's in education at universities in Bogotá. Her experiences in the capital were marked by both her privilege—Fátima brought a local woman with her to watch four daughters, cook, and tend to the house while she studied—and prejudice, as Putumayo was viewed as a backward, violent, and criminal region. She returned to the capital Mocoa and built a career in education, rising to the role of supervisor for the regional office of the Ministry of Education, one of a large network of educated professionals in the Flórez and Muriel families, including members of Congress and other high-ranking politicians. Through education and increasingly urban white-collar jobs, Fátima and her siblings assimilated into the mestizo regional elite, with minimal contact with their Inga extended family, raising their children as college-educated, monolingual Spanish speakers who went on to study English abroad in the United States and London.[11] Fátima's childhood experiences with her extended Inga family and her witness of the discrimination by the Catholic school of her Inga schoolmates imbued her with a concern for fairness and remained a personal touchstone as she moved into a position as part of the region's emerging elite.

National Networks and the Origins of Activism

During the early years of Fátima's career, she was involved in multiple efforts led by women to promote various reform efforts. During this period in the 1970s and 1980s, the FARC were expanding their power, funded in part through the coca bonanza that brought money and migrants into the region. Putumayo at the time was an *intendencia*; governing officials were not elected but appointed by a central body. Regional elite women—wives and daughters of local officials, business owners and ranchers—organized committees to improve local services. One such effort was the women-led civic campaign, organized to advocate for the completion of a road from Mocoa to Pitalito. Despite the fact that Putumayo lacked many basic services, including generally available electricity, they prioritized the road, arguing that "isolation" was the source of Putumayo's issues, and infrastructure would create "more direct connection to the interior to connect us to the country," according to Fátima's sister-in-law Luz, who also participated in the committee. Piedad, another woman who served on the committee, told me that women were required "because the men were too political. This road was made by a women's movement, women went to Bogotá, women spoke to the transportation ministry."[12] While road projects—and their failures—remains a contentious issue in Putumayo, these efforts served to develop women's organizing skills and build political networks in the region.[13]

The teacher's union was another important place where women gained leadership experience during this period. Teachers in Colombia have one of the strongest unions in the country; their national coordinating body, FECODE, has long been active in public policy debates. The Putumayo branch, the Asociación de Educadores del Putumayo (ASEP), also served as a network connecting and supporting women teachers, providing political analysis and education workshops and a national platform for political participation. The ability for women to gain teaching training through the Normal Superior in Sibundoy, and access paid employment through teaching, transformed women's professional prospects and their public role in the region. Women organized the creation of the Secretaría de la Mujer as one of 13 directorates in the union, despite being excluded from all leadership positions within the ASEP. The women who championed the position were even expelled from the union; they were later reinstated but this struggle demonstrated the ongoing resistance to women assuming such roles, as well as the creativity and persistence required to create such opportunities.

In addition to her public advocacy for public infrastructure and institutional organizing for women's leadership in the teacher's union, Fátima led covert efforts to promote women's rights through Catholic workshops as well as school parents' associations. Backed by the institutional power of the Catholic Church, the transformative possibilities of such initiatives were enabled by the charismatic Father Alcides Jiménez, a visionary leader who worked for more than 18 years in the Puerto Caicedo parish, and made social justice ministry in the community his focus. His Liberation Theology-influenced perspective included critique of what he called savage capitalism as well as the coca culture, Colombian patriarchal social norms and the country's political elite. In his many programs, he promoted gender equality and the central role of women in development while emphasizing the importance of an idealized heteronormative peasant family, while using the institutional networks and legitimacy of the Catholic Church for support.

Fátima was one of the leaders of the *"escuela de madres"* program, Catholic workshops for women that included basic literacy, first aid, and health information. In these classes and in parents' meetings she organized through the schools, Fátima used her role as an educator focused on family wellness to disguise her efforts to promote women's rights. Fátima laughed when she described how local guerrilla commanders permitted the class because of its innocuous focus, women teaching other women about domestic matters. Once away from the watchful eyes of the FARC informants, Fátima recalled being able to discuss a wide range of issues of local concern, including the forced recruitment of children, women's rights, and domestic violence. Similarly, in parents meetings convened at rural schools, she recalled working with

> the mothers of the students, we would be talking about things and then someone from one of the [armed] groups would be there and I would quickly change to teaching *alfabetización* [literacy], go from talking about women's rights to basic literacy, that you spell, *mi papá*, the *m*, the *i*, and then they would watch and see what was going on, thinking it was just literacy classes, and get bored and leave, and one of the women would give me a nod, and then we would go back to talking about women's rights.

Fátima fought for the increasing responsibilities and resources of leadership roles within the Ministry of Education that allowed to travel throughout the region even during the height of the conflict. Her professional standing as a state official, first as a public-school teacher and then as a supervisor in the Ministry of Education, offered her the privileges of white-collar middle-class independence, while in practice involved extensive travel by boat, jeep, and horse to remote rural areas in the Amazonian foothills. Proving her competence in these demanding circumstances, including impromptu negotiations with armed actors and building trust with peasant farming communities, was critical for her success as one of the first women supervisors; she was no Bogotá bureaucrat. Her deep networks throughout the region were critical during the years of escalating conflict. These professional opportunities allowed her to travel in cosmopolitan transnational circuits as well, as she was invited to participate in international education training opportunities in Spain, Israel, and Sweden, experiences that contributed to her facility with transnational diplomacy.

Shifting Conflict Dynamics

In the late 1990s, the region was transformed by the arrival of paramilitary forces intend on gaining territorial control away from the FARC, and the U.S.-sponsored fumigation and military counternarcotics operations. Residents had learned hard lessons about the limits of making political claims to the Colombia state from earlier peasant-based organizing of the 1996 marches, when coca growers demanded increased state services and protested counternarcotics operations in the region, only to be decimated.[14] At that same time, local FARC commanders became increasingly abusive in their treatment of the population and suspicious of efforts to autonomously organizing. FARC operatives killed Father Alcides Jiménez while he was conducting mass on September 11, 1998, along with an elderly parishioner. Members of the Southern Bloc of the United Self-Defense Forces of Colombia, AUC, had arrived in 1997 carrying out intelligence operations and selective assassinations; on January 9, 1999, they occupied the small hamlet of El Tigre, killing at least 28 people and disappearing 14. During the following years, paramilitary commanders terrorized the region in order to consolidate their social and territorial control, and exercised governance in small town centers, using violence and brutality but also regulating public space, individual comportment, and interpersonal relationships.[15]

Plan Colombia, a U.S. package passed in 2000, funneled funding into newly created Colombian military counternarcotics battalions to operate in the region, as well as expanding the area sprayed by chemical herbicides.[16] Through the alternative development programs part of Plan Colombia, millions of dollars were spent on alternative livelihood projects that were abandoned or left no trace in the local economy except farmer frustration.[17] Thousands of heads of cattle were distributed, and millions of dollars in seed, credit, and agricultural support were spent. Anthropologist María Clemencia Ramírez's exhaustive study of local development efforts found that USAID programs undermined state legitimacy and eroded public confidence in the state, contradicting their stated goals.[18] At the same time, aerial fumigation destroyed legal crops; thousands of people attempted to register complaints with local ombudsmen in an effort to claim compensation, to no avail. Violence and suspicion from armed actors also prevented local development projects from being realized.

These new armed actors, and the transformation of the conflict, required the women activists to adapt new strategies. Without minimizing the levels of FARC violence experienced in these communities, many leaders and soldiers were from the region, and their kinship and community ties provided Fátima and others critical insight as well as leverage in their efforts to pressure the FARC. The newly arrived paramilitary and Colombian armed forces soldiers had no such links. Plan Colombia and the new U.S. role in the region offered another strategy, increasing transnational solidarity attention. In 1999, as the Colombia analyst for the Washington Office on Latin America, WOLA, a Washington-based human rights advocacy organization, I traveled to Putumayo with a representative from the U.S. Committee for Refugees and four Bogotá-based staff of human rights groups organizations including the Office for Action on Colombia, OIDHACO, which focused on connecting Colombian groups with European solidarity groups and advocacy campaigns in Europe. Witness for Peace (WFP), founded in 1983 to bring Americans to directly witness and experience the impact of U.S. policy beginning in the U.S.-funded Contra War in Nicaragua and then throughout Central America, began bringing educational delegations to Colombia, including Putumayo, in 1999. European solidarity and diplomatic missions also expanded their interest in the region.

The new public possibilities for protest in the region were exemplified by the November 2003 "Journey of Solidarity with Women of the South," which brought 3,500 women in 98 buses from all over the country to Puerto Caicedo. The march was organized by the Women's Path to Peace, known as la Ruta (Ruta Pacífica de las Mujeres), whose Putumayo chapter is the largest and most visible women's organization in the region and is a member organization of the Women's Network. The national organization was founded in 1996 as a nation-wide feminist, pacifist, anti-militarist alliance of 300 organizations, including many of the most important feminist groups in Colombia (including Casa de la Mujer in Bogotá, and Vamos Mujer and Mujeres que Crean in Medellín); they also allow individuals membership. La Ruta has a central office in Medellín and regional branches, including a small store front in Puerto Caicedo. The radical Catholic roots of these efforts are evident in the many members who trace their awakening to Father Alcides' trainings. Their slogan *"Ni guerra que nos mate, ni paz que nos oprima"* (no to a war that kills us, no to a peace that oppresses us) encapsulates their holistic critique of conflict resolution efforts. Within their written documents and workshops, they focus on economic inequality and exploitation as the root cause of conflict, accusing multinational corporations of economic genocide, environmental destruction, and exploiting biodiversity and natural resources, employing the analytic categories of ecofeminism.

Fátima spoke at the march as the literal embodiment of their central demand to end the U.S.-fumigation programs, as she appeared dressed like the woman represented on the poster advertising the march, with her naked torso painted to resemble a fertile jungle on one half, and a desiccated desert following fumigation on the other. She and other march organizers drew on an ecofeminist imagery and discourses and the long history of the feminist visual display of painted naked female bodies in Latin America, legitimating their critique of U.S. counternarcotics policies by positioning themselves as defenders of mother earth, not as criminals defending drug traffickers (a frequent charge from officials following such protests). Critically, they did not call out specific actors in the conflict, calling for a general "demobilization and recovery of civil life," with banners proclaiming "*la fumigación = la miseria*" (fumigation equals misery).

The Emergence of the Women's Alliance: Weavers of Life

Fátima tells the story of the founding of the Putumayo Women's Network (*La Alianza de Mujeres del Putumayo*, herein Alliance) as a gradual, collective realization that women in the department were facing increasing challenges as political violence escalated. As a supervisor in the education department, Fátima was one of the few women who was able to travel in rural areas during this time of escalating conflict. She called teachers in these communities a "*paño de lágrimas*," literally the community's handkerchief for tears, as community members turned to them for support. The network's first retreat was held in November 2003, where the group adopted three central themes to guide their work: women, human rights, and armed conflict; women history and political participation; and women, social, and economic development. The network also provides support for women under threat by using contacts with national and international nongovernmental organizations (NGOs), and attempts to connect women working with specific community development projects with funding possibilities. With ongoing piecemeal funding from a range of national and international allies, the Network has held workshops, forums, and meetings in a retreat center in neighboring Neiva, Bogotá, and throughout the department. The public human rights work of the Alliance focuses on preparing periodic reports about the region and highlighting emblematic cases of violence intended to raise awareness about the ongoing struggle for justice. Their work documenting human rights abuses continues to be a central focus; their human rights work has been largely directed by group advisor Nancy Sánchez, an experienced human rights activists who first came to Putumayo in the early-1990s to staff the region's first municipal human rights organization paid by the Bogotá- based Jesuit progressive think tank CINEP.[19] Threats forced the committee's dissolution in the mid-1990s, but Nancy remained, first working with the state health service, linking Bogotá-based and international human rights organization and then with the Alliance.

Fátima remains the Alliance's president and public face. In her public statements, standing before assembled crowds at commemorative marches or welcoming statements before workshops, she speaks in a general voice as representing all women who have suffered violence. On many occasions, she would draw on her personal experience as a survivor of brutal attacks against male relatives, such as the ones suffered by her brothers and husband. Her focus is not on the perpetrators, who generally remain unnamed allowing her to escape alignment with particular armed actors and to participate in the generic category of victim. Rather, she highlights the experience of loss and grief. She rhetorically casts women as a unified group, listing indigenous, Afro, and peasant women as kinds of women who experience the same suffering, as parts of the whole, united in their experiences in the region and as resourceful family leaders, victims of multiple forms of violence, and marginalized by the state that should work on their behalf.

The increasing public profile of the Alliance was made possible by the gradual ebb of violence during the mid and end of the first decade of the twenty-first century, which also opened space for investment in communities, and intensified efforts to secure international funding for local projects. The most public marking of this shift was the Putumayo paramilitary demobilization ceremony, held on March 1, 2006, for 504 members of the Bloque Bolívar. While the process has been widely critiqued, it did reflect a reduction in paramilitary violence. The FARC was weakened: their troop numbers diminished, leaders killed, and their units forced into strategic retreat. Mobility increased, with Alliance representatives now able to travel freely without fear of kidnapping. Women from the small towns of Putumayo could travel once again to rural areas to visit counterparts in small hamlets who had been isolated for years during the intense conflict of the early 2000s.

In her effort to elevate public recognition of women's suffering, Fátima was the driving force in the creation of memorial walls throughout the department as a form of public collective memory of violence against women, drawing on the Catholic tradition of public shrines. To date, the Alliance has placed three permanent markers placed in the two central plazas to commemorate the deaths of women in Putumayo. The first was the "wall of truth," 170 bricks in a large square of wall in one corner of the central park in Mocoa, the departmental capital. Each brick contains the name of one woman killed violently in the department, occupation, and date of death (often only a year, in some cases the day and month as well) without mention of the perpetrators and circumstances of death. The panel of bricks is set within a pastoral scene of blue sky, rolling hills, and regional flowers. The name of the Alliance runs in large letters across the top, with the slogan "not a single one more!" along the bottom, and the name of the funding institutions on the right. The wall itself was donated by the Diocese of Mocoa, and is located next to the Catholic Church in front of a moto and taxi waiting area. The wall has become a point of pride, encounter, and foreboding for the women of the Alliance, who frequently mention the wall when talking about violence against women. In Villagarzón, a mural of woman's head surrounded by the names of murdered and missing women commemorates local women.

The Alliance has organized public commemorative acts to create space for public memory and mourning as well as public pressure for accountability. These events incorporated a repertoire of symbolic acts drawn from Catholic mourning rites and the public rituals of women's human rights groups from around the globe, including the Women in Black from Israel and the Argentine Mothers of the Plaza de Mayo. These events enact memories of violence as symbolic and emotional rather than simply legal and evidentiary. In workshops and discussions, women refer to *un trabajo lúdico*, which translates as playful but here glosses a much larger field of sensory, sensuous, emotional, and artistic experience and expression. The notions of the importance of *lo lúdico*, and its role in political demands and collective organizing for women, has emerged from a range of ecofeminist and so-called difference feminist writing in Latin America and is employed here to create space for gendered enactment of commemoration and memory. These elements include ambulatory displays of photos of the dead and disappeared, and installations in public plazas of religious funeral objects such as crosses, invitations to funeral masses (often printed on newsprint paper post-sized, plastered on streets as a public invitation, including the name, dates and basic identifying information including family members; invitations to funeral masses have also circulated as a form of death threat), flowers, and candles. In one example, in September 2011, the Women's Alliance organized a march to commemorate the case of four sisters who were abducted, tortured, and murdered by paramilitaries in 2001. This case was a focus of sustained activism by the Alliance, led by their mother, as representative of paramilitary violence in the region while also an extreme spectacle. After the girls' bodies were found, exhumed, and reburied in Bogotá, the Alliance organized the event as a pilgrimage through the town centers of the most populated municipalities. More than 3,000 women participated, vastly more than the few hundred they originally anticipated, following footprints painted in red. In recognition of this work, in 2011, the Alliance won the Antonio Nariño Human Rights prize, from the German and French Embassies. In addition to a commemorative statue, the prize included a trip to Bogotá for a public ceremony, and a European tour of France and Germany to present their work and network among European governmental, NGOs, and solidarity groups. Fátima and two representatives traveled first to Bogotá and then to Europe, in trips that generated both symbolic and material support for their projects.

Peace Activism and Access to E.U. Resources

The 2010 election of Juan Manuel Santos on a peace platform had opened a new area of work for Fátima and the Alliance: Promoting support for a negotiated settlement between the FARC and the Colombian government, and seeking funding for such efforts from the European Union. The talks began in Havana in 2012. Fátima and the Alliance supported the process, in part by continually arguing that women were peacemakers within their communities, and that peace would bring Putumayo possibilities for economic development and prosperity, even while they were part of a chorus of civil society groups arguing for a greater role in the conduct of the negotiations. As a result, Fátima was one of a group of women and LGBTI representatives that traveled to Havana to testify on February 11, 2014, as part of the peace process. Fátima raised multiple issues: Asking the government to suspend aerial fumigation to support peace; asking both sides to end the abuse of women; and asking the FARC to end child recruitment and release 13 youth identified by their families. By the end of the month, the FARC announced they would end recruitment of youth under 17.

The declining levels of political conflict, and the possibility of a peace accord with the FARC, opened up possibilities for more international funding for small-scale economic development projects in the region. During surveys, workshops and protests, women in Putumayo consistently prioritized the need for economic support for their families. Women faced ongoing exclusion from both legal and illegal markets, given difficulties with access to land, and hiring practices that kept women in service roles, usually cooking for male farm workers. Network leaders also discussed Colombian legislation protecting women's rights, and strategized how to make local officials more responsive to the needs of women's and families facing abuse and sexual violence. A 2011 survey of participating women revealed that women faced much more ongoing violence in their daily lives from their domestic partners than from the larger conflict. As they continued with work focused on gender violence, Fátima and others began to describe the situation in Putumayo with the emerging category of femicide, understood as violent murder of women because of their gender and taken up by activists throughout Latin America to draw attention to this undocumented and minimized violence.

The relationships they developed with European Union diplomats and other E.U. funders were vital in their efforts to secure money for women-led projects, although they remained far from sufficient to meet the community demand. One such program was Luz de la Frontera (Light of the Border), organized by women in La Dorada beginning in 2008. Working with advisors from the Alliance, the women identified their priority as primary food security and economic productive projects for women who were heads of households or suffering from severe poverty with their partners. As a result, they first developed a community garden, on the property of one of the members, but continued to express desire for a larger space and land owned by the group through collective title. In 2010, the group obtained a farm, approximately five hectares about ten minutes outside of town. Managing the land was complicated. Conflicts centered on how to deal with collective work, the time and financial demands of the farm, the lack of a full-time caretaker living at the farm, and the need for funding to improve the property and pay for sowing crops. The farm also required various permits and registrations from local officials. I was able to participate in a series of meetings about the farm, its management, and the desired support from the community from 2010–2012, and so witnessed some of the difficulties.

One of the major hurdles was the lack of support from local government agencies and officials, obstacles that the Alliance hoped could be overcome with international pressure. Members had been frustrated that in order to apply for project funding, they need a land title or documents proving their legal standing, but they were unable to get a topographer from the municipal government to survey the land and file the results. Fátima told the group, "Don't blame yourself. Remember that for 17 years we have been trying to get the mayor to help us with the Casa de la Mujer, and we haven't been able to." Part of their strategy to gain access was to work their international connections. "We should get a letter from a German representative to Congress, we could ask them to send a letter." Fátima continued, "We could tell them that if you don't help us with what you promised, Germany will withdraw the money that they promised."

These exchanges revealed several important aspects of the Alliance's struggles and Fátima's leadership skills and shortcomings. First, the ability to gain recognition and respect from local officials was a critical responsibility for the group's leaders. More importantly, it revealed the ways in which local politics continue to be driven by clientelist politics. Personal relationships and political patronage drive the distribution of state resources, including designation of state services (such as the land surveys required for legal documentation of land ownership) and fulfillment of promised resources. In response, Fátima and other Alliance members attempted to position their transnational allies and supporters as powerful patrons who can intervene and support their efforts in response to local state inaction. In her conversations with government officials, international diplomats, and local women, Fátima claimed her position as the scion of a wealthy, politically connected family, comfortable in remote rural communities and in European embassies alike, as a point of connection, legitimacy, and moral authority.

Over the next years, the Antonio Nariño prize facilitated an ongoing relationship between the Alliance and embassy personnel, positioning them as political patrons and eventually economic patrons. The French and German ambassadors visited the region with their staff, in a trip coordinated and hosted by Alliance members (costs were covered by the Embassies). Alliance members were able to participate in meetings with local officials, including the governor and mayors, as the hosts of these powerful transnational guests. The following year, the 18 ambassadors' wives traveled to the region, again on a visit hosted by the Alliance, in which in both private and public meetings, the Alliance was positioned as facilitating powerful political allies. Fátima and two other Alliance members participated in a two-week tour of Europe sponsored by the Embassies, in which they met with European Union officials, funders, and solidarity organizations. Finally, the relationship facilitated direct support of the farm project, when a staff member of the German embassy directed guests at his wedding to make monetary donations to the Luz de la Frontera rather than gifts, collecting approximately U.S.$3,000 for the farm.

The peace agreement, signed on August 26, 2016, was announced in an emotional international ceremony in Cartagena on September 26, with the FARC ratifying the agreement with their base in the 10th Conference in Colombia's southern plains. Fátima and the Alliance campaigned relentlessly for peace, holding community suppers (*sancochos*), forums, and symbolic actions including candlelight vigils. In October, Colombia's peace process stopped in its tracks after the "No" vote won a referendum by a slim margin. The department of Putumayo, however, voted 65% in favor. "It was the cities that defined [the vote]. We continue being vulnerable, and this is the reality that must change," Fátima wrote me in an email after the final results of the vote had been announced. "It represents a form of discrimination and impedes the outer regions from strengthening themselves on their own terms. In Putumayo [the vote] went well, and I know that it is due to the hard work of the women." The No campaign mobilized a backlash against expanded rights for women and LGBTI rights, a repudiation of the gender equity platform advanced by the Alliance and others.[20] The peace agreement between the FARC and the Colombian government under president Juan Manuel Santos was finally ratified on December 1, 2016, and approved by Congress without going before another popular vote.

Other development projects pursued by the Alliance included a 2017 training program in setting up small ecotourism programs for birding trips, offering a "Diploma in Creation of Community Tourism Initiatives" (including technical training in English) for local women, established with the support of the Ministry of Education, the University of Cauca, the Technological Institute of Putumayo, the Women's Alliance Weavers of Life, and the British Council. Also in 2017, German Ambassador Michael Brock toured Putumayo invited by Fátima and the Alliance, and when handed page after page of local projects seeking funding, he vowed to return. On March 20, 2018, Brock and his entourage traveled to Putumayo to announce a new $6 million-euro European Union Fund for Peace development program, which pools E.U. aid for post-conflict development, in the company of Fátima and other representatives of the Alliance.

Conclusion: Tensions and Contradictions

Fátima's activism and role as a political broker attracted controversy and critique as well as support. The most common centered on her role as a public figure, seen as a desire for *protagonismo*, and the ways in which national and international networks channeled benefits and resources. This criticism reflects how Fátima's work has relied on her personal connections and profile without adequately developing a network of women able to take up the project. This situation is not simply the result of Fátima's leadership, however, but reflects the broader systemic issues of the women's lack of education and opportunities in the region. More complex, and beyond my ability to explore here, is the issue of how the ways she mobilized her extensive social network and her family's position in the region to establish her authority sometimes reinforced clientelist class relations. In one example of such ambiguous attachments, I attended a workshop in Fátima's hometown of Puerto Limón and in my fieldnotes noted the ways in which Fátima positioned herself in an ongoing relationship with the women:

> Fátima returns again and again to the point that this is her hometown, that she knows everyone and that they are all friends. She calls out to women by name, recalling things that they had done together. She calls out some women who worked in her family's house, who raised her children, saying that they are more than servants—*de servicio*—they are friends. Later one of the women, an older black woman—all alone, she says, with only one male child, a young granddaughter on leaning against her—says that she used to work in the Muriel kitchen, peeling plantains, she tells me, holding out her hands, swollen knuckles, and strong fingers. Look, this is where I cut my finger, she says, showing me a thin scar across the top of her middle finger just below the nail. They had a big machine to cut the plantains, and it went fast, and cut me right there. Do you know how much they paid me? 20 pesos for the day, she shakes her head. That was good money in that day, her neighbor says. The woman shakes her head again, and I am not sure if she is agreeing or contesting the woman's assessment of her wage.

Fátima undoubtedly possesses the leadership qualities Durkheim categorized as "charisma"—a dynamic public speaker, vibrant storyteller, and shrewd strategist able to draw in multiple allies. My interest here is examining Fátima's life and activism to illuminate how the conditions of possibility shifted, and the ways in which she was able to mobilize a range of strategies during different political moments. Her work dedicated to the women of Putumayo at considerable personal risk allowed Fátima to realize her commitment and Catholic ideals of service at the same time she became personally renown for her leadership; her work with the Ministry of Education allowed her to travel throughout the department at a time when the escalating conflict prevented public outreach. Her position among the emerging frontier elite facilitated her work as a political broker in national and transnational networks, allowing her to channel resources into the region and offering her the opportunity to travel to represent Putumayan women in Bogotá and beyond.

In excavating some of the possibilities and limitations of women's activism, Fátima's life and work offers lessons for the recovery of these ephemeral histories in other regions throughout Colombia, that while different in their particularities struggled with similar dynamics. This story is also important because of the ways in which Fátima's life and activism in Putumayo offers a different narrative from the dominant case of elites supporting paramilitary forces, as they did in the Caribbean Coast and many other regions.[21] In the case of Putumayo, community leaders such as Fátima adeptly fashioned their political claims on mobilized political legitimacy as women, mothers, and peasant farmers, maximizing opportunities presented by fickle transnational networks and leaving a critical legacy of activism for new generations.

Notes

1 Alejandro Reyes, *Guerreros y campesinos: El despojo de la tierra en Colombia* (Buenos Aires: Grupo Editorial Norma, 2009).
2 Michael Edward Stanfield, *Red Rubber, Bleeding Trees: Violence, Slavery, and Empire in Northwest Amazonia, 1850–1933* (Albuquerque: University of New Mexico Press, 1998); Michael Taussig, *Shamanism, Colonialism, and the Wild Man: A Study in Terror and Healing* (Chicago: University of Chicago Press, 1991).
3 Paul Gootenberg and Liliana M. Dávalos, eds., *The Origins of Cocaine: Colonization and Failed Development in the Amazon Andes* (New York: Routledge, 2019); María Clemencia Ramírez, *Between the Guerrillas and the State: The Cocalero Movement, Citizenship, and Identity in the Colombian Amazon* (Durham: Duke University Press, 2011); María Clara Torres Bustamente, *Estado y coca en la frontera colombiana* (Bogotá: Odecofi-CINEP, 2011).
4 For comparative urban cases, see, for Brazil, Teresa P. R. Caldeira, *City of Walls: Crime, Segregation, and Citizenship in São Paulo* (Berkeley: University of California Press, 2001); for El Salvador, see Susan Bibler Coutin, *Nations of Emigrants: Shifting Boundaries of Citizenship in El Salvador and the United States* (Ithaca: Cornell University Press, 2007); and for Bolivia, see Daniel M. Goldstein, *Outlawed: Between Security and Rights in a Bolivian City* (Durham: Duke University Press Books, 2012).
5 Miriam Ticktin, "A World without Innocence," *American Ethnologist* 44, no. 4 (2017): 577–590.
6 Caldeira, *City of Walls*; Coutin, *Nations of Emigrants*; Lisa LaPlante, "The Law of Remedies and the Clean Hands Doctrine: Exclusionary Reparation Policies in Peru's Political Transition," *American University International Law Review* 23, no. 1 (2009): 51–90; Kimberly Theidon, *Intimate Enemies: Violence and*

Reconciliation in Peru (Philadelphia: University of Pennsylvania Press, 2010); James Holston, *Insurgent Citizenship: Disjunctions of Democracy and Modernity in Brazil* (Princeton: Princeton University Press, 2007).
7 For comparative studies of similar gender strategies see Marguerite Guzman Bouvard, *Revolutionizing Motherhood: The Mothers of the Plaza de Mayo* (Wilmington: Scholarly Resources, 1994); Cynthia Cockburn, *From Where We Stand: War, Women's Activism and Feminist Analysis* (London: Zed Books, 2007); Sara Howe, "The 'Madres de La Plaza de Mayo:' Asserting Motherhood; Rejecting Feminism?" *Journal of International Women's Studies* 7, no. 3 (2013): 43–50; Diana Taylor, "Performing Gender: Las Madres de La Plaza de Mayo," in *Negotiating Performance: Gender, Sexuality, and Theatricality in Latin/o America*, ed. Juan Villegas Morales (Durham: Duke University Press, 1994).
8 For more on gender and the emerging white-collar work force in Colombia, see A. Ricardo López-Pedreros, *Makers of Democracy: A Transnational History of the Middle Classes in Colombia* (Durham: Duke University Press, 2019).
9 Donny Meertens, *Elusive Justice: Women, Land Rights, and Colombia's Transition to Peace* (Madison: University of Wisconsin Press, 2019); Roxani C. Krystalli, "Narrating Victimhood: Dilemmas and (in)Dignities," *International Feminist Journal of Politics* 23, no. 1 (2021): 125–146.
10 Winifred Tate, *Drugs, Thugs, and Diplomats: U.S. Policymaking in Colombia* (Stanford: Stanford University Press, 2015).
11 For more on shifting indigenous identity in Putumayo, see Margarita Chaves and Marta Zambrano, "From *Blanqueamiento* to *Reindigenización*: Paradoxes of Mestizaje and Multiculturalism in Contemporary Colombia," *Revista Europea de Estudios Latinoamericanos y del Caribe/European Review of Latin American and Caribbean Studies* 80 (2006): 5–23.
12 Interview by the author, 2008.
13 Simón Uribe, *Frontier Road: Power, History, and the Everyday State in the Colombian Amazon* (Hoboken: Wiley, 2017).
14 Ramírez, *Between the Guerrillas and the State*.
15 María Clemencia Ramírez et al., *Elecciones, coca, conflicto y partidos políticos en Putumayo, 1980–2007* (Bogotá: CINEP/PPP, ICANH, Colciencias, 2010).
16 Tate, *Drugs, Thugs, and Diplomats*.
17 Adam Isacson, "Putumayo's White Elephant, or How Not to Win Hearts and Minds," *Plan Colombia and Beyond* (blog), August 29, 2006.
18 María Clemencia Ramírez, "Maintaining Democracy in Colombia through Political Exclusion, States of Exception, Counterinsurgency, and Dirty War," in *Violent Democracies in Latin America*, eds. Enrique Desmond Arias and Daniel M. Goldstein (Durham: Duke University Press, 2010).
19 Sara Koenders, "The Right to Speak: The Life and Work of Nancy Sánchez of Colombia," Women PeaceMakers Program, Joan B. Kroc School of Peace Studies, University of San Diego 2007. https://www.academia.edu/7212484/The_Right_to_Speak_The_Life_and_Work_of_Nancy_S%C3%A1nchez_of_Colombia
20 Winifred Tate, "No Peace for Colombia," *NACLA*, February 24, 2016; "A Dark Day in Colombia," *NACLA*, October 4, 2016.
21 Mauricio Romero, *Paramilitares y autodefensas, 1982–2003*, 2nd ed. (Bogotá: Editorial Planeta-IEPRI, 2005); Mauricio Romero, *Parapolítica: La ruta de la expansión paramilitar y los acuerdos políticos* (Bogotá: Corporación Nuevo Arco Iris and Intermedio, 2007).

16 Coercive Brokerage

The Rise and Fall of the Colombian Paramilitary Hernán Giraldo, 1976–2006

Francisco Gutiérrez Sanín

Hernán Giraldo was a paramilitary figurehead—and egregious sex offender—who operated in the Sierra Nevada de Santa Marta region, SNSM, between the late 1970s and 2006. He was a *coercive broker*. On the one hand, he established a complex system of intermediation between different territorial levels. On the other, he was a provider of private security to key economic and political elites which in the context of the Colombian state counterinsurgent strategy eventually allowed him to become a major paramilitary player. The use of large means of violence was at the heart of such system revealing that Giraldo was not "peripheral" in any reasonable sense: the type of brokerage he developed was part and parcel of the specific way in which the Colombian state made presence in different territories in the context of the armed conflict.[1] Furthermore, he operated in a coastal borderland that was economically, socially, and politically relevant for the Colombian state. Santa Marta was and is an important departmental capital and a tourism hotspot. Its rural hinterland—the immense SNSM—is incredibly resource-rich. Giraldo coordinated security demands between the city and its hinterland, receiving in the process the support of timber merchants, cattle ranchers, and banana and coffee growers. The SNSM was also the scenario of two major illegal crops bonanzas—marijuana and coca—and Giraldo's control over them allowed him to substantially increase his power.

Based on my book *Clientelistic Warfare: Paramilitaries and the State in Colombia (1982–2007)*, I will show here how Giraldo's brokerage was built upon the access to a variety of sources of power at least at four territorial levels (local, regional, national, and global), and how at the same time, the coordination between them was intrinsically unstable.[2] In the end, Giraldo could not possibly align the central concerns of key coalitions at the different territorial levels at which he operated. For example, it was likely that Giraldo would eventually become a target of the War on Drugs (global level). At the national level, his strictly localistic control over a militarily strategic region eventually became a nuisance for the national

DOI: 10.4324/9781003048152-22

counterinsurgent push. Some of Giraldo's horrid crimes—as a massive sex offender and killer—have been already discussed seriously and in detail by several scholars.[3] The contributions of this chapter to the understanding of Colombian paramilitarism are thus the following. First, I go in depth into the mechanisms underlying Giraldo's territorial control. I show that, contrary to standard expectation, community involvement in this type of control was associated with extreme and frequent violent acts against civilians. Second, and in relation to this, I show that those mechanisms go a long way in explaining his demise. His territorial power was brutal and extraordinary, but at the same time intrinsically unstable. Thus, I put collective action issues at the center of the understanding of "indirect rule," which I think is indispensable.[4] Third, and more generally, I develop the analytical category of *coercive brokerage* to explain how access to large means of violence changed extant political games. Antonio Giustozzi has made the simple and important point that the access to large means of violence by one or many actors deeply transforms already existing political interactions.[5] However, the black box of how this takes place has seldom been opened. I show here that Giraldo used materials coming from the Colombian highly clientelist polity, but at the same transformed such polity. Based on concepts developed by Michael Mann and Anton Blok that I explore in the next section, I analyze how armed intermediaries are different from standard clientelist types.[6]

The chapter proceeds in the following fashion. In the first section, I discuss some key concepts related to brokerage. Then, I sketch the main aspects of the relevant context: On the one hand, the trajectory of the Colombian war(s), and on the other hand, the region where Giraldo operated (the Sierra Nevada de Santa Marta). The next part is dedicated to Giraldo's ascent. After discussing how Giraldo built his communitarian fiefdom and how he inserted it in national and global networks, I describe his decadence and fall. The conclusions return to the tensions triggered by Giraldo's coercive brokerage and the way in which he engaged in the coordination of different territorial levels. I use mainly three types of judicial sources.[7] First, those coming from standard judicial contexts, where there is adversarial evaluation of testimony and proof. There are tens of documents of these dedicated to Giraldo, his associates, his deeds, and his victims. Second, court rulings about notorious paramilitaries, mainly about those who embraced the transitional justice mechanism called Justice and Peace. Here, the evaluation of evidence is not adversarial, as the basic tradeoff upon which Justice and Peace was built was that the paramilitaries would confess their crimes in exchange for reduced jail terms. Third, court rulings about Giraldo's *parapolíticos*, that is, politicians he had in his payroll or with whom he collaborated. In *Clientelistic Warfare*, I discussed some limits and issues related to this kind of source. Fortunately, for what is relevant for this paper the three judicial sources I utilize largely coincide with each other and with national and regional press, specialized web portals and YouTube videos by victims and perpetrators, all of which I used to corroborate basic information. Whenever there are differences, I highlight them.

Mann, Men, and Coercive Brokerage

The standard definition of brokerage revolves around the notion of connecting previously unrelated people.[8] This dictionary definition of broker is good, but it is still too generic. For example, a Weberian bureaucrat acts in a very fundamental sense as the connective tissue between state and citizens, but he would not be considered by the literature as a broker, and rightly so. Brokers in clientelistic political systems as the Colombian are people who connect "social points" (individuals, coalitions, firms, cartels, etc.) to create, transform or regulate, through channels that involve at least significant non-institutional interactions, a flow of services and resources, including symbolic resources. But then what is a *coercive broker*? He is a broker that counts with the capacity of offering actual or threatened violence—coercion—as a crucial asset for establishing such connections. Giraldo operated through the act of putting together influential men—as Michael Mann recognizes, this is a still overwhelmingly male world[9]—at different territorial levels. But the necessary condition to do it was his having access to large means of violence. Actually, this was historically the primary form of brokerage. According to Mann, empires in Antiquity did not have the administrative and logistical clout to govern directly the entities they conquered, so they delegated territorial power and control over large means of violence to an assortment of notables, specialists in violence and go-betweens belonging both to the conqueror and the conquered.[10] Seen from "below," this was brokerage; seen from "above," it was an indirect rule.

Mann's concepts of brokerage and indirect rule have frequently been applied without further ado to contemporary settings, in which even deeply disrupted national states like the Colombian count with administrative and logistical powers, which are orders of magnitude bigger than those of the states that were initially under Mann's scrutiny. So here, we face a problem. On the one hand, students of contemporary "non-Weberian" states have found from the beginning that indirect rule through notables and intermediaries is at the core of the notion of their statehood, and not a supposed "deviation" from the norm. But they have frequently operated upon the implicit assumption that logistics and administration are so thin there that they can simply be discounted. It is here where Anton Blok's classical opus on the Sicilian Mafia diverges.[11] His method of analysis was based on the understanding of the Mafia as the link between local territorial power structures and the administrative apparatus of the state, not as a substitute of the latter.[12] His work, though, is still very much the exception than the rule. Only very rarely, state agencies, rule-makers, and bureaucrats appear in the cast of characters of brokerage or indirect rule narratives.

For the study of the Colombian paramilitaries, however, state agencies, rule-makers, and bureaucrats should be put front and center. The Colombian paramilitaries grew and developed hand in hand with state bureaucracies, rules, and infrastructure. At the same time, they were dealing with wars that were definitely not only national—counterinsurgent and against drugs—so they were also interacting with global actors, including powerful states. In Blok's political economy, the key to opening the black box of the Mafia is to understand how brokers interact with national state bureaucracies, logistics, and categories, and how—*through them*—they connect closed local power structures to global markets. This may also be the key to fully translating the notion of indirect rule to contemporary settings.[13]

And here also lies the explanation of why the power wielded by the Colombian paramilitaries created prohibitive impasses. Drug traffickers, popularly known as *narcos*, were a core component of the paramilitary coalition. At the same time, the state used the paramilitaries to expand its territorial reach—or, correlatively, to undermine guerrilla presence—in the context of a murderous counterinsurgent war. The result was that in such war, narcos could appear publicly as state power wielders and managers at the local and regional levels; however, it was costly to include them explicitly in a national counterinsurgent coalition. This territorial division of labor ended up being very disruptive. By waging a significant part of its counterinsurgent war through the paramilitaries, the Colombian state put itself in a situation in which it could maintain one of the two basic legal notions of a sovereign state, that is, territorial presence and external recognition by key actors, but not both.[14] Furthermore, the construction of closed territorial fiefdoms could crash against the need to launch national counterinsurgent strategies. As will be seen next, Giraldo ended up suffering from both problems. I thus also show that, as in Mann's and Blok's renderings, Giraldo's coercive brokerage was self-undermining, although the mechanisms through which it triggered knotty social impasses is naturally quite different from those reported by them.[15]

Giraldo operated on two interrelated "organizational principles" (as Blok's Mafiosi). On the one hand, those related to the construction of his local fiefdom supported on a coalition of rural elites, such as cattle ranchers, timber traders, politicians, narcos, and "families of respect" and merchants in Santa Marta. Without counting with them, he could not have become part of the national counterinsurgent coalition, which provided crucial sponsorship and access to legal operations by armed and civilian bureaucracies. Once again, like in Blok, being able to close territories through a combination of violence, deference, and social engineering—this is important, these territories are not "naturally" closed, but shut down at gun point—gave the broker crucial advantages to have access to national bureaucracies and global markets. On the other hand, Giraldo operated on organizational principles related to bridging different territorial levels to exchange goods and favors. Here, clientelistic friendship, "gli amici degli amici" ("the friends of my friends," Blok reminds us) was key. It is only through the tensions between coalitions and friends, between different organizational principles and territorial levels, that we can understand Giraldo's demise. Giraldo fell because his coercive brokerage consisted of power transactions based on locally grounded coalitions, which acted within rules specified by national and global coalitions, and eventually, it surfaced that he could not align their respective core interests and abide by the given rules.

The Context: The Colombian Paramilitary War

Two pieces of information are necessary to understand the intermediation function of the Colombian paramilitaries in the last decades. First, the country has gone through at least two prolonged cycles of violence in the past century: *la Violencia*, between the late 1940s and the mid-1960s; and the recent one, which gathered momentum in the late 1970s and have lasted until now. Second, the country has maintained almost without interruption a democratic, or at least a competitive political system throughout. After a short-lived military regime, the leaderships of the two main political parties created the National Front (1958–1974), which established as its explicit objectives the return to democracy and the promotion of peace and development.[16] The National Front aspired to extend the reach of the national state and to prevent violence and revolution through different forms of (soft) social inclusion, one of them being the creation of Community Action Councils (JAC in Spanish) at the neighborhood and county level, which soon became the largest popular organization in the country until today.

It was in this context that—as in other Latin American countries—the first guerrillas appeared. Unlike what happened with its neighbors, though, in Colombia they gradually grew, and after the late 1970s, they morphed into major armed projects.[17] From the beginning, guerrillas were opposed by private security groups in different regions.[18] In reality, a substantial part of the response of the Colombian state to the insurgent challenge was funneled by institutional design through the increasing delegation of access to large means of violence to an assortment of rural rich, regional notables and politicians and their respective areas of intersection.[19] All of them counted with a political "Bogotá tie-in," that is, contacts with key decision makers in the capital, especially through political parties.[20] At the beginning of the 1980s, tight counterinsurgent territorial coalitions that regularly included cattle ranchers, politicians, narcos, or people associated to illegal economies, and were sponsored, even sometimes promoted massively and openly, by the army and other state agencies, started to create and support their paramilitary groups in different regions. By the end of the decade, they had expelled the guerrillas from several highly disputed territories and were growing as fast as any other non-state armed group. They were displaying the most brutal forms of violence against civilians.

In the 1990s, paramilitary activity and territorial presence escalated even further. For one, new paramilitary groups appeared. In 1994, the government approved the creation of security cooperatives named Convivir, which allowed the paramilitaries to establish links with a wide cast of legal actors. The Convivir once again expressed the provision of private security and violence to territorially grounded actors by institutional design, but also revealed in a pristine fashion the intersections and mismatches between the national and regional/local coalitions during the counterinsurgent war. The Convivir were unrelentingly supported by the national federation of cattle ranchers, the association of banana growers, and the main state security agencies, which had clear access to decision-making mechanisms. By design, the Convivir required an initial endowment that guaranteed that they could only be created by wealthy people, and the keys to their regulation were given to radicalized characters coming from the banana-growing sector.[21] Created by cattle ranchers and funded massively by banana grower associations, Convivir worked in coordination with the army and civilian bureaucracies.[22] At the same time, a substantial number of Convivir were created by paramilitaries involved in drug trafficking. Unlike ranchers and banana growers, though, narcos could not appear publicly at the national or global levels. This type of arrangement was intrinsically unstable, and not only for the narcos. There were other national power wielders that had to respond to different audiences, such as the public opinion and international actors. In 1999, a Constitutional Court ruling basically ended the Convivir.

By then, some of the most successful paramilitaries had launched massive expansionist projects. This amounted to a national strategy that hoped to cover larger areas of the territory and evict the guerrillas from there. All this activity converged toward the creation of a national paramilitary federation in 1997 under the name of United Self-Defense Forces of Colombia (AUC in Spanish), a very loose territorial alliance whose main component was the Autodefensas Unidas de Córdoba y Urabá (ACCU). The AUC incessantly created new units, but the largest ones, such as the Bloque

Norte (Northern Bloc) in the Caribbean Coast, soon obtained generous margins of autonomy. The AUC did not only exercised violence against civilians, social movements or "the enemy." The tension between the national, expansionist nature of the AUC and its localist and autonomous components expressed itself also in frequent and bloody intra-paramilitary wars. In 2002, the federation fell into a process of disintegration. In the meantime, a far-right political figure, Álvaro Uribe Vélez, was elected president. The paramilitaries started a peace process under his administration in 2003, which culminated in 2006, and included a substantial number of the paramilitary units.[23] It was also fraught with political turbulences, national and international challenges to its legitimacy, continued recidivism by many paramilitary leaders and scandals surrounding the massive capture of the political system by them. In any case, this was the context in which Giraldo demobilized in 2006 to be extradited two years later to the United States.

The Santa Marta Region

Hernán Giraldo operated mainly in the city of Santa Marta, the capital of the department of Magdalena, and the northern watershed of the Sierra Nevada de Santa Marta (SNSM).[24] Santa Marta is an important city, and the SNSM, an independent mountainous range that comprises nearly 17,000 kilometers in three departments (Magdalena, Guajira, and Cesar), also includes very important roads and communication lines, terrestrial and maritime.[25] The region connects to other mountain systems across the valley, the Serranía del Perijá, which, in turn, gives access to the borderland with Venezuela and other coastal frontiers.[26] Both Santa Marta and the SNSM are places where important economic activities have been developed for decades. They have witnessed the ups and downs of the banana production, intimately linked to transnational capital since the inception of the United Fruit Company in the early 20th century.[27] Other important rural economic activities are cattle ranching and coffee. They are also touristic hotspots. It cannot be said then that the city or the SNSM are peripheral in any reasonable sense, though indeed there is a periphery that is defined in terms of geographical eccentricity and scarce provision of services and public goods.[28] Be it as it may this territorial periphery was not a social or demographical vacuum.[29]

It was there that a substantial part of the first regional bonanza of illegal crops took place: the marijuana boom or *bonanza marimbera*, which involved elites that had already been linked to other legal and illegal economies.[30] The activity involved no less than 10,000 hectares, and probably more.[31] Economies of this size can be illegal but not clandestine: they need substantial complicity by legal operators to thrive. But by 1985, the marijuana economy was already being critically disrupted. According to experts and judicial sources, aerial spraying of herbicides (at enormous environmental costs) and the creation of a prosperous marijuana economy in the United States basically destroyed it.[32] Although there is some divergence between the relevant sources, it is probably the case that already in the early 1990s, the second major illicit bonanza had started: coca crops. Different regional operators had inherited the marijuana and contraband routes, connections, and infrastructure, so they were in an ideal position to develop a bustling coca economy. From the 1980s on, different armed groups established a foothold in the SNSM and in the city. In particular, what would become the main two guerrillas in the country—the FARC and the ELN—developed different armed actions against both the economic base and the personal integrity of banana growers, cattle ranchers, politicians, and narcos, including homicide and kidnapping.

Giraldo's Ascent

As many other peasants from the Andean region of the country, Hernán Giraldo decided to tempt fate in Santa Marta in the mid-1970s.[33] When he arrived there, he met a complex security landscape. The marijuana boom was taking off.[34] This sudden inflow of illegal resources had two effects. On the one hand, it triggered—or escalated—violent competitions between illegal entrepreneurs, or between legal economic actors that had got involved in marijuana cultivation and trafficking.[35] The marijuana business was characterized by an endemic double crossing and cheating among its operators[36] and high levels of risk.[37] The phenomenon affected not only large marijuana traders but also farmers and their workers, who could be assassinated by competitors or neighbors. On the other, it created fresh opportunities to extort or burglarize, rustle, and pick upon the new rich, who, of course, could not resort to the authorities to protect their properties.[38] Taken together, both factors triggered a strong demand for private security.

Giraldo rapidly oriented himself in this world, and with a small team of strongmen started to provide protection to merchants at the Santa Marta market but also to timber traders. His success attracted the attention of other vulnerable elites in the hinterland of the city. These "distinguished families" (*familias prestantes*) also needed protection to fend off different threats.[39] The relationship of Giraldo with this coalition was stable. At the end of his saga, it was still there. For example, Jorge 40—a paramilitary Don who ended up overtaking Giraldo's territory—narrates in his autobiography[40] how a politician and cattle rancher and intimate collaborator of his, José Gnecco,[41] spoke to him about the widespread support of the

SNSM's entrepreneurs and ranchers to the paramilitaries because of the fear of the guerrilla.[42]

It is in this context that the transformation of Giraldo—from a private provider of security into a paramilitary—took place. Indeed, his key role as a protector of vulnerable elites endowed him with strong anti-subversive instincts. Additionally, he might have had personal reasons to politicize.[43] Independently of that he eventually merged with a social cleansing group that had developed in parallel with his team—*los Chamizos*—and this probably allowed him to establish increasingly better links with economic elites and municipal authorities. After the merger, Giraldo extended his grip over new territories, including some that were epicenters of tourism. Since he had already become a prominent figure in the region's underworld the—also growing—Bloque Caribe of the FARC declared him military objective. In 1988, Giraldo lent a hand to the massacre of Las Tangas, led by Fidel Castaño, a paramilitary figurehead that was achieving national standing and that was involved in a ferocious dispute with the guerrillas in his own region, Urabá.[44] At some point, he and his paramilitary associate and rival Adán Rojas were captured by the police at different events. Both were freed soon, probably because of the good offices of well-placed politicians. This is one among many examples of the decisive nature of counting with the "Bogotá tie-in." Giraldo then returned to the SNSM, strengthening his grip over his territory. By the first half of the 1990s, he and some of his closer associates, like Jairo Musso, had already become very rich, basically through two operations: land accumulation through purchase or grabbing, and control of routes and laboratories of the new coca/cocaine boom.[45] Musso also invested in other activities, like transportation.[46] The fact that Giraldo and Musso became significant economic actors in the region allowed them to strengthen and multiply their ties with the elites to which they were providing security, and to cement their territorial control.

The Giraldo's self-defense forces obtained an extraordinary boost when, in 1994, the government created the Convivir cooperatives, which operated in the open and established legal connections with all sorts of actors. Paramilitaries throughout the country started to create Convivir, usually with the support of large landowners. Giraldo indeed set up his own one called Conservar (conserve or preserve). At that moment, Giraldo's power was peaking. He controlled coca production for the processing of cocaine and had already grabbed enough land to become a wealthy cattle rancher. He coordinated the security demands of rural and urban elites, for example, Santa Marta's popular market was under his control. He developed strong links with different state bureaucracies, not only the army and the police but also one of the main intelligence agencies known as DAS, and people inside civilian agencies. Politicians could only act in Giraldo's territory under the condition that they asked him permission to do so. Giraldo's recollection of the amount of political power he had amassed by then does not seem hyperbolic:

> Politicians seek votes wherever they are . . . they seek the votes anywhere, on our part, it is well known that there are plenty of peasants [here], among other things because many people have their land (*finca*) [in the SNSM] and at the same time a house in Santa Marta. There is also a large amount of votes in Santa Marta . . . so we met with the person in question, with the person we were going to vote for, who was the person who always won, then I sat with him and the community leaders so that they posed their requests and expressed their needs. . . . Santa Marta acts as one single people [es *una sola gente*], the large majority of us come from the [same] side of the Sierra Nevada, we produce most of the food for the region . . . everybody knows that I was the boss of the region . . . I cannot deny it because that was true . . . every person whose name I suggested [*que nosotros orientábamos*] was elected, won, that was a secret to nobody.[47]

In these conditions, the regional importance of Giraldo's role as political intermediary grew incessantly, so much as to attract to his network heavyweight politicians that had a saying in national governance issues. The list of Giraldo's so-called *parapolíticos* (politicians allied to the paramilitaries) is rather impressive, as it includes at least three departmental governors, two mayors of important cities, and several municipal councilors.[48] Note, on the other hand, that Giraldo built his intermediation on his ability to act and speak on behalf of his "community" (or communities). This takes me directly to the next section.

Community, Coercion, and Intermediation

Giraldo brokerage was based on two organizational principles: on the one hand, it created a closed-community power base, and on the other, it was a bargaining chip to build long networks with armed and civilian bureaucracies, politicians, and actors in the global markets. I consider in this section the first dimension. The first point to highlight is that the notion of community was fundamental for Giraldo to establish his coercive control—that is, to "close" territorially his fiefdom. According to a witness, he used to say: "We are a community and within communities, people take care of each other. So, wait and see if you bring the enemy here, wait and see. You are not useful here within this community."[49] Not only enemies were banned; there were also strong restrictions on mobility of people and information for inhabitants and even allies. Purported informants were killed. The network of Giraldo's informants constantly maintained a detailed scrutiny of people's lives.⁵⁰ Giraldo's information network included specialists, but also neighbors who kept track of day-to-day activities, who were popularly known as "radios." So, for example, people who spoke badly of "The Boss" during every day chitchat were regularly reported to him and could be assassinated. A system of three strikes, which consisted of successive warnings and finally killing or forced displacement at the fourth episode, was applied to transgressions that did not challenge directly Giraldo's control. Giraldo's information system was also grounded on land tenure. Landowners reported to Giraldo, willingly or not, the names and whereabouts of their workers and were asked to vouch for them if necessary.⁵¹ If it was found that the worker was in some way or another linked to the "enemy," this prompted his immediate killing and maybe also the killing of his employer.⁵² Giraldo maintained strict control over land transactions in his territory; unreported transactions could be punished with the death penalty.

As seen earlier, from the beginning, a central activity of Giraldo was to protect large landowners and cattle ranchers, as well as marijuana and coca farmers, cocaine laboratories, and routes. Giraldo's paramilitaries assassinated not only purported subversives but also cattle rustlers, small-time thieves, drug consumers, and rapists.⁵³ These landowners constituted Giraldo's coalition. Protection, however, was not only delivered to elites. One of the most important reasons for killing small-time delinquents and deviants was to give verisimilitude to his claim of being the protector of the common neighbor against insecurity and crime. He also claimed to be the defender of Evangelical churches and their members against the threat of the FARC.⁵⁴

The selective delivery of violence by Giraldo merged with a system of regulation and patterned allocation of goods and services anchored in the intermediation of both Giraldo and chosen community members. Community leaders who were controlled by Giraldo were charged with routine procedures that lay at the heart of everyday sociability, such as the organization of events, fairs, allocation of resources and rights, and so forth.⁵⁵ They also engaged heavily in conflict resolution between neighbors, families, and friends. Note how communal-based legitimacy and the use of violence were not clearly separable in their everyday mechanisms and expressions. Even part of Giraldo's activity as serial sex offender fell into this twilight zone between violence and communal-based legitimacy, in terms of playing an important role in his coercive brokerage in at least two ways. On the one hand, paradoxical as it may seem, it contributed to the cementing of territorial based alliances and to the strengthening of his network of supporters. To understand this, it must be taken into account that Giraldo's predator activities targeted mainly minors.⁵⁶ He became godfather of the children of many of the girls and women he had attacked in addition of impregnating them, and eventually surrounded himself by a guard of men (godsons, relatives of the victims, *compadres*, etc.) that were linked to him by blood and symbolic ties. This gave relatives and parents of the victims access to high status and goods, and occasionally an entry ticket to Giraldo's armed group and/or businesses. In exchange, Giraldo demanded deference, support, information, and fidelity, as the absence of which could be punished with death.[57] Since the victims were counted in dozens, and the cohesion of Giraldo's group also depended on kinship ties, it is not exaggerated to state that sexual violence was indispensable to maintaining territorial control. Secondly, and possibly as important, sexual violence was used as a punitive tool against sectors of the population that behaved in an "immoral" fashion: prostitutes and supposed subversives, certainly, but also women who allegedly flirted with the husbands of others or who in some way or another acted in manners perceived as "indecent." All of them could be disciplined with death, disappearance, or gang rape. This, in turn, opened the doors to a maddening political economy of denunciation and information delivery, where spotting inappropriate behaviors gave access to sympathies by the armed regulator.[58] Giraldo's sexual violence constituted a very powerful "mechanism of control."[59]

The Insertion of the Communal Fiefdom in Broader Networks

There were three networks and connections in which Giraldo played a fundamental intermediary role between his community and larger actors and processes. These were his territorial control, the political system and agencies of the Colombian state, and narcotrafficking. Politicians knew that Giraldo was trustworthy as an anti-subversive and that he was the "owner" of a non-negligible number of votes. According to one of the politicians in his payroll, Giraldo "determined who would be voted, community meetings were held but with the permission of Hernán Giraldo, so all those that acted politically in the region did so with the permission of mister Hernán Giraldo."[60] It was not only votes, though, which cemented his relationship with politicians. It was also coercion and territory. Giraldo was also the "owner" of a significant portion of territory, which allowed him to woo his politicians with funding for their campaigns or simply economic favors for them and their entourage, but also to decide who could have access to the political and economic resources in his fiefdom. Politicians, on the other hand, provided goods and services for Giraldo's community, protection from any state offensive against his group, and intermediation with yet new actors. Many of them already had the contacts and know-how to do this, because many of their friends and relatives had participated in the marijuana boom. They provided protection from any hostile activity from a state agency, and also public goods to Giraldo's territory.

Symptomatically, the Giraldo personnel in charge of negotiating this provision of goods with politicians could be very active as brokers vis-à-vis illegal global markets of weapons and drugs. Politicians also played a key role in protecting paramilitaries from other paramilitaries or acting as go-betweens when intra-paramilitary conflicts escalated.[61]

Giraldo also established stable interactions with different state officials and agencies. His networking with men in uniform was hugely facilitated by the creation of the Convivir security cooperatives. At the peak of his power, he could boost strong links with at least three security agencies of the state: the Army, the Police, and the intelligence agency DAS. Paramilitary sympathizers within these state bureaucracies, or simply people in Giraldo's payroll, set up a very dense system of exchanges of services and mutual support. Giraldo offered to men in uniform stable anti-subversive control of a key territory, access to rents, and information. He got from them badly needed protection. He was also benefited by strategic blindness, that is, he could move through the territory as if he were invisible, operational support, and information (included who to target in his homicidal attacks). The networking of the Colombian paramilitaries with civilian bureaucrats has somehow fallen below the radar; the foci have been militaries and politicians. However, for Giraldo civilian state agencies were very important. Some civilian bureaucrats could operate in Giraldo's territory, on the condition of submitting to strong informational and access restrictions.[62] At the same time, some bureaucrats that were definitely on his side—like José Gélvez—came to play a key role. As relatively well-connected people and holders of valuable specialized knowledge, they could become an asset that allowed Giraldo to spot business and political opportunities and to find new associates among political and economic elites, local, regional and national.

These connections were enormously important for Giraldo. What did Giraldo offer to actors in global markets? First, as seen earlier, his territory could deliver a significant coca/cocaine production. Second, he had a permanent and well-trained force at his disposal, so he could provide much better protection to cocaine exports than more conventional narcos. Third, he enjoyed the additional and crucial protection of prominent politicians and of a substantial part of the armed bureaucracies of the state. Being protected by key state agencies put him in a much better position than other drug exporters, who had to buy such protection, many times from potentially disloyal intermediaries. Shielded by a triple protection (his own force, politicians, and state agents), Giraldo was in a much better position than conventional narcos, because the product had to be carried to port through dangerous routes due to a "lack of loyalty" (JP1) among traffickers that was conducive to mutual stealing, as well as the presence of rogue contrabandists in the region.

Giraldo's Demise

The administration of overlapping jurisdictions and entities over and within Giraldo's fiefdom required paying attention to "internal" and "external" processes, transactions, and challenges. Internally, as seen earlier, the communitarian support base and "epistemology" of Giraldo were at the core of his specific form of brokerage. He combined it with generous doses of different forms of violence, so that his power was never really challenged in his territory. "Externally" his fiefdom was relatively stable for a long time, due in good measure to state protection. Because of this, the guerrillas rarely posed a problem. The police was not a threat either, though antinarcotics policemen could become a nuisance from time to time. Other paramilitaries, especially the Rojas, were instead a permanent source of concern, among other things, because they competed with Giraldo for the support of the Army and the Police, and political sponsorship.

The moment of breakdown came when a national paramilitary project put into question the strictly localistic perspective that had fed Giraldo and many of his peers. As seen earlier, the Castaño brothers were creating and promoting their national federation, the United Self-defense Forcesof Colombia, AUC. Though the AUC was an extremely unwieldy and unstable federation, it did operate according to a logic of national expansion that put it in conflict with many of the paramilitary setups that had appeared throughout the country.[63] Under the aegis of Castaño-picked regional cattle ranchers (Salvatore Mancuso and Jorge 40), the AUC created the powerful Northern Bloc, which from 1997 on spread throughout the Caribbean Coast. For Castaño and the AUC leadership, the national expansion was necessary in view of the threat that the FARC posed to a state and civilian leadership that they characterized as weak and prone to give way under subversive pressure, especially after a new president elected in 1998 summoned a peace process with the FARC.

Hernán Giraldo was invited by Carlos Castaño to join the AUC, but he turned the offer down. However, he soon got involved in yet another bout of conflict with the Rojas. As regularly happened with such territorial turfs, each paramilitary setup started to try to undermine the social bases of the other through assassinations.[64] The Rojas killed a beloved friend of Giraldo, and Giraldo answered in kind. The battle ended up with the assassination of three antinarcotics policemen and a DEA agent.[65] For Carlos Castaño, this was an unforgivable offense, as it put the paramilitaries under the United States crosshairs. At the same time, the Northern Bloc was fighting against the resistance of more localistic forms of paramilitarism throughout the Caribbean Coast, so the event gave the AUC the pretext it needed to attack Giraldo. Said in other terms, the control that Giraldo exerted over his territory had already changed its character: from being an anti-subversive guarantee, it became an obstacle for the national counterinsurgent strategy. Castaño and Jorge 40 launched in 2001 a major offensive against Giraldo, eventually defeating him. It is important to note that the Giraldo-Northern Bloc crisis was public, and it involved community mass mobilizations promoted by Giraldo against the Northern Bloc and the killing of some of Giraldo's politicians, mayors, and entrepreneurs, without prompting any significant response by the state.[66] After their defeat, the Giraldo's self-defense forces were renamed as an AUC bloc—the Bloque Tayrona—and Giraldo was put under Jorge 40's tutelage. The fact that he was not killed—intra-paramilitary conflicts more often than not ended in the assassination of the leader of the losing side—speaks eloquently about the power that Giraldo had been able to accumulate. For the Northern Bloc, it was better to subordinate Giraldo and milk him (JP9), maintaining at the same time access to his power sources, such as territory, networks, and global markets.[67] Certainly, new conflicts between Giraldo's and the Northern Bloc personnel flared, but Giraldo and Jorge 40 were able to administrate them.[68]

One of the reasons for this is that, by then, Jorge 40 himself was already dealing with much more serious concerns. Castaño had launched the demobilization process. As has come to be known, the paramilitary leaders were feeling seriously uneasy about the outcome. Castaño regretted the "narcotization of the self-defense [forces]," and tried to separate the wheat from the chaff among his ranks to save his own responsibility and skin. It was too late. From the beginning, narcos had played a significant role within the paramilitaries, and Castaño's last-minute attempt to purge the AUC triggered poisonous conflicts among them.[69] Be it as it may, at the end of his term as national paramilitary leader, and of his life, Carlos Castaño begged Jorge 40 to let Giraldo fall. The underlying notion was that Giraldo was already doomed, because he had killed a DEA agent, and would not be pardoned by the United States. "This man—warned Castaño to Jorge 40—will end in the United States and from there he will sweep with everything he has in his path in Colombia."[70] Carlos Castaño was killed by his comrades in an operation ordered by his own brother Vicente in 2004. Jorge 40 and Giraldo were extradited in 2006.

Conclusion

Giraldo relied on four sources of power: his closed territorial fiefdom, his dense network of supporting politicians, his interaction with armed and civilian bureaucracies, and his access to global markets of marijuana, cocaine, and weapons. These sources could work because Giraldo, as a provider of security to rural and urban elites, had become part and parcel of the state's counterinsurgent strategy. Here, the dual nature of indirect rule as a form of governance and war strategy, highlighted by Mann, appears clearly.[71] Lina Britto made the important point about the link between legal and illegal elites in the creation and administration of the marijuana bonanza.[72] Indeed, this fully applies to the political realm. Being a counterinsurgent actor, Giraldo enjoyed key forms of support from the Bogotá tie-in. When jailed, he was released thanks to political intermediation. He was generally shielded from state-hostile activity thanks to his contacts with politicians and security agencies. Between 1994 and 1999, the state created the Convivir security cooperatives, which became for Giraldo a powerful tool for expansion. Note, however, that the Bogotá tie-in was complemented by contacts at different territorial levels: Giraldo counted as well with a Santa Marta tie-in, which allowed him to be at ease in his core territory.

Building upon Blok's work, I have argued that Giraldo operated on two organizational principles. On the one hand, he built a closed fiefdom based on a communitarian perspective, combining sheer violence, including sexual violence, egregious even for paramilitary standards, deference, differential access to services and goods, and control of information.[73] At the heart of this fiefdom was a coalition of legal and illegal elites, to whom Giraldo provided security and business opportunities. But he also built on different mechanisms to create and develop dense networks of support among the inhabitants of his territory. Against standard liberal assumptions, here the exercise of an extraordinarily brutal repertoire of violence against civilians and the effort to create stable forms of territorial control have a relatively broad area of intersection. Giraldo's inability to make compatible his coalitions at different territorial levels eventually destabilized his fiefdom.

From a territorial point of view, Giraldo's power structure resembled a Matryoshka doll. His communitarian perspective was rabidly localistic. He coordinated the relationships between the city's market and its hinterland, and the relationships with departmental authorities. Above this was the Bogotá tie-in. And finally came his global position, which was intrinsically ambiguous. Colombia was wielding two global, U.S.-promoted wars, that is the War on Drugs and the War on Terror. Giraldo was a counterinsurgent ally, but at the same time, a target. And, thanks to his success, he had also become a major economic actor. The protection he enjoyed, and his privileged geographical position put him in a better position vis-à-vis other drug exporters.

Giraldo's fragility stems from the intrinsic contradictions involved in this brokerage. His localism came to be a nuisance when the paramilitaries endowed themselves with a national expansionist strategy that necessarily had to overrule localistic paramilitaries throughout the country. In this sense, Giraldo is only a case among many.[74] The paramilitary federation had a better Bogotá tie-in than Giraldo: it had better connections with the security agencies of the state, it had its own set of politicians, and it had the margin of maneuver to proceed through sheer terror. So, when Giraldo entered a war with the Northern Bloc, the coordination between his fiefdom and regional and national levels was undermined and eventually broken. Such a war was the result of Giraldo's decision to kill a DEA agent in the context of an intra-paramilitary turf, which put him under the United States crosshairs. After that moment, he became more a target than an ally. Certainly, this was the perception of the paramilitary federation leaders, who believed both that the event gave them an ideal pretext to attack Giraldo and that in effect Giraldo was endangering them all.

I have discussed throughout this chapter the specific mechanisms that undergirded both Giraldo's power and his fragility. These mechanisms are marked by the state's administrative rules and presence, which may be a central characteristic of contemporary indirect rule: Giraldo drew his power from administrative structures, acted within administratively set territorial boundaries (departments, municipalities, districts), and developed activities within clearly defined administrative boundaries that included participation in elections, interactions with the Army and other state and non-state bureaucracies.

Notes

1 Francisco Gutiérrez-Sanín, *Clientelistic Warfare: Paramilitaries and the State in Colombia (1982–2007)* (Oxford: Palgrave, 2019).
2 Michael Mann, *The Sources of Social Power: A History of Power from the Beginning to AD 1760* (Cambridge: Cambridge University Press, 2012).
3 See for example, Centro Nacional de Memoria Histórica, CNMH, *La guerra inscrita en el cuerpo: Informe nacional de violencia sexual en el conflicto armado* (Bogotá: CNMH, 2017); Camila Hoyos and Alejandra Londoño, *La violencia sexual. Una estrategia paramilitar en Colombia: Argumentos para imputarle responsabilidad penal a Salvatore Mancuso, Hernán Giraldo y Rodrigo Tovar* (Bogotá: Corporación Humanas, 2013).
4 Gutiérrez-Sanín, *Clientelistic Warfare*.
5 Antonio Giustozzi, *The Art of Coercion: The Primitive Accumulation and Management of Coercive Power* (London: Hurst & Company, 2011).
6 Mann, *The Sources of Social Power*; Anton Blok, *The Mafia of a Sicilian Village, 1860–1960: A Study of Violent Peasant Entrepreneurs* (London: Basil Blackwell, 1974).
7 I cite them in the text in sequential fashion (JP1, JP2, and so on), and give the full reference at the end.
8 Charles Demetriou, "Processual Comparative Sociology: Building on the Approach of Charles Tilly," *Sociological Theory* 30, no. 1 (2012): 51–65; Katherine Stovel and Lynette Shaw, "Brokerage," *Annual Review of Sociology* 38 (2012): 139–158.
9 Mann, *The Sources of Social Power*.
10 Mann, *The Sources of Social Power*.

11 To prevent from the beginning any misunderstanding: I am NOT claiming that the Colombian paramilitaries constituted a Mafia. If this characterization makes any sense, it will demand a separate discussion. My much weaker claim is that the *method* of analysis of the Mafia by Blok provides powerful insights for the understanding of the Colombian paramilitaries.
12 Blok, *The Mafia of a Sicilian Village*.
13 On the unfinished nature of the concept of indirect rule, see Adnan Naseemullah and Paul Staniland, "Indirect Rule and Varieties of Governance," *Governance* 29, no. 1 (2016): 13–30.
14 Gutiérrez-Sanín, *Clientelistic Warfare*.
15 Which of course should not prevent a reflection at a more abstract level about the problems and contradictions underlying indirect rule.
16 Andrés Dávila, *Democracia pactada: El Frente Nacional y el proceso constituyente del 91* (Bogotá: Ediciones Uniandes, 2002); Francisco Gutiérrez-Sanín, *¿Lo que el viento se llevó?: Los partidos políticos y la democracia en Colombia, 1958–2002* (Bogotá: Norma, 2007).
17 Darío Villamizar, *Las guerrillas en Colombia: Una historia desde los orígenes hasta los confines* (Bogotá: Penguin-Random House, 2017).
18 Gonzalo Sánchez and Donny Meertens, *Bandoleros, gamonales y campesinos* (Bogotá: El Áncora, 1983); Villamizar, *Las guerrillas en Colombia*.
19 Gutiérrez-Sanín, *Clientelistic Warfare*; Gutiérrez-Sanín, "Propiedad, seguridad y despojo: El caso paramilitar," *Estudios Socio-Jurídicos* 16, no. 1 (2014): 43–74.
20 Richard Maullin, "The Fall of Dumar Aljure, a Colombian Guerrilla and Bandit," Memorandum RM- 5750-ISA, prepared for the Office of the Assistant Secretary of Defense/International Security Affairs. RAND Corporation, p. V, 1968. www.rand.org/content/dam/rand/pubs/research_memoranda/2008/RM5750.pdf, accessed 15 July 2017.
21 Gutiérrez-Sanín, *Clientelistic Warfare*.
22 Yamile Salinas and Juan Manuel Zarama, *Justicia y paz: Tierra y territorios en las versiones de los paramilitares* (Bogotá: Centro Nacional de Memoria Histórica, 2012).
23 But at the same time leaving out a substantial part of paramilitary membership. See Sarah Zukerman Daly, *Organized Violence after Civil War: The Geography of Recruitment in Latin America* (Cambridge: Cambridge University Press, 2016).
24 Ruling by Magistrate Eduardo Castellanos, Tribunal Superior de Bogotá, July 31, 2015.
25 One of which, the Troncal del Caribe, came under the "total" control of Giraldo (JP11).
26 Police report file 2015–00225, November, 14, 2014 (JEPSM).
27 Ruling by Magistrate Eduardo Castellanos.
28 "Delitos sexuales de Hernán Giraldo," document at the Juzgado de Ejecución de Penas de Santa Marta (JEPSM).
29 As it seems that Giraldo tried to arrive to an accommodation with indigenous people, I will drop the issue here, although of course it deserves a separate consideration.
30 Lina Britto, *Marijuana Boom: The Rise and Fall of Colombia's First Drug Paradise* (Oakland: University of California Press, 2020); Priscila Zúñiga, "Ilegalidad, control local y paramilitares en el Magdalena," in *Parapolítica: La ruta de expansión paramilitar y los acuerdos políticos* (Bogotá: Cerec-Arco Iris, 2007).

31 "Delitos sexuales de Hernán Giraldo;" Ruling by Magistrate Eduardo Castellanos; Supreme Court Ruling Alonso de Jesús Ramírez Torres, SP2230–2016, February 24, 2016.
32 See for example Ruling by Magistrate Eduardo Castellanos.
33 Britto, *Marijuana Boom.*
34 Zúñiga, "Ilegalidad, control local y paramilitares en el Magdalena."
35 Britto, *Marijuana Boom.*
36 Ruling by judge Gustavo Aurelio Roa Avendaño, Tribunal Superior Distrito Judicial Sala de Justicia y Paz Barranquilla, October 21, 2014.
37 Diana Bocarejo, "Thinking with (Il)legality: The Ethics of Living with Bonanzas," *Current Anthropology* 59, no. 18 (2018): S48–59.
38 Fiscalía General de la Nación, file 2009–00044 28, April, 2008 (JEPSM).
39 Ruling by judge Gustavo Aurelio Roa Avendaño.
40 Rodrigo Tovar Pupo, aka Jorge 40, "Mi vida como autodefensa y mi participación como miembro del BN y del BNA," no date. www.webcolegios.com/file/ce06bf.pdf
41 A brother of José, Jorge, supported Giraldo. Eventually Jorge Gnecco was assassinated by Jorge 40.
42 Informe del Alto Comisionado para los Derechos Humanos, Organización de las Naciones Unidas, File 2006–00066, January 26, 2001 (JEPSM); Ruling by the Supreme Court on Enrique Caballero Aduén, March 9, 2011.
43 Apparently, a half-brother of his was assassinated by the guerrillas in 1977. There are different versions about the event, see Ruling by judge José Haxel de la Pava Marulanda, Tribunal Superior Distrito Judicial Sala de Justicia y Paz Barranquilla, June 20, 2017.
44 "Delitos sexuales de Hernán Giraldo."
45 Declaración de Alberto Segundo Manjarrés, file 2014–00189 CUD 5, August 21, 2003 (JEPSM).
46 Judicial Police Report, file 2011–00016 CUD 2, February 22, 2007 (JEPSM).
47 Ruling by the Supreme Court on Enrique Caballero Aduén, March 9, 2011.
48 Verdad Abierta, 2010. https://verdadabierta.com/
49 "Delitos sexuales de Hernán Giraldo."
50 "Delitos sexuales de Hernán Giraldo."
51 "Delitos sexuales de Hernán Giraldo."
52 "Delitos sexuales de Hernán Giraldo."
53 "Delitos sexuales de Hernán Giraldo."
54 Freddy Giraldo, "Autodefensas de Hernán Giraldo S.," YouTube video, 35:53. www.youtube.com/watch?v=ywo-66W14Hk&t=6s
55 At some point these leaderships constituted community boards, but sources diverge regarding when and how.
56 Hoyos and Londoño, "La violencia sexual."
57 "Delitos sexuales de Hernán Giraldo."
58 On the effects of this on terrorizing populations, see Mimmo Franzinelli, *Delatori. Spie e confidenti anonimi: l'arma segreta del regime fascista* (Milano: Feltrinelli, 2012); Gutiérrez-Sanín, *Clientelistic Warfare.*
59 Edna Melissa Osorio, "Dilucidando silencios: Hernán Giraldo y la violencia reproductiva en el conflicto armado colombiano," (BA thesis, Facultad de Ciencias Políticas y Relaciones Internacionales, Pontificia Universidad Javeriana, 2021).
60 Ruling by the Supreme Court on Enrique Caballero Aduén, March 9, 2011.
61 Gutiérrez-Sanín, *Clientelistic Warfare.*

62 "Delitos sexuales de Hernán Giraldo."
63 Gutiérrez-Sanín, *Clientelistic Warfare*; Alfredo Serrano, *Paracos* (Bogotá: Debate, 2009).
64 Gutiérrez-Sanín, *Clientelistic Warfare*.
65 Ruling by the Supreme Court on Miguel Pinedo Vidal, February 1, 2012.
66 Ruling by judge Gustavo Aurelio Roa Avendaño, Tribunal Superior Distrito Judicial Sala de Justicia y Paz Barranquilla, October 21, 2014.
67 Fiscalía General de la Nación, file 2009–00044, April 28, 2008 (JEPSM).
68 Declaración José Gélvez y otros, file 2010–00020 CUD 3, September 24, 2009 (JEPSM).
69 Gutiérrez-Sanín, *Clientelistic Warfare*.
70 Correspondence by Carlos Castaño, Magistrada Uldi Teresa Jiménez, Tribunal de Justicia y Paz, Bogotá.
71 Mann, *The Sources of Social Power*.
72 Britto, *Marijuana Boom*.
73 "Delitos sexuales de Hernán Giraldo."
74 Serrano, *Paracos*.

17 The Conflicts of Coca
Women's Struggles for Economic Autonomy in Colombia's Coca-Growing Regions

Estefanía Ciro[1]

"We also want you to understand that this is where our food comes from," said a peasant woman and leader from Piamonte, in the Bota Caucana region, to a group of Colombian soldiers who, armed with rifles and machetes, had walked into their land to cut down the coca plants. The year was 2017, and the soldiers were there as part of a coca eradication operation led by the National Police in Southern Colombia. In response to the woman's complaint, the sergeant shouted, "Rip it all out! Get rid of it out right now!" The coca leaf, food access or lack thereof, the woman's political stand, and the War on Drugs collided in this angry encounter between a group of peasants and the police. A year later, the woman would receive threats—and was even shot at—due to her leadership in defense of the peasants against the government's coca crop substitution program.[2]

What are the *cocaleras*, or women who grow coca for the processing of cocaine, trying to defy when they are up against a threefold oppression? The ongoing violence exerted on them from an illegalized trade, the hardships that come with rural exclusion, and the violence of a patriarchal society defined their lives and struggles for economic autonomy. In this chapter, I take into consideration a structural element in the lives of the cocaleras in Colombia's Amazon region to answer this question, that is, the three communicating vessels between the economies of the cocaine trade and the repression brought on by the War on Drugs, as a component of the armed conflict. First, how the cocaine market reflects two conflicting realities for these women, condemnation, and salvation. Second, how the blurred distinction between civilians and combatants in the War on Drugs has violent ramifications in the daily lives of rural women. Third, how the peasant agricultural crisis, which explains the emergence of coca plantations, manifests in two main challenges for these women, that is, the difficulties of land ownership and the struggle for their autonomy.

The relation between these communicating vessels is by no means immediate. It is true that some view the War on Drugs as a given condition and an undisputed policy. We find such stance, for example, in the report

DOI: 10.4324/9781003048152-23

¡Basta ya!, published by Colombia's National Center for Historical Memory, which at no point questioned the aerial spraying of glyphosate and forced eradication, or the counterinsurgency exerted in these territories under the guise of an "anti-drug policy."[3] This situation has a few fundamental milestones, such as Ronald Reagan's declaration in 1986 that drug trafficking was a U.S. national security issue, the discursive construct of the Revolutionary Armed Forces of Colombia (FARC) as a drug trafficking cartel in the 1990s, and the signing of Plan Colombia that turned the War on Drugs into a tool for counterinsurgency warfare. In this context, I argue that a closer examination of the transition from the dirty war of counterinsurgency to a "war against narcos" is necessary to understand everyday violence, directed in this case against the bodies, territories, and lives of women.[4]

By listening to the cocaleras, one can find concrete examples of how these communicating vessels informed shifts in Colombia's armed conflict, the cocaine economies, and the War on Drugs.[5] As Rita Segato attests, market economies and war go hand in hand, and in this case, shifting forms of violence against women have been crucial. This line of inquiry could help reassess Colombia's historiographical discourse and our own understanding of its armed conflict. The expansion of the rules of engagement in the fight against an illegal cocaine market and the related dynamics of violence transformed cocaleras into cheap labor for an international business that, despite giving them relative autonomy, actually deepened their inequality and vulnerability. What is like to be a woman in Caquetá's countryside, living in the middle of an illegalized coca/cocaine economy, and being the target of both the War on Drugs and a counterinsurgent doctrine? What were their lives like amid violent contradictions?

My research on the lives of the cocaleras is based on sustained dialogues with several women from Caquetá. My conversations with these women were first undertaken as part of a doctoral research project in 2017, during the first year of the implementation of the peace agreement in Colombia, thanks to a grant from the Instituto Colombiano de Antropología e Historia (ICANH). My aim was to understand gaps between the reality of the post-agreement and the women peasants' hopes for their future in Caquetá, up until 2017.

I analyzed 33 in-depth semi-structured interviews, held between 2014 and 2017 in the towns of La Montañita, San Vicente del Caguán, Florencia, Morelia, Paujil, Belén, and Curillo, in the Caquetá region for a book,[6] and later in an effort to track the transitions brought on by the negotiation, signing, and implementation of the peace agreement signed between the FARC and the Juan Manuel Santos administration (2010–2018) on November 24, 2016. In addition to formal interviews, I also engaged in informal conversations with these women and witnessed their experiences in the streets, at local town meetings, inside their homes, on rural buses (*chivas*), on their plots of land, and other locations where they work and go about with their lives. I also had a chance to learn from their questions, thoughts, and experiences during workshops organized by the communities to discuss the peace agreement in the towns of La Novia, Reina Baja, and La Montañita. The purpose of these workshops was to explain and discuss chapters 1 and 4 of the accords, which deal with integral rural reform and illicit drugs. They came to these workshops with their sons and daughters to see what "all this talk about peace" was about. During this process, I also accompanied women's efforts to denounce the violence and criminalization of coca eradication.

Along the way, "geographies of terror" began to emerge: A sequence of roads, paths, houses, and spaces gleaned during our conversations as everyone would regularly point out the remains of the war, also visible when walking through their communities and Caquetá's hamlets, towns, and landscapes. The everydayness of a war, one that seemed to be ending, came into view during these walks.

There are many ways to address the armed conflict in Colombia and women's experience in it. On the one hand, one can view it as a traditional clash of legal and illegal armed forces that impose orders and regulate the daily life of women peasants. Another approach seeks to understand the conflict from the daily experiences of war and violence, and the ways in which these experiences affect people's lives. The study of women in the coca territories in a state of war is closely related to how violence is used to expand and sustain the country's development model, where armed groups are just one of many actors in this conflict. Studying the experience of women in the armed conflict makes it possible to view these communicating vessels more clearly and help us outline new questions.

The regions in Caquetá where I carried out my fieldwork are complex territories. The FARC has had a historical presence but with key subregional differences.[7] During the first decade of the twenty-first century, two important military bases operated, with support from the United States, and Álvaro Uribe Vélez's counterinsurgency program of Democratic Security, while paramilitary groups regularly carried out bloody attacks. Because Liberal and communist peasant organizations had deep historical roots in the region, many peasant families became victims of counterinsurgent persecution. Additionally, Caquetá has also been one of the historical coca-growing regions in Colombia, although the number of coca crops reduced after the signing of the peace agreement in 2016.

The testimonies I collected during the reintegration of the FARC into civilian life were marked by silences but also reaffirmations of these women who no longer felt threatened by the presence of the armed actor. It was also an opportunity to question the FARC's image as an all-powerful state, as portrayed in various published research. Instead, it allows us to see other conditions of rural daily life and the limits of the rhetoric of the armed social order.

In the first section, I seek to understand how the rural dynamic impacts the lives of women in coca-growing regions, followed by a discussion about what economic autonomy means for these women. I then discuss different forms of violence that take place in the illegalized cocaine trade in the region, and, more specifically, the role of the War on Drugs. I conclude by reflecting on how the violence, dispossession, and inequality that encroach upon the lives of these women manifested through the illegalization of cocaine, the patriarchal structure of rural societies, and the War on Drugs.

Cocaleras and Rural Dynamics in Coca Territories

Women have been protagonists of the colonization of Colombia's Amazon region. Peasant women in Caquetá are daughters of the colonization of the rainforest, which has been a forced one, more often than not. The word "colonization" is often tinged with heroic overtones of adventurous endeavor, such as the stories of colonization of the West in the United States.[8] However, the violence of dispossession is often omitted, such as the stories of peasant "colonizers" who were forced to flee into areas that were unfit for agriculture in order to survive. Histories of displacement, abandonment, and loss of territory and capital, remain hidden. When talking about forced colonization, one must make explicit what women gain or lose from this process.

Like their parents, partners, and siblings, these women were originally from Andean regions like Tolima, Valle, Huila, or the coffee-growing Eje Cafetero, but they were raised in Caquetá's cordilleras and rainforests.[9] A first wave of colonization occurred during the dire period of *la Violencia* in the mid-twentieth century, when people from their family nucleus were murdered or threatened and those who survived fled to the region. Other waves came later when escaping coca crop fumigations in other departments or fleeing the armed conflict.

Thus, colonization in Caquetá must be understood as a relentless process that continues to separate peasants from their means of livelihood, land in particular, drive them out of their territories, and is conducive to the loss of seed capital. What is more, this process is not over when they reach their destination, much to the contrary, it is cyclical. When they arrive, the agricultural market they hoped for never materializes, nor does it offer alternatives for economic stability. Even within Caquetá, peasants are constantly displaced by a cyclical pattern of colonization-conflict-colonization,[10] driven by hunger and violence.[11]

In earlier investigations, I have discussed the particular circumstances under which cocaleras in Caquetá are able to become independent through a detailed analysis of a critical moment in their lives, when they "split from home" or leave their parental home.[12] In this context, it is necessary to review how youth is perceived and understood in the hamlets and towns of Caquetá, since age and gender constitute transversal axes that define how power and violence are exerted, experienced, and resisted by these women.

Research has shown that cocaleras must face conditions of extreme poverty and manual labor at an early age. Unlike men, who leave home to engage in day labor and to colonize, thereby enjoying a wider margin of action and independence, peasant women leave their parents' home when they find a partner or to migrate to the city to become domestic workers. Many women I interviewed expressed interest in studying, but only those who could afford it or rebelled against traditional roles were able to do so. Given the limited range of opportunities, women who end up becoming mothers at a very early age find themselves at a disadvantage.

Those families that have a higher purchasing power send their daughters to school in the bigger towns or the department's capital, seeking to distance them from family obligations and early sexual relations, but at the expense of uprooting them from the countryside. Doña Juana describes the case of her niece, who found a husband at age 13 and went off to live on a farm:

> What can you expect in a farm? I don't like living in the farm, waiting and waiting, just a whole lot of waiting (*una esperadera*) for your husband on Sundays. My dad would head to the so-called market and he would come back drunk; that's what it is like, waiting for him to come back drunk bringing meat that's already gone bad. You see them heading out to the market and the poor wife waiting for them to arrive. "Let's go out together," that never happens.[13]

Women's main mechanism to gain access to land is to start a family. However, this depends on how negotiations, family roles, and relationships evolve within each family, often influenced by a general distrust against women who seek to earn income, and the added hurdles of how women's names are not included on property documents. Although they are involved in the process of clearing the land, tree removal, and tilling the land, there is no legal acknowledgment (when there are property deeds) nor legitimate status (when the sales contract is informally accepted and regionally recognized) for women.

The fundamental spaces of formal interactions in the region are the Community Action Councils (Juntas de Acción Comunal, or JACs), followed by the Community Nuclei (Núcleos Comunales). In the absence of state agencies and procedures for formalizing land ownership, the JACs issue documents that validate sales contracts and property. For example, to implement coca substitution agreements, growers were required to register their land and, toward that end, they had to submit a form signed by the president of their local JAC confirming that they were residents of their *vereda* (a hamlet within a municipality) and owners of the plot, even without a deed. Although for the Colombian state, these are not valid documents, they are legitimate in the regional land market.

Access to land follows a process that begins with daily labor and eventually results in the purchase of a person's own plot. Alternatively, those who cannot do it this way hope to settle somewhere by clearing out land in the rainforest, as part of the colonizing process. The options are limited: working as a day laborer and never securing land, or working on a small, insufficient plot of land until finally being able to buy that property. These circumstances and dynamics are different for men and women. There are much fewer women working as day laborers; it is easier for them to find work as coca leaf pickers (*raspachines*), domestic workers, or in a small business in town, which often means they are forced to migrate from their *hamlet* to a different town.

For example, Blanca was forcibly displaced, lost her plot of land, and had to separate temporarily from her husband, who migrated to the border with Ecuador, driven by hunger. As she put it, "Without a farm, you have nothing, you have to look for day labor, and you need to be where the potatoes are, as my husband likes to say." Magdalena also talked about having to constantly move around, "We just went to wherever there was work." Even single mothers have raised their families through nothing "but day labor," as Dulce explains:

> My mom played both roles of father and mother, just doing day labor. There were eight of us. Three children were from marriage, the other men said they would take responsibility, but then they wouldn't, they would leave and abandon her. She had no education; she barely had a house.[14]

Another way of transitioning from day labor to land ownership is colonizing after women leave their paternal home. Some said in their interviews that when they decided to start a family, they first had to live with their parents or move in with their in-laws, where they would do day labor or find work nearby. Amanda talks about her experience this way:

> I would see my husband in secret, but my mom knew. They didn't agree with me leaving, but I did anyway. I asked my sister to bring my clothes, and we left. We had no clue what to do; we didn't know where we could go or anything. We made it to a hamlet and rented a room, and there we

rented a little soft drinks place. I was already used to that, I knew how it worked, so we were there for two months. Then we went to a *hamlet*, with my in-laws, I helped them a lot, I learned how to milk and take care of the animals. My dad sent for me again, but I stayed with my in-laws and after a month I got pregnant, so then I really had to work for the children. We built a little house on my in-laws' land until I said no, I want a house of my own.[15]

Another possible way of transitioning from day labor to owning property is by managing a plot where coca is grown. Marta, for example, worked with her husband managing a coca plot or *plante*,[16] and on the weekends, they worked on their own plot, which they acquired through their savings.[17] In the best case scenario, women receive a plot of land from their parents, which allows them to own property. This was the case for Celina and Magdalena. The latter, after working in a coca plot, being chased during a police raid, and later by the owner of the plante, found her dad who suggested that they both head to Putumayo, where he had a plot of land for her.[18]

Land ownership thus is achieved through savings as women work as day laborers, coca leaf pickers, colonizers, and plante managers, or through their families or husbands. Dulce was provisionally living in Putumayo, but with the money she and her husband made, they purchased "a little farm, some cattle, and some heifer calves" in Caquetá. The same was possible for Ximena, who used her coca savings—measured in three cows—to purchase a plot of land; and with Tania, who, after converting her coca savings to cows, purchased some land of her own.[19]

Such forms of exchange, swap, or sales agreements are frequently used, even though the properties are not formally legalized. People often talk about swapping one farm for another, being offered land elsewhere, or relatives suggesting that they move to other *hamlets*. Although the peasants are tied to the land, the armed conflict and searching for better opportunities often lead them to migrate and try out new locations.

For older women, grandmothers, widows, or senior women, property may become a burden because they can no longer keep up with a mortgage or because they may need to move to the city once they feel incapable of carrying out the physical labor required to take care of a farm. Andrea's farm, for example, was seized because she was unable to pay a debt after a robbery. As a grandmother and a widow, she now lives in La Unión Peneya and is looking to sell her land.[20]

Armed conflict has drastically impacted access to land, however, whether formal or informal. A male merchant from a hamlet in Curillo told me, "I have gone broke about four times." Peasant families leave, return, wait, abandon, and are forced to leave their property behind with each forced displacement.

The fragmented process of land ownership is influenced by the violence exerted by armed actors in the context of the War on Drugs and the state's failure to provide any guarantees for rural development. Since the cocaine market is not regulated legally, it offers few reasons to formalize property, less so in the case of women; it instead promotes displacement and informality that impact women's independence and economic autonomy. Violence has actively fragmented the cocaleras path toward land ownership in Caquetá, and migration often failed to provide economic security for their families. For instance, when Andrea left from Tolima to Caquetá after her father was murdered, she went, as she put it, "From bad to worse" (*de Guatemala a Guatepior*).

Additionally, as colonization pushes onwards, access to land becomes scarcer. Peasant women point out that each time, they must go farther to find some land, and the department's agricultural frontier is becoming increasingly crowded. Amanda's son, whose crops had been eradicated a few months earlier, was unable to get a farm and, she now noted, "My farm is not enough, we own 30 steers, my son lost every single one of his coca plants, now he is sharing with us, and that is very hard on everyone." The pressure over land leads to greater codependence within families. Plots of land are often divvied up between family members, and this is particularly common with coca crops. Divvying up plantes is used to support and help out family members, as with Mireya, who has divided her four hectares among the family, "Each of my daughters has her own little plot, four of them, because my other daughter does have a small farm of her own. My son also has a small plot, I manage it for him."[21]

The plots become smaller as the families grow bigger, and such dynamic favor coca as a survival crop over others for rural families in Caquetá. In a situation of increased family codependency, coca allows them to get some income out of a small plot, and this is something that no other produce can currently offer.

Throughout several decades of colonization, we find that a violent separation from their main means of subsistence—the land—has been a key factor in the life stories of peasants in the region. Moreover, this affects women at greater levels, since they have specific challenges and obstacles to overcome to gain access to land. The inability to transition from day labor to land ownership lowers opportunities for both men and women to insert themselves into the legal agricultural market. Women, in particular, are at a disadvantage since their options to own land are intimately linked to imposed family roles, forced marriage, and motherhood at an early age. Given the scarcity of legal employment opportunities, and a recurring family hunger crisis, growing coca allows women to narrow the gaps in access to property—although under a structure that keeps them at a disadvantage—and offers them opportunities for economic autonomy.

Being able to grow their own coca and have a stable income usually occurs after overcoming many obstacles.

What Is at Stake for Peasant Women in Coca Income?

This section shows how women experience the tensions for economic autonomy. Cocaleras mentioned several reasons for getting involved in the coca trade: the first was to guarantee food and an education access for their children. They are keenly alert about this since they themselves endured many moments of hunger as a result of the War on Drugs, especially after campaigns of aerial fumigation and eradication. This family priority is voiced by Nancy, who, after being displaced from La Unión Peneya, had to pull her own family ahead without support from the Colombian state or the father of her children, "I have always lived in poverty, and it is a terrible thing to watch your children starve to death."[22]

Another motivation for seeking coca income was the discomfort that came from having to "ask your husband for money," and the possibility of breaking away from that dependency or having to "ask for permission" to buy things for themselves, such as clothing. Within the family dynamic, cocaleras experience a tension between depending and not depending on men, which takes on multiple forms. For example, they view their partner as a provider, "With a man you have food, and you have a bit of support by your side." But they also experience a degree of distrust, as a result of that dependency.[23]

The question of whether to depend or not on a husband critically inflects women's role within this subsistence economy, leading them to engage in various productive activities, including coca. In this context, women who have searched for a certain degree of independence have encountered obstacles, opportunities, and some margin for action, even though their agency continues to be undermined and occasionally denied, even by the women themselves. When asked about their family, many will tell stories about how their fathers made great efforts to get their families ahead, but they have little to say about their mothers. Rubiela, for example, said this about her father who had 18 children with two different women: "They [the mothers] lived on the same farm, he did not abandon any of the children, he kept us all, he took us all in one of his two houses."[24] This invisibility is broken when, in their narratives, cocaleras share their strategies and courses of action, their struggle and leadership to safeguard their projects, interests, and their decision to attain a wider margin of action within their families with regard to income, among other things.

There are few activities and jobs that are economically remunerated or rewarded that women can take on in the farms or elsewhere in rural areas. Coca is an option that grants them this margin of maneuver, and it is considerably attractive to women because it does not require great expanses of land: a little less than a hectare is enough for them to achieve a margin of economic autonomy. Many of the women asked their husbands for a small plot in the farm to grow their own little corner (*codito*); they could also process the harvest themselves or have it processed by someone else, without much trouble. As Paola explains, "I could go over to my mom's, have a crop to sustain myself, it would help me move ahead."[25]

Women's relationship with coca is complex. Mireya told me that she managed her son's coca plantation and that she and her husband decided to grow coca themselves after their banana crop was swept by a plague, leaving them with no income.[26] Often, the labor for the plante requires the participation of their own children, who become the first *raspachines* [coca pickers]. This was the case for Andrea and Magdalena, who were the best coca leaf pickers in their *hamlet*. According to Magdalena, the work was so hard that as soon as she saw her father clearing out ten more hectares for growing coca, she ran away from home.

Often even coca failed to yield enough income, as in the case of Ximena, who could barely make enough to buy food. They were just as exposed as men to the dangers of growing coca or of working at a plante. Magdalena, for example, had to flee from her place of work during a raid, and Marina was imprisoned for six months in an Ecuadorian jail after being captured during a raid on a cocaine lab where she had to work after she was displaced from Peñas Coloradas and could not feed her four children.[27]

Finally, coca also allowed single mothers, who were abandoned by their husbands, to keep the hunger at bay. This was the case for Nancy and Mireya, who had to raise their children with no support from their former partners. The danger of state initiatives of crop substitution that does not offer opportunities for women is vividly described by Rosaura, "If there is no more coca, this will become a shithole."[28]

Some of them work at home while their husbands look over the plantation; other women, when they are young, resort to coca leaf picking to make ends meet for their families, and once they can get some land, they grow coca themselves and learn how to process it. Clara talks about how she has been growing coca for 15 years, and she works alongside her husband growing, processing, and selling the crop.

Another group of women grow a share of their own in their "husband's land," which provides income for their personal expenses. They do not necessarily process the coca into cocaine (which they refer to as *quimiquear*, or "doing chemistry"), instead they pay someone to do it or sell the leaves themselves. Many of them, like their husbands, know the numbers and how much can be earned through this activity. This affords them a greater degree of freedom to control expenses within the family nucleus:

> I started living with him and my mother-in-law herself told me: Save some money on the sly, because behind the door it's your husband and

Figure 17.1 A child guides the author through the plante explaining how to take care of and cultivate coca. Montañita, Caquetá, 2015.

Source: Photo by the author

death. So, I saved up everything that I made through my work. My mother-in-law would say: You don't have to live in fear of humiliation, that's what she would say. You get a small crop and that will give you enough for some business, for the farm, to go to the doctor, for the children. A medical appointment in Florencia costs between 200,000 and 300,000 pesos, if you want to help your children, you have to be independent, without it, it's just not possible. . . . It's very hard to have to ask your husband for money all the time.[29]

Nonetheless, jobs for women in the hamlets and towns in the coca business are scarce, since fear and danger mean that neither coca nor cattle can be counted on as sources of direct remuneration, whether provisional or long-term.[30] Some women have sought formal employment as public servants in local civil authority agencies (*inspecciones*), as school teachers, domestic workers, managers, or employees in neighborhood stores, or other service jobs such as piloting motorboats in the river ports. When there is a booming coca economy, women have enjoyed some access to employment opportunities in the service sector, which have afforded them another degree of independence.

Age restrictions were unclear; many women left their homes as teenagers looking for such jobs and traditionally participated in home labor from an early age. Amanda told me that each time one of her older sisters would leave, the next in line would be left in charge of domestic chores and assist with raising their brothers, until it was her turn.

In a hamlet in San Vicente del Caguán, there was a building that functioned as a pool hall during the day and lodging at night, where I stayed. A young girl, who could not have been older than 12 years, had been serving beer to the pool players since early hours in the morning, among other things. In that same place, Amanda explained how she had worked from a very young age minding her father's restaurant, dry goods store, tavern, and pool hall:

> We had to handle the housework, she [her mother] hardly knew anything about the store and the pool hall. My dad put me in charge of that. I would get up at 3 am, make breakfast for the teachers, clean up, tend the pool hall, the business, make lunch, and take care of the business while the others did domestic chores. I was a smarty-pants for business, along with my brother, with whom I picked coca leaf. I waited the pool halls until midnight; my dad had a very short fuse, you worked and worked, you had no freedom, so I got a husband, at 15 I ran away from home. He would not forgive any of his daughters, but he did forgive me. One time I came home with my future husband and my dad came and asked me to come back, even though I was pregnant. He said that he would take me back because he needed me, he needed someone for the business. But no, I stayed with my husband, my dad stayed home by himself and was killed two or three years after that. The business shut down, was not doing well after that. . . . My dad was an angry person, but I never struggled to get money. Each week I would buy a change of clothes, of course I didn't go out, never went dancing and had no friends, like other people my own age used to.[31]

In addition to working within their family circle, some women also opened their own businesses to sustain their families. In hamlets and towns, women-owned restaurants, trained as hairdressers, ran beauty parlors, sold clothes or shoes, managed pool halls and hostels, and sold catalog beauty products, jewelry, and other care items. Marta's first step on her path to self-employment came when a man offered her credit to start a clothes-selling venture: "I got one million [pesos] from a man to work with clothing, and after two weeks I had already made that million back and I was dressing myself, my daughter, I was even dressing him [her partner]."[32]

Nonetheless, forced eradication of coca makes their outlook quite unpromising, when women's efforts toward economic autonomy are mediated by discussions about how this income should be used. At first glance, one might believe that their minds are set only on money, but this assumption is entirely mistaken. In these territories, given the lack of access to land and an ongoing food sovereignty crisis, the subsistence economy is limited to the purchase and sale of food and basic goods. There are no peasant markets, worker-owned enterprises, nor cooperatives, which generate catastrophic inequality. For economic autonomy to work, such dynamic requires the construction of a strong social fabric, political networks, political awareness, and activism training, and thinking about alternative forms of production and reproduction.

The present dynamic of social reproduction and family subsistence has a direct impact on women's ability to participate in political processes in their rural communities. Women's participation could be a means to change their livelihoods and their ability to influence and organize new spaces of production and reproduction—both politically and economically—thus bringing dignity to these women's lives. However, doing so becomes an impossible privilege under the current circumstances:

> Yes, because of life's rhythm and housework . . . coming to a meeting means getting up early at four o'clock in the morning, leaving everything ready because, one doesn't have the luxury of arriving late and simply making juice or something, is just not possible, because if one has to go fetch water and all that, it requires more time in the house all day long, all day long one works and goes to bed late, and the next day is the same.[33]

The Places of Women in Coca Territories

The previous sections explained how the cocaine economy is interrelated to land ownership and women's economic autonomy. This section explores tensions women face because of how roles are imposed on them by a rural campesino environment and how they find ways to survive from income generated by the coca crops. During the 1970s and 1980s, Colombian drug lords like Pablo Escobar, Gonzalo Rodríguez Gacha (a.k.a. "El mexicano"), Fabio Ochoa, and the Cali cartel came to the Amazon region to open coca plantations and cocaine laboratories like Tranquilandia (on the Yarí River) and El Azul (in the Putumayo region).[34] These plantations provided work for many settlers like María, who being a single mother and pressured by her partner to have an abortion, "went off into the jungle." She survived after finding a job as a cook for the workers in a coca plantation, and that is where her daughter was born:

> That Saturday I was feeling pains. I went to give birth and told the boss. I picked up a piece of rubber that is used to dry coca leaves, I locked myself up in a room and prepared everything that I would need. The girl was born at 10 [a.m.], and just like I did for the other one, I collected the placenta. And at that point everyone began to come down, a bunch of people came down from the stilt houses (*zancos*). I measured her with my hand, and I handed her over to them. She was passed down from one person to the next. Then they told the commander [of the FARC guerrillas] that I had gotten sick, I was still at the plantation. Then a bunch of people from the guerrilla came, and the commander picked up some clothes [on the way there] and brought them all to me.[35]

Women were always present in the rainforest and coca plantations spaces. Hamlets and roads for colonization took shape in the early years, when a regional economy was built up around the cocaine paste. In the words of a cocalero leader, "The town was built at the end of the construction of a road, and this is how towns were founded."

Since the 1980s, life in these hamlets has followed fluctuations in the price of cocaine. Bonanzas and crises were a matter of "life or death" for a hamlet. In their narratives, women and men remember the good and the bad times quite differently, particularly because women were often the victims of sex-trafficking networks and peaks of domestic violence during times of partying and excess.[36]

This explains why interviewees often describe cocaine bonanzas as motors of "social decomposition." The ups and downs of the cocaine trade are measured, for example, by counting how many *chongos* (brothels) can be found in a hamlet. As Marta commented in an interview, there used to be many bars in her town, whereas now, in a time of crisis, there was only one *chongo*, and women sex workers were now brought every 15 days, while before, as many as 40 women would be brought each week.[37] Some of men place the burden of stigma and responsibility on the women themselves:

> The town was a madhouse. We spent every minute drunk in the cantinas, hoping it would never end. I'm not ashamed of anything, everything in life turns around. The women in the town were at the bars, the few

others were married. You would fall in love with them, have children with them. You lived in the present, there was no respect . . . since we were sleeping around with them.[38]

In one town, out of 50 women, 30 of them were whores (*vagabundas*). They knew what it was like having money because every Sunday guys would come to them. They would become "lovers" with some, but when other [lovers] would turn out, they would kill the women because people were sick.[39]

According to these male voices, women's roles in coca territories belonged to the "easy life," synonymous with vice, thus exemplifying the deep violence of a flowing money market that crushed the lives of women, imprisoning them in a state of violence with only two possibilities: either get married or devote themselves to sex work.

Beyond this male narrative, women are made invisible in other lines of work, but they were, in fact, absolutely present. In interviews, they describe their experiences working in restaurants as cooks and servers, waiting tables, as cleaning ladies, beauticians, or saleswomen. Moments of bonanza would very often translate into situations of domestic violence that remain imprinted in their memories and altered the course of their family lives, often leading to separation or divorce. Olga's story illustrates these conflicts:

The thing is that the father of my children wasn't able to enjoy life back then because he drank too much. Whenever he and his cousins went off to sell in Solita,[40] they would go on a Tuesday, and they would keep on drinking until maybe Monday. In those days they would pick up 2 or 3 million, which was enough for the month's expenses, and they would start drinking. Well, back then I didn't have as much experience as I do now, so after I had my second child, you start to grow wiser and take a closer look at your life, so I told him no. I told my dad and mom that I wouldn't go back there. He came looking for me, but I told him that I wasn't going back there.[41]

Although some studies have called attention to the important role of women's income in this economy,[42] that is only one aspect of the whole picture, which must be contextualized within the conflict, since otherwise we are at risk of disregarding the structure of violence against women that pervades in this market. The cocaine economy created spaces of labor and opportunity for women, but these were confined within a precarious and violent dynamic shaped by prohibitionist policies and its cycles, often regulated by the communities themselves, violent mafias, and legal and illegal armed actors. Underpinning it all, we find a layer of patriarchal structures imposed on women.⁴³ The predation of women's bodies in the cocaine economy was continuous, and it is decisively determined by what was at play for them: They could either claim their part of the profit or be at the mercy of predators.

This tension between condemnation and curse is rooted in what Oskar Jansson identifies as the role of coca in the everyday lives of people in Putumayo's rainforest: Coca spares them from hunger, but it also condemns them. It is "cursed money."⁴⁴ The lives of women could be said to exemplify a different version of this tension, placing them between economic autonomy and everyday violence, as analyzed in greater depth and in other regions in several studies.⁴⁵ A sign of success was when women in Caquetá were able to fight for their autonomy by managing their own income, thus taking responsibility for their families.⁴⁶ These decisions allowed families to survive with a greater degree of equality and autonomy, and they also led to the expansion of coca plantations, which under their control gave them a degree of independence. Of course, this also allowed them to escape from or evade sex-trafficking networks. In any case, marriage continued to be their prison: they rarely had the chance of taking a different path.

The War on Drugs in the Lives of Women

One of the main effects of the War on Drugs has been the blurred distinction between civilians and combatants, which promoted indiscriminate warfare in the countryside. For women, the War on Drugs is one more factor of violence against them in the coca-growing territories through militarization, aerial spraying, displacement, paramilitary activity, armed confrontations, and the lack of control over drug use. This situation did not change after the peace agreement signed in 2016.

The women I interviewed told me about their experiences during the Plan Colombia and Plan Patriota years (2000–2006). These two policies amounted to a counterinsurgency strategy, disguised as an antinarcotics effort, that determined the course of the armed conflict through direct U.S. intervention in Colombia's theater of military operations.⁴⁷ This was the clearest evidence that the government was fighting an unconventional war in the country, and it led the FARC to exert stricter territorial control, barring outsiders from the region. In some areas, cell phones and photographs were forbidden, and people were prevented from moving freely into towns. Problems within communities also became more dire due to accusations of betrayal and the handling of information. Moreover, the militarization of the region and counterinsurgency operations were camouflaged as antinarcotics operations, backed by a hefty budget, with a tragic impact on the region.⁴⁸

Militarization by the armed forces was seen as a hostile tactic that delegitimized the state. Interviewees explained that the military presence was problematic because if they exchanged looks with the soldiers or were called in for questioning, it meant being accused of being informants and being forced to leave. Communities also experienced psychological and physical abuse by the Army. The military's withdrawal from the region brought peace of mind, they said. They also noted that the Army seduced young girls and exerted or threatened sexual abuse as part of a wider war strategy.[49]

Aerial spraying with glyphosate was another reason for communities to feel threatened and become mistrustful of the state. Some even claimed that it was a strategy to displace the population since spraying operations would often be followed by the arrival of prospectors from multinational oil corporations. In a case that was reviewed by the Interamerican Court of Human Rights, a pregnant woman was washing clothes and was unable to run or take cover when the planes came. She was showered with glyphosate, her health declined, she lost the baby, and passed away a year later.[50] The impact of aerial spraying on the food sovereignty of these peasant families is probably underestimated, since very few cases for damages made it to court, due to a lack of information, fear of land seizures, if they filed a complaint, and a lack of "scientific" evidence of those farms affected.[51]

The women talked about forced displacement operations by the military as part of the Plan Patriota, leading to an exodus of entire populations in La Unión Peneya (town of La Montañita) and Peñas Coloradas, on the shores of the Caguán River (town of Cartagena del Chairá) in 2004.[52] Nancy's case, for example, illustrates the political persecution of peasants as part of the War on Drugs, when she was displaced from La Unión Peneya. The FARC had warned them that the entire population should flee if the military or paramilitaries arrived, since an armed confrontation was certain. Thus, when the Army came that night, they left everything behind.[53]

For four years, Nancy and her five children wandered between La Montañita and Florencia without any work or government assistance, living off informal jobs that barely allowed them to survive and send the children to school. Moreover, since she had been displaced from La Unión Peneya, she also bore the stigma of being regarded as a guerrilla member. Four years later, they returned to find that a military base set up in the center of the hamlet, but her family never received reparations for what they had lost.

Another violent experience described by many women was the paramilitary incursion in southern Caquetá and Putumayo.[54] They were constantly at the risk of sexual abuse from the paramilitary forces, and their husbands were often forced to work as guides or drivers.[55] They also described the confrontations that took place in their farms and other locations, the impossibility of moving around alone, the fear they experienced at checkpoints, the accusations, and the presence of the paramilitaries in the region's schools, where they would attempt to recruit children and seduce young girls.[56]

In the border region between Caquetá and Putumayo, there were bloody confrontations between the guerrillas and the paramilitaries, who advanced from the mountain toward the Caquetá River, seeking to gain ground on the guerrillas. One hamlet, Puerto Valdivia-La Novia in the town of Curillo, was next to a river in a ravine and the women described how when the paramilitaries would "come down" people would spread the alert, and then they would all run with their children, food, animals, and prized belongings to the other side of the river to take shelter in the rainforest. By the time the paramilitaries arrived, there would be hardly anyone left, they would find pots still on the stove and music playing. Then they would destroy whatever stock was left in the stores, steal food from the houses, and break whatever they could find.[57]

As Magdalena told me, those who were unable to flee would be taken to the communal center (*caseta comunal*) as the armed men yelled: "You, to the *caseta*, right over there . . . we're going to kill you." They would return to their homes when the paramilitaries would leave, but fear would invariably remain: "One time, when I came back, I found a leg in the laundry sink, it was still wearing its boot and everything."[58]

During these moments when I walked around these towns, listening to their stories, I could trace out the geography of this terror:

> From that house they pulled out an old man and a young man who were *false positives* [murdered by the Army and presented as guerrillas]; you can still find skulls up in the mountains; on the other side of that ditch, they left the body of a woman cut up in six parts, they brought her from another town and sometime later her father and her husband came asking for her. And the bodies of the *paracos*? We couldn't bury them, we weren't allowed to, and it was very weird because those bodies wouldn't decompose, they would last forever, it's because they did so much coke. They were all high.[59]

In coca-growing territories, women were subjected daily to horror and death, mistreatment, and abuse. Most of them never received reparations or assistance of any kind from the state.

It is also important to take note of the role of drug use in rural territories. Drug use was strictly regulated by the guerrillas, with the approval of the peasant communities, and it was regarded as an activity of the Army and paramilitaries, who would leave remnants of marijuana behind after breaking into their houses or force children to bring and carry drugs. It is no less important to remark that alcohol intake is not stigmatized or

Figure 17.2 Meeting with government representatives to discuss chapter 4 of the peace agreement on Illicit Crops Substitution with peasant women and cocaleras' organizations. Curillo, Caquetá, 2017.
Source: Photo by the author

looked down on. On the contrary, the lack of control in this regard was one of the communicating vessels that regularly enabled violence against women. Access to doctors or medical attention might have been lacking, but there was never an absence of beer; the market always prevailed over any interest in safeguarding fundamental rights.

The implementation of the peace agreements between the FARC and the Santos administration has not brought an end to conflict in the coca-growing communities, despite the roadmap of substitution crops. Women continue to be key in the peace process, despite not being included in the decision-making nor its implementation, nor being asked how the conflict has affected them directly.

After glyphosate spraying was suspended in 2014, and in direct contradiction with the principles of the peace agreement, the Ministry of Defense issued Resolution 3080 in April 2016, launching a strategy to substitute 50,000 hectares and to eradicate 50,000 more. This created confrontations between peasants and the armed forces in farms all over Caquetá; in La Montañita, San Vicente del Caguán, and Curillo, where women have led protests against governmental contradictions whose programs have promoted coca substitution as a guarantee of no eradication while disregarding their own promises and destroying coca crops, nonetheless. In this context, cocaleras have mobilized to defend coca substitution, their plantes and their neighbors' plantes against crop eradication.[60]

For example, in July 2017, the police attempted to arrest five *raspachines* in San Vicente del Caguán, one of whom was Amanda's daughter. She and the community blocked the road and the police with a large tree trunk to prevent them from taking them away. Eradication tactics used by the Police and the Armed Forces clearly demonstrate the extreme hostility underlying the Ministry of Defense's policies. Amanda told me that she had to pay the Army off with a young bull to keep them from cutting down the coca plants and take her son, who was in the lab. The second time around they went in and set the lab on fire. The third time:

> We went over to them and told them that we wouldn't let them leave, that we wouldn't let them through. It was very hard, they were going to take my daughter, she was working as a cook there, and they said they had four people, but it wasn't true, they only had her and were taking her with them. Finally, they left her there and as they were coming down to the highway we blocked their path, we did that so that we could take her back by force. There were a lot of people there.[61]

Finally, we should not overlook the political dimension of the stigmatization and persecution of women in the War on Drugs. Female leaders and cocaleras have been stigmatized for their affiliation with the Communist Party or their membership in women's or peasant organizations. Several women have been harassed by police or military officers who have accused them of aiding the guerrillas. Nancy is a recent case who, after being displaced from La Unión Peneya and assuming leadership of a women's organization with training from the Communist Party, continued to work with the communities. In 2017, she was involved in creating a "humanitarian fence," a defense mechanism against forced eradication. Their intention was to protect a coca plante belonging to an elderly woman neighbor who had no other source of income. During the ensuing altercation, the community detained 14 policemen, and Nancy, as their spokesperson, demanded that representatives from the National Substitution Program come over to hand the police over safely and listen to their complaints. She was imprisoned for about a year because of her actions.

The roles of civilian women and female combatants are often blurred in the War on Drugs and the counterinsurgency tactics. Cocaleras and the violence inflicted against them are concrete examples of how distinctions can be blurry during war.

Conclusion

The transversal triad of violence against cocaleras presents a diffuse economic-military scenario that is played out in the frontal war between the military, guerrillas, and paramilitary forces.[62] But it is also present in the everyday experiences of these women, their struggle for autonomy, life goals, and plans for their future.

Women see no alternative but to take advantage of an illegalized market that condemns them but also saves them. They do so while the War on Drugs deepens structural violence against women, in a rural coca-growing context where women lack access to land and the means of production of other crops. There is a constant tension over the distribution of income from coca profits that plays a part in these women's quest for autonomy within their families. A fundamental step is land ownership, which affects coca-growing families in a profoundly unequal way compared to the rest of the country's peasants, with women bearing the brunt of this exclusion and disadvantage. To gain access to income from coca, women must fight against a whole apparatus of dispossession directed against them.

This chapter reframes the armed conflict as something more than a confrontation between armed groups, and actors. The violence of economic and military interests and processes involve, for example, the expansion of the cocaine market, the separation of peasant families from their means of subsistence, and the criminalization of Colombian peasants. This new perspective makes the role of peasant women in coca-growing territories visible by studying the communicating vessels between the conflict and the coca for cocaine market. They show that the struggle for land ownership and economic autonomy are central in these women's lives, marked by traditional roles in rural areas and the bittersweet opportunities that the coca market opens up for them. When participating in this market in a War on Drugs framework, they face condemnation, indiscriminate violence, and exploitation.

Notes

1 I am very grateful for the careful comments and valuable feedback by Mary Ryder, María Emma Wills, Lina Britto, and A. Ricardo López-Pedreros. Thanks to Tupac Andrés Cruz and Sofía Jarrin-Thomas for the translation.
2 www.mondialisation.ca/estado-contra-cara-quiebres-de-la-paz-en-colombia-por-la-sustitucion-de-coca/5576575.
3 Centro Nacional de Memoria Histórica, ¡Basta ya!, Colombia: Memorias de guerra y dignidad (Bogotá: Imprenta Nacional, 2013).
4 Carlos Illades and Teresa Santiago, Estado de guerra: De la guerra sucia a la narcoguerra (México, DF: Ediciones Era, 2015).
5 Rita Segato, Las nuevas formas de la guerra y el cuerpo de las mujeres (Puebla: Pez en el árbol, 2014), 16.
6 This part of my research project resulted in a book, Estefanía Ciro, Levantados de la selva: Vidas y legitimidades de la actividad cocalera (Bogotá: Uniandes, 2020).
7 Claudia Alejandra Ciro Rodríguez, "Unos grises muy verracos": Poder político local y configuración del Estado en el Caquetá, 1980-2006 (Bogotá: Editorial

Ingeniería Jurídica, Instituto Jean Piaget, Centro de Pensamiento AlaOrilladelRío, 2016); Teófilo Vásquez, Andrés Vargas, and Jorge Restrepo, *Una vieja guerra en un nuevo contexto: Conflicto y territorio en el sur de Colombia* (Bogotá: Cerac, 2011).
8 Frederick Jackson Turner, *The Frontier in American History* (The Project Gutenberg eBook, 2017). www.gutenberg.org/files/22994/22994-h/22994-h.htm
9 Estefanía Ciro Rodríguez, "Las tierras profundas de la 'lucha contra las drogas' en Colombia: la ley y la violencia estatal en la vida de los pobladores rurales del Caquetá," *Revista Colombiana de Sociología* 41 (2018): 105–133; Graciela Uribe Rendón, *Veníamos con una manotada de ambiciones: Un aporte a la historia de la colonización del Caquetá* (Bogotá: Unibiblos, 1998).
10 Darío Fajardo, "Territorialidad y Estado en la Amazonía colombiana," en *Espacio y sociedad: Formación de las regiones agrarias en Colombia* (Bogotá: Corporación Colombiana para la Amazonia—Araracuara, 1993).
11 Jaime Jaramillo, Leonidas Mora, and Fernando Cubides, *Colonización, coca y guerrilla* (Bogotá: Universidad Nacional de Colombia, 1986); Alfredo Molano, *Aguas Arriba: Entre la coca y el oro* (Bogotá: Debolsillo, 2017).
12 Estefanía Ciro Rodríguez, *Las vidas en disputa: Mujeres cocaleras, violencia y relaciones de producción- reproducción social en la economía regional de la coca en el sur de Colombia* (Caquetá: Informe Etnográfico, Programa de Fomento a la Investigación del ICANH, Subdirección Científica ICANH, 2017).
13 Interview by the author and Juana, hamlet in Curillo, August 2017.
14 Interview by the author and Dulce, hamlet in Curillo, August 2017.
15 Interview by the author and Amanda, hamlet in San Vicente del Caguán, August 2017.
16 A plante is a small plantation, averaging half a hectare.
17 Interview by the author and Marta, hamlet in La Unión Peneya, October 2017.
18 Interview by the author and Magdalena, hamlet in Curillo, August 2017.
19 Interview by the author and Dulce, hamlet in Curillo, October 2017; interview by the author and Ximena, Florencia, September 2016; interview by the author and Tania, hamlet in San José del Fragua, August 2017.
20 Conversation with the author and Andrea, Paujil, August 2017.
21 Interview by the author and Mireya, hamlet in San José del Fragua, August 2017.
22 Conversation with the author and Nancy, Florencia, September 2016.
23 Interview by the author and Amanda, hamlet in San Vicente del Caguán, August 2017.
24 Interview by the author and Rosaura, hamlet in La Montañita, August 2017.
25 Conversation with the author and Paola, hamlet in La Montañita, October 2017.
26 Conversation with the author and Mireya, hamlet in San José del Fragua, August 2017.
27 Interview by the author and Mariela, Florencia, August 2017.
28 Interview by the author and Rosaura, hamlet in La Montañita, October 2017.
29 Interview by the author and Amanda, hamlet in San Vicente del Caguán, August 2017.
30 A study by Gumucio et al. has observed the invisibilization of women in cattle-farming areas of Nicaragua, Costa Rica, and Colombia, as well as the limited access to productive resources for women, a lack of information about gender in the context of cattle production, and how control of crucial assets like

land, livestock, and training remains in the hands of men. Moreover, the study explains that subsistence strategies such as the farming of smaller livestock and poultry farming, and food production in general, are not regarded as important. See Gumucio T., Mora Benard M.A., Twyman J., and Hernández Ceballos M.C., "Género en la ganadería: Consideraciones iniciales para la incorporación de una perspectiva de género en la investigación de la ganadería en Colombia y Costa Rica," *Documento de trabajo CCAFS*, no. 159 (2016). Copenhagen, Denmark.

31 Interview by the author and Amanda, hamlet in San Vicente del Caguán, August 2017.
32 Interview by the author and Marta, hamlet in La Montañita, August 2017.
33 Interview by the author and Tania, Curillo, August 2017.
34 Centro Nacional de Memoria Histórica, CNMH, *El Placer: Mujeres, coca y guerra en el Bajo Putumayo* (Bogotá: Taurus, 2012).
35 Interview by the author and María, Florencia, October 2014.
36 Gabriela Valdivia, "Coca's Haunting Presence in the Agrarian Politics of the Bolivian Lowlands," *GeoJournal* 77, no. 5 (2012): 615–631.
37 Interview by the author and Marta, La Montañita, October 2017.
38 Interview by the author and Jeison, September 2013.
39 Interview by the author and Ramiro, September 2013.
40 A town in southern Caquetá.
41 Interview by the author and Olga, Florencia, October 2017.
42 María Mónica Parada Hernández and Margarita Marín Jaramillo, "Mujeres y coca: Una relación agridulce," *Análisis Político* 32, no. 97 (2019): 45–70.
43 For example, recent reflections about how and why prohibition creates such a precarious context for coca growers in Camilo Acero and Frances Thomson, "'Everything Peasants Do Is Illegal': Colombian Coca Growers' Everyday Experiences of Law Enforcement and Its Impacts on State Legitimacy," *Third World Quarterly* (2021): 1–19.
44 Oskar Jansson, *The Cursed Leaf: An Anthropology of the Political Economy of Cocaine Production in Southern Colombia* (Uppsala: Uppsala Universitet, 2008).
45 Ciro Rodríguez, *Unos grises muy verracos*; Parada and Marín, *Mujeres y coca*; Estefanía Ciro Rodríguez, *Cultivando coca en el Caquetá: Vidas y legitimidades de la actividad cocalera* (Ph.D. dissertation, Programa de Posgrado en Ciencias Políticas y Sociales, Universidad Autónoma de México, 2016).
46 Ciro Rodríguez, *Unos grises muy verracos*.
47 Ciro Rodríguez, "Las tierras profundas"; Diana Marcela Rojas, *El Plan Colombia: La intervención de Estados Unidos en el conflicto armado colombiano (1998–2012)* (Bogotá: Penguin Random House Grupo Editorial, 2015).
48 John Lindsay-Poland, *Plan Colombia: U.S. Ally Atrocities and Community Activism* (Durham: Duke University Press, 2018).
49 Interview by the author and Carolina, La Montañita, October 2017; interview by the author and Belén, La Montañita, October 2017; interview with the author and Teresa, La Montañita, October 2014; conversation with the author and four peasant men and three peasant women, Belén de los Andaquíes, 2015.
50 Comisión Interamericana de Derechos Humanos, CIDH, Informe de Admisibilidad No. 76/18- Petición 1453–08. Approved on June 21, 2018. Abogado Óscar Conde Ortiz. Violación de derechos humanos por aspersión aérea con glifosato, 2018.

51 Interview by the author and a criminal attorney, Florencia, October 2015.
52 A former female combatant with the FARC's 15th Front noted in an interview that the year 2004 had been extremely hard from a military point of view due to the Colombian military's offensive against the FARC's rearguard in Cartagena del Chairá and San Vicente del Caguán.
53 Interview by the author and Nancy, Florencia, October 2016.
54 Centro Nacional de Memoria Histórica CNMH, *Textos corporales de la crueldad: Memoria histórica y antropología forense* (Bogotá: CNMH, 2014).
55 Ciro Rodríguez, *Unos grises muy verracos*.
56 Conversation with the author and a female school teacher, southern Caquetá, September 2017.
57 Conversation and walk with townspeople, hamlet in Curillo, September 2017.
58 Interview by the author and Blanca, hamlet in Curillo, September 2017.
59 Conversation with the author and Magdalena, hamlet in Curillo, September 2017.
60 There have been forced eradications all over the department, even in communities that have already signed an agreement of voluntary substitution, and in spite of the government's commitment to carry out what are known as Immediate Attention Plans (Planes de Acción Inmediata or PAIs). Paujil, for example, signed its PAI on July 21, 2017, and nonetheless eradication operations were carried out on September 8 and October 6. Estefanía Ciro, "Estado contra-cara: Quiebres de la paz en Colombia por la sustitución de coca," *Mondialisation*, February 24, 2017. www.mondialisation.ca/estado-contra-cara-quiebres-de-la-paz-en-colombia-por-la-sustitucion-de-coca/5576575.
61 Interview by the author and Amanda, hamlet in San Vicente del Caguán, September 2017.
62 Segato, *Las nuevas formas de la guerra*.

Part 6

Laboring with Memory

18 Fluctuations and Paradoxes in Colombia's Long Cycle of Historical Memory, 2005–2022

María Emma Wills Obregón
Translated by Jeanine M. Legato

This chapter offers a chronological framework for the battles waged in Colombia by different actors in the field of historical memory since a transitional justice paradigm first gained acceptance and began to frame negotiations between the state and various armed organizations (2003–2021). The last two negotiations—undertaken by the Álvaro Uribe administration with the United Self-defense Forces of Colombia, AUC, between 2003 and 2006, and a second initiated by the Juan Manuel Santos administration with the Revolutionary Armed Forces of Colombia, FARC-EP, between 2011 and 2016—unfolded under this framework, which, unlike previous negotiations, placed the rights of victims to truth, justice, reparations, and non-repetition at the center of state and social efforts to arrive at agreements between the parties.[1] Today, under the auspices of this new paradigm of justice, we know that deals between opponents are insufficient to transition to a common existence unencumbered by socio-political violence. If such violence is to be left behind, the ravages of war have to be faced openly. When articulated publicly, the testimonies of victims escape the private domain and become archives of pain and moral inquiry capable of interrogating not only perpetrators but also neighbors who, in their indifference and silence, tolerated the prolonged suffering of "their brethren."[2] In addition to these moral reflections, transitional justice processes seek to settle central questions: Who gave the orders and planned the strategies that culminated in violent acts? How were they financed? Which interests were served by these strategies? Who were the allies in the shadows? Where are the bodies of the disappeared? Direct victims and their families pose these questions, seeking answers—as do a variety of state entities—through investigation groups, truth commissions, and special jurisdictions responsible for prosecuting and delivering justice.

Both commissions and special jurisdictions are part and parcel of a field that has come to be known as historical memory. Far from a site of unanimity or convergence, historical memory is an arena in which judges,

DOI: 10.4324/9781003048152-25

commissioners, historians, journalists, artists, and diverse victims, among many others, construct representations of the past and dispute the significance of lived experience. While some defend the honor and good name of their deceased relatives, others seek to protect the reputation of the organization to which they belong, to skirt or conceal responsibility, or openly justify their actions.[3] Attempting to periodize the struggles that unfold in this field implies identifying the "agents" of memory, the purpose of their work, the alliances they strike, the resources and power they lose or acquire, and the contingent balance of power reached among them during each period.

In Colombia's case, a field of memory took shape in the 1980s related to the armed conflict and its victims. However, unlike other Latin American countries that undertook memory struggles and campaigns once dictatorships had already ended or when negotiated solutions to armed conflict had been reached, memory agents in Colombia began their struggle in the midst of an ongoing armed conflict. During those years, several authors identified the contours of a historical memory field related to the fate of victims of the armed conflict.[4] The field's central promoters coalesced around the defense of human rights, the denunciation of recurrent human rights violations, and archival preservation. However, even as they acted out of a commitment to challenge prevailing impunity and safeguard the memory of victims, there was still no way to articulate and encapsulate all of their struggles.

It was only 25 years later with the adoption of Justice and Peace Law 975 in 2005 that historical memory was powerfully enunciated in the public sphere and transformed into a site of struggle. From that moment, a multiplicity of social practices converged into broad-based coalitions such as the Movimiento Nacional de Víctimas de Crímenes de Estado (MOVICE) [National Movement of Victims of State Crimes] in 2005, and Hijos e Hijas por la Memoria y Contra la Impunidad [Sons and Daughters for Memory and Against Impunity] in 2006. In parallel, a series of state-led public policies on memory were launched by the government. From that moment on, the representation of the past in the present initiated a turbulent course, attaining prominence in public debate for a period, and then becoming the focal point of bitter controversy. These pages aim to reconstruct that *fluctuating* and *paradoxical* trajectory, in itself demonstrative of the dynamism of a field of memory in which struggles over the meaning of the past never culminate at a definitive end point.[5] I have identified three periods: the first extending from 2005 to 2010, a second encompassing the years of 2011 to 2018, and a final period from 2018 to 2022 that concludes with the auguring of profound changes with the arrival of the first leftist coalition, the Pacto Histórico (Historic Pact), to national power.

Heroic Memories of Powerful Actors and the Plurality of Grassroots Memory Initiatives, 2005–2010

After an unsuccessful negotiation process between the FARC and the Andrés Pastrana administration (1998–2002), public frustration shrouded the 2002 electoral contest, proving victorious for those who offered a radical shift in approach to the armed conflict. Álvaro Uribe, governor of the department of Antioquia in the years prior, arrived to the presidency with a hardline discourse against guerrilla groups. During his years as governor, Uribe had been the principal advocate of the Convivir, state-backed private armed groups charged with securing regions ravaged by violence. This "outsourcing" of security, as well as the support of factions within the State Security Forces (SSF) of clandestine methods of defeating the guerrilla, resulted in the expansion and consolidation of the paramilitary phenomenon. Once elected president, Uribe reconfigured the way the internal armed conflict had come to be codified, disciplining government discourse to articulate the conflict as a terrorist confrontation of guerrillas against society and the state.[6]

In addition to this discursive reconfiguration, the president stunned by initiating dialogue, this time not with the guerrilla but with the AUC, an anti-guerrilla and anti-communist organization founded in 1997 with the purpose of uniting different regional expressions of paramilitarism in the country. In 2004, while the Colombian Congress was discussing the regulatory framework for these negotiations, three paramilitary commanders, Iván Roberto Duque (alias Ernesto Báez), Salvatore Mancuso, and Ramón Isaza, were invited by the House of Representatives Peace Commission to explain their motivations for organizing armed groups. Dressed in ties and dark suits, each of them delivered a speech to the whole country about their version of the past and justified their methods. Hardly remorseful, the commanders were sure that they had made the right decisions, faced as they were with (in their view) an absent state and an unscrupulous enemy (the guerrilla). While they rattled on at the microphone, two victims, Iván Cepeda, son of Manuel Cepeda, a Patriotic Union Party Senator murdered in 1994, and Dilia Solana, representative of NGO Justicia y Verdad, protested alone in the upper galleries of the Oval Room against a ceremony that, according to them, consecrated impunity for paramilitaries and enshrouded victims in silence and oblivion.

Despite their silent but powerful protest, most of those who attended the pronouncements broke into thunderous applause, endorsing the historical explanation offered by the commanders dressed in civilian attire about the emergence and expansion of paramilitarism in Colombia. It did not stop there. A year later, in statements to the Supreme Court, Salvatore Mancuso and Vicente Castaño reaffirmed their declarations to *Semana*

Figure 18.1 Human Rights defender Iván Cepeda with a portrait of his murdered father at the Oval Room while a group of paramilitary commanders addressed a congressional hearing. Photograph by Herminso Ruiz Ruiz, published in *El Espectador*, July 29, 2004.

magazine that they enjoyed the support of 35% of the legislature.[7] These narratives shared a sole historical justification of paramilitarism: "We had to arm ourselves" to "save the homeland." This would later be reiterated in the courts established by Justice and Peace Law 975 of 2005 in which prosecutors enlisted different strategies, some more successful than others, to confront the heroic versions of the commanders.[8] While the accounts voiced resonated with president Uribe's discourse, individuals, families, communities, and movements in the regions honored their victims through memory processes, challenging the justification of the violation of their rights, and demanding justice. Unlike the memories that basked in official absolution and the repetition, if not litany, of a singular heroic narrative, communities and social movements took to the public sphere, sometimes locally, and other times regionally or nationally, to establish for themselves the convergence points among a profound diversity of experiences.[9]

This broad range of expression in terms of emphasis and language attested to diverse subjects acting from their own perspectives, traditions, world views, and aesthetics. These intersected, configuring an increasingly heterogeneous field of memory that was rich in symbolism such as family altars for the deceased, memory gardens, memory murals, school museums, human rights archives and meeting rooms, community memory museums, photography exhibitions, plays, musical compositions, and textile art.[10] All of these memory agents openly or implicitly revolted against the reign of silence that different armed groups imposed through armed control of territory and communities.

These actors promoted memory exercises which gave rise to an explosion of pluralistic expression and from which *emergent archives* of enormous symbolic wealth were produced. In this sense, the past would not solely and exclusively get imprinted on lifeless official documents during a memory reconstruction process but would be recorded in body maps, social cartographies, territorial landmarks, rituals, and ceremonies for the dead, songs, ballads, graffiti, and poems.[11] As these innovations were carried out in increasingly conscious ways by its agents, the field not only acquired new textures and soundscapes but also incorporated unprecedented ways of producing archives. In retrospect, throughout those years, in addition to the existence of the voices of the powerful proposing a hero-versus-villain narrative, it is possible to recognize the simultaneous emergence and consolidation of a social field of historical memory forged in potently diverse languages, genres, varieties, and interpretations.[12] The capacity to go beyond the circles of those who were "already convinced [about the reality of victims' suffering]" marked this period as one in which victims managed to make headway in new settings. Thanks to these inroads, public opinion was forced to recognize an astoundingly diverse nation resisting erasure in thousands of ways and, at the same time, was confronted with the bitter contemporary reality of our country: war atrocities and the suffering of victims.

This discovery, at once revelatory and painful, was produced hand in hand with an unexpected ally, the Historical Memory Group (GMH in Spanish), an ad-hoc team of researchers and academics who had been delegated to produce a narrative of the armed conflict by the National Reparation and Reconciliation Commission (CNRR in Spanish), an entity created by Law 975 to attend to the reparation of victims and the demobilization of AUC combatants. The GMH became a sounding board for victims' claims, indignations, and hopes thanks to the relationships of trust it built with, for example, the Association of Relatives of the Victims at Trujillo (AFAVIT in Spanish), the community of El Salado victims, some of the leaders from Bahía Portete, and the community of Bojayá, to mention a few cases, thus overcoming the resistance of victims' organizations to the Law 975. The GMH's reports tried to adhere to what its team had cautioned since consolidating in 2007: Truth and memory are socially constructed. Consequently, truly participatory mechanisms were vital to its work to guarantee that victims and their organizations be "part of the construction" of truth and memory processes.[13] Unexpectedly, in confronting the country with the horrors of the armed conflict, the GMH and victims' organizations found powerful allies in certain mass media. To name a few, *Semana* magazine and *El Tiempo* and *El Espectador* newspapers shone a light on victims and their memories, which were given center stage at all public launches of GMH reports. Victims' testimonial and narrative traditions consequently shook up the anesthetized conscience of many Colombians.

By the end of the Uribe administration, the context was divided as follows. On the one hand, an executive and cabinet focused on a national policy, Democratic Security, that denied the existence of an armed conflict and sought the military defeat of the guerrilla, branded as terrorists, by means of its Patriot Plan.[14] On the other hand, increasingly powerful victims' organizations were emboldened by the consolidation of their own solidarity and exchange networks, as well as by international and national support.[15] The field of memory in the next period would be configured by the start of negotiations between the FARC and the incoming Santos administration, the passage of Victims' Law 1448 of 2011, and the accompanying creation of institutions charged with state duties of historical memory. In addition, victims would play a fundamental role at the negotiating table in Havana; simultaneously, the leadership of the SSF,[16] the FARC, and rural business sectors such as cattle ranchers would opt to participate in memory-making and become direct memory agents themselves.

Peace Talks in Havana and the Crystallization of a Primal Rift, 2011–2018

With outgoing President Uribe's blessing and the support of the Partido de la U coalition, Juan Manuel Santos was elected in 2010. In his inaugural address, the incoming president signaled profound retreat from the positions of his predecessor. On August 7, 2010, Santos announced that "the key to peace was not at the bottom of the sea," in a nod to imminent negotiations.

With enormous discretion and absent press leaks that could have ruined the effort, a team appointed by the president met with FARC delegates to agree on a negotiation agenda. Negotiating implied recognizing the FARC as an actor with whom it was possible to negotiate and transact on a political agenda. On October 15, 2012, the first joint announcement of the delegations was finally made public.[17] With this gesture began an exhausting and complex road that would culminate on June 23, 2016, with the signing of a Final Peace Agreement. This agreement had to be renegotiated with the opposition led by former president Uribe, who achieved victory for a NO vote in a plebiscite on October 2, 2016, by a narrow margin (50.21% voted No and 49.78% Yes).[18]

While delegations negotiated the terms of an agreement to end the armed conflict throughout these years (2012–2016), Colombian factions across the political divide, separated by rising and seemingly insurmountable differences, led the construction of opposing memory archives and actions. The first milestone to reveal this clash was the Victims and Land Restitution Law. Preceded by several unsuccessful attempts, the law was approved in 2011 when it finally gained majority support thanks to the persistence of its champions, the oversight and contributions of several victims' organizations, and the support provided by president Santos himself.

These face-offs over memory revolved around the thorny question of who could legally be considered victims and, by extension, who would fall in the category of perpetrators. These issues were plumbed by Law 1448, but they generated enormous unease among the Uribe-led opposition (see Table 18.1). The issue of the judicial and historical treatment of responsible parties would later be codified in the Final Peace Agreement signed in 2016,[19] but I include it in Table 18.1 because its dispute came to a head when Uribe acolytes raised their disagreements with Law 1448.

Confrontations over these differences were heated. From one extreme, some asked indignantly how it could be that guerrillas and SSF were treated with the same yardstick when some were criminals and the other heroes. From the opposite side, victims of state agents in particular were horrified and asked themselves how it was possible that their compatriots deny the responsibility of state actors in their victimization, papering over the

Table 18.1 Fault Lines of the Primal Rift of Historical Memory

	Pro-negotiation	Anti-negotiation
How should the past be referenced?	Armed conflict	Terrorism targeted at society and the state
Proposed solution	Negotiation with the FARC	Military defeat
Who should be considered victims?	Those who have suffered harm from acts that constitute "serious violations of International Humanitarian Law (IHL) or gross violations of International Human Rights Law (IHRL)" precisely because they occurred "in the context of armed conflict," according to Article 3 of Law 1448 of 2011.	All those who have suffered any type of harm in connection to the occurrence of terrorist acts committed by criminal guerrilla organizations.
Who among the members of State Security Forces (SSF) are considered victims?	Only those members who have suffered harm by acts in violation of any of the rules established by IHL, the case law that establishes "a series of restrictions on the means of warfare, especially weapons, and methods of warfare, such as certain military tactics," like the use of anti-personnel mines, degrading treatment, or "killing or wounding an adversary who has surrendered weapons or who is not in combat."[i]	State Security Forces officers can only be categorized as victims and never as perpetrators, and all SSF members who have suffered harm should be considered victims, without distinction, with rights to all reparation measures.
Who is responsible for the reparation of members of the SSF who have suffered harm in combat circumstances that *did not infringe* on IHL?	Such SSF members are not considered victims, but can access the special arrangements established in the country's legal codes, for which the corresponding institutions are responsible.	All members of the SSF who have suffered harm are considered victims with rights to all reparation measures. The Victims' Unit should therefore assume their reparation.
Who are considered perpetrators/victimizers/responsible parties (as defined in the Peace Agreement)?	Third parties, members of guerrilla organizations, SSF, and officials of other state institutions if they were involved in acts that constitute violations of IHL or human rights. If proven guilty, they must be held accountable to victims, society as a whole (Truth Commission), and the Special Jurisdiction for Peace (JEP) for their acts, decisions or dereliction of duty.	Only guerrillas.

[i] Comité Internacional de la Cruz Roja. (2004). *¿Qué es el derecho internacional humanitario?* Available at: www.icrc.org/es/doc/assets/files/other/dih.es.pdf Accessed November 22nd, 2021.

undeniable accountability that the state ought to assume. In both cases, the differences were not merely legal technicalities. In these discussions, values, notions of justice, and deep loyalties to the deceased and aggrieved were aired. The actors involved recognized that their own reputation and rights, as well as the honor and dignity of victims, were at stake. In a closed-door meeting in his office, an army general expressed it succinctly: "What will my children and grandchildren think of us?"[20] As for family members, many mothers and fathers asked that processes to elucidate truth establish that their children were not criminals and did not deserve the fate inflicted on them by their perpetrators under any circumstances. As the weight of each side's claims became clearer, more memory agents became involved in these battles; they saw a way to rally their peers behind memory work, pay homage to their own victims, and convince other audiences of the righteousness of their struggle.

This section focuses on two examples of sectors involved in memory work: FARC members who were already aware of the centrality of memory to their struggle and who promoted their own initiatives more publicly during the peace negotiation, and the Colombian Federation of Cattle Ranchers (FEDEGAN in Spanish). Both of them defended their own versions of the past. Both outlined strategies to compile archives about their experiences, elaborate narratives of the past, use various vehicles of memory,[21] and share their reading of events through the consecration of different memory sites.[22]

In the FARC's case, the guerrilla group began to bring its "well-guarded memories" into the public sphere after "awaiting . . . more favorable conditions."[23] In 2013, for example, Inty Maleywa, at the time an active FARC combatant, decided to put her drawing skills at the service of the reconstruction of the past from the perspective of her organization because, according to her, "today's artist must be aware that her mission is that of a historian par excellence. Her quest is [to decide] which stories need telling and which stories need crafting."[24] Moreover, these illustrations took on educational and informational significance when, for the celebration of the 50th anniversary of the FARC's founding, the artist joined her talents with those of musician Martín Batalla. Together they created an exhibition set to music called *Desenterrando memorias* [unearthing memories]. Both artists dedicated the work to "thousands and thousands of invisible victims." Their focus was a decade-by-decade reconstruction of the most prominent "popular struggles" in the country's history. Tracing the birth of the contemporary armed conflict, the artists went back to the historic massacre of the banana fields in the United Fruit Company enclave in 1928, as the origin point for the story, followed by the peasant and union movements of the 1930s, the assassination of Jorge Eliécer Gaitán and the Bogotazo crisis of 1948, forced migration to flee "the inclemency of power" in the 1950s, and culminating with the "dignified resistance" and "watershed of memory" in Marquetalia, where the FARC-EP was founded.[25] Plainly, this memory is painted with the brush of heroism in which the victims are those who undertook years of popular struggle, unbeknownst to official history.

From the opposite camp, in opposition to these memories, the Colombian Federation of Cattle Ranchers (FEDEGAN) promoted the construction of a counter-memory. As the FARC had done, the guild made a timeline of commemorative dates,[26] put together groups dedicated to gathering and analyzing archives and testimonies,[27] and launched publications[28] compiling accounts of the lived experience of cattle ranchers, thus emphasizing their victimization, particularly at the hands of the FARC. In 2013, the second edition of the book *Acabar con el olvido* [An End to Oblivion] was published by the Colombian Cattle Farmer Foundation (FUNDAGAN in Spanish). FEDEGAN president José Félix Lafaurie affirmed in the prologue that the initiative sought to shine a light on cattle ranchers "to honor our past, and look towards the construction of the future."[29] Both he and María Fernanda Cabal, FUNDAGAN director, referred to violence and criminal violence in their texts, avoiding any allusion to the existence of an armed conflict. The FUNDAGAN director's prologue also highlighted:

> The country's magnification of some victims for political ends, in the face of the literal anonymity of others, including cattle rancher victims of violence. . . . There are no first or second-class victims. . . . That is why from the outset we posit an "end to silence to end the oblivion" of cattle rancher victims of violence. Because cattle rancher victims are no less victims.[30]

As with the memories of FARC members, a claim is made to supposed official amnesia, which, in the eyes of cattle rancher victims, overlooks them and offers preferential treatment to other victims. As a counterweight to the guerrillas' memories identifying the "inclemency of power," in the FUNDAGAN narrative, widespread victimization is "the determinant role of international communism in the context of the Cold War," which "exports armed revolt to Latin America."[31]

The argument of first- and second-class victims resonated deeply in other sectors, breeding discontent with the peace negotiation process. In October 2014, this disapproval was expressed at a forum titled *Colombia abraza a las víctimas de las FARC* [Colombia embraces victims of the FARC], organized by Senator Sofía Gaviria—president of the Senate Human Rights Commission, codirector of the Liberal Party, and a victim of the FARC[32]— and journalist Herbin Hoyos, producer of the radio program *Voces del secuestro* [Voices of the kidnapped ones]. With 1,500 people in attendance at the Jiménez de Quesada Convention Center, the participants booed the minister of interior Juan Fernando Cristo, one of the proponents of the Victims Law, and issued a public statement announcing the creation of the National Federation of Victims of the FARC (FEVCOL in Spanish) to guarantee "the right to freedom of expression [of these victims], so that they might combat stigmatization, accusations, and revictimization, no matter their position on the peace process" and to prevent "our victimizers from qualifying or disqualifying us as victims."[33] They further added, "the fact that there are some victims of the FARC present at the negotiations in Havana does not make their presence a unified, coordinated, or authoritative voice. They can only speak on their behalf." This final document would be disseminated and replicated in anti-peace agreement coalitions, and in particular on the website of the Colombian Association of Retired Officers of the Military Forces (ACORE in Spanish),[34] demonstrating an affinity between both organizations.[35]

Despite the traction of clashing positions, attempts to build bridges between the memories of the victims of the FARC and the memories of victims of paramilitaries and the state cannot be overlooked. One of these efforts was led by delegations of victims who traveled to Havana to be heard and who, as a unit, were representative of the majority of typical crimes, perpetrators, and regions.[36] In some of the delegations, it was possible for the victims to overcome the fractures that divided them and act as a "community in suffering" united in their defense of peace.[37] Likewise, in Havana, the negotiation teams carefully planned rituals to avoid any hint of revictimization of the aggrieved. The victims were able to freely recount their experiences and openly rebuke the representatives of the organization or institution presumed to be responsible for their suffering. None of the participants in the delegations, whether from the FARC, government, state institutions, or guarantor countries in attendance could retort; the only thing that the shared protocol allowed them to do was to listen in silence and take in the condemnation of victims. Victims were able to communicate in sober environments what they had experienced. Paradoxically, by listening to emotionally intimate stories about the interruption of everyday aspirations, as well as of grief and absence, the victims and perpetrators were able to connect with their own pain and the suffering of others to overcome the rifts imposed by political positions and to recreate, even for a short while, a sense of communion.

This unexpected fraternity allowed some of the perpetrators to take accountability for the damage done and apologize from a place of acknowledgment of their responsibility:

> The death of the [Valle de Cauca] deputies [during a hostage crisis] was the most absurd thing I have experienced in the war, the most shameful

episode. May it never be a source of pride. Today, with sincere humility, we ask for forgiveness. We hope you can forgive us.[38]

Several of the negotiators recognized that this was a turning point in the peace talks. Both delegations stated their firm belief that neither the victims' suffering nor the degradation of the war as witnessed in the recounting of their memories could continue. There was therefore an ethical imperative to arrive at an agreement that could facilitate an opening toward peace in the country.

But the images of perpetrators distressed at the testimonial memory of victims quickly gave way to division and bitter recrimination in Colombia, when plebiscite campaigning began in 2016. Despite the warnings of different experts and politicians about the dangers of plebiscites, president Santos insisted on carrying out the referendum to fulfill his word and to legitimize the pact signed in Havana with a popular endorsement. Even though the highest rate of abstention in the last 20 years won the day on October 2, 2016, news cameras captured jubilant shouts in the halls of the Uribe-led "No" campaign and, conversely, the inconsolable cries of the defenders of the "Yes" vote. Having seen themselves in these images, Colombians were forced to contend with the undeniable reality of the schism dividing the country. Most of the opposition, in particular the Democratic Center party, questioned among other issues the Comprehensive Rural Reform expressed in the first point of the peace agreements. From their standpoint, the pact did not explicitly recognize "the contribution of business production to rural development," did not specify the scope of the concept of "extinguishing propriety entitlement" and, therefore, did not guarantee "legitimate landed property rights" or the "good-faith land occupation" of unoccupied state lands.[39]

Although at first glance these issues did not relate to disputes over narratives of the past, in reality, the controversies surrounding the first point of the agreement do have to do with memory. The FARC, as previously mentioned, constructed a narrative of the past and of themselves in relation to the country's peasant movements. Precisely because of its condition as a peasant organization, the first point of the negotiation was to establish ground rules to guarantee land access for its members, as well as other conditions essential for their sustenance, without disputing the right of the business class to rural property. History seemed to be repeating itself, however, replicating what happened in 1936 when Law 100 was passed under the Alfonso López Pumarejo administration, triggering strong reactions and fueling the Liberal-Conservative confrontation known as *la Violencia*, as well as what happened in the 1960s, when Liberal Carlos Lleras Restrepo defended an agrarian reform that was approved by Congress. In the 1970s, this led to the Chicoral Pact, an agreement between government and landowners to revoke the reformist measures that had been approved a few years earlier. As in prior iterations, the proposal in point 1 of the 2016 peace agreements once again turned out to be intolerable to some powerful sectors organized behind the "No" campaign.

In this sense, this discussion was particularly illustrative of how memory articulates positions about the past whereby their promoters assume positions in the present that are at once symbolic and material, political and socio-economic. In summary, during this period (2011–2018), while delegations in Havana arrived at formulas to tackle crucial issues,[40] in Colombia, tension and polarization divided sectors of the citizenry and, in particular, of the political and social elite. In the midst of this confrontation were not only the rules and agreements to be applied in the future undoubtedly at stake for central actors but also the moral reading of the past that would prevail and be passed on to future generations. These conflicts dovetailed with disputes over the economic policy that would structure the Colombian countryside and had their root in battles that had already fissured Colombian society at critical junctures.

Therefore, from 2011 to 2018, the gaps separating different readings of the past, rather than diminishing or becoming less pronounced, crystallized into a "primal rift" configured by two irreconcilable readings of the past, the present and, of course, the future. During this period, elites and political leaders built two opposing readings of reality that articulated (inherited or current) differences, organizing an interpretative mold from which to construct an "us" that not only rivaled but was totally antagonistic to the "other" with whom it became increasingly difficult to negotiate and coexist, giving way to pernicious polarization.[41] This schism was plain in the subsequent presidential election. As preluded by the electoral results of the plebiscite, after eight years of an administration that had promoted peace talks within a framework that recognized the existence of an armed conflict, the country would now return to Uribe-style management at the helm of Iván Duque, elected to the presidency in a run-off on June 17, 2018.

Counter-Memory and a Newfound Pulse, 2018–2021

With the return of Uribe's doctrine to power, the view of the present (and therefore the past) changed course, reconfiguring around other priorities. A discourse of legality and security became the throughline of public policy, pushing victims, reparations, and peace to the margins. From the day Duque was inaugurated on August 7, 2018, his message was clear. Before national and international guests in the Plaza de Bolívar, surrounded by export-grade roses and flanked on all sides by uniformed soldiers from all branches of the Armed Forces and the Police, the elected president made it explicit that to him the grandeur of the state and its power resided above all else in its security apparatus. Unsurprisingly, Duque's administration (2018–2022) hardly mentioned victims. With the exception of Colombia +20, the section of the *El Espectador* newspaper funded by the UN Development Program, most mass media stopped focusing on issues of memory and reparations. Then the pandemic arrived and, like a hurricane, leveled other stories, turning the news into an endless death toll of those lost to COVID-19. Simultaneously, the administration sought to bottleneck the work of certain institutions in charge of elaborating accounts of the past, like the National Center for Historical Memory (CNMH in Spanish), just as it had marginalized from its agenda any efforts to favor conditions for a stable and lasting peace, for victims, and for their memories. In a series of failed attempts, Duque tried to appoint individuals, not for their academic qualities, but for their ideological sympathies, causing scandal after scandal. The president finally succeeded in appointing professor Darío Acevedo as director of the CNMH, someone who had not hidden his vexation with the peace process in his public addresses and tweets and who ardently criticized those who spoke of the past in terms of an armed conflict. As soon as he assumed the role, Acevedo espoused a series of controversial positions that put him at the center of the maelstrom. While some victims' organizations demanded the return of their archives claiming a loss of trust,[42] other sectors like the military and police arranged meetings between the director and high-level officials.[43]

Then, a script at the National Memory Museum (MNM in Spanish) broke the camel's back. The director tried to change parts of the exhibition *Otras voces para transformar a Colombia* [Other Voices to Transform Colombia], a script elaborated for the MNM with the participation of victims, arguing that he considered some "propagandist"[44] and others because he deemed metaphors about bodies, water, and land lacking in rigor.[45] Acevedo censored the words he considered inappropriate. These actions were leaked to the press and provoked a new scandal, prompting Senator Iván Cepeda to petition that the Special Jurisdiction for Peace (JEP in Spanish), the transitional justice system tribunal created by the peace agreements, establish precautionary measures to protect the museum archives and script. The JEP's Peace Tribunal Section on Absence of Acknowledgment of Truth and Responsibility for Facts and Conduct, after hearing from both current and previous officials of the CNMH and museology experts, issued several orders granting these precautionary measures. It further dictated that the Center carry out "actions to guarantee the intangibility of the *Voces para transformar a Colombia* collection" and submit to the Tribunal a "program and schedule to have the collection returned to its original state and guarantee it NOT be modified, altered, eliminated, or diminished in terms of accepted methodology and content."[46] It is clear that the administration's intention of promoting counter-memories at the CNMH faced resistance, so much so that for the time being, it seems to have failed.

At the same time, despite the indifference shown them by the Executive, victims found other settings to have their memories heard. They attended and contributed their testimonies and knowledge in the JEP and the Commission for the Clarification of Truth, Coexistence, and Non-Repetition, also known as the Truth Commission, to share their memories publicly and contribute to the elucidation of the past.

Throughout these four years, there have been extraordinary moments at the JEP, which speak to the possibility of profound transformations in the country. For example, in Macro-case 01 on kidnappings, demobilized members of the FARC secretariat, each dressed in civilian clothes, stripped of their nom de guerre, and identifying themselves by their legal names and national identification cards, appeared before the Recognition Section[47] to render their version of the events.[48] While they fell short of recognizing all the damages caused by the kidnapping policy they enforced for years, their respectful attitude and conduct adhered to the strict protocol established by the Section, showing that these men, seasoned in violent confrontation during the armed conflict, were willing to recognize and bow to the authority of state jurisdiction. In other JEP hearings and in some truth dialogues organized by the Truth Commission, perpetrators have shown true remorse; some go so far as to cry inconsolably, wondering if they will one day be able to make amends for all the harm they caused.[49] In other cases, victims become indignant at the canned speeches of their perpetrators and resort to the hope that those responsible will one day choose a different path and "cry together with their victims to become human again."[50] There have also been moments of historical lucidity, such as when, during a meeting on the perspective of indigenous peoples, a former member of the FARC recognized that "we were able to make many mistakes with Indigenous communities by trying to impose our ideology, our criteria [because] we could not understand their worldview, their way of doing things, and we were wrong."[51]

All of these examples provide glimpses of alternative approaches to the past, freed of heroics. Such alternatives, for those who listen, provide the keys to understanding the plotlines, alliances, interpretative frameworks, and inner workings that drive human misery. In Colombia, these keys enabled the snowballing of events that would horrify the humanitarian consciousness over centuries of violent conflict. In this sense, these encounters become emergent archives allowing us to break away from the heroic construction of memories—which perhaps inevitably leads to the constitution of two hate-filled, antagonistic camps—and to opt for more worthy memory constructions. The latter kind, much more lucid and self-critical, opens a pathway inasmuch as the narrator and listener are able to situate events within the historical conditions that made them possible, and to extract lessons for action in the present from that understanding.[52]

In summary, if the configuration of power in the field of memory in the previous period (2011–2018) crystallized a primal rift in which memory became an articulating node for different social and political conflicts, in this last period (2018–2021), memory ceased to be a central site of public debate as a consequence of the president's oppositional stance to the peace agreement. However, despite the efforts of the Duque administration, "loose" or untamed memories[53] did not disappear, but were circumscribed to specific settings like the JEP and Truth Commission—entities founded by the final agreement—and to the communitarian and grassroots sites of memory production that struggled to survive in the regions.

A New Period in the Making: The Peace Agreement Bears Fruit

After the election of president Gustavo Petro and Vice President Francia Márquez in 2022, we entered a new period: memory is once again associated with the fate of victims, the Final Peace Agreement, and the elucidation of the truth. This orientation, far from aiming at a protracted war or revenge by "wielding the same weapons, only now as words," is "one of the pillars of peace, [and] the possibility of reconciliation, and national and social coexistence."[54] These words, spoken by the newly elected president during the launch ceremony of the Truth Commission's Final Report on June 27, 2022, augur a new period in the field of memory, as do the recognition hearings at the JEP in which victims or their surviving relatives and perpetrators meet publicly in front of the bench. Victims appear in these scenarios to recount their suffering before those who inflicted it, and to demand truth, for example, the names of civilian third parties involved in the events, as well as economic reparations from their perpetrators. They rebuke the guilty ones without granting them forgiveness or, to the contrary, offer pardon. To access the special protections and measures contemplated by the law, perpetrators must recognize "factually, legally and restoratively" the damage caused to their victims[55] and assume the reparation measures demanded by the victims themselves.

In these hearings as well as in the truth dialogues organized by the Truth Commission, moral transformations are taking place in which perpetrators assume their responsibility, without equivocation. For example, as Figure 18.2 shows, members of the defunct FARC-EP secretariat recognized that they were "breeders of despair" and that the kidnapping policy adopted by the leadership was "a grave error that in no way matched the objectives and principles that led us to take up arms. . . . [These] demented attitudes [show] that we lost our political compass and that we, the commanders, are responsible [for it]." These settings have become sites where, simultaneously, judges gather evidence and hand down sentences, historians compile testimonies and formulate explanations, and victims and perpetrators exercise catharsis and confront their past with raw emotion. As eloquently said by a victim, these moments speak to the opportunity of being "face to face with one another to recognize each other's humanity," above and beyond impassive objectivity. Amid this convergence of mixed emotions, even the staging within the courts of justice acquires a different property. Photographs of absent victims, displayed in the style of altars with succinct explanations of the spirit of the victim and who they were, turn these formal places into ritual memorial sites that dignify those who are no longer with us. In turn, by being recorded for future generations, the hearings and truth dialogues become vestiges of an ongoing present, that is, emergent archives that account for the historical moment in which we live.

Finally, the Truth Commission's findings and the accountability assumed by those appearing before the JEP are increasingly, robustly, and overwhelmingly confirming some of the long-held explanations in the work of academics and human rights organizations, the essays of the Historical Commission on the Conflict and its Victims, and the reports of the Historical Memory Group and the National Center for Historical Memory.

Figure 18.2 Some of the FARC commanders at the first acknowledgment of responsibility hearing, Special Jurisdiction for Peace (JEP), Macro-case 01, Biblioteca Virgilio Barco, Bogotá, June 22, 2022. Photograph by the author.

In this sense, in addition to an inheritance of arresting testimony in the form of Truth Commission and CNMH archives, increasingly irrefutable patterns are uncovered and the conditions and decisions that gave rise to them identified. To the power of memory itself is then added an ever more indisputable elucidation of truth, a legacy that lays the foundation for a more accurate understanding of the country we have inherited, molded, and still yearn to become.

Notes

An early version of this chapter was published under the edition of Yvon Le Bot, *Sortir de la violence: Ce que nous enseigne l'Amérique latine* (Maison des Sciences de l'Homme, Paris, 2021). Thanks to Gonzalo Sánchez for his reading and suggestions which have undoubtedly improved the chapter.

1. Félix Reátegui, ed., *Justicia transicional: Manual para América Latina* (Brasilia: Comisión de Amnistía, Ministerio de Justicia; Nueva York: Centro Internacional para la Justicia Transicional, 2011).
2. Francisco de Roux, *Convocatoria a la paz grande*, discurso en el lanzamiento del Informe Final de la Comisión de la Verdad, Teatro Jorge Eliécer Gaitán, Bogotá, 27 de junio, 2022.
3. Elizabeth Jelin, *Los trabajos de la memoria* (Lima: IEP Ediciones, 2012).
4. Gonzalo Sánchez, *Memorias, subjetividades y política: Ensayos sobre un país que se niega a dejar la guerra* (Bogotá: Planeta-Crítica, 2020); Winifred Tate, *Counting the Dead: The Culture and Politics of Human Rights Activism in Colombia* (Oakland: University of California Press, 2007); Alcaldía Mayor de Bogotá, *Debates de la Memoria: Aportes de las organizaciones de víctimas a una política pública de memoria* (Bogotá: Centro de Memoria, Paz y Reconciliación, 2010).
5. Michael H. Bernhard and Jan Kubik, *Twenty Years after Communism: The Politics of Memory and Commemoration* (New York: Oxford University Press, 2016).
6. Sergio Jaramillo Caro, "La posibilidad de la paz," in *El inicio del proceso de paz: La fase exploratoria y el camino del Acuerdo General* (Bogotá: Oficina del Alto Comisionado para la Paz, 2018).
7. "Mancuso: 'el 35 por ciento del Congreso fue elegido en zona de influencia de las AUC'," Caracol Radio, August 4, 2005. http://caracol.com.co/radio/2005/08/04/judicial/1123166760_191922.html This account that the paramilitary apparatus was a dense network of allies from sectors with economic and political power was reiterated by Salvatore Mancuso in his voluntary contribution to the Truth Commission on August 8, 2021. See: www.facebook.com/ComisionVerdadC/videos/contribuci%C3%B3n-a-la-erdad-y-reconocimiento-de-responsabilidad-de-parte-de-salva/523286322281910/
8. Centro Nacional de Memoria Histórica (CNMH) et al., *Justicia y paz: ¿Verdad judicial o verdad histórica?* (Bogotá: Taurus, 2012).
9. Grupo de Memoria Histórica (GMH) and María Victoria Uribe, *Memorias en tiempo de guerra: Repertorios de iniciativas* (Bogotá: Comisión Nacional de Reparación y Reconciliación, 2009).
10. This updated record is available at: https://centrodememoriahistorica.gov.co/iniciativas-de-memoria/
11. GMH and Uribe, *Memorias en tiempo de guerra*.

12 Nancy Fraser, *Iustitia Interrupta: Reflexiones críticas desde la posición "postsocialista"* (Bogotá: Universidad de los Andes- Facultad de Derecho y Siglo del Hombre Editores, 1997).
13 Comisión Nacional de Reparación y Reconciliación, CNRR, *Plan de acción 2007, 2008* (Bogotá: CNRR, 2007).
14 Francisco Leal Buitrago, "La política de seguridad democrática: 2002–2005," *Análisis Político*, no. 57 (May-August 2006): 3–30.
15 Among aid agencies and embassies, the following merit mention: the United Nations (UN), UN Women, the European Union, Federal Department of Foreign Affairs of the Swiss Confederation, USAID, and the United States Institute of Peace (USIP).
16 María Emma Wills, "An Unorthodox Relationship: Colombian Public Forces and the National Center for Historical Memory (2012–2019)," in *How the Military Remembers: Countermemories and the Challenges to Human Rights in Latin America*, eds. Cynthia E. Milton and Michael J. Lazzara (forthcoming).
17 Biblioteca abierta del Proceso de Paz. https://bapp.com.co/, accessed July 4, 2018:
18 Registraduría Nacional de Estado Civil, "Plebiscito 2 de octubre 2016, República de Colombia."
19 The full title of the agreement is *Final Agreement for the Termination of the Conflict and the Construction of a Stable and Lasting Peace.*
20 Meeting at the Ministry of Defense, Bogotá, 2014.
21 Jelin, *Los trabajos de la memoria.*
22 Pierre Nora, *Les lieux de mémoire* (Paris: Editions Gallimard, 1997).
23 Rafael Quishpe, "Los excombatientes y la memoria: Tensiones y retos de la memoria colectiva construida por las FARC en el posconflicto colombiano," *Análisis Político* 31, no. 93 (2018): 93–114.
24 Valeria Posada, "Historia Rev(b)elada: La voz guerrillera que narra el conflicto en *Desenterrando memorias*," *Cuadernos de Curaduría*, no. 16 (Bogotá: Museo Nacional de Colombia, 2020).
25 Inti Maleywa and Martín Batalla, *Desenterrando memorias*, Part I, Comité Comunicaciones La Guajira, February 27, 2017, YouTube video, 3:58. www.youtube.com/watch?v=D2CeXtaF6Hc
26 FEDEGAN created on September 30, 2005, the National Appreciation Day for Cattle Ranchers in honor of José Raimundo Sojo Zambrano, "viciously murdered by the FARC."
27 Fundación Colombiana de Ganaderos (FUNDAGAN) which founded the Observatory of Human Rights and International Humanitarian Law.
28 Fundación Colombiana de Ganaderos, *Acabar con el olvido* (Bogotá: Fundagán, 2012).
29 FUNDAGÁN, *Acabar con el olvido*, segundo informe (Bogotá: Fundagán, 2013), 16, 17.
30 FUNDAGÁN, *Acabar con el olvido*, segundo informe, 21–22.
31 FUNDAGÁN, *Acabar con el olvido*, segundo informe, 22.
32 Her brother, Guillermo Gaviria, was governor of Antioquia and an ardent supporter of the peace cause. In a symbolic march with the movement for nonviolence, he was kidnapped by the FARC and killed by the same armed group thirteen months later.
33 "Declaración conjunta de víctimas de las FARC," Asociación Colombiana de Oficiales en Retiro de las Fuerzas Militares, ACORE, November 11, 2014. www.acore.org.co/boletin-acore/declaracion-conjunta-de-victimas-de-las-farc/
34 "Declaración conjunta."

35 On FEVCOL's page, it is possible to trace the Federation's openly declared support of Iván Duque, the candidate who "does care about victims" in 2018.
36 The delegations elaborated selection criteria that was enacted by the UNDP, the Episcopal Conference, and the National University of Colombia, following a series of regional meetings. According to an analysis by *Verdad Abierta*, the aim of including "victims of all kinds of perpetrators was fulfilled in general terms. Military, businesspeople, trade unionists, religious, academics, journalists, and ordinary people were present in Havana. Of the sixty of them, not only did victims of state security forces and the FARC participate, but also [victims] of paramilitaries, the ELN, criminal gangs, and a single case of a community affected by mining multinationals." See https://verdadabierta.com/victimas-en-la-habana-los-que-fueron-y-los-que-faltaron/
37 In Colombia, there is widespread discussion of new cycles of violence being fueled by inherited hate. Elkin Rubiano proposes that "instead of inherited hatred, we promote accounts of inherited pain. Hatred divides, while pain equalizes, creating bonds of solidarity." Elkin Rubiano, "Las cenizas y los rastros: La emergencia forense en el arte colombiano," in *Narrativas artísticas del conflicto armado colombiano: Pluralidad, memorias e interpelaciones*, ed. María Emma Wills (Bogotá: Ediciones Uniandes, 2021), 27–64.
38 "La increíble fuerza del perdón en el proceso de paz" [The Incredible Power of Forgiveness in the Peace Process], *Semana*, September 16, 2016.
39 Fundación Ideas para la Paz, "Radiografía del nuevo acuerdo. ¿Qué tanto se renegoció?" 2016. www.ideaspaz.org/especiales/nuevo-acuerdo/
40 The six negotiation points were (1) comprehensive rural reform, (2) political participation and democratization, (3) the end of the conflict, (4) illicit drugs, (5) victims of the armed conflict, (6) implementation, verification and public endorsement. See: www.portalparalapaz.gov.co/publicaciones/811/explicacion-puntos-del-acuerdo/, accessed October 6, 2021.
41 Jennifer McCoy and Murat Somer, "Toward a Theory of Pernicious Polarization and How It Harms Democracies: Comparative Evidence and Possible Remedies," *Annals of the American Academy of Political and Social Science* 681, no. 1 (2019): 234–271.
42 "Víctimas retiran sus archivos del Centro de Memoria por nuevo director" [Victims Take Back Their Archives from the Center for Memory Because of Director] *El Tiempo*, February 21, 2019.
43 Diego Alarcón, "El Centro Nacional de Memoria Histórica está en crisis (y el Museo de Memoria también)" [The National Center for Historic Memory is in Crisis (and the Memory Museum, too)], *Arcadia*, February 25, 2020.
44 "Así censuró Darío Acevedo a la Unión Patriótica" [How Darío Acevedo Censored the Patriotic Union], *Noticias Uno*, November 4, 2019. www.youtube.com/watch?v=fW53WmL4eoA
45 "Saying a river can speak . . . forgive me folks, that is well and good for a literary work, for poetry. Let's remember how Maduro was mocked for talking to a little bird." According to audio that was later leaked by *Noticias Uno*, this is how Darío Acevedo expressed his disagreement with the victims' metaphors. Mario Figueroa, "Para matar de nuevo a las víctimas" [Killing the Victims Again], *Un Periódico*, November 7, 2019.
46 AUTO AT 031–2021, Peace Tribunal Section on Absence of Acknowledgment of Truth and Responsibility for Facts and Conduct, JEP, Bogotá, MARCH 5, 2021.

47 The full Spanish name is "sala de reconocimiento, de verdad, de responsabilidad y de determinación de los hechos y conductas de reconocimiento" [Acknowledgement of Truth and Responsibility of Facts and Conduct Section]. See a list of JEP sections and chambers at: www.jep.gov.co/JEP/Paginas/Salas-de-la-JEP.aspx
48 See www.youtube.com/watch?v=p3HO61AyOGA&t=2483s
49 See www.youtube.com/watch?v=y3iKE7peqt8&t=269s
50 See https://comisiondelaverdad.co/actualidad/noticias/ingrid-betancourt-comission-verdad-secuestro-colombia-sin-guerra
51 Although the indirect "we were able" sounds distant from the "we committed" utterance expected in an Acknowledgement of Responsibility process, Ubaldo Zúñiga, a former member of the FARC's 57th Front acknowledged that the FARC, far from representing the interests of indigenous communities from their own alterity, violently imposed themselves and inflicted irreparable damage. *Truth Dialogue: Truth from an Indigenous Perspective*, streamed on October 23, 2020. www.youtube.com/watch?v=kBox7JPTfPw&t=38s
52 Tzvetan Todorov, *La memoria, ¿un remedio contra el mal?* (Barcelona: Arcadia, 2013).
53 Steve Stern, "De la memoria suelta a la memoria emblemática: Hacia el recordar y el olvidar como proceso histórico (Chile, 1973–1998)," in *Las conmemoraciones: Las disputas en las fechas "in-felices,"* comp. Elizabeth Jenin (Madrid: Siglo XXI editores, 2002), 11–33.
54 Gustavo Petro, Discurso en el lanzamiento del Informe Final de la Comisión de la Verdad, Teatro Jorge Eliécer Gaitán, 27 de junio, 2022.
55 Lemaitre, Alape, Londoño and Arandia participated in the Hearing of Recongnition of Macro-case 01 (kidnappings by FARC-EP) that took place in Bogotá beginning on June 21. For day 1: www.youtube.com/watch?v=KckiSIEZRcY; day 2: www.youtube.com/watch?v=yhy5DP1s_R4; for day 3: www.youtube.com/watch?v=Q1T1Gr_AanU.

19 Rendering the Unheard-of Believable

On *Fragmentos* by Doris Salcedo and *Duelos* by Clemencia Echeverri

María del Rosario Acosta López

In the following pages I would like to tackle a question that has surfaced now and again in my work for several years, namely: What role has contemporary art played in Colombia by consistently denouncing the various forms of institutional oblivion wrought by the normalization of violence during the country's armed conflict? On different occasions, I have tried to show how specific artworks, in determinate contexts, have managed to envision plausible ways of giving shape to and materializing alternative, non-institutional modes of memorialization and resistance to forgetting.[1] I have framed my efforts in this direction as contributions to a project that I describe, in broad terms, as the production of alternative grammars of listening. By which I mean that, in view of the various levels and kinds of silencing that violence is known to produce, we should urgently question the criteria that determine what is and is not made audible, and thereby, what is and is not considered memorable, politically recognizable, and historically indexable.[2]

Considering the difficulty of finding ways of representing what has been excluded from the historical record and, most importantly, the effects of such modes of silencing, I have argued that art introduces new *frameworks of meaning* ("grammars") through which we may be able to bring *the unheard of* into audibility. My use of the expression "the unheard-of" in this context is informed by the double meaning of the Spanish adjectival noun "*lo inaudito*," which denotes both something that resists being integrated into any narrative, such that, for that very reason, it remains to some extent beyond the reach of perception (inaudible)—even for an ear that is willing to listen for and to it; and something that exceeds everything that we accept as possible and ethically tolerable (something outrageous or inadmissible).

In the first section, I begin by explaining in further detail why I regard this notion of "listening to the unheard-of" as a crucial conceptual framework for reflecting on memory and memorialization in the context of the Colombian armed conflict. In the second and third sections, I take this

DOI: 10.4324/9781003048152-26

framework as a point of departure for approaching two artworks that brilliantly give voice, body, and materiality to this idea—two works that, moreover, came at a decisive moment in Colombia, both from a historical and from a political point of view.[3] These are *Fragmentos* (Fragments, 2018), the counter-monument designed by Doris Salcedo as the first of three monuments commissioned as part of the Havana peace agreement between the FARC guerrillas and the Colombian government;[4] and *Duelos* (Mournings, 2019), a video installation by Clemencia Echeverri selected to inaugurate Salcedo's counter-monument as an exhibition space.[5]

I should mention that *Fragmentos* was inaugurated during the early days of Iván Duque's administration, after he won the elections by openly criticizing the peace agreement signed by his predecessor Juan Manuel Santos,[6] and consequently both the agreement and the memorialization initiatives attached to it came under the threat of being dismantled during his government. Given these circumstances, I am unable, in my analysis of these works, to set aside the political commitments that stem from my own stance against any political attempt to discredit the agreement and undermine its implementation. For these reasons, I also find it important, at this very moment, to attend to the singular gestures to which both Salcedo and Echeverri introduce us with their works, and to examine, as I intend to do in the following pages, how each explores the possibility of providing a site and a body to a kind of memory that is able to resist two equally dangerous pitfalls: that of forgetting and erasing and that of the urge to shape remembrance as something closed and definitive. I am interested, then, in a kind of memory work that understands the task of remembrance as the constitution of *a site where open forms of listening may occur* and where the repercussions and implications of this openness are to be embraced.

Memory as a Site for Listening: "To Render Our Lives Believable"

In his acceptance speech for the 1982 Nobel Prize in Literature, Gabriel García Márquez depicted Latin American reality as caught in a "crux of solitude" that set specific conditions for writers like himself:

> I dare to think that it is this outsized reality, and not just its literary expression, that has deserved the attention of the Swedish Academy of Letters. A reality not of paper, but one that lives within us and determines each instant of our countless daily deaths. . . . Poets and beggars, musicians and prophets, warriors and scoundrels, all creatures of that unbridled reality, we have had to ask but little of imagination, for our crucial problem has been *a lack of conventional means to render our lives believable*. This, my friends, is the crux of our solitude.[7]

What could these words mean to us today in Colombia, after more than 50 years of armed conflict and 70 years of "unbridled" violence, of "countless daily deaths," whose excesses seem to defy in each case any conventional schemata and all of our conceptual resources? Given its oblique and prolonged nature, the conflict is in itself already a complex historical artifact, not to mention the different modes of silencing that have been institutionalized by violence and the ensuing theoretical quandaries surrounding its historicization. But that is not all. The construction of memory in Colombia must also deal with the fact that the reality that awaits and demands to be told—to be heard and remembered—exceeds in each case the mechanisms by which we usually account for and represent the world.[8] This, we might say, is the contemporary form of the "crux" described by García Márquez: How can we render *believable* lives that would otherwise seem so implausible?

When it is extreme, as it often has been in Colombia, violence has that strange quality that Hannah Arendt described as a "horrific originality."[9] That is, there are moments when violence goes beyond *destruction* and brings about something *entirely new*, something previously unimagined—realities so unheard of that we must grapple with the absence of conceptual mechanisms that might allow us to apprehend, represent, and make sense of them. In other words, extreme violence does not simply destroy whatever it touches but also our capacity to name it—and, beyond that, to think, imagine, and understand it. This is what Arendt expounds at the end of her book *The Origins of Totalitarianism*, where she herself takes upon the difficult exercise of listening to and attempting to make sense of testimonies from the Nazi concentration camps that overwhelmed—at the time, as they still do now—the powers of imagination.[10]

The reality these testimonies struggle to convey is, writes Arendt, "too monstrous," so much that those who try to offer an account of the horror of the camps will have:

> an inherent tendency to run away from the experience; instinctively or rationally . . . [they] are so much aware of the terrible abyss that separates the world of the living from that of the living dead, that they cannot supply anything more than a series of remembered occurrences that must seem just as incredible to those who relate them as to their audience.[11]

As Arendt puts it, "the peculiar unreality and *lack of credibility* that characterize all reports from the concentration camps" is such that even those who speak from experience are "often assailed by doubts with regard to [their] own truthfulness, as though [they] had mistaken a nightmare for reality."[12] Although these remarks are made in a context that differs from the specifically colonial and postcolonial varieties of violence to which García Márquez refers in his speech,[13] they are helpful in drawing our attention back to the singular *incredibility* of the stories that emerge out of unbridled manifestations of the reality of violence. These struggles with credibility are not simply the result of a voluntary skepticism on the part of those who listen to such stories; they can also be seen as an almost inevitable reaction—which, as Arendt shows, is shared even by those who have survived and attempted to tell their own experiences—to the *unheard-of* nature of the harm, the pain, and the damage that violence can cause.

Arguably, *the unheard-of*, as a concept spanning the distance between the two meanings outlined earlier, can be said to capture what is at stake in both Arendt's analysis and in the words of García Márquez: It is because we still lack categories to name, think, and denounce such degrees of violence that we refuse to acknowledge their possibility—to hear them as something *believable*—and, for precisely this reason, they are ultimately classed under the category of the "unbelievable." Extreme violence, in its horrific originality, both outrages and renders us incapable of listening by depriving us of the resources—semantic, aesthetic, and even bodily—through which we might hope to grasp it. Such violence can, at best, paralyze us or, worse, leave us incredulous, for accepting its reality, would entail the vanishing of the world as we understand and perceive it, along with its meanings. As Arendt explains:

> There are no parallels to the life in the concentration camps. Its horror can never be fully embraced by the imagination for the very reason that it stands outside of life and death. It can never be fully reported for the very reason that the survivor returns to the world of the living, which makes it impossible for him [or her] to believe fully in his [or her] own past experiences.[14]

Stories that come from environments that have been produced and reproduced by extreme violence remind us of those pages from *One Hundred Years of Solitude* where a plague of insomnia overtakes an entire town, bringing about a state of permanent hallucination in which things become progressively detached from the names that single them out:

> The most fearsome part of the sickness of insomnia was not the impossibility of sleeping, for the body did not feel any fatigue at all, but its inexorable evolution toward a more critical manifestation: a loss of memory. . . . [W]hen the sick person became used to their state of vigil, the recollection of their childhood began to be erased from their memory, then the name and notion of things, and finally the identity of people and even the awareness of their own being.[15]

In places like those described by Arendt and García Márquez, where it is impossible to distinguish reality from nightmare, where the problem is not simply that dreams may be mistaken for reality, but that reality is dreamed and imagined both in the name and in the company of others, the present comes to be inhabited by the clamor of the living and the dead in a state of "hallucinated lucidity" where the excess of images and the lack of words ultimately bring about, as the novel puts it, an "idiocy that has no past."[16]

This dearth of resources for *rendering our lives believable* entails that whatever remains inaudible is confined to a region beyond memory. Oblivion is therefore, in these cases, not only the result of a conscious decision to silence, erase, and cover our ears when confronted with the stories that horror produces. Where violence has destroyed all available frameworks of meaning, and thus all the dimensions through which we might perceive and apprehend the world, oblivion also embodies an induced paralysis of our capacity to so much as *imagine* a site, a point of encounter, a mode of communication that could actively enable an attentive listening, not only of something that we are told but precisely of that which does not let itself be told—and yet must be remembered. "Only the fearful imagination," Arendt tells us, "can afford to keep thinking about"—and I would add here: listening to—"horrors."[17] It is imagination that allows us to find within ourselves, precisely in a place where "we have lost the yardsticks by which to measure, and rules with which to subsume the particular," the possibility "to understand without preconceived categories and to judge without the set of customary rules."[18] The imagination alone is capable of understanding "something that has damaged our categories of thought and our standards of judgment."[19]

In my view, this unique set of conditions that García Márquez and Arendt articulate in different ways can prove extremely useful in our efforts to understand the crucial challenge faced by those who engage in the work of memory in Colombia. Instead of placing the focus on the "truthfulness" of a reality that will not allow itself to be proven or verified, they suggest that we attune ourselves to the difficulties that adhere in the *representation* of a violence that radically overtaxes all conventional means. They both invite us to think of the task of *listening* without pre-conceived frames of sense as a responsibility; that is, if to listen is to strive for representation in an encounter with something that is seemingly un-representable. When we lack the resources with which to render those stories into "believable lives," we should not be looking for ways to confirm, corroborate, or insert them into a linear chronology so as to invest them with a traditional (conventional) intelligibility and historicality. The question is rather how to create sites—imaginary, if necessary—where these stories may be told without being excluded as unbelievable.[20] The question, then, is whether we can understand memory—and thus history, which will now have little

Rendering the Unheard-of Believable 403

to do with "monumental" history—as the task of conceiving and enabling real and active forms of listening.[21] How can we produce the conditions, the frameworks of meaning, the resources that would render *believable*—and therefore truly audible, even in their silences and erasures—the lives and stories of violence, and the truths (understood as plural and as possible precisely under different conditions of enunciation) that emerge from the conflict. How, ultimately, can we offer companionship to those who endure unspeakable loss, and a space for mourning, remembrance, and grieving for horrors that do not always allow themselves to be told, but that nonetheless demand to be listened to.

I would like to take these questions as guidelines as I now turn my attention to *Fragmentos* and *Duelos*. I aim to explore the way in which these two individual works imagine and shape other modes of making memory and building history; more than anything else, I am interested in their capacity to make us aware of the need to create sites and temporalities where these tasks can be carried out under the imperative of a radical listening. Spaces and times where the fragments of memory can be heard as fragments without being compelled into a univocal order and appearance, because their legitimacy is no longer grounded on an objective correspondence, proven and tested against reality, but on the evidence (as clear as can be) of the ethical claim that constitutes them: That we must urgently find a grammar for them—a framework of meaning, both perceptual and semantic—that may allow them to become audible in their contradictions, excesses, and breaks. Most importantly, these grammars should convey the strength by which such fragments call to us from out of that place, between life and death, from whence the testimonies of the survivors speak to us, reminding us that there can be no future—indeed, that there cannot even be a present—unless we are able to sense that irregular ground that seems to open beneath our feet; the ground where the pain, the excess, the multiple silences, and the damaged spellings transform into strength, into a point of departure and the hinge of a promise—contentious, always open to dispute, barely murmured—of a different future and a different way of listening.[22]

Fragmentos: To Forge Pain into Strength

Now, how can all of this be constructed within and translated into a material register? What kind of gestures could make available this mode of listening by configuring it, testing it out, and drawing us both to enact it and to heed the risks it entails? Upon walking into *Fragmentos*, one gets a sense of the space's eloquence and of its potential pull on those who have the privilege of visiting it. Whoever crosses the threshold is first welcomed by the ruins of the old nineteenth-century house that hosts Salcedo's counter-monument.²³ Carefully preserved, these ruins mark out the space as a site that is itself already an in-between: A space that remains somewhere between the past and the present, life and death, the ruin and something that dwells on within. The space thus demarcated by ruins is divided into three areas, two of which are to be used as exhibition spaces and one equipped for video projection, although they all merge through connecting glass walls, as if to remind us that there is no inside or outside of violence, just as there is no inside or outside of pain. When we decide to enter this space—exposing ourselves by accepting its invitation to exit the outside—we discover that it is not simply an interior to be in, for we also feel ourselves called upon to experience what it is like to be *on* it, to let the place hold our weight and be moved by the uneven floor tiles whose folds compel us to mind each step to avoid tripping, thus barring the possibility of strolling idly around the room. The past here is not simply a support, it also propels us toward the present—with a thrust that is no less measured, careful, conscious of the risks entailed by making one's way through an unstable, broken, and fragmented terrain.

There is no way to describe what it is like to walk into *Fragmentos* without quoting the figures that welcome us silently with a discrete but incisive presence: This jagged horizontal plane is made out of 1,296 individual tiles, themselves made out of 70 tons of melted weapons that were then molded into 50 zinc sheets hammered and shaped by 12 women, survivors of sexual violence during the armed conflict, who projected onto the metal the resilience with which they, after enduring so many hardships, decided to remain strong in the face of atrocity. Ángela Escobar, one of these 12 women, describes her experience in a video that meets visitors as they enter the space: She tells us:

> We hammered for days powered by the hatred that sexual violence left in us and by the anger of war. But through this we were able to free ourselves of those feelings. Now we are standing on the weapons, and the weapons are no longer a weight on the country.²⁴

When I first visited *Fragmentos*, before it had officially opened to the public, the place was still under construction and the video was not yet part of the visit. There is, on the one hand, something very moving about the video. The women's testimonies compel us to hear what the floor on its own might not manage to convey; the shot of an expansive white cloth covered with each of the weapons turned in by the guerrilla fighters, captured by a drone that slowly rises (it is interesting to note how here a mechanism of war has been appropriated for and invested with an ethical-testimonial task), effectively conveys the true scale of the surrender; the undeniably beautiful images of the weapons melting and being poured into the molds

Rendering the Unheard-of Believable 405

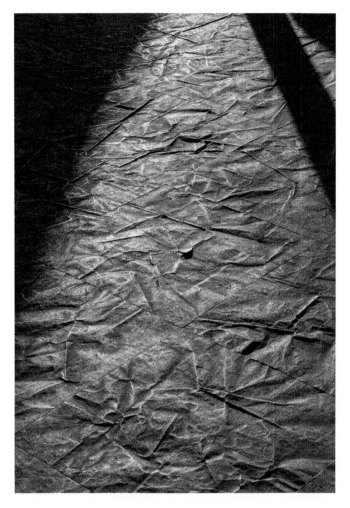

Figure 19.1 Detail of Doris Salcedo's *Fragmentos*, thousands of FARC's weapons melted and recast as 1296 tiles. Courtesy of Doris Salcedo.

that yield the sheets allow us to confirm—although to dwell on it may paradoxically lead us to doubt—that the memorial was indeed made out of the weapons turned in by the FARC. The video, however, can instill a kind of cynical distance in the viewer precisely through its explicit attempts to move: The carefully curated music, the slightly staged images of the women who, after working at the studio, now find themselves literally "put on display"—like museum objects—between the ruins of the house, the police commander who is filmed uttering "wise" words as an example of a job well done. Not to mention the fact that no former guerrilla member is interviewed or speaks in the video, we just see a few shots of FARC members without ever listening to them—this is one of the many ways in which *Fragmentos* silences their voices. Their arms melted and fused into one is a powerful image, as the aforementioned quote reveals, but it also risks burying in those tiles the individual stories that each of those weapons would have told otherwise.[25]

The video also reinforces a critique raised by philosopher Luciana Cadahia when Salcedos's counter-monument opened its doors: *Fragmentos*, Cadahia argued, replays the most traditional and patriarchal division of gender roles in both war and peace—while the men sign the peace treaty and turn in their weapons, the women are left to deal with the process of "mourning." It is undoubtedly an insightful reading—all the more so if we bear in mind that *Duelos*, whose title refers directly to mourning, is also the work of a woman artist who, as we will see, likewise developed her piece in collaboration with women whose sons were victims of forced disappearance. From a certain point of view, then, the video does seem to corroborate Cadahia's suspicions with respect to the memorial.[26]

And yet, these suspicions are not enough to dim completely the work's reverberations. To experience *Fragmentos* is to tread on a floor forged with and through pain and tenacity—the tenacity of survival—and to hear the sounds of the hammers striking the tiles as they echo through the room. To move across this space is to live in it and to lend an ear to its silences. In their many folds, the tiles preserve the *mark* of a pain now *inscribed* onto a material that was once the very source and means of violence, and which now sustains a powerful act of resistance ("now we are standing on the weapons"). What is thus *written* in this space is something that cannot be said aloud but whose eloquent silence nonetheless communicates, forcefully, through the very act of deforming and reshaping these tiles. There is something here, in the quiet dialogue between the space, the inside and outside of the gallery, and the uneven tiles that overwhelm us in their spectacular presence, that no longer represents war and that lays an uneven ground for the possibility of a present that is committed to its remembrance.

Here, then, Colombia's history of violence is translated into a history of resistance, of tenacity and resilience. The story told here is that of a capacity to stand over that history of violence, even if what comes from it is something other than words, perhaps simply the very gesture of having survived. Like the floor that shapes it, this can be a form of survival that persists quietly and patiently without drawing attention to itself. Because the memorial both is and is not there, these tiles, which at first may have been the sole protagonists of the space, are now to be inhabited by other modes of representation, by multiple ways of telling the history of Colombian conflict and of dealing with the difficulties of its memorialization

Figure 19.2 Fragmentos, room view. Courtesy of Doris Salcedo.

and the challenges of its remembrance. Dozens of artists will be invited to exhibit in these rooms during the next 53 years—equivalent to the officially recognized duration of the conflict—and they will be able to use the space to forge history and memory in other ways, to produce remembrance and find ways of resisting its disappearance. The temporality of the space is thus structured by a sustained engagement with an open form of listening, one that the Colombian state must support (and the National Museum must guarantee).[27] The effort required for elaborating a memory and a counter-memory of the conflict will thus become audible, visible, and perceptible here in its myriad forms of representation.

Salcedo has often stated that the purpose of a counter-monument is not to tell History, with a capital H, to offer a triumphalist account of the facts or to establish a range of valid meanings in advance. Instead, it should aim to make the present sensitive to a plurality of pasts that resist disappearance, including those that do not let themselves be told, represented, or collected in official narratives. The floor tiles and the open space demarcated by *Fragmentos* are there to enable other modes of resonance for sounds that might otherwise remain unheard. Thus, by stressing the idea of a counter-monument, Salcedo reminds us that when we are dealing with a past yet to be produced, we should not aspire to the monumentality of history understood as a discursive regime that settles on a *true* account and a *single* meaning. Instead, we should cultivate the kind of gesture that she has often accomplished herself in her artworks: that of *denouncing* the fact that there still are unheard-of voices (even if no one can hear them anymore), of *being there for* those whose mourning has been stolen from memory, and of *inscribing* the very mark of oblivion, for in Colombia, history is not just erased but also made and remade by oblivion.[28]

Although Salcedo has enacted this gesture in many different ways throughout her works, her way of doing so in *Fragmentos* is singular. The work responds to its historical moment and takes sides in a present that, all uncertainty notwithstanding, has placed its trust in the end of the war. In that sense, there is a telling distinction to be made between *Fragmentos* and other works by Salcedo. Let's take one among many to gauge the significance and singularity of the decisions taken by Salcedo in developing *Fragmentos* vis-à-vis the main corpus of her work, and the awareness therefore that this piece seems to enact with regards to the concrete role of the counter-memorial and of Salcedo's own role as an artist in this context—a role she has consistently embraced in ways that may often warrant some qualms, but which are unequivocally political.

In *Disremembered III* (2014), conceived in preparation for Salcedo's first major retrospective at Chicago's Museum of Contemporary Art, we see thousands of burnt needles that pierce and tear a piece of barely perceptible silk, clinging to a ghostly shirt-like body as it hovers from the wall. The work lends itself to view and yet conceals itself, putting its own visibility into question. One doubts whether it is there, present; from certain angles, it can be mistaken for a drawing sketched in pencil—and from others, it seems to vanish from view completely. The curator of the retrospective, Julie Rodríguez, told me that Salcedo produced the piece in response to her encounters with mothers from Chicago's South Side who had lost their children to "gang violence"—a euphemism often used to obscure the structural nature of police violence against African-Americans in this city where historical racism is paradigmatically instantiated and translates into alarming statistics. In *Disremembered* a pain that cannot be shed covers the body like a second skin—it is worn *a flor de piel* (to use a Spanish expression that points back to another of Salcedo's works and which signals the point at which emotions can be said to "bloom" onto the skin) while also taking on the potential role of a protective layer, a shield against any attempt at external contact, for this shirt is as painful to touch as it is to wear. The work speaks to us about that state of latency brought on by loss and mourning that cannot be worked through, when the unresolved nature of violent deaths prevents those afflicted by them from even remembering them, from grasping them as part of the past, which, in turn, leads the loss to repeat itself over and over, obsessively, as a present. The fragility of the fabric, along with its painful and yet imperceptible presence, the sculptural quality that places the piece somewhere between a drawing and a carving, an inscription that at once marks out and distances itself from a field of tangibility; everything in this work speaks to us about something that Salcedo has described, on multiple occasions, as the core of her work as an artist: "the work of mourning and its topology."

Although *Fragmentos* also places itself at this interstice between loss and its working through, its mode of appeal seems different. When we enter this site and walk on these tiles, as our imagination turns to the places inhabited by the voices of those who are no longer with us, and of those of us who will now have to make a place for ourselves, here, by taking on the responsibility of an attentive listening, we sense that Salcedo is no longer summoning a pain that "blooms onto the skin." What we have here is not an image of a mourning trapped in its own impossibility, nor even the timid promise of life that sometimes peaks through some of her works. Instead, we sense an affirmation, or at least a wager in favor of the possibility that one day we might no longer bear and wear this pain on our skin—that we will no longer have to. *Fragmentos* seems to suggest that the marks this pain leaves on the body and the repetition of its occasionally insatiable demands do not exhaust the sense of the present, and that, like Ángela Escobar, we may yet be able to say that the pain is now beneath our feet, that it grounds us and sustains us—that we are standing on it.

The robustness of a ground that holds us is connected to the gesture by which a material so deeply charged with a history of violence has been transformed into beauty. This beauty compels us to occupy and redistribute the space of our own present; it dares us to translate and transform, materialize, and forge pain into strength, summoning us into memory and into the memory of that strength. Of course, there is no denying that Salcedo runs the risk of aestheticization, and that further risks are entailed by the symbolism of a molten pain poured into a homogeneous structure that is ultimately too full, we might say, to make room for anything other than itself. The weightiness, the solidity, the ultimate monumentality of the tiles, which can almost be said to stand out from the ground, might not be enough for—and might even contradict—the kind of resistance needed to counter the temptation to monumentalize memory.[29]

These are indeed some of the risks that Salcedo has taken by producing a memorial like *Fragmentos*. Perhaps what I have described as an almost self-effacing floor that draws attention away from itself can be perceived nonetheless as the excess of a presence that, by being too grounded, too stable, too assured of its own strength, might hinder the sensitivity to fragmentation that is required for any real and open experience of listening. It may indeed be inaccurate to describe a work like *Fragmentos* as instilling a sense of disorientation. But it would be just as inaccurate to say that the counter-monument leaves us with a sense of definite resolution and closure. It is rather an invitation to enter what I am calling a "site for believability," where the truth is not something to be proven but rather something to be experienced as the possibility and opening of the very act that could convey it, with all the interruptions, subversions, and contradictions that populate those sites that remain at the threshold between life and death, past and present, pain and resilience, as we wait and search for the appropriate grammars to render such truths audible.

Duelos: The Sound of Disappearance

If the floor in *Fragmentos* can strike us as all too solid, something in the work might yet unsettle the sense of a misplaced firmness beneath our feet. This is exactly what Clemencia Echeverri taps into in her work *Duelos*, the first installation to take over *Fragmentos* as an exhibition space. In complete darkness, we see a video projected onto the floor where mounds of earth seem to rise out of the cold tiles, abruptly transforming the room into a space inhabited by specters. Still at first, the earth slowly begins to speak to us. We hear a rumor, a murmur, whispers that gradually become louder—or maybe it is just that it is getting harder and harder not to hear them—and whose shrill—feminine?—intensity and fragmented, interrupted—although stubborn and insistent—texture contrast with a masculine background voice, a low, clean, even chanting that reminds us of the gravity of Gregorian choirs.[30] The voices—reduced to their "essential phonetic elements"[31]—are fragments of the testimonies of the women relatives of those who lie buried under a field of rubble and who can no longer take up a place in the space of the sonorous.

These images and sounds over which we stand refer to those who disappeared and whose bodies lie buried in La Escombrera, a place in Medellín that is literally known as "The Rubble Dump." The site of La Escombrera is a conspicuous scar on the city landscape.[32] A dumping ground for ruins and residues hides the ghastly secret—an all-too-open secret—of a series of "operations" (code-named Mariscal, Potestad, Antorcha, and Orión) during which Colombia's Army, National Police, and Air Force, in collaboration with paramilitary groups, disappeared a number of young people yet to be determined from the Comuna 13 neighborhood (the figure is somewhere between 100 and 300, though the official count is 138). After a series of failed attempts by the Attorney General Office, the authorities have still not been able to retrieve the remains of those whose mutilated bodies were dumped on this site.

A relentless murmur whispers without saying anything, seemingly rising from the earth as it gradually begins to shift under our feet—shaking with the rhythms of the mumbling voices, as if heeding their injunction to unbury, to remove, to scratch the earth that hides the bodies for which this choir of voices is calling. Suddenly, these voices are overshadowed by

Rendering the Unheard-of Believable 411

Figure 19.3 Detail of dump truck in Clemencia Echeverri's *Duelos*, video installation. Courtesy of Clemencia Echeverri/Studio 2019.

a thundering noise: in videos now projected on the walls, we see a dump truck about to unload its contents onto that lifeless mountain, and we hear the sudden, clattering sound of debris falling on the heap followed by the sound of rubble falling on rubble, piling layer upon layer of waste. Likewise, these layers of noise now pile over the sound of the voices, preventing us from understanding what they might be saying beneath the mountain's deafening clamor. As the projections multiply—first one, then two, and eventually one for every wall in the room—one cannot help but feel surrounded by this tumultuous and repeated collapsing, crashing, and booming through which the work aims perhaps to create an audible counterpart to the experience of silencing it aims to denounce.[33]

We realize then that this shifting earth, which loosens the tiles of *Fragmentos* and makes them resonate above the empty metal of which they are made (and which itself shelters so many lifeless voices), is not moving so as to overturn, dig out, or release something that lies buried there and calls out for visibility. It is rather an earth that swallows us, gives us vertigo, and confirms what La Escombrera silences out loud: The disappearance of those bodies that, known to be there, will not be found; the impossibility of a mourning for those voices that call for these bodies; and the impotence that comes with feeling in your own body if only an inkling of the awareness of that impossibility.[34] Thus, the earth from which nothing emerges

Figure 19.4 Detail of stones in Clemencia Echeverri's *Duelos*, video installation. Courtesy of Clemencia Echeverri/Studio 2019.

becomes a host of stones that now heap over one another, absent tombstones for those graves, a proper name for each but an epitaph for none.

With this installation, Echeverri has found a way to invest disappearance with a body and a voice, a sound of its own. Walking into that dark room is like entering the digestive apparatus of Colombia's ghastly state and parastate system that has fostered the atrocity of forced disappearance. As we stand in the middle of the room—assuming we are able to stay on our feet, the feeling of dizziness is unavoidable—we feel little by little how these bodies that we do not see, but that we know are lying there, beneath our feet, around us, are "digested," as if there were a gigantic stomach churning and revolving us[35] as it tries to cast from itself what it has decided to brand as disposable—dispensable, "killable."[36]

La Escombrera is the perfect symbol—perfectly horrifying—of what Banu Bargu, coining a new category by which to understand the workings of state power in the postcolonial context, describes as the "sovereignty of erasure."[37] According to Bargu, in the postcolony, the state's absence of legitimacy paradoxically coincides with its nearly paranoid urge to become legitimate, or better, to compensate for that absence of legitimacy with the excessive spectacle of its power. What is publicly displayed in this spectacle, however, is no longer the state's right to punish, but its capacity to erase—albeit spectacularly—the traces of its own violence.[38] An erasure that displays itself as spectacular, there can be no better way to describe La Escombrera. The mountain could not be said to hide—on the contrary, it rises gigantically for everyone to see, concealing a secret that "everybody knows" but nobody dares to proclaim. And if an accusation was made, or a suit filed, there is not even any need to play deaf: Even when the state agrees to a forensic inquiry—an operation that Echeverri tracks with her camera, lucidly picking up what is paradoxical about such a search—there is no way of proving what happened there. The very spectacle of the state's capacity to render invisible, to obliterate—not only to take life and to brand as *killable* but to disappear the body—and to thereby erase from itself all trace of that dark and ghastly side is thus constitutive of and essential to its operation.[39]

And yet, as Juan Diego Pérez argues in his reading of Echeverri's work, the rubble as a notion entails a resistance to any will and attempt to vanish. Something about the rubble outstrips this power to erase and obliterate, a remainder that will not allow itself to be disposed of

> as an abandoned remainder, piled up and exposed to degradation like fistfuls of dust in the air, the rubble is nonetheless always an obstacle, however precarious and obstinate in its precarity, to the consummation of the violence of disappearance; and so, an obstacle that reminds us of the impossible erasure. . . . [T]he presence of the rubble reminds us that there is no body, no matter how vulnerable its appearance in the world, whose matter can (be made to) disappear outright, without remainder.[40]

Indeed, if *Duelos* manages to communicate the modes in which disappearance, in the ghastliest of its forms, is carried out through a visible theatricality, the work simultaneously stages an effective resistance to the spectacle of disappearance by turning to the register of sound in order to interrupt the mode of functioning by which power has come to monopolize the grammar of the visual. *Duelos* audibly presents what is not seen, presents it as something that never ceases to make itself heard, to resonate. No matter how thunderous the rumor of the falling rubble, the voices are, if not noisier, more persistent in their murmuring. They return, they fill up the empty space—the voice here becomes space, as though to inhabit the place that the body of the disappeared can no longer occupy.

"How does one speak to a disappeared person?" wonders José Roca in his reading of *Duelos*.[41] I think that the work rather allows us to imagine how those who are disappeared can speak to us from out of that place of resistance to oblivion, calling out for a place in the regime of the audible, since the most that the state and its mechanisms can and mean to do is to keep them from *view*. How, then, does the disappeared person speak to us?—or, if one prefers—and ultimately this is perhaps what makes the work so powerful—how is it that disappearance becomes audible and resonant, and will not desist in sounding? What is the sound of its unforgivable erasure? What is the sound of the voices of those who do not cease to look for the bodies? What is the resonance of the state's efforts (and those of the parastate, the legal and paralegal violences that have forged such a singularly sinister alliance in Colombia) to silence them? And how is it that nonetheless their resonant noise is both indigestible and impossible to ignore?

I think, then, that the work calls us not with the demand to utter a discourse, a claim, or a reply. Instead, it summons us to listen, to imagine how we can receive and interpret the voice that speaks from out of that place between life and death, which in radically challenging all the categories available to us for making sense of the world, runs the danger of going unperceived amidst the rubble that, in such a case, would finally manage to bury definitively what the work so powerfully endeavors to exhume. This may not yet be a resource by which we could finally grasp those seemingly impossible lives as something believable, lives whose impossibility is framed by a visual narrative that the state controls and struggles to perpetuate. But it is at least our first glimpse of a sonorous grammar that could be powerful enough to render them audible—and thereby to interrupt and disarticulate the regime that, try as it might to hide them, will not be successful in silencing them forever.

Notes

The following is an edited version of a text of the same title published in Spanish in Rodrigo Parrini and María Victoria Uribe, eds., *La violencia y su sombra: Reflexiones desde Colombia y México* (Mexico City and Bogotá: Universidad Autónoma Metropolitana and Universidad del Rosario, 2021), 227–265. I have made considerable changes and adapted the text before and after its translation into English, to make it a contribution to this volume. A briefer version was read during an opening event for *Fragmentos* organized by Colombia's National Museum. I thank its former director, Daniel Castro, and the event's co-organizer, Carolina Vanegas, for inviting me to contribute. This version was translated by Tupac Cruz, additional copyediting by Benjamin Brewer. Julian Rios-Acuña also worked on the translation of the first two sections, which were taken as point of departure for Cruz's final translation. Many thanks go to all of them for rendering my work so faithfully and beautifully into English.

1 See, among others, María del Rosario Acosta and Grupo Ley y Violencia, *Resistencias al olvido: Memoria y arte en Colombia* (Bogotá: Universidad de los Andes, 2016), and the special issue of *Diálogo: A Journal for Latin American Studies* 22, no. 2 (2019), titled "Art and Memory in Colombia: Resistance to Forgetfulness," which I edited in collaboration with A. Duarte and J. D. Pérez.

2 I develop this in further detail in my forthcoming book *Gramáticas de la escucha: Pensar la memoria después del trauma* (Barcelona: Herder, 2022). See also María del Rosario Acosta López, "*Gramáticas de lo inaudito* as Decolonial Grammars: Notes for a Decolonization of Memory," *Research in Phenomenology* 52, no. 2 (2022): 203–222. Even though the content of her research is very different, Ana María Ochoa Gautier's *Aurality* (Durham: Duke University Press, 2014) has been an inspiration for my own project, which is also in tune

with attending to other "ontologies and epistemologies of the acoustic," (3) as she describes it in her book, and to the kinds of silencing that can come from hegemonic constitutions of what counts or not as a voice worthy of register.
3 I do not mean to suggest that these works by Salcedo and Echeverri "exemplify" the thoughts I outline here. Instead, in a kind of reverse exercise, I would argue that the idea of a grammar of the unheard-of can only gain purchase through the existence of spaces that, by virtue of their materiality and temporality, create the uniquely potent opening of which certain artworks are capable.
4 As stated in the text of the Final Peace Agreement, article 3.1.7: "*the weapons surrendered by the FARC-EP will be used to build 3 monuments: one located in the United Nations building, one in the Republic of Cuba, and one in Colombian territory, in a site to be determined by the political organization that will emerge from the transformation of the FARC-EP, in agreement with the National Government.*" In an official announcement issued on April 27, 2018, the Ministry of Culture named Mario Opazo as the artist selected to work on the New York monument. The person who will create the monument in Cuba is yet to be decided.
5 Alongside Echeverri's installation a work by Felipe Arturo titled *Antibalas* [Bullet-proof] was also selected. I will not discuss Arturo's work in this text.
6 Since his arrival in office, Duque conspicuously endeavored to disassemble many key components of the peace agreement, ignoring the time-sensitive implementation of many of the points agreed upon and appointing officials to lead key institutions like the National Center for Historical Memory who clearly intended to cement an official and unilateral memory of Colombia's armed conflict. I do not have space here to dwell on these specific circumstances, but it is crucial to bear this context in mind if we are to understand the important role that works such as Salcedo's counter-monument have to play in Colombia's current political environment.
7 Gabriel García Márquez, "The Solitude of Latin America," Nobel Lecture, December 8, 1982. www.nobelprize.org/prizes/literature/1982/marquez/lecture/. My italics.
8 I have argued this point in detail in my discussion of the structural challenges that constrain the construction of historical memory in Colombia in my essay "Gramáticas de la escucha: Aproximaciones filosóficas a la construcción de memoria histórica," *Ideas y valores* LXVIII, supplement no. 5 (2019): 59–79. See also Acosta López, "*Gramáticas de lo inaudito* as Decolonial Grammars."
9 Hannah Arendt, *Essays in Understanding* (New York: Schocken, 1994), 309.
10 See also the powerful reading Didi-Huberman proposes of Arendt's dictum in relation to the question of the representability/imaginability of the camps; Georges Didi-Huberman, *Images in Spite of All: For Photographs from Auschwitz* (Chicago: The University of Chicago Press, 2008).
11 Hannah Arendt, *The Origins of Totalitarianism* (New York: Harcourt, 1967), 441.
12 Arendt, *Origins*, 438, 439. My italics.
13 It could be said, moreover, that to conceive the violence of the camps as "paradigmatic," as Arendt does, is yet again to erase and deny the magnitude of colonial violence. I have analyzed García Márquez's statement in relation to this particular concern in "*Gramáticas de lo inaudito* as Decolonial Grammars," 211.
14 Arendt, *Origins*, 444. For a more detailed reading of these passages by Arendt, where I draw further links to the question of listening that I will also address below, see my essay "Arendt on Totalitarianism as Structural Violence: Towards

New Grammars of Listening," in *Logics of Genocide: The Structures of Violence and the Contemporary World*, eds. Anne O'Byrne and Martin Shuster (Bloomington: Indiana University Press, 2020), 173–186. On García Márquez and the conception and enactment of aesthetic resources to denounce and represent the impossibility of a complete apprehension of violence, see my essay "One Hundred Years of Forgottenness: Aesth-Ethics of Memory in Latin America," *Philosophical Readings* XI, no. 3 (2019): 163–171.

15 Gabriel García Márquez, *One Hundred Years of Solitude*, translated by Gregory Rabassa (New York: Harper Perennial, 2006), 43–44. Trans. modified.
16 García Márquez, *One Hundred Years*, 44.
17 Arendt, *Origins*, 441.
18 Arendt, *Essays in Understanding*, 321.
19 Arendt, *Essays in Understanding*, 321.
20 On the connections between history and invention, and the idea of an "invention of history" in the double sense of the genitive as an essential task for a decolonization of memory, see Acosta López, "*Gramáticas de lo inaudito* as Decolonial Grammars," 218ff.
21 My remarks should not be taken to imply that the juridical and historical dimensions of listening are not fundamental. My claim is rather that what cannot meet these conditions of "truthfulness" should not therefore be cast aside into oblivion.
22 Even though I cannot work out explicitly here all the sources and authors who inform my approach to the question of memory building in Colombia, it is important for me to acknowledge the immense influence that many of the researchers working for the Grupo de Memoria Histórica (GMH), and then the Centro Nacional de Memoria Histórica, have had over my work. The works of María Emma Wills, Pilar Riaño-Alcalá, María Victoria Uribe, Alejandro Castillejo, and Gonzalo Sánchez, to name just a few, are essential points of reference for my own inquiry into the challenges of theorizing memory in the context of Colombia's current political and historical situation. The work done by the Truth Commission, as can be consulted in their recently issued final report (2022), is also a fundamental reference for what it means to "listen" as an end in itself in the context of the state's duty to repair. For a retrospective analysis of memory work in Colombia, from the GMH to the present, see the book I have edited with support of the World Humanities Report, funded by the Mellon Foundation, María del Rosario Acosta López, *Memory Work in Colombia: Past and Present Experiences, Legacies for the Future* (The World Humanities Report: South America [CHCI], 2023).
23 The concept of a counter-monument emerged out of debates around the possibility and ethics of representing the Nazi holocaust. I have opted not to contextualize Salcedo's counter-monument along these lines precisely to avoid inscribing *Fragmentos* within a conceptual framework that is rooted in European history and cannot give an account or elaborate the specific discursive position required for a discussion of violence in Colombia. For just this reason, I have turned to García Márquez's way of arguing for the necessity of anti-monumental and fragmentary forms of representation. For a classical account of the notion of counter-monument, see James Young, "Teaching German Memory and Countermemory: The End of the Holocaust Monument in Germany," in *Teaching the Representation of the Holocaust*, eds. M. Hirsch and I. Kacandes (New York: The Modern Languages Association of America, 2014), 274–285.
24 A version of the video can be seen here: www.youtube.com/watch?v=d7rAb2O0JV8

25 I have to thank Íngrid Johanna Bolívar for pointing to this silenced side of the work. Her own research on what she calls the "emotional value" of the discourses articulated by both former paramilitary members and FARC ex-combattants emphasizes the importance of listening to those stories in their singular historical contexts. See *Discursos emocionales y experiencias de la política* (Bogotá: Universidad de los Andes, 2006).

26 Most of Cadahia's criticisms were shared through her twitter and facebook accounts, and I have reproduced them here with her authorization. For a very suggestive proposal for subverting that gender division—based on a reading of *Antigone* understood as the classical locus of its interruption, see Luciana Cadahia, "Su voz desatará tu lengua: Antígona, lo femenino y lo plebeyo," *Ideas y valores* LXVIII, supplement no. 5 (2019): 129–149.

27 That this is a government-administered space is symbolically important but also opens the space to a political instrumentalization of which we have already started to see some instances. In the context of the 2021 National Strike (the continuation of the 2019 "paro nacional," known as "el estallido" for some of its most important actors), Iván Duque decided to utilize the space to stage a dialogue with religious leaders and victims of the conflict, in order to exemplify a "peaceful dialogue" vis-à-vis his interpretation of the National Strike as unnecessarily violent and conducted by criminal forces. Artist Doris Salcedo denounced the fact and the scandalous implications of using the space—which at the time had also an ongoing exhibition by the artist Francis Alÿs, who decided then to withdraw his work from the space. See among others the note in *El Espectador* and in *Hyperallergic*.

28 See my essay "Las fragilidades de la memoria: Duelo y resistencia al olvido en el arte colombiano (Muñoz, Salcedo, Echavarría)," in Acosta López, ed., *Resistencias al olvido*, 23–48.

29 See the responses to my reading of *Fragmentos*, in particular those by Isabella Vergara and Gwendolen Pare, compiled in "Debates," *Ideas y valores* LXVIII, supplement no. 5 (2019): 224–262.

30 The male voice parts were performed by Negro Billy, an Afro-Colombian musician who recently passed away. As Echeverri told me, he sang "as if for his own burial."

31 See David Medina, "Una imagen resonante," in the exhibition catalog *Duelos*, ed. Clemencia Echeverri (Bogotá: Museo Nacional de Colombia and Mincultura, 2019), 106. The final voice arrangement by singer Ximena Bernal is a musical composition, a spectral analysis, a sort of whispered funeral chant.

32 This is how Laura Flórez described it in a symposium on *Duelos* of which I was a participant, held in *Fragmentos* on November 16, 2019.

33 "Resistance is unlikely: One can always close one's eyes to avoid getting involved with the unnameable; to cover one's ears is much harder," José Roca, "¿Y cuándo vuelve el desaparecido? Cada vez que lo trae el pensamiento," in *Duelos*, 28.

34 According to estimates, it would take over four million dollars to exhume what may be Latin America's largest shallow grave. See Roca, "¿Y cuándo vuelve el desaparecido?," 36.

35 I owe the image of *Duelos* as a gigantic digestive apparatus to Rafik Neme, who shared his experience of the work with me after our joint visit.

36 The expression comes from Giorgio Agamben, though I bring it up mostly in light of recent work by Adriana Cavarero as it is taken up by Jaime Santamaría, who has built on ideas also by Achille Mbembe and Rita Laura Segato to

analyze Colombia's unique modality of *necropolitics*, the result of a ghastly alliance between the state and paramilitary organizations. See for instance Jaime Santamaría, "La masacre de El Salado como paradigma de violencia soberana paramilitar," *Eidos* 34 (2020): 161–190.
37 See Banu Bargu, "Sovereignty as Erasure: Rethinking Enforced Disappearances," *Qui Parle: Critical Humanities and Social Sciences* 23, no. 1 (2014): 35–75.
38 According to Bargu "sovereignty is not the absence of violence or domination but the ability to assert their *erasability* as the ultimate proof of power;" see "Sovereignty as Erasure," 62.
39 In the postcolonial state, as Mbembe has accurately shown, the exercise of necroviolence is not accidental but constitutive of sovereignty. See Achille Mbembe, "Necropolitics," *Public Culture* 15, no. 1 (2002): 11–40.
40 Juan Diego Pérez, "Escombros sonoros, afectos dolientes," in *Duelos*, 82.
41 Roca, "¿Y cuándo vuelve el desaparecido?" 36.

20 "We Gave Them Names"
Exhumations, Peace Agreement, and Social Reparation in Bojayá, Chocó, Colombia

Pilar Riaño-Alcalá in collaboration with José de la Cruz Valencia, Natalia Quiceno Toro, and Camila Orjuela Villanueva

On November 11, 2019, the remains of 102 *Bojayaceños* [people of Bojayá], massacred in the church of Bellavista on May 2, 2002, and associated events, returned to their territory. As a large United Nations helicopter carrying 49 white coffins for the dead children, and 53 brown coffins for the dead adults, landed in the Middle Atrato town of Vigía del Fuerte, relatives, *cantadoras* [singers of *alabaos*, traditional Afro-Colombian funerary songs], elders, and members of the Committee for the Rights of the Victims of Bojayá witnessed their return to the territory and to finally conduct a proper burial.[1] One by one, the coffins were carried and ceremonially placed on the wooden platform built for the occasion in a large boat dressed with white flowers. Then, as the air and river filled with the powerful voices of the cantadoras intoning alabaos for the dead, they began their last river journey. Four other boats, where hundreds of relatives, community members, and institutional companions traveled, accompanied the river journey that first brought them to the church where they were killed, and later to the town of Bellavista Nueva for their wake and final burial.

The reunion between the living and the dead was part of the forensic and accompaniment process undertaken by the community to properly identify, care, and bury their dead. It resulted from years of struggle and the constant interpellation of the Committee for the Rights of the Victims of Bojayá before the Colombian state, transitional justice institutions, and the international community. I examine here how the demand to exhume, identify, and properly bury those massacred in 2002 became a critical component of the peace negotiations (2011–2016) and agreement (2016) between the Revolutionary Armed Forces of Colombia (FARC) and the Colombian government of Juan Manuel Santos. The chapter discusses the search and exhumation of victims of mass violence as practices of historical clarification, peace sustainability, and justice in the afterlives of mass violence.

DOI: 10.4324/9781003048152-27

This chapter illustrates how, due to its magnitude and technical and political complexity, the forensic process in Bojayá constitutes a pioneering and unprecedented one in Colombia. It required working with the remains of 102 people, searching and excavations in eight different sites and the challenges in identification resulting from the high level of mixing and fragmentation of bones, deterioration of the soft tissue due to the humidity and acidity of the land and soil in a rainforest jungle, and ongoing armed violence in the region. The process was also unprecedented in the scope of inter-institutional commitment and coordination with over 15 national and international institutions involved and hundreds of experts and professionals,[2] and the active engagement of more than 2,000 family members, knowledge keepers, and social leaders from the region. The process in Bojayá involved, in similar unprecedented ways, extensive inter-institutional coordination, governmental and non-governmental organizations, as well as the United Nations, and a commitment to resources and to work from an ethnic territorial perspective.[3] The process in Bojayá was also the first one to incorporate the recognition of the cultural and political autonomy and self-determination of Black and Indigenous communities in exhumation, identification, and burial protocols that seek to respond to communities' standards of comprehensive reparation and restitution of dignity, their ancestral knowledges, and practices to care for the dead.[4]

In a collaborative research exercise, I worked with leader José de la Cruz Valencia, 22 community members and knowledge keepers, and researchers Natalia Quiceno Toro (associate professor at the Universidad de Antioquia) and Camila Orjuela Villanueva (independent researcher) to document this process and examine what happens when community-based memory processes, mortuary rituals, and ancestral knowledge intersect with forensic procedures, transitional justice interventions, and scientific expertise. I first came to Bojayá in 2008 as an investigator and co-rapporteur of the historical memory report on the massacre by the Historical Memory Group (GMH in Spanish).[5] Since then, I have conducted ethnographic work in the region, examining sound memory and the labor of cantadoras as practices of social repair,[6] and exhumation and burial processes as practices of prolonged wake in the afterlives of mass violence.[7]

Questions on how to properly search and exhume victims of political violence are critical today as the discovery of mass and unmarked graves and the search for the missing worldwide give evidence of past and ongoing colonial and political violence through genocide, war, torture, land dispossession, and forced displacement. However, forensic knowledge and practice remain problematically tied to Western scientific standards and disregard the affected communities' knowledge, needs, and mortuary

Figure 20.1 Boat on the Atrato river carrying the coffins of the victims of the massacre of Bojayá. Courtesy of Comité por los Derechos de las Víctimas de Bojayá.

practices. This observation is critical in present times as the search for the missing and exhumations have become a centerpiece of transitional justice and human rights processes worldwide.[8] In a 2015 global survey on mass graves and exhumations, Ferrándiz, Robben, and Wilson concluded that measures of success in exhumations after mass violence remained tied to Western scientific standards of proper identification and disregard the knowledge, needs, and mortuary practices of the communities affected by mass violence.[9] Similarly, a 2014 report by Equitas—a non-governmental organization accompanying forensic processes in Colombia—highlighted the existing conflict in current methods of exhuming mass graves between standardized forensic procedures based primarily on scientific data collection and the knowledge and cultural traditions of Indigenous and Black communities.[10]

In Colombia, between 2005 and 2022 alone, 6,695 graves were found, and 99,235 people have been identified as missing in the context of a war spanning five decades.[11] A disproportionate number of these victims are from Indigenous and Black communities. Today, elders, leaders, and memory keepers from these communities are leading processes on the rightful ceremonies and practices to exhume, identify, and bury their dead, sometimes clashing with forensic scientific teams. I aim to show here how, within a transitional justice context, the community's vision of cultural and political autonomy combined with ancestral knowledge reframed forensic procedures of searching, exhuming, and identifying bodies into moments of caring and remembering the dead, repairing relationships with the territory, the families, and the dead, and as moments of evidence collecting for historical clarification.

The process was led by the Committee for the Rights of the Victims of Bojayá (the Committee, from now on). The incorporation of the Committee's vision of political and cultural autonomy, ancestral and scientific knowledge exchange, funerary rituals, and spiritual practices of care for the living and the dead showed a way to work toward decolonizing forensic, psychosocial, and judicial protocols. The process is evidence of work to decolonize transitional policies through enrichment of forensic and judicial protocols with local ways of dealing with death and spirits and horizontal collaboration. Scientific knowledge and mortuary ancestral knowledge met in a creative and sometimes conflictive tension that managed to promote measures of satisfaction for the survivors and relatives while transforming the logics of participation by actively involving the extended family, cantadoras, *rezanderos* [those leading the prayers for the dead during funerary rituals], midwives, traditional Emberá doctors, as well as local leaders and authorities. The story is one of the living restoring the identity and memory of their loved ones and memorializing their presence as an integral component of a scientific, reparative, and truth-seeking process.

The chapter is organized into three parts. The first provides a brief historical background to the modalities of violence in the Middle Atrato region since the 1980s. It also contextualizes death and disappearances in such region, the recurrence of violent deaths, known as "bad deaths," and their profound impacts due to the impossibility of conducting proper funerary rituals, and the unresolved presence of the dead in dreams and the territory. A second section examines how the community increased their demands for the exhumation after the case of the massacre of Bojayá became a central component of the peace negotiations between the FARC and the government in Havana, Cuba. The last section turns to the exhumation, identification, and return of the victims' remains to the territory, describing how knowledge keepers guided the process and the ritual, spiritual, and accompaniment practices they brought in dialogue with forensic procedures and protocols.

War in the Middle Atrato

The municipality of Bojayá in the Middle Atrato, department of Chocó, is located in a region rich in biodiversity in a mostly humid tropical forest that borders Panama and the Caribbean and Pacific coasts. The Pacific littoral is the largest contiguous area of Black presence in the Americas and the ancestral territory of the Indigenous Emberá peoples.[12] Between the 1980s and 2000s, towns along the Middle Atrato river lived in constant fear and under a critical humanitarian situation. The armed confrontations between the guerrillas and paramilitaries for the territorial control

"We Gave Them Names" 423

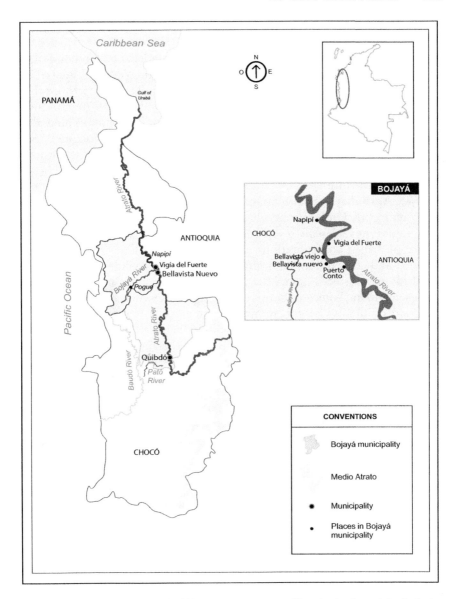

Map 20.1 Bojayá and the Middle Atrato Region, Chocó. Author: María Luisa Moreno.

of the region increased in the mid-1990s, as did the forced displacement, disappearances, selective assassinations, confinement, forced recruitment, and critical food insecurity of the Afro-Colombian and Indigenous inhabitants of the Middle Atrato. The territorial dispute reached a critical turn in April 2002 with the violent takeover of the town of Vigía del Fuerte by the FARC (across the river from Bojayá). Twenty-two policemen and nine civilians were killed and the paramilitary, under the command of "El Alemán," began to plan the takeover of Bojayá and Vigía del Fuerte. The dispute for territorial control was part of a broader dispute to establish strategic corridors toward the Caribbean and the interocean Atrato canal[13] for the drug and arms trades, resource-extraction, including mining along the Atrato, Baudó, and San Juan rivers,[14] and commercial logging.[15] Such a repertoire of violent interventions took place in a region that registered one of the highest rates of poverty, structural marginalization, and lack of basic infrastructure.

Since April that year, the communities of the Middle Atrato, the Diocese of Quibdó, the Ombudsman Office, and the United Nations had sent the Colombian government seven early warnings alerting them of the imminence of armed confrontations in Bellavista, as well as the confinement, hunger, and critical humanitarian situation of the civilian population. But the Colombian state ignored the urgent warnings, and the population was exposed and unprotected. In this context of mass violence, one of the deadliest war crimes in Colombian history, the massacre of Bojayá, occurred.[16] On May 2, 2002, after 12 days of infighting between the leftist Frente José María Córdoba of the FARC guerrilla and the right-wing Bloque Élmer Cárdenas of the paramilitary United Self-Defense Forces of Colombia (AUC), the FARC seized Bellavista, where the paramilitary had temporarily established their base of operations. As the confrontations intensified, over 300 Afro-Colombian elders, adults, youths, and children took refuge in the church. While the paramilitary barricaded themselves behind the church of Bellavista, using the civilians as a human shield, the FARC fired several homemade bomb cylinders. Before noon one of the cylinders landed and exploded in the church.[17] The sacred place of refuge became a scenario of horror, death, and injury.

The explosion killed 79 Bojayaceños, half children, and injured more than a hundred.[18] There were no Indigenous victims at the church because many Emberá who lived in the town of Bellavista had been displaced before the massacre. Those few remaining in town fled as the confrontations increased. They followed their displaced brothers and sisters traveling north of Bojayá River to seek refuge in the head of the rivers where they have ancestrally lived.[19] Afro-Colombian survivors massively fled the town amid the crossfire, leaving their dead and injured behind. After the pleas and demands from survivors to be allowed to return to the church and bury their dead, the FARC ordered that only a small delegation could return, giving them 24 hours. On May 3, a group of five volunteers, including the two town gravediggers, returned to the church to hastily bury their dead. Amid the crossfire, they collected the bodies of their dead, mangled and decomposing, and buried them in a mass grave. No relatives or mourners were present, and no rituals accompanied them. In the following days, thousands of people from the surrounding river communities were forcibly displaced. At the same time, the armed confrontation and assassinations continued, at least eight people were killed in the days that followed.[20] Nine days after the massacre, a forensic team from the Attorney General Office arrived with the plan to collect, identify, and bury the dead, but after a few days and with only three exhumed, they hurriedly left due to the intense crossfire and ongoing armed violence against the remaining population (disappearances, selective assassinations, and throwing of bodies in the rivers continued). A month later, another forensic team returned and exhumed the mass grave's remains, conducted in-site identifications and inspection, and buried the majority in the cemetery of Bellavista in an area highly exposed to river flooding. Once again, no relatives or community members were informed, present, or consulted. The results of the autopsies were not shared with the people of Bojayá.

The year 2002 marks a turning point in the war regionally and nationally, particularly in the government's discourse toward peace negotiations. In February 2002, Conservative president Andrés Pastrana—who won the elections in 1998 on the promise of signing a peace agreement with the leftist guerrilla—officially ended the fractured and failing peace talks with the FARC. The massacre in May 2002, a few months after the peace talks failed, was timely used by president Pastrana and the government of the United States to demonstrate a "global terrorist threat."[21] Pastrana used it too to pressure the European Union to include the FARC in their terrorist groups' list. Then, in June 2002, right-wing politician Álvaro Uribe won the elections and became president on an antiterrorism and anti-FARC agenda in the context of an international scenario dominated by a War on Terror after the events of September 11, 2001, in the United States.[22] Francisco Giraldo discusses various political uses of this emblematic massacre by three consecutive presidents. He shows Pastrana's discursive shift from one of peace dialogues as a way forward for Colombia to one of fighting terrorism through all the possible means.[23] Uribe maintained this discourse alive. By the time Juan Manuel Santos came into power in 2010, the discourse gradually shifted to respond to the Santos government's agenda to reach a peace agreement with the FARC. Santos' speeches and interventions often turned to Bojayá to speak about reconciliation, forgiveness, and victims' support and commitment to peace negotiations and future agreement. When he was awarded the Nobel Peace Prize in 2016, days after the failure of the peace referendum, he invited Leyner Palacios, leader of Bojayá, to join the delegation. Santos brought the personal story of Palacios in his Nobel speech to demonstrate the commitment of Colombian victims to peace. Months later, he and his wife went to Bojayá to announce the donation of the Nobel Prize's money to the reparation of the victims.[24]

Bad Deaths

The danger and climate of terror, massive forced displacement, and the constant surveillance and restrictions on locals gathering and traveling on the rivers hindered the possibility of taking proper care of the dead and the disappeared. The increasing number of "bad deaths"—a sudden violent death away from home or without the proper wake, protection, and burial rituals—in the late 1990s and during the 2000s fractured the relationship between the living and the dead that funerary practices maintain. For the Afro-Colombian communities, a nine-day wake, procession, burial, and rituals facilitate a harmonious departure of the soul.[25] The disturbance of these ancestral practices created collective angst over the lack of resolution for the dead.[26] Although there were no Indigenous victims in the massacre of Bojayá, these communities also experienced the increase in "bad deaths" of leaders and community members as a result of the killings, torture, and disappearances in the region and the dramatic increase in suicide among the young Emberá population in the Middle Atrato. These scenarios created deep angst and collective anxiety, and as Emberá leader and anthropologist Manyulo Apicana explains, fear for the harmful effects (including death and attacks) that the spirits of those who suffered a bad death and did not receive burial rituals may have on the living and the *jaibanas* [people with the power and knowledge to heal and protect life].[27]

Death, for the Afro-Colombian communities along the Atrato river, is a journey involving both the living and the dead. Afro-Colombian intellectual and cultural worker Ana Gilma Ayala explains that death does not break the ties between the living and the deceased but rather strengthens them.[28] This connection is sealed by a complex set of rituals that turns the dead into a living ancestor and the social character of the wake and burial. Similarly, for the Emberá, death is a journey and the dead possess a force that impacts the living and the territory. Funerary rituals among the Emberá ensure a "good death" and a journey across land and water that facilitates the departure and transition into the "world below." Emberá and Committee leader Delmiro Palacios explains the dead presence in the world of the living: "They listen to what we are talking about, the spirit of a dead person exists for us, for we the Emberá [they] exist as human beings." Leyner Palacios, leader of the Committee during the exhumations and one of the current commissioners of the Truth Commission of Colombia, remembers a young woman's testimony of her nightly dreams with her father and mother, who were killed in the massacre, asking her for water. The knowledge keepers explained that when a dead person asks for water in a dream, this reveals a demand for prayers. The problem with those who died in the massacre, they said, is that they were buried without proper rituals.

The force behind the struggle for the exhumation and proper identification of the victims of Bojayá results from a sense of shared responsibility among relatives and community members to properly care for their dead. This practice would allow them to repair the interrupted relation with their ancestors and reconnect the living and the dead worlds disrupted by violence. This vision of the rights and duties toward the survivors and the dead are part of a complex web of responsibilities that was clearly stated as a condition and core element in peacebuilding.

The Peace Process and Exhumations

The demand to know the location and identities of the victims in the events that took place between April and May 2002 remained unattended for over a decade. By the tenth commemoration of the massacre and as the exploratory phase of the peace negotiations began, the various organizations of Bojayá renewed the demands. They pressured the Colombian government to provide access to information about those killed in the massacre and related events. They approached the Attorney General Office and the National Institute of Legal Medicine and Forensic Sciences, demanding a response to the many unresolved questions and existing information gaps.[29] The Attorney General Office refused to provide access to information under the argument it was "reserved." In 2014, as the peace negotiations in Havana, Cuba, began to include and consult the victims, and Leyner Palacios came with the first delegation of victims, the FARC approached him, communicating their desire to make a formal apology. There were several reasons to select Bojayá as the site of their first public act of acknowledging responsibilities. First, FARC's legitimacy after the massacre was shattered. An act of recognition of responsibilities during negotiations carried a strong political and symbolic weight and demonstrated their commitment to the peace process, truth-telling, and accountability. In what has been referred to as the "age of apologies,"[30] the need to apologize forms a central component and condition to access transitional justice benefits worldwide. Similarly, apologies are a central feature of the various transitional justice laws implemented in Colombia since the 2005 Justice and Peace Law, later in the 2011 Victims Law, and in the 2016 Peace Agreement that created the Integral System of Truth, Justice, Reparation and No Repetition.[31] A key expectation is that the apology is offered in a public manner, is unequivocal, and includes a recognition of responsibilities.

Leyner Palacios shared the FARC's message when he returned to Bojayá and consulted with leaders and local organizations. Months later, a delegation representing various territorial organizations and victims from the region traveled to Havana. The representatives from Bojayá made it clear to the FARC and the High Commissioner for Peace that they would not consider the apology without the FARC committing first to stop all forms of armed harassment to the communities of the Middle Atrato. They also agreed that the leaders of Bojayá would consult with the Indigenous and Afro-Colombian communities about the intended apology and that the event of recognition would take place in Bojayá. The consulted communities agreed to listen to the FARC but demanded that all forms of armed harassment and restrictions on circulation, food access, and gathering be stopped immediately. On December 6, 2015, a FARC delegation led by Félix Antonio Muñoz Lascarro (alias Pastor Alape), then a member of the FARC secretariat and its spokesperson in the peace negotiations, traveled to Bojayá to recognize their responsibility for the massacre and present their apology. A total of eight members of the FARC came in the delegation. They came from Cuba and were unarmed.[32] The place of the symbolic event was the ruins of the building adjacent to the church of Bellavista Viejo, where the explosive artifact fell. The Committee invited the Indigenous Guard, an unarmed security force of Indigenous women and men from the Cauca region in southern Colombia, and the recently created Black Guard of Chocó to accompany and provide protection to the event as the community prohibited any armed presence. Hundreds of community members came, with several hoping it would become the opportunity to learn whether their relatives were alive or dead, where were they buried, or if there was any firm evidence of their disappearance.

On this day, Leyner Palacios spoke on behalf of the people of Bojayá. He read a statement with their vision for peace "from our territories." He reminded everyone that the massacre was a war crime with three responsible actors: the FARC that advanced the combat against the paramilitary amid the civilian population and threw several gas cylinders; the paramilitary that took the civilian population as a human shield; and the Colombian state that did not attend to the early alerts sent. A key element of their vision was that peacebuilding starts from acknowledging the painful memories of the horror in the region, mainly the uncertainty felt around those lost in the massacre. Palacios said:

> Our souls cannot find peace because we have not been able to mourn the little angels we lost, the pregnant women, mothers, fathers, brothers, sisters, cousins, nephews, grandparents, uncles, and aunts who were torn from our territory, because to this date, more than 13 years after this misfortune occurred, we have not been able to be certain which are their mortal remains, because the identification made by the Attorney General Office was insufficient and inefficient, to the point that we do not know if the names that appear on the graves in the Bellavista cemetery really correspond to each of our relatives. There are people

who died and do not appear there, nor do the children who died in the mothers' wombs. That is why we continue to cry and with this lament we demand the state to fulfill its duty.[33]

Calling upon FARC and the Colombian state to respect their autonomy as "ethnic peoples," they demanded the location and proper identification of all the victims, their rightful return and burial with dignity in their territory, and the construction of a memorial place where they could rest together. There was no doubt for the people of Bojayá that creating conditions for peace, reconciliation, and living together was intimately linked to acknowledging and acting upon their debt to their dead, and for this, they reiterated their demands for the search and identification of the victims. Death and the dead became vital agents in the process of building conditions for peace and for the negotiations. The FARC and the government committed to working toward this goal at the meeting. Thus, on October 17, 2015, the negotiating parties released a joint statement (Comunicado #62) that outlined initial steps for the "humanitarian search, location, identification and dignified return of the remains of persons given as disappeared in the context and due to the internal armed conflict." In the statement, they also announced a plan to strengthen the search, location, identification, and dignified return of the remains of the disappeared. The National Commission for the Search of Disappeared Persons was asked to outline recommendations to achieve this goal. In this context, the director of the National Institute of Legal Medicine, Carlos Valdés, was invited to work with the Commission in formulating a plan. The director, who earlier met with members of the Committee and recognized the errors and problems of the forensic work conducted in 2002, raised the need to "work in the cemetery of Bojayá and the need to respond to the victims in an organized and joint manner."[34]

In 2016, as steps were taken to implement these protocols, the Attorney General Office created the Transitional Justice Unit. The Unit took on coordinating the process with Bojayá, giving more momentum to the search, exhumation, and burial process.[35] Bojayá became the first case that resulted from the peace negotiations. Later in November 2016, in a tense and emotionally challenging meeting with hundreds of relatives, knowledge keepers, and Committee members, forensic experts from the Attorney General Office and Legal Medicine finally presented the results from the 2002 and 2004 necropsies.[36] The information and the questions and challenges posed by the relatives confirmed to community members the many errors, gaps, and difficulties of previous work: the high level of mixing of bodies and remains in the graves, the mistakes in the identification and individualization of the bones and in the location of the place where they were buried, the loss of bones and clothing, the discrepancies between written information and oral communications, the confirmation that several of the victims remain disappeared, and the many technical and procedural problems. Forensic experts acknowledged that only a new exhumation and individualization effort may provide proper answers.

The reports left everyone devastated and angry. Of particular concern was that people who were in the church and supposedly buried in the grave were now disappeared and that people may be praying to the wrong person in the cemetery. Argenio, the father of a boy who died in the church, voiced his concerns and demands when he learned that there was no trace or documentation on where his son may have been buried, saying, "the truth is that I want to see that you are going to solve the case of my boy who does not appear anywhere." Toward the end of the meeting, María Pascuala, who lost her parents and brother in the massacre and is one of the Committee leaders, concluded that the information provided at the meeting confirmed that "the Colombian state is definitely still in debt to us." María Pascuala said:

> You can see that in all the information presented, there are shortcomings, anguish, gaps, and we are left with everything. Why do I say this? Because they downloaded the information and María Pascuala's brother, Edison Palacios, is still totally disappeared, that is to say that the only thing we as a family have is his name on a piece of paper.

In a closed-door meeting, relatives and Committee members discussed whether or not to move forward with the exhumations. Leader José de la Cruz Valencia explained that the decision was difficult. They were fully aware that the search and exhumation will, hauntingly, "call back the pain," mainly because exhumations and second burials are not practiced in Afro-Colombian funerary rituals in the Middle Atrato region, and they are rare among the Emberá communities as well.[37] Nevertheless, the assembly decided they have a collective responsibility to their dead ancestors and that all the massacre's victims should be exhumed. "We," said Committee member Yuber Palacios, "decided to do something that in the history of the Atrato has never been seen before: Exhume our dead."

By 2017 when the exhumations began in Bojayá, the search for the disappeared and unidentified and clandestine graves had grown exponentially in Colombia. Women and relatives organized in over 100 collectives—such as the Madres de la Candelaria, Madres de los Falsos Positivos, or the women of the town of San Carlos—advanced the search for their missing relatives and were fighting against impunity and for the truth on what happened to them.[38] Additionally, the hints provided in confessions and declarations from former paramilitary and guerrilla commanders contributed to this growth. As a result, the search for the missing and exhumation gained momentum these years, becoming vital elements in the struggle for justice and truth. The exhumations in Bojayá were initiated by relatives and community members, as is the case with most of the exhumations of victims of political violence in Latin America.[39] It follows a pattern of participatory and politically engaged organization generally led by women that search for the missing, seeking any traces of their loved ones, and accompanying exhumation processes.[40] Additionally, the Bojayá case brought attention to the centrality of exhumations and restoring identity to the missing in creating and maintaining conditions for peace and as practices of repair.

Prolonged Wake and How to Properly Care for the Dead

By the time the exhumations began in May of 2017, the Committee and knowledge keepers shared with the institutions and stakeholders involved a vision and a set of principles that framed the exhumations in two intersecting lenses. First, a process inscribing forensic procedures and protocols of exhuming, identifying, and returning the remains of the dead in funerary rituals and traditional ceremonial practices of caring for the dead (I refer to this process as *forensics of care*). Second, an autonomous political movement of truth-seeking, historical clarification, and memorialization led by the community under the guidance of their knowledge keepers. Since they began the journey to identify and bury their dead, Black and Indigenous ways of understanding life and death and the responsibilities toward their dead guided the Committee's work. This inscription in a worldview and caring practices ensured the ethical, cultural, and political integrity of the process and conceived the exhumation process as a *prolonged wake*.

By deciding to exhume the remains of their loved ones, the communities of Bojayá made clear their demand that things had to be "done the right way" and respectfully. For this reason, as soon as the exhumation becomes viable, a group of *personas sabedoras* [knowledge keepers] is formed who, as Indigenous Emberá leader Delmiro Palacios says, assume the "great responsibility of spiritual accompaniment." According to leader and researcher José de la Cruz Valencia, the personas sabedoras are knowledgeable people experts in one or several specialties of ancestral knowledge, such as knowledge of plants and their uses; times of the moon, human anatomy, and climate; and deep understanding of the surrounding territory, the power of the secret word, and communicating with human and nonhuman spirits and sentient beings, such as the rivers, trees, and land.

In an unprecedented way, Afro-Colombian knowledge keepers advised and participated in the design of each process component. They trained forensic anthropologists, physicians, and other forensic experts as well as psychosocial and social work professionals on Afro-Colombian ways of understanding death and relating to dead people in the Middle Atrato

432 *Pilar Riaño-Alcalá et al.*

Figure 20.2 Ritual performed in Pogue before the exhumation begins. Courtesy of Comité por los Derechos de las Víctimas de Bojayá.

region, according to their age and manner of death and respectful forms and protocols to handle their remains. These manners of knowledge exchange between ancestral knowledge keepers and forensic science professionals accompanied the entire process up to the final burial. The intercultural dialogue highlighted how protection is one of the central elements of their accompaniment in both knowledges. For the first time in a mortuary ritual for Afro-Colombians in the Middle Atrato, the knowledge keepers saw it necessary to bring the spiritual work of the Indigenous brothers and sisters due to the spiritual risks that could be generated by removing the bodies of the dead and intervening in sacred spaces.

On the days of the exhumations, while the forensic team organized information, videos, and other types of records on the previous burials and necropsies in preparation for the exhumation, the Emberá *sabios* [wise person] and the jaibanas [with the power and knowledge to heal and protect life] conducted protection rituals of the exhumation sites. Jaibana Cresencio Dumaza, sabios herbalists Héctor Chami and Balbino Palacios brought their ancestral knowledge of the territory, the plants, and the spirits and conducted ceremonies that ensure the work is, in Héctor Chami's words, "positive and obtains the needed information." The ritual furthermore acknowledges the community's expectations for truth and is understood as creating the conditions to find needed information and evidence. Héctor Chami explains that in these moments, the deceased person's spirit or soul "can reveal what we are looking for." Such revelation will also "affect the site, and they [the forensic team] can access and do the relevant work." In this vision, protective rituals generate the affective and spiritual conditions needed to seek truth and justice and advance a proper exhumation.[41]

The praying and singing alabaos by Black cantadoras and rezanderos follow. Ereiza Palomeque, rezandera and cantadora, explains the meaning of this ritual work as accompanying the pain of the living and the dead and facilitating the transition to the "other world":

> We know that songs are for us like going to the other world, and prayer is like anything spiritual. . . . We believe that with prayer, that person will feel a moment of tranquility when arriving in the presence of the Lord.

Afro and Indigenous knowledge and ritual practices complement each other to guarantee protection. The work of the Indigenous knowledge keepers aims to protect the living from the spirits, understanding that there are good and bad spirits. As Emberá anthropologist Manyulo Chanapicama explains, the rituals conducted by the jaibana and the sabios in the cemeteries and exhumation places were "to protect the spirit of the people who are alive, since it can harm us if we do not do this ritual that the jaibana does."[42] The work of the Emberá knowledge keepers is fundamental since they carry out the work of preparing the territory and providing adequate and safe conditions for any intervention by the Afro-Colombian knowledge keepers and the forensic professionals. On the other hand, the work of Afro-Colombian knowledge keepers ensures the care of the souls and their proper resting, accompanying, and taking emotional and spiritual care of the family members. After the rituals, the anthropologists, topographers, photographers, and technicians begin their work of locating the graves, removing materials, and excavating with the help and guidance of local gravediggers. In this space of exhumation and cultural and knowledge exchange, family members and community members act as eyewitnesses of the conditions in which their relatives are found, how their search is carried out, and who remains disappeared. They attest to the proper recovery of their dead and accompany them throughout the excavation and procession to the temporary vaults. Days later, family members carry them in another march to the helicopter that will take them to the city of Medellín to start the appropriate identification and individualization process.

Similarly, during the days of the final burial, forensic professionals presented, in technical-scientific sessions with each family, the information on the circumstances and causes of death of their relatives, the traumatism suffered, and the results of the forensic analysis of the bodies that confirm

Figure 20.3 Relatives carrying the remains of their loved ones toward the temporary vaults. Courtesy of Comité por los Derechos de las Víctimas de Bojayá.

their identity. The families—who, throughout this process, provided their DNA, family trees, photos, stories, and documents—listen, ask questions, highlight inconsistencies and unanswered questions, and prepare messages they will place inside each coffin before closing. Cantadoras and rezanderos/as make themselves available to the families, aware of the sorrow generated by the description of the injuries and circumstances of the violent death of their family member, and later in the opening of coffins and first encounter with the remains, including pieces of clothing and accessories. In consultation with the families, they sing and pray to the dead and carefully wrap the bones and remains according to tradition: In white fabrics for the adults and colorful ones for children. These are reparative moments of mourning, encountering, and restoring individual and collective ties with the dead that illustrate forensics of care to challenge what Isaias Rojas describes as the narrow focus of transitional justice programs on "how to prevent the repetition of mass violence rather than the problem of how to dispatch the dead."[43] The meanings, temporalities, and knowledge at the base of the mortuary rituals and collective actions that repair the balance and maintain the movement of life in places like the Middle Atrato have a central place in transitional justice work and the construction and strengthening of peace processes.

Dignifying Their Name and Memory

One of the primary purposes of forensic work is the restitution of the identity of nameless bodies and those that disappear in the face of violence and atrocity.[44] But forensic procedures risk dehumanizing the dead through their practices of cataloging, storing, and referring to human remains. The view during the exhumations was rows of crosses whose only inscription was a number corresponding to the case number under which the records of each person are registered in forensic and legal archives. Erasing their names denied their agency and personhood, dehumanized them, and deepened a sense of mistreatment of the dead. As Committee members and relatives immersed themselves in the documents and information on each person killed and reviewed available information and forensic-related procedures with forensic experts, they became deeply unsettled with the use of numbers to refer to and speak about their dead.

An ethical principle in Afro-Colombian mortuary practices in the Middle Atrato region is to call a person by their name. Through the exhumations and later identification of the remains, the Committee continued to question how to relate and refer to those who died a violent death by stressing the use of names. Using their names was critical to the ethnic territorial perspective that the institutions agreed to respect and to the organization, protocols, and reimagining of exhumations as forensics of care. When knowledge keepers trained the forensic experts in Bogotá, they spoke about how the care for the dead and living is anchored in their territory, rivers and the forest, and, significantly, in naming the dead. Rezandero and cantador, Saulo Enrique Mosquera explains, "we told them how we considered that we had to call the dead; we gave them names." Saying their names, for the people of Bojayá, is an ethical and cultural duty. Leader and cantadora Máxima Asprilla reflects:

> Many people are sure that the number [in the cross] is their family [member] when in fact, it is not. So that served us as a tool so that they [the forensic professionals working on their identification] would give us a clearer reality, that they would individualize us, that even if it were a little tooth, they would not refer to it as a "miscellaneous" [as referred in forensic labs] about such a person. Because even if he is a hundred years old, we mention that person's name.

The names of those exhumed are first recalled during the day; before the exhumations begin, the communication team recorded their names with video and tape recorders. They also finish their daily register with a recording saying their names. Their names are recalled in each ritual happening during the day: In the signs that the children prepared and carried in the procession to the temporary vaults and in the quilt on the wall of the temporary vault where the women of the collective Guayacán wove the names of each person killed in the massacre so that, as cantadora Oneida Orejuela says, "they appear with their name." Naming is about restoring their presence and marking their absence in everyday action by infusing the territory and landscape with an audible presence: Say their names.

During the identification phase, the Committee and the advisory organization Equitas began a process of documentation and interviewing with 22 extended families to collect antemortem information.[45] The reconstruction exercise turned to orality and family memory—using memory, mapping, and storytelling sessions—and to recovering personal and family archives. This memory work contributed to and streamlined forensic procedures since non-Afro and non-Indigenous professionals faced many challenges understanding what constitutes a family, family relationships, levels of consanguinity, uses of surnames, the relationship between names and nicknames, and the forms of relatedness between Afro-Colombian families in the Middle Atrato. This innovative exercise of incorporating oral history and ancestral knowledge in gathering antemortem information offered a cultural perspective and a way of gathering information that resists the dehumanizing that occurs when the dead are registered with a number. It also challenged the assumption that historical clarification, identification, and evidence gathering are merely "technical" or "scientific" matters.

The documentation and material collected contributed enormously to the identification and recovery of the memory and identity restitution of those killed in the massacre. The collected information makes a critical contribution to the case, to the decisions on whose DNA samples may provide the needed information. It transforms their antemortem and overall identification protocols, as recognized by doctor Jennifer García:

> Taking those family trees is a spectacular job, yes? It has helped us so much to identify, as to say: "Look, I can't say who this person is, but she is a daughter of this man, because he has so many daughters of the same age," . . . if you have that family tree you can realize it and this for genetics is very important. Because you look at the family tree and say "this sample is more useful to me than this one.". . . And it has been an impressive help . . . we can differentiate them by sex, by age, and then one begins to look, that is, that information has been a wonderful thing.

Committee members continued to remind forensic experts that restoring the identity of the dead is not solely about probing DNA samples or dental cards, nor the result of a scientific assessment of the various facts and sources that provide evidence of whose bones are those. It is also about naming, caring, singing, and praying to them to restore their connection and status as *living ancestors*. In the context of such knowledge exchange and the innovations and cultural renewal it activated, death and the dead became critical sites and agents for the sustainability of peace processes and reconstituting life and death worlds. In this perspective, peacebuilding and gestures of repair constitute dynamic and active moments that require the engagement and agency of both the living and the dead.

Closing

The torture, gunshots, screams, threats, and the disposal of bodies in clandestine graves or rivers by the paramilitary, guerrilla, and the Army carved in the region a landscape of fear. It aimed to strip the missing and killed of humanity and identity. These forms of deafening violence and their imposed silences, according to Adriana Cavarero, seek to dehumanize the victim by turning their voices into unidentifiable screams or muteness or, in the case of disappearance and death, the eradication of any audible trace.[46] The many gestures of naming the dead and saying their names in Bojayá generated an affective space for being together as it marked a political act against silencing and dehumanizing practices. These acts inscribed the process of exhumations in a prolonged wake, that is, as a memorial practice that re-established the conditions for properly mourning the dead.[47] It acknowledged the political claims and vision of the knowledge keepers, Committee members, and the families on the conditions and forms to relate to the dead and the living together.[48] However, this is not a closed process nor a success story. Six people remain disappeared and several unresolved questions about the loss of bones and unclear information in necropsies remain. Up to 2022, only the FARC has acknowledged their responsibility for the war crime, and the judicial process on responsibilities has advanced little. In May 2022, on the 20th anniversary of the massacre, community leaders of Bojayá denounced the ongoing selective assassinations, forced recruitment, confinement, threats, racism, and climate of terror in the Middle Atrato and their fear that "another Bojayá" could happen anytime.

The search for the disappeared and the process of reassembling bodies, probing their identity, and returning them to the land and relatives are at the core of struggles for justice and against silencing in Latin America and many other regions of the world. It is also a growing area of practice by forensic sciences and communities that, as Anne Huffschmid has documented in Mexico, Argentina, and Guatemala, seek to contribute to restoring the person to the social world.[49] For the knowledge keepers, relatives, and members of the Committee, it was not enough to prove the identity of the dead and establish who the bones belong to, how they died, and returning them to their families. The reconstitution of their dead embedded a moral and reparative duty that goes beyond restoration into the social world of the living to confirm their identity and dignify their memory. It materialized an imaginative politics of cultural renewal rooted in the processes of becoming living ancestors and their recuperation in the worlds of the dead. In this manner, exhumation, identification, and burial processes were inscribed in the forensics of care and as components of a prolonged wake. The return into the social world was a political, moral, territorial, and ritual act that, as Isaias Rojas has argued for the Quechua women of Ayacucho, redraws the ontological boundaries between life and death.[50] It shows how questions of proper identification and burial are an ontological problem rather than a symbolic one. To reconstitute the dead into the social world is to reclaim their place as living dead in the complex ecology of the forest, the river, and the community. This view continues to inform the work of the Committee and their perspectives on peace, reparation, and senses of justice.

Notes

1 The municipality of Bojayá in the department of Chocó and the municipality of Vigía del Fuerte in the department of Antioquia make up the region known as the Middle Atrato.
2 For a description of the forensic, transitional justice, academic, and religious institutions involved and the roles that professionals mainly from the Victims Unit, the Attorney General Office, Legal Medicine, the United Nations, the National Center for Historical Memory and the Quibdó Diocese played in the process, see Comité por los Derechos de las Víctimas de Bojayá and Pilar Riaño, Natalia Quiceno and Camila Orjuela, *Los muertos de Bojayá son nuestros muertos: Exhumar, identificar, enterrar y acompañar en Bojayá, Chocó*, 2021. https://bojayacuentaexhumaciones.com/
3 Oficina en Colombia del Alto Comisionado de las Naciones Unidas, "Sistematización del acompañamiento y documentación de la participación de las víctimas de Bojayá, de la articulación interinstitucional y de la cooperación internacional en el proceso de búsqueda, exhumación, identificación, individualización y entrega digna" (Unpublished document, 2019).
4 The guidelines from government institutions responsible for exhumation and identification processes in the context of the armed conflict (up to 2019) instruct professionals to become familiar with local "uses and customs" and direct them to reach agreements with "traditional authorities." The directives rest on the knowledge, authority, expertise, and decision-making of the forensic teams and government institutions.
5 Centro Nacional de Memoria Histórica, *Bojayá: La guerra sin límites* (Bogotá: Ediciones Semana and Taurus, 2010).
6 See Pilar Riaño, "Poetics and Politics of Sound Memory and Social Repair in the Afterlives of Mass Violence: The Cantadoras of the Átrato River of Colombia," in *Remembering and Memorializing Violence: Transnational Feminist Dialogues*, eds. A. Crosby, M. de Alwis, and H. Evans (forthcoming); and Pilar Riaño-Alcalá and Ricardo Chaparro, "Cantando el sufrimiento del río: Memoria, poética y acción política de las cantadoras del Medio Atrato chocoano," *Revista Colombiana de Antropología* 56, no. 2 (2020): 79–110.

7 We conducted a participatory action research project, "Exhumations and Burial in Colombia: Strengthening Forensic Practices through Knowledge Exchange." It was supported by a University of British Columbia Wall Solutions award and led by José de la Cruz Valencia from the Committee for the Rights of the Victims of Bojayá and Pilar Riaño-Alcalá from the Institute for Social Justice, University of British Columbia.
8 Elizabeth Gessat-Anstett and Jean M. Dreyfuss, *Destruction and Human Remains: Disposal and Concealment in Genocide and Mass Violence* (Manchester: Manchester University Press, 2014); Francisco Ferrándiz, Antonious Robben, and Richard Wilson, *Necropolitics: Mass Graves and Exhumations in the Age of Human Rights* (Philadelphia: University of Pennsylvania Press, 2015).
9 Ferrándiz, Robben, and Wilson, *Necropolitics*.
10 Equitas, "Caso Bojayá, Informe de análisis de contexto: Análisis forense de los decesos asociados a la estrategia militar para el control territorial entre el grupo paramilitar Élmer Cárdenas de las Autodefensas Unidas de Colombia (AUC) y el grupo guerrillero del Bloque José María Córdoba de las Fuerzas Armadas Revolucionarias de Colombia-Ejército del Pueblo (FARC-EP)," April–May 2002–2014, 2018.
11 According to the Direction of Transitional Justice of the National Attorney Office, 6,605 graves have been identified, 8,135 bodies exhumed, and 4,547 returned to their relatives as of May 2022 (see www.fiscalia.gov.co/colombia/wp-content/uploads/2022-05-31-grube-estadistica.pdf). As of July 2022, The National Unit to Search for the Disappeared of Colombia records that 99,235 people have been reported as missing in the context of the armed conflict, and 90,088 have not been found (see https://ubpdbusquedadesaparecidos.co/sites/portal-de-datos/universo-de-personas-dadas-por-desaparecidas/).
12 Kiran Asher, *Black and Green: Afro-Colombians, Development and Nature in the Pacific Lowlands* (Durham: Duke University Press, 2009).
13 Martha Nubia Bello et al., *Bojayá, memoria y río: Violencia política, daño y reparación* (Bogotá: Universidad Nacional de Colombia, 2005).
14 Daniel Tubb, *Shifting Livelihoods: Gold Mining and Subsistence in the Chocó, Colombia* (Seattle: University of Washington Press, 2020).
15 Asher, *Black and Green*.
16 CNMH, *Bojayá: La guerra sin límites*; Equitas, "Caso Bojayá, Informe de análisis de contexto"; Oficina en Colombia del Alto Comisionado, "Sistematización."
17 A gas cylinder is a nonconventional and prohibited weapon built with a cylinder used for home cooking and filled with fuel and shrapnel inside a tube replete with dynamite. CNMH, *Bojayá: La guerra sin límites*.
18 Comité, *Los muertos de Bojayá*.
19 CNMH, *Bojayá: La guerra sin límites*; Comité, *Los muertos de Bojayá*.
20 Equitas, "Caso Bojayá, Informe de análisis de contexto."
21 Rojas quoted by Francisco Giraldo, "La masacre de Bojayá: Usos políticos de un recuerdo violento," *Anuario Colombiano de Historia Social y de la Cultura* 47, no. 2 (2020): 50.
22 See www.senalmemoria.co/articulos/conflicto-colombia-2002
23 Giraldo, "La masacre de Bojayá."
24 For a detailed description see Comité, *Los muertos de Bojayá*; and Giraldo, "La masacre de Bojayá."
25 Comité, *Los muertos de Bojayá*; Daniel Ruiz-Serna, *When Forests Run Amok: War and Its Afterlives in Indigenous and Afro-Colombian Territories* (Durham: Duke University Press, 2023).

26 Diego Cagüeñas Rozo, "Almas dañadas, rostro, perdón y milagro: Reflexiones a propósito de Bojayá, Chocó," *Estudios Políticos* 61 (2021): 48–71; Comité, *Los muertos de Bojayá*; Mauricio Pardo, "Movimentos negros na região do Pacífico colombiano: Organizações, violencia e territorio" (Florianópolis: Universidade Federal de Santa Catarina, 2016); Natalia Quiceno Toro, *Vivir sabroso: Luchas y movimientos afroatrateños en Bojayá, Chocó, Colombia* (Bogotá: Universidad del Rosario, 2016).
27 Anne M. Losonczy, "Murderous Spirits: Shamanic Interpretation of Armed Violence, Suicide, and Exhumation in the Economy of Death of the Emberá (Chocó, Antioquia, Colombia)," in *Amerindian Socio-Cosmologies between the Andes, Amazonia and Mesoamerica*, ed. E. Halbmayer (New York: Routledge, 2020), 330–344; Rodrigo Sepúlveda, "'Vivir las ideas, idear la vida': Adversidad, suicidio y flexibilidad en el ethos de los Emberá y Wounaan de Riosucio, Chocó," *Antípoda* 6 (January–June 2008): 245–269.
28 Ana Gilma Ayala, *Rituales mortuorios afroatrateños en el alto y medio Atrato* (Quibdó: Editorial Mundo Libro, 2011).
29 A detailed reconstruction of the steps taken can be found in Comité, *Los muertos de Bojayá*.
30 Nayanika Mookherjee et al., "The Ethics of Apology: A Set of Commentaries," *Critique of Anthropology* 29, no. 3 (2009): 345–366.
31 See www.minjusticia.gov.co/programas/justicia-transicional/colombia
32 *El Colombiano*, "Las FARC oyeron las peticiones de Bojayá," December 6, 2015.
33 Statement read by Leyner Palacios. Bojayá, Chocó, December 6, 2015.
34 Interview for the Committee, 2017.
35 Specifically, Grupo de Orientación y Registro de Casos de Víctimas de Justicia Transicional, GRUBE, assumes the task and responsibility.
36 In Colombia, until 2017, three government units were responsible for forensic processes related to the search for the disappeared and graves, exhumation, and identification. They were the National Attorney General Office (FGN), the National Institute of Legal Medicine and Forensic Science, and the police unit DIJIN. These units have a judicial mandate and character. The creation of the Unit to Search for Disappeared People (UBPD in Spanish) in 2017 as part of the Integral System of Transitional Justice constitutes a fourth one. The UPBD has an extrajudicial, humanitarian, and autonomous character and is expected to work in support of the victims and relatives. See https://ubpdbusquedadesaparecidos.co/
37 Although exhumations and second burials are practiced among the Emberá as part of a complex ritual that involves the jaibana, elders and relatives, they are only practiced under exceptional circumstances and/or in response to a demand from the dead. Manyulo Chanapicama explained that "the Emberá people as such does not practice exhumations; it is only practiced when there is a need" (personal communication). They avoid touching the remains of the dead for their harmful effect. The decision to conduct the exhumation and second burial require the careful interpretation of the signals, identification of the proper time to do it and a special type of ritual; see, *El segundo entierro de Alejandrino*, directed by Raúl Soto Rodríguez and Verdad Abierta, 75 min., 2011.
38 International Commission on Missing Persons, ICMP, "The Participation of the Families of Missing Persons as a Key to Progress: Recommendations to Strengthen the Efforts of Colombian Institutions," 2021. www.icmp.int/wp-content/uploads/2021/09/icmp-gr-col-099-1-doc-

"We Gave Them Names" 441

    participation-of-colombian-families-of-the-missing-as-key-to-progress.pdf. According to a 2019 report by the Commission, out of 36 organizations of relatives of the disappeared, 30 in Colombia are led by women; see multimedia by the Truth Commission of Colombia. https://www.comisiondelaverdad.co
39 Pamela Colombo, "Exhumations in Latin America," *Human Remains and Violence* 2, no. 2 (2016): 1–2.
40 ICMP, "The Participation."
41 Isaias Rojas-Perez, *Mourning Remains: State Atrocity, Exhumations, and Governing the Disappeared in Peru's Postwar Andes* (Stanford: Stanford University Press, 2017).
42 Personal communication with the author and Manyulo Chanapicama, August 1, 2023.
43 Rojas-Perez, *Mourning Remains*, 10.
44 Anne Huffsschmid, "Huesos y humanidad: Antropología forense y su poder constituyente ante la desaparición forzada," *Athenea Digital* 15, no. 3 (2015): 195–214.
45 The documentation of antemortem information is central to identifying bodies and remains. In this phase, data from the body on which forensic analysis is carried out is compared with biographical and other information on the deceased person.
46 Adriana Cavarero, *For More Than One Voice: Toward a Philosophy of Vocal Expression* (Stanford: Stanford University Press, 2005).
47 Memory Biwa, "'Weaving the Past with Threads of Memory': Narratives and Commemorations of the Colonial War in Southern Namibia" (Ph.D. dissertation, University of the Western Cape, 2012).
48 Biwa, "Weaving the Past"; Rojas-Perez, *Mourning Remains*.
49 Huffschmid, "Huesos y humanidad." See also Ferrándiz et al., *Necropolitics*; Victoria Sanford, *Buried Secrets: Truth and Human Rights in Guatemala* (New York: Palgrave Macmillan, 2004).
50 Rojas-Perez, *Mourning Remains*.

Bibliography

Abad Colorado, Jesús. "Jesús Abad Colorado: ¿Hasta cuándo la guerra? Es necesario trabajar por la paz." Published May 29, 2019. Video, 34:55. https://youtu.be/3m-62xqrW28.

Abosede George, Clive Glaser, Margaret D. Jacobs, Chitra Joshi, Emily Marker, Alexandra Walsham, Wang Zheng, Bernd Weisbrod. "AHR Conversation: Each Generation Writes Its Own History of Generations." *The American Historical Review* 123, no 5 (December 2018): 1505–1546.

Acero, Camilo, and Frances Thomson. "'Everything Peasants Do Is Illegal': Colombian Coca Growers' Everyday Experiences of Law Enforcement and Its Impacts on State Legitimacy." *Third World Quarterly* (2021): 1–19.

Acevedo Osorio, Álvaro, and Nathaly Jiménez Reinales, eds. *Agroecología: Experiencias comunitarias para la agricultura familiar en Colombia*. Bogotá: Universidad del Rosario, 2018.

Acosta López, María del Rosario. "Las fragilidades de la memoria: Duelo y resistencia al olvido en el arte colombiano (Muñoz, Salcedo, Echavarría)." In *Resistencias al olvido: Memoria y arte en Colombia*, edited by María del Rosario Acosta and Grupo Ley y Violencia, 23–48. Bogotá: Ediciones Uniandes, 2016.

———. *Resistencias al olvido: Memoria y arte en Colombia*, edited by María del Rosario Acosta and Grupo Ley y Violencia. Bogotá: Ediciones Uniandes, 2016.

———. "Gramáticas de la escucha: Aproximaciones filosóficas a la construcción de memoria histórica." *Ideas y valores* LXVIII, supplement no. 5 (2019): 59–79.

———. "One Hundred Years of Forgottenness: Aesth-Ethics of Memory in Latin America." *Philosophical Readings* XI, no. 3 (2019): 163–171.

———. "Arendt on Totalitarianism as Structural Violence: Towards New Grammars of Listening. In *Logics of Genocide: The Structures of Violence and the Contemporary World*, edited by Anne O'Byrne and Martin Shuster, 173–186. Bloomington: Indiana University Press, 2020.

———. "El arte como resistencia a lo inaudito: Sobre *Fragmentos* de Doris Salcedo y *Duelos* de Clemencia Echeverri." In *La violencia y su sombra: Aproximaciones desde Colombia y México*, edited by Rodrigo Parrini and María Victoria Uribe, 227–265. México City and Bogotá: Universidad Autónoma Metropolitana and Universidad del Rosario, 2021.

———. "*Gramáticas de lo inaudito* as Decolonial Grammars: Notes for a Decolonization of Memory." *Research in Phenomenology* 52, no. 2 (2022): 203–222.
———. *Gramáticas de lo inaudito: Pensar la memoria después del trauma*. Barcelona: Herder, 2022.
———. *Memory Work in Colombia: Past and Present Experiences, Legacies for the Future*. The World Humanities Report: South America [CHCI], 2022.
Acosta López, Juana and María del Rosario Acosta López, eds. *Justicia transicional en Colombia: Una mirada retrospectiva*. Bogotá: Ariel/Universidad de la Sabana, 2023.
Agudelo, Carlos. *Retos del multiculturalismo en Colombia: Política y poblaciones negras*. Medellín: Ed. IEPRI, IRD, ICANH, La Carreta, 2005.
Agudelo Patiño, Luis Carlos. "Campesinos sin tierra, tierra sin campesinos: Territorio, conflicto y resistencia campesina en Colombia." *Revista NERA* 16, no. 13 (2013): 81–95.
Agudo Sanchíz, Alejandro, and Marco Antonio Estrada Saavedra, eds. *Transformaciones del estado en los márgenes de Latinoamérica: Imaginarios alternativos, aparatos inacabados y espacios transnacionales*. México: El Colegio de México; Universidad Iberoamericana, 2011.
———, eds. *Formas reales de la dominación del Estado: Perspectivas interdisciplinarias del poder y la política*. México: El Colegio de México, 2014.
Ahmed, Sarah. *On Being Included: Racism and Diversity in Institutional Life*. Durham: Duke University Press, 2012.
Alcaldía Mayor de Bogotá. *Debates de la memoria: Aportes de las organizaciones de víctimas a una política pública de memoria*. Bogotá: Centro de Memoria, Paz y Reconciliación, 2010.
Alessandrini, Anthony Charles. *Frantz Fanon and the Future of Cultural Politics: Finding Something Different*. London: Lexington Books, 2014.
Alleman, Nathan F., Cara Cliburn Allen, and Don Haviland. "Collegiality and the Collegium in an Era of Faculty Differentiation." *ASHE Higher Education Report* 43, no. 4 (2017): 7–122.
Almario, Javier. "Colombia: The Genesis of the World's First Narco-Democracy." *Executive Intelligence Review* 9, no. 30 (1992): 41–42.
Álvarez Murena, Héctor. *El Pecado original de América*. Buenos Aires: Editorial Sudamericana, 1957.
Álvarez, Sonia. "Introduction to the Project and the Volume: Enacting a Translocal Feminist Politics of Translation." In *Translocalities/Translocalidades: Feminist Politics of Translation in the Latin-a Américas*, edited by Sonia Álvarez, Claudia de Lima Costa, Veronica Feliu, Rebecca Hester, Norma Klahn, and Millie Thayer with Cruz C. Bueno, 1–18. Durham: Duke University Press, 2014.
Anaya Hernández, Antonia. "Mientras cada uno siga jalando por su lado la isla seguirá estancada." In *Textos y testimonios: crisis y convivencia en un territorio insular*, edited by Socorro Ramírez and Luis Alberto Restrepo, 17–20. San Andrés Isla: Universidad Nacional de Colombia sede San Andrés, 2002.
Anderson, Mark. *Black and Indigenous: Garifuna Activism and Consumer Culture in Honduras*. Minneapolis: University of Minnesota Press, 2009.
Andrade, Susana. "Ethos evangélico, política indígena y medios de comunicación en el Ecuador." *Revista Cultura y Religión* 4, no. 1 (2010): 1–14.

Angarita Cañas, Pablo Emilio. *Seguridad Democrática: Lo invisible de un régimen político y económico*. Bogotá: Siglo del Hombre Editores, 2011.
Anrup, Roland. "La paz y las zonas de reserva campesina." *Ciudad Paz-ando* 6, no. 1 (2013): 103–122.
Aparicio Cuervo, Juan Ricardo, and Manuela Fernández Pinto, eds. Neoliberalismo en Colombia: Contexto, complejidad y política pública. Bogotá: Ediciones Uniandes, 2022.
Appelbaum, Nancy. *Muddied Waters: Race, Region, and Local History in Colombia, 1846–1948*. Durham: Duke University Press, 2003.
Apter, Emily. "Forward" to Gayatri Chakravorty Spivak Living Translation, edited by Emili Apter, Avishek Ganguly, Mauro Pala, and Surya Parekh. London: Seagull Books, 2022.
Appelbaum Nancy P, Anne S. Macpherson, and Karin Alejandra Rosemblatt. *Race and Nation in Modern Latin America*. Chapel Hill: University of North Carolina Press, 2003.
Aranguren Romero, Juan Pablo. *Cuerpos al límite: Tortura, subjetividad y memoria en Colombia, 1977–1982*. Bogotá: Ediciones Uniandes, 2023.
Arboleda, Santiago. *Le han florecido nuevas estrellas al cielo: Suficiencias íntimas y clandestinización del pensamiento afrocolombiano*. Cali: Poemia, 2016.
Archila, Mauricio. "Introducción." In *"Hasta cuando soñemos": Extractivismo e interculturalidad en el sur de La Guajira*, edited by Mauricio Archila et al., 25–43. Bogotá: Centro de Investigación y Educación Popular, Programa por la Paz, 2015.
Archila, Mauricio, et al. *"Hasta cuando soñemos": Extractivismo e interculturalidad en el sur de La Guajira*. Bogotá: Centro de Investigación y Educación Popular, Programa por la Paz, 2015.
Archila Neira, Mauricio, ed. *Violencia contra el sindicalismo, 1984–2010*. Bogotá: CINEP/Programa por la Paz, 2012.
Ardila, Martha. *¿Cambio de Norte? Momentos críticos de la política exterior colombiana*. Bogotá: Tercer Mundo Editores, IEPRI—Universidad Nacional de Colombia, 1991.
Arendt, Hannah. *Essays in Understanding*. New York: Schocken, 1994.
Arendt, Hanna. *The Origins of Totalitarianism*. New York: Harcourt, 1967.
Arias Gómez, Diego H. "Pasado cercano de la enseñanza de la historia reciente en Colombia: Los ochenta y noventa del siglo XX." In *Pasados violentos en la enseñanza de la historia y las ciencias sociales: Colombia, Argentina y Chile*, edited by Diego H. Arias Gómez, Sandra Patricia Rodríguez Ávila, María Paula González, and Graciela Rubio, 1–42. Bogotá: Editorial Universidad del Rosario, 2022.
Arjona, Ana. *Rebelocracy: Social Order in the Colombian Civil War*. Cambridge: Cambridge University Press, 2016.
Arias Trujillo, Ricardo. *Historia de Colombia contemporánea, 1920–2010*. Bogotá: Ediciones Uniandes, 2019.
Asher, Kiran. *Black and Green: Afrocolombians, Development and Nature in the Pacific Lowlands*. Durham: Duke University Press, 2009.
Asher, Kiran. "Spivak and Rivera Cusicanqui on the Dilemmas of Representation in Post-Colonial and Decolonial Feminism." *Feminist Studies* 43, no. 3 (2017): 512–524.

Astorga, Luis A. *Mitología del narcotraficante en México*. México D.F.: Plaza y Valdés, 1995.
Ayala, Ana Gilma. *Rituales mortuorios afroatrateños en el alto y medio Atrato*. Quibdó: Editorial Mundo Libro, 2011.
Ayala Diago, César Augusto. "Colombia en la década de los años setenta del siglo XX." *Anuario Colombiano de Historia Social y de la Cultura* 30 (2003): 319–338.
Badia I. Dalmases, Francesc, and Andrés Bernal Sánchez. "Fiebre eólica en La Guajira." *OpenDemocracy*, December 16, 2021. www.opendemocracy.net/es/fiebre-eolica-guajira-colombia/.
Bailey, Zinzi, Nancy Krieger, Madina Agénor, Jasmine Graves, Natalia Linos, and Mary T. Bassett. "Structural Racism and Health Inequities in the USA: Evidence and Interventions." *The Lancet* 389, no. 10077 (2017): 1453–1463.
Bair, Nadia. *The Decisive Network: Magnum Photos and the Postwar Image Market*. Oakland: University of California Press, 2020.
Ballvé, Teo. *The Frontier Effect: State Formation and Violence in Colombia*. Ithaca: Cornell University Press, 2020.
Ballvé, Teo, and Kendra McSweeney. "The 'Colombianisation' of Central America: Misconceptions, Mischaracterisations and the Military-Agroindustrial Complex." *Journal of Latin American Studies* 52, no. 4 (2020): 805–829.
Bargu, Banu. "Sovereignty as Erasure: Rethinking Enforced Disappearances." *Qui Parle: Critical Humanities and Social Sciences* 23, no. 1 (2014): 35–75.
Barrera, Victor, Camila Carvajal and Andrés Aponte."*La sustitución de cultivos de uso ilícito. Entre la represión y la radicalización.*" *Revista 100 días*. Febrero-Marzo, 90, 2017. Bogotá: CINEP., 19–20.
Beigel, Fernanda. "Crítica y teoría en el pensamiento social latinoamericano." In *Crítica y teoría en el pensamiento social latinoamericano*, edited by Fernanda Beigel et al., 287–326. Buenos Aires: CLACSO, 2006.
Bello, Martha Nubia, Elena Martín, Constanza Millan, Becky Pulido, and Raquel Rojas. *Bojayá, memoria y río: Violencia política, daño y reparación*. Bogotá: Universidad Nacional de Colombia, 2005.
Beltrán, Luis Ramiro. "Social Structure and Rural Development Communication in Latin America: The Radiophonic Schools of Colombia." Paper presented at the Summer Conference on Communication and Group Transformation for Development, Honolulu, Hawaii, June 29–July 11, 1975. https://idl-bnc-idrc.dspacedirect.org/handle/10625/1663.
Beltrán, Luis Ramiro, and Jaime Reyes. "Radio popular en Bolivia: La lucha de obreros y campesinos para democratizar la comunicación." *Diálogos de la Comunicación* 35 (1993): 14–31.
Benavides, Carlos Alberto. "Sujeto y vida campesina: Reflexiones en torno al texto para la caracterización del campesinado." In *Conceptualización del campesinado en Colombia: Documento técnico para su definición, caracterización y medición*, edited by Marta Saade Granados, 103–118. Bogotá: Instituto Colombiano de Antropología e Historia, ICANH, 2020.
Benlloch Castellar, Manuel. *San Andrés y Providencia: Cincuenta años de misión bien cumplida*. Bogotá: Editorial Andes, 1976.

Bent Hooker, Randy. "Si nos unimos nos iría mucho mejor y viviríamos en paz." In *Textos y testimonios: Crisis y convivencia en un territorio insular*, edited by Socorro Ramírez and Luis Alberto Restrepo, 35–40. San Andrés Isla: Universidad Nacional de Colombia Sede San Andrés, 2002.

Bernhard, Michael H., and Jan Kubik. *Twenty Years After Communism: The Politics of Memory and Commemoration*. New York: Oxford University Press, 2016.

Bergquist, Charles, Ricardo Peñaranda, and Gonzalo Sánchez, eds. *Violence in Colombia: The Contemporary Crisis in Historical Perspective*. Wilmington: Scholarly Resources, 1992.

Bergquist, Charles, Gonzalo Sánchez, and Ricardo Peñaranda, eds. *Violence in Colombia, 1990–2000: Waging War and Negotiating Peace*. Wilmington: Rowman & Littlefield Publishers, 2001.

Bértola Luis, and José Antonio Ocampo. *The Economic Development of Latin America since Independence*. Oxford: Oxford University Press, 2012.

Besant, John. *Narrative of the Expedition under General Mac Gregor against Porto Bello: Including an Account of the Voyage; and of the Causes Which Led to Its Final Overthrow*. London: T. & J. Allman, 1820.

Beverley, John. *The Failure of Latin America: Postcolonialism in Bad Times*. Pittsburgh: University of Pittsburgh Press, 2019.

Bieliauskaité, Jolanta. "Solidarity in Academia and its Relationship to Academic Integrity." *Journal of Academic Ethics* 19 (2021): 309–322.

Biwa, Memory. "'Weaving the Past with Threads of Memory': Narratives and Commemorations of the Colonial War in Southern Namibia." Ph.D. dissertation, University of the Western Cape, 2012.

Black, Edwin. "The Second Persona." *Quarterly Journal of Speech* 56, no. 2 (1970): 109–119.

Blok, Anton. *The Mafia of a Sicilian Village, 1860–1960: A Study of Violent Peasant Entrepreneurs*. London: Basil Blackwell, 1974.

Bocarejo, Diana. *Tipologías y topologías indígenas en el multiculturalismo colombiano*. Bogotá: ICANH, Pontificia Universedad Javeriana, Universidad del Rosario, 2015.

———. "Thinking with (Il)legality: The Ethics of Living with Bonanzas." *Current Anthropology* 59, no. S18 (2018): 48–59.

Bocarejo, Diana, and Eduardo Restrepo. "Introducción: Hacia una crítica del multiculturalismo en Colombia." *Revista Colombiana de Antropología* 47, no. 2 (2011): 7–13.

Boccara, Guillaume. "The Government of 'Others': On Neoliberal Multiculturalism in Latin America." *Actuel Marx* 50, no. 2 (2011): 191–206.

Boff, Leonardo, and Clodovis Boff. *Como Fazer Teologia da Libertação*. São Paulo: Livraria Vozes, 1986.

Bolívar, Ingrid. *Discursos emocionales y experiencias de la política*. Bogotá: Ediciones Uniandes, 2006.

———. "El Oficio de los futbolistas colombianos en los años 60 y 70: Recreación de las regiones, juegos de masculinidad y vida sentimental." Ph.D. dissertation, Department of History, University of Wisconsin, 2016.

Bonilla, Yarimar, and Jonathan Rosa. "# Ferguson: Digital Protest, Hashtag Ethnography, and the Racial Politics of Social Media in the United States." *American Ethnologist* 42, no. 1 (2015): 4–17.

Bonilla-Silva, Eduardo. "The Invisible Weight of Whiteness: The Racial Grammar of Everyday Life in America." *Michigan Sociological Review* 26 (Fall 2012): 1–15.

Bonilla Vélez, Jorge Iván. *La barbarie que no vimos: Fotografía y memoria en Colombia*. Medellín: Editorial EAFIT, 2019.

Bonilla Vélez, Jorge Iván, and Ancízar Narváez Montoya. "The Media in Colombia: Beyond Violence and a Market-Driven Economy." In *The Media in Latin America*, edited by Jairo Lugo-Ocando, 78–99. New York: Open University Press, 2008.

Borda, Sandra *¿Por qué somos tan parroquiales?: Una breve historia internacional de Colombia*. Bogotá: Crítica, 2019.

Botero Villa, Juan José. *Adjudicación, explotación y comercialización de baldíos y bosques nacionales: Evolución histórico-legislativa, 1830–1930*. Bogotá: Banco de la República, 1994.

Bourdieu, Pierre. "L'essence du néolibéralisme." *Manière de Voir* 8, no. 112 (2010): 11. www.cairn-int.info/magazine-maniere-de-voir-2010-8-page-11.htm

Boyer, Christopher. *Political Landscapes: Forests, Conservation and Community in Mexico*. Durham: Duke University Press, 2014.

Brachet-Márquez, Viviane. *El pacto de la dominación: Estado, clase y reforma social en México*. México: El Colegio de México, 1996.

Brachet-Márquez, Viviane, and Mónica Uribe Gómez, eds. *Estado y sociedad en América Latina: Acercamientos relacionales*. México, D. F.: El Colegio de México, 2016.

Brando, Carlos. "The Political Economy of Financing Late Development, Credit, Capital and Industrialization, Colombia 1940–67." Ph.D. thesis, The London School of Economics and Political Science, 2012.

Britto, Lina. "The Drug Wars in Colombia." *Oxford Research Encyclopedia*, September 28, 2020. https://doi.org/10.1093/acrefore/9780199366439.013.504.

———. *Marijuana Boom: The Rise and Fall of Colombia's First Drug Paradise*. Oakland: University of California Press, 2020.

———. "Generation War." *NACLA. Report of the Americas*, October 18, 2016.

Britton, Raymond Howard. "Religión y política eran una sola cosa." In *Textos y testimonios del archipiélago: Crisis y convivencia en un territorio insular*, edited by Socorro Ramírez and Luis Alberto Restrepo, 108–110. San Andrés Isla: Universidad Nacional de Colombia, 2002.

Brown, Matthew. "Inca, Sailor, Soldiers, King: Gregor MacGregor and the Early Nineteenth-Century Caribbean." *Bulletin of Latin American Research* 24, no. 1 (2005): 44–70.

Brown, Wendy. *Politics Out of History*. Princeton: Princeton University Press, 2001.

———. *Undoing the Demos: Neoliberalism's Stealth Revolution*. New York: Zone Books, 2015.

Brusco, Elizabeth E. *The Reformation of Machismo: Evangelical Conversion and Gender in Colombia*. Austin: University of Texas Press, 1995.

Buenaventura Gómez, Laura Alejandra, Andrés Jiménez Ángel, and Sven Schuster. *Colombia Conectada: El "Tibet" de Sudamérica" en perspectiva global, siglos XIX y XX*. Bogotá: Universidad del Rosario, 2023.

Buitrago Londoño and Stephen Ferry, graphic editor. *EL 9, Albeiro Lopera: Un fotógrafo en guerra*. Medellín: Tragaluz Editores, 2015.

Buitrago Restrepo, Felipe, and Iván Duque Márquez. *The Orange Economy: An Infinite Opportunity*. Washington, DC: IDB, 2013.

Burbano de Lara, Felipe. "El nacimiento de un nuevo sujeto político," *Íconos: Revista de Ciencias Sociales*. No. 15 (January 2003): 6–10.

Bushnell, David. *The Making of Modern Colombia. A Nation in Spite of Itself*. Berkeley: University of California Press, 1993.

———. "The Development of the Press in Great Colombia." *The Hispanic American Historical Review* 30, no. 4 (November 1950): 432–452.

Caballero Argáez, Carlos. Economía colombiana en el siglo XX: Un recorrido por la historia y sus protagonistas. Bogotá: Debate, 2016.

Caballero Argáez, Carlos, Mónica Pachón Buitrago y Eduardo Posada Carbó, eds. Cincuenta Años De Regreso a La Democracia: Nuevas Miradas a La Relevancia Histórica Del Frente Nacional. Bogotá: Ediciones Uniandes, 2012.

Cabeza Meza, Olga Fabiola. "Agua y conflictos en la zona bananera del Caribe colombiano en la primera mitad del siglo XX." MA thesis, Instituto de Estudios Ambientales, Universidad Nacional de Colombia, 2014.

Cabrera, Gabriel. "El monumento al colono en tres localidades de la Amazonía colombiana. Historia de un objeto, representaciones de una idea." *Cadernos do LEPAARQ* 18, no. 36 (2021): 203–228.

Cabrera Ortiz, Wenceslao. *San Andrés y Providencia: Historia*. Bogotá: Editorial Cosmos, 1980.

Cadahia, Luciana. "Su voz desatará tu lengua: Antígona, lo femenino y lo plebeyo." *Ideas y valores* LXVIII, Supplement no. 5 (2019): 129–149.

Cadahia, Luciana, and Valeria Cornel. "Volver al archivo: De las fantasias decoloniales a la imaginación republicana." In *Teorías de la república y prácticas republicanas*, edited by Macarena Marey, 59–98. Barcelona: Herder, Coleción Contrapunto, 2021.

Cagüeñas Rozo, Diego. "Almas dañadas, rostro, perdón y milagro: Reflexiones a propósito de Bojayá, Chocó." *Estudios Políticos* 61 (2021): 48–71.

Caicedo Estela, Andrés. *¡Que viva la música!* Bogotá: Grupo Editorial Norma, 2001.

Caldeira, Teresa P. R. *City of Walls: Crime, Segregation, and Citizenship in São Paulo* Oakland: University of California Press, 2001.

Camacho, Juana, and Natalia Robledo. "Indivisos, esquema colectivo y prácticas de propiedad campesina en Colombia." *Antípoda. Revista de Antropología y Arqueología* 40 (July 2020): 29–51.

Camacho Guizado, Álvaro and Andrés López Restrepo. "Perspectives on Narcotics Traffic in Colombia." *International Journal of Politics, Culture, and Society* 14, no. 4 (2000): 151–82.

Cárdenas, Roosbelinda. "Multicultural Politics for Afro-Colombians: An Articulation 'Without Guarantees'." In *Black Social Movements in Latin America: From*

Monocultural Mestizaje to Multiculturalism, edited by J. M. Rahier, 113–134. New York: Palgrave Macmillan, 2012.

———. "The Anti-Racist Horizon in Colombia's Peace Process." *NACLA*, March 23, 2017. https://nacla.org/news/2017/03/23/anti-racist-horizon-colombia%E2%80%99s-peace-process.

Cardona, César Alejandro. "Proceso organizativo de las comunidades negras rurales de Antioquia: Ancestralidad, etnicidad y política pública afroantioqueña." *Estudios Políticos* 50 (2017): 180–202.

Cardona, Ramiro, and Sara Rubiano de Velásquez, eds. *El éxodo de colombianos: Un estudio de la corriente migratoria de los Estados Unidos y un intento para propiciar el retorno*. Bogotá: Ediciones Tercer Mundo, 1980.

Caro, Catalina. "Horizontes y sentidos de las transiciones: Agendas y propuestas desde los territorios." Presented at Diálogos del Caribe: Trayectorias extractivas y transiciones. Sesión 6: Transiciones para un Caribe post-extractivista, November 13, Facebook live, 1:13, 2020. www.facebook.com/915836611798896/videos/2561867754104422/.

———. "Soñando futuros en la tierra del olvido: Trayectos co-laborativos para imaginar la transición." In *Energías para la transición: Reflexiones y relatos*, edited by Tatiana Roa Avedaño, 85–102. Bogotá: CENSAT Agua Viva, Fundación Heinrich Böll, 2021.

Caro Jaramillo, Sergio. "La posibilidad de la paz." In *El inicio del proceso de paz: La fase exploratoria y el camino del Acuerdo General*. Bogotá: Oficina del Alto Comisionado para la Paz, 2018.

Carse, Ashley. "Nature as Infrastructure: Making and Managing the Panama Canal Watershed." *Social Studies of Science* 42, no. 4 (2012): 539–563.

Cavarero, Adriana. *For More than One Voice: Toward a Philosophy of Vocal Expression*. Stanford, CA: Stanford University Press, 2005.

Caviedes, Mauricio. "Solidarios frente a colaboradores: Antropología y movimiento indígena en el cauca en las décadas de 1970 y 1980." *Revista Colombiana de Antropología* 38 (2002): 237–260.

———. "Obstáculos al desarrollo: La influencia del lenguaje del Frente Nacional en *El Campesino* (1961)." *Anuario Colombiano de Historia Social y de la Cultura* 49, no. 2 (2022): 159–186.

Celis Ospina, Juan Carlos, ed. *Estallido social 2021*. Bogotá: Siglo Editorial, Editorial Universidad del Rosario, Collectivo La Maria Cano, Rosa Luxemburg Stiftung, 2023.

Centro Nacional de Memoria Histórica. *Bojayá: La guerra sin límites*. Bogotá: Ediciones Semana and Taurus, 2010.

———. *El Placer: Mujeres, coca y guerra en el Bajo Putumayo*. Bogotá: Taurus, 2012.

———. *Textos corporales de la crueldad: Memoria histórica y antropología forense*. Bogotá: CNMH, 2014.

———. *La guerra inscrita en el cuerpo: Informe nacional de violencia sexual en el conflicto armado*. Bogotá: Centro Nacional de Memoria Histórica, 2017.

Centro Nacional de Memoria Histórica et al. *Justicia y paz: ¿Verdad judicial o verdad histórica?* Bogotá: Taurus, 2012.

Céspedes-Báez, Lina, and Felipe Jaramillo Ruiz. n.d. "Peace without Women Does Not Go!' Women's Struggle for Inclusion in Colombia's Peace Process with the FARC." *Colombia Internacional* 94: 83–109.

Chakrabarty, Dipesh. *Provincializing Europe: Postcolonial Thought and Historical Difference.* Princeton: Princeton University Press, 2008.

Chaney, Elsa M. "América Latina en los Estados Unidos: Colombianos en Nueva York." In *El éxodo de Colombianos*, edited by Ramiro Cardona Gutiérrez and Sara Rubiano de Velásquez. Bogotá: Tercer Mundo, 1980.

Chaparro, Camilo. *Historia del cartel de Cali.* Bogotá: Intermedio Editores, 2005.

Charry Joya, Carlos Andrés. "Movilización social e identidad nacional en el Caribe insular colombiano: Una historia social contada desde el diario de campo." *Historia Crítica* no. 35 (ene.– jun. 2008): 58–81.

Chaves Margarita, and Marta Zambrano. "From Blanqueamiento to Reindigenización: Paradoxes of Mestizaje and Multiculturalism in Contemporary Colombia." *Revista Europea de Estudios Latinoamericanos y del Caribe/European Review of Latin American and Caribbean Studies* 80 (2006): 5–23.

Ciro Rodríguez, Claudia Alejandra. "*Unos grises muy verracos*": *Poder político local y configuración del Estado en el Caquetá, 1980–2006.* Bogotá: Editorial Ingeniería Jurídica, Insituto Jean Piaget, Centro de Pensamiento AlaOrilladelRío, 2016.

Ciro Rodríguez, Estefanía. "Cultivando coca en el Caquetá: Vidas y legitimidades de la actividad cocalera." Ph.D. dissertation, Universidad Autonoma de México, 2016.

———. *Las vidas en disputa: Mujeres cocaleras, violencia y relaciones de producción- reproducción social en la economía regional de la coca en el sur de Colombia.* Informe Etnográfico, Programa de Fomento a la Investigación del ICANH, Subdirección Científica ICAHN, Caquetá, 2017.

———. "Estado contra-cara: Quiebres de la paz en Colombia por la sustitución de coca." *Mondialization*, 2017. www.mondialisation.ca/estado-contra-cara-quiebres-de-la-paz-en-colombia-por-la-sustitucion-de-coca/5576575.

———. "Las tierras profundas de la 'lucha contra las drogas' en Colombia: La ley y la violencia estatal en la vida de los pobladores rurales del Caquetá." *Revista colombiana de sociología* 41 (2018): 105–133.

———. *Levantados de la selva: Vidas y legitimidades de la actividad cocalera.* Bogotá: Uniandes, 2020.

Clay, Kevin L. "'Despite the Odds': Unpacking the Politics of Black Resilience Neoliberalism." *American Educational Research Journal* 56, no. 1 (2019): 75–110. https://doi.org/10.3102/0002831218790214.

Cockburn, Cynthia. *From Where We Stand: War, Women's Activism and Feminist Analysis.* London: Zed Books, 2007.

Colby, Gerard, and Charlotte Dennett. *Thy Will Be Done: The Conquest of the Amazon: Nelson Rockefeller and Evangelism in the Age of Oil.* New York: HarperCollins, 1996.

Colombian Institute of Rural Development, INCODER. "Reforma agraria y desarrollo rural para los grupos étnicos en Colombia." Paper presented in the International Conference on Land Reform and Rural Development. Porto Alegre, Brazil, March 7–10, 2006.

Colombo, Pamela. "Exhumations in Latin America." *Human Remains and Violence* 2, no. 2 (2016): 1–2.

Comisión de Seguimiento, Impulso y Verificación a la Implementación (CSIVI-FARC), and Centro de Pensamiento y Diálogo Político (CEDIPO). *Estado general de la implementación del acuerdo de paz en Colombia. En claroscuro.* Bogotá: Gentes del Común, CSIVI-FARC, CEDIPO, 2020.

Comisión Nacional de Reparación y Reconciliación, CNRR. *Plan de acción 2007–2008.* Bogotá: CNRR, 2007.

Comisión para el Esclarecimiento de la Verdad, la Convivencia y la No Repetición, Hay futuro si hay verdad. Bogotá: CEV, 2022.

Comisión para el Esclarecimiento de la Verdad, la Convivencia y la No Repetición, No matarás. Bogotá: CEV, 2022.

Comité Internacional de la Cruz Roja. (2004). "¿Qué es el derecho internacional humanitario?" www.icrc.org/es/doc/assets/files/other/dih.es.pdf. Accessed November 22, 2021.

Comité por los Derechos de las Víctimas de Bojayá; Riaño-Alcalá, Pilar, Quiceno, Natalia Quiceno and Camila Orjuela. *Los muertos de Bojayá son nuestros muertos: Exhumar, identificar, enterrar y acompañar en Bojayá, Chocó.* Bojayá, 2021. https://bojayacuentaexhumaciones.com/.

Comunidad de Playa Güío, et al. "La historia de Beto y la selva (cuento para niños)." In *Playa Güío: Ecoturismo y esperanza.* Bogotá: Editorial Pontificia Universidad Javeriana, 2016.

Cortés, Diego Mauricio. "Era mejor cuando éramos ilegales." *Journal of Alternative and Community Media* 4, no. 3 (2019): 28–42.

———. "Foes and Allies: The Catholic Church, Acción Cultural Popular (ACPO), and the Emergence of the Indigenous Movement in Cauca, Colombia." *Latin American and Caribbean Ethnic Studies* 1, no. 2 (2019): 171–193.

———. "Evangelical Indigenous Radio Stations in Colombia: Between the Promotion of Social Change and Religious Indoctrination." *Global Media and Communication* 16, no. 3 (2020): 313–328.

———. "The Quest for Indigenous Autonomy: Communication Media, Internal Conflicts, and Policy Reform in Colombia." *Journal of Latin American and Caribbean Anthropology* 26, no. 1 (2021): 84–103.

———. "Radio indígenas y estado en Colombia ¿Herramientas 'políticas' o instrumentos 'policivos'?" *Chasqui. Revista Latinoamericana de Comunicación.* 140 (April–July 2019) 59–74.

Coutin, Susan Bibler. *Nations of Emigrants: Shifting Boundaries of Citizenship in El Salvador and the United States.* Ithaca: Cornell University Press, 2007.

Crawford, Shakira. "Panama Fever and Colombian Fears of Secession on San Andrés and Providencia Islands, 1903–1913." *The Global South* 6, no. 2 (Fall 2013): 15–38.

Cruz, Edwin. "La rebelión de las ruanas: El paro nacional agrario en Colombia." *Revista Análisis* 49, no. 90 (2017): 83–109.

Currie, Lauchlin. *Reorganización de la rama ejecutiva del gobierno de colombia.* Bogotá: Imprenta Nacional, 1988 [1952].

Damonte, Gerardo, Astrid Ulloa, Catalina Quiroga Manrique, and Ana Paula López. "La apuesta por la infraestructura: Inversión pública y la reproducción de la escasez hídrica en contextos de gran minería en Perú y Colombia." *Estudios Atacameños* 68 (2022): 1–32.

Dargent, Eduardo. *Technocracy and Democracy in Latin America: The Experts Running Government.* Cambridge: Cambridge University Press, 2015.
Das, Veena. "Ordinary Ethics: The Perils and Pleasures of Everyday Life." In *A Companion to Moral Anthropology*, edited by Didier Fassin, 133–148. Hoboken: John Willey & Sons, 2012.
Dau, Yasmine. "El lamento sustituye afán de pensar el futuro." In *Textos y testimonios del archipiélago: crisis y convivencia en un territorio insular*, edited by Socorro Ramírez and Luis Alberto Restrepo, 67–74. San Andrés Isla: Universidad Nacional de Colombia sede San Andrés, 2002.
Dawson, Diane (DeDe), Esteban Morales, Erin McKiernan, Lesley A. Schimanski, Meredith T. Niles, and Juan Pablo Alperin. "The Role of Collegiality in Academic Review, Promotion and Tenure." *PLoS ONE* 17, no. 4 (2022):1–17.
Dávila, Andrés. *Democracia pactada: El Frente Nacional y el proceso constituyente del 91.* Bogotá: Ediciones Uniandes, 2002.
Deas, Malcom: *Del poder y la gramática y otros ensayos sobre historia, política y literatura colombianas.* Bogotá: Taurus, 2006.
———. *Intercambios violentos y dos ensayos más sobre el conflicto en Colombia.* Bogotá: Taurus, 2015.
De Almeida, Ronaldo. "Bolsonaro presidente: Conservadorismo, evangelismo e a crise Brasileira." *Novos Estudos CEBRAP* 38, no. 1 (2019): 185–213.
De Casanova, Erynn Masi. "Beauty Ideology in Latin America." *DObra [s]: Revista Da Associação Brasileira de Estudos de Pesquisas Em Moda* 11, no. 23 (2018): 10–21.
De Cruz, Helen. "Perplexity and Philosophical Progres." *Midwest Studies in Philosophy* 45 (2021): 209–221.
De Roux, Francisco. *Convocatoria a la paz grande*: discurso en el lanzamiento del Informe Final de la Comisión de la Verdad, Teatro Jorge Eliécer Gaitán, Bogotá, 27 de junio, 2022. www.elespectador.com/colombia-20/informe-final-comision-de-la-verdad/en-vivo-entrega-del-informe-final-de-la-comision-de-la-verdad-sobre-el-conflicto-armado-en-colombia-noticias-hoy/, consultado 19 de julio de 2022.
Dejusticia. "Acción de tutela de asociaciones campesinas contra la ANT y del Consejo Directivo de la ANT ante la dilación en el proceso de constitución de las ZRC de Sumapaz, Losada—Guayabero y Güejar—Cafre." December 18, 2020. www.dejusticia.org/wp-content/uploads/2020/12/Tutela-ZRC-Sumapaz-Gu%CC%88ejar-Cafre-y-Losada-Guayabero_compressed.pdf.
———. "Presentamos una tutela para exigir que se garantice el derecho al territorio campesino." December 22, 2020. www.dejusticia.org/presentamos-una-tutela-para-exigir-que-se-garantice-el-derecho-al-territorio-campesino/.
———. "Corte Constitucional selecciona tutela para constituir tres ZRC." September 20, 2021. www.dejusticia.org/corte-constitucional-selecciona-tutela-para-constituir-tres-zrc/.
Del Cairo, Carlos. "Tucanos y colonos del Guaviare. Estrategias para significar el territorio." *Revista Colombiana de Antropología* 34 (1998): 66–91.
———. "Las jerarquías étnicas y las retóricas del multiculturalismo estatal en San José del Guaviare." *Revista Colombiana de Antropología* 47, no. 2 (2011): 123–149.

———. "Environmentalizing Indigeneity: A Comparative Ethnography of Multiculturalism, Ethnic Hierarchies, and Political Ecology in the Colombian Amazon." Ph.D. dissertation, The University of Arizona, 2012.

———. "Selvas y gentes (in)cultas: políticas de la cultura y poblaciones amazónicas en los diseños de intervención estatal." In *Cultura: Centralidad, artilugios, etnografía*, edited by Stuart Hall, Eduardo Restrepo and Carlos del Cairo, 107–147. Popayán, Colombia: Asociación Colombiana de Antropología, 2019.

Del Cairo, Carlos, and Iván Montenegro-Perini. "Espacios, campesinos y subjetividades ambientales en el Guaviare." *Memoria y Sociedad* 19, no. 39 (2015): 49–71.

Del Cairo, Carlos, Iván Montenegro-Perini, and Juan Sebastián Vélez. "Naturalezas, subjetividades y políticas ambientales en el noroccidente amazónico: Reflexiones metodológicas para el análisis de conflictos socioambientales." *Boletín de Antropología* 29, no. 48 (2014): 13–40.

Delgado Rozo, Juan David. "La difícil instauración del gobierno republicano en el espacio local: Las municipalidades y los alcaldes parroquiales en la provincial de Bogotá, 1821–1830." In *La Independencia en Colombia: Miradas transdisciplinares*, edited by John Jairo Cárdenas Herrera, and Julián Augusto Vivas García. Bogotá: Universidad Antonio Nariño, 2015: 19–50.

Demera Vargas, Juan Diego. "Católicos y protestantes entre los indígenas guambianos: La adopción y transformación de nuevas colectividades." *Ciências Sociais e Religião* 5, no. 5 (2007): 173–190.

Demetriou, Charles. "Processual Comparative Sociology: Building on the Approach of Charles Tilly." *Sociological Theory* 30, no. 1 (2012): 51–65.

Departamento Administrativo Nacional de Estadística (DANE). *Censo nacional de población y vivienda*. Bogotá: DANE, 2018.

Diamond, Larry Jay, Juan J. Linz, and Seymour Martin Lipset, eds. *Democracy in Developing Countries: Latin America*, vol. 4. Boulder, CO: Lynne Rienner, 1999.

Díaz Galindo, Félix. *Monografía del archipiélago de San Andrés*. Bogotá: Ediciones Medio Pliego, 1978.

Didi-Huberman, Georges. *Images in Spite of All: For Photographs from Auschwitz*. Chicago: The University of Chicago Press, 2008.

Dietze, Carola. "Toward a History on Equal Terms: A Discussion of Provincializing Europe." *History and Theory* 47 (2008): 69–84.

Domínguez, Camilo, and Augusto Gómez. *La economía extractiva en la Amazonía colombiana*. Bogotá: Tropenbos-Araracuara, 1990.

Domínguez, Marta Isabel. "Comunidades negras rurales de Antioquia: Discursos de ancestralidad, titulación colectiva y procesos de "aprendizaje" del Estado." *Estudios Políticos* 46 (2015): 101–123.

———. *Territorios colectivos: Procesos de formación del Estado en el Pacífico Colombiano (1993–2009)*. Medellín: Fondo Editorial FCSH de la Universidad de Antioquia, 2017.

Dorfman, Ariel. "If Only We All Spoke Two Languages." *The New York Times*, June 24, 1998.

———. *Heading South, Looking North: A Bilingual Journey*. New York: Penguin Books, 1999.

———. "The Nomads of Language." *The American Scholar* 71, no. 1 (Winter 2002): 89–94.

Duarte, Carlos. "(Des)encuentros en lo público: Gobernabilidad y conflictos interétnicos en Colombia." Ph.D. dissertation, Université Sorbonne Paris Cité, 2015. https://tel.archives-ouvertes.fr/tel-01485413/document.

Duarte, Carlos, and Camilo Montenegro. "Campesinos en Colombia: Un análisis conceptual e histórico necesario." In *Conceptualización del campesinado en Colombia: Documento técnico para su definición, caracterización y medición*, edited by Marta Saade Granados, 119–171. Bogotá: ICANH, 2020.

Dumenil Gerard, and Domique Levy. *The Crisis of Neoliberalism*. Cambridge: Harvard University Press, 2013.

Duncan, Gustavo. *Más que plata o plomo: El poder político del narcotráfico en Colombia y México*. Bogotá: Debate, 2014.

———. *Los señores de la guerra: De paramilitares, mafiosos y autodefensas en Colombia*. Bogotá: Planeta, 2006.

Dunham, Jacob. *Journal of Voyages: Containing an Account of the Author's Being Twice Captured by the English and Once by Gibs the Pirate*. New York: Huestis & Cozans, 1850.

Dunlap, Alexander. *Renewing Destruction: Wind Energy Development, Conflict, and Resistance in a Latin American Context*. London: Rownan & Littlefield, 2019.

Dussel, Enrique. *El encubrimiento del Otro: Hacia el origen del mito de la modernidad*. Quito: Editorial Abya Yala, 1994.

Duffy, Bobby. The Generation Myth. *Why When You're Born Matters Less than You Think*. New York: Basic Books, 2021.

Echeverri, Lina María, Eduardo J. Rosker, and Martha Lucía Márquez Restrepo, "Los orígenes de la marca país Colombia es pasión," *Estudios y perspectivas en turismo* 19, no. 3 (2010): 409–421.

Eitón, Emilio. *El Archipiélago lejano*. Barranquilla: Mogollón, 1913.

Ekers, Michael, and Scott Prudham. "Towards the Socio-Ecological Fix." *Environment and Planning A: Economy and Space* 47 (2015): 2438–2445.

Eley, Geoff. Forging Democracy: *The Left and the Struggle for Democracy in Europe, 1850–2000*. Oxford: Oxford University Press, 2002.

Ellner, Steve, ed. *Latin America's Pink Tide: Breakthroughs and Shortcomings*. New York: Rowman and Littlefield, 2020.

Equitas. "Caso Bojayá: Informe de análisis de Contexto: Análisis forense de los decesos asociados a la estrategia militar para el control territorial entre el grupo paramilitar Élmer Cárdenas de las Autodefensas Unidas de Colombia (AUC) y el grupo guerrillero del Bloque José María Córdoba de las Fuerzas Armadas Revolucionarias de Colombia-Ejército del Pueblo (FARC-EP)." April-May 2002, 2018.

Escobar, Arturo. *La invención del Tercer Mundo: Construcción y deconstrucción del desarrollo*. Bogotá: Editorial Norma, 1998.

Escobar, Arturo, and Sonia E. Alvarez. "Introduction: Theory and Protest in Latin America Today." In *The Making of Social Movements in Latin America: Identity, Strategy, and Democracy*, edited by Arturo Escobar and Sonia E. Alvarez, 1–18. New York: Routledge, 1992.

Espinosa, Nicolás. *Política de vida y muerte: Etnografía de la violencia diaria en la Sierra de la Macarena*. Bogotá: ICANH, 2010.

Estrada Álvarez, Jairo. "Las reformas estructurales y la construcción del orden neoliberal en Colombia." In *Los desafíos de las emancipaciones en un contexto militarizado*, edited by Ana Esther Ceceña, 247–284. Buenos Aires: CLACSO, 2006.

Estrada, Fernando. "La retórica del paramilitarismo: Análisis del discurso en el conflicto armado." *Análisis Político* 44 (2001): 39–57.

Estupiñán, Juan Pablo. "Marimba en 'la nevera': Tránsitos sonoros de la música afropacífica colombiana." *Revista de Estudos e Investigações Antropológicas* 6, no. 2 (2019): 102–131.

Etter, Andrés, Clive McAlpine, and Hugh Possingham. "A Historical Analysis of the Spatial and Temporal Drivers of Landscape Change in Colombia since 1500." *Annals of the American Association of Geographers* 98, no. 1 (2008): 2–23.

Fajardo, Darío. *Espacio y sociedad: Formación de las regiones agrarias en Colombia*. Bogotá: Corporación Colombiana para la Amazonía-Araracuara, 1993.

———. "Territorialidad y Estado en la Amazonía colombiana." In *Espacio y sociedad: Formación de las Regiones Agrarias en Colombia*. Bogotá: Corporación Colombiana para la Amazonía—Araracuara, 1993.

———. "Colombia: Dos décadas en los movimientos agrarios." *Cahiers des Amériques latines* 71 (2012): 145–168. https://doi.org/10.4000/cal.2690.

———. "El punto agrario del acuerdo de paz: una larga historia." In *El acuerdo de paz en Colombia: Entre la perfidia y la potencia transformadora*, edited by Jairo Estrada, 93–108. Buenos Aires: Consejo Latinoamericano de Ciencias Sociales, 2019.

Fals Borda, Orlando. *Ciencia propia y colonialismo intelectual*. Bogotá: Editorial Nuestro Tiempo, 1970.

_____, ed. *La insurgencia de las provincias*. Bogotá: Siglo Veintiuno, 1988.

Fanon, Frantz. *Black Skin, White Masks*. London: Pluto Press, 1986 [1952].

FAO. *Organización para la producción y comercialización*. Bogotá: FAO, n. d.

———. *Las Zonas de reserva campesina: Retos y experiencias significativas en su implementación*. Bogotá: FAO, 2019.

Farnsworth-Alvear, Ann. *Dulcinea in the Factory: Myths, Morals, Men, and Women in Colombia's Industrial Experiment, 1905–1960*. Durham: Duke University Press, 2000.

Farnsworth-Alvear, Ann, Marco Palacios, and Ana María Gómez López, eds. *The Colombian Reader: History, Culture, Politics*. Durham: Duke University Press, 2017.

Fattal, Alexander L. Guerrilla: *Marketing: Counterinsurgency and Capitalism in Colombia*. University of Chicago Press, 2018.

———. *Guerrilla marketing: Contrainsurgencia y capitalismo en Colombia*. Bogotá: Universidad del Rosario, 2019.

Ferguson, James, and Akhil Gupta. "Spatializing States: Toward an Ethnography of Neoliberal Governmentality." *American Ethnologist* 29, no. 4 (2002): 981–1002.

———. "The Uses of Neoliberalism." *Antipode* 41 (2009): 166–184.

———. *Give a Man a Fish: Reflections on the New Politics of Distribution*. Durham: Duke University Press, 2015.

Fernández L'Hoeste, Héctor D. "Rodrigo D. No Futuro by Víctor Gaviria and Focine." *Film Quarterly* 48, no. 2 (Winter 1994–1995): 48–51.

———. "On How Bloque de Búsqueda Lost Part of its Name: The Predicament of Colombian Rock in the U.S. Market" in Rockin' Las Américas: The Global Politics of Rock in Latin/o America, edited by Deborah Pacini Hernandez, Héctor Fernández L'Hoeste and Eric Zolov, 179–299. Pittsburgh: University of Pittsburgh Press, 2004.

Ferrándiz, Francisco, Antonious Robben, and Richard Wilson. *Necropolitics: Mass Graves and Exhumations in the Age of Human Rights* (First ed.). Philadelphia: University of Pennsylvania Press, 2015.

Field, Les W. "Who Are the Indians? Reconceptualizing Indigenous Identity, Resistance, and the Role of Social Science in Latin America." *Latin American Research Review* 29, no. 3 (1994): 237–248. www.jstor.org/stable/2503952.

Figueiredo, Angela. "Fora do jogo: a experiência dos negros na classe média brasileira." *Cadernos Pagu*, no. 23 (2004): 199–228.

Finnegan, Cara. *Picturing Poverty: Print Culture and FSA Photographs*. Washington, DC: Smithsonian Institution Scholarly Press, 2003.

FLACSO (Quito, Ecuador), and Camilo Mongua Calderón. "Caucho, frontera, indígenas e historia regional: Un análisis historiográfico de la época del caucho en el Putumayo–Aguarico." *Boletín de Antropología* 33, no. 55 (2018): 15–34.

Flórez Enciso, Luis Bernardo. "Colombia: Economy, Economic Policy and Economists." In *Economists in the Americas*, edited by Verónica Montecinos and John Marko, 197–226. Cheltenham: Edward Elgar, 2009.

Franco Restrepo, Vilma Liliana. *Orden contrainsurgente y dominación*. Bogotá: Siglo del Hombre, 2009.

Franzinelli, Mimmo. *Delatori. Spie e confidenti anonimi: l'arma segreta del regime fascista*. Milano: Felitrinelli, 2012.

Fraser, Colin, and Sonia Restrepo-Estrada. *Communicating for Development: Human Change for Survival*. New York: Bloomsbury Academic, 1998.

Fraser, Nancy. *Iustitia Interrupta: Reflexiones críticas desde la posición "postsocialista."* Bogotá: Universidad de los Andes- Facultad de Derecho y Siglo del Hombre Editores, 1997.

Fraser, Nancy, Hanne Marlene Dahl, Pauline Stoltz, and Rasmus Willig. "Recognition, Redistribution and Representation in Capitalist Global Society: An Interview with Nancy Fraser." *Acta Sociologica* 47, no. 4 (2004.): 374–382.

Freeman, Carla. *Entrepreneurial Selves: Neoliberal Respectability and the Making of a Caribbean Middle Class*. Durham:Duke University Press, 2014.

Friedrich Nietzsche. *Thus Spoke Zarathustra*. London: Penguin, 1971.

Fundación Colombiana de Ganaderos, FUNDAGÁN. *Acabar con el olvido*. Bogotá: Fundagán, 2012.

Fundación Compartir. *Nuestros mejores maestros*. Bogotá: Nomos Impresores, 2011.

Fundación Ideas para la Paz. "Radiografía del nuevo acuerdo: ¿Qué tanto se renegoció?" 2016. www.ideaspaz.org/especiales/nuevo-acuerdo/

FUNDAGÁN. *Acabar con el olvido: Segundo informe*. Bogotá: Fundagán, 2013.

Gago, Verónica. *Neoliberalism from Below: Popular Pragmatics and Baroque Economies*. Durham: Duke University Press, 2017.

Galeano, Eduardo. *Colombiando: Palabras sentipensantes sobre un país violento y mágico*. Bogotá: CEPA Editores, 2016.

Gamba Cubides, Néstor Javier. "Agua, energía eléctrica y caña de azúcar: Declaración de reservas forestales en el Valle del Cauca entre 1938 y 1943." Trabajo para optar al título de maestría en geografía, modalidad profundización. Universidad de los Andes, 2018.

———. "El Bosque Municipal de Piedras Blancas: Primera iniciativa estatal de conservación de la naturaleza en Colombia." Unpublished manuscript.

García, Andrea. "Mujeres campesinas, afrodescendientes e indígenas en Colombia: Prácticas políticas y cotidianas del cuidado." *Pensares y Quehaceres: Revista de Políticas de la Filosofía* 4 (2017): 131–152.

García, Antonio. "Las clases medias y la frustración del Estado representativo en América Latina." *Cuadernos americanos* 1 (January-February 1967): 7–40.

García Canclini, Néstor. *Culturas Hibrídas: Estrategias para entrar y salir de la modernidad*. Buenos Aires: Editorial Paidos SAICF, 2001.

García Isaza, Mario. "La perfectura apostólica de Tierradentro." In *Quinientos años de evangelización*, edited by Hernando Escobar, 384–398. Bogotá: CLAPVI-Conferencia Latinoamericana de Provincias Vicentinas, 1992.

García Márquez, Gabriel. "The Solitude of Latin America." Nobel Lecture, December 8, 1982. www.nobelprize.org/prizes/literature/1982/marquez/lecture/.

———. *One Hundred Years of Solitude*, translated by Gregory Rabassa. New York: Harper Perennial, 2006.

García Taylor, Sally. "Los Half & Half o Fifty Fifties de San Andrés: Los actores invisibles de la raizalidad." Master's thesis, Universidad Nacional de Colombia sede San Andrés Isla, 2010.

García Villegas, Mauricio, Nicolás Torres, Javier Revelo, José R. Espinosa and Natalia Duarte, *Los territorios de la paz: La construcción del Estado local en Colombia*. Bogotá: Dejusticia, 2016.

Gatehouse, Mike. "State Violence, Policing, and Paramilitaries." In *Voices of Latin America: Social Movements and the New Activism*, edited by Tom Gatehouse, 173–197. Rugby, UK: Practical Action Publishing, 2019.

Gaviria, Alejandro and Daniel Mejía, eds. *Anti-Drug Policies in Colombia: Successes, Failures, and Wrong Turns*. Nashville: Vanderbilt University Press, 2016.

Gessat-Anstett, Élizabeth, and Jean M. Dreyfus. *Destruction and Human Remains: Disposal and Concealment in Genocide and Mass Violence*. Manchester, New York: Manchester University Press, 2014.

Gibson, William. *Constitutions of Colombia*. Bogotá: Biblioteca Popular de Cultura Colombiana, 1951.

Gill, Lesley. *A Century of Violence in a Red City: Popular Struggles, Counterinsurgency and Human Rights in Colombia*. Durham: Duke University Press, 2016.

Giraldo, Francisco. "La masacre de Bojayá: Usos políticos de un recuerdo violento." *Anuario Colombiano de Historia Social y de la Cultura*. 47, no. 2 (2020): 43–84.

Gilroy, Paul. *Darker than Blue: On the Moral Economies of Black Atlantic Culture*. Cambridge: Harvard University Press, 2010.

Giraldo, Sol Astrid. "Si los héroes fueran negros: Liliana Angulo y los debates de la masculinidad afrocolombiana." In *La negritud y su poética: Prácticas artísticas y miradas críticas contemporáneas en Latinoamérica y España*, edited by Andrea Díaz Mattei, 295–310. Montevideo/Sevilla: BMR Cultural/Publicaciones Enredars, 2019.

Giraldo Moreno, Javier, Leonardo Luna Alzate, Ferdinad Muggenthaler, and Stefan Peters, eds. *¿Del paramiltarismo al paramilitarismo? Radiografías de una paz violenta en Colombia*. Quito: Rosa Luxemburg Stifung, 2023.

Giustozzi, Antonio. *The Art of Coercion: The Primitive Accumulation and Management of Coercive Power*. London: Hurst & Company, 2011.

Grupo de Memoria Histórica. *¡BASTA YA! Colombia: Memorias de guerra y dignidad*. Bogotá: Imprenta Nacional, 2013.

———. *Bojayá: la guerra sin límites*. Bogotá: Taurus, 2010.

Gobernación de La Guajira. *Plan de desarrollo para La Guajira. Un nuevo tiempo 2017-2019*. La Guajira, Colombia: Gobernación de La Guajira, 2017. https://guajira360.org/wp-content/uploads/2018/09/PDG-Final-2017-2019.pdf.

Golash-Boza, Tanya. "Does Whitening Happen? Distinguishing between Race and Color Labels in an African-Descended Community in Peru." *Social Problems* 57, no. 1 (2010): 138–156.

Goldstein, Daniel M. *Outlawed: Between Security and Rights in a Bolivian City*. Durham: Duke University Press Books, 2012.

Gomes, Nilma. "Trajetórias escolares, corpo negro e cabelo crespo: reprodução de estereótipos ou ressignificação cultural?" *Revista Brasileira de Educação*, n° 21 (2002): 40–51.

Gómez-Barris, Macarena. *The Extractive Zone: Social Ecologies and Decolonial Perspectives*. Durham: Duke University Press, 2017.

Gómez Buendía, Hernando. "Décalogo para entender este país." *El Malpensante* No. 125, Nov 2011.

———. *Entre la independencia y la pandemia: La guerra más larga del mundo y la historia no contada de un país en construcción*. Bogotá: Fundación Razón Pública and Rey Naranjo Editores, 2021.

Gómez Correal, Diana Marcela. *Dinámicas del movimiento feminista bogotano: historias de cuarto, salón y calle, historias de vida (1970–1991)*. Bogotá: Universidad Nacional de Colombia, 2011.

Gómez, Juan Guillermo. Colombia es una cosa impenetrable: Raíces de la intolerancia y otros ensayos sobre historia política y vida intelectual. Medellín: Diente de León, 2006.

González Barrera, Laura Carolina. "¿Desarrollo rural en tensión? La ZRC Cuenca del Río Pato y Valle de Balsillas: una historia de resistencia por la dignidad humana y la paz, el plan nacional de desarrollo y los acuerdos de paz (2012–2017)." Master's thesis, Pontificia Universidad Javeriana, Colombia, 2018. https://doi.org/10.11144/Javeriana.10554.37009.

González Casanova, Pablo. *Explotación, colonialismo y lucha por la democracia en América Latina*. CDMX: Ediciones Akal, 2013.

González Perafán, Leonardo. "Líderes afrodescendientes asesinados." *INDEPAZ*, August 13, 2020. www.indepaz.org.co/lideres-afrodescendientes-asesinados/.

González Posso, Camilo. "Guajira 1. Las verdades ocultas del único parque eólico instalado: 'Renovables Sí, pero no así,' dicen comunidades." *Revista Sur*, January 24, 2022. www.sur.org.co/guajira-1-las-verdades-ocultas-del-unico-parque-eolico-instalado-renovables-si-pero-no-asi-dicen-comunidades/.

González Posso, Camilo, and Joanna Barney. *El viento del este llega con revoluciones: Multinacionales y transición con energía eólica en territorio Wayúu*. Bogotá: Indepaz, Fundación Heinrich Böll, 2019.

González, Fernán E. "¿Colapso parcial o presencia diferenciada del Estado en Colombia? Una mirada desde la historia." *Colombia Internacional* 58 (2003): 124–157.

———. *Poder y violencia en Colombia*. Bogotá: Observatorio Colombiano para el Desarrollo Integral, la Convivencia Ciudadana y el Fortalecimiento Institucional, 2014.

Goodale Mark and Nancy Postero, eds. *Neoliberalism Interrupted: Social Change and Contested Governance in Contemporary Latin America*. Stanford: Stanford University Press, 2013.

Gootenberg, Paul, and Liliana M. Dávalos, eds. *The Origins of Cocaine: Colonization and Failed Development in the Amazon Andes*. New York: Routledge, 2019.

Gordon, Lewis R. *What Fanon Said: A Philosophical Introduction to his Life and Thought*. New York: Fordham University Press, 2015.

Goswami, Manu. "The Modular Nation Form: Toward a Sociohistorical Conception of Nationalism." *Comparative Studies in Society and History* 44, no. 4 (October 2002): 770–799.

Grandin, Greg. *The Last Colonial Massacre: Latin America in the Cold War*. Chicago: The University of Chicago Press, 2011.

———. *Empire's Workshop: Latin America, the United States, and the Rise of New Imperialism*. New York: Holt, Henry& Company, 2007.

———. "The Instruction of Great Catastrophe: Truth Commissions, National History and State Formation in Argentina, Chile and Guatemala." *The American Historical Review* 110, no. 1 (February 2005): 46–67.

Gros, Christian. "Evangelical Protestantism and Indigenous Populations." *Bulletin of Latin American Research* 18, no. 2 (1999): 175–197.

———. "¿Cuál autonomía para los pueblos indígenas de América Latina?" In *Utopía para los excluidos: El multiculturalismo en África y América Latina*, edited by Jaime Arocha. Bogotá: Universidad Nacional de Colombia, Facultad de Ciencias Humanas, Departamento de Antropología, Centro de Estudios Sociales, 2004: 205-230.

Grupo de Memoria Histórica (GMH) and María Victoria Uribe. *Memorias en tiempo de Guerra: Repertorios de iniciativas*. Bogotá: Comisión Nacional de Reparación y Reconciliación, 2009.

Guerra Curvelo, Weilder. "Ontología wayuu: Categorización, identificación y relaciones de los seres en la sociedad indígena de la península de La Guajira, Colombia." Ph.D. dissertation, Universidad de los Andes, Bogotá, 2019. http://hdl.handle.net/1992/41315.

Guevara Jaramillo, Natalia. "Redes isleñas del archipiélago a la capital." Unpublished manuscript, 2009.

Guillén Martínez Fernando. *El poder político en Colombia*. Bogotá: Planeta, [1979] 1996.

Guilluy, Christopher. *No Society: El fin de la clase media occidental*. Barcelona: Taurus, 2019.

Güiza, Diana, Ana Bautista, Ana Malagón, and Rodrigo Yepes. *La constitución del campesinado: Luchas por reconocimiento y redistribución en el campo jurídico.* Bogotá: Colección Dejusticia, 2020.
Gumucio, Tatiana, María Alejandra Mora Benard, Jennifer Twyman, and María Camila Hernández Ceballos. "Género en la ganadería: Consideraciones iniciales para la incorporación de una perspectiva de género en la investigación de la ganadería en Colombia y Costa Rica." *Working Paper CCAFS*, no. 159, (2016).
Gumucio Dagron, Alfonso. "Call Me Impure: Myths and Paradigms of Participatory Communication." In *Community Media. International Perspectives*, edited by Linda K. Fuller, 197–207. New York: Palgrave Macmillan, 2007.
Gutiérrez Sanin, Francisco. "Fumigaciones, incumplimientos, coaliciones y resistencias." *Estudios Socio-Jurídicos* 22, no. 2 (2020). https://doi.org/10.12804/revistas.urosario.edu.co/sociojuridicos/a.9146.
———. *¿Lo que el viento se llevó? Los partidos políticos y la democracia en Colombia, 1958–2002.* Bogotá: Norma, 2007.
———. "Propiedad, seguridad y despojo: El caso paramilitar." *Estudios sociojurídicos* 16, no. 1 (2014): 43–74.
———. *Clientelistic Warfare? Paramilitaries and the State in Colombia (1982–2007).* Oxford: Palgrave, 2019.
———. *El orangutan con sacoleva: Cien años de democracia y represión en Colombia, 1910–2010.* Bogotá: Debate, 2013.
Guzman Bouvard, Marguerite. *Revolutionizing Motherhood: The Mothers of the Plaza de Mayo.* Wilmington: Scholarly Resources, 1994.
Hale, Charles R. "Rethinking Indigenous Politics in the Era of the 'Indio Permitido'." *NACLA*, September 25, 2004. https://nacla.org/article/rethinking-indigenous-politics-era-indio-permitido.
———. "Neoliberal Multiculturalism: The Remaking of Cultural Rights and Racial Dominance in Central America." *Political and Legal Anthropology Review* 28, no. 1 (2005): 10–28.
Hall, Gillette, and Harry Anthony Patrinos. "Indigenous Peoples, Poverty and Human Development in Latin America." In *Indigenous Peoples, Poverty and Human Development in Latin America, 1994–2004.* New York: World Bank, 2004: 35–48.
Hall, Stuart. "Cultural Identity and Diaspora." In *Contemporary Sociological Thought*, edited by Sean P. Hier, 443–454. Toronto: Canada Scholars' Press, 2005.
———. "The Neoliberal Revolution." *Soundings* 48, no. 1 (2011): 9–28.
———. et al. *Policing the Crisis: Mugging, the State, and Law and Order.* London: Macmillan, 1978.
Hallin, Daniel C., and Stylianos Papathanassopoulos. "Political Clientelism and the Media: Southern Europe and Latin America in Comparative Perspective." *Media, Culture & Society* 24, no. 2 (2002): 176–182.
Harrison, Robert Pogue. *Forests: The Shadow of Civilization.* Chicago: The University of Chicago Press, 1992.
Harvey, David. *El enigma del capital y las crisis del capitalismo.* Madrid: Ediciones Akal, 2012.
———. *A Brief History of Neoliberalism.* Oxford: Oxford University Press, 2007.
Hawkins, John. *The Creative Economy: How People Make Money from Ideas.* London: Allen Lane, 2001.

Hellebrandová, Klára. "Escapando a los estereotipos (sexuales) racializados: el caso de las personas afrodescendientes de clase media en Bogotá." *Revista de Estudios Sociales*, no. 49 (mayo, 2004): 87–100.
Hemmings, Clare. *Why Stories Matter: The Political Grammar of Feminist Theory*. Durham: Duke University Press, 2011.
Henderson, James. *Modernization in Colombia. The Laureano Gómez Years, 1889-1965*. Gainsville: University of Florida Press, 2001.
Hernández Salgar, Óscar. *Los mitos de la música nacional: Poder y emoción en las músicas populares colombianas*. Bogotá: Universidad Javeriana, 2016.
Herrera, Marta. *Ordenar para controlar: Ordenamiento espacial y control político en las llanuras del Caribe y en los Andes centrales neogranadinos, siglo XVIII*. Bogotá: Ediciones Uniandes, 2002.
Herrera Huérfano, Eliana, and Francisco Sierra Caballero. "Comunicación y pueblos indígenas en Colombia: Apuntes sobre la necesidad de una política pública." In *Miradas Propias: Pueblos indígenas, comunicación y medios en la sociedad global*, edited by Claudia Magallanes Blanco and José Manuel Ramos Rodríguez, 45–57. Quito: CIESPAL, 2016.
Hibou, Béatrice, ed. Privatizing the State. New York: Columbia University Press, 2004.
Hoffmann, Odile. "Divergencias construidas, convergencias por construir: Identidad, territorio y gobierno en la ruralidad colombiana." *Revista Colombiana de Antropología* 52, no. 1 (2016): 17–39.
Holbraad, Martin, and Morten Axel Pedersen. *The Ontological Turn: An Anthropological Exposition*. Cambridge: Cambridge University Press, 2017.
Holmes, Jennifer, Sheila Amin Gutiérrez de Piñeres, and Kevin M. Curtin. Guns, Drugs and Development in Colombia. Austin: University of Texas Press, 2009.
Holston, James. *Insurgent Citizenship: Disjunctions of Democracy and Modernity in Brazil*. Princeton: Princeton University Press, 2007.
Hommes, Rudolph. *Memoria al Congreso Nacional, 1990-1991*. Bogotá: Ministerio de Hacienda y Crédito Público, 1991.
Hooker, Juliet. "Afro-descendant Struggles for Collective Rights in Latin America: Between Race and Culture." *Souls* 10, no. 3 (2008): 279–291.
Howard Britton, Raymond. "Religión y política eran una sola cosa." In *Textos y testimonios del archipiélago: Crisis y convivencia en un territorio insular*, edited by Socorro Ramírez and Luis Alberto Restrepo, 107–116. San Andrés Isla: Universidad Nacional de Colombia sede San Andrés, 2002.
Howard Livingstone, Keisha. *San Andres: A Herstory*. San Andres Island: Casa Editorial Welcome, 2014.
Howe, Sara. "The 'Madres de La Plaza de Mayo': Asserting Motherhood; Rejecting Feminism?" *Journal of International Women's Studies* 7, no. 3 (2013): 43–50.
Hoyos, Camila, and Alejandra Londoño. *La violencia sexual. Una estrategia paramilitar en Colombia: Argumentos para imputarle responsabilidad penal a Salvatore Mancuso, Hernán Giraldo y Rodrigo Tovar*. Bogotá: Corporación Humanas, 2013.
Hristov, Jasmin. Paramilitarism and Neoliberalism: Violent Systems of Capital Accumulation in Colombia and Beyond. New York: Pluto Press, 2014.
Hudson, Rex. Colombia: A Country Study. Washington, D.C: Federal Research Division, Library of Congress, 2010.

Huber, Evelyn, and Frank Safford, eds. Agrarian Structure and Political Power: Landlord and Peasant in the Making of Latin America. Pittsburgh: University of Pittsburgh Press, 1995.

Huffschmid, Anne. "Huesos y humanidad: Antropología forense y su poder constituyente ante la desaparición forzada." Athenea Digital 15, no. 3 (2015): 195–214.

Hylton, Forrest. "Plan Colombia: The Measure of Success." The Brown Journal of World Affairs 17, no. 1 (Fall 2010): 99–115.

Hylton, Forrest. Evil Hour in Colombia. London: Verso, 2006.

Illades, Carlos, and Teresa Santiago. Estado de guerra: De la guerra sucia a la narcoguerra. México DF: Ediciones Era, 2015.

Inclán, Daniel. "La historia en disputa: El problema de la inteligibilidad del pasado." In Piel blanca, máscaras negras: Crítica de la razón decolonial, edited by Gaya Makaran and Pierre Gaussens, 45–66. Ciudad de México: Bajo Tierra, 2020.

Inglehart, Ronald, and Christian Welzel. "Changing Mass Priorities: The Link between Modernization and Democracy." Perspectives on Politics 8, no. 2 (2010): 551–567.

Instituto Colombiano de Antropología e Historia, ICANH. Elementos para la conceptualización de lo "campesino" en Colombia. Bogotá: ICANH, 2017. www.dejusticia.org/wp-content/uploads/2017/11/Concepto-t%C3%A9cnico-del-Instituto-Colombiano-de-Antropolog%C3%ADa-e-Historia-ICANH.pdf

Instituto Colombiano de Reforma Agraria, INCORA. La colonización en Colombia: Una evaluación del proceso Tomos I and II. Bogotá: Instituto Interamericano de Ciencias Agrícolas, IICA, 1974.

Instituto de Hidrología, Meteorología y Estudios Ambientales [IDEAM]. Reporte de avance del estudio nacional del agua ENA. Bogotá: IDEAM y Ministerio de Ambiente y Desarrollo Sostenible, 2018.

International Commission on Missing Persons. "The Participation of the Families of Missing Persons as a Key to Progress. Recommendations to Strengthen the Efforts of Colombian Institutions." 2021. www.icmp.int/wp-content/uploads/2021/09/icmp-gr-col-099-1-doc-participation-of-colombian-families-of-the-missing-as-key-to-progress.pdf

Isacson, Adam. "Putumayo's White Elephant, or How Not to Win Hearts and Minds." Plan Colombia and Beyond (blog). August 29, 2006.

Jackson Turner, Frederick. The Frontier in American History. The Project Gutenberg eBook, 2007. www.gutenberg.org/files/22994/22994-h/22994-h.htm

Jansson, Oscar. The Cursed Leaf: An Anthropology of the Political Economy of Cocaine Production in Southern Colombia. Uppsala: Uppsala Universitet, 2008.

Jaramillo, Jaime, Leonidas Mora, and Fernando Cubides. Colonización, coca y guerrilla. Bogotá: Universidad nacional de Colombia, 1986.

Jaramillo Marín, Jefferson. Pasados y presentes de la violencia en Colombia: Estudio sobre las comisiones de investigación, 1958–2001. Bogotá: Editorial Pontificia Universidad Javeriana, 2014.

Jaramillo, Pablo. Las servidumbres de la globalización: Viento, créditos de carbono y regímenes de propiedad en La Guajira, Colombia. Buenos Aires: Centro de Estudios Legales y Sociales, 2013.

Jaramillo Caro, Sergio. "La posibilidad de la paz." En *El inicio del proceso de paz: La fase exploratoria y el camino del Acuerdo General*. Bogotá: Oficina del Alto Comisionado para la Paz, 2018: 35–57.
Jaramillo Correa, Luis Fernando. *Memoria al Congreso Nacional, 1990–1991*. Bogotá: Ministerio de Relaciones Exteriores, 1991.
Jaramillo Vélez, Rubén. *Colombia: La modernidad postergada*. Bogotá: Editorial Temis, 1998.
Jelin, Elizabeth. *State Repression and the Labors of Memory*. Minneapolis: University of Minnesota Press, 2003.
———. *Los trabajos de la memoria*. Lima: IEP Ediciones, 2012.
Jiménez Burillo, Pablo Eduardo, Eduardo Posada Carbó, Jorge Orlando Melo, and Alejandro Gaviria. *La búsqueda de la democracia, 1960–2010*. Taurus: Madrid, 2016.
Jiménez Ramos, Luis Miguel. "Unas montañas al servicio de Bogotá: Imaginarios de naturaleza en la reforestación de los cerros orientales, 1899–1924." In *Fragmentos de historia ambiental colombiana*, edited by Claudia Leal. Bogotá: Ediciones Uniandes, 2020.
Jiménez, Jonnathan, Juan Sebastián Bernal, and David Leonardo Carmona, "La amenaza terrorista en el postconflicto." In *Políticas públicas de seguridad y defensa: Herramientas en el marco del postconflicto en Colombia*, edited by Carlos Alberto Ardila Castro and Vicente Torrijos Rivera, 57-82. Bogotá: Libros Escuela Superior de Guerra, 2017.
Jordan, Robert. "Neoliberalism and Free Trade in Latin America." *Oxford Research Encyclopedia of Latin American History*. Published online on September 29, 2016. https://doi.org/10.1093/acrefore/9780199366439.013.227.
Junguito, Roberto and Carlos Caballero. "La otra economía." *Coyuntura Económica* 8, no. 4 (1978): 103–139.
Karl, Robert A. *Forgotten Peace: Reform, Violence, and the Making of Contemporary Colombia*. Oakland: University of California Press, 2017.
Kaspersen, Lars Bo, and Jeppe Strandsbjerg. "The Spatial Practice of State Formation: Territorial Space in Denmark and Israel." *Journal of Power* 2, no. 2 (2009): 235–254.
Katra, William H. *The Argentine Generation of 1837: Echeverría, Alberdi, Sarmiento, Mitre*. London: Associated University Presses, 1996.
Katz, Stephen. "Generation X: A Critical Sociological Perspective." *Generations: Journal of the American Society of Aging* 41, no. 3 (Fall 2017): 12–19.
Keane, Webb. "Minds, Surfaces, and Reasons in the Anthropology of Ethics." In *Ordinary Ethics: Anthropology, Language, and Action*, edited by Michael Lambek, 64–83. New York: Fordham University Press, 2010.
Keddie, Amanda et al. "Beyond Culturalism: Addressing Issues of Indigenous Disadvantage through Schooling." *Australian Educational Researcher* 40, no. 1 (2013), 91–108.
Kellaway, Victoria, and Sergio J. Liévan. *Colombia: A Comedy of Errors* Independently Published, 2020.
Kelley Robin D. G. *Freedom Dreams: The Black Radical Imagination*. Boston: Beacon Press, Twentieth anniversary ed., 2022.
Klein, Naomi. *The Shock Doctrine: The Rise of Disaster Capitalism*. New York: Henry Holt and Company, 2010.

Kline, Harvey. "Review of Violence, Conflict, and Politics in Colombia by Paul Oquist." *The Journal of Politics* 44, no. 1 (February 1982): 282–283.

———. Colombia: *Democracy under Assault*. London: Routledge, 2020.

Klubock, Thomas Miller. *La Frontera: Forests and Ecological Conflict in Chile's Frontier Territory*. Durham: Duke University Press, 2014.

Koenders, Sara. "The Life and Work of Nancy Sánchez of Colombia." 2007, 70. https://www.academia.edu/7212484/The_Right_to_Speak_The_Life_and_Work_of_Nancy_S%C3%A1nchez_of_Colombia

Köhrsen, Jens. "Pentecostal Improvement Strategies: A Comparative Reading on African and South American Pentecostalism." In *"Pastures of Plenty": Tracing Religio-Scapes of Prosperity Gospel in Africa and Beyond*, edited by Andreas Heuser, 49–63. Frankfurt: Peter Lang, 2015.

Krystalli, Roxani C. "Narrating Victimhood: Dilemmas and (in)Dignities." *International Feminist Journal of Politics* 23, no. 1 (2021): 125–146.

Kupperman, Karen Ordahl. *Providence Island, 1630–1641: The Other Puritan Colony*. New York: Cambridge University Press, 1995.

Laclau, Ernesto. "Identidad y hegemonía: El rol de la universalidad en la constitución de lógicas políticas." In *Contingencia, hegemonía y universalidad: Diálogos contemporáneos en la izquierda*, edited by Judith Butler, Ernesto Laclau and Slavoj Zizek. Buenos Aires: FCE, 2003: 49–93.

Lakshmanan, Indira A. R. "Colombia Sets an Example for Peace and Reconciliation." *The Boston Globe*, September 29, 2016.

Lambek, Michael. *Ordinary Ethics: Anthropology, Language, and Action*. New York: Fordham University Press. 2010.

Lane, Jill. "Hemispheric America in Deep Time." *Theatre Research International* 35, no. 2 (2010): 111–125.

Laó-Montes, Agustín. "Neoliberalismo racial y políticas afrolatinoamericanas de cara a la crisis global." In *Afrodescendencias: Voces en Resistencia*, edited by Rosa Campoalegre Septien, 245–265. Buenos Aires: CLACSO, 2018.

———. *Contrapunteos Afrodiaspóricos: Cartografías políticas de Nuestra Afroamérica*. Bogotá: Universidad Externado de Colombia, 2020.

LaPlante, Lisa. "The Law of Remedies and the Clean Hands Doctrine: Exclusionary Reparation Policies in Peru's Political Transition." *American University International Law Review* 23, no. 1 (2009): 51–90.

LaRosa, Michael J., and German Mejía. *Colombia: A Concise Contemporary History*. Lanham: Rowman & Littlefield, 2017.

Larraín, Jorge. "Modernidad e identidad en América Latina." *Revista Universum* (1997): 12–31.

———. "Globalización e identidad nacional." *Revista chilena de humanidades* 20 (2000): 21–42.

———. "Modernity and Identity: Cultural Change in Latin America." In *Latin America Transformed: Globalization and Modernity*, edited by Robert N. Gwynne and Kay Cristobal, 22–38. London: Routledge, 2004.

Laurent, Virgine. "Multiculturalism in Colombia: Twenty-Five Years." *Global Center for Pluralism*. Universidad de los Andes (January 2008): 1–26.

Leal, Claudia. "From Threatening to Threatened Jungles." In *A Living Past: Environmental Histories of Modern Latin America*, edited by John Soluri, Claudia Leal, and José Augusto Pádua, 115–137. New York: Berghahn Books, 2018.

———. *Landscapes of Freedom: Building a Postemancipation Society in the Rainforests of Western Colombia.* Tucson: The University of Arizona Press, 2018.

———. "National Parks in Colombia." In *The Oxford Research Encyclopedia of Latin American History.* New York: Oxford University Press, 2019 [online].

———. "Un tesoro reservado para la ciencia: El inusual comienzo de la conservación de la naturaleza en Colombia (décadas de 1940 y 1950)." *Historia Crítica*, no. 74 (2019): 95–126.

Leal Buitrago, Francisco. "La política de seguridad democrática: 2002–2005." *Análisis Político*, no. 57 (mayo–agosto, 2006): 3–30.

Lebot, Yvon. *Sortir de la violence. Ce que nous enseigne l' Amérique latine.* Paris: Maison des Sciencies de l'Homme, 2021.

LeCain, Timothy. *The Matter of History: How Things Create the Past.* Cambridge: Cambridge University Press, 2017.

LeGrand, Catherine. *Frontier Expansion and Peasant Protest in Colombia, 1850–1936.* Albuquerque: University of New Mexico Press, 1986.

———. *Colonización y protesta campesina en Colombia (1850–1950).* Bogotá: Ediciones Uniandes, Universidad Nacional de Colombia, CINEP, 1988.

Leguízamo Barbosa, Alberto, ed. *Historia y aportes de la ingeniería forestal en Colombia*, Vol. I. Bogotá: Asociación Colombiana de Ingenieros Forestales, 2009.

León, Juanita. Country of Bullets: Chronicles of War. Albuquerque: University of New Mexico Press, 2009.

Lewis, Marvin A. *Literatura afrocolombiana en sus contextos naturales: Imperialismo ecológico y cimarronismo cultural.* Cali: Editorial Universidad del Valle, 2019.

Lewy, Guenter. *Why America Needs Religion: Secular Modernity and its Discontents.* Cambridge, UK: Cambridge University Press, 1996.

Lindsay-Poland, John. *Plan Colombia: U.S. Ally Atrocities and Community Activism.* Durham: Duke University Press, 2018.

Liévano Aguirre, Indalecio. *Los grandes conffictos sociales y económicos de nuestra historia.* Vols. 1 and 2. Bogotá: Imprenta Nacional, [1960, 1966] 1996.

Loker, William M. "'Campesinos' and the Crisis of Modernization in Latin America." *Journal of Political Ecology* 3, no. 1 (1996): 69–88.

Londoño Hoyos, Fernando. *Con licencia para hablar.* Bogotá: Penguin Random House, 2004.

López, Augusto Javier Gómez. n. d. "El valle de Sibundoy: El despojo de una heredad. Los dispositivos ideológicos, disciplinarios y morales de dominación." *Anuario de Historia Social y de la Cultura*, 32 (2005): 51–73.

López, Manuel Francisco, Julian Bommer, and Patricia Méndez. "The Seismic Performance of Bahareque Dwellings in El Salvador." Presented at the 13th World Conference on Earthquake Engineering, Vancouver, Canada, August 1–6, 2004. www.iitk.ac.in/nicee/wcee/article/13_2646.pdf.

López-Pedreros, A. Ricardo. " 'Nosotros también somos parte del pueblo': Gaitanismo, empleados y la formación histórica de la clase media en Bogotá, 1936–1948." *Revista de Estudios Sociales* 7 (December 2007): 84–105.

———. *Makers of Democracy: A Transnational History of the Middle Classes in Colombia.* Durham: Duke University Press, 2019.

López-Pedreros, A. Ricardo with Barbara Weinstein. "We Shall Be All." In *The Making of the Middle Class: Toward a Transnational History*, edited by A. Ricardo López-Pedreros and Barbara Weinstein, 1–11. Durham: Duke University Press, 2012.

López Restrepo, Andrés. "Narcotráfico, ilegalidad y conflicto armado en Colombia." In *Nuestra guerra sin nombre: Transformaciones del conflicto in Colombia*, edited by Francisco Gutiérrez Sanín, María Emma Wills y Gonzalo Sánchez, 405–440.Bogotá: IEPRI, Universidad Nacional, 2006.

Losonczy, Anne. M. "Murderous Returns: Armed Violence, Suicide and Exhumation in the Emberá Katío Economy of Death (Chocó and Antioquia, Colombia)." *Human Remains and Violence: An Interdisciplinary Journal* 2, no. 2 (2016): 67–83.

———. "Murderous Spirits: Shamanic Interpretation of Armed Violence, Suicide, and Exhumation in the Economy of Death of the Emberá (Chocó, Antioquia, Colombia)." In *Amerindian Socio-Cosmologies between the Andes, Amazonia and* Mesoamerica, edited by Ernst Halbmayer, 330–344. New York: Routledge, 2020.

Lyons, Kristina M. *Vital Decomposition: Soil Practitioners and Life Politics*. Durham, NC: Duke University Press, 2020.

Maisuria, Alpesh and Sveja Helmses. *Life for the Academic in the Neoliberal University*. New York: Routledge, 2000.

MacLean, Nancy. *Democracy in Chains: The Deep History of the Radical Right's Stealth Plan for America*. New York: Penguin Books, 2017.

Maleywa, Inti, and Martín Batalla. "Desenterrando memorias." Part I, Comité Comunicaciones La Guajira. February 27, 2017. YouTube video, 3:58. www.youtube.com/watch?v=D2CeXtaF6Hc

McLean, Philip. "Colombia: Failed, Failing or Just Weak?" *The Washington Quarterly* 25, no. 3 (Summer 2002): 123–134.

Mann, Michael. *The Sources of Social Power: A History of Power from the Beginning to AD 1760*. Cambridge: Cambridge University Press, 2012.

Marino, Katherine M. *Feminism for the Americas: The Making of an International Human Rights Movement*. Chapel Hill: The University of North Carolina Press, 2019.

Marras, Sergio. "Comedia de equivocaciones: Entrevista a Mario Vargas Llosa." In *América Latina: Marca registrada*. Santiago de Chile: Editorial Andrés Bello, 1992.

Marrero, Raúl. *El Señor de la salsa*. Sello Salson 07(1431) 00006, LP, Álbum Colombia, 1987.

Martín-Barbero, Jesús. *De Los medios a las mediaciones: Comunicación, cultura y hegemonía*, 6th ed. México D.F: Anthropos: Universidad Autónoma Metropolitana Azcapotzalco, 2010.

Martínez-Echazábal, Lourdes. "*Mestizaje* and the Discourse of National/Cultural Identity in Latin America, 1845–1959." *Latin American Perspectives* 25, no. 3 (1998): 21–42.

Martini, Stella. *Periodismo, noticia y noticiabilidad*. Buenos Aires: Grupo Editorial Norma, 2000.

Masi de Casanova, Erynn. "Beauty Ideology in Latin America." *DObra [s]: Revista Da Associação Brasileira de Estudos de Pesquisas Em Moda* 11, no. 23 (2018): 10–21.

Mays, Kyle T. *City of Dispossessions: Indigenous Peoples, African Americans, and the Creation of Modern Detroit*. Philadelphia: University of Pennsylvania Press, 2022.

Mbembe, Achille. "Necropolitics." *Public Culture* 15, no. 1 (2002): 11–40.
———. *Critique of Black Reason*. Durham: Duke University Press, 2017.
———. "The Banality of Power and the Aesthetics of Vulgarity in the Postcolony." *Public Culture* 4, no. 2 (1992): 1–30.
McCarthy, James. "A Socioecological Fix to Capitalist Crisis and Climate Change? The Possibilities and Limits of Renewable Energy." *Environment and Planning A: Economy and Space* 47, no. 12 (2015): 2485–2502.
McCombs, Maxwell E., and Donald L. Shaw. "The Agenda-Setting Function of Mass Media." *Public Opinion Quarterly* 36, no. 2 (1972): 176–187.
McCoy, Jennifer and Murat Somer. "Toward a Theory of Pernicious Polarization and How It Harms Democracies: Comparative Evidence and Possible Remedies." *Annals of the American Academy of Political and Social Science* 681, no. 1 (2019): 234–271.
Medina, David. "Una imagen resonante." In *Duelos*, edited by Clemencia Echeverri. Bogotá: Museo Nacional de Colombia and Mincultura, 2019. Exhibition Catalog, 82–85.
Meertens, Donny. *Elusive Justice: Women, Land Rights, and Colombia's Transition to Peace*. Wisconsin: University of Wisconsin Press, 2019.
Meillassoux, Claude. *Mujeres, graneros y capitales*. México: Siglo XXI, 1987.
Meisel Roca, Adolfo. "La continentalización de San Andrés Islas, Colombia: Panyas, Raizales y Turismo, 1953–2003." In *Economía y medio ambiente del archipiélago de San Andrés, Providencia y Santa Catalina*, edited by Adolfo Meisel Roca and María Aguilar Díaz, 19–45. Bogotá: Banco de la República, 2016.
Mejía, William. "Casi dos siglos de migración colombiana a Estados Unidos." *Papeles de Población* 24, no. 98 (2018): 65–101.
Mejía Villa, Julián. "La fotografía violenta: Dispositivo alegórico y construcción emblemática de la masacre de Bojayá." MA Thesis, Universidad Nacional de Colombia, 2017.
Melo, Jorge Orlando. Colombia: Una historia mínima. Una mirada integral al país. Bogotá: Crítica, 2021.
Mendoza, Breny. Colonialidad, género y democracia. Madrid: Akal, 2023.
Miano, Léonor. *Vivir en la frontera*. Madrid: Los libros de la catarata, 2016.
Mignolo, Walter D. "Enduring Enchantment: Secularism and the Epistemic Privileges of Modernity." In *Postcolonial Philosophy of Religion*, edited by Purushottama Bilimoria and Andrew B. Irvine, 273–292. Dordrecht, Netherlands: Springer, 2009.
Mignolo, Walter D., and Catherine E. Walsh. *On Decoloniality: Concepts, Analytics, Praxis*. Durham: Duke University Press, 2018.
Mina Aragón, William. "Manuel Zapata Olivella: Escritor y humanista." *Afro-Hispanic Review* 25, no. 1 (Spring 2006): 25–38.
———. "Manuel Zapata Olivella: A Wandering Thinker (1920–2004)." In *Routledge Handbook of Afro-Latin American Studies*, edited by Bernd Reiter and John Antón Sánchez. New York: Routledge, 2022: 540–544.
———, ed. *Manuel Zapata Olivella: Un legado intercultural. Perspectiva intelectual, literaria y política de un afrocolombiano cosmopolita*. Bogotá: Fundación Universitaria de Popayán, Ediciones Desde Abajo, 2016.

———. "Estudio introductorio: Alienación y desalienación de la novela." In *Deslumbramientos de América*. Cali: Universidad del Pacífico, 2017: 169–172.
———, ed. *Deslumbramientos de América, Manuel Zapata Olivella: humanista afrodiaspórico*. Bogotá: Universidad del Pacífico, Asociación Iberoamericana de Filosofía Práctica, 2020.
———. "Manuel Zapata Olivella: intelectual afrodiaspórico." *Revista Communitas* 5, no. 10 (April/June 2021): 63–78.
Mina Aragón, William, George Palacios, and Cristina Cabral. "Intelectualidad, literatura y multiculturalismo in Manuel Zapata Olivella (1920–2020)." Wokrshop for the Certificate in African American Studies at Harvard University, Cambridge, MA, 2020.
Ministerio de Agricultura. *Agricultura Campesina, familiar y comunitaria ACFC*. Bogotá: Ministerio de Agricultura y Desarrollo Rural, Unión Europea, 2012. www.minagricultura.gov.co/Documents/lineamientos-acfc.pdf.
Ministerio de Cultura de Colombia. *Informe de gestión. Enero—diciembre 2019*. Ministerio de Cultura. www.mincultura.gov.co/prensa/noticias/Documents/Patrimonio/INFORME%20GESTION%202019%20MINCULTURA%20V31012020.pdf. Accessed August 20, 2020.
———. "Entrevista: La *playlist* de la ministra." *Facebook*, June 4, 2020. www.facebook.com/MinisterioCultura/videos/entrevista-la-playlist-de-la-ministra/254784129274605/. Accessed August 20, 2020.
———. "Mincultura lanza listado de '100 canciones #ColombiaCreaTalento' para promover a los artistas nacionales." Ministerio de Cultura, July 2, 2020. www.mincultura.gov.co/prensa/noticias/Paginas/Mincultura-lanza-listado-de-%E2%80%98100-canciones-ColombiaCreaTalento%E2%80%99-para-promover-a-los-artistas-nacionales-.aspx. Accessed August 20, 2020.
———. *Sistema de información musical* (SIMUS). Ministerio de Cultura. https://simus.mincultura.gov.co/. Accessed August 20, 2020.
Ministerio de Minas y Energía. *Transición energética: Un legado para el presente y el futuro de Colombia*. Bogotá: Banco Interamericano de Desarrollo, 2021.
Mirowski, Philip. "The Political Movement that Dared Not Speak its own Name: The Neoliberal Thought Collective Under Erasure." *Institute for New Economic Thinking Working Paper Series*. No. 23 (September 2014).
Molano, Alfredo *Aguas arriba: Entre la coca y el oro*. Bogotá: Debolsillo, 2017.
Mollison, James, and Rainbow Nelson. *The Memory of Pablo Escobar*. London: Chris Boot, 2007.
Mongey, Vanessa. *Rogue Revolutionaries: The Fight for Legitimacy in the Greater Caribbean*. Philadelphia: University of Pennsylvania Press, 2020.
Montaña, Vladimir, Natalia Robledo, and Soraya Maite Yie. "La categoría campesino y sus representaciones en Colombia: Polisemia histórica y regional." *Revista Colombiana de Antropología* 58, no. 1 (2022): 9–24.
Montenegro Lancheros, Hernán C. "Ampliaciones y quiebres del reconocimiento político del campesinado colombiano: Un análisis a la luz de la Cumbre Agraria, Campesina, Étnica y Popular (Cacep)." *Revista Colombiana de Antropología* 52, no. 1 (2016): 169–195.
Montoya-Londoño, Catalina. "In Search of a Model for the Colombian Media System Today." In *Media Systems and Communication Policies in Latin America*,

edited by Manuel Alejandro Guerrero and Mireya Márquez-Ramírez, 66–81. New York: Palgrave Macmillan, 2014.
Montoya Correa, Jonathan Andrés. "¿Profesión? ¡Colombianistas!" El Efaitense no. 109 (2015–2): 168–173.
Mookherjee, Nayanika, Nigel Rapport, Lisette Josephides, Ghassan Hage, Lindi Renier Todd, and Gillian Cowlishaw. "The Ethics of Apology: A Set of Commentaries." *Critique of Anthropology* 29, no. 3 (2009): 345–366.
Moraes Silva, Graziella, Luciana Souza Leão, and Barbara Grillo. "Seeing Whites: Views of Black Brazilians in Rio de Janeiro." *Ethnic and Racial Studies* 43, no. 4 (2020): 632–651.
Morales, Lorenzo, and Martha Ruiz. *Hechos para contar: Conversaciones con diez periodistas colombianos*. Bogotá: Penguin Random House, 2013.
Moreno Figueroa, Mónica, and Peter Wade, eds. *Against Racism: Organizing for Social Change in Latin America*. Pittsburgh: Pittsburgh University Press, 2022.
Moser, Walter. "Eulogy for Bolívar Echeverría." *Anales del Instituto de Investigaciones Estéticas* 32, no. 97 (2010): 195–203.
Mouffe, Chantal. "Política y pasiones: Las apuestas de la democracia." In *Pensar este tiempo: Espacios, afectos, pertenencias*, edited by Leonor Arfuch. Buenos Aires: Paidós, 2005: 75–100.
Moutinho, Laura. "Raza, género y sexualidad en el Brasil contemporáneo." In *Raza, etnicidad y sexualidades: Ciudadanía y multiculturalismo en América Latina*, edited by Peter Wade, Fernando Urrea Giraldo, and Mara Viveros Vigoya, 223–245. Bogotá: Universidad Nacional de Colombia, Facultad de Ciencias Humanas, Centro de Estudios Sociales (CES), Escuela de Estudios de Género, 2008.
Mudimbe, V. Y. *The Invention of Africa: Gnosis, Philosophy, and the Order of Knowledge*. Bloomington: Indiana University Press, 1988.
Muñoz, Catalina. *A Fervent Crusade for the National Soul: Cultural Politics in Colombia, 1930–1946*. Lanham: Lexington Books, 2022.
Murillo, Mario A. "Weaving a Communication Quilt in Colombia: Civil Conflict, Indigenous Resistance, and Community Radio in Northern Cauca." In *Global Indigenous Media: Cultures, Poetics, and Politics*, edited by Pamela Wilson and Michelle Stewart. Durham: Duke University Press, 2008: 145–159.
Murillo Posada, Amparo. "La modernización y las violencias." In *Historia de Colombia: Todo lo que hay que saber*, edited by Luis Enrique Rodríguez Baquero et al., 278–325. Bogotá: Editorial Taurus, 2007.
Murray, Pamela. "Foreword" to Michael LaRosa and Germán Rodrigo Mejía Pavony. *Colombia: A Concise Contemporary History*, xiii–xvi. Lanham: Rowman & Littlefield, 2017.
Musto, Stefan A. *Los medios de comunicación social al servicio del desarollo rural: Análisis de eficiencia de "Acción Cultural Popular—Radio Sutatenza."* Bogotá: Acción Cultural Popular, 1971.
Naseemullah, Adnan, and Paul Staniland. "Indirect Rule and Varieties of Governance." *Governance* 29, no. 1 (2016): 13–30.
Naylor, Robert. *Penny Ante Imperialism: The Mosquito Shore and the Bay of Honduras. A Case Study of British Informal Empire*. Rutherford, NJ: Fairleigh Dickinson University Press, 1989.

Ng'weno, Bettina. "¿Puede la etnicidad reemplazar lo racial? Afrocolombianos, indigenidad y el Estado multicultural en Colombia." *Revista Colombiana de Antropología* 49, no. 1 (2013): 71–104.

Nora, Pierre. *Les Lieux de mémoire*. Paris: Editions Gallimard, 1997.

Nugent, James Patrick. "Ontario's Infrastructure Boom: A Socioecological Fix for Air Pollution, Congestion, Jobs, and Profits." *Environment and Planning A: Economy and Space* 47, no. 12 (2015): 2465–2484. https://doi.org/10.1068%2Fa140176p.

Obertreis, Julia, Timothy Moss, Peter Mollinga, and Christine Bichsel. "Water, Infrastructure, and Political Rule: Introduction to the Special Issue." *Water Alternatives* 9, no. 2 (2016): 168–181.

Ocampo, José Antonio. *Colombia y la economía mundial*. Bogotá: Siglo XXI-Fedesarrollo, 1984.

Ochoa Escobar, Juan Sebastián. *Sonido sabanero y sonido paisa: La producción de música tropical en Medellín durante los años sesenta*. Bogotá: Pontificia Universidad Javeriana, 2018.

Ochoa Gautier, Ana María. *Aurality*. Durham: Duke University Press, 2014.

O'Connor, Alan. *Community Radio in Bolivia: The Miners' Radio Stations*. Lewiston: Edwin Mellen Press, 2004.

Oficina en Colombia del Alto Comisionado de las Naciones Unidas para los Derechos Humanos. "Sistematización del acompañamiento y documentación de la participación de las víctimas de Bojayá, de la articulación interinstitucional y de la cooperación internacional en el proceso de búsqueda, exhumación, identificación, individualización y entrega digna." 2019. Unpublished document.

———. "Informe de la Oficina en Colombia del Alto Comisionado de las Naciones Unidas para los Derechos Humanos sobre su Misión de Observación en el Medio Atrato." Mayo 2002. https://www.ohchr.org/es/countries/colombia

Offner, Amy. *Sorting Out the Mixed Economy: The Rise and Fall of Welfare and Development State in the Americas*. Princeton: Princeton University Press, 2020.

Ojeda, Diana. "Green Pretexts: Ecotourism, Neoliberal Conservation and Land Grabbing in Tayrona National Natural Park, Colombia." *Journal of Peasant Studies* 39, no. 2 (2012): 357–375.

Ojeda, Diana and Eloísa Berman-Arévalo., "Ordinary Geographies: Care, Violence, and Agrarian Extractivism in 'Post-Conflict' Colombia." *Antipode* 52, no. 6 (2020): 1583–1602.

———. "War and Tourism: The Banal Geographies of Security in Colombia's 'Retaking.'" *Geopolitics* 18, no. 4 (2013): 759–778.

Ordóñez, Freddy. *Zonas de reservas campesinas: Elementos introductorios y de debate*. Bogotá: Instituto Latinoamericano para una Sociedad y un Derecho Alternativos, 2012.

Organisation for Economic Co-operation and Development, OECD. "A Broken Social Elevator? How to Promote Social Mobility." Paris: OECD Publishing, 2018. https://doi.org/10.1787/9789264301085-en.

Ortiz, Yaneth, et al. *Agua y mujer: Historias, cuentos y más sobre nosotras, la Púlooi y Kasouolü en el resguardo Wayúu Lomamato*. Bogotá: Centro de Investigación y Educación Popular [CINEP], 2018.

Osejo Varona, Alejandra, et al. "Zonas de Reserva Campesina en el escenario del posconflicto: Una herramienta comunitaria para el manejo de la biodiversidad." In *Biodiversidad 2017: Estado y tendencias de la biodiversidad continental de Colombia*, edited by L. A. Moreno, C. Rueda, and G. I. Andrade. Bogotá: Instituto de Investigación de Recursos Biológicos Alexander von Humboldt, 2018: 403–405.

Osei-Kofi, Nana. "Junior Faculty of Color in the Corporate University: Implications of Neoliberalism and Neoconservatism on Research, Teaching and Service." In *The Truly Diverse Faculty: New Dialogues in American Higher Education*, edited by Stephanie A. Fryberg and Ernesto Javier Martínez, chapter 3. New York: Palgrave Macmillan, 2014.

Oslender, Ulrich. Geographies of the Social Movements: Afro-Colombian Mobilization and the Aquatic Space. Durham: Duke University Press, 2016.

Osorio, Edna Melissa. "Dilucidando silencios: Hernán Giraldo y la violencia reproductiva en el conflicto armado colombiano." Masters Thesis, Facultad de Ciencias Políticas y Relaciones Internacionales, Universidad Javeriana, Bogotá, 2021.

Owen, Diana. "El papel de los nuevos medios en la política." In *La era de la perplejidad: Repensar el mundo que conocíamos*. Madrid: BBVA, 2017.

Pablo Escobar, Ángel o Demonio. Directed by Jorge Granier. Netflix, Sierralta Entertainment and Angostura Film Company, 2007.

Padilla, Nelson. "Jesús Abad Colorado: La mirada por excelencia." *Festival Gabo*, September 10, 2019. https://premioggm.org/noticias/2019/09/jesus-abad-Abad Colorado-la-mirada-por-excelencia/.

Padilla, Raymond V. and Rudolfo Chávez Chávez. *The Leaning Ivory Tower: Latino Professors in American Universities*. Albany: SUNY Press, 1995.

Palabras Más. "Palabras más con Jesús Abad Colorado (2/2)." Published June 18, 2017. Video, 24:27. https://youtu.be/ZAk7Qve9MD8.

Palacio Castañeda, Germán A. *Territorios improbables: Historias y ambientes*. Bogotá: Editorial Magisterio, 2018.

Palacios, George. *Manuel Zapata Olivella (1920–2004): Pensador político, radical y hereje de la diáspora africana en las Américas*. Medellín: Editorial Universidad Pontificia Bolivariana, 2020.

Palacios, Marco. *Between Legitimacy and Violence: A History of Colombia, 1875–2002*, translated by Richard Stoller. Durham: Duke University Press, 2006.

Paley, Julia. "Introduction." In *Democracy: Anthropological Perspectives*, edited by Julia Paley. 3–20. Santa Fe: School for Advanced Research Press, 2008.

———. ed. *Democracy: Anthropological Approaches*. Santa Fe: School of Advance Research Press, 2008.

Paley, Dawn. *Drug War Capitalism*. Oakland: AK Press, 2014.

Parada Hernández, María Mónica, and Margarita Marín Jaramillo. "Mujeres y coca: Una relación agridulce." *Análisis Político* 32, no. 97 (2019): 45–70.

Pardo, Diana, and Diego Cardona. "El procedimiento de la certificación y las relaciones entre Colombia y los Estados Unidos." *Colombia Internacional* 29 (1995): 3–6.

Pardo, Mauricio. *Movimentos negros na região do Pacífico colombiano: organizações, violencia e territorio*. Florianópolis, SC: Universidade Federal de Santa Catarina, 2016.

Pardo, Neyla G. "The Dual Causes of Fragmentation: Democratic Security and the Communitarian State in Colombian Politics." In *Discourse & Society* 31, no. 1 (2020): 64–84.
Parra, Mayra, and Alexandra Urán. "Parentesco y precariedad en la minería de oro en Chocó, Colombia." *Revista Mexicana de Sociología* 80, no. 4 (septiembre-diciembre, 2018): 801–826.)
Parrini, Rodrigo, María Victoria Uribe. *La violencia y su sombra: Reflexiones desde Colombia y México*. Mexico City and Bogotá: Universidad Autónoma Metropolitana and Universidad del Rosario, 2021.
Parsons, James J. *San Andrés and Providencia: English-Speaking Islands in the Western Caribbean*. Berkeley: University of California Press, 1956.
———. *Antioqueño colonization in Western Colombia*, revised ed. Berkeley: University of California Press, 1968.
Paschel, Tianna S. *Becoming Black Political Subjects: Movements and Ethno-Racial Rights in Colombia and Brazil*. Princeton: Princeton University Press, 2016.
Pattillo, Mary, Rosa Emilia Bermúdez, and Ana María Mosquera. "Estamos distanciados: The Black Middle Class and Politics in Cali, Colombia." *Du Bois Review* (2021): 1–24.
Paz, Octavio. *The Labyrinth of Solitude*. New York: Grove Press, 1985.
Pearce, Jenny. *Colombia inside the Labyrinth*. London: Latin America Bureau, 1990.
Peck, Jamie. "Explaining (with) Neoliberalism." *Territory, Politics, Governance* 1, no. 2 (2013): 132–157.
Pécaut, Daniel. *Orden y violencia: Colombia 1930–1954*. Bogotá: Siglo XXI, 1987.
———. *Crónica de dos décadas de política colombiana, 1968–1988*. Bogotá: Siglo Veintiuno Editores, 1989.
Pedraza Torres, Hilario. "El proceso de paz en Caquetá (El caso del Caguán)." Unpublished manuscript, 1986.
Pennycook, Gordon, and David G. Rand. "Fighting Misinformation on Social Media Using Crowdsourced Judgments of News Source Quality." *Proceedings of the National Academy of Sciences* 116, no. 7 (2019): 2521–2526.
Peralta, Laly Catalina. "Curules especiales para comunidades Negras: ¿Realidad o ilusión?" *Estudios Socio-Jurídicos* 7, no. 2 (2005): 147–172.
Peralta, Manuel. *Límites de Costa Rica y Colombia: Nuevos documentos para la historia de su jurisdicción territorial, con notas, comentarios y un examen de la cartografía de Costa Rica y Veragua por Manuel María de Peralta*. Madrid Hernández, 1890.
Peralta, Victoria and Michael LaRosa, *Los colombianistas: Una completa visión de los investigadores extranjeros que estudian Colombia*. Bogotá: Planeta, 1997.
Pérez, José Gregorio. *Operación Cali Pachanguero*. Bogotá: Editorial Planeta, 2005.
Pérez Morales, Edgardo. *La obra de Dios y el trabajo del hombre: Percepción y transformación de la naturaleza en el virreinato del Nuevo Reino de Granada*. Medellín: Universidad Nacional de Colombia sede Medellín, 2011.
Petersen, Walwin G. "Cultura y tradición de los habitantes de San Andrés y Providencia." In *San Andrés y Providencia: Tradiciones culturales y coyuntura política*, edited by Isabel Clemente. Bogotá: Ediciones Uniandes, 1989.
———. *The Province of Providence*. Nashville: R.H Boyd Publishing, 2002.

Petro, Gustavo. "Discurso en el lanzamiento del Informe Final de la Comisión de la Verdad." Teatro Jorge Eliécer Gaitán, 27 de junio, 2022. www.youtube.com/watch?v=VIfiEPBF8S8, consultado el 19 de julio de 2022.
Pisano, Pietro. "Triunfadores, desplazados sociales y Cenicientas: Representaciones sobre raza y ascenso social en la segunda mitad del siglo XX." *Universitas Humanística* 77 (marzo 2014): 95–119.
Pizano, Eduardo. Plan Colombia: The View from the Presidential Palace. Carlisle: Strategic Studies Institute of the U.S. Army War College, 2001.
Plazas Vega, Luis Alfonso. ¿Desaparecidos? El negocio del dolor. Bogotá: Dipon, 2011.
Pomare Howard, Martin Alonso. *Clamor of the Islands: Saint Andrew and Old Providence under Colombian Rule*, edited by Jorge Duchesne Winter. Pittsburgh: Instituto Internacional de Literatura Iberoamericana, 2021.
Ponce de León, Carolina, and Jesús Abad Colorado. *Mirar de la vida profunda*. Bogotá: Paralelo 10 Ltda., 2015.
Posada, Valeria. "Historia rev(b)elada: La voz guerrillera que narra el conflicto en desenterrando memorias." In *Cuadernos de Curaduría no. 16*. Bogotá: Museo Nacional de Colombia, 2020.
Posada Carbo, Eduardo. *La nación soñada: Violencia, liberalismo y democracia en Colombia*. Bogotá: Grupo Editorial Norma, 2007.
Polit Dueñas, Gabriela. *Narrating Narcos: Culiacán and Medellín*. Pittsburgh: University of Pittsburgh Press, 2013.
Price, Thomas J. "Algunos aspectos de estabilidad y desorganización cultural en una comunidad isleña del Caribe Colombiano." *Revista Colombiana de Antropología* III (jul.–dic. 1954): 11–54.
Pulleiro, Adrian. *La radio alternativa en América Latina: Debates y desplazamientos en la década de 1990*. Buenos Aires: Universidad de Buenos Aires, 2012.
Pusey, Enrique. "Los eventos de 1822. Vistos por un raizal." In *Memorias, historias y olvidos: Colonialismo, sociedad y política en el archipiélago de San Andrés y Providencia*, edited by Raúl Román Romero and Antonino Vidal Ortega, 243–250. Bogotá: Editorial Universidad Nacional de Colombia, 2019.
Quiceno, Natalia. *Vivir sabroso: Luchas y movimientos afroatrateños, en Bojayá, Chocó, Colombia*. Bogotá: Editorial Universidad del Rosario, 2016.
Quijano, Aníbal. "Coloniality of Power and Eurocentrism in Latin America." *International Sociology* 15, no. 2 (2000): 215–232. https://doi.org/10.1177%2F0268580900015002005.
Quintero Rivera, Ángel G. *La danza de la insurrección: Para una sociología de la música latinoamericana: textos reunidos*. Buenos Aires: CLACSO, 2020.
Quishpe, Rafael. "Los excombatientes y la memoria: Tensiones y retos de la memoria colectiva construida por las FARC en el posconflicto colombiano." *Análisis Político* 31, no. 93 (2018): 93–114.
Radcliffe, Sarah A. "Development for a Postneoliberal Era? Sumak Kawsay, Living Well and the Limits to Decolonisation in Ecuador." *Geoforum* 43, no. 2 (2012): 240–249.
Raid, Michael. *The Forgotten Continent: A History of the New Latin America*. New Haven: Yale University Press, 2017.

Ramírez Bacca Renzo, and León Darío Marín Arenas. "Seguridad e ideología en Colombia, 1978–1982: Análisis crítico del discurso de Julio César Turbay Ayala." *Anuario de Historia Regional y de las Fronteras* 20, no. 2 (July–December 2015): 241–269.

Ramírez, Carlos Andrés. "Indigenismo de derecha. La formación de la OPIC como 'revolución pasiva'." *Revista de Estudios Sociales* 51 (2015): 89–104.

Ramírez, María Clemencia. "Maintaining Democracy in Colombia through Political Exclusion, States of Exception, Counterinsurgency, and Dirty War." In *Violent Democracies in Latin America*, edited by Enrique Desmond Arias and Daniel M. Goldstein. Durham: Duke University Press, 2010: 84–103.

———. *Between the Guerrillas and the State: The Cocalero Movement, Citizenship, and Identity in the Colombian Amazon*. Durham: Duke University Press, 2011.

———. "Genealogía de la categoría de colono: Imágenes y representaciones en las zonas de frontera y su devenir en campesino colono y campesino cocalero." *Revista Colombiana de Antropología* 58, no. 1 (2022): 29–60.

Ramírez, María Clemencia, Íngrid Bolívar, Juliana Iglesias, María Clara Torres, and Teófilo Vásquez. *Elecciones, Coca, Conflicto y Partidos Politicos en Putumayo, 1980–2007*. Bogotá: CINEP/PPP, ICANH, Colciencias, 2010.

Ramírez, Socorro, and Luis Alberto Restrepo. *Textos y testimonios del archipiélago: Crisis y convivencia en un territorio insular*. San Andrés Isla, Col.: Universidad Nacional de Colombia Sede San Andrés, 2002.

Rancière, Jacques. *The Names of History: On the Poetics of Knowledge*. Minneapolis: University of Minnesota Press, 1994.

Randall, Stephen J. *Colombia and the United States: Hegemony and Interdependence*. Athens: University of Georgia Press, 1992.

———. *Frente a la estrella polar: Colombia y los Estados Unidos desde 1974*. Bogotá: Taurus, 2017.

Ranocchiari, Dano. "Música urbana en San Andrés Isla: ¿Hacia una etnicidad más inclusiva." *Cuadernos del Caribe* 19 (ene.–jul. 2015): 11–23.

Rappaport, Joanne. *Cowards Don't Make History: Orlando Fals Borda and the Origins of Participatory Action Research*. Durham: Duke University Press, 2020.

Rausch, Jane. *Colombia: Territorial Rule and the Llanos Frontier*. Gainesville: University of Florida Press, 1999.

Reátegui, Félix, ed. *Justicia transicional: Manual para América Latina*. Brasilia: Comisión de Amnistía, Ministerio de Justicia; Nueva York: Centro Internacional para la Justicia Transicional, 2011.

Registraduría Nacional de Estado Civil. "Plebiscito 2 de octubre 2016, República de Colombia." https://elecciones.registraduria.gov.co/pre_plebis_2016/99PL/DPLZZZZZZZZZZZZZZZZZZ_L1.htm

Restrepo, Eduardo. "Imaginando comunidad negra: Etnografía de la etnización de las poblaciones negras en el Pacífico sur colombiano." In *Acción colectiva, Estado y etnicidad en el Pacífico colombiano*, edited by Mauricio Pardo, 41–70. Bogotá: ICANH, Colciencias, 2001.

———, ed. *Estudios afrocolombianos hoy: Aportes a un campo transdisciplinario*. Popayán, Colombia: Editorial Universidad del Cauca, 2013.

———. *Etnización de la negridad: La invención de las comunidades negras como grupo étnico en Colombia*. Popayán: Universidad del Cauca, 2013.

Restrepo, Eduardo, and Alejandra Gutiérrez. *Misioneros y organizaciones campesinas en el río Atrato, Chocó*. Medellín: Uniclaretiana, 2017.
Reyes, Alejandro. *Guerreros y campesinos: El despojo de la tierra en Colombia*. Buenos Aires: Grupo Editorial Norma, 2009.
Rhenals Doria, Ana Milena, and Francisco Javier Flórez Bolívar. "Marginados, pero no marginales: Negros, mulatos y sus disputas por la autonomía en Chocó, Colombia (1903–1947)." *Anuario de Historia Regional y de las Fronteras* 24, no. 2 (2019): 125–149.
Riaño-Alcalá, Pilar. "Poetics and Politics of Sound Memory and Social Repair in the Afterlives of Mass Violence: The Cantadoras of the Atrato River of Colombia." In *Remembering and Memorializing Violence: Transnational Feminist Dialogues*, edited by A. Crosby, M. de Alwis, and H. Evans. Forthcoming.
Riaño-Alcalá, Pilar, and Ricardo Chaparro. "Cantando el sufrimiento del río: Memoria, poética y acción política de las cantadoras del Medio Atrato chocoano." *Revista Colombiana de Antropología* 56, no. 2 (2020): 79–110.
Richani, Nazih. "Caudillos and the Crisis of the Colombian State: Fragmented Sovereignty, the War System and the Privatisation of Counterinsurgency in Colombia." *Third World Quarterly* 28, no. 2 (2007): 403–417.
Riordan, Patrick. "Crisis of Democracy: Practice and Theory," *An Irish Quarterly Review* 106, no. 423 (Autumn 2017): 298–307.
Rivas Gamboa, Angela. "Anansi en el mar de los siete colores: historia, memoria y cultura en el Archipiélago." BA thesis, Universidad de los Andes, 1995.
Rivera Cusicanqui, Silvia. "Ch'ixinakax utxiwa: A Reflection on the Practices and Discourses of Decolonization." *South Atlantic Quarterly* 111, no. 1 (2013): 95–109.
Robertson, Morgan. "Measurement and Alienation: Making a World of Ecosystem Services." *Transactions of the Institute of British Geographers* 37, no. 3 (2012): 386–401.
Robinson Abrahams, Hazel. *No Give Up, Maan!* Bogotá: Editorial Unibiblos, 2002.
Robinson, Cedric. *Marxismo negro: La formación de la tradición radical negra*. Madrid: Traficantes de Sueños, 2019.
Robinson, James A. "Another 100 Years of Solitude." *Current History* (February 2013): 43–48.
———. "La miseria en Colombia." *Desarrollo & Sociedad* 76 (January–June 2016): 9–88.
Rodríguez, Becerra. *Memoria del Ministerio de Agricultura al Congreso Nacional, 1959*. Bogotá: Imprenta Nacional, 1959.
Rodríguez, Clemencia, and Jeanine El Gazi. "The Poetics of Indigenous Radio in Colombia." *Media, Culture & Society* 29, no. 3 (2007): 449–468.
Rodríguez Abadía, William. *No elegí ser el hijo del cartel*. Madrid: Ediciones Temas de Hoy, 2015.
Rodríguez Becerra, Manuel. "Ecología y medio ambiente." In *Nueva Historia de Colombia vol. IX: Ecología y Cultura*, edited by Álvaro Tirado Mejía. Bogotá: Editorial Planeta, 1998.
Rodríguez Rueda, Álvaro. *Cómo vivían nuestros mayores*. Santander de Quilichao, Colombia: Asociación de Cabildos Indígenas de la Zona Norte del Cauca, 2001. https://isbn.cloud/pt/9789589704202/catedra-nasa-unesco/.

Rojas, Axel. "Subalternos entre los subalternos: presencia e invisibilidad de la población negra en los imaginarios teóricos y sociales." In *Conflicto e (in)visibilidad: Retos en los estudios de la gente negra en Colombia*, edited by Eduardo Restrepo and Axel Rojas, 157–172. Popayán: Editorial Universidad del Cauca, 2004.

Rojas, Diana Marcela. *El Plan Colombia: La intervención de Estados Unidos en el conflicto armado colombiano (1998–2012)*. Bogotá: Penguin Random House Grupo Editorial, 2015.

Rojas Álvarez, Jorge. "'Campesinos y Radios': Aspectos Sociales de la Tecnología Escuelas Radiofónicas de Radio Sutatenza (1950–1970)." Master's tesis, Universidad de los Andes, Colombia, 2014. https://repositorio.uniandes.edu.co/handle/1992/12820.

Rojas Gómez, July Carolina. "Conflictos ambientales por medidas de mitigación al cambio climático en territorio Wayuu: El Parque Eólico Jepirachi, 1999–2011, Colombia." Master's tesis, Universidad Nacional de Colombia, Bogotá, 2012. https://repositorio.unal.edu.co/handle/unal/9676.

Rojas-Pérez, Isaias. *Mourning Remains. State Atrocity, Exhumations, and Governing the Disappeared in Peru's Postwar Andes*. Stanford: Stanford University Press, 2017.

Roldán, Mary. *Blood and Fire: La Violencia in Antioquia, Colombia, 1946–1953*. Durham: Duke University Press, 2002.

Roldán, Mary. "Radio y Cultura Nacional: Años 30 y 40." In *Música, Radio y Documentos Sonoros*, 16–25. Bogotá: Radio Nacional de Colombia, 2009. www.academia.edu/37247156/memorias_musica_radio_pdf?email_work_card=title.

Román Romero, Raúl, and Antonino Vidal Ortega. "Imperio y poder a finales del siglo XVIII: Las disputas en el interior del imperio español por el control de la costa misquita y el archipiélago de San Andrés y Providencia." en *Memorias, historias y olvidos: Colonialismo, sociedad y política en el archipiélago de San Andrés y Providencia*, 23–44. Bogotá: Editorial Universidad Nacional de Colombia, 2019.

Romero, Jazmín. "¿Qué pasaría si se desvía el arroyo Bruno?" Interview by CINEP, Programa por la Paz, 2015. YouTube video, 1:58–2:52. www.youtube.com/watch?v=7jDDOaaOPCU. Accessed June 1, 2021.

Romero, Mauricio. *Paramilitares y autodefensas, 1982–2003*, 2nd ed. Bogotá: Editorial Planeta-IEPRI, 2005.

———. *Parapolítica: La ruta de la expansión paramilitar y los acuerdos políticos*. Bogotá: Corporación Nuevo Arco Iris and Intermedio, 2007.

Romero Epiayu, Jakeline. "La movilización y la resistencia desde distintas latitudes: Reflexiones y herramientas para la acción colectiva." Presentation at Quinto Conversatorio de la Universidad del Magdalena, 2020. YouTube video, 14:54, 16:08. www.youtube.com/watch?v=2XBL9YAxuW4.

———. Panelist at *Diálogos Caribe 6: Transiciones para un Caribe post-extractivista*, produced by Censat. Agua Viva podcast. February 18, 2021. MP3 audio, 14:35. https://transiciones.info/podcast/dialogos-caribe/dialogos-caribe-6-transiciones-para-un-caribe-post-extractivista/.

———. "Mujeres amigas del Viento." *Noti Wayuu*, produced by Fuerza Mujeres Wayuu and Oxfam, June 29, 2022. YouTube video, 0:07–0:38. www.youtube.com/watch?v=gOd1toz_G_w.

Rosen, Jonathan. *The Losing War: Plan Colombia and Beyond*. SUNY Press, 2014.

Rosette, Ashleigh, and Tracy Dumas. "The Hair Dilemma: Conform to Mainstream Expectations or Emphasize Racial Identity." *Duke Journal of Gender Law & Policy* 14, no. 1 (2007): 407–422.

Ross, James. "Routes for Roots: Entering the 21st Century in San Andrés Island, Colombia." *Caribbean Studies* 35, no. 1 (January–June 2007): 3–36.

Roy, Arundhaty. *Field Notes on Democracy: Listening to Grasshoppers*. Chicago: Haymarket Books, 2009.

Roseberry, William. "Hegemony and the Language of Contention." In *Everyday Forms of State Formation: Revolution and the Negotiation of Rule in Modern Mexico*, edited by Gilbert Joseph and Daniel Nugent, 355–366. Durham: Duke University Press, 1994.

Rubiano, Elkin. "Las cenizas y los rastros: La emergencia forense en el arte colombiano." In *Narrativas artísticas del conflicto armado colombiano. Pluralidad, memorias e interpelaciones*, edited by María Emma Wills. Bogotá: Ediciones Uniandes, 2021, 27–64.

Ruiz, María Margarita. "Vivienda, asentimientos y migración en San Andrés Isla, 1950–1987." In *San Andrés y Providencia: Tradiciones culturales y coyuntura política*, edited by Isabel Clemente, 209–238. Bogotá: Uniandes, 1989.

Ruiz-Serna, Daniel. "El territorio como víctima: Ontología política y las leyes de víctimas para comunidades indígenas y negras en Colombia." *Revista Colombiana de Antropología* 53, no. 2 (2017): 85.

———. *When Forests Run Amok: War and Its Afterlives in Indigenous and Afro-Colombian Territories*. Durham: Duke University Press, 2023.

Saade, Marta, ed. *Conceptualización del campesinado en Colombia: Documento técnico para su definición, caracterización y medición*. Bogotá: ICANH, 2020.

Sáenz Rovner, Eduardo. "La participación de los cubanos, los colombianos y los chilenos en las redes del narcotráfico en Nueva York durante los años sesenta." *Innovar* 17, no. 30 (2007): 133–144.

———. "Entre Carlos Lehder y los vaqueros de la cocaína: La consolidación de las redes de narcotraficantes colombianos en Miami en los años 70." *Cuadernos de Economía* 30, no. 54 (2011): 105–126.

———. *Conexión Colombia: Una historia del narcotráfico entre los años 30 y los años 90*. Bogotá: Crítica, 2021.

Safford, Frank, and Marco Palacios. *Colombia: Fragmented Land, Divided Society*. New York: Oxford University Press, 2002.

Salgado, Juliano, and Wim Wenders, dirs. *The Salt of the Earth*. 2014; Cannes, France: Decia Films, 2015.

Salinas, Yamile, and Juan Manuel Zarama. *Justicia y paz: Tierra y territorios en las versiones de los paramilitares*. Bogotá: Centro Nacional de Memoria Histórica, 2012.

Sanabria Diago, Olga Lucía, and Arturo Argueta Villamar. "Cosmovisiones y naturalezas en tres culturas indígenas de Colombia." *Etnobiología* 13, no. 2 (2015): 5–20.

Sánchez, Gonzalo. *Memorias, subjetividades y política: Ensayos sobre un país que se niega a dejar la guerra*. Bogotá: Planeta-Crítica, 2020.

Sánchez, Gonzalo, and Donny Meertens. *Bandoleros, gamonales y campesinos*. Bogota: El Áncora, 1983.

Sánchez Cristo, Julio. *Óscar Naranjo: El General de las mil batallas*. Bogotá: Editorial Planeta, 2017.

Sanford, Victoria. *Buried Secrets: Truth and Human Rights in Guatemala*. New York: Palgrave Macmillan, 2004.

Santamaría, Jaime. "La masacre de El Salado como paradigma de violencia soberana paramilitar." *Eidos* 34 (2020): 161–190.

Santamaría Chavarro, Ángela. "Lorenzo Muelas y el Constitucionalismo Indígena 'desde Abajo': Una Retrospectiva Crítica sobre el Proceso Constituyente de 1991." *Colombia Internacional* 79 (2013), 77–120. https://doi.org/10.7440/colombiaint79.2013.04.

Schulman, Bruce J. *The Seventies: The Great Shift in American Culture, Society and Politics*. New York: Free Press, 2001.

Segato, Rita. *Las nuevas formas de la guerra y el cuerpo de las mujeres*. Puebla: Pez en el árbol, 2014.

Sekaquaptewa, Denise. "On Being the Solo Faculty Member of Color: Research Evidence from Field and Laboratory Studies." *In The Truly Diverse Faculty: New Dialogues in American Higher Education*, edited by Stephanie A. Fryberg and Ernesto Javier Martínez, chapter 4. New York: Palgrave Macmillan, 2014.

Semper, Frank. "Los derechos de los pueblos indígenas en Colombia en la jurisprudencia de la corte constitucional." In *Anuario de Derecho Constitucional Latinoamericano 2006, Tomo II*. Berlin: KONRAD-ADENAUER-STIFTUNG E.V.

Sepúlveda, Rodrigo. "'Vivir las ideas, idear la vida:' Adversidad, suicidio y flexibilidad en el ethos de los embera y wounaan de Riosucio, Chocó." *Antípoda* 6 (January–June 2008): 245–269.

Serrano, Alfredo. *Paracos*. Bogotá: Debate, 2009.

Sevilla Peñuela, Manuel, Juan Sebastián Ochoa, Carolina Santamaría Delgado, and Carlos Eduardo Cataño Arango. *Modernity and Colombian Identity in the Music of Carlos Vives y La Provincia*. Lanham: Lexington Books, 2020.

Shadmi, Erella. "Between Resistance and Compliance, Feminism and Nationalism: Women in Black in Israel." *Women's Studies International Forum* 23, no. 1 (2000): 23–34.

Sierakowski, Robert. "Central America's Caribbean Coast: Politics and Ethnicity." *Oxford Research Encyclopedia of Latin American History*, September 29, 2016. https://oxforde.com/latinamericanhistory/view/10.1093/acrefore/9780199366439.001.0001/acrefore-9780199366439-3-372. Accessed July 1, 2022.

Silva Prada, Diego F. "Construcción de territorialidad desde las organizaciones campesinas en Colombia." *Polis* 15, no. 34 (2016): 633–654.

Skocpol, Theda. "Bringing the State Back In: Strategies of Analysis in Current Research." In *Bringing the State Back In*, edited by Peter Evans, Dietrich Rueschemeyer, and Theda Skocpol. New York and Cambridge: Cambridge University Press, 1985: 3–38.

Slobodian, Quinn. Globalists: *The End of Empire and the Birth of Neoliberalism*. Cambridge: Harvard University Press, 2018.

Soto Rodríguez, Raúl, director. *El segundo entierro de Alejandrino*. 75 min. Verdad Abierta, Bogotá, Colombia, 2011.

Spivak, Gayatri. *An Aesthetic Education in the Era of Globalization*. Cambridge: Harvard University Press, 2012.

Stanfield, Michael Edward. *Red Rubber, Bleeding Trees: Violence, Slavery, and Empire in Northwest Amazonia, 1850–1933*, 1st ed. Albuquerque: University of New Mexico Press, 1998.

Stavenhagen, Rodolfo. "Indigenous Peoples: Land, Territory, Autonomy, and Self-Determination." In *Promised Land: Competing Visions of Agrarian Reform*, edited by Peter Roser, Raj Patel, and Michael Courville, 208–211. Oakland: Food First Books, 2006.

Stern, Steve. "De la memoria suelta a la memoria emblemática: Hacia el recordar y el olvidar como proceso histórico (Chile, 1973–1998)." In *Las conmemoraciones: Las disputas en las fechas "in-felices,"* compiled by Elizabeth Jenin, 11–33. Madrid: Siglo XXI editores, 2002.

———. *Remembering Pinochet's Chile: On the Eve of London 1998*. Durham: Duke University Press, 2003.

Sternbach, Nancy Saporta, Marysa Navarro-Aranguren, Patricia Chuchryk, and Sonia E. Alvarez. "Feminisms in Latin America: From Bogotá to San Bernardo." *Signs* 17, no. 2 (1992): 393–434.

Stirling, Andrew. *Emancipating Transformations: From Controlling 'the Transition' to Culturing Plural Radical Progress*. STEPS Working Paper 64. Brighton: STEPS Centre, Economic & Social Research Council, 2014.

Stovel, Katherine, and Lynette Shaw. "Brokerage." *Annual Review of Sociology* 38 (2012): 139–158.

Stross, Brian. "The Hybrid Metaphor: From Biology to Culture." *Journal of American Folklore* 112, no. 445 (1999): 254–267.

Suárez, Felix. "Prólogo." In *Africanidad, indianidad, multiculturalidad*, edited by William Mina Aragón. Cali: Universidad del Valle, 2017.

Suleiman, Ezra. *Dismantling Democratic States*. Princeton: Princeton University Press, 2013.

Sweeney, John. "Colombia's Narco-Democracy Threatens Hemispheric Security." *The Heritage Foundation Backgrounder*, no. 1028 March 21, 1995.

Tate, Winifred. *Counting the Dead: The Culture and Politics of Human Rights Activism in Colombia*. Berkeley: University of California Press, 2007.

———. *Drugs, Thugs, and Diplomats: U.S. Policymaking in Colombia*. Stanford: Stanford University Press, 2015.

———. "No Peace for Colombia." *NACLA*, February 24, 2016. https://nacla.org/news/2016/02/24/no-peace-colombia.

———. "A Dark Day in Colombia." *NACLA*, October 4, 2016. https://nacla.org/news/2016/10/04/dark-day-colombia-0.

———. "Post-Accord Putumayo." *The Journal of Latin American and Caribbean Anthropology* 22, no. 1 (2017): 164–173.

———. "A Precarious Peace in Putumayo." *NACLA*, May 4, 2018. https://nacla.org/news/2018/05/04/precarious-peace-putumayo.

Tauss, Aaron, Daniel Pardo, and David Graaff. "El bloque de poder contrainsurgente en Colombia y su papel en el resurgimiento de la derecha en América Latina." *Colombia International* 99 (2019): 63–90.

Taussig, Michael. *Shamanism, Colonialism, and the Wild Man: A Study in Terror and Healing*. Chicago: University of Chicago Press, 1991.

Taylor, Diana. "Performing Gender: Las Madres de La Plaza de Mayo." In *Negotiating Performance: Gender, Sexuality, and Theatricality in Latin/o America*, edited by Juan Villegas Morales. Durham: Duke University Press, 1994: 275–305.

Telles, Edward, and Tianna Paschel. "Who Is Black, White, or Mixed Race? How Skin Color, Status, and Nation Shape Racial Classification in Latin America." *American Journal of Sociology* 120, no. 3 (2014): 864–907.

Temper, Leah, et al. "A Perspective on Radical Transformations to Sustainability: Resistances, Movements and Alternatives." *Sustainability Science* 13 (2018): 747–764.

Theidon, Kimberly. *Intimate Enemies: Violence and Reconciliation in Peru*. Philadelphia: University of Pennsylvania Press, 2014.

Thomson, Sinclair. "Self-Knowledge and Self-Determination at the Limits of Capitalism." In René Zavaleta Mercado. xvi-xxxv. *Towards a History of the National-Popular in Bolivia*. New York: Seagull Books, 2018.

Thoumi, Francisco E. *Illegal Drugs, Economy, and Society in the Andes*. Baltimore: The Johns Hopkins University Press, 2003.

Thurner, Mark and Andrés Guerrero eds. *After Spanish Rule: Postcolonial Predicaments of the Americas*. Durham: Duke University Press, 2003.

Tickner, Arlene. "U.S. Foreign Policy in Colombia. Bizarre Side Effects of the 'War on Drugs'." In *Peace, Democracy, and Human Rights in Colombia*, edited by Christopher Welna and Gustavo Gallón. Notre Dame: University of Notre Dame Press, 2007.

Ticktin, Miriam. "A World without Innocence." *American Ethnologist* 44, no. 4 (2017): 577–590.

Tirado Mejía, Alvaro. *Los años 60: Una revolución en la cultura*. Bogotá: Debate, 2014.

———. "Presentación." In *Colombia: Una nación a pesar de sí misma*. David Bushnell, 11–14. Bogotá: Crítica.

Tinsman, Heidi. *Buying into the Regime: Grapes and Consumption in Cold War Chile and the United States*. Durham: Duke University Press, 2014.

Tocancipá-Falla, Jairo. "El retorno de lo campesino: una revisión sobre los esencialismos y heterogeneidades en la antropología." *Revista Colombiana de Antropología* 41 (January/December 2005): 7–43.

Todorov, Tzvetan. *La memoria: ¿Un remedio contra el mal?* Barcelona: Arcadia, 2013.

Tomba, Massimiliano. *Insurgent Universality: An Alternative Legacy of Modernity*. Oxford: Oxford University Press, 2021.

Torres, Silvia Elena. "Los raizales: Cultura e identidad angloafrocaribeña en el Caribe Insular colombiano." *Revista Cuadernos del Caribe* 16, no. 1 (2013): 11–26.

Torres Bustamente, María Clara. *Estado y coca en la frontera colombiana*. Bogotá: Odecofi-CINEP, 2011.

Torres del Río, César Miguel. *Colombia siglo XX: Desde la Guerra de los Mil Días hasta la elección de Álvaro Uribe*. Bogotá: Grupo Editorial Norma, 2010.

Tovar Pupo, Rodrigo aka Jorge 40. "Mi vida como autodefensa y mi participación como miembro del BN y del BNA." n. d. www.webcolegios.com/file/ce06bf.pdf

Trejo, Guillermo. "Religious Competition and Ethnic Mobilization in Latin America: Why the Catholic Church Promotes Indigenous Movements in Mexico." *American Political Science Review* 103, no. 3 (2009): 323–342.

Tremble, Alfred. "Among the Cocoanuts: A Jaunt through the Island of St. Andrews." *Leslie's Popular Monthly* (1877): 691–698.
Troyan, Brett. "Ethnic Citizenship in Colombia: The Experience of the Regional Indigenous Council of the Cauca in Southwestern Colombia from 1970 to 1990." *Latin American Research Review* 43, no. 3 (2008): 166–191.
Trouillot, Michel-Rolph. *Silencing the Past: Power and the Production of History*. New York: Beacon Press, 1995.
———. "The Vulgarity of Power." In *Trouillot Remixed*, edited by Yarimar Bonilla, Greg Beckett, and Mayanthi L. Fernando, 97–102. Durham: Duke University Press, 2021.
———. "The Odd and the Ordinary: Haiti, the Caribbean and the World." In *Trouillot Remixed*, edited by Yarimar Bonilla, Greg Beckett, and Mayanthi L. Fernando, 85–96. Durham: Duke University Press, 2021.
Trujillo Irurita, Orlando Javier. "Integración nacional y pluralismo cultural en la radio y la televisión de San Andrés Isla: La configuración histórica del campo periodístico." *Historia Crítica* no. 28 (2004): 153–169.
Tubb, Daniel. *Shifting Livelihoods: Gold Mining and Susbistence in the Chocó, Colombia*. Seattle: University of Washington Press, 2020.
Turek, Lauren Frances. "To Support a 'Brother in Christ': Evangelical Groups and U.S.-Guatemalan Relations during the Ríos Montt Regime." *Diplomatic History* 39, no. 4 (2015): 689–719.
Turnage, Loren. *Island Heritage: A Baptist View of the History of San Andrés and Providencia*. Cali: Colombian Baptist Mission, 1975.
Ulloa, Alejandro. *La salsa en Cali*. Cali: Editorial Universidad del Valle, 1992.
———. *La salsa en tiempos de "nieve." The Cali-New York Latin Connection (1975–2000)*. Cali: Editorial Universidad del Valle, 2020.
———. *Salsa, drogadicción y oralidad en la narrativa de Andrés Caicedo: Un estudio sobre la transgresión social en la novela ¡Qué Viva la música!* Popayán: Editorial Universidad del Cauca, 2022.
Ulloa, Astrid. "Geopolíticas del cambio climático." *Revista Anthropos: Huellas del conocimiento* 227 (2010): 133–146.
———. "Controlando la naturaleza: ambientalismo transnacional y negociaciones locales en torno al cambio climático en territorios indígenas en Colombia." *Iberoamericana* 13, no. 49 (2013): 117–133.
———. "The Geopolitics of Carbonized Nature and the Zero-Carbon Citizen." *South Atlantic Quarterly* 116, no. 1 (2017): 111–120.
———. "Perspectives of Environmental Justice from Indigenous Peoples of Latin America: A Relational Indigenous Environmental Justice." *Environmental Justice* 10, no. 6 (2017): 175–180.
———. "The Rights of the Wayúu People and Water in the Context of Mining in La Guajira, Colombia: Demands of *Relational Water Justice*." *Human Geography* 13, no. 1 (2020): 6–15.
———. "Transformaciones radicales socioambientales frente a la destrucción renovada y verde, La Guajira, Colombia." *Revista de Geografía Norte Grande* 80 (2021): 13–34.

Unidad de Radio del Ministerio de Cultura. *Memorias del Encuentro Internacional de Radios Indígenas de América.* Bogotá: Ministerio de Cultura, 2002.

Unigarro Caguasango, Daniel E. "Los campesinos de la Amazonía noroccidental colombiana: Entre la coca, el conflicto y la construcción de paz." *Antípoda: Revista de Antropología y Arqueología* 40 (May 2020): 175–200.

Uribe de Hincapié, María Teresa. *Nación, ciudadano y soberano.* Medellín: Corporación Región, 2001.

Uribe, Simón. *Frontier Road: Power, History, and the Everyday State in the Colombian Amazon*, 1st ed. Hoboken: Wiley, 2017.

Uribe Rendón, Graciela. *Veníamos con una manotada de ambiciones: Un aporte a la historia de la colonización del Caquetá.* Bogotá: Unibiblos, 1998.

Urrea Giraldo, Fernando, Carlos Viáfara López, and Mara Viveros Vigoya. "From Whitened Miscegenation to Tri–Ethnic Multiculturalism. Race and Ethnicity in Colombia." In *Pigmentocracies: Ethnicity, Race, and Color in Latin America*, edited by Edward Telles. Chapel Hill: The University of North Carolina Press, 2014.

Urrea Giraldo, Fernando, Jeanny Lucero Posso Quiceno, and Nancy Motta González. "Sexualidades y feminidades de mujeres negras e indígenas: Un análisis de cohorte generacional y étnico-racial." Informe Técnico Final. Cali: Centro de Investigaciones CIDSE, Facultad de Ciencias Sociales y Económicas, Universidad del Valle, 2010. http://etnicoraciales.univalle.edu.co/InfinalSexualidades.pdf.

Urzúa, Raúl and Felipe Agüero, eds. *Fracturas en la gobernabilidad democrática.* Santiago de Chile: Universidad de Chile, 1998.

Valderrama, Carlos A. "La diferancia cultural negra en Colombia. Contrapúblicos afrocolombianos." *Revista CS* 29 (septiembre 2019): 209–242.

Valdivia, Gabriela. "Coca's Haunting Presence in the Agrarian Politics of the Bolivian Lowlands." *GeoJournal* 77, no. 5 (2012): 615–631.

Valencia, Inge Helena P. "Identidades del caribe insular colombiano: Otra mirada hacia del caso isleño-raizal." *CS* no. 2 (jul.–dic. 2008): 51–73.

———. "Impactos del reconocimiento multicultural en el Archipiélago de San Andrés, Providencia y Santa Catalina: entre la etnización y el conflicto social." *Revista Colombiana de Antropología* 47, no. 2 (jul.–dic. 2011): 69–95.

———. "Lugares de las poblaciones negras en Colombia: La ausencia del afrocaribe insular." *CS*, no. 7 (ene.–jul. 2011): 313–349.

Vallejo Mejía, Maryluz. *A plomo herido: Una crónica del periodismo en Colombia (1880–1980).* Bogotá: Planeta, 2006.

Van Ausdal, Shawn. "Pasture, Power and Profit: An Environmental History of Cattle Ranching in Colombia, 1850–1950." *Geoforum* 40, no. 5 (2009): 707–719.

Van Cott, Donna Lee. "Constitutional Reform in the Andes: Redefining Indigenous-State Relations." In *Multiculturalism in Latin America: Indigenous Rights, Diversity and Democracy*, edited by Rachel Sieder, 45–73. London: Palgrave Macmillan, 2002.

Vandergeest, Peter, and Nancy Peluso. "Territorialization and State Power in Thailand." *Theory and Society* 24, no. 3 (1995): 385–426.

Vanegas, Isidro. *Todas son iguales: Estudios sobre la democracia en Colombia.* Bogotá: Universidad Externado de Colombia, 2011.

Varela, Jairo. "No muero mañana." In *Señales de Humo* by Grupo Niche, CD, recorded at Estudios Niche. Cali: Sony Music Colombia, 1998.
Vargas Guevara, Óscar Santiago, et al. *Impulsos desde abajo para las transiciones energéticas justas: Género, territorio y soberanía*. Santa Marta: Fundación Friedrich Ebert Stiftung, 2022.
Vasconcelos, José. *La raza cósmica*. México DF: Espasa-Calpe Mexicana, 1977.
Vásquez, Édgar. "Los Caleños, por qué somos así." *Revista Cali-Artes* 1 (1983): 3–14.
Vásquez, Mateo, María Galvis, and Diana Bocarejo. *Sumapaz: Zona de Reserva Campesina*. Bogotá: Universidad del Rosario, Sintrapaz, 2019.
Vásquez, Teófilo, Andrés Vargas, and Jorge Restrepo. *Una vieja guerra en un nuevo context: Conflicto y territorio en el sur de* Colombia. Bogotá: Cerac, 2011.
Vega Cantor, Renán. *Gente muy rebelde*, vol. 3, *Mujeres, artesanos y protestas cívicas*. Bogotá: Ediciones Pensamiento Crítico, 2002.
———. *La oligarquía colombiana: Una belicosa marioneta del Tío Sam*. Bogotá: Teoría and Praxis, 2022.
———. *Capitalismo y despojo: Perspectiva histórica sobre la expropiación universal de bienes y saberes*. Bogotá: Impresol Ediciones, 2013.
———. *Los economistas neoliberales-Nuevos criminales de guerra: El genocidio económico y social del capitalismo contemporáneo*. Bogotá: CEPA, 2010.
Vega Rodríguez, Alejandra, ed. *Las zonas de reserva campesina: Retos y experiencias significativas en su implementación*. Bogotá: FAO, 2019. www.fao.org/3/CA0467ES/ca0467es.pdf.
Velasco, Juan David, Gustavo Duncan, and Felipe Lopera. "Oligarquía, poder político y narcotráfico en Colombia: Los casos de Medellín, Santa Marta y Muzo." *Colombia Internacional* 95 (2018): 167–201.
Vélez, Juan. "Entre la selva y el estado: Políticas públicas medioambientales, comunidades campesinas y prácticas cotidianas en la Amazonía noroccidental colombiana." Undegraduate thesis, Pontificia Universidad Javeriana, Bogotá, 2015.
Vergara, Isabella, and Gwendolen Pare, compiled in "Debates." *Ideas y valores* LXVIII, supplement no. 5 (2019): 224–262.
Verlot, Marc. "Understanding Institutional Racism." In *Europe's New Racism: Causes, Manifestations, and Solutions*, edited by The Evens Foundation, 27–42. New York: Berghahn Books, 2002.
Viáfara López, Carlos Augusto, Alexander Estacio Moreno, and Luisa María González Aguiar. "Condición étnico-racial, género y movilidad social en Bogotá, Cali y el agregado de las trece áreas metropolitanas en Colombia: un análisis descriptivo y econométrico." *Revista Sociedad y Economía*, no. 18 (junio 2010): 113–136.
Viana, Manuela Trindade. *Postconflict Colombia and the Global Circulation of Military Expertise*. Gewerbestrasse: Palgrave Macmillan, 2022.
Vidal Ortega, Antonino. "Noticias de San Andrés e islas vecinas 1789." *Memorias: Revista digital de Historia y Arqueología desde el Caribe colombiano* 8, no. 14 (jun. 2011): 277–282.

Villagra, Luis Rojas, ed. *Neoliberalismo en América Latina: Crisis, tendencias y alternativas*. Buenos Aires: CLACSO, 2015.
Villamizar, Darío. *Las guerrillas en Colombia: Una historia desde los orígenes hasta los confines*. Bogotá: Penguin-Random House, 2017.
Villarreal Benítez, Kristell Andrea. "Trenzando la identidad: cabello y mujeres negras." Master's thesis, Universidad Nacional de Colombia, 2017. https://repositorio.unal.edu.co/handle/unal/63160.
Villaveces Izquierdo, Santiago. "¿Por qué erradicamos? Entre bastiones de poder, cultura, y narcotráfico." *Journal of Latin American Anthropology* 7, no. 1 (2008): 226–253.
Viveros Vigoya, Mara. "Más que una cuestión de piel: Determinantes sociales y orientaciones subjetivas en los encuentros y desencuentros heterosexuales entre mujeres y 'negros' y no 'negros' en Bogotá." In *Raza, etnicidad y sexualidades. Ciudadanía y América Latina*, edited by Fernando Urrea, Peter Wade, and Mara Viveros Vigoya, 247–279. Bogotá: Universidad Nacional de Colombia, 2008.
Viveros Vigoya, Mara. "La interseccionalidad: Una aproximación situada a la dominación." *Debate Feminista* 52 (October 1, 2016): 1–17.
———. "Social Mobility, Whiteness, and Whitening in Colombia." *The Journal of Latin American and Caribbean Anthropology* 20, no. 3 (2015): 496–512.
———. *Les couleurs de la masculinité*. Paris: La Decouverte, 2018.
Viveros Vigoya, Mara, and Krisna Ruette-Orihuela. "Care, Aesthetic Creation, and Anti-racist Reparations." In *Care and Care Workers: A Latin American Perspective*, edited by Nadya Araujo Guimaraes and Helena Hirata. New York: Springer, 2020: 107–124.
Viveros Vigoya, Mara, Franklin Gil Hernández, Pietro Pisano, and Klara Hellebrandová. "Grandes Esperanzas: Memorias de raza, género y clase en familias afrodescendientes del siglo XX." Manuscript for the Orlando Fals Borda research grant—2017, Apoyo a Proyectos de investigación docentes, 2019.
Vollmer, Lorraine. *La historia del poblamiento del Archipiélago de San Andrés y Vieja Providencia y Santa Catalina*. San Andrés: Ediciones Archipiélago, 1997.
Von Hildebrand, Martín, and Vincent Brackelaire. *Guardianes de la selva: Gobernabilidad y autonomía en la Amazonía colombiana*. Bogotá: Fundación Gaia Amazonas, 2012.
Wade, Peter. *Blackness and Race Mixture: The Dynamics of Racial Identity in Colombia*. Baltimore: Johns Hopkins University Press, 1993.
———. "Colombia." In *Africana: Encyclopedia of the African and African American Experience*, edited by Kwame Anthony Appiah and Henry Louis Gates Jr., 475–477. New York: Basic Civitas Books, 1999.
———. *Music, Race, and Nation: Música Tropical in Colombia*. Chicago: The University of Chicago Press, 2000.
———. *Race and Ethnicity in Latin America*. London: Pluto Press, 2010.
———. "Mestizaje, Multiculturalism, Liberalism, and Violence." *Latin American and Caribbean Ethnic Studies* 11, no. 3 (2016): 323–343.
Wagner, Peter. *A Sociology of Modernity: Liberty and Discipline*. London: Routledge, 2002.

Waisanen, Don J., and Amy B. Becker. "The Problem with Being Joe Biden: Political Comedy and Circulating Personae." *Critical Studies in Media Communication* 32, no. 4 (2015): 256–271.
Walde Erna von der. "La novela de sicarios y la violencia en Colombia." *Iberoamericana* 1, no. 3 (2001): 27–40.
Washburne, Christopher. *Sounding Salsa: Performing Latin Music in New York City*. Philadelphia: Temple University Press, 2008.
———. "Salsa y drogas en Nueva York: Estética, prácticas performativas, políticas gubernamentales y tráfico ilegal de drogas." In *Cocinando suave: ensayos de salsa en Puerto Rico*, edited by César Colón Montijo. Caracas: Ediciones Callejón, 2016.
Waxer, Lise A. *The City of Musical Memory: Salsa, Records Grooves, and Popular Culture in Cali, Colombia*. Middletown: Wesleyan University Press, 2002.
Wilder, Gary. *Concrete Utopianism: The Politics of Temporality and Solidarity*. New York: Fordham University Press, 2022.
Wills, María Emma. "An Unorthodox Relationship: Colombian Public Forces and the National Center for Historical Memory (2012–2019)." In *How the Military Remembers: Countermemories and the Challenges to Human Rights in Latin America*, edited by Cynthia E. Milton and Michael J. Lazzara. (in press).
Yie, Maite. *Del patrón-Estado al Estado-patrón: La agencia campesina en las narrativas de la reforma agraria en Nariño*. Bogotá: Pontificia Universidad Javeriana, Universidad Nacional de Colombia, 2015.
———. "Aparecer, desaparecer y reaparecer ante el estado como campesinos." *Revista Colombiana de Antropología* 58, no. 1 (2022): 115–152.
Yie Garzón, Soraya Mayte " '¡Vea, los campesinos aquí estamos!' Etnografía de la (re) aparición del campesinado como sujeto político en los Andes nariñenses colombianos." Ph.D. dissertation in Social Science, Institute of Philosophy and Human Sciences, Universidad Estadual de Campiñas, Brazil, 2018.
Young, James. "Teaching German Memory and Countermemory: The End of the Holocaust Monument in Germany." In *Teaching the Representation of the Holocaust*, edited by M. Hirsch and I. Kacandes. New York: The Modern Languages Association of America, 2014.
Zacipa Infante, Ingrid. *La mujer pentecostal de la etnia Misak en Guambía, Cauca: El caso de la comunidad Alianza Cristiana Misionera Indígena Guambiana Colombiana*. Bogotá: Universidad Nacional de Colombia, 2019.
Zapata Olivella, Manuel. *El hombre colombiano*. Cali: Universidad del Valle, 1974.
———. *La rebelión de los genes*. Bogotá: Altamir, 1997.
———. "Pensamiento, mestizaje e imaginación política." In *El árbol brujo de la libertad*. Bogotá: Ediciones Desde Abajo, 2014.
———. *Deslumbramientos de América*, compiled by William Mina Aragón. Cuernavaca: AIFP, 2017.
Zavaleta Mercado, René. *Towards a History of the National-Popular in Bolivia, 1879–1980*. New York: Seagull Books, 2018.
Zubiría Samper, Sergio. "Dimensiones políticas y culturales en el conflicto colombiano." In *Contribución al entendimiento del conflicto armado en Colombia*, ed.ited by Comisión Histórica del Conflicto y sus Víctimas, CHCV, 197–248. Bogotá: Ediciones Desde Abajo, 2015.

Zuleta, Estanislao. *Elogio a la dificultad y otros ensayos*. Bogotá: Ariel, 2020.
Zuckerman Daly, Sarah. *Organized Violence after Civil War: The Geography of Recruitment in Latin America*. Cambridge: Cambridge University Press, 2016.
Zuluaga Gil, Ricardo. *De la expectativa al desconcierto: El proceso constituyente de 1991 visto por sus protagonistas*. Bogotá: Editorial Universidad Pontificia Javeriana, 2006.
Zúñiga, Priscila. "Ilegalidad, control local y paramilitares en el Magdalena." In *Parapolítica: la ruta de expansión paramilitar y los acuerdos políticos*, edited by Mauricio Romero. Bogotá, Cerec-Arco Iris, 2007.

Index

Note: Page numbers in *italic* indicate a figure or map and page numbers in **bold** indicate a table on the corresponding page.

Abad Colorado, Jesús 252–254, 267–269, *258, 262–263*; moral performance 264–267; moral vision 259–264; photographer as a young man 254–259
Acción Cultural Popular Radio Sutatenza (ACPO) 273–274, 276–279, *278*
ACPO *see* Acción Cultural Popular Radio Sutatenza (ACPO)
activism: origins of 317–319; *see also* gendered activism
Afro-Caribbean heritage 65–66, 78–79; brief history 66–71
Afro-Colombians: drafting a law for 129–130; as ethnic group 132–136; as owners of the rural Pacific 140–142
Afrodiasporic humanism 23–26; interview 26–42
agrarian ideal 113–115
Amazonian Forest Reserve 109–112, *111*, 115–119, *117*, 123–124; agrarian ideal 113–115; ethnic territories 121–123; national parks 119–121
Anglophone heritage 65–66, 78–79; brief history 66–71
armed conflict: coercive brokerage 331–347; economic autonomy in coca-growing regions 351–371; gendered activism and elite formation 313–329

art *see* contemporary art
autonomy *see* economic autonomy

Black population 4, 46–50; and middle class 53–56
Black upward mobility 44–46, 58–60; and middle class 53–56; and neoliberal multiculturalism 46–53; resistance to white cultural domination 56–58; and social whitening 50–53
blue energies 148–150; asymmetries of power 153–156; radical socio-environmental transformations 160–162; structural inequalities and institutional transitions 156–159; territorial and cultural dispossession 150–152; transformations for the continuation of life 162–163
Bogotá 24–25, 36, 44–46, 51–53, 71, 76, 116, 120–121, 123, 172–173, 175, 207–213, 256, 300–302, 304, 317–318, 321–322, 324, 346–347, 435; Bogotazo 385
Bojayá 419–422, *421, 423,* 437–438; bad deaths 426–427; dignifying name and memory 435–437; peace process and exhumations 427–431; prolonged wake and how to properly care for the dead 431–434; war in the Middle Atrato 422–425
brokerage *see* coercive brokerage

488   Index

Cali 6–7, 24, 45, 56, 133, 139–140, 214–220; Cali Cartel 172–173, 189, 363
Cali-New York connection 185–186, 198, 202–203; Cali Cartel in New York 193–199, 198; Colombian migration to New York 190–193; historical context 187–190; Larry Landa 199–202, 201
campesinos 84–86, 99–101; Constitution of 1991 90–92; as a contested category 86–90; culture and local strategies of territorial management 92–94; Zonas de Reserva Campesina and socio-environmental agenda 95–99, 98
carbon extraction 148–150; radical socio-environmental transformations 160–162; structural inequalities and institutional transitions 156–159; territorial and cultural dispossession 150–152; transformations for the continuation of life 162–163
Catholicism 11, 14; and collective land titling 141; and gendered activism 314–319, 321, 323–324, 329; and indigeneity 71–77; and the media 240, 254, 268, 273, 273–279, 281–285
Cauca 273–174, 285–286; Catholic ACPO 276–279, 278; Evangelical indigenous radio stations 282–285; indigenous peoples as modern subjects 274–276; state-sponsored indigenous radio stations 279–282
Chócolo (Harold Trujillo) 207–213, 210, 226
class formation xxiii, xxx, xxxiii, 11, 41, 86, 101, 256–257, 273, 281, 285, 295, 298, 300, 316–317, 328
coca 86–88, 96, 118, 173, 207, 215, 217–219, 338, 351–357, 370–371; coca eradication and substitution 278, 281, 351–353, 356, 360, 363, 369–370; Cocaine xxxiv, 6, 185, 189–191, 193–194, 212, 219, 234, 237, 239, 339, 341, 343, 352, 364; coca paste 93, 189, 192, 314; peasant women and coca income 359–363; places of women in coca territories 363–366; War on Drugs 366–370
cocaleras 351–352, 354–359, 369–370, 369; cocaleras and rural dynamics 354–359
coercive brokerage 331–333; communal fiefdom 342–343; community and intermediation 340–342; context 335–337; Hernán Giraldo 338–346; and Michael Mann 333–335; Santa Marta region 337–338
collective land titling 127–129; Afro-Colombians as owners of the rural Pacific 140–142; drafting a law for Afro-Colombians 129–130; hegemonic language of participation 130–131; "projectism" and grassroots neoliberalism 143–145; recognition of Afro-Colombians as ethnic group 132–136; territorial effects 136–140
commercial advantages 170–171
community radio stations 273–174, 285–286; Catholic ACPO 276–279, 278; Evangelical indigenous radio stations 282–285; indigenous peoples as modern subjects 274–276; state-sponsored indigenous radio stations 279–282
conflict: of coca 351–354, 357, 365–366, 369, 371; conflict dynamics 320–322; see also armed conflict
Constitution of 1991 xxxiv, 4–5, 45–46, 66, 78, 90–92, 99, 121–122, 130, 137, 169, 273, 277, 280, 295–297, 306–308
contemporary art 206–207, 225–226; Bogotá 207–213; Cali 214–220; Medellín 220–225
cooptation 10, 282, 292–296; flawed strategy 305–306; Mincultura 292, 294–296, 299–305, 309; music and hegemony 296–298; role of the state 306–309
counter-memory 385–386, 389–392, 398–399, 407; see also memory
cultural dispossession 150–152
cultural domination, white 33, 56–59

culture: and the role of the state 306–309; and territorial management 92–94

democracy xxvi–xxxiii, xxix, 1–4, 10–11, 15, 25, 100–101; *see also* mestizaje; racial democracy
dignity 24, 157, 363, 385, 420, 429, 435–437
diplomacy 169–170; commercial advantages 170–171; domestic economic agenda 173–174; negotiation with drug traffickers 171–173; state violence 174–178
disappearances 177–178, 406–407, 410–414, 422–426
dispossession 150–152
domestic economic agenda 171–174
drug trafficking: and César Gaviria's administration 169–178; and contemporary art 206–226; and salsa music 185–203
Duelos (Echeverri) 399, 403, 406, 410–414, *411–412*

Echeverri, Clemencia 399, 403, 406, 410–414, *411–412*
economic agenda, domestic 171–174
economic autonomy 351–354, 370–371; *cocaleras* and rural dynamics 354–359; peasant women and coca income 359–363; places of women in coca territories 363–366; War on Drugs 366–370
elites 313–316, 328–329; Antioquia's elite 209; Black elite 55, 58; Cali's white elite 188; cultural 295–298, 302–304; elite control of the press 257, 264; elite discourses 274, 280–281; elite sources 256; emergence of the Women's Alliance 322–324; illegal 346; indigeneity and class formation 316–317; elite islanders 73; national networks and the origins of activism 317–319; peace activism and access to E.U. resources 324–327; and race 46–50; rural 334–339; shifting conflict dynamics 320–322; tensions and contradictions 328
ELN 257, 265, 268, 338

entrepreneurs *see* narco-entrepreneurs
environmental agenda *see* socio-environmental agenda
environmental transformations *see* radical socio-environmental transformations
Escobar, Pablo 229–231, *235, 238, 241,* 247–248; accidental persona 245–247; journalism routines 242–245; the narco 236–242; the Robin Hood 231–236
ethnic group: Afro-Colombians as 132–136; rights of ethnic group 45, 57; Raizal as 77; recognition of 90–91, 121–122, 131–136
ethnic territories 112, 121–123, 141, 420, 435
Evangelical indigenous radio stations 282–285
exhumations 419–422, 437–438; bad deaths 426–427; dignifying name and memory 435–437; and peace process 427–431; prolonged wake and how to properly care for the dead 431–434; war in the Middle Atrato 422–425
extraction, carbon *see* carbon extraction
extractivism 148–150; radical socio-environmental transformations 160–162; structural inequalities and institutional transitions 156–159; territorial and cultural dispossession 150–152; transformations for the continuation of life 162–163

FARC xxx–xxxii; and campesinos 85–87; and coca 352–354, 364–369; and coercive brokerage 338–341; and drug trafficking 174–176; and gendered activism 314–320, 323–327; and the media 255–261, 264–269; and memory 377–379, 382–388, 391–393, *393,* 405–406, *405,* 422–425, 427–429
fiefdom 332, 334, 340, 342–346
forests 109–112, *111,* 123–124; agrarian ideal 113–115; ethnic territories 121–123; forest reserves 115–119, *117;* national parks 119–121

Fragmentos (Salcedo) 399, 403–410, *405*, *407*
frontier region 313–316, 328–329; emergence of the Women's Alliance 322–324; indigeneity and class formation 316–317; national networks and the origins of activism 317–319; peace activism and access to E.U. resources 324–327; shifting conflict dynamics 320–322; tensions and contradictions 328

Gaviria, César 169–170; commercial advantages 170–171; domestic economic agenda 173–174; negotiation with drug traffickers 171–173; state violence 174–178
gendered activism 313–316, 328–329; emergence of the Women's Alliance 322–324; indigeneity and class formation 316–317; national networks and the origins of activism 317–319; peace activism and access to E.U. resources 324–327; shifting conflict dynamics 320–322; tensions and contradictions 328
Giraldo, Hernán 331–335, 337–347
grassroots memory initiatives 379–382, 435–438; construction of memory 400–402; counter-memory 385–386, 389–392, 398–399, 407
grassroots neoliberalism 143–145
green energies 148–150; asymmetries of power 153–156; radical socio-environmental transformations 160–162; structural inequalities and institutional transitions 156–159; territorial and cultural dispossession 150–152; transformations for the continuation of life 162–163
Guajira 148–150; asymmetries of power 153–156; radical socio-environmental transformations 160–162; structural inequalities and institutional transitions 156–159; territorial and cultural dispossession 150–152; transformations for the continuation of life 162–163
Guaviare 86–90

hashtags 10, 292, 295, 299–305
Havana 383–389
hegemony 292–296; flawed strategy 305–306; hegemonic language 130–131; Mincultura 292, 294–296, 299–305, 309; and music 296–298; role of the state 306–309
historical memory 377–378; counter-memory 385–386, 389–392, 398–399, 407; grassroots memory initiatives 379–382; new period in the making 392–394; primal rift of 383–389, **384**
humanism xxvii, 23–26, 253; interview 26–42

identity 23–25, 47, 88, 91, 95, 100; Black 51–54, 77; Campesino 88–91, 100; collective cultural 84, 95, 131–133; hybrid 274–275; Indigenous 283; National xxxvi–xxxvii, 3, 50, 276, 294–296, 304–306, 309; Raizal 56; restoring 422, 431, 434–437
immigration 185–186, 202–203; Cali Cartel in New York 193–199, *198*; Colombian migration to New York 190–193; historical context 187–190; Larry Landa 199–202, *201*
income 5, 47, 143, 218, 355, 359–363, 356–366, 370–371; National 129
indigeneity 65–66, 78–79, 273–174, 285–286; brief history 66–71; Catholic ACPO 276–279, *278*; and class formation 316–317; Evangelical indigenous radio stations 282–285; indigenous peoples as modern subjects 274–276; National Intendancy 71–78; state-sponsored indigenous radio stations 279–282
indigenous peoples 8, 25, 36, 49, 66, 87, 90–91, 122, 132–133, 149–150, 391; ancestral territories 214; coca and 215–217; as modern subjects 274–276; new technologies 285–286; rights of 154, 163, 280–282
inequalities, structural 156–159
infrastructure 121–149, 154, 157–159, 306–309, 318, 334, 338, 424

institutional transitions 156–159
intermediation 340–342

Jacanamijoy, Benjamín 207–213, 226
Jaibana 426, 432–434
journalism 242–245, 252–259, 267–269; moral performance 264–267; moral vision 259–264; *see also* media

Kuchimba, Mauricio 214–220, 226

Landa, Larry 199–202, *201*
land titling *see* collective land titling
language, hegemonic 130–131
law 71, 78, 91–92, 96, 99, 113–114, 116, *117*, 119, 129–130, 200; Justice and Peace Law 378, 381–382, 427; Law 70 of 1993 47, 122, 128–142; Victims and Land Restitution Law 383, 387, 427
life, continuation of 162–163
listening 352, 368, 387, 399–403, 407, 409
local strategies of territorial management 92–94
Lorenzo Tunobalá, Taita 214–220, 226

map (SIMUS interface) 301–302, 304
Medellín 220–225
media: community radio stations 273–286; and Jesús Abad Colorado 252–269; and Pablo Escobar 229–248; social media and music 292–309
memory: exhumations, peace agreement, and social reparation 419–438; fluctuations and paradoxes 377–394; rendering the unheard-of believable 398–414
mestizaje 3, 23–27, 30–32, 35–36, 46–50
methods xxxiv–xxxix
Middle Atrato 122, 142, *262*, 419, 422–425, *423*, 428, 430–432, 434
middle class xxxii–xxxiii, 4, 11, 44–46, 48–49, 51–52, 53–56, 187–188, 254, 308; Black 58–59, 133
migration 190–193

modern indigeneity 273–174, 285–286; Catholic ACPO 276–279, *278*; Evangelical indigenous radio stations 282–285; indigenous peoples as modern subjects 274–276; state-sponsored indigenous radio stations 279–282; *see also* indigeneity
Mona®co 206–207, 225–226; Bogotá 207–213; Cali 214–220; Medellín 220–225
moral performance 264–267
moral vision 259–267
motivations xxxiv–xxxix
multiculturalism xxviii, 3–5, 23, 25, 85, 90, 92, 129, 137, 273, 280, 297; and Anglophone Afro-Caribbean heritage 65–79; and Black upward mobility 44–60; and campesinos 84–101; and Manuel Zapata Olivella 23–42
Muñoz, Víctor 220–225, 226
Muriel, Fátima 313–316, 328–329; emergence of the Women's Alliance 322–324; indigeneity and class formation 316–317; national networks and the origins of activism 317–319; peace activism and access to E.U. resources 324–327; shifting conflict dynamics 320–322; tensions and contradictions 328
music 292–296; flawed strategy 305–306; and hegemony 296–298; Mincultura 292, 294–296, 299–305, 309; role of the state 306–309; salsa 185–203

narco 8, 208–210, 220, 222–223, 230–231, 234, 236–242, 246–247, 334, 336, 343, 345; narco-democracy xxvi, 173
narco-entrepreneurs 190–193, 199, 202
narco-phenomena 206–207, 225–226; Bogotá 207–213; Cali 214–220; Medellín 220–225
narcotrafficking 185–186, 202–203; antinarcotics xxxii, 7, 87, 172, 177, 344, 366; Cali Cartel in New York 193–199, *198*; Colombian migration to New York 190–193; historical context 187–190; Larry Landa 199–202, *201*

national networks 317–319
national parks 119–121
native islanders 71–78
neoliberalism xxviii, 2–3, 7, 45, 58, 127–129, 293–294, 296; Afro-Colombians as owners of the rural Pacific 140–142; drafting a law for Afro-Colombians 129–130; hegemonic language of participation 130–131; "projectism" and grassroots neoliberalism 143–145; recognition of Afro-Colombians as ethnic group 132–136; territorial effects 136–140
neoliberal multiculturalism 44–46, 58–60; and *mestizaje* 46–50; and middle class 53–56; resistance to white cultural domination 56–58; and social whitening 50–53
networks: and communal fiefdom 342–343; national 317–319
New York *see* Cali-New York connection

Pacific region 127–129; Afro-Colombians as owners of the rural Pacific 140–142; drafting a law for Afro-Colombians 129–130; hegemonic language of participation 130–131; "projectism" and grassroots neoliberalism 143–145; recognition of Afro-Colombians as ethnic group 132–136; territorial effects 136–140
Pacto Histórico 60, 378
paradox xxx–xxxiii, 378, 387
paramilitary 10–14, 93–94, 175–177, 255–261, 266–269, 323–324, 331–333, 366–368, 379–381, 422–424, 428–430; communal fiefdom 342–343; community and intermediation 340–342; context 335–337; Hernán Giraldo 338–347; and Michael Mann 333–335; Santa Marta region 337–338
participation, language of 130–131
peace activism 324–327; *see also* activism; gendered activism
peace agreement xxxii, xxxiv, 49, 85, 98–99, 327, 352–353, 369, 383, 388–389, 392–394, 419–422, 437–438; bad deaths 426–427; dignifying name and memory 435–437; peace process and exhumations 427–431; prolonged wake and how to properly care for the dead 431–434; war in the Middle Atrato 422–425
peace process 427–431
peace talks 383–389, **384**
peasant women 359–363
persona 229–231, 247–248; accidental 245–247; journalism routines 242–245; the narco 236–242; the Robin Hood 231–236
photojournalism 252–259, 267–269; moral performance 264–267; moral vision 259–264; *see also* media
Plan Colombia xxxii, xxxvi, 6, 320–321, 352, 366
playlist 394–395, 299–306, 308–309
political repression 169–170; commercial advantages 170–171; domestic economic agenda 173–174; negotiation with drug traffickers 171–173; state violence 174–178
political subjectivities 90–92; *see also* subjectivities
primal rift 13, 383–389, *384*, 392
"projectism" 143–145
Providencia 65–66, 75, 78–79; brief history 66–71; National Intendancy 71–78

Quiñones, Edinson 214–220, 226

racial democracy and mestizaje 25, 46
racism xxxiii, 4, 44, 47–49, 56–60, 275, 408, 437
radical socio-environmental transformations 148–150; asymmetries of power 153–156; radical socio-environmental transformations 160–162; structural inequalities and institutional transitions 156–159; territorial and cultural dispossession 150–152; transformations for the continuation of life 162–163
radio stations *see* community radio stations

Raizals 65–66, 78–79; brief history 66–71; National Intendancy 71–78
reparation *see* social reparation
repression *see* political repression
reserves, forest 115–119, *117*
resistance to white cultural domination 56–58
Revolutionary Armed Forces of Colombia *see* FARC
Rincón, Omar 207–213, 226
Robin Hood 231–236
rural dynamics in coca territories 354–359
rural Pacific 140–142

Salcedo, Doris 399, 403–410, *405*, *407*
salsa music 185–186, 202–203; Cali Cartel in New York 193–199, *198*; Colombian migration to New York 190–193; historical context 187–190; Larry Landa 199–202, *201*
San Andrés 65–66, *78*, 78–79; brief history 66–71; National Intendancy 71–78
Santa Catalina 65–66, 78–79; brief history 66–71; National Intendancy 71–78
Santa Marta region 337–338; Sierra Nevada de Santa Marta (SNSM) 12, 94, 116, 150, 223, 331–332, 339, 340
Santos, Juan Manuel xxx, 13, 84, 303, 324, 327, 352, 377, 383, 399, 419, 425
sexual violence 14, 325, 342, 346, 404
social media 292–296; flawed strategy 305–306; Mincultura 292, 294–296, 299–305, 309; music and hegemony 296–298; role of the state 306–309
social reparation 419–422, 437–438; bad deaths 426–427; dignifying name and memory 435–437; peace process and exhumations 427–431; prolonged wake and how to properly care for the dead 431–434; war in the Middle Atrato 422–425
social whitening 50–53, 59
socio-environmental agenda 95–99, *98*
socio-environmental transformations *see* radical socio-environmental transformations
state, territorial *see* territorial state
state building *see* territorial state building
state-sponsored indigenous radio stations 279–282
state violence 55, 60, 159, 174–178, 314
storytelling 15, 254–255, 267–269, 436
structural inequalities 156–159
subjectivities 84–85, 90, 101
Sumapaz 96–98

taita 213–215, 277, 284
territorial dispossession 150–152
territorial effects of collective land titling 136–140
territorial management 92–94
territorial state: and collective land titling 127–145; and forests 109–124; and radical socio-environmental transformations 148–163
territorial state building 109–112, *111*, 123–124; agrarian ideal 113–115; ethnic territories 121–123; forest reserves 115–119, *117*; national parks 119–121
territories, ethnic 121–123
titling *see* collective land titling
trafficking *see* drug trafficking
Trujillo, Harold *see* Chócolo

unheard-of, the 398–399; *Duelos* 410–414, *411–412*; *Fragmentos* 403–410, *405*, *407*; memory as a site for listening 399–403
upward mobility 44–46, 58–60; and middle class 53–56; and neoliberal multiculturalism 46–53; resistance to white cultural domination 56–58; and social whitening 50–53
Uribe Vélez, Álvaro 172, 174, 261, 264, 268, 337, 377, 379, 425; Democratic Security xxxii, 353, 382
Uribe, Carlos 220–225, *222*, 226

violence *see* sexual violence; state violence

wake, prolonged 431–434
War on Drugs xxxvi, 7, 12, 87, 169–170, 242–243, 280, 331, 346, 351–352, 358–359, 366–370

white cultural domination 33, 56–59
whitening, social *see* social whitening
wind energy 148, 150–163
women 151, 160–161, 193, 197, 260, 284–285, 313–316, 318–319, 322–325, 328–329, 351–371, 404, 430–431, 436; Black 52–53, 56–57; and coca income 359–363; *cocaleras* and rural dynamics 354–359; places of women in coca territories 363–366; War on Drugs 366–370
Women's Alliance Weavers of Life 315, 322–324, 327

Zapata, Jorge Alonso 220–225, 226
Zapata Olivella, Manuel 1–2, 15, 23–26, 26; interview 26–42
Zonas de Reserva Campesina 4, 85, 91, 95–99, 98